Common Places

Bridge to College English

Lisa Hoeffner and
Kent Hoeffner

Mc
Graw
Hill
Education

COMMON PLACES: BRIDGE TO COLLEGE ENGLISH

1 2 3 4 5 6 7 8 9 DOW 21 20 19 18 17 16

ISBN: 978-0-07-680732-1 (student edition)
MHID: 0-07-680732-0 (student edition)

ISBN: 978-0-07-680733-8 (teacher's edition)
MHID: 0-07-680733-9 (teacher's edition)

Senior Vice President, Products & Markets: *Kurt L. Strand*
Vice President, General Manager, Products & Markets: *Michael Ryan*
Vice President, Content Design & Delivery: *Kimberly Meriwether David*
Managing Director: *David S. Patterson*
Executive Brand Manager: *Kelly Villella*
Director, Product Development: *Meghan Campbell*
Senior Market Development Manager: *Suzie Flores*
Senior Marketing Manager: *Jaclyn Elkins*
Marketing Manager: *Nancy Baudean*
Executive Director of Development: *Lisa Pinto*
Director, Content Design & Delivery: Terry Schiesl

Program Manager: *Jennifer Gehl*
Content Project Manager: *Sandy Wille*
Buyer: *Susan K. Culbertson*
Design: *Trevor Goodman*
Content Licensing Specialists: *Shawntel Schmitt*
Cover Image: Joe Josephs Photography/Getty Images
Bridge to College English: Digital Essentials
   Cover Image: ©Swapan Jha/Getty Images
Compositor: *Laserwords Private Limited*
Printer: *R. R. Donnelley*
All credits appearing on page or at the end of the book are considered to be an extension of the copyright page.

Library of Congress Cataloging-in-Publication Data

Hoeffner, Lisa, author.
   Common Places : integrated reading and writing / Lisa Hoeffner, McLennan Community College ; Kent Hoeffner, McLennan Community College.
      p. cm
   Includes bibliographical references and index.
   ISBN 978-0-076-80732-1 (student edition : alk. paper) — ISBN 0-076-80732-0 (student edition: alk. paper) — ISBN 978-0-076-80733-8 (instructor's edition) — ISBN 0-076-80733-9 (instructor's edition) 1. English language—Rhetoric—Problems, exercises, etc. 2. Report writing—Problems, exercises, etc. 3. Reading comprehension—Problems, exercises, etc. 4. College readers. I. Hoeffner, Kent, author. II. Title.
   PE1413.H553 2015
   808'.042076—dc23

2014022177

www.mheducation.com

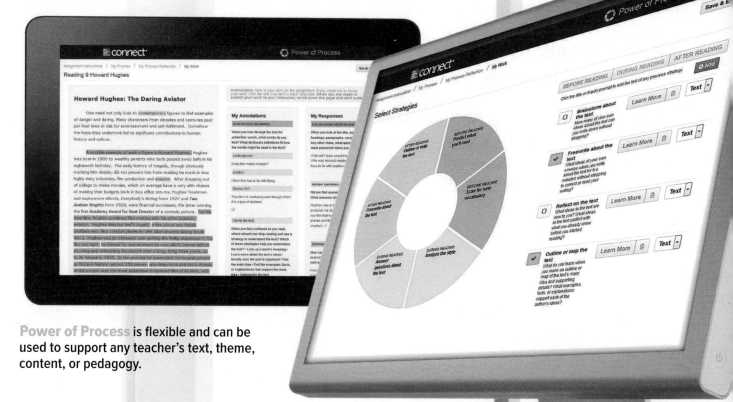

BRIEF CONTENTS

ABOUT THE AUTHORS

Lisa Hoeffner

Lisa Hoeffner earned a PhD in English with a specialization in rhetoric from the University of Houston. She has taught a wide range of courses over the past twenty-five years, including English composition and rhetoric, reading, critical thinking, American and British literature, world literature, humanities, and business writing. Since 1998, Dr. Hoeffner has served in two positions—professor of English and professor of reading—at McLennan Community College in Waco, Texas.

In addition to her teaching role, Dr. Hoeffner is focusing on curricular redesign in developmental education. She serves as grant director for a Texas Higher Education Coordinating Board grant awarded for work on improvement and innovation in developmental education. With the advent of integrated reading and writing in Texas, she has provided leadership for colleges and universities across the state that are creating integrated reading and writing (INRW) programs. She has designed and led training workshops and webinars to prepare faculty to teach INRW and to help institutions create INRW programs. She has also provided leadership to public school districts implementing INRW programs as college preparatory classes.

Dr. Hoeffner has a passion for teaching and for innovative technologies. She designed and taught her first online freshman composition class in 1999 and has since developed and taught online courses for developmental students. She is thrilled that she is able to bring both passions to bear in her development of *Common Places* and the Connect IRW: *Common Places* Master Course.

Dr. Hoeffner is a recipient of several awards, including the National Institute for Staff and Organizational Development (NISOD) Excellence Award. She has written and published scholarly articles and poetry, and she has presented her work in developmental education nationally. A native Texan, Dr. Hoeffner enjoys exploring the flora and fauna of regional ecosystems, cooking, and dreaming about living off the grid.

Kent Hoeffner

Kent Hoeffner earned a BA from Texas A&M University in College Station, an MDiv from Golden Gate Seminary in Mill Valley, California, and a PhD from Southern Seminary in Louisville, Kentucky. Before working in higher education, Dr. Hoeffner was employed in the mental health field, working primarily with adolescents with social and emotional difficulties. During that time, he also taught adult basic education and GED preparation classes.

Dr. Hoeffner has served at McLennan Community College since 2001, first as the division director for liberal arts and currently as a professor of philosophy. In addition to teaching introductory courses in philosophy, he has also taught and developed courses in critical thinking and logic. In 2007, he developed McLennan's first online philosophy course, and since then he has continued to develop and teach various online courses.

Recently, Dr. Hoeffner renewed his long-standing involvement in academic advising by joining a group of faculty in a grant-funded intensive advising program focused on improving the success of developmental students. He regularly mentors students who need help in the areas of successful academic behaviors, self-advocacy, and the development of college-level reading and writing skills.

His background in foreign languages and logic contributed to his talents for creating the sentence-combining and grammar units in *Common Places*, and his expertise in teaching critical thinking and in student mentoring has helped to shape the text. When he is not teaching, advising, or writing, Dr. Hoeffner enjoys following the Dallas Cowboys, reading, and traveling.

CONTENTS

PART 1

Planning for Success

CHAPTER 1

PART 2

Reading and Writing as Integrated Processes

CHAPTER 7

Organizing, Drafting, and Summarizing 222

CHAPTER 9

Inferences and Tone 277

PART 3

Additional Skills

 2

Spelling and Word Choice 428

UNIT 3

Punctuation and Mechanics 450

Available only in create

Project 4: Reading and Writing Summaries

Motivations and Mindsets

Project 5: Reading and Writing to Solve Problems

Problem-Solving Skills

Available only in create

THE LEARNING SUPPORT SYSTEM OF *COMMON PLACES*

The *Common Places* Text

- Quick Start Guide to Bridge to College English Assignments: an overview of steps in the integrated reading and writing process necessary for success in college English composition courses
- Text chapters: eleven foundational chapters and three handbook units

Bridge to College English Connect Course

- *LearnSmart Achieve*
- *Power of Process*
- Writing assignment type with peer review capability

Lisa Hoeffner has created the following assignments to align with chapters in *Common Places*:

- Chapter quizzes
- Chapter vocabulary quizzes

Teaching Resources and Digital Support

- *Annotated Teacher's Edition* with on-page teaching tips
- *Instructor's Manual*
- Handouts, exercises, and graphics
- Chapter quizzes and vocabulary quizzes
- Topical *PowerPoint* presentations

Additional Content in Connect

- Three Integrated Reading and Writing Projects
- Four Thematic Anthologies of Readings

Additional Content in MHE Create

- Three additional Integrated Reading and Writing Projects
- Two additional skills and practice chapters
- Two additional Thematic Anthologies of Readings

PREFACE

Why *Common Places?*

Common Places teaches students to *read from a writer's point of view* by considering the choices writers make when presenting their content. It also encourages students to *write from a reader's point of view* as they face the same choices with their own writing. Students immediately and continually emulate recursive reading and writing processes as they work through the text. As the teaching of developmental, college-level reading and writing is finding its way to high schools across the country, teachers and instructors are coming together in *common places* to find effective methods for teaching both sets of strategies as an interdependent reading and writing process. The title *Common Places* celebrates this interdependence and the thoughtful common ground that teachers and instructors are finding with this integration.

The *Common Places* Instructional Framework

A leader in developmental education redesign, Lisa Hoeffner has created for *Common Places* an innovative instructional framework that includes step-by-step modeling for integrated reading and writing processes, a unique series of purpose-oriented projects, a fresh approach to grammar, and a compelling set of thematic, leveled readings. Hoeffner incorporates the powerful concepts of metacognition, reflection, and critical thinking using practical exercises. Offering unsurpassable flexibility with customizable content, *Common Places* is backed by a thoughtful learning support system, envisioned and developed by Hoeffner.

Features of the Learning Support System of *Common Places*

Common Places and the components of Connect Bridge to College English (Connect BCE) address the specific needs of integrated reading and writing courses.

- **A fully integrated and flexible solution for the integrated reading and writing course.** *Common Places* provides a strong instructional framework for intertwining the skills of reading and writing. The Learning Resources in Connect BCE *LearnSmart Achieve* provide students with integrated skills instruction in the form of visual slides with narrated coach text and video resources, within an adaptive platform that targets areas in which students need remediation.

- **Multiple features to promote metacognitive skills.** These features, including Thinking from an Instructor's Point of View exercises and end-of-chapter activities in emotional intelligence, cultural literacy, critical thinking, and metacognition, help students develop an awareness of multiple points of view as readers, writers, students, and citizens. Features in Connect BCE *LearnSmart Achieve* and *Power of Process* assignments also support the development of students' metacognitive awareness.

- **A methodical, step-by-step approach for modeling integrated reading and writing processes.** The logical and clear framework presented in *Common Places* provides an abundance of models that help build students' confidence in their ability to master specific skills as they work through the chapters and the projects. The Learning Resources in Connect BCE *LearnSmart Achieve* display annotated examples as good models for students.

- **A fresh approach to grammar.** The handbook takes a positive, highly effective approach to grammar, with a strong emphasis on sentence combining and grammar in context. Grammar Focus features within chapters reinforce the integrated nature of reading and writing. Students have ample opportunity for additional, targeted grammar practice in any of the eighteen *LearnSmart Achieve* grammar and mechanics topics in Connect BCE.

- **Unique, purpose-oriented projects for upper-level and lower-level BCE courses (available in Connect and MHE Create).** Each project within the set emphasizes a particular writing purpose: to inform, to analyze and evaluate, or to persuade. Each upper-level project features four readings on a specific topic and requires students to read and analyze the selections and then integrate them effectively in their own source-based, documented essay. The lower-level projects, available only in Create™, require students to read critically a single source and complete a purpose-oriented writing assignment appropriate for the earlier course in the sequence.

- **The Quick Start Guide to Bridge to College English Assignments.** This brief guide at the start of the text articulates the steps in the reading and writing process and enables students to engage in the process immediately.

- **A wealth of highly engaging readings across a range of themes.** With the readings in *Common Places* and in Connect BCE *Power of Process*, teachers will find readings for any student audience or Lexile range. Themes and readings have all been chosen to include topics that are of high interest to students and most prevalently used in BCE courses. All readings come with a variety of assessments and assignments. Connect BCE *Power of Process* makes visible to students their own reading and writing process as they analyze readings within the toolset. Essay-writing assignments and reading-based writing assignments may be assigned through the Connect BCE *Writing Assignment* toolset to support rubric assessment and peer review.

- **Examples of how purpose and patterns work together.** *Common Places* treats patterns of development (rhetorical modes) as tools for creating support in texts, not as ends in themselves. Students are guided to select and combine patterns of development that fit writing purposes—informing, analyzing, evaluating, and persuading—and provide the best support for particular audiences. For teachers who teach only particular text patterns, *Common Places* Chapter 6 may be customized to include only the text patterns desired.

- **An abundance of opportunities to practice skills.** *Common Places* provides students with extensive practice in reading and writing skills. Exercises interspersed throughout the text build individual skills, and more-comprehensive activities appear at the end of each chapter. Connect BCE *LearnSmart Achieve* provides additional practice of those skills in an adaptive, individualized learning experience. *Power of Process* supports more holistic practice and assessment of the integrated reading and writing process.

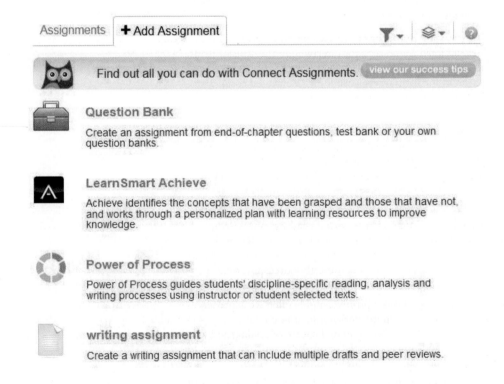

Teaching Resources

As an early adopter of the integrated reading and writing approach, Dr. Hoeffner created the annotations in the *Annotated Instructor's Edition*, as well as all the textbook supplements. These resources work hand-in-hand with the digital tools available in Connect Bridge to College English.

Connect for *Common Places: Bridge to College English*

Connect BCE addresses the specific needs of integrated reading and writing courses and various redesign models of instruction. It teaches reading and writing skills as a *complementary* process by contextualizing the material within thematic disciplinary readings and authentic writing models. In addition to the innovative content, revolutionary learning technology drives the integration of reading and writing skills through a selection of corresponding toolsets:

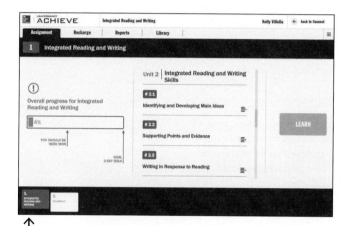

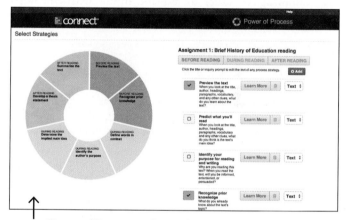

- *LearnSmart Achieve* offers students an adaptive, individualized learning experience designed to ensure the efficient mastery of reading and writing skills in tandem. By targeting students' particular strengths and weaknesses, *LearnSmart Achieve* customizes its lessons and facilitates high-impact learning at an accelerated pace.

- *Power of Process* guides students through performance-based assessment activities using the pedagogy of strategies instruction, in which students use strategies to read and respond to the text, and then teachers can assess students' depth of engagement with the text.

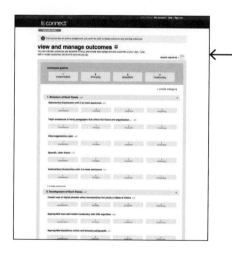

- *Writing Assignments* with **Outcomes Based Assessment** allow teachers to assess written assignments with custom rubrics built around learning outcomes and to generate detailed reports that support formative assessment and improve efficacy at the student, section, and program levels.

- **An integrated digital ebook,** available in Connect®, allows students to access their textbooks on the go from any Internet-connected computer or tablet. Students can take notes and make annotations in their ebooks as they read, and access them later for study and review.
- Connect Insight™ is an analytics tool that provides a series of visual data displays—each framed by an intuitive question—to provide instructors at-a-glance information regarding how their classes are doing

Annotated Teacher's Edition: On-Page Teaching Tips

The author draws on her extensive experience in the classroom—as well as the experiences of many other seasoned college English faculty—to offer pedagogical ideas that are effective and easy to use. Marginal tips suggest innovative ways to present the topics in each chapter. The *Annotated Teacher's Edition* also alerts instructors to teaching resources such as handouts, quizzes, and *PowerPoint* presentations, as well as to assignments and resources in Connect BCE.

The following resources are available in the Instructor Resources area in Connect.

Instructor's Manual

The *Instructor's Manual* is written with the diverse needs of BCE teachers in mind. Those new to teaching a Bridge to College course will appreciate the brief presentations of theory that accompany the reading pedagogy in the textbook, as well as the suggestions for how to teach some of the more difficult reading skills. They may also find helpful the suggestions for grading strategies, managing the paper load, addressing grammatical issues, and teaching MLA and APA styles.

Handouts, Exercises, and Graphics

These documents may be used for in-class, hands-on practice. These copy-and-go pages make preparing for class easier, and they give teachers a way to present material to students whose learning styles benefit from kinesthetic activities.

Chapter Quizzes

The chapter quizzes test students' literal comprehension of chapter content. They can be used to motivate students to read the chapters, and they were designed to be easily administered and graded.

Topical *PowerPoint* Presentations

The *PowerPoint* presentations for *Common Places* are short, fun for students, and powerful. Unlike traditional textbook-supplied *PowerPoint* presentations that simply provide chapter outlines, *Common Places* presentations are topical and highly visual. For instance, the *PowerPoint* presentation "Broad or Narrow?" starts with photos and transitions to text in order to teach students to recognize differences in the breadth of ideas.

A Word from the Lead Author, Lisa Hoeffner

Many recent high school graduates are surprised when they learn that they do not have the necessary skills to take college-level classes. They are dismayed by the prospect of taking remedial courses their first semester in college. Not only are these classes a set-back in terms of time and money, but they affect the spirit, too.

As a college instructor who has taught these courses for over twenty years, I believe in remediation. Yet I also know that if we can prepare students for college before they enroll, students will inevitably do better. The national movement to provide this remediation during high school simply makes sense. Wouldn't it be great if we could identify and remediate every developmental student in high school? Even those students who do not go on to college will certainly benefit.

As Kent (my husband and co-author) and I wrote this text, we sought to present a pedagogy that would equip students for college-level reading and writing tasks. To this end, Common Places presents the most important reading and writing skills students will need for college coursework. The goal of the pedagogy we have used is to save valuable instruction time by integrating these skills. Instead of teaching reading as a separate course from writing, we present both reading and writing at the same time. Many of the learning objectives for each course mirror each other: identify a thesis statement/ write a thesis statement, identify various types of support/create various types of support, and so on. The natural way to integrate is to teach the reading skill and then teach the mirrored writing skill.

This point is important to me as an instructor. We have so little time to remediate in so many areas that I needed a book that would really support an integrated process to accelerate student learning. My hope is that Common Places provides the best integration of reading and writing possible and that it makes the learning of both subjects not only feasible in a shorter time frame, but also enjoyable.

To write a book is a humbling experience. The process reminded me of just how much I am indebted to all the people around me who have stimulated my thoughts, shared their own great ideas, and encouraged me to keep going. I would like to thank a few people without whom this book simply would not exist. I am entirely grateful for Paul Banks and the faith he had in this project from the beginning. Also, *Common Places* owes much of its visionary content to Kelly Villella. She has been a dynamic source of ideas, energy, and drive and has often been the engine that has propelled me forward. And I cannot imagine finding a more personable, professional, and gifted editor than Linda Stern. Linda has a real knack for seeing the possibilities in a text and making them come to life. Lisa Pinto has also been crucial to our team; her calm, can-do attitude and logical ideas have brought reassurance to our team meetings. I am also grateful for the many people who worked tirelessly and cheerfully on various aspects of *Common Places*: Wes Hall, who managed the text permissions; Shawntel Schmitt, who handled the photo program; Trevor Goodman, who created the beautiful cover and design; Dana Wan, who handled administrative details; Judith Riotto, who copyedited the manuscript; Debra DeBord and Martha Ghent, who proofread the pages; Nancy Ball, who prepared the index; Suzie Flores, who managed market development activities; Jaclyn Elkins and Nancy Baudean, who carefully crafted marketing plans; and Sandy Wille, who oversaw the entire production process masterfully.

To my colleagues at McLennan, I owe a debt of gratitude. In particular, Linda Crawford, Lorraine Stansel, Charlotte Laughlin, Bill Matta, and Fred Hills have not only offered great ideas, but have been supportive of this project from the beginning. I would also like to thank the crucial work of all the faculty reviewers. Without their guidance and creativity, *Common Places* would be a different book: Susan Achziger, *Community College of Aurora*; Marian Anders, *Alamance Community College*; Joe Antinarella, *Tidewater Community College–Chesapeake*; Deva Arumugam, *El Centro College*; Jenny Beaver, *Rowan Cabarrus Community College*; Erica Bertero, *Del Mar College*; Michael Boyd, *Illinois Central College*; Kimberly Britt, *Horry Georgetown Technical College*; Robyn Browder, *Tidewater Community College–Virginia Beach*; Sarah Bruton, *Fayetteville Technical Community College*; Kellie Cannon, *Coastal Carolina Community College*; James Carranza, *College of San Mateo*; Judith Carter, *Amarillo College*; Susan Chism, *Greenville College*; Thomas Connolly, *Suffolk University*; Michael Cox, *Mitchell Community College*; Christy Cutshaw, *Allen County Community*

College; JoAnn Davis, *Saint Philips College;* Patricia Davis, *Houston Community College–Southwest;* Kelly Dedmon, *Isothermal Community College;* Brian Dickson, *Community College of Denver;* Alicia Dominguez, *Saint Philips College;* Tammy Donaldson, *Del Mar College;* Barbara Doyle, *Arkansas State University–Jonesboro;* Mary Dubbe, *Thomas Nelson Community College;* Patricia Dungan, *Austin Community College–Rio Grande;* Christi Duque, *Tarrant Community College;* Justin Eatmon, *Coastal Carolina Community College;* Crystal Edmonds, *Robeson Community College;* Jason Ellis, *Cincinnati State Technical and Community College;* Dell Smith Enecks, *Beaufort Community College;* Ruth Engel, *Tarrant Community College;* Betty Evans, *University of Arkansas–Monticello;* Ellen Feig, *Bergen Community College;* Marianne Friedell, *College of the Mainland;* Jacquelyn Gaiters-Jordan, *Pikes Peak Community College;* Julie Garner, *Tri-County Community College;* Debbie Gilmore, *Temple College;* Brent Green, *Salt Lake Community College;* Dustin Greene, *Caldwell Community College;* Karen Hackley, *Dominican College;* Beth Hammett, *College of the Mainland;* Curtis Harrell, *Northwest Arkansas Community College;* Michelle Hawkins, *Bryant and Stratton College;* Michael Hedges, *Horry Georgetown Technical College;* Kathleen Hickey, *Dominican College;* Amy Holly, *Front Range Community College–Fort Collins;* Judy Hubble, *Austin Community College–Round Rock;* Elizabeth Hudspeth, *Northeast Lakeview College;* Jill Hughes, *Casper College;* Blanche Hunt, *Arkansas Northeastern College;* Sharyn Hunter, *Sinclair Community College;* Janis Innis, *Houston Community College–Southwest;* Danen Jobe, *Pikes Peak Community College;* Alyssa Johnson, *Horry Georgetown Community College;* Leah Jones, *College of the Albemarle;* Kimberly Koledoye, *Houston Community College–Northwest;* Mary Ann Landino, *Housatonic Community College;* Jeff Landon, *John Tyler Community College;* Kina Lara, *San Jacinto College–South;* Alice Leonhardt, *Blue Ridge Community College;* Thomas Lilly, *Georgia Gwinnett College;* Tiffany Lofton, *Horry Georgetown Technical College;* Breanna Lutterbie, *Germanna Community College–Locust Grove;* Carol Manciel, *Wayne County Community College–Western;* Elizabeth Marsh, *Bergen Community College;* Lori Massey, *Tarrant County College;* Brook Mayo, *Asheville Buncombe Technical Community College;* Kathy McCoskey, *Butler Community College;* Kerry McShane-Moley, *Cape Fear Community College–North Camp;* Kim Meeks, *Oconee Fall Line Technical College–Dublin;* Marti Miles-Rosenfield, *Collin College Plano;* Kathleen Mollick, *Tarleton State University;* Robbi Muckenfuss, *Durham Technical Community College;* Maureen Murphy-Smolka, *Sussex County Community College;* Alice Newsome, *Tarleton State University;* Hilda Ollmann, *Austin Community College–Eastview;* Diane Payne, *University of Arkansas–Monticello;* Emily Peebles, *San Jacinto College–Pasadena;* Betty Perkinson, *Tidewater Community College–Portsmouth;* Cara Potter, *Durham Technical Community College;* Jeanni Pruitt, *Northeast Texas Community College;* Sandra Reinhardt, *Catawba Valley Community College;* Nancy Risch, *Caldwell Community College;* Jackie Roberts, *Richland Community College;* Kathleen Ross, *Asheville Buncombe Technical Community College;* Kay Ruth, *Wake Technical Community College;* Maria Salinas, *Del Mar College;* Robert Sandhaas, *San Jacinto College–South;* Esther Sapell Rachelson, *Devry University–South Florida;* Tracy Schneider, *Solano Community College;* Jim Schrantz, *Tarrant County College;* Linda Shieff, *Wake Technical Community College;* Mary Sizemore, *Lamar State College–Orange;* Debra Slaton, *Cisco College–Abilene;* Cheryle Snead-Greene, *Prairie View A&M University;* Mae Spicer, *Richland College;* Tanya Stanley, *San Jacinto College–Pasadena;* Kelly Terzaken, *Coastal Carolina Community College;* Alexandr Tolj, *John Tyler Community College–Midlothian;* Ernie Tsacalis, *San Antonio College;* Joan Valichnac, *Northland Pioneer College;* Dustin Wenrich, *Wright State University–Dayton;* Tina Willhoite, *San Jacinto College–South;* Katherine Winkler, *Blue Ridge Community College;* Michelle Zollars, *Patrick Henry Community College.*

I am grateful for the contributions of my brother, Richard Wright, my mother, Gail Wright, and my sister-in-law, Margie Hoeffner. For bearing with Kent and me throughout the process of "the book," I must also thank our kids, Abby, Hannah, and Seth, and our parents, Richard and Gail Wright and Vondee Hoeffner. Our families have patiently stood by us, offering encouragement and helping us as they could.

Finally, I must thank my husband and coauthor, Kent Hoeffner. I now look back with fondness at the many days we sat in our study researching together, writing and rewriting, fussing, and laughing. Kent's incredible writing gifts, intelligence, and creativity mark many of the pages of *Common Places,* and his constant encouragement brought this project to fruition.

Lisa Hoeffner

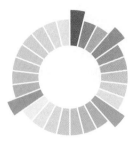

QUICK START GUIDE
to Bridge to College English Assignments

This brief reference guide will walk you through the integrated reading and writing process so important to success in college-level English courses that you have guidance for your reading and writing assignments from the first day of class. The first column lists the tasks as steps. The second column briefly explains each task. While these steps are listed in order, most people go back to previous steps during the reading and writing process. For instance, the first step—analyze your assignment— is something you will likely do more than once. Reviewing the assignment at various points in the process will help guide your reading and will help keep you on track as you write. Notations suggest steps to review if you need more ideas, support, or information as you work.

Not all assignments require you to use every step presented here. Choose the steps that will best help you complete each assignment.

GETTING STARTED

Analyze your assignment.	Ask yourself: Is the assignment clear and complete? Is research required? What are the formatting and length guidelines? Highlight or underline key words. For additional clarity, reword the topic as a question to be answered.
Identify your purpose.	Ask yourself: What is my purpose as I read the assigned texts? When I write, will my purpose be to inform, to entertain, to evaluate or analyze, or to persuade?

WORKING WITH READINGS

Preview the reading and think about the topic.	Examine the title, headings, illustrations, and context to determine the topic. Make a guess about what the writer will say about the topic. Consider how the new information will fit into what you already know about the topic.
Read and annotate the text.	Annotate the thesis statement, major supporting points, and supporting details. Annotate any key words associated with the issue. Mark at least three potential quotes.
Outline and summarize each reading.	Write a brief outline that includes the thesis statement and major supporting points. Summarize the article in two or three sentences. In your summary, include the source's bibliographic information (author's name, title, and publication information), the topic, the writer's main idea, the major supporting points, and the significant supporting details.

(continued)

Prepare an information sheet for each reading.	List the source's bibliographic information and any other general notes. Add your outline, your brief summary, a list of issues addressed in the reading, a list of key words, and the quotes you have identified. *For more ideas, go back to "Read and annotate the text" and "Outline and summarize each reading."*

DEVELOPING YOUR ESSAY

Synthesize your sources.	If you are using several sources, organize the ideas from all the sources. Determine the points the sources have in common and where the sources differ. Use a graphic organizer, such as a chart, to categorize and organize the ideas.
Prewrite to develop your ideas.	Use prewriting strategies (discussion, simple listing, clustering, journalistic questions, freewriting, and freetalking) to come up with topics, major supporting points, and supporting details. *For more ideas, go back to "Analyze your assignment."*
Construct a thesis statement.	Write a thesis statement, a complete sentence in which you articulate your topic and your main point about the topic. Check that your thesis statement is not a statement of fact, a question, or an announcement and that it is not too broad.
Develop support for your thesis statement.	Determine your major supporting points. Develop supporting details for each major supporting point as content for your essay. Select text patterns (narration, definition, illustration, classification, comparison-contrast, cause and effect, process analysis) and features (such as examples and facts) to express the supporting details. *For more ideas, go back to "Prewrite to develop your ideas."*
Create an outline to organize your essay.	Start with your topic and thesis statement. Express each major supporting point in a complete sentence. Add supporting details. Jot down ideas for the introduction and conclusion.
Add source materials to your outline.	Add to your outline references to where you might use information from the summaries you wrote, the quotes you identified, and any other source information you plan on using. *For more ideas, go back to "Read and annotate the text" and "Prepare an information sheet for each reading."*
Write a complete draft of your essay.	Using your outline for guidance, write an introduction, body paragraphs, and a conclusion. Use the major supporting points as topic sentences for body paragraphs. Write as many paragraphs as you need to develop fully the essay's main idea. Decide where to place your thesis statement. Keep your audience's needs in mind as you write. Frequently reread your paper from the beginning to check the flow of ideas, to add needed information, and to reword passages for clarity.

(continued)

Integrate ideas and quotes from sources correctly.	Follow these rules: (1) Copy direct quotations exactly from the source. (2) Integrate a quoted fragment grammatically into a complete sentence. (3) Use an attributive tag to integrate a quotation into your writing. (4) Start and end a quotation with quotation marks. (5) Place the sentence's period inside the quotation marks; if a parenthetical reference ends the quotation, place the period after the reference. *For more ideas, go back to "Read and annotate the text" and "Prepare an information sheet for each reading."*

FINISHING YOUR ASSIGNMENT

Check that you have met assignment requirements.	Review your annotated assignment to make sure the content of your essay meets the requirements of the assignment. *For more ideas, go back to "Analyze your assignment."*
Revise for organization and unity.	Ask yourself: Is the essay's organization logical? Do all the paragraphs relate to the main idea? Have I used transitions effectively? Make any necessary changes. *For more ideas, go back to "Create an outline to organize your essay."*
Revise for development.	Ask yourself: Have I answered readers' potential questions? Have I included enough support for my thesis statement? Have I explained unfamiliar terms? Make any necessary changes. *For more ideas, go back to "Prewrite to develop your ideas."*
Revise for clarity.	Ask yourself: Are the words I use concrete and specific? Is the tone appropriate? Are all pronoun references clear?
Create a works cited or references list.	If you used sources, create an MLA works cited list or an APA references list. *For more ideas, go back to "Integrate ideas and quotes from sources correctly."*
Check for plagiarism.	Make sure you have given credit to sources: (1) Check that each summary, quotation, and idea from a source is credited with an attributive tag (*Jones said, . . .*) or a parenthetical reference. (2) Check that each source cited in your essay is listed correctly in the works cited or references list.
Edit your essay using SMART TRACS.	Check for grammatical errors that you have had trouble with in the past. Run a spell-checker. Use other methods, such as SMART TRACS, to find errors. S = Spelling T = Tense consistency M = Missing words R = Rhythm A = Accurate punctuation A = Active voice R = Repeated words C = Confusing words T = Terminal punctuation S = Sources
Put your essay in the proper format.	Follow your instructor's directions for formatting your paper in MLA style or APA style.

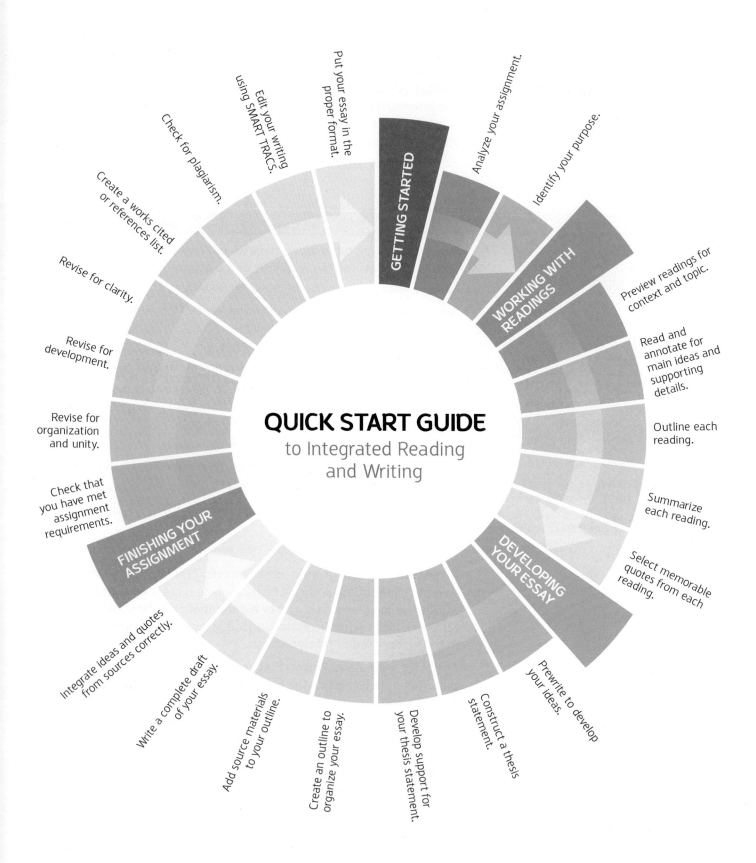

QUICK START GUIDE
to Integrated Reading
and Writing

GETTING STARTED

- Put your essay in the proper format.
- Analyze your assignment.
- Identify your purpose.

WORKING WITH READINGS

- Preview readings for context and topic.
- Read and annotate for main ideas and supporting details.
- Outline each reading.
- Summarize each reading.
- Select memorable quotes from each reading.

DEVELOPING YOUR ESSAY

- Prewrite to develop your ideas.
- Construct a thesis statement.
- Develop support for your thesis statement.
- Create an outline to organize your essay.
- Add source materials to your outline.
- Write a complete draft of your essay.
- Integrate ideas and quotes from sources correctly.

FINISHING YOUR ASSIGNMENT

- Check that you have met assignment requirements.
- Revise for organization and unity.
- Revise for development.
- Revise for clarity.
- Create a works cited or references list.
- Check for plagiarism.
- Edit your writing using SMART TRACS.

PART 1

Planning for Success

1 Critical Thinking Skills
and Success Strategies

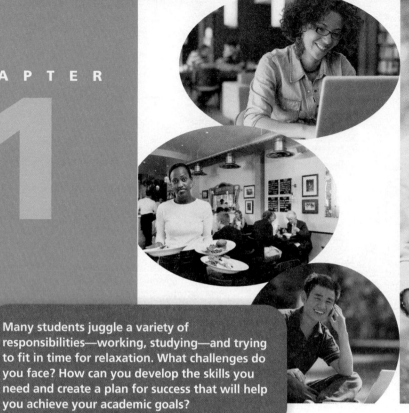

Many students juggle a variety of responsibilities—working, studying—and trying to fit in time for relaxation. What challenges do you face? How can you develop the skills you need and create a plan for success that will help you achieve your academic goals?

Critical Thinking Skills and Success Strategies

What are the two most important skills needed for success in college and at work? Computer literacy? A good attitude? A knack for doing research?

These skills are important, but they are not the *most* important ones. To succeed in college and at work, you must be able to read critically and write clearly. Every college course requires reading, and often your knowledge and abilities are assessed through writing assignments. Additionally, most jobs require employees to read carefully and critically, and many jobs require competent writing ability. In short, your ability to read and write well is a life skill.

The foundation for strong reading and writing skills is the ability to think clearly and critically. As you develop your critical thinking ability, your reading and writing skills will also improve. Picture thinking, reading, and writing as connected skills that continually reinforce one another:

- The more you practice critical thinking, the better you can read critically.
- The more you read critically, the better you can write.

Success in college and at work depends on building and improving these important skills.

CHAPTER OBJECTIVES

After completing this chapter, students will be able to do the following:

- **Explain the importance and interdependence of critical reading and writing skills.**
- **Define and practice critical thinking.**
- **Describe the foundations for college success.**

READING CRITICALLY TO WRITE WELL

Reading critically—that is, reading the way students are expected to read in college—goes beyond basic reading in a number of ways. Reading critically means understanding relationships among the elements in a text. For example, when you read a chapter in a college textbook critically, you must determine which ideas are more important and which ideas are less important. You must also figure out whether ideas are contradictory or similar, and whether they are related. More complex tasks, such as understanding **inferences** (the unstated but suggested ideas in a text), are also part of critical reading. These are only a few of the important reading skills you will develop as you practice reading critically.

Strong writing skills are also necessary for college and career success. Your writing is often the primary way professors get to know you and your work. In a business class, for example, your instructor might come to know you by reading your ideas for improving a failed business. In a nursing class, your instructor might get to know you by reading the annotations you write on a patient's chart. The ability to write well often makes a difference when employees are considered for promotions. More importantly, strong writing reflects clear thinking. Because people get to know us through our writing, clear thinking and competent writing can profoundly affect our lives, choices, and opportunities.

How exactly does reading critically help you write better?

- When you read critically, you no longer see a static page of words: reading becomes a dialogue between you and the writer. Likewise, your own writing becomes a conversation between you and your reader. As a reader, you become aware of the information you need a writer to supply. For example, if a writer does not provide enough background information about a topic, you may feel frustrated.

- As you read critically, you begin to think about your needs as a reader. Thus, as you become more aware of what it takes to communicate with a reader, you write texts that better meet your reader's needs and expectations.

- When you read critically, you develop vocabulary skills. You learn new words and new forms of expression that you can employ later on in your own writing. As your vocabulary develops, your ability to think and write about complex issues increases.

- When you read critically, you learn to distinguish between more effective and less effective writing. You can tell whether writers have successfully made their points—or not. In turn, you become more adept at assessing the effectiveness of your own writing.

> I like the way the writer explains the background information.

> I'm going to explain some background information readers might need to know.

■ Reading critically leads to writing more carefully and competently.

- When you read critically, you discover models for good writing. As you become a more critical reader, you find writing techniques worth emulating in your own writing. For example, after noticing how convincingly a writer has used a comparison to make a point, you may decide to use a comparison in an essay of your own.

■ When you look at the same city from two different perspectives, what insights can you gain?

Learning to read critically takes practice. It helps to set aside regular times to read and to make sure your surroundings are comfortable and free of distractions. Keep reading material with you when you travel so that you can practice reading in spare moments. Remember to ask yourself questions as you read, and if possible, read with a pencil in hand and take notes. Finally, also take the time to read for fun—even magazines, gossip Web sites, and graphic novels.

Like reading, writing is a skill that is developed through practice. Many people think that writing well is a mysterious ability possessed from birth by lucky people like novelists and scholars. Anyone who has struggled to get words down on a page has had days when the words seem barely to drip out. Those same people, however, also experience times when the words seem to pour onto the page without effort. Even the best writers have both types of days. The more time you spend practicing writing, the more comfortable you will get with the ebb and flow of ideas. You will eventually develop a writing process that works—whether you are having a good day or a bad day.

By focusing on texts from the perspectives of both a reader and a writer, we become better thinkers in general. And when we think more critically, we understand and communicate better.

PRACTICE ❶ Predicting Reading and Writing Tasks for Your Future Career

Make a list of five careers you think might be interesting, such as being a national park ranger, a veterinarian, a small business owner, an event planner, or an environmental activist. On a separate sheet of paper, jot down the reading and writing tasks that might be involved in each career. If you cannot identify possible reading and writing tasks, discuss the career with someone in the field. Alternatively, consult the US Bureau of Labor Statistics' *Occupational Outlook Handbook* (available online) to determine the duties involved in each career.

1. _____
2. _____
3. _____
4. _____
5. _____

WHAT IS CRITICAL THINKING?

Critical thinking is the practice of forming and asking key questions about the texts you read and the situations you encounter in life. Critical thinkers go on to answer these key questions in order to form rational judgments and find creative solutions to problems.

One way to understand critical thinking is to consider examples of thinking that are *not* critical. For example, anyone who has children knows that kids do not always think critically, as the following dialogue illustrates:

TIMMY:	Mommy, I want this toy. Why can't I have it?
MOM:	I don't have the money for it.
TIMMY (digging through his mother's purse):	Look! Here's your credit card! You *do* have money, Mommy!

It's easy for adults to chuckle at this scene. Timmy is hopelessly naive about how money works. He assumes that having a credit card means having money. He cannot even think of the right questions—Will we have money to pay the credit card bill? Does the credit card even "work"?—much less ask them.

As adults, however, we can be equally naive. You would be in a situation similar to Timmy's. If you did not know that the amount of random access memory (RAM) in a computer affects the tasks it can accomplish, you would not know to ask about a computer's RAM. Similarly, if you had not figured out the tasks you would be doing on the computer, you could not ask the right questions about the components the computer should have.

An Example of Critical Thinking

While critical thinking sometimes relies on having background knowledge, it also involves being able to predict difficulties, question assumptions, and solve problems. In the workplace, being able to think critically often separates managers from lower-level employees.

Consider this scenario: Monica is a clerk at a rental car agency. It is a busy Friday afternoon, and lines of people are waiting to pick up rental vehicles for weekend travel. Monica's supervisor, Fred, who is the store manager, has to leave suddenly to handle a family emergency. Monica and Jill, another entry-level employee, are the only rental clerks available. They are managing to keep the lines moving and keep customers happy, much to Monica's relief.

A customer whom Monica recognizes—an administrative assistant for the local university's sports program—comes in the door. He greets Monica by name; he has done so much business with the rental agency that he has developed a warm relationship with all the employees. In fact, the agency relies on the university's business to meet its sales goals each month.

He bypasses the line of customers and asks to have a private word with Monica. An unexpected situation has come up, he says, and the basketball team needs three vans immediately. Monica doesn't even have to look at her computer to know that the agency's last three vans have already been reserved by customers who are waiting in line. She checks anyway, and sure enough, the vans are reserved. Pulling Jill aside, she asks her advice. Jill has no idea what to do. Monica texts Fred, but she gets no answer. She calls a nearby agency, but they have no vehicles of any sort available.

What should Monica do? Should she lease the vans to the loyal university customer and turn away the people who already have reservations? Surely, the company would do better financially to retain the university's business than to satisfy three casual customers. But would such an action be fair? What would her boss do, she wonders? What are the things she should consider to make this decision? What Monica needs is the ability to think critically—to weigh all of her options, think creatively about possible solutions, predict the consequences of her actions, and make an informed decision.

Health-care professionals use critical thinking to ask questions that lead them to a correct diagnosis. For example, if a patient presents with seizures, a nurse or physician's assistant might ask him whether he has taken drugs or has a history of neurological disorders. Knowing the right questions to ask requires critical thinking.

This same kind of thinking is required in college courses. Sometimes courses will require you to simply memorize information, a task that does *not* involve thinking critically. Often, however, your instructors will push you to think critically by requiring you to use that information in unpredictable ways. For example, on a math test, you may see problems that are not like the ones you studied and reviewed but whose solutions are possible if you apply the knowledge you have learned. In applying your knowledge to solve these problems, you are thinking critically, the way Monica has to think.

How Critical Thinking Affects Reading and Writing Skills

Just as there is more to running a rental car agency than following a list of instructions for checking out cars, there is more to comprehending a text than merely understanding its literal meaning. Critical reading requires us to ask questions: What does this writer want me to believe? How might this writer benefit if I believe what he has to say? What assumptions is he making? Do I agree with those assumptions?

Good writing also depends on critical thinking. We can teach a computer to construct grammatically correct sentences, but a computer cannot write convincing essays. It cannot analyze its audience, and it cannot analyze its own assumptions. It cannot think of the critical questions that need to be asked. Such questions include much more complex inquiries than simply "How many pages should this essay be?" Effective writers ask a variety of questions that help them focus their writing. For example, a writer might ask herself whether she should use the term *woman* or *lady* in a composition. She might wonder if an audience is likely to respond more positively to one term than the other. Her analysis can help her choose the more appropriate term for her purpose. This kind of critical questioning will help her anticipate readers' responses and consequently become a better writer. Just as Monica's questions can help her determine the right course of action, critical thinking about your writing will help you determine how to word your ideas and communicate your thoughts effectively. Practice your critical thinking skills by completing the exercise that follows.

PRACTICE ② Thinking Critically

The following passage describes a scheduling problem for Lin, a freshman in college. Read the passage, and then use critical thinking to answer the questions on a separate sheet of paper.

Lin lives with his parents and is in his second semester in college. He is considering renting an apartment with his best friend. The apartment is within walking distance from campus, so Lin believes he will save on gasoline and make better use of campus resources if he lives in the apartment. Lin would need to work about twenty-five hours a week to afford the apartment and related expenses. His part-time job offers him only fifteen hours a week, but he plans to ask his supervisor for more hours. He has three weeks to decide whether he wants to rent the apartment or remain at his parents' house.

1. List the questions Lin should ask before making this decision.
2. List the potential problems that could arise if Lin were to rent the apartment with his friend.
3. Which of these potential problems could Lin prevent or overcome?
4. If these problems were to occur, how would they affect Lin?
5. Based on your critical thinking, is this a risk worth taking? Why or why not? What advice would you give Lin? Explain in a paragraph.

THE FOUNDATIONS FOR COLLEGE SUCCESS

Researchers who study the reasons for college success and the obstacles preventing it have identified several characteristics of successful students:

- Students who succeed are self-directed.
- Students who succeed use resources effectively.
- Students who succeed manage their time well.
- Students who succeed are self-reflective.

Students Who Succeed Are Self-Directed

People who are self-directed are in charge of their own learning experiences. They find a way to learn. They do not depend solely on a textbook or on an instructor or on having the perfect learning situation. They do not wait for an instructor's advice to go to a tutoring center. They take the initiative to find the resources they need for success.

Consider, for example, the situation of Jenny, a self-directed learner. She makes sure to buy her textbooks before the semester begins so she is prepared for class, and she reviews her class notebook or folder before each class session. This semester Jenny is taking an algebra class. She begins to realize that every time her instructor discusses multiplying and dividing fractions, she gets lost. As a self-directed learner, Jenny goes to the library, checks out a book on basic mathematics, and reviews the rules for working with fractions. She could also do a quick Internet search for information, visit a learning center, or talk to her instructor.

One way to work on being self-directed is to use a learning journal. A **learning journal** is a place to record your thoughts and goals, any obstacles to those goals, and new insights. By writing down these reflections, you are better able to analyze them. Journaling is a way to think about the things that happen to you, beyond just experiencing them. It is a way to take a step back and view yourself as a learner.

The goal in keeping a learning journal is to reflect on the concepts you are encountering and to learn about yourself. The goal is not to write perfect sentences, so do not be overly concerned with grammar. To start a learning journal, find a dedicated space to keep your writing, such as a spiral notebook or a computer file. Some students use smartphones with digital voice recording to keep track of their thoughts. By periodically reviewing your journal, you will become aware of just how much you are learning.

Students Who Succeed Use Resources Effectively

Resources are the tools that are available to you as you work on a task. To succeed in college, you need to use a variety of tools: your textbooks, the learning labs on campus, your supportive friends and family, computer software, Web sites, and so on. Identifying the correct tools to use for academic tasks requires careful thinking, and it also requires that you know what tools are at hand. Two categories of tools, in particular, can assist your academic journey: human resources and content resources.

Human Resources

Human resources are the people around you who can provide help:

- Your instructors are your best resources. Do not hesitate either to visit your instructors during their office hours or to e-mail them. Instructors welcome their students' questions and office visits.

- Look around your classes to identify peers with whom you might be able to connect. Consider swapping e-mail addresses with one or two classmates so you can discuss assignments or keep up with class notes in case of absences. Of course, always use care about giving your personal information to anyone. A school e-mail address is a fairly safe way to chat with a classmate, but it might *not* be wise to give out your phone number or address.

We learn from tutors in many areas of our lives. Find a tutor with whom you feel comfortable, and develop a working relationship with him or her.

- You can also form study groups to discuss course assignments. Such groups can meet on a regular basis or only when necessary.

- Lab instructors or tutors can also be excellent resources for professional feedback on papers or for help with complex assignments.

- If your school has a writing center, use it. Writing center instructors or tutors are specially trained to help with reading and writing assignments. Do not hesitate to ask a writing center instructor for help with your reading course.

- Additionally, student success counselors and librarians have been trained to help students succeed.

Once you have identified the available human resources, take the next step—use them! Regularly interacting with instructors and others at school who are there to help will make a significant difference to your academic success.

PRACTICE ③ Finding Human Resources

Using school directories, the Internet, and conversations with your instructors and classmates, construct a list of human resources available to you.

Type of Resource	Name	Phone/E-mail	Hours/Location
Instructor			
Classmate			
Librarian			
Tutor			
Lab instructor			
Others			

Content Resources

Textbooks, library reference books, *YouTube* and *TeacherTube* videos, reading comprehension Web sites, online writing labs (OWLs), and search engines are only a few of the content resources that can help you succeed academically. These resources can often help you with questions you have about coursework and careers. Librarians can help you locate a wealth of valuable content resources. In addition, textbooks on writing and carefully chosen Internet sites can be useful.

When choosing Internet content resources, be careful. Some Web sites that appear at first to be helpful are actually commercial sites that exist to sell educational products— or plagiarized essays. Use these principles to guide your search for credible Internet study resources:

- **Check to see whether the Web site is associated with a college or university.** Usually, *.edu* in a Web address tells you the source is housed at a college or university. Often instructors post helpful study information on their personal college Web pages. Be aware, though, that student Web sites may also have an *.edu* address; these sites are less likely to provide credible resources than instructor-created Web pages.

- **Use the online resources that are available from your textbook publisher.** Many publishers make available study resources on the Internet free of charge. For example, if you search for "sentence fragments" and "McGraw-Hill" (the publisher of this textbook), you will find a variety of Web resources, such as tutorials, *PowerPoint* slides, and practice quizzes.

> Purdue OWL: **Sentence Fragments**
> owl.english.purdue.edu › OWL › General Writing › Mechanics ▾
> Feb 21, 2013 - This handout provides an overview and examples of
> **sentence fragments**.
>
> **Sentence Fragments** - Guide to Grammar and Writing
> grammar.ccc.commnet.edu/grammar/fragments.htm ▾
> **Sentence Fragments**: How to Find and Repair them.

■ A search on *Google* for "sentence fragments" brings up a long list of sites. The information in the Web addresses can help you identify credible and potentially helpful Web sites.

PRACTICE ④ Finding Online Resources

Using a computer search engine such as *Google* or *Yahoo,* find a Web site that provides the particular type of information listed for each item.

Information Needed	Web Site You Found	Features of Web Site
For a psychology class: help understanding a reference to "Pavlov's dogs"		
For a geology class: help understanding how the Richter scale works		
For a health careers class: practice quizzes to help you learn medical terminology		
For a math class: a video that reviews exponents		

- **When you open a Web site, click on a few items to see how thoroughly the information is covered.** For example, students post questions to social media sites, but the answers are often not very helpful, as you will see when you read the postings. Look for Web sites that do not allow users to post their own answers to questions.

Students Who Succeed Manage Their Time Well

Time management is a necessity in almost every area of life. Good time management starts with assessing your time commitments honestly and carefully. Logging your commitments on a calendar—whether on paper, on a computer, or on your smartphone—is one way to realistically view what you need to get done. There are a variety of ways to sync online calendars to smartphones. Use technology to help you when possible, but make sure that you manage your electronic devices and that they do not manage you:

- Turn off your phone when you study.
- Use your phone's alarm and calendar to keep track of due dates.
- Reward yourself with *Facebook* and other social media *after* you have finished your course work for the day.

To make a time management system, use a simple chart that lists the days of the week and the hours of each day. Input your commitments, and schedule your study time.

Time	Sun.	Mon.	Tues.	Wed.	Thurs.	Fri.	Sat.
6 a.m.							
7							
8							
9							
10							
11							
Noon							
1 p.m.							
2							
3							
4							
5							
6							
7							
8							
9							
10							

Dana's Time Management Plan

KEY
Class
Family
Lab/study time
Study time
Work

Be sure to leave some hours open for flexibility. Also, be aware of your habits and preferences. If you are not a "morning person," do not schedule study time before morning classes. For example, see Dana's Time Management Plan above, which was created by a student who works part-time and cares for other family members.

Another way to make sure you have time for everything in your life is to predict the circumstances that will affect your time and inhibit your success. For example, commitments to family and employers can unexpectedly interfere with your best intentions to study. By predicting these situations, you can find ways to deal with them. One way to make sure you have uninterrupted study time is to be intentional about constructing a plan that allows time for each aspect of your life, and then stick to your plan. Make others aware of your plan so they can help you follow it.

Making small changes can be a good strategy for improving time management. You may not be able to spend three hours each day studying, but you may be able to find an hour in the morning and an hour at night. Similarly, if you have downtime during your day—for example, waiting in line or commuting to work on public transportation—use it to read and work on assignments. Keep energy bars, earplugs, and any other helpful items in your backpack so that you can make the most of your time. Planning ahead and using your time wisely can result in major benefits.

PRACTICE 5 Creating a Time Management Plan

Follow these directions to create a time management plan.

1. On a separate sheet of paper, list small changes that will help you be a successful student.

(Continued)

2. Choose two or three of these changes, and come up with an action plan to implement them. Some examples are waking up earlier, studying during a certain time period every day, packing a lunch for the day, and avoiding procrastination.

3. Fill in the chart with the changes you selected and how you will make them.

Small Change	How I Will Make This Change

Students Who Succeed Are Self-Reflective

Reflecting is simply taking time to think about something in order to understand it or learn from it. *Self-reflection* is looking at your behaviors and feelings from the outside so that you can see yourself more objectively.

We can all think of someone—perhaps an acquaintance, a friend, or even a family member—who makes the same mistakes repeatedly. Perhaps this person is always late or cannot maintain a relationship. It is easy to see the person's faults, and most likely, we can see what causes his failures. But it is much more difficult for us to view ourselves as objectively. Self-reflection is an attempt to do just that.

To practice self-reflection, imagine yourself floating to the top of a room and looking down at yourself, noting the things you are saying and doing. The goal is to be able to see yourself as others see you. Think about yourself as a student. Which of your behaviors sabotage your success? Which behaviors work for you? Self-reflective analysis will help you view your strengths and weaknesses more objectively so you can become the kind of learner and person you want to be.

Writing a Self-Reflective Analysis

One way to become a successful learner is to use self-reflection to assess your strengths and weaknesses. Below is a list of questions that one student, Monty, used as a guide in writing a self-reflective analysis.

QUESTIONS FOR SELF-REFLECTION

1. How would you describe your personality?
2. Think of three previous instructors you have had. How might each instructor describe you as a learner?
3. When you reflect on yourself as a learner, do you find yourself agreeing with your former teachers' descriptions? If not, what would you say these teachers did not know about you?
4. How would you describe yourself—at your best—as a student?
5. At your worst, what kind of student are you?
6. How would you finish the following sentence? "[Your name] will be very successful in college and in life if [she/he] . . ."

What follows is the self-reflective analysis written by Monty in response to these questions. Notice how most of Monty's analysis is written in third person. Instead of saying "I" or "me," he writes from the perspective of another person so that he can see himself more objectively.

According to Plato, the ancient Greek philosopher Socrates said that "the unexamined life is not worth living." What do you think Socrates meant?

Monty's Self-Reflection

1. Monty is a really nice guy. He is easy to get along with and funny sometimes, and he will offer help to anyone who needs it. He has never been afraid of hard work, although he likes to be lazy on the weekends. He is a great Web page designer, a good driver, and a pretty good cook.

2. Previous teachers might describe Monty like this:

   - "He is shy when it comes to answering questions in class or even asking questions. He is not shy about cracking a joke and can make us laugh sometimes."

   - "He is an average student, but he does not always turn in his work on time. I know he could make higher grades if he took more interest in the subject and turned work in on time."

   - "I like Monty but wish he would take school more seriously."

3. I would agree with most of the teachers' statements, but I would disagree about not being interested in the subject. I am usually interested but just do not have the confidence to speak up in class, or maybe I just have not done all the reading, so I do not feel very sure of myself. I do not want to be asked questions. The last teacher's comment is right: I could take school more seriously.

4. At best, Monty is a great student. He does the reading for class, gets to every class on time, listens to everything the teacher says, and does not cut up in class too much.

5. At worst, Monty can almost be depressed. He can oversleep and stay in bed too long, put off doing his homework assignments, and feel as if school does not matter.

6. Monty will be very successful in college and in life if he takes school seriously and does the things he knows he should do—study, wake up on time, be in class, and maybe ask questions or make comments in class on occasion. He will also be more successful if he limits his time creating Web pages, his favorite hobby.

Complete the following exercise about Monty's self-reflective analysis. Then use Monty's questions to write your own analysis.

PRACTICE ⑥ Writing a Self-Reflective Analysis

Write a self-reflective analysis about yourself as a student, using Monty's analysis as a guide.

1. To begin, answer the following questions about Monty's analysis.

   a. Which strengths does Monty identify about himself?

   b. Which weaknesses does Monty identify about himself?

   c. Does Monty's self-reflection seem believable? In other words, does it seem as though he is being truly honest about his strengths and weaknesses? Why or why not?

   d. What can Monty learn from his self-reflection? What would be the best insights he could gain from it?

2. Now, using Monty's self-reflection as a model, compose your own. Use the same questions and instructions Monty used to compose his analysis.

CHAPTER ACTIVITIES

A READING AND WRITING ASSIGNMENT

The critical thinking, reading, and writing skills we discuss in this text not only apply to college success but also affect workplace success. What follows is an article entitled "Employability Skills: Your Trump Card." As you read the article, underline at least three important pieces of advice that you will use to prepare for a future career. A writing assignment follows the article.

Employability Skills: Your Trump Card

Two guys—let's call them Ace and Joker—have associate's degrees from the same community college. They have obtained basically the same level of academic knowledge and the same technical skills. They both held jobs while in high school and in college. Yet Ace is a much more attractive job candidate to managers who are recruiting workers. Why?

Everyone would agree that having basic knowledge and stock technical abilities is essential for career readiness. However, in addition to academic and technical competencies, a third category of abilities is critical for career readiness: employability skills.

Employability skills, sometimes called *work-readiness* or *job-readiness skills,* are a set of competencies and behaviors that are necessary for *every* type of job. Acquiring them *and* being able to demonstrate to prospective employers that you possess them are crucial to employment success.

Foundational Skills

Being a good employee depends on some very basic, foundational skills. While these qualities may seem too obvious to be highlighted, employers express frustration at how few workers possess them.

Joker pads his time sheet by adding a half-hour here and fifteen minutes there. Ace is totally honest about the hours that he works.

Honesty and trustworthiness are indispensable qualities in the workplace. If an employer cannot trust a worker, every aspect of the work environment becomes overly complicated.

Ace shows up for work on time every single day. Joker comes in on time some days but straggles in a few minutes late about as often. Ace finishes his assignments on time; Joker frequently has excuses about why he was unable to get an assigned project completed by the deadline.

Dependability is vital. Employees need to show up on time every day (unless they have a valid excuse). Completing every task is another dimension of dependability. A staff member who completes tasks as assigned, without prompting and by the deadline, is a very valuable employee.

When Ace goofs up, he admits it; when he borrows an idea from coworkers, he gives them credit. Joker, on the other hand, frequently tries to blame others when things go wrong, and he regularly takes credit for the insights and accomplishments of others.

Employers greatly appreciate staff members who take responsibility for their own decisions and actions. If you make a mistake, own it. If someone else came up with a worthwhile idea, give credit where credit is due.

Ace is aware of the benefits of his job, and he remembers all too well the frustration and discouragement he felt when he was unemployed. Joker, on the other hand, seems to consistently see only the negative side of his job.

Having a positive attitude toward work is a wonderful characteristic. You don't have to "whistle while you work," but being upbeat matters. Nobody relishes working with a grumbler; coworkers and supervisors alike appreciate someone with a can-do attitude.

Joker catches on to new tasks quickly, but he often tires of doing the work and fails to complete assignments. If Joker is the hare, Ace is the tortoise. He sees every project through to the end.

Workers need to exert high levels of effort and persistence. Working hard and keeping at it will not only enable you to accomplish more, but your persistence will be noticed by colleagues and superiors. To some employers, a college degree is more important as evidence of perseverance than of knowledge.

Whenever an unexpected crisis occurs, Joker freaks out and has a hard time recovering. Ace, however, rolls with the punches; he is able to adjust on the fly.

Flexibility is highly valued by employers. Many of us like routine; however, in every work environment, unanticipated events occur, often upsetting the regular order of affairs. Workers who can adapt to changing situations are especially valuable.

Ace "looks the part." He comes to work dressed and groomed appropriately. Joker, conversely, will often show up for work looking disheveled, lacking some part of his uniform, and generally resembling a slob.

Understanding and following the dress code or uniform guidelines should be a given in every work context. Employees must always be presentable and pay attention to personal hygiene.

Interpersonal Skills

In most work environments, there are three groups with whom a person interacts: customers or clients, coworkers or colleagues, and managers or supervisors. Relating well to all three groups is vital for success in the workplace.

Many of Joker's customers view him as a jerk. Ace's goal, on the other hand, is to help all his customers feel better about their day after their encounter with him.

Anyone who works with customers must be friendly and polite and must respond appropriately to their requests. Although it is not always the case that "the customer is always right," that assumption is an excellent beginning point in dealing with customers.

Everybody likes a team player, and that is how Ace's colleagues characterize him. Joker's associates, in contrast, comment about how they often have to do his part of an assignment.

Good employees respect and work well with coworkers, even those they do not like. It's crucial to be compatible enough with everyone in the workplace to make a successful team. Consider basketball as an analogy. Although it would be great if the players on a team liked one another, it is not really necessary. As long as they communicate with one another and each player performs his or her role, they can be successful as a team.

Joker always seems to be in conflict with his supervisor. Different jobs, different managers—it doesn't seem to matter; there's always tension between Joker and his boss.

The manner in which employees relate to their supervisors is absolutely critical to job success. Employees must treat their supervisors with respect, despite their personal feelings toward them. As an employee, you must respect the *role* even if you do not respect the *individual.*

If Ace's boss tells him that he could do better work, Ace views it as a "gift" from his supervisor. Ace wants to be better at what he does, so he appreciates guidance in that regard—even if he doesn't necessarily enjoy being corrected.

Effective employees take constructive criticism to heart and consider it carefully. No one enjoys being criticized, but effective employees understand that their supervisors offer criticism to guide, not to insult. Good workers don't reflexively reject criticism. Rather, they use it to gain insight and improve their performance on the job.

Whether relating to customers, coworkers, or supervisors, employees inevitably encounter conflict at work. Being able to resolve conflict successfully is a very important interpersonal skill. The successful resolution of conflict lies between two extremes. One extreme is to react to a clash defensively and aggressively. The other extreme is to respond by withdrawing and acting as though no issue exists. Neither of those reactions is productive. If conflict is respectful, honest, sincere, and kind, then it isn't confrontational at all—and it can be very fruitful!

Problem-Solving Skills

Every job involves problem solving: How can we produce our goods or provide our services faster, better, more efficiently? How do we address the roadblocks that inevitably arise? It's not surprising that problem-solving skills routinely rank at the top of the list of desirable traits for prospective staff members. Problem solving involves both critical thinking and creative thinking.

When Joker sees a problem at work, he criticizes his supervisors for not having solved it. On the rare occasions when Joker has a suggestion, he throws out an idea without having thought it through. He skips steps—he tends to go from A to C without explaining how to get there, and then he is unhappy when no one thinks his plan is worthwhile. Ace constructs a plan with his audience in mind—whether that is customers or his boss or someone else. He realizes that they cannot fill in unexplained gaps.

Critical thinking involves recognizing and clarifying a problem. What issue, precisely, is it that needs to be addressed? Identifying possible solutions and then ranking them in terms of preferability is a next step. Constructing a step-by-step explanation as to how the approach selected would be implemented is the final stage. (You can see how courses in math and science provide students with training in critical thinking;

although the particular issues in a job setting may not be algebra problems or chemistry experiments, the *method* learned in these academic courses can be applied in a multiplicity of situations.)

> *Joker never seems to come up with any fresh ideas. He offers the same, tired approaches even when they have not worked in the past or when new issues arise on the job. Ace, in contrast, thinks creatively.*

While critical thinking emphasizes the rigorous, analytical type of thinking that we associate with math and science, creative thinking is just as important. Innovative thinking is highly valued in most work environments. Just as the relationship between critical thinking and courses in math and science is clear, so too is the parallel between creative thinking and "artistic" academic courses. Courses in the visual and performing arts—drama, music, art, dance—provide examples of how artists conceive new and imaginative creations. Moreover, academic study in areas less commonly thought of as creative can be very helpful as well. Engineering, marketing, and education courses—to name a few—promote innovative thinking, too.

Conclusion

The skills described here are the attributes that workforce managers repeatedly indicate they desire in their employees. People who are looking for employment opportunities—or better jobs than they currently hold—must possess both employability skills and specific job skills. Additionally, when applying for a job, people need to convey their employability skills in the application process. Employability skills can be added to a résumé, discussed in an interview, or demonstrated while networking. Perhaps most importantly, a person who demonstrates these employability skills in every aspect of his life will impress potential employers as unique.

Who would not want to hire Ace?

Questions for Consideration

1. What are employability skills? Write two to three sentences defining them.
2. How do employability skills differ from academic and technical skills?
3. Read through the section describing the foundational skills employees should have. In what other contexts are these skills important? Explain.
4. On the left side of a sheet of paper, list all the employability skills discussed in the article. Next to each skill, write a sentence explaining whether you possess the skill, are working on acquiring the skill, or have not developed the skill yet. How would an employer view your abilities as a potential employee on the basis of the list you created? Which of these skills do you plan to work on developing? Explain in a paragraph.

Responding to the Reading

1. Reread Monty's self-reflection. Compare his strengths and weaknesses to the employability skills discussed in "Employability Skills: Your Trump Card." If Monty had to choose two areas to work on immediately, which two should they be? Write

two or three paragraphs defending your answer. Use the Quick Start Guide to Integrated Reading and Writing Assignments for guidance.

2. Choose three employability skills that you need to develop more fully. Write a paragraph about each skill in which you do the following:
   - Explain why you believe you need to develop the skill.
   - Provide an example of a time when you would have been more successful if you had possessed the skill.
   - Finish the paragraph with ideas for how you can develop the missing skill.

3. Using the "Employability Skills" article for ideas, write an essay in which you identify the top five employability skills required for a job in which you are interested. Explain why each skill is important for the job you choose. For example, if you would like to be a nurse, you might discuss the importance of problem solving.

⊙ THINKING FROM AN INSTRUCTOR'S POINT OF VIEW

Instructors know they are preparing students not only for academic success but also for proficiency in the workplace. Consequently, most instructors expect workplace behaviors from their students. The behaviors employers expect from workers include the following:

- Arrive on time to work and stay until the shift is finished.
- Listen carefully to directions.
- Do the work correctly.
- Stay focused and productive (no personal calls, texts to friends, or excessive conversing with coworkers).
- Use a respectful tone and respectful language.

You can probably think of several other behaviors that employers expect. Now, try thinking from an instructor's point of view. You are responsible for teaching your students the course content, but you also want to prepare them for workplace success. Additionally, you want your students to use behaviors that will help them succeed in college.

If you were an instructor, what kinds of policies would you create to make sure your students' behaviors contributed to their learning and to their future workplace success? Answer in three or four paragraphs, explaining how each of your ideas would contribute to success in college and at work.

⊙ ADDITIONAL ASSIGNMENTS

1. Think of a job or a class you had in the past in which discipline and behavior were not good. What was the problem? What could your employer or instructor have done differently to make student or worker behaviors more acceptable? Write two or three paragraphs to explain.

2. Think of a time when you made a decision without thinking critically about it. Perhaps you told a lie to a person you loved or bought something expensive on an impulse. What decision did you make? What process did you use to make the decision? Why do you think you made the decision without thinking critically? What steps should you have taken to make a better, more-informed decision? Write two or three paragraphs to explain.

3. If you made a time management chart in response to Practice 5, exchange charts with a classmate. Ask your classmate questions that might help her think critically about her time planning. For example, if you notice she has scheduled a study

session from 5:00 a.m. to 6:00 a.m., you might ask her if such an early hour is reasonable for her. (Some people could not consistently wake up that early, while others are naturally early risers.) Find potential areas of time conflict, and ask her about them. Have your classmate do the same for you. Revise your time management chart as needed.

4. Earlier in this chapter, you read about four characteristics that make students successful. Here is a restatement of the list:

   - Students who succeed are self-directed.
   - Students who succeed use resources effectively.
   - Students who succeed manage their time well.
   - Students who succeed are self-reflective.

   For each of these four characteristics, write a brief paragraph in which you do the following:

   a. Explain what the characteristic means. For example, what does it mean to be self-directed?
   b. Make a judgment about yourself regarding the characteristic. To what extent are you self-directed?
   c. Provide an example of a time you exhibited the characteristic. When were you self-directed?
   d. Finally, describe one way you plan to exhibit the characteristic this semester. For example, you might say that this semester, if you receive a failing grade on an assignment (or a grade you do not like), you will figure out why you received the grade and will make a plan to do better on the next assignment.

EMOTIONAL INTELLIGENCE

We all have good moods and bad moods. People who are "emotionally intelligent" can explain their moods and the likely reasons for them. They can do something else, as well: they can find ways to regulate their moods when doing so is desirable. Psychologists suggest that people who can control their moods have much better relationships and are happier and more successful than people who cannot. Have you ever intentionally *controlled* a mood? For example, perhaps you went to work one day feeling irritated and snapped at your coworkers. Realizing the effects of your mood on others, you decided to breathe deeply, relax, and say only kind things the rest of the day. If you have managed to control a mood, what methods worked for you? What might have happened if you had not taken control of your mood? Explain in a paragraph.

CULTURAL LITERACY

A culture consists of the behaviors, expectations, customs, and rules (both written and unwritten) of a group of people. Schools have their own cultures. Think about your school. What are some ways students are expected to act? What are some unwritten rules and behaviors on campus? Here are some examples, comparing high school to college:

- In college, students take out their class materials without being instructed to do so by the professor.
- Most college students act more politely in class than many high school students do.

Make a list of at least five behaviors, expectations, customs, or rules you have found in the culture of your school.

CRITICAL THINKING

Attending college is an experience that many students will find new and challenging. Nevertheless, college is in some ways similar to each of the situations below—although some of the comparisons are better than others. Think about each of the following comparisons. Which is most likely to help you succeed in college? Why?

- Going to college is like going to high school.
- Going to college is like going to a job.
- Going to college is like going to a new country.
- Going to college is like going to a doctor.

Write a few sentences explaining your answer.

METACOGNITION

Think about a high school class that you found very difficult. Imagine that you can watch a video of how you behaved (studied, attended, listened, questioned, spoke, read, and so on) during that class. What would the video show you doing? Describe the video in a paragraph. What insight can you gain by looking at yourself *from outside*?

PART 2

Reading and Writing as Integrated Processes

One way to learn new skills and techniques is to emulate the skills and techniques of experts. What skills—physical or mental—have you practiced or even perfected by observing other people at work?

Annotating Texts and Developing Vocabulary

The writer Stephen King has said, "If you don't have time to read, you don't have the time (or the tools) to write. Simple as that." What King means is that to become a good writer, you have to read. And the more you read, the better you can write.

Why does reading play such a significant role in writing ability? Reading and writing processes are two sides of the same coin. When we read actively and critically, paying close attention to the text, we cannot help but learn how writing works.

To help with paying close attention, we can use annotation—making notes on a text. In addition, we can use strategies to develop our vocabulary. These two techniques—learning to annotate and building vocabulary—are foundational for becoming both a better reader and a better writer.

CHAPTER OBJECTIVES

After completing this chapter, students will be able to do the following:

- **Use reading to improve their writing.**

- **Annotate a text for its content and features.**

- **Determine the meanings of words and build vocabulary.**

USING READING TO IMPROVE WRITING

Whether we are reading for analysis or for pleasure, reading has an effect on our writing ability through unintentional and intentional emulation. *Emulation* means doing the same thing as someone else. A high school basketball player, for example, may emulate the moves of his favorite NBA star.

Unintentional Emulation

When you read, you begin to understand on an unconscious level how language works. Have you ever started using a word you learned from a friend?

If so, you probably did not make an intentional decision to use that word; the word just began to appear in your vocabulary. Although you are not consciously aware of it, your brain records information such as words and phrases. (Think about all the clichés you have learned unintentionally—for example, *seeing eye to eye, easy as pie, love is blind.*)

Our brain also records information about the features of texts we read. For example, if we read several texts that begin with questions, we sometimes find ourselves writing a text that starts with a question. This process is called **unintentional emulation.** People who read frequently often write well because they have a wealth of information to draw on from unintentional emulation.

Intentional Emulation

We can also use our reading to study texts purposefully and use them to become better writers. This method is **intentional emulation.** It involves carefully analyzing the techniques writers use to communicate effectively. Once we analyze the techniques, we can then practice using them in our own writing. The purpose of intentional emulation is to develop a toolbox of writing strategies we can use as we compose our own texts.

Imagine you are taking a business communications class. Your instructor asks you to read and analyze a memo, which you will then use as a model for a writing assignment. In the memo, a company is recalling an unsafe product. To use the memo as a model, you would start by noticing its key features and the kinds of information it includes.

Recall Notice	Title
Industrial Food Products, Inc.	Company name
January 16, 2014	Date
Name of product: Industrial Honey Mustard, 12-oz. plastic bottles	Name of product and important descriptive information
Hazard: The sealing mechanism on certain bottles of mustard did not work properly, posing a risk of contaminated product.	Reason for recall
Remedy: Consumers should immediately stop using Industrial Honey Mustard if purchased in 12-oz. plastic bottles between June 15, 2013, and January 16, 2014. Consumers may obtain a full refund by returning the product to the place of purchase or by contacting Industrial Food Products.	What consumers should do
Consumer Contact: Industrial Food Products, 11114 Ellison Blvd., Hannington, IL 56565. Toll-free number: (800) 555-0199 from 8 a.m. to 5 p.m. CST, Monday through Friday.	Contact information

Vocabulary Collection Word:
mechanism

Your in-context definition:

_____

_____

A dictionary definition:

_____

_____

Try your hand at intentional emulation by completing the following practice exercise.

PRACTICE Using Intentional Emulation

Imagine your company, Eft Toy Company, has created an unsafe product, the Tough and Ready Tool Belt. The belt has small parts that can come off and pose a choking hazard to young children. The toy was sold at Aim retail stores between June 13, 2013, and October 15, 2013.

Using the model from Industrial Food Products, write a memo issuing a product recall notice for Eft Toy Company, 14500 Nelson Dr., Winnipeg, LA 87777, phone 800-555-0199, hours 8 a.m. to 5 p.m. CST, Monday through Friday.

DEVELOPING ANNOTATION SKILLS

Like most people, you read for a variety of reasons: to find an answer, to study, to learn, to relax, and to be entertained. Developing your reading and writing skills for college requires you to go a step beyond casual reading: it requires you to practice reading critically. Reading critically is reading to determine not only *what* writers are saying but also *how* they communicate their messages.

One way to start reading critically is to begin annotating. **Annotation** is reading a text and marking points that are important and items about which you have questions. Most students have experience highlighting words or phrases. While this is one way to annotate, it is not the only way or even the best way. Annotating is a way of reading actively. When you read actively, or critically, you are engaged in a conversation with the writer. Think of annotation as a way to deepen that conversation.

Annotation Tips

Many of the annotation tips shown here require that you write in your books. You may not be comfortable writing in books because you have always been told that marking books ruins them (true for a library book!), but writing in your books is one of the best ways to make sure that you're getting the most out of the time you spend reading.

Tips for Annotating Readings	
Mark new information	Mark only information that is new to you. If you already know something, there's no need to mark it.
Use highlighters sparingly	If the page is covered with yellow by the time you're done reading, the important information won't stand out. Only about 20 percent of a page should be annotated, and even less than that should be highlighted.
Focus on vocabulary	Save the yellow highlighter for definitions. That will make them really stand out. Circle words you do not know. Look them up and write the definition in the margins.
Use different colors	Use different colored pens for different types of information. For example, underline the main idea of a paragraph in red and write "main idea" in the margin. Use a blue pen to write your questions in the margins.

(continued)

Tips for Annotating Readings *(continued)*	
Talk to the text	Ask the writer questions: "Why true?" "Always the case?" Note when you agree or disagree with the text. Make connections between different parts of a text: "Said something different on p. 50." Make connections between the text and your experience: "Just like M's habits."
Make comparisons	Start a dialogue between the text you are marking and others you have read. Do the authors agree with one another? Make shorthand notes in the margins about other writers' views: "Smith disagrees; says air pollution is only getting worse."
Develop a system of codes	Use a question mark for something you aren't sure about, an exclamation point for something you find particularly interesting, and a star next to the main idea.
Use sticky notes	Write a word or two on a sticky note so you can quickly find the important information you have flagged: "Stats about pollution." Use these sticky notes sparingly, like a highlighter. Too many notes make it hard to identify what is important.
Summarize	When you're finished reading, put the main ideas in your own words. Summarizing is an excellent way to make sure you've understood what the reading is about.

Think about how convenient it would be to have the writers of the texts we read sit next to us during the reading process. We could ask a variety of questions, such as these:

- What did you mean by that phrase?
- How do you know this information?
- Why did you choose to include an example in this spot but not in this spot?
- Is this story true?
- Would you please define that term for me?

These are the kinds of questions it is valuable to think about and note in the margins of the texts you read. By "voicing" your questions in annotations, you become more aware of needing answers to those questions; consequently, you will be more likely to look for possible answers as you continue reading. Marking significant features or content in a text will also help you remember those items.

PRACTICE ② Assessing the Value of Annotations

Look at each example of annotation below, and determine whether the annotation is likely or unlikely to be useful to you as you learn the material. Explain your reasoning.

1. Is this annotation useful? Explain why or why not. _____

_____

The amygdala is the part of the brain responsible for processing and regulating emotions and for storing and retrieving memories. Part of the limbic system, the amygdala is located deep within the two hemispheres of the brain. It is a small, almond-shaped mass of tissue.

Isn't the limbic system related to nerves? (go back and check)

(continued)

2. Is this highlighting useful? Explain why or why not. _____

_____

The amygdala is the part of the brain responsible for
processing and regulating emotions and for storing
and retrieving memories. Part of the limbic system, the
amygdala is located deep within the two hemispheres
of the brain. It is a small, almond-shaped mass of tissue.

Vocabulary Collection Word:
hemisphere

Your in-context definition:

_____

3. Is this annotation useful? Explain why or why not. _____

_____

A dictionary definition:

_____

The amygdala is the part of the brain responsible for
processing and regulating emotions and for storing
and retrieving memories. Part of the limbic system, the
amygdala is located deep within the two hemispheres
of the brain. It is a small, almond-shaped mass of tissue.

Amygdala
1. regulates emotions
2. retrieves memories

4. Is this annotation useful? Explain why or why not.

_____

The amygdala is the part of the brain responsible for
processing and regulating emotions and for storing
and retrieving memories. Part of the limbic system, the
amygdala is located deep within the two hemispheres
of the brain. It is a small, almond-shaped mass of tissue.

DEF:
Amygdala: part of
brain, processes
emotions/memories/
almond shaped/deep
inside 2 hemispheres

Annotating a Text's Content

Annotations that concern the **content** of a text are about the ideas the writer presents.
Your primary responsibility as a reader is to understand the content of the text. It is usually a good idea to start the reading process with these questions in mind:

- What is this text about? (What is the topic?)
- What is the writer's main point?

As you think about the topic and the writer's point, you may also wonder *why*
the topic is important or *how* the content of the text relates to you. When you are
reading for a particular assignment, you will probably also wonder which parts of the
reading are more important than others. These are additional content questions to
keep in mind as you read. When you find an answer to such a question, jot down an
annotation.

Content annotations concern anything in the text that helps you understand its meaning. For example, if the first paragraph defines a term, make a note of the definition in the margin. You will probably need to know that term as you read through the text. If you find an idea later in the text that you believe is important, make an annotation by jotting down "impt. idea" or putting a star in the margin. If a part of the reading is confusing, jot down a question mark or simply note "confusing." Later you can reread the confusing sections and see if they make more sense or ask for help in understanding them. These kinds of content annotations will help you better understand and remember the text.

The following example shows how Zoe, a student, annotated a textbook passage for content. The passage is from *Foundations of Parasitology*, 9th edition, by Larry Roberts, John Janovy, Jr., and Steve Nadler.

Parasitology is largely a study of symbiosis, or, literally, "living together." Although some authors restrict the term symbiosis to relationships wherein both partners benefit, we prefer to use the term in a wider sense, as originally proposed by the German scholar A. de Bary in 1879: Any two organisms living in close association, commonly one living in or on the body of the other, are symbiotic, as contrasted with free living. Usually the symbionts are of different species but not necessarily.

Symbiotic relationships can be characterized further by specifying the nature of the interactions between the participants. It is always a somewhat arbitrary act, of course, for people to assign definitions to relationships between organisms. But animal species participate in a wide variety of symbiotic relationships, so parasitologists have a need to communicate about these interactions and thus have coined a number of terms to describe them.

Margin annotations:

DEF *parasitology* (like parasites)
DEF: symbiosis (a relationship where both parties get something/depend on the other)
A. de Bary (1879) (gave def.)

Def: symbionts—the organisms in the symbiotic relationship
Parasitology: study of symbiotic relationship (betw 2 symbionts)

Huh? the nature of the interactions?
What does this mean?

(random)

Animals (organisms) have parasitic (symbiotic) relationships with other animals (organisms).

Zoe annotated definitions, made note of a question she had, and summarized her understanding of the passage. Notice how she reserved yellow highlighting only for definitions. She used green highlighting for material that she did not fully understand. Developing a simple system will help ensure that your annotations make sense to you when you go back to review them later.

Annotating a Text's Features

Annotating a text's features makes you more aware of the choices a writer has made to communicate her message. This awareness of writing features, in turn, can open up a world of possibilities for your own writing.

Writers make choices about the ways they communicate their messages to particular audiences. They may use **analogies** (comparisons), **anecdotes** (stories), **rhetorical questions** (questions for which the writer provides an answer or for which the answer is obvious), and other techniques to communicate their points. The chart Common Text Features presents some of the features often used by writers. Don't worry if you do not know what all of these are. As you learn more about the features of texts, you will feel more comfortable finding these features and using these terms.

Common Text Features	
Main ideas	**Thesis statement:** The main idea of an essay. **Topic sentence:** The main idea of a paragraph.
Organizing strategies	**Conclusion:** One or more paragraphs at the end of an essay that bring the essay to a close. **Introduction:** One or more paragraphs at the beginning of an essay that introduce the topic and create interest in the reader. **Sequence of information:** Use of time, space, and level of importance to organize information.
Details and text patterns	**Analogy:** An example that explains something unfamiliar by comparing it with something more familiar. **Anecdote:** A brief story that illustrates a specific point. **Cause and effect:** How one circumstance brought about or resulted from another. **Comparison and contrast:** How one item or event is similar to or different from another. **Concrete example:** Specific information that helps the reader understand the writer's point. **Definition:** An explanation of the meaning of a word or concept. **Explanation:** A description of how something is constructed, how a task is performed, or how something works. **Hypothetical example:** An example that asks the reader to imagine something that is not currently true. **Use of sources:** Citing experts so the reader knows where the information is coming from and can evaluate its validity.
Language features	**Questions:** Use of questions to focus readers' attention or engage their emotions. **Repetition:** Use of a word or a phrase several times for emphasis. **Rhetorical question:** A question that the writer asks to make a point but does not expect the reader to answer. The answer may be provided in the text, or it may be self-evident. **Sentence variety:** Use of sentences of different lengths and types to create interest. **Tone:** Use of specific language to convey the emotion the author feels or wants the reader to feel. **Transition:** A word, phrase, or sentence that moves the reader from one idea to another, such as *first, next,* and *after that.* **Wit, sarcasm:** Use of humor to get the point across. Sarcasm is a kind of humor that relies on saying one thing and meaning the opposite.

Annotating features means looking not so much at *what the text says* but at *how the writer writes.* The more you learn about the strategies writers use to convey their ideas in texts, the more you will find to annotate. The passage that follows, called "Why I Am a Vegan," presents one of the major supporting reasons the author decided to change her diet. This passage has been annotated in different colors to point out the text features. (Your annotations as a student should look more like the sample annotations shown earlier in the chapter—and you might not annotate every feature indicated in this example. The color annotations shown here are used throughout the text to demonstrate important points in the examples.)

Why I Am a Vegan

I did not begin my life as a vegan. Like many other children, I dutifully drank the creamy white milk my mother poured for me at breakfast. Rarely did my family not have a

Introduction paragraph

Detail: example of childhood eating habits

(continued)

Using Word Parts

One way to increase your vocabulary is to learn the meanings of individual word parts. You already know many word parts. For example, *-ology* is an ending with which you are familiar. Considering words like *astrology*, *geology*, and *biology*, what do you think *-ology* means? (Check a dictionary to see if you are correct!) You will be surprised at how many word parts you already know. If you memorize the word parts in the Common Prefixes, Common Suffixes, and Common Roots charts, you will be well equipped to figure out the meanings of many of the new words you encounter.

Prefixes and **suffixes** are syllables that can be added to a word to change its meaning; prefixes and suffixes cannot stand alone as complete words. Prefixes appear at the beginning of a word, and suffixes appear at the end of a word. **Roots** are syllables that convey the basic meaning of a word. They can appear in the beginning, middle, or end of a word, and sometimes they can stand alone as complete words.

Example of a Word with a Prefix, Root, and Suffix		
Word: microscopic		
Prefix: micro- **Meaning:** small, tiny	**Root:** scop **Meaning:** to see	**Suffix:** -ic **Meaning:** relating to, characterized by
Definition: Relating to something too tiny to be seen by the unaided eye.		

Study the charts of common prefixes, suffixes, and roots, and complete the practice exercises that follow.

Common Prefixes

PREFIX	MEANING	EXAMPLE
anti-	against, opposite	antisocial
auto-	self	autobiography
bi-	two	bicycle
com-, con-	with, together	communicate, context
dis-	not, opposite of	dislike
em-, en-	to cause to be, to put into or onto, to go into or onto	embattle, enable
ex-, exo-	out of, from	exoskeleton
fore-	earlier	foreshadow
hom-, homo-	same	homogeneous
hype-	over, too much	hyperactive
im-	not	impatient
in-, il-, im-	not	insufficient, illiterate, immature
inter-	between	interstate
micro-	small, tiny	microchip
mid-	middle	midline
mis-	bad, wrong	misbehave

(continued)

Common Prefixes   *(continued)*

PREFIX	MEANING	EXAMPLE
neo-	new, recent, revived	neonatal
poly-	many, much	polygon
pre-	before	pregame
pro-	forward	proceed
quad-	four	quadrilateral
re-	again, back	rejoin
retro-	back, backward	retroactive
se-	apart	separate
semi-	half	semisolid
sub-	under, beneath, secondary	subterranean
super-	above, on top of, beyond	superimpose, superintendent
tele-	far, distant	telephone
trans-	across, change, through	transfer, transmit
tri-	three	tricycle
un-	not, opposite of	unhappy
uni-	one, single	unicycle

Common Suffixes

SUFFIX	MEANING	EXAMPLE
-able, -ible	can be done	laughable, edible,
-age	result of an action/collection	manage
-al, -ial	related to, characterized by	parental, trivial
-an, -ian	one having a certain skill, relating to, belonging to	artisan, Haitian
-ation, -ion, -ition, -tion	act of, state of	graduation, isolation
-en	made of, to make	brighten, wooden
-ence, -ance	act or condition of	governance
-ent, -ant	an action or condition, causing a specific action	obedient, inhabitant
-er, -or	person connected with, comparative degree	competitor, greater
-fy	to make, to form into	liquefy
-hood	state, quality, condition of	adulthood
-ic	relating to, characterized by	historic
-ice	state or quality of	cowardice
-ide	chemical	peroxide

(continued)

Common Suffixes   *(continued)*

SUFFIX	MEANING	EXAMPLE
-ish	like, having the characteristics of, inclined or trending to	childish
-ity, -ty	state of, quality of	beauty, prosperity
-ive, -ative, -tive	inclined or tending toward an action	active, inquisitive
-ize	to make, to cause to become	energize
-less	without	homeless
-logy, -ology, -ologist	science of, study of, one who studies	psychology, ecologist
-ment	act, process	torment, replacement
-ness	condition, state of	happiness
-ous, -eous, -ious	full of or characterized by	joyous, rambunctious
-ward	characterized by a thing, quality, state, or action	backward, inward
-ways	in what manner	sideways

Common Roots

ROOT	MEANING	EXAMPLE
amo, amatum	love	amorous
aqua	water	aquatics
aud, audi, aus	to hear, listen	audiophile
bene, boun, bon	good, well	benefit
biblio	book	bibliography
bio	life	biological
chrom, chron	time	synchronous
dico, dictum, dict	to say, tell, speak	dictation
fact	make, do	manufacture
geo	earth, ground, soil	geological
graph	writing	biography
inter	between	interrelated
junct	join	junction
log, logos	word or study	dialogue
magnus	large	magnificent
meter, metron	measure	thermometer
path, pathos	feeling, suffering	sympathy
phone	sound	phonetics
populous	people	population
pro	for	proponent
scribe, script	to write	transcribe
sol	sun	solar

(continued)

Common Roots   *(continued)*

ROOT	MEANING	EXAMPLE
sonus	sound	sonogram
spectro, spect, spec	to see, watch, observe	prospect
struct	to build	destruction
syn, sym	the same, alike	sync, synonym
terra	land	subterranean
trans	across	translate
visum, video	to see	videographer
vivo	live	vibrant

PRACTICE 5 Using Word Parts to Speculate about Meanings

Use the Common Prefixes, Common Suffixes, and Common Roots charts to make an educated guess about the meaning of each of the following words. Write the meaning in the provided space. Then consult a dictionary, and write the dictionary meaning in the appropriate space.

1. Word: *bioconcentrates*

    Your best guess: _____

    Dictionary definition: _____

    _____

2. Word: *excommunicate*

    Your best guess: _____

    Dictionary definition: _____

    _____

3. Word: *contamination*

    Your best guess: _____

    Dictionary definition: _____

    _____

4. Word: *benefactor*

    Your best guess: _____

    Dictionary definition: _____

    _____

5. Word: *transcribe*

    Your best guess: _____

    Dictionary definition: _____

    _____

Using Context Clues

A **context** is an environment. The context of a particular word is the sentence in which it appears and sometimes the sentences nearby.

You may have already noticed Vocabulary Collection Words in the margins of this chapter like the example shown at the right. This feature is designed to call attention to words you

---

Vocabulary Collection Word:
mechanism

Your in-context definition:

_____

_____

A dictionary definition:

_____

_____

may not know. When you see a vocabulary box for a word in the text, first attempt to figure out the word's meaning using the context clues described in the steps that follow. Finish the paragraph you are reading, and then fill in the definitions for the word in the vocabulary box.

These three steps can help you use context clues effectively to determine definitions.

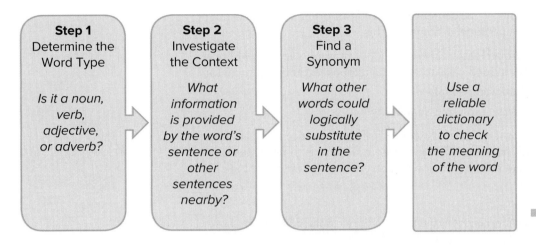

Step 1
Determine the Word Type

Is it a noun, verb, adjective, or adverb?

Step 2
Investigate the Context

What information is provided by the word's sentence or other sentences nearby?

Step 3
Find a Synonym

What other words could logically substitute in the sentence?

Use a reliable dictionary to check the meaning of the word

▨ Using context clues to determine a word's meaning

Context Clue Step 1: Determine the Word Type

The sentence in which the word appears and the surrounding sentences are context clues. The first point to notice when you are using context clues is the *type of word*. In the following example, we will consider the word *precipitates*, a word unfamiliar to many people.

Example: Transported through the air, mercury *precipitates* in water supplies . . .

Precipitates describes something that mercury *does*, so it is an action word. Thus, *precipitates* is a verb.

Context Clue Step 2: Investigate the Context

Now that you know the word is a verb, think of other verbs you are familiar with, such as *jumps*, *runs*, and *sits*. Can you come up with another verb that might mean the same thing as *precipitates*? To do so, investigate in more depth to determine what happens before mercury precipitates.

Example: Currently the most widespread toxic metal contamination in North America is mercury released from incinerators and coal-burning power plants. Transported through the air, mercury precipitates in water supplies, where it bioconcentrates in food webs to reach dangerous levels in top predators.

- Since mercury is released from incinerators and coal-burning power plants, it is not on the ground: it is coming out of smokestacks. Thus we can conclude that the mercury is in the air.
- The word *transported* gives us another clue: mercury moves through the air before ending up in water supplies.
- The mercury *precipitates* from the air into water supplies. That must mean it somehow gets from the air into the water below.
- You may already be familiar with a similar word, *precipitation*, which is often used in weather forecasts. You know *precipitation* means rain. Rain is a *thing*—the actual water that falls from the sky—but *to rain* is a verb. Precipitation is a thing—the actual wet weather—but it can also be used as a verb, *to precipitate*. Thus, maybe *to precipitate* is like *to rain*.
- Conclusion: *Precipitates* very likely means "falling from the sky like rain."

Context Clue Step 3: Find a Synonym

Once you have used the context to understand the writer's point, you can find a synonym to help you define the new word. A **synonym** is a word that means the same thing as another word. For example, *house*, *home*, and *residence* are synonyms; all three words mean roughly the same thing.

Take the unfamiliar word out of the sentence, and plug in other words that might make sense. Think through each potential synonym in this way.

Example: Transported through the air, mercury _____ in water supplies, where it bioconcentrates in food webs to reach dangerous levels in top predators.

Try this: Mercury *falls* into water supplies.

Or this: Mercury *rains down* into water supplies.

If the synonym makes sense *and* if it fits in the context of the sentence and paragraph, you may have found the word's meaning. The only way to be sure is to use a dictionary to check your hunch. Here's what part of a dictionary entry for *precipitate* might look like.

---

pre•cip•i•tate 🔊)) (pri-ˈsi-pə-tāt)

v. **1. METEOROLOGY** To cause water to condense and fall from the air in the form of rain, snow, sleet, or hail.

2. CHEMISTRY To cause a solid to separate from the solution in which it is contained.

Precipitate means "to condense and fall from the air." That is exactly what the mercury is doing. There is also a second definition from chemistry that fits: mercury, which is a solid, is being separated from the smoke released from incinerators and coal-burning power plants and falling into the water. The context clues were successful in leading us to the right meaning. Context clues will not always lead you to the exact meaning of a word, but they can help you get close.

Try your hand at using context clues to figure out the meanings of unfamiliar words by completing the following exercise.

PRACTICE 6 Using Context Clues

Use context clues to guess the meaning of each of the *italicized* words in the passages below. Follow the three context clue steps described above. Next, use a dictionary to see if your definition is correct. Record your answers.

1. Mike, the lodge owner, gave us a *convoluted*, hand-drawn map that was impossible to follow.

   Context-based guess: _____

   Dictionary definition: _____

2. The map was intended to lead us to a gold mine that had long been abandoned by *prospectors.*

   Context-based guess: _____

   Dictionary definition: _____

3. After hiking for half an hour, we decided that the *pragmatic* thing to do would be to walk back to the lodge and ask for clearer instructions.

   Context-based guess: _____

   Dictionary definition: _____

4. Mike laughed and gave us a list of *enumerated* instructions. We could easily follow the ten instructions he gave us.

   Context-based guess: _____

   Dictionary definition: _____

Acquiring New Vocabulary

You now have three tools—using a dictionary, using word parts, and using context clues—to help you understand unfamiliar words you encounter as you read. These tools are great at leading you to a temporary understanding, but to actually acquire new vocabulary that you will remember, you have to be much more intentional than merely noting a definition.

The key to expanding and adding to your vocabulary is *using* the words you learn. One way to do this is to keep a log of all the vocabulary words that are new to you. You can keep the log in a notebook or, better yet, on note cards. Make a note card each week with new vocabulary words. Include the words that are annotated as vocabulary words in each chapter of this textbook, and add any other new words you find in your reading. Your vocabulary log will give you a collection of words to study and to practice using in daily conversation and writing.

- When you write e-mails, use as many of the words on your note card as you can.
- Think about situations in your life that would provide the right context for the new word. For example, if the new word is *stringent* ("strict; severe"), a discussion about rules or laws may be a good situation in which you can use the word *stringent*.
- When you write assignments for your classes, find a way to weave in new vocabulary words.

At the end of each chapter, you will find an Adding to Your Vocabulary activity that will challenge you to use the new vocabulary from the chapter in your day-to-day activities.

CHAPTER ACTIVITIES

READING AND ANNOTATING

As you know, intentional and unintentional emulation help us learn new skills. However, emulation alone is not always enough to help us become fully competent in a new craft or skill. Perhaps the most important ingredient in accomplishing any goal is motivation.

In the selection that follows, you will read about how motivation and emulation led Frederick Douglass to true accomplishment. Douglass was born into slavery around 1818 in Maryland. Around the age of twelve, his master's wife began teaching him the alphabet. After being reprimanded by her husband, she stopped her lessons, but Douglass was determined to read. In his remarkable story, he explains how learning to read and write was a major factor in his desire to become free. Douglass eventually escaped slavery and became a greatly respected thinker, speaker, and writer. In addition to other writings, lectures, and accomplishments, he told the story of his life in *My Bondage and My Freedom* (1855) and *Life and Times of Frederick Douglass* (1881).

What follows is a paraphrase of a passage from *Narrative of the Life of Frederick Douglass, an American Slave*, published in 1845 by the Anti-Slavery Office in Boston. Read and annotate the paraphrased selection. As you read, think about the character traits Frederick Douglass had. He was a very patient man, but he had many other character traits that helped him succeed in life. Make notes about these traits when you read about Douglass's strategies to learn to read and write.

Learning to Read and Write

By Frederick Douglass

I lived in Master Hugh's family about seven years. During this time, I succeeded in learning to read and write. In order to accomplish this, I was compelled to resort to various strategies because I had no regular teacher.

YOUR ANNOTATIONS

The plan which I adopted, and the one by which I was most successful, was that of making friends of all the little white boys whom I met in the street. I "converted" as many of these boys as I could find into "teachers." With their kind assistance, obtained at different times and in different places, I finally succeeded in learning to read.

When I was sent to run errands, I always took a book with me and by doing one part of my errand quickly, I found time to get a lesson in before my return. Bread was always available to me at the house but not so for many of the poor white children in our neighborhood. So I would bring extra bread with me on my errands and give some to these hungry little urchins. In return, they gave me the much more valuable bread of knowledge.

I am strongly tempted to give the names of two or three of those little boys as a testimonial of the gratitude and affection I have toward them. However, I believe it is wiser not to do so—not because so doing would injure me but because it might embarrass them in that teaching slaves to read is an almost unpardonable offense in this Christian country. It is enough to say of the dear little fellows that they live on Philpot Street, very near Durgin and Bailey's shipyard.

On occasion, I would sometimes talk the matter of slavery over with them. Sometimes I would tell them that I wished I could be as free as they would be when they became men. "You will be free as soon as you are twenty-one, but I am a slave for life! Do I not have as much right to be free as you have?" These words troubled them; they would express deep sympathy for me and console me with the hope that something would occur by which I might be free.

At this point I was about twelve years old, and the thought of being a slave for life began to weigh heavily on my heart. Just about this time, I obtained a book entitled *The Columbian Orator.* I read it at every opportunity. Among its many interesting ideas, I discovered in it a dialogue between a master and his slave. The slave had run away from his master three times. The book presented the conversation that took place between the two of them after the slave was recaptured the third time. In this exchange, the master presented every pro-slavery argument, and the slave addressed every point. The slave was characterized as saying some very smart, impressive things in reply to his master. The slave was both surprised and delighted regarding the effect of the argument he presented—the master decided voluntarily to emancipate the slave!

In the same book, I encountered some of the powerful arguments that Richard Sheridan made regarding the oppression of Catholics in Britain. I read his ideas over and over again because they were so interesting. He expressed some of my own thoughts, which had frequently flashed through my mind but which died away because I could not put them into words. The key insight that I gained from his works was that truth could have power over even the conscience of a slaveholder. What I learned from Sheridan was a bold denunciation of slavery and a powerful vindication of human rights.

Reading these documents enabled me to express my own thoughts and to address the arguments offered for the continuation of slavery. While they relieved me of one difficulty, they brought on another even more painful understanding. The more I read, the more I was led to abhor and detest my enslavers. I could regard them as nothing other than a band of successful robbers, who had left their homes, gone to Africa, and stolen us from our homes, reducing us to slavery in a strange land. I loathed them as being the meanest as well as the most wicked of men.

The Columbian Orator was a collection of poems, political essays, and other writings. It was widely used in American schoolrooms in the early nineteenth century to teach reading and speaking.

After the Reformation in Great Britain, Roman Catholics were subjected to many restrictions. They could not own land, hold government offices or seats in Parliament, or practice their religion freely without being fined or prosecuted. Richard Sheridan was a writer and member of Parliament who actively supported the expansion of rights for British Catholics.

As I writhed under this pain, I would at times feel that learning to read had been a curse rather than a blessing. Learning to read had given me a view of my wretched condition but without any cure. It opened my eyes to the horrible pit of my circumstances but offered no ladder with which I could get out. In moments of agony, I envied the unawareness of my fellow slaves. I have often wished that I myself were an animal and thus ignorant of my plight. I thought that I would prefer to be the lowliest reptile rather than myself. Anything—no matter what—to escape from thinking! The contemplation of my situation tormented me. There was no getting rid of it. It was pressed upon me by every object within sight or hearing, animate or inanimate. The silver trumpet of freedom had roused my soul to eternal wakefulness. Freedom now appeared, to disappear no more forever. It was heard in every sound and seen in every thing. It was ever present to torment me with a sense of my wretched condition. I saw nothing without seeing it; I heard nothing without hearing it; and I felt nothing without feeling it. Freedom—it looked from every star, smiled in every calm moment, breathed in every wind, and moved in every storm.

I often found myself regretting my own existence and wishing that I were dead. If it had not been for the hope of being free, I have no doubt but that I would have killed myself—or done something for which I would have been killed. While in this state of mind, I was eager to hear anyone speak about slavery. I was a ready listener. From time to time, I would hear a reference to the "abolitionists." However, it was some time before I learned what the word meant. It was always used in a context that caused it to be an interesting word to me. If a slave ran away and succeeded in getting clear, or if a slave killed his master, or set fire to a barn, or did anything very wrong in the mind of a slaveholder, it was referred to as the fruit of abolition. Hearing the word in this connection very often, I set about to learn what it meant. The dictionary offered me little help. I found it was "the act of abolishing," but then I did not know what it meant for something to be abolished. So I was perplexed.

I did not dare to ask anyone about its meaning, for I was confident that it was something they wanted me to know very little about. After waiting patiently, I came across one of our city newspapers that contained an account of the number of petitions from the North pleading for the abolition of slavery in the District of Columbia and of the slave trade between the States. From this time forward, I understood the words "abolition" and "abolitionist" and always drew near when that word was spoken, expecting to hear something of importance to myself and fellow-slaves. The light broke in upon me by degrees.

One day I went down on the wharf, and seeing two Irishmen unloading stone from a scow, I went, unasked, and helped them. When we had finished, one of them came to me and asked me if I was a slave. I told him I was. He asked, "Are ye a slave for life?" I told him that I was. The good Irishman seemed to be deeply bothered by the statement. He said to the other that it was a pity that so fine a little fellow as I should be a slave for life. He said it was a shame to hold me. They both advised me to run away to the North; they said that I would find friends there, and that I would be free. I pretended not to be interested in what they said and acted as though I did not understand them because I feared they might be treacherous. White men have been known to encourage slaves to escape, and then, to get the reward, catch them and return them to their masters. I was afraid that these seemingly good men might use me so; but I nevertheless remembered their advice, and from that time onward I resolved to

Scow: a large flat-bottomed boat.

run away. I looked forward to a time at which it would be safe for me to escape. I was too young to think of doing so immediately; besides, I wished to learn how to write, as I might have occasion to write my own pass. I consoled myself with the hope that I should one day find a good chance. Meanwhile, I would learn to write.

The idea as to how I might learn to write was suggested to me by being in Durgin and Bailey's shipyard. I would frequently see the ship carpenters, after hewing and getting a piece of timber ready for use, write on the timber the name of that part of the ship for which it was intended. When a piece of timber was intended for the larboard side, it would be marked thus—"L." When a piece was for the starboard side, it would be marked thus—"S." A piece for the larboard side forward would be marked thus—"L. F." When a piece was for starboard side forward, it would be marked thus—"S. F." For larboard aft, it would be marked thus—"L. A." For starboard aft, it would be marked thus—"S. A." I soon learned the names of these letters and understood their meaning when written on a piece of timber in the shipyard. I immediately began copying them and in a short time was able to make these four letters.

Hew: to cut wood coarsely.

After that, whenever I met any boy whom I knew could write, I would tell him I could write as well as he. The next word would be, "I don't believe you. Let me see you try it." I would then make the letters which I had been so fortunate as to learn and ask him to beat that. In this way I got a good many lessons in writing, which I could not possibly have gotten in any other way. During this time, my copy-book was the board fence, brick wall, and pavement; my pen and ink was a lump of chalk. With these, I learned how to write.

Copy-book: a blank tablet for practicing handwriting.

I continued by copying the advanced spelling words in *Webster's Spelling Book* until I could make them all without looking at the book. By this time, my little Master Thomas had gone to school and learned how to write and had filled a number of copy-books with his handwriting. He had brought these home and shown them to some of our near neighbors and then laid them aside. My mistress would leave the house every Monday afternoon and require me to take care of the house. While she was gone, I used the time writing in the blank spaces left in Master Thomas's copy-book, copying what he had written. I continued to do this until I could write in a manner very similar to that of Master Thomas. Thus, after a long, tedious effort for years, I finally succeeded in learning how to write.

Master Thomas: the child of Frederick Douglass's master.

Questions for Consideration

1. What effect did reading have on Frederick Douglass initially?
2. Why was Douglass so motivated to learn to read? Why was he motivated to learn to write?
3. What role did emulation play in Douglass's education?
4. In what ways was Douglass's reading of *The Columbian Orator* important in his intellectual and emotional development?
5. How did reading and writing separate Douglass from the other slaves?
6. Write a paragraph in which you speculate about what life would have been like for Frederick Douglass had he never learned to read or write. Use your imagination.
7. Why do you think slave owners prohibited slaves from learning to read and write?

USING MODELS TO PRACTICE COMPOSING

Shaun read Frederick Douglass's "Learning to Read and Write" in his English class and was given an essay assignment. Read Shaun's assignment on the next page and notice his annotations.

Essay Assignment

In "Learning to Read and Write," we learn not only how Frederick Douglass became literate, but also about the character traits that helped him eventually become a free man. Write an essay in which you discuss the character traits that drove Douglass to become literate. Discuss at least three character traits and their effects on Douglass's life in your essay. Use examples from the reading to support your discussion.

SHAUN'S ANNOTATIONS

Assignment turned into a question: What are the character traits that drove Douglass to become literate?

Discuss character traits (3 or more).

Discuss their effects.

Use examples from the reading.

To respond to the assignment, Shaun reread the narrative and marked every possible character trait he could think of. Here are the first four paragraphs Shaun annotated with Douglass's character traits.

Resourceful

Flexible & persistent

Hardworking

Thankful

Aware, concerned for others

I lived in Master Hugh's family about seven years. During this time, I succeeded in learning to read and write. In order to accomplish this, I was compelled to resort to various strategies because I had no regular teacher.

The plan which I adopted, and the one by which I was most successful, was that of making friends of all the little white boys whom I met in the street. I "converted" as many of these boys as I could find into "teachers." With their kind assistance, obtained at different times and in different places, I finally succeeded in learning to read.

When I was sent to run errands, I always took a book with me and by doing one part of my errand quickly, I found time to get a lesson in before my return. Bread was always available to me at the house but not so for many of the poor white children in our neighborhood. So I would bring extra bread with me on my errands and give some to these hungry little urchins. In return, they gave me the much more valuable bread of knowledge.

I am strongly tempted to give the names of two or three of those little boys as a testimonial of the gratitude and affection I have toward them. However, I believe it is wiser not to do so—not because so doing would injure me but because it might embarrass them in that teaching slaves to read is an almost unpardonable offense in this Christian country. It is enough to say of the dear little fellows that they live on Philpot Street, very near Durgin and Bailey's shipyard.

Determined

Friendly

Creative

Cooperative

Wise

When Shaun finished annotating the entire reading, he made a list of all the character traits he found. Next, he grouped together character traits that were similar, as you can see from the circled numbers in this excerpt from Shaun's prewriting.

Character Traits

- ② determined
- ① resourceful
- friendly
- ① flexible
- ③ persistent
- ③ patient
- thankful
- ① creative
- ② hardworking (diligent)
- cooperative
- wise
- concerned for others

After identifying the character traits he would discuss in his essay, Shaun wrote a simple outline that included his thesis statement and the major supporting points he planned to use. He decided his essay would be structured like this:

Introduction paragraph

Thesis statement: Frederick Douglass's success in learning to read and write was a result of his resourcefulness, diligence, and persistence.

Major supporting point 1: Without resourcefulness, Douglass would probably not have ever become literate.

Major supporting point 2: While resourcefulness was necessary, diligence and hard work were also important.

Major supporting point 3: Most importantly, Douglass's persistence is the character trait that eventually gave rise to his success.

Conclusion paragraph

After drafting his essay, Shaun revised and edited it, making sure he gave credit to the sources he used. Notice the features of Shaun's writing in the first body paragraph of his essay.

Body Paragraph 1 from Shaun's Essay

Without resourcefulness, Douglass would probably not have ever become literate. Douglass had to come up with his own teachers and his own materials. With the exception of learning the alphabet from his master's wife, every bit of Douglass's reading education was a result of his own resourcefulness. For example, Douglass would get the boys in his neighborhood to teach him by giving them bread and befriending them. He used both bread and the young boys as resources for education. To learn to write, Douglass had to be especially resourceful. Noticing the letters used on wood in the shipyard, Douglass began to copy the letters by writing them with chalk on sidewalks and fences. Another example of Douglass's resourcefulness was in his use of the young Master Thomas's educational materials. Douglass would wait until his	Main idea of the paragraph (a topic sentence) Detail: resourcefulness required to learn to read Example Detail: resourcefulness required to learn to write Example Example

(continued)

mistress left the house and would then use blank spots in Master Thomas's used spelling-books. Because Douglass was resourceful, he was able to use non-traditional methods for learning to read and write.

A READING AND WRITING ASSIGNMENT

Try your hand at writing the remaining paragraphs of Shaun's essay. Using the first body paragraph Shaun wrote as a model, write the remaining two body paragraphs based on Shaun's outline. Alternatively, choose two other items on Shaun's prewriting list to write about. Add an introduction paragraph and a conclusion paragraph to complete the essay. Use the Quick Start Guide to Integrated Reading and Writing Assignments for assistance.

THINKING FROM AN INSTRUCTOR'S POINT OF VIEW

Emulation exercises like the one in this chapter based on "Why I Am a Vegan" can sometimes be worrisome for instructors. No instructor wants to convey the idea that it is OK to use another writer's composition after changing a few words. However, many writing instructors understand the importance of using models for study and practice.

Think about this issue from the perspective of an instructor for a moment. What is the difference between plagiarizing and practices like the emulation exercise in this chapter? How would you explain the difference to students? Write two or three paragraphs in which you answer these questions.

ADDING TO YOUR VOCABULARY

This chapter's vocabulary words appear below.

mechanism	hemisphere	minute
internalize	speculate	transient

Choose five of the vocabulary words from this chapter that you would like to add to your vocabulary, and think about how you can use them this week. For example, one of this week's words is *speculate*. You can often substitute *speculate* for *guess*, as in the examples that follow.

Example: I don't know if this soup is fattening, but I'd *guess* that it is because it tastes so good.

I don't know if this soup is fattening, but I'd *speculate* that it is because it tastes so good.

List each of the five words you plan to use this week, and make note of a context in which you could use each word.

Example: *Speculate*. I can use this word when I predict what will be on tests or what we'll do in class.

⊙ ADDITIONAL ASSIGNMENTS

1. Reading and writing were arguably the most important skills Frederick Douglass ever acquired. Being literate opened new worlds for Douglass, and eventually he found a way to free himself from slavery. Think about your own life. Have you developed a skill that has made a difference in your world? Perhaps you have developed a friendship that has been highly influential, or maybe you have had an experience—such as a job or a vacation—that had a profound effect on you. Write two or three paragraphs about a positive, powerful influence you have had in your life. Explain why this influence affected you, and provide examples of its positive influence.

2. Using Frederick Douglass's essay and your own life experiences, reflect on these questions: What were the effects of hardship on Douglass? What have been the effects of hardship in your life? Write a few paragraphs in which you explain your answer.

3. In a variety of career fields, emulating the skills of others is a way to learn. For example, nursing students spend time as interns emulating the skills of professional nurses in clinics and hospitals. In disciplines such as music, art, and theater, students learn by emulating the masters of their crafts. And in sales and marketing, students learn by emulating the successful techniques of those in the field. Choose a career in which you are interested. How might emulation help you master the content or skills required in this career? Write two or three paragraphs to explain.

❤ EMOTIONAL INTELLIGENCE

One skill that is important for getting along with others is social awareness. Management experts have defined social awareness as "the ability to perceive and understand the social relationships and structures in which you and those around you are operating. It involves being able to understand how other people are feeling—and validating those feelings. . . . And it means understanding that individual happiness is dependent upon assisting others to achieve their own happiness as well."

Write two or three paragraphs explaining what social awareness is. Put the ideas into your own words. Provide an example of a person who is socially aware in a particular situation. Provide another example of a person who is socially *unaware* in a particular situation. For example, a socially aware person may recognize that when the conversation turns to romantic relationships, one of her friends becomes uncomfortable. A person who is socially *unaware* might speak too loudly in class or might dominate a conversation without knowing how he is being perceived by those around him. Finish by offering suggestions for becoming more socially aware.

🌐 CULTURAL LITERACY

"Learning to Read and Write" is chapter 7 of Frederick Douglass's story. The entire text is available at www.gutenberg.org/ebooks/23. Select at least one additional chapter from Douglass's narrative. Read the chapter and write a paragraph in which you summarize the information it presents. Use the Quick Start Guide for assistance.

CRITICAL THINKING

A valuable way to use critical thinking is to analyze the models we emulate, especially the people in our lives. It's easy to identify the emulation mistakes of other people. We have all observed a young person who falls in with the wrong crowd and makes poor choices. Seeing our own emulation mistakes, however, requires critical thinking about our lives.

Think about the people you have emulated—whether consciously or unconsciously. Often, they are the people closest to you, such as parents, friends, and relatives. Some people even emulate celebrities. Select the person who has had the greatest effect on you. Has it been a wise choice to emulate this person? Why or why not? Write two or three paragraphs that reveal critical thinking about your conscious or unconscious emulation of this person.

METACOGNITION

What do you remember after having read this chapter? Without looking back at the chapter, list the major topics this chapter covered. Then review the chapter to see what you missed. Write a short paragraph about how well you remembered the content for each topic.

When you finish, assess your understanding and memory of this chapter. Was it difficult to recall the information you read? Why? What particular material did you remember from the chapter? Why do you think you remembered those items and not others? Did you remember what you annotated better than what you did not annotate? What strategies might you use in the future to better remember the contents of what you read?

3

In many careers, previewing materials is essential to getting a job done well. Previewing strategies also help readers and writers keep focused as they work with and create texts.

Previewing Texts and Working with Topics

Sometimes the way you do a job really affects the final result. For example, a high school senior decided to paint his old worn-out car. Not being the mechanical—or artistic—type, he washed his car and dried it, and then he painted it with nine cans of red, high-gloss, bargain-brand spray paint. You can probably imagine the outcome. The painting process he used resulted in the creation of what he and his friends came to call The Bloodmobile. Indeed, the process he used affected the quality of the outcome.

The same principle is true for reading and writing. The early steps are important. Carefully following these steps will help you confidently begin the integrated reading and writing journey.

CHAPTER OBJECTIVES

After completing this chapter, students will be able to do the following:

- **Examine a reading's context.**
- **Preview a reading to identify its topic.**
- **Work with assigned writing topics.**
- **Develop and narrow a topic for an essay.**
- **Use prewriting strategies to generate ideas.**

EXAMINING A READING'S CONTEXT

When we **preview** a reading, we look it over and notice key elements rather than read it word for word. One key element is the reading's context. The context of a reading consists of *where* it was published, *who* wrote it, and *for whom* it was written. Let's consider some specific types of texts, their characteristics, and the insights we can gather from their contexts.

Types of Text

	NEWSPAPER ARTICLES	ARTICLES IN GENERAL-INTEREST MAGAZINES	ARTICLES IN SPECIAL-INTEREST MAGAZINES	ARTICLES IN ACADEMIC JOURNALS	BOOKS
Author	Journalists, whose primary task is to report news and ideas	General-interest writers who are not necessarily subject experts	People with experience or background in the subject	Highly qualified experts with extensive background in the subject	Experts and nonexperts
Audience	General public	Wide range of readers	Readers interested in the subject	Experts in the subject	General or specialized audiences
Purpose	To inform or analyze (news articles) or persuade (editorials)	To inform, analyze, evaluate, or persuade	To inform, analyze, evaluate, or persuade	To inform, analyze, evaluate, persuade, or present new research	Varied purposes
Length	Often short	Varied	Varied	Varied, but generally long (3,000+ words)	Varied
Language and style	Journalistic (multiple short paragraphs)	Very little jargon or technical language, always explained and defined	Likely to include jargon and technical language	Likely to include jargon and technical language	Classifiable into genres (novels, textbooks); may use jargon and technical language
Examples	Articles in *The New York Times, The Washington Post,* and *The Wall Street Journal*	Articles in *Time, Newsweek, The Atlantic,* and *Salon.com*	Articles in *Psychology Today, Fortune,* and *Scientific American*	Articles in *American Journal of Nursing* and *Journal of Engineering and Technology Research*	*The Grapes of Wrath* by John Steinbeck; *Managerial Accounting,* 14th ed., by Ray Garrison

Vocabulary Collection Word:
editorial

Your in-context definition:

_____

_____

A dictionary definition:

_____

_____

By thinking about the publication, its intended audience, and the writer's purpose, you can develop insights about texts before reading them.

Practice examining contexts by completing the following exercise.

PRACTICE ① Examining the Contexts of Readings

Read the titles of the publications in the left column, and read the descriptors in the right column. Match each publication to the correct descriptor.

_____ 1. Journal: *Journal of Chemical Physics*

_____ 2. Book: *Money Management Principles That Work*

_____ 3. Journal: *Journal of Applied Psychology*

_____ 4. Newspaper: *The New York Times*

_____ 5. Specialty magazine: *GamePro*

_____ 6. Newspaper: *The Loyaltown Gazette*

_____ 7. Book: *Invisible Man* by Ralph Ellison

_____ 8. Specialty magazine: *Texas Monthly*

a. Source most likely to report a Labor Day parade

b. Source most likely to appeal to regional readers

c. Source most likely to use technical jargon for mental health professionals

d. Source most likely to appeal to a hobby or interest group

e. Source most likely to provide practical advice to a general audience

f. Source most likely to offer high-quality news for a general but educated audience

g. Source most likely to require readers to know scientific concepts

h. Source most likely to provide pleasurable reading for a general audience

PREVIEWING A READING TO IDENTIFY ITS TOPIC

A careful preview of the reading can help you figure out what the reading is about—its **topic.** Being able to determine the topic of a reading is one of the most important reading skills. The topic can be expressed in a word or a short phrase. It will not be a complete sentence because a topic does not express a complete thought; it is only the subject or content with which the text is concerned.

Example of a topic: iPads in education

Not a topic: Although many schools are rushing to purchase iPads for their students, little research shows that learning on iPads is more effective than other methods of learning.

The second example is not a topic because it is a complete thought and is thus presented in a complete sentence.

A few techniques can help you determine the topic of a reading.

Consider the Reading's Title

A title like "Five Weight-Training Techniques" is very helpful, as it clearly describes the topic of the reading. Not all titles, however, are as revealing. A title like "Alternatives" does not give us much information about the topic.

Examine the Reading's Headings

Flipping through the text to examine its headings and subheadings will give you clues about the topic. Consider the textbook chapter headings in the illustration that follows.

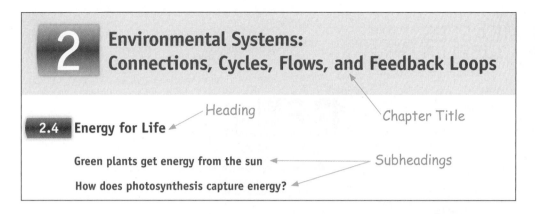

2 **Environmental Systems:
Connections, Cycles, Flows, and Feedback Loops**

Heading   Chapter Title

2.4 **Energy for Life**

Green plants get energy from the sun   Subheadings

How does photosynthesis capture energy?

The title tells us that the chapter is about environmental systems. Since section 2.4 is about energy, we can reasonably conclude that energy is an environmental system or is part of an environmental system. Looking at the subheadings, we have good reason to expect to learn about the connection between green plants and the sun. More specifically, we will learn about photosynthesis.

Look at the Reading's Illustrations

A preview should also involve looking at any photos or illustrations. The illustration labeled "Figure 2.2" (below) from the same textbook chapter can help us predict content. Reading the caption is a quick way to see how the illustration connects to the headings and subheadings. In this case, the illustration gives us an example of a food chain. This picture helps us get a better idea of what the chapter title means when it refers to "environmental systems."

From a simple preview of the chapter, we know we will be learning about systems such as those involving photosynthesis and the food chain. We can then think about what we already know about photosynthesis and the food chain so that when we encounter new information about those systems, we can have a frame of reference for the new knowledge, a place to plug the information into what we already know.

Figure 2.2 A system can be described in very simple terms.

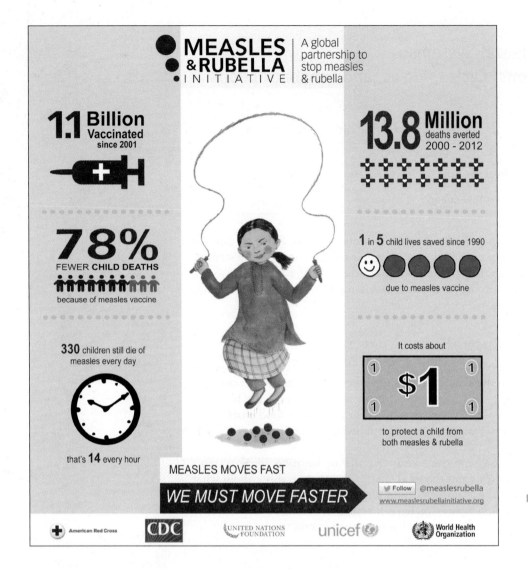

If you found this infographic in a text, what would you think the text's topic might be?

As you preview readings, you may find **infographics,** which are illustrations that combine artwork and text to convey information or explain topics. Maps are a common type of infographic. When you find infographics, take a minute to read through them. Look at the infographic "Measles & Rubella Initiative." A good infographic can provide quality information about a text's content.

To preview an infographic, you can use strategies similar to those that you use for text.

- **Read the title and subtitle for a clue to the topic.** In the infographic the title is followed by a subtitle, "A global partnership to stop measles & rubella." What clues do the title and subtitle give you about the topic?

- **Notice the different visual elements.** How are the elements grouped together? Do they have explanatory captions or headings?

- **Check how colors and sizes are used.** Bright colors and large shapes are often used to draw the reader's attention to aspects of the graphic that the creator thinks are important. Notice the use of the color red in this graphic. Why do you think red is used for some information?

- **Identify familiar images and what they mean.** One image used in the graphic is a syringe. What might readers think of when they see this image? What other images do you see? Do these images help you understand the graphic's content and meaning?

- **Look for elements that are essentially traditional charts and graphs in disguise.** For example, the graphic that shows a row of children and has "78%" written above it could be expressed as a statistic on a chart.

PRACTICE ❷ Previewing a Textbook Chapter

Study the title, headings, and photo below, taken from a chapter of a textbook entitled *Criminal Investigation.* Then answer the questions that follow.

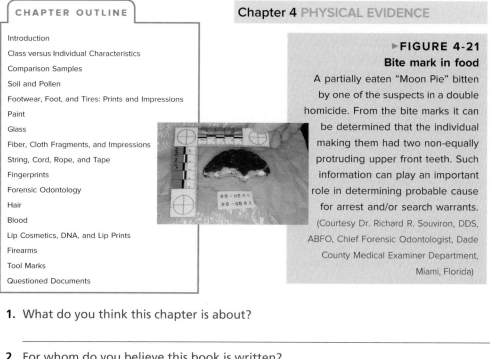

CHAPTER OUTLINE

Introduction

Class versus Individual Characteristics

Comparison Samples

Soil and Pollen

Footwear, Foot, and Tires: Prints and Impressions

Paint

Glass

Fiber, Cloth Fragments, and Impressions

String, Cord, Rope, and Tape

Fingerprints

Forensic Odontology

Hair

Blood

Lip Cosmetics, DNA, and Lip Prints

Firearms

Tool Marks

Questioned Documents

Chapter 4 PHYSICAL EVIDENCE

▶FIGURE 4-21
Bite mark in food
A partially eaten "Moon Pie" bitten by one of the suspects in a double homicide. From the bite marks it can be determined that the individual making them had two non-equally protruding upper front teeth. Such information can play an important role in determining probable cause for arrest and/or search warrants.
(Courtesy Dr. Richard R. Souviron, DDS, ABFO, Chief Forensic Odontologist, Dade County Medical Examiner Department, Miami, Florida)

1. What do you think this chapter is about?

   _____

2. For whom do you believe this book is written?

   _____

3. What do you think the purpose of this chapter is?

   _____

   _____

4. The chapter outline lists a number of items, such as hair, blood, and lip cosmetics. What are these? What information do you think the chapter will present about these items?

   _____

   _____

   _____

Once you've skimmed over the graphic, you should be able to identify its topic. How does the topic of the infographic relate to the topic of the entire reading? Use the other information you've gleaned from previewing the reading to answer that question.

Look for Repeated Words and Phrases

Another method for identifying the topic is to briefly scan the reading. *Scanning*, or *skimming*, simply involves glancing at each paragraph, perhaps reading a sentence or two on each page, and getting a sense of the kind of content and the kind of writing in the text. As you scan the reading, note any words that come up again and again. Look also for synonyms. Imagine skimming over an article and seeing these words constantly repeated:

flying	phobia	fear	nervousness
flights	paranoia	calm	worry
fear of flying	travel	anxiety	uneasiness

These words suggest that the reading's topic is the fear of flying. Notice that some of the words are synonyms. *Anxiety, worry, uneasiness, nervousness, fear*—these words are all somewhat related in meaning. Finding the recurring words and synonyms will help you identify the topic at a glance.

Find Common Ideas

Some readings present a number of different elements, any one of which could be the topic. In such readings, asking what all these elements share may give you the topic of the reading. For example, consider these subheadings from a magazine article:

Biodiesel Engines

Hydrogen-Based Automobiles

Natural Gas Vehicles

Electric Cars

All the subheadings refer to vehicles that use alternative forms of energy. Thus the topic of the article is likely to be alternative-fuel vehicles.

PRACTICE ③ Identifying Topics

Read each passage that follows, and identify its topic. Use the context information to help you, and circle any repeated words and synonyms.

1. Context: A short paragraph found in a community newspaper's opinion section. The writer is a citizen of the community.

Our town is woefully ill-prepared for flash floods. We do not have a recycling program. Our library has struggled to keep its doors open and has not had funds for new books for two years. In spite of these facts, the City Council is considering installing a new, expensive fence around the city park baseball field. The projects we need the most are not even being discussed. City Council members need to get their priorities in order and consider projects that will benefit all of the citizens in our town, not just sports enthusiasts.

What is the topic? _____

2. Context: A short reading from a general-interest magazine.

Although anxiety disorders are common, they often go undiagnosed for years. One reason for this delay in diagnosis is that the symptoms of anxiety can appear to be symptoms of other illnesses.

In particular, anxiety disorders often produce physical symptoms such as intestinal discomfort, nausea, dizziness, shortness of breath, hyperventilation, and rapid heartbeat. Since these symptoms *can* be caused by physical ailments, people with anxiety often assume their disorder is physical. This assumption can lead them to even greater anxiety and worry because they fear there is something wrong with them and that they may die.

All of the physical symptoms of anxiety—racing heartbeat, shortness of breath, hyperventilation, dizziness, nausea, and intestinal cramps—can converge on a sufferer at one time. This onslaught of physical symptoms can be terrifying. It can be hard for the victim to believe that the cause is "only anxiety" since the physical symptoms are so real.

What is the topic? _____

WORKING WITH ASSIGNED WRITING TOPICS

Much of the writing you will do in college and the workplace will be based on topics assigned by your instructors or supervisors. Sometimes you will receive very specific topic information. For other writing assignments, you may be given a range of topic choices and will need to narrow the topic you choose. You will also encounter writing assignments that require you to supply your own topic.

In some ways, when an instructor selects the topic, the writing process is easier since the first step has already been completed for you. Nonetheless, you should plan to use four strategies to make sure that the paper you write fits the assignment.

Create an Assignment Page

Ideally, you will be provided with written instructions that tell you exactly what the topic is and how to approach it. If you do not have written directions, then you need to create your own page of instructions. Record all of the information about the assignment available to you. Here are some questions you should use to collect information for your assignment sheet:

- What is the topic?
- Is research required? If so, what kind of research is expected?
- Is research (or the use of sources such as the Internet) prohibited?
- What is the writing purpose—to inform, to analyze and evaluate, or to persuade?
- What is the due date?
- What is the length requirement?
- What formatting is expected? Has the instructor specified font type and size, spacing, and heading format? Do you need to include a word count? Do you need to use a particular documentation style, such as MLA (Modern Language Association) style or APA (American Psychological Association) style?

Finally, take note of who will be reading your paper. You will need to consider your audience as you make decisions about what to include and how to word your ideas. Often with academic writing tasks, the instructor is the only person who will read what you write. Even though the instructor is just an audience of one, keeping in mind that you are writing for your instructor is very important, as it will help you choose content, terminology, and a style appropriate for academic writing. Academic writing assignments always require formal writing, so avoid contractions and slang, use correct grammar and mechanics, and use third person.

Read and Reread the Assignment

A common writing mistake is to write about something that does not address the topic well enough. Understanding the assignment is imperative. Read the assignment instructions twice, making annotations to highlight each particular requirement. Merely reading through assignment instructions in a **cursory** fashion can lead to disastrous results. For example, students in a writing class were asked to write an essay about the morality of physician-assisted suicide. One student wrote a paper on why physicians' assistants should not commit suicide. A second reading of the assignment instructions would have helped this student avoid the embarrassment of misunderstanding the topic and, as a result, receiving a low grade.

Vocabulary Collection Word:
cursory

Your in-context definition:

_____

_____

A dictionary definition:

_____

_____

State the Paper's Topic in the Form of a Question

If the topic is not offered to you in the form of a question, transform the instructions into a question, as in the following example.

> **Original instructions:** Write an essay in which you examine how credit card companies exploit college students. Include a consideration of the various problems that result for students as a consequence of this exploitation.

> **Instructions reworded as a question:** How do credit card companies exploit college students, and what are the problems that result from this exploitation?

Seek Help If You Need It

The best way to find help is to talk to your instructor. If your instructor is not available, work with a staff member at a writing lab or tutoring center. If you are confused about the topic or unsure how to begin, seek help before you go any further with your writing.

DEVELOPING AND NARROWING A TOPIC FOR AN ESSAY

Some assignments require you to generate your own topic. The best place to start this process is on a blank sheet of paper. Brainstorm about the subject by writing down everything that comes to mind. Do not evaluate your ideas at this time. Just allow yourself the freedom to write them down.

Brainstorming for Topics

On the next page are some strategies you can use to brainstorm ideas for possible topics.

One way to find a topic is to consider an interesting scene, such as a photo of a street in New York City (top), and think of a question like "What advantages are there to living in a major city?" As you look at these photos, what questions come to mind? Can you think of a question that would lead you to a good essay topic?

- **Start with your own interests.** If you were not writing this paper, what would you be doing right now? What are your interests? What are you passionate about? Make a list.

- **Free your imagination.** If you had the time, money, energy, and ability, what activities would you pursue?

- **Reflect on the world around you.** Which world events affect or interest you? Are there issues about which you are passionate? Could you write an essay on one aspect of a particular world event?

- **Think about your life and your history.** You have a history of experiences and memories. What are some of these experiences or memories that are worthy of being recorded? Does your family tell the same stories again and again because they are fun to listen to? Have you learned lessons about life that might interest or benefit readers?

- **Visit your school's or a virtual writing lab or tutoring center or your school or local library.** Librarians can help by guiding you to the resources that are available for topic selection. Some librarians will even help you think through topics that interest you and that would be suitable for your writing assignment. Writing center and tutoring center staff members are also good resources for topic development.

- **Use an online database available through your school or local library.** An **online database** is a collection of articles, studies, and other types of research information. Often, databases will also offer topic guides, such as "hot topics" or "current issues." Ask a reference librarian where you should start. Remember that you are using the database for ideas about subjects, not to find actual sources. If you use an actual source, you must give credit to the source in your essay. Unless your instructor requires you to find a source, use the database for topic searches.

- **Use an Internet search engine like *Google* or *Yahoo*.** Search engines can be powerful and quick tools for generating information. However, be aware that information found on the Internet is not always reliable. Avoid sites that offer papers for sale. Those kinds of Web sites often pop up when you are browsing for topics. Your instructors are familiar with the kinds of papers these Web sites sell or give away, and using a paper written by someone else for your writing assignment is plagiarism.

PRACTICE ④ Finding Topics of Interest

Imagine that your writing instructor asks you to choose a current event or issue that is important for your classmates to consider. The assignment is to select the issue and write an informative essay about it. What event or issue would you choose? Use one or more of the topic-selection techniques to choose a topic.

1. Your topic: _____

2. What process did you use for choosing this topic? Explain in one or two sentences:

_____

_____

Narrowing Topics

The topic you choose for an essay or other writing assignment (and sometimes even a topic that is assigned to you) needs to be adequately narrowed. For example, Raphael was considering majoring in music. When his instructor asked students to write an essay that discusses the daily activities involved in a job of interest to them, he decided to write about a job in the music industry. Though Raphael plays several instruments, he did not want to pursue a career as a performer. So he focused on finding jobs that do not include performing music.

To narrow the topic, Raphael started by breaking the subject into parts or types.

Next, he chose one type of music career—being a teacher—to discuss in his essay. After choosing "teacher," Raphael identified the following three kinds of teachers.

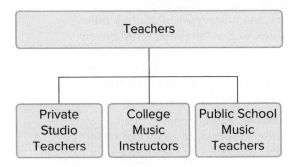

At this point, Raphael determined that these topics could be narrowed even further. Thus he identified three types of "college music instructors."

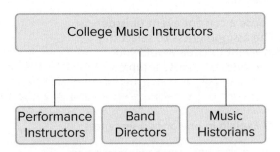

Raphael was then able to choose a narrower topic—the daily job activities of a band director—that was suitable for his assignment. To check whether he had sufficiently narrowed his topic to fit the scope of an essay, Raphael asked himself the questions that follow:

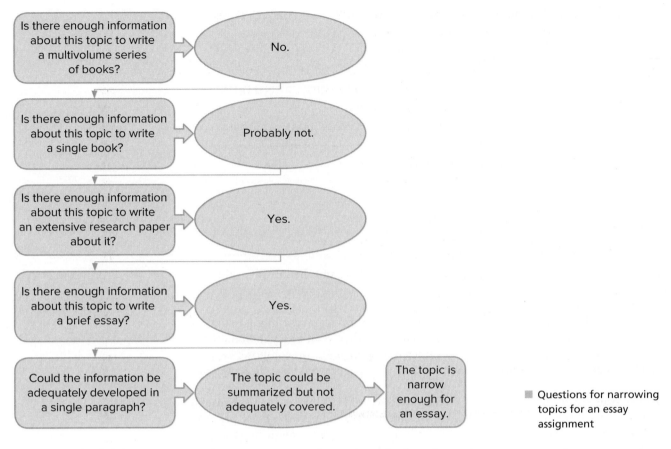

■ Questions for narrowing topics for an essay assignment

As Raphael did, you can use these questions to determine whether the topics you select are suitable for essays.

PRACTICE ⑤ Narrowing Topics for Essays

Use the "Questions for Narrowing Topics for an Essay Assignment" to consider each topic that follows. If the topic is suitable for an essay, write "Suitable for an essay." If the topic is too broad, narrow it so that it would be suitable for an essay.

1. The programming on cable television

_____

2. The importance of healthy lunches for schoolchildren

_____

3. Dentistry

_____

4. Why teens drop out of high school

_____

5. Sleep

_____

6. Stress

_____

7. Homelessness

_____

(continued)

8. Why tattoos are so popular

_____

9. Religious tolerance in the United States

_____

10. Cell phones

_____

USING PREWRITING STRATEGIES TO GENERATE IDEAS

Writers do not start at the beginning, go through the middle, and then finish at the end all in a straight line. They might get partway through the writing process only to realize they need to return to an earlier step to clarify their ideas.

Masterful writers go back and forth constantly, often throwing out entire paragraphs or pages as they figure out what they want to say and how they want to say it. Sometimes they go back to texts they were reading to gather more ideas. As you compose, be willing to go back and revise, rethink, and rewrite when your paper would benefit from your doing so.

Prewriting strategies—methods for coming up with ideas—are particularly useful techniques to employ again and again. Once you determine a topic, you can use prewriting to generate ideas. You may find yourself returning to different prewriting strategies to develop more ideas as you write.

As you experiment with prewriting methods, suspend judgment; that is, do not be critical about what you write. Write everything that comes to mind. You can weed out unsuitable ideas after you finish prewriting.

Practice using the following prewriting methods to find one or two of them that work well for you. You might find that some strategies work better than others for a particular topic.

Prewriting Strategy: Discussion

Discussing ideas with others can be a useful prewriting strategy. Meet with other students—in person, online, or by phoning or texting—and talk about your ideas for the assignment. While classmates make good discussion partners, family members and friends can also help you with ideas. Tell your discussion partners about your writing task, and ask them how they would proceed. Take notes so that you can revisit the ideas later when you are developing an outline.

PRACTICE ⑥ Using Discussion for Prewriting

Imagine your task is to write an essay about a current trend, such as getting a tattoo or wearing a certain style of clothing. You must determine why the trend is popular and how it developed. Use discussion to (1) identify a trend, (2) make a list of the possible reasons for its popularity, and (3) determine, if possible, how the trend developed. Jot down your answers on a separate sheet.

Prewriting Strategy: Simple Listing

Some people love to make lists. Even if you are not one of those people, you might still find that **listing** is a helpful prewriting strategy. The best way to use listing is to first turn the topic into a question.

For example, Luisa's topic for a writing assignment was the following: *strategies for increasing exercise.* First, she rewrote the topic as a question: What are some ways people can get more exercise? Next, she simply made a list of ways people could increase the amount of their daily exercise. Notice how her list, which follows, includes a wide variety of items. She did not censor any ideas at this stage; she wrote them all down and chose the best ones later on.

What are some ways people can get more exercise?

- go for a walk every day
- park farther away from entrances
- take stairs when possible
- join a gym
- join a community team (such as volleyball, baseball, and so on)
- find an exercise partner
- let their children be their "trainers"
- buy an exercise machine, such as an elliptical or treadmill
- buy a video and exercise with it
- use an online program for motivation
- hire a personal trainer
- do chores that require physical exertion, such as washing a car by hand
- find activities that combine exercise with fun, such as visiting and hiking in parks
- do the things they liked in childhood, such as bike riding, playing kickball, and so on

PRACTICE 7 Using Listing for Prewriting

Drawing on your own experience as a student, think about the following question: "What changes could be made in the public school system to increase student learning?" On a separate sheet, list at least ten ideas in response to the question.

Prewriting Strategy: Clustering

Clustering, or *mapping*, is a visual method of prewriting, illustrated on the next page. To use clustering, draw a circle in the middle of a sheet of paper, and in that circle write your paper's topic. As you think of an idea related to the topic, put the new idea in a new circle. Use lines to show relationships among ideas. Do not censor any ideas during this process, and do not worry if your result is messy. The example on the next page shows how Samuel used clustering for an essay about common rites of passage for American youth. (A *rite of passage* is an event or ritual that marks the change from one life stage to another.)

PRACTICE ⑧ Using Clustering for Prewriting

Use clustering to come up with examples or illustrations for an essay. The topic for this essay is *family traditions.* On a separate sheet, draw a clustering chart to prewrite about this topic. Some items you might consider are types of traditions, problems with traditions, and feelings about traditions.

Prewriting Strategy: Journalistic Questions

The six **journalistic questions** used by reporters can help you generate ideas about your topic. Think about your topic, and then consider these questions:

    Who?   What?   Where?   When?   Why?   How?

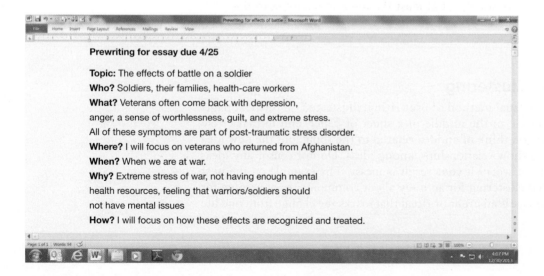

PRACTICE ⑨ Using Journalistic Questions for Prewriting

Consider the issue of cheating on tests. Use the six journalistic questions to explore this issue. Write your answers for the following questions on a separate sheet.

Topic: Cheating on tests

1. Who is involved?
2. What happens?
3. Where does it happen?
4. When does it happen?
5. Why does it happen?
6. How does it happen?
7. What can we do to prevent it?

Keep in mind that you may not need to use all the information these questions will produce. At this stage, do not censor any information. If you wish, use a computer to type in your ideas. The example at the bottom of the previous page shows Carolina's questions and answers about a particular topic.

Prewriting Strategy: Freewriting

Freewriting is one of the simplest prewriting methods. To freewrite, simply think about your topic and write everything that comes to mind for a limited period of time, such as three minutes. You do not need to write in complete sentences; it is fine to jot down phrases and words that come to mind. If you cannot think of anything to write, then type or write the topic's key words over and over. The point is not to censor ideas during this stage of writing. The example below shows Anita's freewriting. Notice how she simply recorded everything that came to mind.

Topic: sleep deprivation

makes it hard to concentrate, makes it hard to stay awake at work and school, can't live life well if you don't get enough sleep, must take time for yourself, set a good example for your kids by going to bed on time, sleep, sleep, deprivation, not enough of it, why, because too much is going on, eat dinner too late, too many activities, maybe should cut down on activities, eat a simple dinner like sandwiches, make a time you must go to bed every night, stick to it, teach kids the same, sleep, make room comfortable, nice atmosphere, comfy bed, fluffy pillows

Vocabulary Collection Word:
deprivation

Your in-context definition:

_____

_____

A dictionary definition:

_____

_____

PRACTICE ⑩ Using Freewriting for Prewriting

Imagine that you are required to write an essay about the decline of manners in public. Give yourself two to three minutes to freewrite. On a separate sheet, write down everything that comes to mind during this time period. If you get stuck, write a key word like *rude* or *polite* or *manners* over and over until you think of new ideas.

Prewriting Strategy: Freetalking

Freetalking is just like freewriting, except you use speech instead of a pen and paper. For two to three minutes, simply talk out loud to yourself about the topic. Consider using a cell phone that records your voice or a small digital recorder. Take your time and think out loud. It might be helpful to imagine you are talking to a friend about the topic. If you get stuck, repeat the topic over and over again. Jot down new ideas as they come to mind.

PRACTICE 11 Using Freetalking for Prewriting

Find a quiet place where you can talk to yourself or to your cell phone or digital recorder without distraction (or embarrassment!). Imagine that you have been assigned a paragraph or an essay on a social issue about which you are very concerned. More specifically, your assignment is to explain why this issue is worth our time and our attention. Examples of such issues are global warming, the **eradication** of poverty in a certain place, and the improvement of every elementary school. Use freetalking to explore why your chosen social issue is important. Write down at least three ideas you discover.

Vocabulary Collection Word:
eradication

Your in-context definition:
_____
_____

A dictionary definition:
_____
_____

CHAPTER ACTIVITIES

READING AND ANNOTATING

Below is a passage from the textbook *Environmental Science: A Study of Interrelationships* by Eldon Enger and Bradley Smith. This is the kind of textbook reading you will frequently encounter in college courses. Using the strategies in this chapter, preview the passage and jot down what you think the passage will be about. As you preview the text, identify the topic and try to predict what the main idea of the passage will be. Use annotations to mark key ideas. Additionally, mark any ideas that you find interesting. You will use your annotations for a later assignment.

Your Observations from Previewing

_____
_____
_____
_____

Potential Consequences of Global Warming and Climate Change

It is important to recognize that although a small increase in the average temperature of the Earth may seem trivial, such an increase could set in motion changes that could significantly alter the climate of major regions of the world. Computer models suggest that rising temperature will lead to changes to the **hydrologic** cycle, sea level, human health, the survival and distribution of organisms, and the use of natural resources by people. Furthermore, some natural ecosystems or human settlements will be able to withstand or adapt to the changes, while others will not.

YOUR ANNOTATIONS

Vocabulary Collection Word:
hydrologic

Your in-context definition:
_____
_____

A dictionary definition:
_____
_____

Poorer nations are generally more vulnerable to the consequences of global warming. These nations tend to be more dependent on economic activity that is climate-sensitive, such as **subsistence** agriculture, and lack the economic resources to adjust to the changes that global warming may bring. The Intergovernmental Panel on Climate Change has identified Africa as "the continent most vulnerable to the impacts of projected changes because widespread poverty limits adaptation capabilities."

Disruption of the Hydrologic Cycle

Among the most fundamental effects of climate change is disruption of the hydrologic cycle. Rising temperatures are expected to result in increased evaporation, which will cause some areas to become drier, while the increased moisture in the air will result in greater rainfall in other areas. This is expected to cause droughts in some areas and flooding in others. In those areas where evaporation increases more than precipitation, soil will become drier, lake levels will drop, and rivers will carry less water. Lower river flows and lake levels could impair navigation, hydroelectric power generation, and water quality and reduce the supplies of water available for agricultural, residential, and industrial uses.

Some areas may experience increased flooding during winter and spring, as well as lower supplies of water during summer. In California's Central Valley, for example, melting snow provides much of the summer water supply; warmer temperatures would cause the snow to melt earlier and thus reduce summer supplies, even if rainfall increased during the spring. More generally, the tendency for rainfall to be more concentrated in large storms as temperatures rise would tend to increase river flooding, without increasing the amount of water available.

Rising Sea Level

A warmer Earth would result in rising sea levels for two different reasons. When water increases in temperature, it expands and takes up more space. In addition, a warming of the Earth would result in the melting of glaciers, which would add more water to the oceans. Rising sea level erodes beaches and coastal wetland, inundates low-lying areas, and increases the vulnerability of coastal areas to flooding from **storm surges** and intense rainfall. By 2100, sea level is expected to rise by 15 to 90 centimeters (6–35 inches). A 50-centimeter (20-inch) sea-level rise will result in substantial loss of coastal land in North America, especially along the southern Atlantic and Gulf coasts, which are subsiding and are particularly vulnerable. Many coastal cities would be significantly affected by an increase in sea level. The land area of some island nations and countries such as Bangladesh would change dramatically as flooding occurred. The oceans will continue to expand for several centuries after temperatures stabilize. . . .

Changes to Ecosystems

Some of the most dramatic projections regarding global warming involve natural systems:

- Geographic distribution of organisms could be significantly altered by climate change. As climates warm, organisms that were formerly restricted to warmer regions will become more common toward the poles. The tundra biomes [habitats] of the world will be greatly affected because of the thawing of the permafrost, which will allow the northward migration of species. Similarly, mountainous areas will have less snow and earlier melting of the snow that does accumulate during the winter.

YOUR ANNOTATIONS

Vocabulary Collection Word:
subsistence

Your in-context definition:

_____

_____

A dictionary definition:

_____

_____

Vocabulary Collection Word:
storm surge

Your in-context definition:

_____

_____

A dictionary definition:

_____

_____

- Coral reefs are especially challenged because they are affected both by an increase in water temperature and by an increase in the acidity of the ocean. When carbon dioxide dissolves in water, it forms an acid. An increase in acidity would cause the skeletons of corals and the shells of many other organisms to tend to dissolve. This would make it more difficult for these organisms to precipitate calcium salts from the ocean to construct their skeletons and shells.

- Low-lying islands and shorelines will be especially impacted by rising sea level. Mangrove forests and marshes will be inundated and subjected to violent weather and storm surges.

Challenges to Agriculture and the Food Supply

Climate strongly affects crop yields. Yields will fall in regions where drought and heat stress will increase. In regions that will receive increased rainfall and warming temperatures, yields should increase. However, episodes of severe weather will cause crop damage that will affect yields. A warmer climate would reduce flexibility in crop distribution and increase irrigation demands. Expansion of the ranges of pests could also increase vulnerability and result in greater use of pesticides. Despite these effects, total global food production is not expected to be altered substantially by climate change, but negative regional impacts are likely. Agricultural systems in the developed countries are highly adaptable and can probably cope with the expected range of climate changes without dramatic reductions in yields. It is the poorest countries, where many already are subject to hunger, that are the most likely to suffer significant decreases in agricultural productivity.

Questions for Consideration

1. What is the topic of this textbook passage—global warming or rising sea levels? Explain and defend your answer in a paragraph.

2. How can global warming affect the growth of crops? Explain your answer in a paragraph.

3. Why should we be concerned with the issues raised in this reading? Explain your answer in two or three paragraphs.

4. What is the *hydrologic cycle*? Explain it in a paragraph.

5. What do the writers want students to know after reading this passage? Make a list of important items.

USING MODELS TO PRACTICE COMPOSING

The model essay that follows was written by Kendra, a student in an environmental science class. Kendra's assignment was to select a topic the instructor discussed in class and to explain why people should know more about that topic. Kendra remembered her instructor's discussion of the effects of rising sea levels and chose to write her essay on why people need to know about rising sea levels. For support, she planned to use information from her in-class lecture notes and information from her textbook. The passage "Potential Consequences of Global Warming and Climate Change" you read in the Reading and Annotating activity is from Kendra's textbook.

Follow the instructions below to see how Kendra used her text to write an essay.

1. Read the textbook selection below that Kendra used as a source, observing the types of annotations she created.

Potential Consequences of Global Warming and Climate Change
from *Environmental Science: A Study of Interrelationships*

Rising Sea Level

A warmer Earth would result in rising sea levels for two different reasons. When water increases in temperature, it expands and takes up more space. In addition, a warming of the Earth would result in the melting of glaciers, which would add more water to the oceans. Rising sea level erodes beaches and coastal wetland, inundates low-lying areas, and increases the vulnerability of coastal areas to flooding from storm surges and intense rainfall. By 2100, sea level is expected to rise by 15 to 90 centimeters (6–35 inches). A 50-centimeter (20-inch) sea-level rise will result in substantial loss of coastal land in North America, especially along the southern Atlantic and Gulf coasts, which are subsiding and are particularly vulnerable. Many coastal cities would be significantly affected by an increase in sea level. The land area of some island nations and countries such as Bangladesh would change dramatically as flooding occurred. The oceans will continue to expand for several centuries after temperatures stabilize.

KENDRA'S ANNOTATIONS

2 reasons for rising sea levels: expanding water, melting glaciers

Negative effects (good quote)

√ Prediction (good info)

Result: loss of land in North America (good quote)

Flooding and loss of land in other areas

2. Kendra wrote the following essay. Read Kendra's essay and the supplied annotations, which point out content and features. Insert your own annotations to mark writing strategies you would like to use in your essay.

Hayworth 1

Kendra Hayworth

Dr. Miller

INRW 0402

13 November 2013

The Effects of Rising Sea Levels

Somewhere in the world a steady *drip*, *drip*, *drip* sound can be heard. The sound comes from a massive glacier, slowly melting as

Introduction paragraph

Hayworth 2

the sun's rays penetrate the thinning ozone layer and warm the ice.

How can a little drip hurt? Multiply that single drop by millions

across the world and soon the melting ice will form enough water to

cause problems. In fact, scientists predict that the sea level will rise   **Information from textbook**

by 6-35 inches by 2100 (Enger). Global warming has already begun   **Kendra's thesis statement**

to increase the sea levels, and more people should be concerned

about this potentially deadly phenomenon.

As sea levels rise, beaches and their communities are affected. An   **Major supporting detail 1:** coastal regions affected

increase in sea level "erodes beaches and coastal wetland, inundates

low-lying areas, and increases the vulnerability of coastal areas to   **Quote:** used as support

flooding from storm surges and intense rainfall" (Enger). Beaches

are thin strips of land. It does not take much erosion to cause a   **Explanation**

narrow strip of land to disappear completely. Sand dunes can be

washed out when sea water rises, and then sea water can easily flood

the low-lying areas. When Hurricane Sandy hit the eastern region of   **Example**

the United States, entire beach communities were destroyed.

While the human cost of this destruction is apparent, there   **Transition sentence**

is also an ecological cost. When marshes and wetlands disappear,   **Major supporting detail 2:** species threatened

the species that live in those areas are threatened. As Dr. Miller

has explained, whenever one species decreases, there are chain   **Explanations and examples**

reactions such as increases in other species. For example, if marsh

birds disappear because the environment has changed, mosquito

populations could increase. Eventually, the spread of diseases would

Hayworth 3

also increase since mosquitos carry disease. Ultimately, human life would be affected by these changes.

Rising sea levels will be a challenge for cities on the coast. In the United States, many major cities are on coastlines. Miami, New York, Los Angeles, New Orleans, Houston, Boston, and Seattle are among many cities that would be impacted by a rise in sea level. An increase in sea level of 20 inches "will result in substantial loss of coastal land in North America, especially along the southern Atlantic and Gulf coasts, which are subsiding and are particularly vulnerable" (Enger).

Major supporting detail 3: major cities on coasts threatened

Examples: cities on coastlines

Quote: used as proof

The impact of sea level rise could be devastating for coastal cities. The costs of relocating coastal populations and industries would be enormous, not to mention the social upheaval such changes would cause.

Causes and effects

A rising sea level may not sound as alarming as a potential nuclear disaster or the threat of a disease like avian flu. However, the increase in sea level that is occurring right now is quite serious. More people need to know about the dangers that await if we do not make changes to stop the rise of the oceans.

Conclusion paragraph

A READING AND WRITING ASSIGNMENT

Using Kendra's essay as a model, write your own essay about a topic you have recently learned about in one of your classes and consider important. Consult your textbook for that class as a source.

Alternatively, use a different portion of the textbook passage "Potential Consequences of Global Warming and Climate Change" as a source for an essay on another aspect of climate change about which people should be concerned.

Refer to the Quick Start Guide to Integrated Reading and Writing Assignments for help as you write this essay.

◉ THINKING FROM AN INSTRUCTOR'S POINT OF VIEW

In a classroom setting, listening is important in at least two ways. For one, students have to focus on their instructors to learn the content covered in the course. Also, students must understand the instructions for assignments—what to read for homework, what to do for the next class, and so on. These tasks require basic listening tasks, yet some students have trouble with them.

If you were a college instructor, how would you help students learn to listen? Consider this scenario. The semester is fifteen weeks long, and it is week 9. Each week you have talked about the research essay due in week 10. There is a "no late work" policy in your class, so it is really important that students understand the assignment and its due date.

You leave some time during the last class of week 9 to answer students' last-minute questions. A few students stay after class to get clarification about the assignment.

On the research essay's due date, seven students out of twenty-five turn in their papers. That means only seven students will be eligible to pass because submitting the research essay is a requirement for passing. What follows are tears, apologetic e-mails, explanations about elderly relatives who died, and so on.

You do not want students to fail, but on the other hand, learning to listen and follow instructions is such an important life skill that you cannot send students the wrong message about listening. How do you proceed?

Write a paragraph or two explaining what you would say to students who failed to turn in their research papers. Write another paragraph or two presenting what you would say to your supervisor to explain why more than half your class failed.

◉ ADDING TO YOUR VOCABULARY

This chapter's vocabulary words appear below.

editorial	cursory	deprivation	eradication
hydrologic	subsistence	storm surge	

Choose five of the vocabulary words from this chapter that you would like to add to your vocabulary, and think about how you can use them this week. For example, one of this chapter's words is *cursory*. You can often substitute *cursory* for *hasty*, as in the examples that follow.

Example: I didn't have time to study, so I looked over my notes in a *hasty* fashion.

I didn't have time to study, so I looked over my notes in a *cursory* fashion.

List each of the five words you plan to use this week, and make note of a context in which you could use the new word.

Example: *Cursory*. I can use this word to teach my little brother the difference between cleaning his room thoroughly and cleaning his room in a *cursory* way.

⊙ ADDITIONAL ASSIGNMENTS

1. In Practice 7, you wrote down ideas in response to this question: "What changes could be made in the public school system to increase student learning?" Using your prewriting, select two to four changes you believe would transform public education. Write an essay in which you present your ideas.

2. Study the infographic "Measles & Rubella Initiative," which appeared earlier in this chapter. First, determine its topic. Then complete the following assignments.

   a. Why is measles and rubella prevention important enough for the federal government to create posters and campaigns? Use a prewriting method to generate a page of thoughts to answer this question.

   b. Select a health or environmental issue you believe people should be concerned about. Create your own infographic poster in which you present the topic, your point about the topic, and information to help you prove your point. Use color and images to emphasize information. For additional infographic models, go to www.google.com, click on "images," and type in "infographics." Hit the enter key and you will see a screenful of various infographics you can use as models.

EMOTIONAL INTELLIGENCE

A recent experiment shows the importance of *optimism*, a tendency to feel hopeful and positive about the future. A psychologist tested students at the University of Pennsylvania to determine whether optimism had an effect on grades. The experiment showed that by analyzing the level of optimism students had, researchers could more accurately predict the students' college success than by analyzing their SAT scores! Students who were on the optimistic end of the scale earned better grades than did students who were pessimistic.

Think about optimism, pessimism, and how they affect a person's success. Think of someone you know who is always optimistic. Has optimism made this person a better student or worker? Think of a pessimistic person you know. Has pessimism decreased this person's effectiveness? Write a paragraph in which you speculate on this topic.

CULTURAL LITERACY

Many of the readings in this book concern issues in the fields of psychology and interpersonal communications. What are these two fields? Do some Internet research to determine what experts in these areas study. Write a paragraph explaining what the experts in each field focus on. Give credit to the sources you consult.

CRITICAL THINKING

To find the best solution to a problem, we must consider all of the possible solutions. An enjoyable way to practice this kind of critical thinking is to find an answer to a problem.

To start, select a simple but irritating situation that needs a solution. For example, a disorganized pile of papers in your house might be a problem. How could you solve the problem? What solutions might you use that would help you eliminate the problem? Cleaning up the pile of papers is a good start, but it is not a permanent solution to the problem. Keeping the pile from coming back requires a daily organization routine.

Find a minor problem in your life that needs a solution. Think critically and creatively about how you might be able to solve the problem. If you wish, work with a classmate and see how many creative solutions you can devise. Write a paragraph in which you explain the problem and the solution you believe will work.

METACOGNITION

Did you know that students can change their learning ability over time? If you were never successful in math in the past, that does not mean you cannot learn to do math well now. Your ability to learn can develop and increase over time. What seemed unattainable last year might prove quite achievable this year.

Make a list of your assumptions about your strengths and weaknesses as a learner. Note any subjects about which you have thought, "I'm just not good at that." Next, think of a skill you found difficult at one time but later came to master. Write a paragraph explaining how you learned the skill. Finally, write a paragraph about whether you believe you can learn one of the weak subjects or skills you listed earlier. In your paragraph, explain the reasons for your beliefs.

If you were blindfolded and could touch only one part of an elephant—trunk, tusk, or leg, for example—what would you guess you were touching?

Main Ideas

In an old parable from India, several blind people each examine a single part of an elephant. Unable to see the whole, the person examining the tail assumes that the item in question is a rope. The person examining a tusk, meanwhile, determines that he is feeling a spear. The body is thought to be a wall, the trunk is mistaken for a snake, and the legs are assumed to be tree trunks. Without any knowledge of the whole—the elephant!—the investigators are led astray.

A written text can also be seen as a whole made up of various parts. While appreciating the individual parts is important, grasping how the parts make up the whole message—the writer's main idea—is crucial to comprehension.

Both reading and writing require us to work with main ideas. In reading, we must be able to identify main ideas, and in writing we must be able to communicate them. Our focus in this chapter is to see how the identification of particular parts of a reading can lead us to an understanding of the whole—the reading's main idea.

CHAPTER OBJECTIVES

After completing this chapter, students will be able to do the following:

- **Identify topic sentences and implied main ideas in paragraphs.**
- **Compose topic sentences for paragraphs.**
- **Identify main ideas in essays.**
- **Find implied main ideas in essays.**
- **Compose effective thesis statements.**
- **Use parallel structure in thesis statements.**

IDENTIFYING TOPIC SENTENCES
AND IMPLIED MAIN IDEAS IN PARAGRAPHS

The purpose of a paragraph is to communicate a main idea to the reader. The main idea of a paragraph is expressed in a **topic sentence,** and additional sentences in the paragraph are called **supporting sentences.** These additional sentences provide explanations, examples, and other kinds of support to help readers understand the topic sentence.

A topic sentence generally has these characteristics:

- **A topic sentence expresses the most important point in the paragraph.** If a writer could point to only one sentence that communicates her message, it would be the topic sentence.

- **A topic sentence presents an idea that requires support.** The idea is complex enough to require additional explanation.

    Acceptable: High blood pressure can do more damage to health than many people realize.

    What damage can high blood pressure cause? We need more information.

    Inadequate: Many people have high blood pressure.

    This simple fact does not require any more explanation.

- **A topic sentence expresses an idea that is broader than the ideas in supporting sentences.** To support a topic sentence, other sentences must provide narrower and more detailed information.

    Topic sentence: High blood pressure can do more damage to health than many people realize.

    Supporting sentences: *In the supporting sentences, the writer will describe the specific types of damage high blood pressure can cause, such as weakening of arterial walls, enlargement of the heart, and scarring of the kidneys.*

- **A topic sentence is not a question.** A topic sentence makes a **claim**—an assertion that requires support—and that claim is backed up by details in the other sentences in the paragraph.

Keeping in mind these characteristics will help you both identify and compose topic sentences.

Identifying Topic Sentences

In addition to recognizing topic sentences based on their characteristics, you can also identify topic sentences by means of this four-step process.

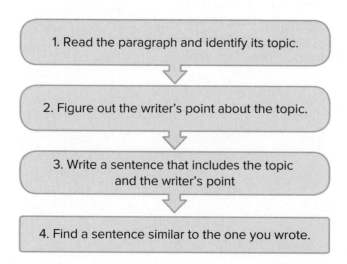

1. Read the paragraph and identify its topic.

2. Figure out the writer's point about the topic.

3. Write a sentence that includes the topic and the writer's point

4. Find a sentence similar to the one you wrote.

▪ Steps for identifying topic sentences

Study the following paragraph to see how the four-step process works. The **bold** print shows repeated words that suggest the topic.

Stress management is an emotional intelligence skill that increases the value of employees in a workplace. Personnel who have methods for relieving **stress** are much less likely to lash out at either coworkers or customers. Additionally, the ability to **control stress** helps workers be more efficient because they are not distracted by tension and worry. Staff who are successful at **keeping their stress levels down** will often rise to a higher level and become especially valued employees.

Topic: stress management

Detail: makes people less likely to lash out

Detail: helps with efficiency

Detail: makes employees more valued

Since managing stress is repeatedly mentioned in the paragraph, we can reasonably guess that the topic of the paragraph is stress management. The details in the paragraph suggest that stress management has benefits for employees. Once we identify the topic and the details about the topic, we can use the four steps to identify the topic sentence.

1. Read the paragraph and identify its topic.
   Topic: stress management

2. Figure out the writer's point about the topic.
   Writer's point: importance of stress management skills for workers

3. Write a sentence that includes the topic and the writer's point.
   Your sentence: Stress management is important for workers.

4. Find a sentence similar to the one you wrote.
   Topic sentence: Stress management is an emotional intelligence skill that makes employees valuable.

By using these four steps, we created a sentence with a meaning similar to the sentence we found in the original paragraph. If you can correctly identify the topic and the point the writer is making about the topic, you can find the paragraph's topic sentence.

Additionally, you can check to see whether the sentence you've identified has the qualities that topic sentences generally have. In this case, the sentence we have identified has the following characteristics.

Characteristics of an Effective Topic Sentence

- It expresses the most important point in the paragraph.
- It presents an idea that requires support.
- It expresses an idea that is broader than the ideas in supporting sentences.
- It is not a question.

In this example, the topic sentence is the first sentence in the paragraph. While a topic sentence is often placed first, it does not have to be. It may be placed in the body of a paragraph or even at the end. The key to finding a topic sentence is not to focus on where it is placed; rather, you need to put the main idea communicated in the paragraph into your own words and then find a sentence that corresponds to that idea. Complete the following exercise to see if you can find the topic sentence of a paragraph.

PRACTICE Finding Topic Sentences

Annotate the following paragraph to determine its main idea and topic sentence. Fill in the answers below.

YOUR ANNOTATIONS

What is the difference between a credit card and a debit card? Both can be used instead of cash or checks to make purchases online as well as at places of business. Debit cards are often associated with major credit card companies such as MasterCard

(continued)

and Visa. Yet debit cards function quite differently from credit cards. The fundamental difference is that when you use a credit card, you are actually borrowing money from a bank (the credit card company). That money must be paid back at the end of the grace period (usually about a month), or interest will be charged to you on the amount of the loan. With a debit card, you are spending your own money. Most often the money comes directly out of your checking account. While there are other dissimilarities, the principal difference between a credit card and a debit card is the difference between taking out a loan and spending money that you already have "on hand."

1. Read the paragraph and identify its topic.

   Topic: _____

2. Figure out the writer's point about the topic.

   Writer's point: _____

3. Write a sentence that includes the topic and the writer's point.

   Your sentence: _____

   _____

   _____

4. Find a sentence similar to the one you wrote.

   _____

   _____

   _____

Conclusion: If your analysis is correct, you have very likely identified the topic sentence.

_____

Finding Implied Main Ideas in Paragraphs

Some paragraphs do not include a stated topic sentence. In such paragraphs, the main idea is **implied**—suggested by the ideas in the paragraph but not explicitly stated. Readers must figure out the main idea and put it into their own words. When they do so, they are composing an **implied topic sentence.** Use this modified four-step process to identify the implied main idea, put it into your own words, and create an implied topic sentence.

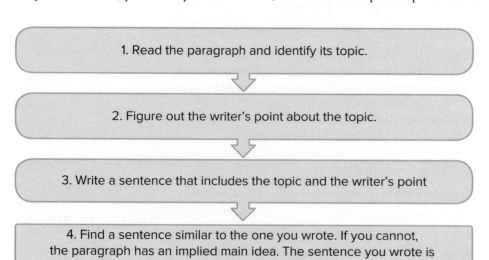

Steps for identifying an implied topic sentence

What follows is a paragraph from a psychology textbook. This paragraph does not have an explicit topic sentence. To find the paragraph's implied main idea, we must first identify the topic. The repetition, in **bold** print, of the terms *middle school* and *children* suggests that the topic involves middle school children. The terms *obsess, being scrutinized, being judged,* and *self-consciousness* help sharpen the focus of the topic. Other details will help us determine the writer's point about the topic.

In the **middle school** years, **children** may obsess over perceived personal flaws such as their height, weight, hair color, style of clothing, and even the types of music they choose. They believe that they are being scrutinized by everyone around them, and many **middle school children** feel that they are constantly being judged by their peers. **Children** in **middle school** can focus so much on their image that their grades suffer, they get depressed, or they are unable to maintain friendships. This self-consciousness can also result in dangerous or tragic behaviors.	**Topic:** middle school children Detail: They obsess over perceived personal flaws. Detail: They believe they are being watched. Detail: They feel they are being judged. Effect: Their self-focus can have negative results. Effect: Their self-consciousness can even have dangerous effects.

We can use the four-step process to figure out the implied main idea and to write an implied topic sentence.

1. Read the paragraph and identify its topic.
   Topic: the self-consciousness of middle school children
2. Figure out the writer's point about the topic.
   Writer's point: detrimental effects self-consciousness can have
3. Write a sentence that includes the topic and the writer's point.
   Your sentence: Middle school children may experience detrimental effects due to extreme self-consciousness.
4. Find a sentence similar to the one you wrote. If you cannot, the paragraph has an implied main idea. The sentence you wrote is the implied topic sentence.
   There is no similar sentence in the paragraph. Thus, the sentence from step 3 is the implied topic sentence.

Notice that each of the sentences in the paragraph above presents a type of difficulty middle school children experience. No single sentence sums up these difficulties, so the main idea is implied, not stated. We could write the implied topic sentence in a variety of ways, each of which is effective:

- Middle school children are at a difficult stage of life because of social stress.
- The extreme self-consciousness of middle school children makes this stage of life a challenge.
- The middle school years present social challenges for children because of self-consciousness.

When you encounter a paragraph with an implied topic sentence, write your own implied topic sentence in the margin. You will then be able to go back to the paragraph and read your implied topic sentence to get a quick summary of the paragraph's point.

A well-written paragraph always has a main idea. It may be stated explicitly in a topic sentence, or it may be implied, in which case you will have to write the implied topic sentence in your own words. Practice determining topic sentences in the exercise that follows.

PRACTICE ② Finding Implied Main Ideas in Paragraphs

The following paragraph has an implied main idea, not an explicit topic sentence. Use annotations to determine the topic and the writer's point, and then compose your own topic sentence for the paragraph.

> Banks frequently make credit cards available to college students. Some people are critical of this practice, pointing out that many college students are not mature enough—in terms of financial wisdom—to handle the borrowing potential that easy credit offers. Despite these criticisms, such cards do offer benefits to college students. Having a credit card can provide a student with an emergency fund. Not many college students have the luxury of a robust savings account. In the event of an emergency, such as a serious health issue, a wrecked vehicle, or stolen textbooks, having a credit card might be a real advantage. Having a credit card also enables a student to begin the process of building credit, which can have long-term benefits. The careful use of credit cards throughout college may mean the student will have built enough credit history to qualify for a home mortgage after graduation.

YOUR ANNOTATIONS

1. Read the paragraph and identify its topic.

   Topic: _____

2. Figure out the writer's point about the topic.

   Writer's point: _____

3. Write a sentence that includes the topic and the writer's point.

   Your sentence (implied topic sentence): _____

   _____

   _____

Finding Topic Sentences in Journalistic Style Paragraphs

Articles that appear in newspapers and popular magazines often have many very short, often single-sentence, paragraphs, even when the content could logically be combined into one longer paragraph. The use of short paragraphs is a feature of journalistic writing—a less formal style of writing intended to be read by a **diverse** general audience.

When you read essays that contain short, journalistic style paragraphs, group together the paragraphs that address the same topic. Use the grouped set of paragraphs to determine the explicit or implied topic sentence. For example, consider these paragraphs from a college newspaper article.

Vocabulary Collection Word:
diverse

Your in-context definition:

_____

_____

A dictionary definition:

_____

_____

> One program that is funded by the student use fee at Suntown College is the Academic Tutoring Project.
>
> Students can enroll in Academic Tutoring and do not have to pay anything out-of-pocket for the services.
>
> The student use fee is also used to help fund the Suntown Mental Health Clinic, a resource students can use free of charge for counseling and other mental health services.

Detail: Student use fee pays for tutoring.

Detail: Tutoring is free.

Detail: The student use fee funds Mental Health Clinic.

Detail: Counseling is free.

Although this passage consists of three very short paragraphs, these paragraphs are unified. They are all about the student use fee, and they all answer the question "What does the student use fee cover?"

Topic: student use fee

Writer's point: what the student use fee is used for

Your sentence: The student use fee at Suntown College funds free tutoring and free mental health services for students.

After you group together short paragraphs that are related, use the four-step process for finding the topic sentence. Keep in mind that the topic sentence may be explicit (stated) or implied (unstated).

PRACTICE ③ Analyzing Journalistic Style Paragraphs

Read and annotate the paragraphs that follow. Determine the topic sentence. If the topic sentence is stated, underline it. If not, write it in your own words.

YOUR ANNOTATIONS

Apartheid was a legal system of segregation and institutionalized racism in South Africa. It began officially in 1948, although South Africa had discriminated against people of color since the Dutch colonial period.

One of the most prominent and influential critics of apartheid was Nelson Mandela. Born in 1918, Mandela came of age during the institutionalization of apartheid. Mandela practiced nonviolent resistance to apartheid. He was a natural leader.

Although he spent twenty-seven years in prison for an alleged plot to overthrow the racist government, he eventually became president of South Africa in 1994. Nelson Mandela was instrumental in ending apartheid in South Africa.

1. Topic: _____

2. Writer's point: _____

3. Topic sentence or implied main idea: _____

_____

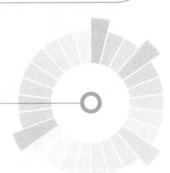

COMPOSING TOPIC SENTENCES FOR PARAGRAPHS

As you use the four-step process to identify topic sentences in readings, you are—at the same time—learning how to write topic sentences. When you compose a topic sentence, it should have the same four characteristics we described earlier.

- A topic sentence expresses the most important point in the paragraph.
- It presents an idea that requires supporting sentences.
- It expresses an idea that is broader than the ideas in supporting sentences.
- It is not a question.

You can follow a three-step process, shown on the next page, for composing a topic sentence.

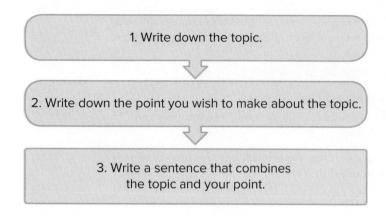

1. Write down the topic.

2. Write down the point you wish to make about the topic.

3. Write a sentence that combines the topic and your point.

■ Steps for composing a topic sentence

For example, suppose you are assigned an essay in which you are to identify and discuss the core college courses that are most important for being a well-informed person in today's world. You decide to consider three courses—World Geography, Public Speaking, and American Government. Here's how you might compose a topic sentence for your paragraph on the geography course.

1. Write down your topic.
   Topic: college course in World Geography

2. Write down the point you wish to make.
   Your point: what taking World Geography means for understanding world events

3. Write a sentence that combines your topic and your point.
   Your topic sentence: Because it is so important for understanding world events, World Geography should be a required course for all college students.

You can check the quality of your topic sentence by considering whether it has the characteristics of topic sentences.

- **Does it express the most important point in the paragraph?** Yes. The other sentences will help prove the point that college students should take World Geography.

- **Does it present an idea that requires supporting sentences?** Yes. Readers will want to know why the course is so important.

- **Does it express an idea that is broader than the ideas in supporting sentences?** Yes. The supporting sentences will give specific reasons why the course is important enough to be required of all college students.

- **Is it a question?** No.

Practice writing your own topic sentences in the exercise that follows.

PRACTICE ④ Writing Topic Sentences

Below you will find sets of topics and points about those topics. For each set, write a topic sentence by combining the topic and the point to be made about it. Use the characteristics of topic sentences to check your work.

1. Topic: choosing a career

   Point: how aptitude tests can help

   Your topic sentence: _____

2. Topic: home water filters

   Point: how they help the taste of tap water

   Your topic sentence: _____

(continued)

3. Topic: easing mental depression

Point: how a new hobby can help

Your topic sentence: _____

4. Topic: volunteering

Point: four steps for choosing appropriate volunteering opportunity

Your topic sentence: _____

_____

You can also practice composing topic sentences as you analyze readings. This kind of practice helps you understand what you are reading. Making it a habit to write out the topic sentences of the paragraphs you read yields two additional benefits. First, you improve your ability to write your own topic sentences. Second, you can use the topic sentences you write to grasp the broader idea that unites all of the paragraphs, as you will see later in this chapter.

PRACTICE 5   Identifying and Writing Topic Sentences

The following textbook passage contains three body paragraphs. For each body paragraph, identify the topic and the writer's point about the topic. Write a sentence that combines the topic with the writer's point. If the main idea is expressed in a topic sentence, write the topic sentence.

PARAGRAPH A

Guilt both alerts us to and motivates us to correct a wrong we have committed. Guilt is a lot like pain. When you cut yourself, you feel pain at the site where the injury occurred. The pain motivates you to repair the injury before it becomes infected and festers. Guilt also motivates us to avoid harming ourselves and others. We refrain from cheating on an exam or from stealing someone's laptop—even when no one is around to see us take it—because the very thought of doing so makes us feel guilty.

1. Topic: _____

2. Writer's point: _____

3. Topic sentence in your words: _____

4. Topic sentence from paragraph or implied topic sentence: _____

_____

PARAGRAPH B

Guilt is frequently regarded as a barrier to personal freedom and happiness. Some of us respond to guilt with resistance, either trying to ignore it entirely or getting angry at the person who "made" us feel guilty. But at the same time, we generally regard a person who feels no guilt—such as a sociopath—as inhuman and a monster.

(continued)

1. Topic: _____

2. Writer's point: _____

3. Topic sentence in your words: _____

4. Topic sentence from paragraph or implied topic sentence: _____

_____

PARAGRAPH C

Guilt is often broadly defined to include shame. However, the two are different. Guilt results when we commit a moral wrong or violate a moral principle. Shame, on the other hand, occurs as a result of the violation of a social norm, or not living up to someone else's expectations for us. Teenagers who are lesbian, gay, or bisexual may feel shame for not living up to the expectations of their family, church, or society—but they may not feel moral guilt. Rather than motivating us to do better, shame leaves us feeling inadequate, embarrassed, and humiliated. As good critical thinkers, it is important that we distinguish between guilt and shame.

1. Topic: _____

2. Writer's point: _____

3. Topic sentence in your words: _____

4. Topic sentence from paragraph or implied topic sentence: _____

_____

IDENTIFYING MAIN IDEAS IN ESSAYS

Just as a paragraph is a group of sentences that expresses and supports one main idea, an *essay* is a set of paragraphs that work together to support a main idea. Essays can take many forms, including magazine articles, scholarly journal articles, brief academic papers, and personal reflections.

Essays vary widely in depth, coverage, and use of technical language, depending on their context, purpose, and audience. An essay written for a medical journal, for example, is likely to be a well-researched piece of writing because of the expectations of its readers—doctors and professors—who require proof of careful research and reasoning in the essays they read. On the other hand, an essay written for an introductory biology course will be much shorter and will not go into much depth. The instructor will expect far less research and detail since the students reading the piece are just beginning to study the subject.

A common thread uniting all essays is that each one uses multiple paragraphs to communicate a main idea to an audience. Usually, a writer introduces the topic, states the main idea, supports or explains the main idea in a series of paragraphs, and offers a conclusion. Not all essays follow this pattern, but most essays include all four elements:

- Introduction
- Statement of the main idea (thesis statement)
- Supporting paragraphs
- Conclusion

Recognizing the Characteristics of Thesis Statements

The main idea of an essay is its **thesis statement.** The thesis statement provides the writer's topic and the point the writer wishes to make about the topic. Often, a thesis statement is expressed in a single sentence, but sometimes it will span two or three sentences. To help readers understand or accept a thesis statement, the writer must provide support. Each of the body paragraphs in an essay provides such support.

Like a topic sentence, a thesis statement has particular characteristics.

- **A thesis statement expresses the most important point of an essay.** While an essay may contain a great deal of information, all of that material is used to support a central point: the thesis statement.

- **A thesis statement presents an idea that requires support.** The idea or opinion demands explanation, evidence, or discussion in the essay.

    Acceptable: The Americans with Disabilities Act (ADA) has significantly helped disabled people, but more changes are needed to ensure that equal opportunities are available for people with disabilities.

    How has the ADA helped people, and what changes still need to be made? The thesis statement needs support to answer these questions.

    Inadequate: Some college students have physical disabilities.

    This simple fact does not require any more explanation.

- **A thesis statement expresses an idea that is broader than the ideas in supporting paragraphs.** To support a thesis statement, narrower and more detailed information is required.

    Thesis statement: The Americans with Disabilities Act (ADA) has significantly helped disabled people, but more changes are needed to ensure that equal opportunities are available for people with disabilities.

    Supporting paragraphs: *The writer will use some supporting paragraphs to discuss areas in which the ADA has improved life for disabled people, such as public transportation and access to public places. In other supporting paragraphs, the writer will discuss the changes that still need to be made, such as greater employment opportunities and more independent living options.*

- **A thesis statement is not a question.** A thesis statement makes a point that the writer believes and wants readers to believe or understand; thus, a thesis statement will not be a question.

Comparing Thesis Statements and Topic Sentences

You may have noticed that the characteristics of thesis statements are similar to those of topic sentences. In fact, thesis statements and topic sentences are similar in that they both communicate main ideas. The difference between them lies in their functions within an essay. If you have only a single paragraph, you will have only one single main idea, expressed either in an explicit topic sentence or in an implied topic sentence. You already know the purpose of the topic sentence: it tells you the most important point of the paragraph.

What happens when paragraphs are put together in an essay? These paragraphs still have topic sentences, and each topic sentence still tells the reader the most important point of its paragraph. However, the paragraphs in an essay serve to support the thesis statement. In the case of the thesis statement concerning the Americans with Disabilities Act given earlier, we might write four paragraphs to support the thesis statement. Each paragraph's main idea, stated in its topic sentence, would provide evidence for the thesis statement, as the diagram on the next page shows.

Thesis statement: The Americans with Disabilities Act (ADA) has significantly helped disabled people, but more changes are needed to ensure that equal opportunities are available for people with disabilities.

Body paragraph 1	Body paragraph 2	Body paragraph 3	Body paragraph 4
Topic sentence:	Topic sentence:	Topic sentence:	Topic sentence:
The ADA has improved the public transportation opportunities for people with disabilities.	Additionally, the ADA has given people with disabilities improved access to public places.	However, employment opportunities are still hard to find for many people with disabilities.	Also, people with disabilities continue to need better housing options.

Notice how the thesis statement in the preceding illustration presents a broader idea than each of the topic sentences. Just as a topic sentence presents a broader idea than the supporting sentences in a paragraph, the thesis statement of an essay presents a broader idea than the topic sentences of the supporting paragraphs. Try your hand at distinguishing thesis statements from topic sentences by completing the exercise that follows.

PRACTICE 6 Distinguishing Thesis Statements from Topic Sentences

In each group below, you will find a thesis statement and several topic sentences. Put an X in the blank for the sentence that is the thesis statement.

1. _____ Cooking at home saves money.

   _____ Knowing how to cook is advantageous in terms of savings, food safety, nutrition, and relaxation.

   _____ Cooking can be a relaxing activity.

   _____ The nutritional value of homemade meals is superior to that of fast food.

   _____ Home cooks can be assured their food is safely prepared.

2. _____ Some people take risks because of a need for sensory stimulation.

   _____ Risk taking is associated with aggression and hostility.

   _____ People who are impulsive are more likely to be risk takers.

   _____ Risk taking is a result of a complex set of human needs, behaviors, and emotions.

3. _____ Attending college with people of all backgrounds helps ease social tensions between groups.

   _____ Diversity on campus leads to diversity in the workforce, which has been shown to benefit businesses.

   _____ As individuals become more educated, their income generally rises.

   _____ Supporting affirmative action in college admissions is in the national interest.

Identifying the Thesis Statement in an Essay

Like topic sentences, thesis statements express a main idea by providing the *topic* and the *writer's point about the topic.* Thus, you can use a process for finding thesis statements that is similar to the one you used for finding topic sentences. These five steps will help you identify thesis statements.

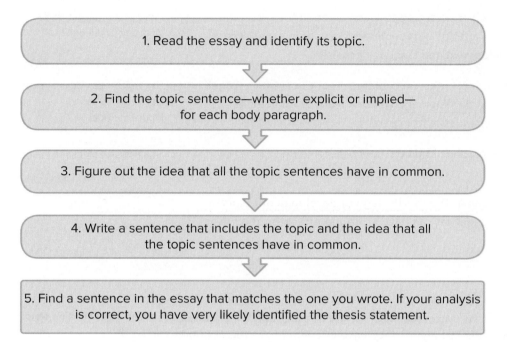

1. Read the essay and identify its topic.

2. Find the topic sentence—whether explicit or implied— for each body paragraph.

3. Figure out the idea that all the topic sentences have in common.

4. Write a sentence that includes the topic and the idea that all the topic sentences have in common.

5. Find a sentence in the essay that matches the one you wrote. If your analysis is correct, you have very likely identified the thesis statement.

■ Steps for identifying a thesis statement

Now we will examine in more detail each step in the process of identifying thesis statements.

Step 1: Read the essay and identify its topic.

Identify the essay's topic by analyzing the title, introduction, and context of the publication. Titles often reveal the writer's focus. We can guess reasonably well the topic of an essay entitled "The Benefits of Acupuncture." Of course, such guesses can be wrong, so it is important to follow guesses with a close reading of the essay.

Sometimes introduction paragraphs provide important clues to the topic of the essay. If "Surprises in Vermont" begins with a story of a couple finding gold in their backyard, you might reasonably guess that the surprise in question is that gold exists in Vermont.

Consider also the context of the reading. If an article titled "A Step Forward in New Mexico" is published in a journal written for high school principals, you might guess the article would concern good things happening in education in New Mexico. Reading the introduction paragraph would help confirm your guess.

Step 2: Find the topic sentence—whether explicit or implied—for each body paragraph.

Each body paragraph in an essay will have a main idea—either expressed in a topic sentence or implied. Read and carefully annotate each body paragraph, underlining the topic sentence or expressing the implied topic sentence in your own words.

Earlier in this chapter, we found an implied main idea in the paragraph about middle school children (see "Finding Implied Main Ideas in Paragraphs"). Now we will return to that paragraph and put it into the context of an essay. The paragraph about middle school children is only one of four body paragraphs in an essay about the theories of Jean Piaget, a well-known Swiss psychologist. By examining the topic sentences for all of the body paragraphs, you can figure out the idea that unites them. The example below displays the topic sentence for the paragraph about middle school children. It also displays the topic sentences for the other three body paragraphs, with student annotations.

Topic sentence of body paragraph 1: According to Jean Piaget, in the <u>first stage of development</u>, which occurs in infancy and toddlerhood, children experience challenges in their motor development and language **acquisition**.

First stage (motor and language challenges)

Topic sentence of body paragraph 2: In the elementary school years, which Piaget designates as the <u>second stage of development</u>, children learn to think more logically and practice more independence from parents.

Second stage (logical thinking and more independence)

Implied main idea of body paragraph 3: Middle school children may experience <u>extreme social stress.</u>

Third stage (social stress)

Topic sentence of body paragraph 4: <u>The fourth stage of development</u> occurs in high school when children's experiences can have profound effects on their lives as adults.

Fourth stage (experiences with profound consequences)

Once you have determined the topic sentence for each paragraph in an essay, highlight ideas and words (including synonyms) they have in common, as the example above illustrates.

Vocabulary Collection Word: acquisition

Your in-context definition:
_____
_____

A dictionary definition:
_____

Step 3: Figure out the idea that all the topic sentences have in common.
Reread the topic sentences, asking yourself, "What point do all of these sentences support?" In the paragraphs shown in step 2, the topic sentences all concern *chronological stages* in a child's development. Additionally, the topic sentences focus on what children *experience* during these stages.

Step 4: Write a sentence that includes the topic and the idea that all the topic sentences have in common.
Now you are ready to combine the essay's topic and the common point made by the supporting paragraphs into one sentence.

>   **Topic:** Jean Piaget's description of children's life stages
>
>   **Writer's point:** each stage and the experiences in it
>
>   **Your sentence combining the topic and the writer's point:** Children progress through four developmental stages and have different experiences in each stage, according to Jean Piaget.

Step 5: Find a sentence in the essay that matches the one you wrote. If your analysis is correct, you have very likely identified the thesis statement.
Read through the essay looking for a sentence that, like your sentence, contains the essay's topic and the writer's point about the topic. Do not expect the sentence you find to match your sentence precisely. In fact, sometimes you will find the thesis statement and then realize that the sentence you wrote was off-track. The goal is to identify the writer's point about the topic. When you understand the writer's point, you will be able to determine the thesis statement.

PRACTICE ⑦ Using Topic Sentences to Find the Main Idea of an Essay

Below you will find an essay's topic sentences. Use the topic sentences to make an educated guess about what the essay's thesis statement might be. Put the thesis statement into your own words.

Topic sentence of body paragraph 1: Movement—physical activity of any kind—changes the brain's structure and reduces depression.

Topic sentence of body paragraph 2: Certain types of therapy, especially cognitive behavioral therapy, can help with depression.

Topic sentence of body paragraph 3: Learning a new skill, even something as minor as using a new recipe, can lessen depression.

Topic sentence of body paragraph 4: Biofeedback, meditation, and deep breathing contribute to a calmer, less depressed mood.

Write the main idea in a complete sentence: _____

_____

Vocabulary Collection Word:
cognitive

Your in-context definition:
_____
_____

A dictionary definition:
_____
_____

Example of Identifying an Essay's Thesis Statement

The following essay contains a paragraph you analyzed earlier in this chapter. Read the essay to see how one student, Sarit, uses the steps you just learned to identify the main idea and thesis statement of the essay.

First, Sarit determines what the essay's topic is by highlighting key words in the title and words that are repeated throughout the essay. Then she identifies and underlines the topic sentence of each paragraph.

Why Emotional Intelligence Matters—At Work

Do you know anyone who is not necessarily the smartest member of a work group but who is a great team player and always seems to contribute significantly? On the other hand, do you know someone who is "book smart" but seems to have a difficult time getting along with coworkers? The first person has high "emotional intelligence." The second person does not. Emotional intelligence (EI) refers to how well people understand their own feelings as well as the emotions of others. Surprisingly, perhaps, being "book smart" is not sufficient for career success. We have learned in recent years that successful employees—those who move the most quickly up the ladder—possess greater emotional intelligence skills than their coworkers.

Awareness of your emotions is one way EI makes you a better employee. Intentionally thinking about how you are feeling is a crucial skill. For example, if you are irritable, you may have a harder time with a planning session at the office than you otherwise would. Realizing that you are grumpy does not instantly make you happy, but it does give you a heads-up that you need to be especially careful as you relate to your coworkers or customers or supervisors. Sometimes people with low emotional intelligence will think their moods justify bad behavior. You may even have heard comments like "Don't mind Jessica; she's always moody." The truth is, Jessica won't be the one getting the promotion.

Sarit's Annotations

Step 1—Identify topic.
Emotional intelligence?

Can't be thesis statement—these are questions.

Definition. Maybe the entire essay's main idea is to define emotional intelligence.

Topic—EI and career success?

Step 2—Find the topic sentences.

Topic sentence

Topic:—being a better employee??

Emotional intelligence again—topic?

(continued)

Empathy means putting yourself in another person's shoes emotionally. <u>Beyond being self-aware, employees who interpret the emotions of others by being empathetic are assets in the workplace.</u> Can you imagine how the other person feels in a given situation? If one of your colleagues has just come from an evaluation with his supervisor and snaps at you when you say "Hello," he might be feeling upset because of what his boss had to say. Recognizing your coworker's emotional situation would help smooth over hurt feelings. Similarly, a salesperson who can empathize with customers will have more pleasant interactions with them; as a consequence, she might even make more sales!

Topic sentence

A benefit of emotional intelligence

<u>Stress management is another EI skill that makes employees more valuable.</u> A person who has methods for relieving her stress is much less likely to blow up at a coworker or a customer. One who can control her stress is also a more efficient employee because she is not distracted by the tension that has built up inside her psyche. Controlling stress is not always an easy thing to do; people who are successful at keeping their stress level down can rise above their colleagues and become more valued employees.

Topic sentence

Topic—how emotional intelligence benefits you?

Unpleasant or difficult situations inevitably occur in the workplace. Workers who are able to adapt fairly quickly when frustrations or disappointments occur will be able to proceed with occupational tasks. Employers can trust employees who are adaptable; such employees will make the adjustments needed to get the work done. Workers who are prone to "drama" over frustrations or disappointments will be labeled "difficult" and will not be the ones on the promotion list. <u>Employees who have emotional flexibility are considered more dependable than those who do not.</u>

Topic—emotional intelligence at work?

Topic sentence at end of paragraph

<u>Teamwork is crucial in almost every vocation, and EI makes employees better team players.</u> Working well with clients or customers is also critically important in many occupational settings. Being able to recognize and relate to the feelings of others and being aware of your own feelings will increase your ability to work well with others. That is why people with high EI are more successful in their careers than people with low EI.

Topic sentence

EI is tied to career success.

Sarit must now figure out what all the topic sentences have in common. Her annotations show her that two principal things are going on in this essay:

- The topic sentences discuss four components of emotional intelligence: awareness of emotions, empathy, stress management, and emotional flexibility.
- The topic sentences also show that emotional intelligence is valuable to employees because workers who have EI skills are more valuable than those who lack them.

Thus, Sarit has found both the topic—components of emotional intelligence—and the writer's point: that these components make workers more valuable.

With this information, Sarit continues with the fourth step—combining the topic and the point made by the topic sentences. Here is the sentence she wrote:

<u>Having emotional intelligence skills</u> <u>helps people in their careers.</u>

        Topic   Writer's point about the topic

To complete the last step, Sarit rereads the essay to find a sentence that matches the main idea she has identified. She is able to locate two sentences that match the main idea. One is in the introduction:

We have learned in recent years that successful employees—those who move the most quickly up the ladder—possess greater emotional intelligence skills than their coworkers.

And one is in the conclusion:

> That is why people with high EI are more successful in their careers than people with low EI.

Sarit decides that the first statement, which more fully expresses the main idea, is the thesis statement and that the sentence in the conclusion simply **reiterates** the main idea.

Not all essays will include repeated thesis statements as this example does. As a flexible reader, you need to be aware that essays do not follow a strict formula. Some writers will place the thesis statement in the middle of an essay, and sometimes the thesis statement occurs only at the very end.

Vocabulary Collection Word:
reiterate

Your in-context definition:

_____

_____

A dictionary definition:

_____

_____

PRACTICE Finding the Thesis Statement of a Textbook Passage

Read and annotate the following passage from *Lesikar's Business Communication,* a textbook by Kathryn Rentz, Marie Flatley, and Paula Lentz. Use your annotations and the five-step process for identifying a thesis statement. Fill in the answers below.

The Importance of Communication Skills to You

YOUR ANNOTATIONS

Because communication is so important in business, businesses want and need people with good communication skills. Evidence of the importance of communication in business is found in numerous surveys of executives, recruiters, and academicians. Without exception, these surveys have found that communication (especially written communication) ranks at or near the top of the business skills needed for success.

For example, NFI Research, a private organization that regularly surveys over 2,000 executives and senior managers, recently found that 94 percent of the members "rank 'communicating well' as the most important skill for them to succeed today and tomorrow." A study of skills and competencies needed by accountants strongly supports the value of writing, speaking, and listening, and Deloitte & Touche, ranked by *BusinessWeek* in 2007 as the best place to launch a career, cited communication skills as the "most desirable trait" in a job candidate. Employers surveyed for the National Association of Colleges and Employers' *Job Outlook 2009* also cited "communication skills" and the related traits of "a strong work ethic, ability to work in a team, and initiative" as highly prized qualities in job applicants. Recruiters who participated in *The Wall Street Journal*'s latest ranking of MBA programs agreed. They rated "interpersonal and communication skills, a teamwork orientation, personal ethics and integrity, analytical and problem-solving abilities, and a strong work ethic" as most important.

Unfortunately, business's need for employees with good communication skills is all too often not fulfilled. Most employees, even the college trained, do not communicate well. In fact, surveys show that, in the opinion of their employees, even managers and executives who think they communicate well actually fall short. Effective communicators are, therefore, in high demand. Not surprisingly, there is a high correlation between communication skills and income. Even among college graduates, those with higher scores in literacy (use of printed and written information) earn significantly more than lower scoring graduates earn. A study by Office Team revealed that technology magnifies the exposure of one's communications skills, forcing workers to communicate more effectively and articulately because these skills will be showcased

(continued)

more. Email often results in a sender's language skills being placed in front of different people simultaneously, while audio and video will reveal the caliber of one's verbal and diplomacy strengths as well.

The communications shortcomings of employees and the importance of communication in business explain why you should work to improve your communication skills. Whatever position you have in business, your performance will be judged largely by your ability to communicate. If you perform and communicate well, you are likely to be rewarded with advancement. And the higher you advance, the more you will need your communication ability. The evidence is clear: Improving your communication skills improves your chances for success in business.

1. Write the essay topic: _____

_____

2. Underline the topic sentence for each paragraph, or write the implied topic sentences here: _____

_____

3. Write the idea that all the topic sentences have in common: _____

_____

4. Write your own sentence that includes the essay topic and the idea that the topic sentences have in common: _____

_____

5. Underline the thesis statement and write it here: _____

_____

FINDING IMPLIED MAIN IDEAS IN ESSAYS

Just as some paragraphs do not have explicit topic sentences, some essays do not contain explicit thesis statements. The main idea—and thesis statement—in such essays is implied. Readers must figure out the main idea through the essay's content. We can use steps from the same process to find implied thesis statements as we use to find explicit ones.

Lucas needs to analyze an essay to determine its thesis statement for an assignment in his sociology class. He determines that the essay is on the topic of learning disorders in children. To identify the writer's point about the topic, he first annotates the function of each topic sentence.

Topic sentence for paragraph 1: Parents often notice physical difficulties with fine motor skills first.	One symptom of a learning disorder
Topic sentence for paragraph 2: Trouble in particular classes—such as math or reading—is a symptom that may indicate particular learning disabilities.	Another symptom of a learning disorder
Topic sentence for paragraph 3: Some learning disabilities are identified by a child's social behaviors.	Social behaviors—also symptoms
Topic sentence for paragraph 4: Language difficulties can also signal learning disorders.	Language difficulties—another symptom

By looking for a common point that unites all four paragraphs, Lucas can see that they all concern symptoms of learning disorders. Now he is ready to write a sentence combining the writer's topic and main point. Here is Lucas's statement of the essay's implied main idea:

<u>Four types of symptoms are associated with</u> <u>learning disorders in children.</u>

        Writer's point about the topic   Topic

Lucas's sentence expresses the implied main idea of the essay. When the thesis statement is implied, write out the thesis statement yourself, as Lucas did. You will have an easier time remembering the essay's main idea if you write it down in your own words.

PRACTICE ⑨ Finding an Implied Thesis Statement in an Essay

The following essay has an implied main idea. Annotate the essay to determine its topic and topic sentences. On the basis of your analysis, complete the questions that follow.

Summer. The Kenai Peninsula. Wow.

YOUR ANNOTATIONS

When we leave Dallas, it is 98°F. It is an amazing 68°F when we land in Alaska. It's almost midnight when we pick up the rental car. We proceed to drive the length of the Kenai Peninsula, from Anchorage to Seward, amazed by the amount of daylight. On summer evenings in this part of the world, the sky never grows entirely dark. The sun dips just below the horizon, creating a lingering dusk, and then an hour or two later, the sun gradually peeks above the horizon again. Dusk and dawn are buddies, pals, hanging out together.

Green—everything is green. The mountains are green; the valleys are green; even the water in the dozens of lakes and rivers and creeks that we drive past is emerald green. The mountaintops are the only exception: they are white. Even in July, the mountain crests are still covered with glistening snow.

Salmon are running in the creeks. We stop along the highway and take a few steps to a stream to watch them. In water that is only a couple of feet deep, we see dozens, scores, hundreds of salmon struggling upstream to spawn. During their trek from the ocean, the color of their bodies has been transformed from silver to deep scarlet.

More than once, we come around a curve and happen upon moose beside the road. The size of these animals is startling. They just chew their cud and watch us go by.

At one point, we exit the highway. We drive a few miles and come face-to-face with an ancient—millions of years old—glacier and the icebergs that it calves. We see icebergs as big as houses in a just-above-freezing lake within walking distance of the highway.

Alaska. The Kenai Peninsula. Summer. Wow.

(continued)

1. Write the essay topic: _____

   _____

2. Underline the topic sentence for each paragraph or write the implied topic sentences here: _____

   _____

   _____

3. Write the idea that all the topic sentences have in common: _____

   _____

4. Write your own sentence that includes the essay topic and the idea that the topic sentences have in common: _____

   _____

COMPOSING EFFECTIVE THESIS STATEMENTS

When you put the main idea of a reading into your own words, you are not only learning how to find thesis statements; you are also learning how to write them. Remember that to find the thesis statement of an essay, you must focus on determining the topic and identifying the point the writer is making about the topic. Similarly, when you compose a thesis statement, you write a sentence that includes your topic and your point about the topic.

Thesis Statements That Are Too Narrow or Too Broad

Because a thesis statement provides the main point of an essay, it must be broad enough to cover everything the writer will include in the essay. For example, imagine you are writing an essay about ways to conquer stage fright. In the essay, you plan to discuss how practice, relaxation techniques, and planning for mistakes can help a person conquer stage fright. If the thesis statement focuses on only one of the suggestions you will be discussing in your essay, the thesis statement will be too narrow.

> **Overly narrow thesis statement:** Stage fright can be conquered by setting aside time each day to practice.
>
> **Effective thesis statement:** Stage fright can be conquered by practicing, using relaxation techniques, and planning for mistakes.

Thesis statements can also be too broad. "Stage fright is a very common experience," for example, is too broad to really focus in on your main idea—that there are several specific ways to conquer stage fright. The key is to write a thesis statement that is just broad enough to cover every point you will be making in your essay.

PRACTICE ⑩ Creating Effective Thesis Statements

Below are sets of topic sentences that go with the body paragraphs of different essays. Construct a thesis statement for each set of topic sentences, making sure your thesis statement is neither too broad nor too narrow.

(continued)

EXAMPLE

Topic sentences:

- A common effect of recession is unemployment.
- Additionally, businesses lose money in recessions.
- In a recession, most people have less money to spend.

Your thesis statement: *Recessions have negative effects on businesses and individuals.*

SET 1

Topic sentences:

- Online courses require students to be self-motivated.
- Additionally, online classes are best for students who have a functional knowledge of computer operations.
- Students who take online courses should have a learning style that is consistent with independent learning.

    Your thesis statement: _____

    _____

    _____

SET 2

Topic sentences:

- Studying economics results in greater knowledge about how consumer goods are priced.
- A course in economics also benefits students by showing how financial decisions have long-term consequences.
- An economics course provides an understanding of how investments work.
- Studying economics helps students understand the **implications** of political decisions on the economy.

    Your thesis statement: _____

    _____

    _____

Vocabulary Collection Word:
implications

Your in-context definition:

_____

A dictionary definition:

_____

_____

SET 3

Topic sentences:

- Students need basic Internet skills to be able to succeed in college.
- Students need to know how to do word processing for a variety of tasks.
- The ability to use e-mail and to handle e-mail attachments is another requirement for students.

    Your thesis statement: _____

    _____

    _____

Prewriting and Thesis Statements

You have already learned some methods for prewriting. Prewriting will help you generate ideas about topics, and from your prewriting, you can decide on the main idea you want to communicate. Prewriting will also help you determine the ideas you will use to support your thesis statement.

In the example of prewriting that follows, we see a list of ideas generated by Ben, a student in a writing class, in response to an essay assignment. He has crossed out the ideas he does not want to address and has made notes next to the ones he will include in his essay.

Assignment: Write an essay in which you discuss how failure can be a positive experience.
Ideas from prewriting:

- helps people learn about their strengths and weaknesses   *(helps people with self-discovery)*

- ~~teaches people to not give up can be motivational~~

- ~~makes people stronger~~

- is actually a way we learn new skills   *(bike riding, for example)*

- teaches people life lessons   *(when people fail because of not listening to wise advice or by breaking the law)*

Because of his prewriting, Ben knows what he wants to discuss in his essay. He is ready to write a thesis statement. To write a thesis statement, Ben can follow these steps.

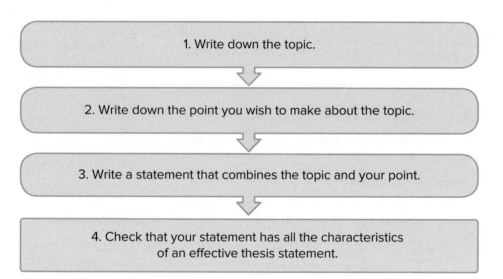

1. Write down the topic.

2. Write down the point you wish to make about the topic.

3. Write a statement that combines the topic and your point.

4. Check that your statement has all the characteristics of an effective thesis statement.

■ Steps for composing a thesis statement

Here's what Ben did to compose his thesis statement.

1. Write down the topic.
   Topic: the value of failure

2. Write down the point you wish to make about the topic.
   Ben's point: encourages self-discovery, is a way of learning new skills, teaches life lessons

3. Write a statement that combines the topic and the point you wish to make.
   Ben's thesis statement: Failure is valuable because it encourages self-discovery, provides a way to learn new skills, and teaches life lessons.

Ben believes that in the long run, it is more important for people to learn life lessons, so he decides to emphasize that idea by putting it last. In his thesis statement, he puts the ideas in the order in which he will present them in the essay.

Ben's thesis statement provides the main idea of the essay. It also gives readers a clue to the kind of information the essay will contain and the order in which it will be presented.

To make sure his thesis statement is acceptable, Ben must do one more task. He needs to make sure his thesis statement has all the characteristics of an effective thesis statement.

Characteristics of an Effective Thesis Statement

- It combines the topic of the essay with your point about the topic.
- It expresses the main idea you are making in the essay.
- It requires supporting details, supplied in the essay's paragraphs.
- It is broad enough to unify the ideas in the supporting paragraphs.
- It is a statement, not a question or an announcement.

After evaluating his thesis statement, Ben finds that it has the characteristics of an effective thesis statement. Refer to this list of characteristics to complete the following exercise.

PRACTICE 11 Critiquing Thesis Statements

Imagine you are guiding Sharon, who is writing an essay about why people choose to be vegetarians. She plans to discuss these three reasons:

- Some people believe vegetarian diets are healthier than meat-based diets.
- Others choose vegetarianism because of their ethical beliefs regarding the treatment of animals.
- A third reason for choosing a vegetarian diet is concern about the effects of meat production on the environment.

Sharon has written several sentences and wants to know which one would make the best thesis statement, based on the characteristics of thesis statements. Read each numbered sentence, and explain why it would or would not be the best thesis statement. Finally, write your own thesis statement for Sharon's essay.

1. Why is it a good idea to be a vegetarian?

   Your comments: _____

   _____

   _____

2. Because a vegetarian diet is healthier than a meat-based diet, becoming a vegetarian is a good idea.

   Your comments: _____

   _____

3. People must decide for themselves whether a vegetarian diet is the right choice.

   Your comments: _____

   _____

4. Your thesis statement: _____

   _____

   _____

Open and Closed Thesis Statements

Not all thesis statements are explicit about the support the writer will present. Some thesis statements lead the reader to expect to learn about "several reasons" or "important aspects," or they use some other phrase to let the reader know the essay will address a variety of similar elements. These kinds of statements are **open thesis statements.**

Example: Making firearms illegal on college campuses is the right policy.

We call this an open thesis statement because it does not reveal the writer's reasons for his position or the kinds of support he will present in the essay. The rest of the essay is left *open*, so to speak.

On the other hand, **closed thesis statements** tell the reader exactly what support will be used in the essay.

Example: Making firearms illegal on college campuses will reduce the potential for violence, keep campuses focused on education, and foster a community of trust.

Closed thesis statements reveal the reasons or supporting points that will be in the essay; thus, the essay is *closed* to other reasons or support.

Open thesis statements are appropriate for essays with body paragraphs that are similar to one another in function. For example, an essay setting out causes of **insomnia** lends itself to a thesis statement such as this one.

Open thesis statement: Insomnia can be caused by a variety of conditions.

               Topic   Writer's point about the topic

The following chart gives examples of open thesis statements.

TYPE OF ESSAY	OPEN THESIS STATEMENT
An essay showing how the differences between the public school systems of the United States and Canada affect learning	A comparison of the public school system in the United States with the public school system in Canada reveals significant differences that affect student learning.
An essay offering solutions to the problem of homelessness	Communities can reduce the negative consequences of homelessness by using six strategies that have been proved effective.
An essay in support of making college education free	Making a college education free and available to all citizens makes sense for several reasons.

Closed thesis statements are appropriate when it is important or helpful to readers to reveal the content of the essay in advance. The disadvantage is that such thesis statements can be difficult to compose since they list the specific support that will appear in the body paragraphs. For instance, to convert the open thesis statement about reasons for insomnia to a closed thesis statement, we would need to include particular causes of insomnia.

Closed thesis statement: Insomnia can have many causes, but the most common ones are stress, medications, and environmental distractions.

The topic is insomnia, and the three causes presented in this closed thesis statement are stress, medications, and environmental distractions.

One key to writing a good closed thesis statement is using parallelism. The Grammar Focus that follows will help you write closed thesis statements that demonstrate parallelism.

Vocabulary Collection Word:
insomnia

Your in-context definition:

_____

_____

A dictionary definition:

_____

_____

■ The design of this room demonstrates parallelism in that both of the columns are parallel to each other. Can you find other elements that are parallel?

Parallelism

Thesis statements often contain a series of elements that are part of the writer's main idea. For example, in the thesis statement that follows, three phrases are used to communicate parents' responsibilities.

Parents' primary duties are to nurture, to protect, and to educate their children.

The sentence lists three duties in a series connected by and. *Notice that each item in the series takes the form* to + main verb.

In the following thesis statement, a series of elements is presented in parallel form.

Life coaches should model successful living, provide good advice, and teach effective planning to their clients.

Each item in the series consists of a verb and an object:

model (*verb*) ⟶ successful living (*object*)

provide (*verb*) ⟶ good advice (*object*)

teach (*verb*) ⟶ effective planning (*object*)

The sentence contains a series of three verbs (model, provide, teach). Each verb is followed by an adjective that modifies a noun (successful living, good advice, effective planning).

Parallelism is the use of consistent structure for all elements in a series of two or more elements. (Hint: Look for a conjunction such as *and* that links the items.)

Bullying in schools is a serious problem because it can cause extreme anguish to victims *and* result in serious physical harm.

The two reasons for the seriousness of bullying are presented in parallel form.

(continued)

Knowledge of geography is <u>necessary for jobs in commerce</u>, <u>important for careers in sales</u>, and <u>essential for careers in international business</u>.

The three items in the series are presented in parallel form; each contains an adjective followed by a prepositional phrase.

Because thesis statements often present series of elements, always check to ensure that your thesis statement is in parallel form. While parallelism is especially important in thesis statements, *every* sentence that presents a series of elements should reflect parallel form.

To use parallelism in sentences, follow these guidelines:

- Identify items in the sentence that could be put in parallel form, usually a series of two or more similar elements joined by a coordinating conjunction (*for, and, nor, but, or, yet, so*).

- Make sure the items in the series are alike in their parts of speech.

  Example: During college, Micah liked <u>skiing</u>, <u>jogging</u>, and ~~to skateboard~~ <u>skateboarding</u>.

- Make changes in wording, if necessary, to achieve parallelism.

  Example: Trinity teaches special-needs adults to manage their money, practice good hygiene, and ~~the ability to make breakfast, lunch, and dinner~~ prepare their own meals.

COMBINING SENTENCES

The examples that follow show how to combine ideas to create thesis statements with parallelism.

Ideas to combine:

- <u>Time</u> is required to open a new business.
- Having <u>patience</u> is part of opening a business.
- Opening a business requires <u>an initial investment</u>.

Parallel thesis statement: To open a business requires <u>time</u>, <u>patience</u>, and <u>money</u>.

Ideas to combine:

- <u>A college education should be free in the United States</u>.
- An alternative to making college free is <u>making student loans available to anyone who wants one</u>.

Parallel thesis statement: Either <u>a college education in the United States should be free</u> or <u>student loans should be available to anyone who wants one</u>.

EXPANDING THE CONCEPT

Parallelism is used in sentences, but it is also used in headings and lists, in sets of instructions, and within paragraphs and compositions.

EXERCISES

Combine each set of sentences below into a thesis statement that demonstrates parallelism.

(continued)

1. Ideas to combine:

- Global warming affects sea levels.

- Global warming creates changes in precipitation patterns.

- Ecosystems are also affected by global warming.

   Answer: _____

   _____

2. Ideas to combine:

- One reason to require college algebra for college degrees is to teach students to think **sequentially**.

- The improved use of logic in thinking is another reason college algebra should be required.

- Algebra also creates more flexibility in the way people think.

   Answer: _____

   _____

   _____

3. Ideas to combine:

- The use of drones reduces casualties for the military that uses them.

- The cost of military engagement is decreased when drones are used.

- Drones do less damage to cities than traditional warfare does.

   Answer: _____

   _____

   _____

4. Ideas to combine:

- Because tablet computers are more expensive than desktop computers, schools should purchase desktop computers rather than tablets.

- Regular desktop computers offer greater functionality than tablets.

- Tablets are much more likely to be stolen than desktop computers.

   Answer: _____

   _____

   _____

Vocabulary Collection Word:
sequentially

Your in-context definition:

_____

_____

A dictionary definition:

_____

_____

PRACTICE ⑫ Writing Parallel Closed Thesis Statements

Combine each of the essay topics below with the point being made about the topic to write a parallel closed thesis statement.

1. Topic: learning a new skill

   Writer's point: helps you grow intellectually, can discover new talents, can be fun and relaxing.

(continued)

Closed thesis statement: _____

_____

_____

2. Topic: wind technology

   Writer's point: advantages—it is renewable; cost of energy production is relatively low; environment is not harmed

   Closed thesis statement: _____

   _____

   _____

3. Topic: reasons to shop in thrift stores

   Writer's point: fun, save money, might be rewarded by finding valuable items

   Closed thesis statement: _____

   _____

4. Topic: advantages of using e-mail instead of other forms of communication

   Writer's point: can control your emotional responses to ideas, time is available to think about the ideas involved, discussion of the issue is recorded in the e-mail

   Closed thesis statement: _____

   _____

   _____

   _____

CHAPTER ACTIVITIES

READING AND ANNOTATING

The following is an excerpt from a brief essay published in the journal *Perspectives in Biology and Medicine*. Like many professional essays, this one includes a wide variety of support.

1. Analyze the body paragraphs. Some of the body paragraphs are quite short, so when necessary, use the strategies provided in this chapter for finding the topic sentences for journalistic paragraphs.

2. Identify the topic sentences—whether explicit or implicit—for each paragraph (or set of journalistic paragraphs) in this article.

3. Use the five-step process described in this chapter to determine the essay's main idea. Find the thesis statement in the text, or if the thesis statement is implied, write it in a sentence.

Be sure to annotate the essay as you read.

Adapting to the Situation

by Peter J. McDonnell, MD

> Be yourself; everybody else is already taken.   —Oscar Wilde
>
> Whatever you do, don't be yourself.   —Unknown

Many years ago, one of my younger sisters worked for a U.S.-based international corporation. It's an enormous company; they make all kinds of things. You probably have something made by them around your house.

To develop (and test) their young executives, the company would send them to head up a division in another country. If they performed well, they were brought back to the United States in a few years and moved into a high-level position at corporate headquarters.

Mary was sent to Europe and was doing very well in a glamorous but high-pressure position despite all the cultural and linguistic challenges.

"Running a business here in Europe is very different [from] back home," she told me.

I, of course, was proud of her. During a visit to Europe, Mary and I celebrated her success. We had dinner at a wonderful restaurant in Munich, enjoying the fantastic draft beer and delicious German sausages. There was a musician playing a guitar and singing Simon and Garfunkel songs.

A terrible singer myself, I admire people who are talented at it. "He is really good," I said to my sister, who agreed and suggested that I tell him. Mary laughed, as it was clear the musician had absolutely no idea what I was saying.

"There are musicians like this all over Europe," she said, "unable to understand a word of English but singing American songs as though they had grown up in New Jersey."

I was reminded of this story recently while attending a U2 concert. To me, the lead singer, Bono, sings pretty much without a discernible accent, but when he speaks to the audience between songs he sounds like the quintessential boy from the streets of Dublin. A couple weeks after the concert, I did an experiment with someone who has had a lot of musical training, but whose taste runs to classical and jazz (but not rock).

"I'll give you $20 if you can tell me what country this singer is from," I said.

"America?" was the guess.

Behaviors and Mannerisms

My thought is that really talented musicians are so adaptable that they can learn new manners of speech to entertain their audiences better. Similarly, successful businesspeople learn what it takes to be successful in whatever situation they find themselves. Physicians also do the same, as they adopt certain mannerisms and speech patterns to meet their patients' expectations.

Sir William Osler, MD, a famous American physician, wrote a book called *Aequanimitas*. In it, he argued that physicians should cultivate a persona of cool detachment from patients and calmly accept what comes, so that the difficulties and sufferings of patients do not cause emotional reactions and cloud the physician's scientific judgment.

Some have criticized Dr. Osler and this approach as reducing physicians' empathy for patients. Right or wrong, it suggests that good physicians can serve their patients best by adopting behaviors that might be different from their normal attributes in the rest of their lives.

The bottom-line impression I have is that success in many fields involves being good at pretending to be someone or something you are not.

Questions for Consideration

1. The writer thinks pretending can be a useful method for adapting to different situations. Think of someone you know who is successful—perhaps a relative, a friend, a teacher, or a doctor. In what ways do you think this person has used *pretending* as an effective strategy? Explain in a paragraph.

2. We all know people who try to excuse bad behaviors or bad habits by saying, "That's just how I am." Consider a situation in which saying, "That's just how I am," would have negative effects. Reflect on job situations, college responsibilities, and relationships. Write a paragraph in which you examine a particular situation.

3. Think about the career you aspire to have. In what ways might pretending help you when you start this career? For example, when teachers begin their careers, they have to project confidence in the classroom. Most inexperienced teachers are worried and insecure about their ability to teach well, especially in the first year. When teachers project confidence, parents and students can relax, believing that the teacher has everything under control. In what way will pretending help you adapt to the career you plan to pursue? Write a paragraph to explain.

4. Although we may be unaware of it, we adapt to situations all the time. If we feel ill, for example, and a coworker asks, "How are you?" many of us will say, "Just fine." These minor acts of pretending make interactions with colleagues more positive. In what ways have you pretended today or in the last few days? Why did you pretend? Did it help your relationships with others go more smoothly? Describe one of your experiences in a paragraph.

USING MODELS TO PRACTICE COMPOSING

What follows is a model essay written by Xavier, a student in an English class. Read through the assignment instructions that Xavier's professor provided.

> **Essay assignment:** In the conclusion paragraph of Peter J. McDonnell's essay "Adapting to the Situation," the author writes, "The bottom-line impression I have is that success in many fields involves being good at pretending to be someone or something you are not."

To start this assignment, Xavier used the prewriting technique of clustering as a method for considering new situations that many people experience.

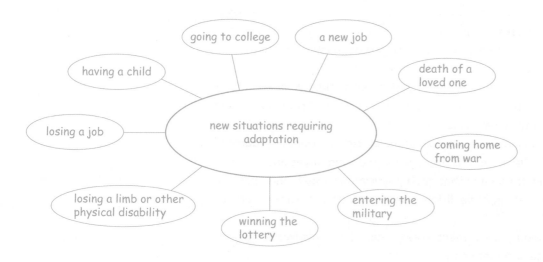

Next, Xavier chose a topic derived from his prewriting and examined how pretending might be advantageous and disadvantageous in his particular context. He used prewriting to make lists.

Situation: Death of a loved one

Benefits of pretending:

- Pretending life is normal helps people do the necessary things (wake up, get ready for work, deal with children, go to the job site).

- Pretending can help children feel like their lives are in control, even if their parents don't feel in control.

- Pretending will give you more privacy; other people won't always be asking if they can help or what is wrong.

Disadvantages of pretending:

- Pretending takes a lot of energy and effort.

- Pretending might keep you from grieving and experiencing the sorrow so that you can work through it.

- Pretending might set a poor example for children by teaching them to cover up their feelings of sorrow.

Once Xavier finished his prewriting, he created a brief outline that included his thesis statement and the topic sentences for each of his body paragraphs. Notice that he chose not to include all the advantages and disadvantages that he came up with.

Thesis statement: Pretending is a way to adapt to the loss of a loved one, and as a coping strategy, it offers advantages as well as disadvantages.

Body paragraphs:

1. Topic sentence: Pretending life is normal helps people do the things necessary for everyday life (wake up, get ready for work, deal with children, go to the job site).

2. Topic sentence: By pretending everything is okay, parents can provide a more stable living environment for their children.

3. Topic sentence: Pretending might set a poor example for children by teaching them to cover up their feelings of sorrow.

4. Topic sentence: Pretending takes a great deal of energy and effort.

After creating an outline that includes his thesis statement and topic sentences, Xavier drafted his essay, revised it, and checked it for errors. Read Xavier's final essay, and annotate at least three features in the essay. For example, if you see sentences that demonstrate parallelism, annotate them. If you find a passage that you believe is worded particularly well, annotate it. Also, annotate the thesis statement and notice where it is placed, and mark the topic sentences.

Xavier Lewis

INRW 0402

Dr. Wright

20 February 2014

The Role of Pretending in Times of Grief

New situations can easily throw us off balance. A new job, a new baby, or a new living situation can be hard to handle. However, most people find methods for adjusting to these new circumstances. One method that can be helpful is pretending. Sometimes by pretending, people can reduce the stress involved in making the transition to a new situation. This is especially true in the case of grief. Pretending is a way to adapt to the loss of a loved one, and as a coping strategy it offers advantages, although there are disadvantages as well.

Pretending that everything is normal helps a grieving person do the things necessary for dealing with everyday life. By pretending that nothing is out of the ordinary, a person is more likely to wake up on time, bathe, tend to chores, go to work, and so on. Pretending, in this case, is a good way to deal with grief. It keeps the grieving person busy, and it allows him or her to do the things that have to get done. Without pretending that life is normal, grieving people might merely stay in bed and cry or quit their jobs out of despair. These actions would add even more complications to adjusting to life without the loved one. Therefore, pretending that nothing has changed is a good way to keep going.

Pretending can help children feel that their lives are in control, even if their parents don't feel in control. Children need stability in their lives. This need for stability doesn't change, even though a parent's life may have drastically changed with the loss of a loved one. Parents who recognize their children's need for stability can use pretending as a way to keep their children on an even keel. When parents act as if life goes on as usual, continuing with typical daily activities, children can be comforted and can continue their own lives with fewer disruptions.

While pretending is helpful in many ways, people who are adjusting to grief must realize that pretending, if not used carefully, can have some disadvantages. For one thing, pretending might set a poor example for children by teaching them to cover up their feelings of sorrow. While children need the stability that comes from pretending life is normal, children also need to know it is OK to feel sorrow and to grieve. Therefore, pretending should be used to help life go on, but it should not be used so extensively that there is no room for sorrow.

In addition, pretending takes a lot of energy and effort. It is hard to act as if everything is OK when everything in life has changed so drastically. There must be times of release when those who are grieving can take off the mask of pretending and admit they are exhausted and sad. Having periods of sorrow and periods of productive pretending helps those who are grieving. By reserving energy and effort for only those times when pretending to be normal is necessary, people can reap the advantages of pretending without the disadvantages of it.

No one asks for the sorrow that death brings, but most people go through it sometime in their lives. By pretending that life is normal, people who are grieving can find a way to go on with life—until life really does become normal again, or at least as normal as it can be after a deep loss.

A READING AND WRITING ASSIGNMENT

Now that you have read and annotated Xavier's essay, use the same assignment instructions Xavier received to write your own essay on the topic. Follow these steps.

1. Reread Xavier's assignment from "Using Models to Practice Composing," repeated here:

   In the conclusion paragraph of Peter J. McDonnell's essay "Adapting to the Situation," the author writes, "The bottom-line impression I have is that success in many fields involves being good at pretending to be someone or something you are not."

2. Use prewriting to think about situations in which a person could benefit from using pretending as a coping strategy.

3. Choose one of those situations, and use a prewriting method to determine ways in which pretending might be advantageous and disadvantageous.

4. Use prewriting to write a thesis statement and compose topic sentences for body paragraphs. Plan as many paragraphs as you need to support your thesis statement.

5. Using Xavier's essay as a model, write a complete essay, including an introduction paragraph, body paragraphs, and a conclusion paragraph. Use the thesis statement and topic sentences you have already composed.

6. Follow the Quick Start Guide to Integrated Reading and Writing Assignments to help you with this process.

⊙ THINKING FROM AN INSTRUCTOR'S POINT OF VIEW

One method for understanding assignments is to look at them from your instructor's point of view. Focus on getting inside your instructor's mind. Your instructor cares about your learning. She has written assignments so that you can demonstrate your progress. When you read an assignment, ask yourself, "How will this assignment enable me to demonstrate my knowledge and skills?"

In the exercise below, excerpts from a possible essay assignment are provided. Read each excerpt and ask yourself, "What does my instructor want me to do when she says . . . ?" The first exercise has been completed as an example. Remember, you don't have to actually do the assignments in the left column. Your task is to interpret the assignments and to write about how you think the instructor wants you to respond to them.

WHAT MY INSTRUCTOR WROTE	WHAT I THINK MY INSTRUCTOR MEANS OR WANTS FROM ME
Example: While you may not be familiar with additional parts of the writing process, such as choosing supporting details and writing effective introductions and conclusions, try your hand at writing a complete essay by doing the assignment that follows.	**Example:** *She wants me to write an entire essay without worrying too much about the parts we have not covered.*
Write an essay in which you choose a situation in your life that required adaptation. In your essay, write about your own experiences with adjusting to this situation.	
In the conclusion, comment on this statement in Peter J. McDonnell's essay "Adapting to the Situation": "The bottom-line impression I have is that success in many fields involves being good at pretending to be someone or something you are not." From your experience, is he correct? Why or why not?	
Next, write a closed thesis statement that makes use of your prewriting ideas and categories. Be sure to combine the topic and your point about the topic into your thesis statement, and be sure your thesis statement demonstrates parallelism.	
For examples of complete essays, look through this chapter.	

⊙ ADDING TO YOUR VOCABULARY

This chapter's vocabulary words appear below.

diverse	acquisition	cognitive	reiterate
implication	insomnia	sequentially	

Choose five of the vocabulary words from this chapter that you would like to add to your vocabulary, and think about how you can use them this week. For example, one of this chapter's words is *diverse*. You can often substitute *diverse* for *varied* or *assorted*.

Example: This college offers a *varied* course selection.

This college offers a *diverse* course selection.

List each of the five words you plan to use this week, and make note of a context in which you could use each word.

Example: *Diverse.* I can use this in talking about the career opportunities in the field of information technology.

⊙ ADDITIONAL ASSIGNMENTS

1. Look up the word *adaptation* in a dictionary. You will find more than one definition for this term. Which definition of *adaptation* is the most appropriate one for the term as Peter McDonnell uses it in his essay?

2. Reread the textbook passage entitled "The Importance of Communication Skills to You" in Practice 8 in this chapter. After you reread it, focus on this excerpt:

   A study of skills and competencies needed by accountants strongly supports the value of writing, speaking, and listening, and Deloitte & Touche, ranked by *BusinessWeek* in 2007 as the best place to launch a career, cited communication skills as the "most desirable trait" in a job candidate. Employers surveyed for the National Association of Colleges and Employers' *Job Outlook 2009* also cited "communication skills" and the related traits of "a strong work ethic, ability to work in a team, and initiative" as highly prized qualities in job applicants. Recruiters who participated in *The Wall Street Journal*'s latest ranking of MBA programs agreed. They rated "interpersonal and communication skills, a teamwork orientation, personal ethics and integrity, analytical and problem-solving abilities, and a strong work ethic" as most important.

   List the qualities employers value. Which of these qualities do you have? Which ones do you lack? Explain actions you can take so that you will have all the qualities employers desire. Write a paragraph or two presenting and explaining your answers.

3. Consider the qualities you explored in assignment 2 above. Now imagine you are writing an essay in which you present four qualities you would like to develop while you are in college. Write a thesis statement for an essay in which you combine the following ideas.

   Topic: qualities employers desire in workers

   Your point about the topic: qualities you would like to develop for your own advancement

   You may write an open or closed thesis statement.

EMOTIONAL INTELLIGENCE

Earlier in this chapter, you read "Why Emotional Intelligence Matters—At Work." In that essay, you read about emotional flexibility. How is emotional flexibility like adaptation? How is it different? Write a paragraph explaining your answers.

CULTURAL LITERACY

Some of the readings in this chapter come from the fields of psychology, sociology, and economics. What is the focus of each of these fields? How are they different, and how are they similar? Skim over the readings in this chapter. Name one reading that comes from each of the three fields. (Not all of the readings in this chapter come from these fields.)

CRITICAL THINKING

Figuring out implied main ideas requires critical thinking. You have to look at clues and contexts, and you have to read critically. Analyzing cartoons and examining advertisements are two ways to practice identifying implicit main ideas. Both cartoons and advertisements are intended to communicate an idea without stating it explicitly. What is the implied main idea of the advertisement that follows? Explain your answer in a paragraph.

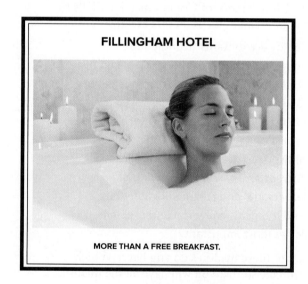

FILLINGHAM HOTEL

MORE THAN A FREE BREAKFAST.

METACOGNITION

One way to learn about your strengths and weaknesses as a student is to analyze your graded exams. Find a graded exam on which you received a lower grade than you had expected. On a separate sheet of paper, answer these questions about that exam.

1. What study methods did you use to prepare for the exam?
2. Based on your exam grade, did your study methods work?
3. Look at the questions you missed on the exam. Do the question types have anything in common? For example, on a math test, perhaps you missed the word problems or the problems that require multiplying fractions. On a history test, you may have missed questions based on instructor lectures.
4. Based on the type of questions you missed, what study strategies might have helped you prepare better for these questions?
5. In general, what can you do differently next time to earn an even higher grade?

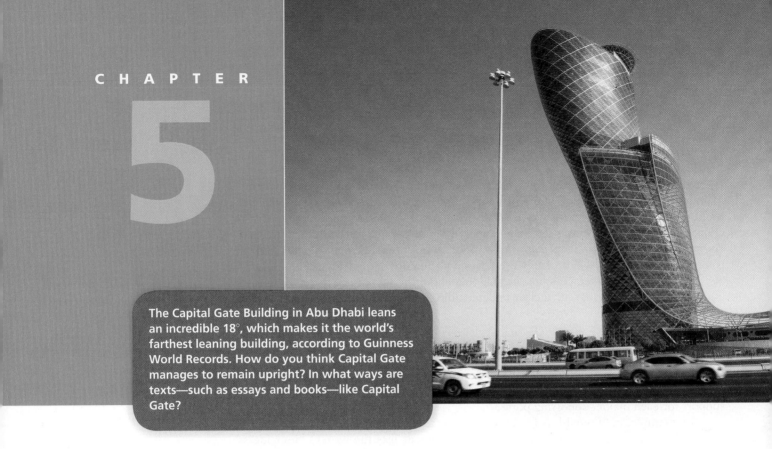

CHAPTER

5

The Capital Gate Building in Abu Dhabi leans an incredible 18°, which makes it the world's farthest leaning building, according to Guinness World Records. How do you think Capital Gate manages to remain upright? In what ways are texts—such as essays and books—like Capital Gate?

Support for Main Ideas

At about the age of four, children begin to ask a particular question: "Why?" If you have spent much time with four-year-olds, you probably know the frustration of having to explain *everything:* why broccoli is green, why cars need gasoline, why dinosaurs no longer exist, why it is not OK to talk with your mouth full of food. A part of the maturation process is to wonder about the reasons for things. Curious children need more than a main idea; they need support for that idea, and they will ask "Why?" until they get that support!

As adults, we are not all that different from these curious four-year-olds. We may recognize a writer's main idea, but we may not fully understand why the writer believes as he or she does. We may not understand why the main point is important. We may not even entirely understand the main point unless the writer gives us explanations and examples. A major responsibility for writers is to provide the support needed to communicate their ideas effectively. Readers must also be able to identify supporting details in order to understand a writer's main point correctly.

CHAPTER OBJECTIVES

After completing this chapter, students will be able to do the following:

- **Recognize major supporting points and supporting details in texts.**

- **Use outlining or graphic organizers to identify major supporting points and supporting details.**

- **Identify and use transitions.**

- **Use specific types of supporting details in writing.**

RECOGNIZING MAJOR SUPPORTING POINTS AND SUPPORTING DETAILS IN TEXTS

The thesis statement of an essay is a strong sentence because it provides the writer's main idea. However, it cannot stand on its own. It requires support, and this support comes in the form of body paragraphs.

Support consists of all the information readers need to fully understand a writer's main idea. Supporting details come in a variety of types: examples, analogies, explanations, short anecdotes (stories), reasons, statistics, quotations, and so on. The support you choose depends on your thesis statement and writing purpose. If you are informing readers, you might use *data* and *explanations* to support your thesis statement. If your purpose is to define a term, you will probably use *definitions* and *examples*.

To be a critical reader, you must be able to identify the supporting materials in texts. This identification begins with a clear understanding of how support provides the structure for an essay.

Major Supporting Points in Essays

In an essay, the **major supporting points** are the ideas that explain, develop, or prove the thesis statement. A common way writers structure essays is to create a paragraph of support for each major supporting point.

For example, in "Four Ideas for How Obama Could Really Transform the Cost of College," an essay by Bryce Covert, the thesis statement lists the writer's "four ideas." These four ideas are the major supporting points of the thesis statement, and each is discussed in its own body paragraph. Moreover, the topic sentence for each paragraph states the major supporting point that is explored in the paragraph.

The diagram that follows illustrates the support structure for Covert's essay. Notice that each body paragraph presents a different major supporting point—one of the writer's four ideas—for the thesis statement.

Thesis statement: There are four ideas for how to radically transform the way Americans pay for college that stand a chance of truly shaking up the system.

Paragraph 1 Major supporting point 1 Topic sentence: First, we should allow graduates to discharge student loans in bankruptcy.	Paragraph 2 Major supporting point 2 Topic sentence: A second significant idea is to encourage and finance college savings accounts.	Paragraph 3 Major supporting point 3 Topic sentence: Third, we should cover the cost of tuition with an income-based payment plan post-graduation.	Paragraph 4 Major supporting point 4 Topic sentence: And finally, we could simply make college free.

Supporting Details in Essays

Within each of Covert's paragraphs, other sentences help readers understand the major supporting point (topic sentence). These other sentences provide supporting details that relate directly to the topic sentence. The supporting details offer further information (examples, explanations, statistics, quotations, anecdotes, and facts) for the topic sentence.

Here is one of the body paragraphs of Covert's essay. Notice that some supporting details are themselves expanded upon by additional sentences with details.

> Third, we should cover the cost of tuition with an income-based payment plan post-graduation. In July, Oregon passed a bill that allows students to attend a community college or public university at no cost if they agree to pay a certain portion of their income after they graduate. One model proposed that for 20 years after graduation, community college students would have to pay 1.5 percent of their incomes and four-year public university students would pay 3 percent. Those are much more favorable terms than what many go through with student loans. And while income-based repayment plans exist for student loans, the Consumer Financial Protection Bureau has found that few are making use of them.

Major supporting point (topic sentence)

Supporting detail: presents Oregon's bill as a solution

Details: info about Oregon's bill

Supporting detail: makes a new point to support the topic sentence

One way to visualize the support structures of an essay is to label them in a diagram.

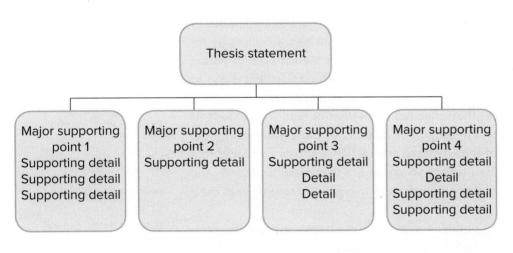

■ Major supporting points can have varying numbers of supporting details.

Now that you are familiar with the levels of support used in essays, read Covert's essay and study the annotations that point out the various types of support in it.

Four Ideas for How Obama Could Really Transform the Cost of College
by Bryce Covert

As part of his summer bus tour, President Obama will be making speeches this week that will include proposals for tackling the problem of college affordability. As the *New York Times* reports, ahead of those speeches he told supporters in an email, "To create a better bargain for the middle class, we have to fundamentally rethink about how higher education is paid for in this country. We've got to shake up the current system."

The value of a college degree is clear: University graduates make 85 percent more than high school graduates on average and have just a 3.8 percent unemployment rate, compared to 7.6 percent for those with high school degrees. The factors behind the sharp increases in college tuition and mounting load of student debt are complex.

(continued)

But tinkering with student loan rates, while important, doesn't actually change the way Americans pay for higher education. There are four ideas, however, for how to radically transform the way Americans pay for college that stand a chance of truly shaking up the system.

Thesis statement

First, we should allow graduates to discharge student loans in bankruptcy. While nearly all forms of debt can be discharged in bankruptcy proceedings, letting a borrower start anew financially, rules put into place by Congress in the 1970s make it nearly impossible to do so with student loans. Joe Valenti and David Bergeron of the Center for American Progress have proposed changing this system by allowing loans with unbearable repayment conditions or taken out to attend schools with poor track records on graduates finding employment to be eliminated in bankruptcy. This would not only combat the sky-high default rate and give graduates a way to build back their finances, it would incentivize lenders to offer better terms and schools to improve the employment prospects for students.

Major supporting point 1 (topic sentence)
Supporting detail: background info

Supporting detail: a proposal

Detail: info about proposal

A second significant idea is to encourage and finance college savings accounts. The Assets and Education Initiative at the University of Kansas has proposed a plan that would automatically enroll every child in a college savings account at birth, publicly finance initial deposits, and provide public matching funds to help families pay for college costs. This would allow many more families to pay for the costs out of pocket and rely less on student loans that have to be paid back with interest. But doing so wouldn't just make college more affordable—it would make it vastly more accessible to many people. The report notes that while just 45 percent of high school students without college savings ever enroll, nearly three-quarters of those with savings do. Meanwhile, just seven percent of those without savings will graduate compared to a third of those who have them. Even college savings of less than $500 means low- and moderate-income students will be three times as likely to enroll and four times as likely to graduate.

Vocabulary Collection Word:
initiative
Your in-context definition:

_____

_____

A dictionary definition:

_____

_____

Major supporting point 2 (topic sentence)

Supporting detail: Univ. of Kansas plan

Details: info about Kansas plan—results, statistics

Supporting detail: general statistic

Supporting detail: general statistic

Third, we should cover the cost of tuition with an income-based payment plan post-graduation. In July, Oregon passed a bill that allows students to attend a community college or public university at no cost if they agree to pay a certain portion of their income after they graduate. One model proposed that for 20 years after graduation, community college students would have to pay 1.5 percent of their incomes and four-year public university students would pay 3 percent. Those are much more favorable terms than what many go through with student loans. And while income-based repayment plans exist for student loans, the Consumer Financial Protection Bureau has found that few are making use of them.

Major supporting point 3 (topic sentence)

Supporting detail: Oregon's bill

Details: info about Oregon's bill

Supporting detail: other plans

And finally, we could simply make college free. It may sound like a radical idea, but it wouldn't have to be a huge expense. The Roosevelt Institute's Mike Konczal ran the numbers and found that the government already spends $22.75 billion through tax breaks and incentives that are aimed at making student loans or the cost of college more manageable. The government also spends $104 billion on student loans. The cost of providing free public higher education has been estimated to come to $127 billion—not far from what it's already shelling out. Not only would this create an entirely affordable and accessible option for all students, but private universities would likely be pressured to reduce costs to better compete with the free option.

Major supporting point 4 (topic sentence)

Supporting detail: view of cost

Details: facts about cost

Supporting detail: effects on private universities

To distinguish the types of support in a paragraph, keep in mind that secondary support always elaborates on the idea provided in primary support. Here is a very simple example:

Major supporting point (topic sentence): Our cafeteria serves great Italian food.

Supporting detail: The homemade lasagna is one of the specialties.

Additional details: Rachel, the head cook, uses her own family recipe to make the lasagna, and she uses herbs from her own garden!

To distinguish major supporting points from supporting details, examine the relationships the idea has with the ideas around it.

PRACTICE ① Recognizing Major Supporting Points and Supporting Details in Essays

In the following essay, the thesis statement has been annotated for you. Read the essay, and underline the topic sentences (major supporting points) of the body paragraphs. Highlight or underline the supporting details that go together.

The Footprint That Does Not Fade

Anyone who uses a cell phone, posts to social media sites such as *Facebook* or *Twitter*, posts comments on Web sites, uploads photos, or even uses a credit or debit card has a digital footprint—a trail left behind by all of the digital activity in which the person has been involved. A digital footprint provides small bits of information about a person, and all of that information—together—is used to generate a picture of the person's character. Should people be concerned that this information is so readily available to almost anyone who wants it? Probably. Digital footprints can affect a person's reputation, opportunities in life, and personal safety.

The nature of social networking encourages people to freely post their on-the-spot and **off-the-cuff** comments or photos without thinking carefully about what the information they post says about them. Postings can have serious consequences for one's reputation. For instance, Justine Sacco, a senior director of corporate communications, was sending off-the-cuff tweets while on a trip from New York to South Africa. On the final leg of her trip, she tweeted, "Going to Africa. Hope I don't get AIDS. Just kidding. I'm white!" By the time she landed, her tweet had exploded on social media, where she was pilloried as a bigot, and she had lost her job, too. Another high-profile person affected by his digital footprint is Anthony Weiner, former US representative from New York. Weiner sent compromising texts and photos unbecoming of a public office holder, and then denied having sent them. Weiner eventually confessed—ashamedly—for both lying and having sent the photos and texts, according to CNN. The scandal ultimately resulted in his resignation as a congressman.

In addition to affecting one's reputation, a digital footprint can have serious implications for a person's opportunities in life. It is now commonplace for employers to check out the *Facebook* pages or *Twitter* histories of potential employees. A photo that

YOUR ANNOTATIONS

Thesis statement

Vocabulary Collection Word:
off-the-cuff

Your in-context definition:

_____

_____

A dictionary definition:

_____

_____

(continued)

was meant for only friends to see or an offhand comment about hating one's job can give potential employers an impression that can be damaging. Ashley Payne, a twenty-four-year-old teacher in Georgia, recently lost her job when a parent complained about a photo Payne posted of herself at a party, according to CBS News. Payne said she tried to make the photo private when she posted it on Facebook but apparently did not succeed. Payne's situation demonstrates how simple postings can have disastrous results.

Perhaps more frightening than the potential for damaged reputations or the loss of a job is the possibility of losing one's life. Alicia Ann Lynch, a twenty-three-year-old from Michigan, made the unfortunate choice to dress up for Halloween as a victim of the Boston Marathon bombing. After she posted a picture of herself in "costume" on *Tumblr,* outraged people sent her death threats, dug up embarassing photos she had posted on the Web, and even harassed her parents. Lynch also lost her job, and she probably will not have an easy time finding another one because of the infamous digital footprint she now has.

Educators are now beginning to teach children from a young age to guard their digital footprint. Before the Internet, people could erase their history and start anew. Photos could be ripped up and destroyed; people had the chance to change their reputation if they had made mistakes in the past. These days, a thoughtless posting or photo may be on the Web forever. It is far easier to protect one's reputation than to re-establish it. *Caveat usor* [Latin for "user beware"].

Multiparagraph Support

So far, we have seen how an essay might be structured by presenting each major supporting point in its own body paragraph. What happens, however, if one of the major supporting points requires more than one paragraph of explanation?

In professional essays, writers sometimes use several paragraphs to explain one of the major supporting points. For example, one of the major supporting paragraphs in Covert's essay proposes the use of income-based payment plans for college graduates. The paragraph discusses Oregon's bill for such a plan. The writer could also discuss another state's ideas to provide further explanation of income-based payment plans. If he chooses to talk about another state's income-based payment plan, he would very likely create another paragraph. The new paragraph would *not* be a new major supporting point. It would simply be a continuation of the point that income-based repayment plans are a good idea.

For the sake of example, we can write a hypothetical paragraph to show what an additional support paragraph might look like. The first paragraph below is from Covert's essay. The second paragraph shows what an additional paragraph with new details might look like. (The details in this example are purely fictional.)

Covert's paragraph:

Third, we should cover the cost of tuition with an income-based payment plan post-graduation. In July, Oregon passed a bill that allows students to attend a community college or public university at no cost if they agree to pay a certain portion of their income after they graduate. One model proposed that for 20 years after graduation, community college students would have to pay 1.5 percent of their incomes and four-year public university students would pay 3 percent. Those are much more favorable terms than what many go through with student loans. And while income-based repayment plans exist for student loans, the Consumer Financial Protection Bureau has found that few are making use of them.

> Major supporting point 3 (topic sentence)
>
> Supporting detail: Oregon's bill
>
> Details: info about Oregon's bill
>
> Supporting detail: other plans

Hypothetical additional paragraph:

Another example of an income-based repayment plan has been proposed in Montana. The Montana plan would require graduates to pay a small percentage of their yearly taxable wages as part of their annual state taxes for a period of either ten or twenty years. Graduates would be able to choose the repayment period. Montana's plan has the additional advantage of making the collection of repayments easier since it would be built into the state tax system.

> Supporting detail (topic sentence): Montana's bill
>
> Details: info about Montana's bill

Notice that while the topic sentence in Covert's paragraph is a major supporting point, the topic sentence in the paragraph that we have added is just a supporting detail, like this.

Major supporting point: Third, we should cover the cost of tuition with an income-based payment plan post-graduation.

- Supporting detail: In July, Oregon passed a bill that allows students to attend a community college or public university at no cost if they agree to pay a certain portion of their income after they graduate.

- Supporting detail: And while income-based repayment plans exist for student loans, the Consumer Financial Protection Bureau has found that few are making use of them

- Supporting detail: Another example of an income-based repayment plan has been proposed in Montana.

Writers provide an additional paragraph of supporting details when the point they are making needs significant explanation or discussion. Try your hand at identifying different types of support by completing the following exercise.

PRACTICE ② Identifying Support in Essays

Read the following essay, which provides an opinion on tar sands oil. You will notice that the thesis statement has been identified. The essay presents three major supporting points, but you will find more than three body paragraphs. Figure out where each major supporting point is, and put brackets around the paragraphs that provide support for the major supporting point.

(continued)

The Most Deadly Oil Yet

The United States is **on the cusp** of an oil-importing contract that will provide us with endless gallons of cheap crude oil, and we won't have to depend on oil from Saudi Arabia, Venezuela, or other oil-rich countries with whom we have tenuous relationships. How will we make this miracle happen? The answer, we have been told, is to import tar sands oil from our neighbor and friend, Canada. Tar sands oil has been touted as the answer to our oil problems. A close look at what tar sands oil is and the devastation it wreaks, however, will reveal the truth: the use of tar sands oil is an impending disaster, not a miracle.

Canada's countryside, particularly in Alberta, is full of oil. The trouble is that the oil is trapped in sand. Extracting oil from sand is an extremely dirty and environmentally harmful process. To free the sticky oil from the sand, vast amounts of steam (and sometimes toxic solvents) are used. It is a process that increases greenhouse gases by 5%–15%, according to IHS CERA, a research firm. Burning tar sands oil has been shown to produce 20% greater emissions, according to David Strahan.

In addition to the environmental price of tar sands oil, people and animals also pay a high price—with their health, and sometimes with their lives. A number of substances that are linked to cancers and serious diseases, volatile organic compounds, have been found in the area of tar sands oil production at levels of six thousand times normal, according to Think Progress. Cancer levels in the area of tar sands production are now higher than normal, and the Athabascan people who live north of the vast area of tar sands oil production are fearful for their health.

While people worry about cancer, the animals in the area are sick and dying. Kevin Timoney writes in a peer-reviewed article that in the tar sands oil-production areas, large numbers of animals died between 2000 and 2008, including black bears, deer, red foxes, coyotes, and moose. The National Wildlife Federation points out that the tar fields are directly in the path of scores of migratory birds, including American songbirds and the endangered whooping crane. The Athabascans will not eat the local fish because of the potential that the fish contain toxins.

If devastating the environment, endangering animals, and causing cancers in humans is not enough, the dangers posed by transporting tar sands oil might be. TransCanada Corporation, a major producer of tar sands oil, has petitioned the United States to allow the development of a pipeline that would sends tar sands oil components from Canada to Port Arthur, Texas, to be refined. This pipeline would literally run through the backyards of thousands of Americans. It would intersect major rivers and the Ogallala **Aquifer**, a water supply that is used by one-fourth of the irrigated land in America and provides drinking water for two million people, according to Friends of the Earth.

(continued)

YOUR ANNOTATIONS

Vocabulary Collection Word:
on the cusp

Your in-context definition:

_____

_____

A dictionary definition:

_____

_____

Thesis statement

Vocabulary Collection Word:
aquifer

Your in-context definition:

_____

_____

A dictionary definition:

_____

_____

What would happen if the pipeline leaked or a major break occurred? The oil sands product flowing in the pipeline is a heavy, sludgy material, Friends of the Earth points out. If a leak occurs in water, the oil sands material will sink, unlike traditional crude oil. Cleanup efforts would be extremely costly and complicated. Our supply of water may become more valuable than oil itself.

It would be wonderful to do business with our Canadian neighbors and solve our oil problems at the same time—but not at the risk of ruining the environment and endangering our lives and livelihood. The ecological and human costs far outweigh any of the touted benefits of this deadly oil.

USING OUTLINING OR GRAPHIC ORGANIZERS TO IDENTIFY MAJOR SUPPORTING POINTS AND SUPPORTING DETAILS

One of the best ways to visualize a reading's support is to create a simple outline. The outline should include the reading's title and author, thesis statement, major supporting points, and supporting details. What follows is an informal outline of Bryce Covert's essay on college costs from earlier in this chapter.

Title: "Four Ideas for How Obama Could Really Transform the Cost of College" by Bryce Covert

Thesis statement: "There are four ideas, however, for how to radically transform the way Americans pay for college that stand a chance of truly shaking up the system."

Major supporting point 1: "First, we should allow graduates to discharge student loans in bankruptcy."

  Supporting detail: Bankruptcy law now

  Supporting detail: What the Center for American Progress proposes—allowing bankruptcy forgiveness

- Would lower default rate
- Would benefit graduates
- Would incentivize lenders to offer better loan terms
- Would encourage colleges to develop career-placement strategies

Major supporting point 2: "A second significant idea is to encourage and finance college savings accounts."

  Supporting detail: Example—University of Kansas Assets and Education Initiative

- Would allow families to rely less on student loans and would provide other benefits

Vocabulary Collection Word:
default

Your in-context definition:

_____

_____

A dictionary definition:

_____

_____

(continued)

Supporting detail: Savings accounts associated with higher graduation rate

Supporting detail: Even low savings associated with higher graduation rate

Major supporting point 3: "Third, we should cover the cost of tuition with an income-based payment plan post-graduation."

    Supporting detail: Introduces Oregon's income-based payment plan

- Details of Oregon's plan
- Comparison of Oregon's plan to existing student loan repayment plans

    Supporting detail: Few make use of existing income-based repayment plans.

Major supporting point 4: "And finally, we could simply make college free."

Supporting detail: Would be more affordable than appears

- Roosevelt Institute cost data
- Comparison of Roosevelt data with current costs
- Projections based on Roosevelt data

Supporting detail: Results—college available for all; private universities may reduce costs.

Notice that the outline includes complete sentences for each of the major supporting points. If the major supporting points are stated directly in the reading, you can simply copy them into your outline. Always use quotation marks around any words you quote directly so that you can easily tell which words are from the source and which are yours. If a major supporting point is implied, you will have to use your own words to express it. For each supporting detail, write a short phrase or sentence summarizing the idea. The goal is to express—very briefly—what these details say.

An outline allows you to reduce the content of a reading into a short, easy-to-read map. In fact, some people create actual maps or graphic organizers to take the place of an outline. If you prefer a more visual representation of the information in a reading, you can create a simple graphic organizer. What follows is a graphic organizer showing the ideas used to support the first major supporting point.

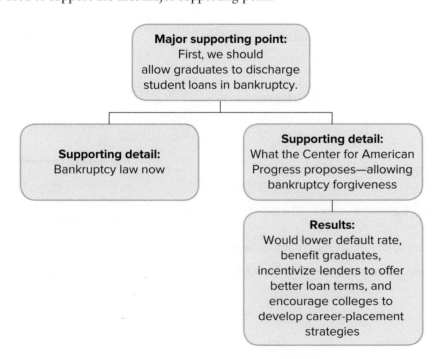

To create a graphic organizer of a paragraph, write the major supporting point in a box at the top of the page. Place the major supporting details in the next row of boxes. Place any additional details below. Attach all the boxes with lines to show how they are connected.

The purpose of a graphic organizer is to show the relationships among supporting details. Because each essay presents ideas in its own unique way, graphic organizers will not look the same. For example, the graphic organizer for an essay with six major supporting points will look different from one for an essay with four major supporting points.

Hand-drawn graphic organizers are effective for showing relationships among ideas, and they are easy to draw. The hand-drawn organizer below demonstrates the relationships among ideas in a essay on the benefits of encouraging farmers' markets. Notice that the student found it easier to draw the diagram from left to right rather than from top to bottom.

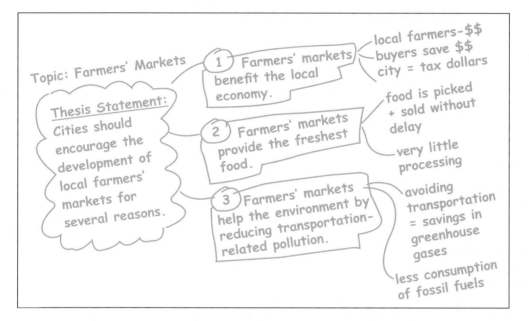

An especially good occasion for using outlining is when you are reading complex material and studying. By putting a reading's major supporting points and supporting details in order, you will be better able to understand the relationships among ideas and remember them later for tests.

PRACTICE ❸ Outlining a Reading

Earlier in this chapter, you read "The Footprint That Does Not Fade." Create an outline or graphic organizer for this essay. Use the outline or a graphic organizer presented in this chapter as a model.

GRAMMAR FOCUS   Transitions

In good writing, the sentences used for support are clearly related to one another. One way to make sure that the relationships between sentences are evident is to use words or phrases that help readers follow the ideas in a text and help writers move smoothly from one idea to another. Notice how the use of the phrase *for example* helps readers see the relationship between the two following sentences.

Even cell phone use leaves a digital footprint. <u>For example</u>, a person's cell phone records can reveal that he was traveling between Austin and San Antonio on May 15, 2014, when he made a phone call.

(continued)

The phrase for example *reveals that the second sentence is meant to elaborate on the first sentence.*

Words and phrases that help the reader move from one sentence to another or from one paragraph to another are called **transitions.** Transitions also help readers recognize a sequence of ideas. If each major supporting point in a text starts with a transition, it is easy to recognize the points. Note the transitions (underlined) in the following example.

Three factors are important to consider in choosing a career. The <u>first</u> factor to consider in choosing a career is personal interest. . . .

The <u>second</u> factor is aptitude. . . .

The <u>third</u> factor that comes into play is the training and education requirements of the career. . . .

When sentences related by transitions indicate a series, the sentences often function in the same way. In this case, the sentences are all major supporting points.

Often, the logic of the supporting details is easier to follow when transitions are used, as in this example.

Good reasons exist on both sides of the debate about whether it is wise to take out student loans. <u>On the one hand,</u> taking out student loans seems logical. College graduates, <u>after all,</u> statistically earn much more than those who do not have degrees. <u>Thus,</u> it seems likely that college graduates will be able to pay off their loans. <u>On the other hand,</u> taking out student loans is fraught with risk. <u>Clearly,</u> college students cannot be certain they will find good jobs after graduation. <u>Additionally,</u> even if they do find good jobs, their entry-level salaries may not be high enough for both a comfortable life and the repayment of student debt.

Transitions show the logical relationships among ideas in this supporting paragraph.

One way to think about transitions is to identify them by their functions, as this table demonstrates.

COMMON TRANSITION WORDS AND PHRASES

CLARIFICATION		
for example	in reality	to demonstrate
for instance	put another way	to explain further
indeed	that is	to illustrate
in fact	to clarify	simply stated
in other words		specifically

SEQUENCES OR TIME ORDER		
about	immediately	previously
after	in the future	simultaneously
as	later	soon
as soon as	meanwhile	to begin
at the same time	next	until
during	now	when
final	often	while
first, second, . . . last	one, another	

(continued)

COMMON TRANSITION WORDS AND PHRASES

SIMILARITY OR ADDITION

additionally	equally important	in the same way
again	for another thing	likewise
along with	for example	moreover
also	for instance	next
another	furthermore	plus
as well	in addition	similarly
besides		

CONTRAST

although	in spite of this	otherwise
conversely	nevertheless	still
counter to	on the contrary	yet
despite	on the one hand, on the	
even though	other hand	
however		

CONCLUSION OR SUMMARY

accordingly	in summary	the bottom line
in closing	in the end	the final point
in short	lastly	to conclude

CAUSE AND EFFECT

as a consequence	because	so then
as a result	consequently	therefore
at last	resulting in	thus

DIRECTION

above	here	overhead
across	nearby	there
against	next to	to the left
behind	opposite	to the right
below	over	
beyond		

SENTENCE COMBINING

The example that follows shows the major supporting points that appear as topic sentences in an essay. Notice how the added transitions clarify that these sentences are giving the three main ideas in the essay. In some cases, the writer has to rewrite the sentences slightly to make the transitions work.

Main supporting points needing transitions:

- Using tar sands oil will reduce the US presence in the Middle East. Canada will provide the majority of the oil the country imports.

- Developing tar sands oil production will greatly benefit the economies of both Canada and the United States.

- Innovations in its production are reducing the potential environmental effects of manufacturing it.

(continued)

Main supporting points using transitions:

- <u>One reason</u> to support using tar sands oil is that it will reduce the US presence in the Middle East; <u>indeed</u>, Canada will provide the majority of the oil the country imports.

- <u>An equally important reason</u> for developing tar sands oil production is that it will greatly benefit the economies of both Canada and the United States.

- <u>A final reason</u> for using tar sands oil is that innovations in its production are reducing the potential environmental effects of manufacturing it.

In the following example, the sentences give the supporting details for the final major supporting point of the essay. Notice how the added transitions connect the sentences to one another and provide clues about meaning. Note also that while transitions most commonly appear at the beginning of a sentence, they can also be effective in the middle or even at the end of a sentence.

Supporting details needing transitions:

- Innovations in its production are reducing the potential environmental effects of manufacturing it.

- Producers use less water now. A process that used to take ten barrels of water to produce a barrel of bitumen (the valuable product that is turned into oil) now takes about half of that.

- Some companies plan to recycle water. They plan to share water among themselves to protect the area's aquifer.

- Extraction companies are now beginning to use another method of reaching the bitumen. This method, called THAI (toe-to-heel air injection) does not affect the water supply.

Supporting details using transitions:

- <u>A final reason</u> for using tar sands oil is that innovations in its production are reducing the potential environmental effects of manufacturing it.

- <u>To begin</u>, producers use less water now. A process that used to take ten barrels of water to produce a barrel of bitumen (the valuable product that is turned into oil) now takes about half of that, <u>for example</u>.

- <u>Additionally</u>, some companies plan to recycle water. They plan, <u>in fact</u>, to share water among themselves to protect the area's aquifer.

- <u>Moreover</u>, extraction companies are now beginning to use another method of reaching the bitumen. This method, called THAI (toe-to-heel air injection) does not affect the water supply.

Try your hand at using transitions to add clarity to supporting ideas.

EXERCISES

Insert appropriate transitions into the sentences that follow. Reword the sentences if necessary.

1. Major supporting points (topic sentences) needing transitions:

   a. Federal student loans are a good financing option. College graduates have the choice of not repaying them. Graduates can work in the Peace Corps. They can participate in Teach for America. They can take part in other loan-forgiveness programs.

(continued)

Vocabulary Collection Word:
accruing

Your in-context definition:

_____

_____

A dictionary definition:

_____

_____

   b. Students do not have to pay back federal student loans immediately. Students can wait until after graduation.

   c. Federal student loans do not start accruing interest immediately. Interest begins when the student graduates.

   d. The interest rate on federal student loans is generally 3 to 7 percent. This is much lower than that of private student loans.

Answers:

a. _____

_____

_____

_____

b. _____

_____

c. _____

_____

d. _____

_____

2. Supporting details needing transitions:

   a. There is a Teacher Loan Forgiveness Program. It is a way to help teachers pay back student loans. Not every teacher is eligible for the program.

   b. The program is available only to teachers. Only teachers with Stafford Loans can participate.

   c. There are eligibility requirements. A teacher must have worked for five years at a school. The school must be eligible to participate in the program.

   d. The teacher must have taken the student loan prior to or during the five years of teaching.

Answers:

a. _____

_____

b. _____

c. _____

_____

d. _____

_____

3. Sentences needing transitions:

   a. Obesity has become a major health problem in the U.S. Health experts and researchers warn of it as an epidemic.

   b. Some lawmakers are trying to discourage dietary habits contributing to obesity. They are targeting large consumption of sugary drinks.

   c. They have proposed taxing soda. Some have included diet sodas in their legislation.

   d. Diet sodas are low-calorie items. Beginning studies are giving some evidence linking diet sodas to obesity.

   e. Supporters of the soda tax point to the growing public costs of treating medical conditions related to obesity. Opponents argue that the tax impinges on personal freedom.

Answers:

a. _____

_____

_____

(continued)

Reading and Writing as Integrated Processes

b. _____
   _____
   _____

c. _____

d. _____
   _____

e. _____
   _____
   _____

4. Sentences needing transitions:

   a. The new law allows students to graduate from high school with fewer math courses. The law requires only two years of high school math.

   b. College students whose entrance scores are too low will not be able to take college math. They will have to master high school math skills at off-campus facilities. They will then be allowed into college math classes.

   c. Students should learn how much mathematics preparation they will need for college. They may have to add semesters to their degree plans. This may be the only way for them to finish their math requirements.

   Answers:

   a. _____
      _____

   b. _____
      _____
      _____
      _____

   c. _____
      _____
      _____

USING SPECIFIC TYPES OF SUPPORTING DETAILS IN YOUR WRITING

Although you may not be aware of it, you use supporting details in your conversations all the time. For instance, in a casual conversation with a friend, you may comment about a movie you saw: "That movie was fantastic!" Your friend is likely to ask why you liked it so much. Your response will include supporting details. Notice how your conversation can be outlined in a way similar to an essay.

Thesis statement: That movie was fantastic!

Support:

- It was a classic epic. (*classification of the movie type*)
- It was so much better than the first movie in the series because the main character, Kudu, didn't win every battle. He seemed much more realistic. (*comparison*)
- The whole movie was in sepia-colored tones, which really added to the oddness of the scenery. (*description*)

We use support without even thinking about it. Moreover, these supporting details come in a wide variety of types.

Recognizing Types of Supporting Details

As you read, become aware of the various types of support writers use and that you have available to you as a writer. The chart that follows lists some of the most common types of supporting details.

Common Types of Supporting Details	
Analogy	An example that explains something unfamiliar by comparing it with something more familiar
Cause and effect	How one circumstance brought about or resulted from another
Comparison and contrast	How one item or event is similar to or different from another
Concrete example	Specific information that helps the reader understand the writer's point
Definition	An explanation of the meaning of a word or concept
Description	Sensory information that helps the reader understand a thing or concept
Explanation	A description of how something is constructed, how a task is performed, or how something works
Fact	A statement that is verifiably true
Figurative language	Language that expresses ideas in an indirect way, such as metaphors, similes, personification, and hyperbole
Hypothetical example	An example that asks the reader to imagine something that is not currently true
Observation	An account of phenomena or field research
Reason	The rationale or justification for an assertion or claim
Rhetorical question	A question that the writer asks to make a point but does not expect the reader to answer; the answer may be provided in the text, or it may be self-evident
Summaries	A brief recounting of the content of a source
Steps, stages, or phases	A discussion of sequential actions or time periods to depict a process
Testimony	A person's firsthand account of something
Use of sources	Citing external sources, often to prove something: • Citing experts or authorities so the reader knows where the information is coming from and can evaluate its validity • Citing reference books so the information can be considered factual • Citing statistics to provide mathematical information or proof • Citing witnesses to provide evidence or acknowledgments
Visual aid	A photo, diagram, chart, cartoon, or any other graphic representation of content

Writers select the type of supporting details to use based on the point they are making. To develop supporting details, think about each major supporting point as if you were the reader, not the writer. What questions would you have? What information would you want the writer to add to the paragraph?

For instance, to show that a movie is worth seeing, you might provide a brief *summary* of the plot, *compare* the movie to another movie, and *cite* the reviews of expert film critics. You would probably *not* use statistics, visual aids, or hypothetical examples. The following guidelines may help you select appropriate and effective details.

- Use concrete examples of real events and situations to convey trustworthiness.
- Use hypothetical examples—that is, fictional examples—to illustrate a point.
- Use short narratives—stories—to make a point.
- Imagine a reader who says "So what?" Make sure you show the importance of the point you are making.
- Use journalistic questions to think of content: who, what, where, when, why, and how. Only include the information generated by these questions if that information is relevant and truly strengthens the major supporting point.

Let's examine the kinds of support used in a specific essay. Below you will find the first part of an article written by a senior journalism major, Brittany Horn, at Penn State University. Horn does not provide a direct thesis statement, but an implied thesis statement might be worded like this: "In certain villages in China, pollution is causing cancer, and little is being done to change the situation." Read Horn's article, paying particular attention to the support she uses. The supporting details are highlighted, and they are annotated in the right column.

Recovery Is Slow in Rural China's "Cancer Villages"
by Brittany Horn

NANMEN, China—In this small village about 25 miles from Shanghai, the smell of paint and gasoline hangs heavy in the stagnant afternoon air. Small dogs run in streets wide enough for only a small car. Children with worn Disney backpacks walk home from school, avoiding the trash tossed into the street gutters.

Example (Nanmen as an example of a cancer village)

Description

It seems to be a village much like any other in rural China. But there is something different about Nanmen that weighs on villagers' minds.

Comparison and contrast

Nanmen is one of more than 400 so-called "cancer villages," areas so polluted by waste and factory runoff that its citizens are in danger of contracting the deadly disease. The villages are part of the dark underside of China's industrial might—places that critics, environmentalists and foreign experts believe the government has sacrificed in its rush to prosperity.

Definition

"Many cancer villages can be proven, even though the government may choose to not acknowledge it," said Dong Jiang, an environmental activist who has studied the link between pollution and cancer in places like Nanmen.

Citation from environmental activist offered as proof

In the first four paragraphs, Horn uses an example, a description, comparison and contrast, a definition, and a quote from an environmental activist. These forms of support are all appropriate, yet diverse. The rest of the article appears in the practice below.

Vocabulary Collection Word:
activist

Your in-context definition:

_____

_____

A dictionary definition:

_____

_____

PRACTICE ④ Identifying Types of Supporting Details

Identify the support in the remainder of Horn's essay. Underline each supporting detail and identify its type in the column on the right.

	YOUR ANNOTATIONS
The term "cancer village" is not widely recognized by the academic world, but it's a phrase that's been used by the media, citizens and, most recently, the Chinese government to describe the poor living conditions.	

The term "cancer village" is not widely recognized by the academic world, but it's a phrase that's been used by the media, citizens and, most recently, the Chinese government to describe the poor living conditions.

Government officials and some academic experts argue that because the exact causes of cancer are so difficult to trace, there's no direct correlation between the cancer in rural villages and pollutants. But environmentalists like Dong say that the connection is clear, if people look.

And for those who've lost loved ones, there is no doubt.

It's been more than two years since Wang Qin said goodbye to her 22-month-old daughter, who died five months after she was diagnosed with leukemia. A day doesn't pass, Wang Qin said, when she doesn't think of her baby.

"I think of my lovely daughter all the time," she said. "She could say (the words) mom and dad, grandpa . . . she was quite smart."

Wang and her husband, Lu Weiming, spent thousands of dollars in medical bills and travel expenses to get their daughter, Wang Bole, the care she needed. But nothing worked. Their daughter slipped away in front of them, never recovering from the fever that took her life.

Today, more than two years later, Wang is still fighting the Chinese government for compensation for her loss and for recognition that a nearby waste collection factory be held accountable for its pollution.

She remembers the man who became blistered and fainted soon after touching the runoff water from the factory. Wang said the elderly are most susceptible, as the government can often overlook their deaths or blame them on natural causes. Other families tried to move away before the disease could take them, too, but not all were that lucky.

Part of Wang's struggle is getting the government and the scientific community to acknowledge the relationship between specific pollutants and cancer villages like Nanmen.

Professor Song Weimin, of Fudan University in Shanghai, said the connection between the cancer villages and pollutants is hard to prove, as the list of physical, chemical and biological factors continues to grow. Song, who specializes in environmental health, also said that the Chinese government is investigating the village pollution but hasn't released any official statistics as of yet.

"It's hard to find evidence," Song said. "Some organizations are afraid of getting in trouble because if they find that a factory is linked to cancer, it will lead to a lawsuit."

Activists like Dong Jian, vice president and secretary general of the Future Green Youth Leadership Council, say the proof exists, but the government chooses to ignore it.

"There is a direct connection," Dong insisted. "You have to compare the cancer rates before the factory has been built versus after the factory was built. Then you can see the rise."

(continued)

Progress may be slow, but there has been some movement. In a report released Feb. 20 by the Ministry of Environmental Protection, the government for the first time acknowledged the existence of cancer villages clustered around the outskirts of major cities and factories.

Dong says it's not enough. "Although the government has the responsibility to acknowledge cancer villages and pollution, sometimes they don't do what they say they will," he said.

Nanmen villagers know this story well. A village that was once removed from the rest of China became suddenly transformed into a place filled with pollution and disease.

Villagers first noticed a change in 2002, when a small landfill began to take shape in the middle of Nanmen and soon gave way to a waste collection factory that virtually appeared overnight, Wang said.

"The water was colorful, all kinds of colors," Wang said. "The water smelled terrible. Creatures couldn't live there anymore."

The Zhaohong waste collection factory moved out more than two years ago, but Dong Jian said the negative effects on the environment and people remain.

Take Wang Qin's elderly father. He can't afford to move from the village, nor does he want to. The streets he has called home since he was a child aren't something he's ready to give up for the sake of his health.

The pond that once housed fish and wildlife is now home to a toilet basin with thick, black mud and leftover trash. Residents can no longer swim in the polluted water that scarcely resembles the place Wang Qin once swam.

Villagers say conditions are getting better, but the effects of the longtime pollution are hard to gauge. Trees are only beginning to resume growth two years after the factory's removal, and the site where the Zhaohong waste collection factory once stood is barren and avoided.

Home is no longer a place Wang Qin can stomach.

Student Example: Selecting Appropriate Types of Support

To determine the best types of support to use in your own writing, use the three-step process shown here.

1. Write down the point that needs support.

2. Make a list of the types of details that could reasonably support your point.

3. Choose the types of details you believe will best meet the needs of your audience.

◼ Steps for selecting types of support

We will follow the writing process of Trey, a college student writing an essay for a biology class. Trey's assignment is to select an issue in biology that affects public health, to form an opinion on the issue, and to write an essay expressing his opinion. He must offer solid support for his point of view.

Trey goes through the steps of analyzing his assignment, reading and annotating sources for ideas, and prewriting to develop his ideas. As a result of his prewriting, he chooses to write about the reasons why antibacterial products should no longer be sold to the general public, and he constructs a thesis statement.

Write Down the Points That Need Support

Trey decides to use four major supporting points to support his thesis statement.

Thesis statement: The sale of antibacterial products to the general public should be prohibited.

Major supporting points:

- First, the widespread use of antibacterial products is helping superbugs get stronger.
- Second, antibacterial products prevent helpful bacteria from doing their jobs, which results in a weakened immune system.
- Third, antibacterial products are no more effective at killing bacteria than regular soap and water.
- Finally, scientists now believe that antibacterial agents have negative health effects on people, especially pregnant women and children.

Now Trey must figure out the best types of details to use for each major supporting point.

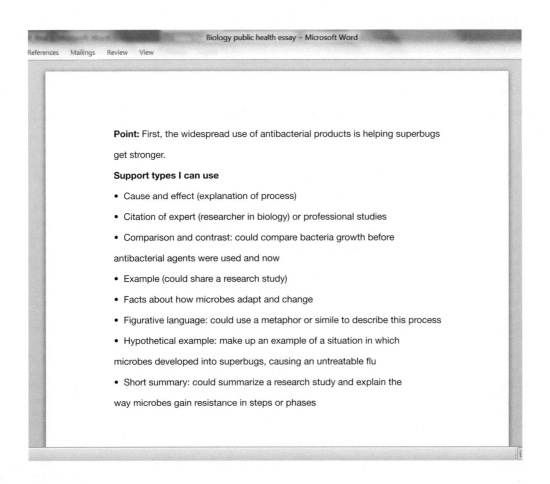

Biology public health essay - Microsoft Word

References   Mailings   Review   View

Point: First, the widespread use of antibacterial products is helping superbugs get stronger.

Support types I can use

- Cause and effect (explanation of process)
- Citation of expert (researcher in biology) or professional studies
- Comparison and contrast: could compare bacteria growth before antibacterial agents were used and now
- Example (could share a research study)
- Facts about how microbes adapt and change
- Figurative language: could use a metaphor or simile to describe this process
- Hypothetical example: make up an example of a situation in which microbes developed into superbugs, causing an untreatable flu
- Short summary: could summarize a research study and explain the way microbes gain resistance in steps or phases

List Details That Could Support the Points

Trey decides to do more prewriting, so he opens a document on his computer and creates a simple list for his first major supporting point.

Choose Details That Will Best Meet the Audience's Needs

Trey knows that he cannot use all of these different types of support. He must choose the ones that will be most convincing to his audience, and he should choose the details he has learned the most about. After thinking about his list, Trey decides to use the following supporting details:

- Cause and effect (explanation of process). *This detail will give readers the information on how antibacterial agents can cause antibiotic-resistant microbes.*
- Citation of expert (researcher in biology) or professional studies. *This information will lend credibility to Trey's ideas.*
- Hypothetical example: make up an example of a situation where microbes developed into superbugs, causing an untreatable flu. *This information will help readers see how serious an issue antibacterial resistance is.*

When you are selecting types of support for a point you are making, use the same three-step process as Trey did. Always keep in mind how your audience will respond to the support you plan to offer. Choose the most compelling support available to you.

PRACTICE ⑤ Selecting Appropriate Types of Support for Your Writing

What follows is a simple essay outline containing a thesis statement and the major supporting points to develop the thesis statement. For each major supporting point, determine the best types of supporting details to use. Jot down your ideas in a fashion similar to Trey's. Use a bullet point for each type of supporting detail you will use.

Topic: College instructors carrying firearms on campus

Thesis statement: Instructors should not have the option of bringing their personal firearms to campus.

Major supporting points:

1. Most teachers do not have enough training to use a firearm with the kind of precision required to stop an attacker.

   Support:_____

   _____

2. The more weapons that are on campus, the more dangerous campus will be.

   Support: _____

   _____

   _____

   _____

3. Other solutions to campus violence are better options.

   Support: _____

   _____

   _____

Student Example: Developing an Essay from Prewriting to Outlining

Creating the kind of support that will help readers fully understand your thesis statement is an essential part of writing an essay. Usually, when you generate ideas in prewriting, you are already beginning to think about the kinds of information you will use in your body paragraphs. What follows is an example of how Sienna, a high school student, generated supporting details for her assignment.

Analyze the Assignment

Sienna is taking a class in anthropology, and her instructor has given the class an essay assignment. Sienna's first task is to fully understand the assignment. She reads the assignment and makes annotations.

Assignment: Write an essay in which you *discuss* a rite of passage you have experienced; *show* readers *why* this rite of passage was significant.

SIENNA'S
ANNOTATIONS
What is this?

By reviewing her class notes, she learns that a rite of passage is an important transitional experience in a person's life, such as marriage, graduation, childbirth, divorce, or even a particular birthday celebration. That information helps her rephrase the assignment as a question.

Sienna's question: What significant rite of passage have I experienced, and why was it important?

Identify the Purpose

Three other words in the assignment that Sienna annotated are *discuss, show,* and *why.* From these terms she concludes that the purpose of her essay is to tell about her rite of passage and discuss the reasons it was important. Moreover, she is not to discuss just any rite of passage. She must choose one from her own experience. So her purpose is to *inform* her readers about a rite of passage she experienced and *evaluate* its importance.

Prewrite to Develop Ideas

From class discussions, Sienna discovers that a rite of passage can typically be thought of as consisting of three phases:

Separation, in which an individual experiences separation from his or her former life or "world"

Transition, in which an individual is in between "two worlds," no longer really a part of his or her "old world," but not fully incorporated into the new one either

Reincorporation, in which the individual is re-introduced into his or her community, which acknowledges the new status of the individual (in their "new" world)

Because she spent the summer working in a restaurant in a tourist town, Sienna decides to write about how that job was an important rite of passage for her. With that in mind, Sienna rewrites the question her essay will answer:

Sienna's revised question: Why was working at Beach Bistro a significant rite of passage?

Then, using the three phases of a rite of passage, Sienna does some *freewriting*—writing quickly on a subject without pausing to make corrections. During her freewriting, she comes up with ideas about how waitressing was a significant experience for her. Afterward, rereading her freewriting, she underlines the important details for each phase. She realizes that the last line of her freewriting answers the question "Why?" so she highlights that line.

Why was working at Beach Bistro an important rite of passage?

Separation: I had to leave my hometown and go stay at the beach all summer with no one I knew except my one friend who I went there with. Then she got sick and went home, and I stayed there. I had to leave my boyfriend, who then broke up with me. I left all of my friends behind, and my family, too. I was in a new world that revolved around the restaurant.

Transition: I had the wrong clothes. I had to learn everything I knew about waitressing over because it was all different. Double shift made me cry—I couldn't handle the pressure. Had to learn to work with different people and solve problems like with silverware rolls. And for a lot of problems, they didn't tell you what to do; you had to figure out what to do.

Reincorporation: In anthropology, that's re-entering society with a new status. I have new status as a member of the Bistro family, and I belong on the island too—people there recognize me and smile at me. Now qualified to work dinner shift—better tips. More independent and I can handle more stress. I feel more mature—ready for college next year. I look and dress differently now, too.

Construct a Thesis Statement

Using the material she developed in her prewriting, Sienna constructs a thesis statement.

> **Thesis statement:** Waitressing at a restaurant in a tourist town was a rite of passage that changed my life forever.

Notice that Sienna has written an *open thesis statement*: it does not reveal an explicit plan for her essay. Sienna also considered this *closed thesis statement*, which lists the stages she will discuss in each major supporting point:

> Waitressing at a restaurant in a seaside resort town was a rite of passage that involved the stages of separation, transition, and reincorporation.

Develop Support for the Thesis Statement

Sienna plans to use each stage in her rite of passage as a major supporting point. Her next task is to create topic sentences for each major supporting point.

Writing Topic Sentences for Major Supporting Points Using the three rite of passage phases from her prewriting, as well as the details she developed in the prewriting, Sienna writes topic sentences for her major supporting ideas.

Thesis statement: Waitressing at a restaurant in a tourist town was a rite of passage that changed my life forever.

Major supporting point 1 (topic sentence): When a friend asked me to be her roommate and work at a restaurant on an island with her for the summer, I didn't think about how I'd have to leave behind my family, friends, boyfriend, and dog, and separate from my old life. I just said, "Okay."

Major supporting point 2 (topic sentence): Things weren't at all how I thought they would be once I got settled in, and the transition period included a lot of learning on my feet.

Major supporting point 3 (topic sentence): By the end of the summer, I felt like a new person, and I looked that way, too.

Sienna uses transitions while she writes her topic sentences. Notice her use of *When, once, By the end*.

When a friend asked . . . I didn't think about . . . I just said . . .

Things weren't how I thought they would be once I got settled in . . .

By the end of the summer . . .

Both the transitions and the similarities in wording tell readers that these details are the major phases in Sienna's rite of passage.

Anticipating an Audience's Questions Sienna needs to make sure the supporting details she has developed in prewriting will provide enough information to meet the needs of her readers. One way to do this is to spend time thinking about what readers might want or need to know. By putting herself in the place of the reader, she can predict some of the needs of her audience. The chart below shows some of the audience questions Sienna asks herself about her second major supporting point.

Topic sentence for major supporting point 2: Things weren't at all how I thought they would be once I got settled in, and the transition period included a lot of learning on my feet.	
Supporting details:	**Audience questions:**
• I brought the wrong clothes	• What is the wrong clothing and why did you bring it? Can you tell me what it looked like? • How did you figure out what to wear—did someone tell you? • How did you get the right clothes?
• The way we worked was completely different from Waffle Barn, and much harder	• What did you do differently? • What do you mean by "the way we worked"—can you give a specific example of what you had to do? What was hard about it?
• I had to solve problems on my own instead of being told what to do	• What kind of problems did you have to solve? Can you give examples of what you figured out to do?

Listing and Choosing Supporting Details for Each Major Supporting Point Sienna returns to her prewriting to find effective supporting details. Although Sienna has already identified some of the supporting details she will use—personal anecdotes and facts about the restaurant business—she takes time to remember even *more specific* examples as she continues thinking about her audience's needs. She plans to add a very short anecdote and some concrete examples to make her essay more informative and enjoyable.

Create an Outline to Organize the Essay

Sienna now writes a simple outline for her essay. She jots down her three major supporting points—written out as full topic sentences. Under each point, she adds the supporting details she will use. When the supporting details themselves need more explanation or support, she adds them as "details."

Sienna's Simple Outline

Title: Summer at Beach Bistro: My Rite of Passage

Introduction paragraph

Thesis statement: Waitressing at a restaurant in a tourist town was a rite of passage that changed my life forever.

Major supporting point 1: When a friend asked me to be her roommate and work at a restaurant on an island with her for the summer, I didn't think about how I'd have to leave behind my family, friends, and boyfriend, and separate from my old life. I just said, "Okay."

  Supporting detail: Friend left right away and I was alone

  Supporting detail: boyfriend broke up with me

  Supporting detail: tiny apartment I shared with 3 other girls I didn't know

Major supporting point 2: Things weren't at all how I thought they would be once I got settled in, and the transition period included a lot of learning on my feet.

  Supporting detail: I had the wrong clothes

    Detail: I brought white shirts and heels. Everyone wore sandals and tie dye.

    Detail: Went thrifting to find "island" clothes

  Supporting detail: work was different and much harder

    Detail: double shift was too hard at first

  Supporting detail: I had to solve problems on my own instead of being told what to do

    Detail: story about rolling napkins

Major supporting point 3: By the end of the summer, I felt like a new person, and I looked that way, too.

  Supporting detail: look different: tan, happy, wearing island clothes

  Supporting detail: more confident, able to work dinner shift and earn more

  Supporting detail: part of the Bistro family

    Detail: party on last day

Conclusion paragraph

Notice that not all of the body paragraphs have the same number of details. Some writers aim to have supporting paragraphs that are roughly the same length, and that is a good goal. However, body paragraphs can have minor variations in the number of details they include and still be effective.

Notice also how coming up with supporting details leads naturally into creating a simple, informal outline for your writing. It is always wise to create an outline before drafting.

PRACTICE **6**   Planning Support Paragraphs for an Essay

Using Sienna's work as a model, generate ideas and an outline for an essay on a rite of passage you have experienced. You will use your outline in a later assignment to draft the essay. Follow these instructions.

1. **Start by reading the assignment.** For this assignment, you will write an essay in which you discuss a rite of passage you have experienced; your essay must show readers why this rite of passage was significant. For details, see A Reading and Writing Assignment at the end of this chapter.

2. **Prewrite to develop your ideas.** Choose a prewriting method, such as listing or freewriting, and use it to generate ideas for the topic. First, prewrite about some of the experiences in your life that were rites of passage. Write down each experience, and note why it was significant to you. Do this for at least three experiences.

   Once you have written about three or more rites of passage, choose one to discuss in an essay. If you need to, spend more time prewriting to think of the ways this experience changed you.

3. **Construct a thesis statement.** Write a sentence in which you express the main point you wish to make about the rite of passage you selected for your essay.

4. **Develop support for your thesis statement.** Write a topic sentence for each major supporting point. Consider creating a major supporting point for each significant effect this rite of passage had. Once you have written topic sentences for your major supporting points, list the questions a general audience might have about them. Next, jot down the minor supporting details that would help readers understand each of your major supporting points.

5. **Create a simple outline to organize your essay.** Use Sienna's outline as a model. Include your thesis statement, major supporting points, and supporting details.

CHAPTER ACTIVITIES

READING AND ANNOTATING

What follows are excerpts about rites of passage from two different scholarly works. The first reading begins with a list of details. The second reading begins by setting the sociological context for rites of passage.

Preview the excerpts. What point do you think the writers are making about rites of passage? Make some notes based on your observations from previewing. Then read the excerpts, and annotate the major supporting points. You may have an easier time analyzing the reading, if you identify the major supporting points before you try to figure out the thesis statement.

When you are finished, answer the questions that follow.

(Note: The first selection contains parenthetical references to sources the author has used. Full information about these sources, listed in the author's text, is not given here.)

Your observations from previewing:

_____

_____

_____

_____

YOUR ANNOTATIONS

The Life Course
by Richard T. Schaefer

Among the Kota people of the Congo in Africa, adolescents paint themselves blue. Mexican American girls go on a daylong religious retreat before dancing the night away. Egyptian mothers step over their newborn infants seven times, and graduating students at the Naval Academy throw their hats in the air. These are all ways of celebrating **rites of passage**, a means of dramatizing and validating changes in a person's status. Rites of passage can mark a separation, as in a graduation ceremony, or an incorporation, as in an initiation into an organization (Van Gennep [1909] 1960).

Rites of passage are a worldwide social phenomenon. The Kota rite marks the passage to adulthood. The color blue, viewed as the color of death, symbolizes the death of childhood. Hispanic girls celebrate reaching womanhood with a *quinceañera* ceremony at age 15. In the Cuban American community of Miami, the popularity of the *quinceañera* supports a network of party planners, caterers, dress designers, and the Miss Quinceañera Latina pageant. For thousands of years, Egyptian mothers have welcomed their newborns to the world in the Soboa ceremony by stepping over the seven-day-old infant seven times.

These specific ceremonies mark stages of development in the life course. They indicate that the process of socialization continues through all stages of the life cycle. . . .

Several life events mark the passage to adulthood. Of course, these turning points vary from one society and even one generation to the next. In the United States, the key event seems to be the completion of formal schooling. . . . On average, Americans expect this milestone to occur by a person's 23rd birthday. Other major events in the life course, such as getting married or becoming a parent, are expected to follow three or four years later. . . .

One result of these staggered steps to independence is that in the United States, unlike some other societies, there is no clear dividing line between adolescence and adulthood. Nowadays, few young people finish school, get married, and leave home at about the same age, clearly establishing their transition to adulthood.

The terms *youthhood, emerging adulthood*, and *not quite adult* have been coined to describe the prolonged ambiguous status that young people in their 20s experience (Côté 2000; Settersten and Ray 2011; Christian Smith 2007).

The following is an excerpt from a work, The Andaman Islanders, *by A.R. Brown, a social anthropologist, on his study in the early 20ᵗʰ century of native Andaman islanders. In the excerpt, Brown is providing an analysis of the Andaman initiation ceremonies (rites of passage). The Andaman Islands are located in the Bay of Bengal, between India and Myanmar.*

The Interpretation of Andamanese Customs and Beliefs: Ceremonial

The position in the social life occupied by a child is different from that of an adult; the child is dependent upon and closely united to his parents, and is not an independent member of the community. . . . As the child grows up a change takes place in his position in the social life, and this must be accompanied by a change in the emotional dispositions of the child himself . . . and by a change in the attitude towards the child [by] the other members of the group. The initiation ceremonies are the means by which these changes are brought about, and by which, therefore, the child is made an independent member of the society.

The ceremonies have two aspects. . . . For the society they are to be described as the recognition of the change of status of the initiate. . . . For the initiate they constitute a sort of moral or social education.

. . . Since in the life of the Andamans by far the most important social activity is the getting of food, . . . it is therefore appropriate that it should be through his relation to food that the child should be taught his relation to the society. . . . During his infancy the child is almost entirely unrestrained and acts with great comparative freedom. He does not realise, in any adequate manner, that the food with which he is freely provided . . . is only obtained by skill and effort, nor does he realise that he will one day be required to labour to supply food for others.

There follows a period of restraint, during which the growing boy or girl has to give up eating certain relished foods, and has to pass through a number of ceremonies, some of them painful, and all solemn and awe-inspiring. Through a series of years, just at what is . . . the most impressionable age, the individual learns to subordinate his own desires to the requirements of the society or of custom, as explained to him by his elders. He is thus impressed, in a forcible manner, with the importance of the moral law, and at the same time he is impressed with a sense of the social value of food. The ceremonies thus afford a moral education adapted to the requirements of life as it is lived in the Andamans.

. . . As stated . . . the ceremonies teach the boy or girl self-control or self-restraint, and they do so in relation to one of the two fundamental human instincts,—hunger. . . . Secondly the ceremonies teach the initiate, for the first time in life, to view life and its duties and obligations seriously. . . . the ceremonies awaken and develop in the adolescent that fear of unseen danger which . . . has a very important place in the mental life of the Andamanese and an important function in their moral life. Finally, the whole series of abstentions and ceremonies serves to develop in the mind of every new member of the society that sense of the social value of foods, . . . which may be briefly described as being a realisation that food is a possession of the society, that not only the power to obtain food, but also the power to use it without danger is something that the individual owes to the society, and that the bestowal upon him of this power involves the acceptance on his part of corresponding obligations.

We may say, to look at the matter under another aspect, that the initiation ceremonies teach the youth or girl to realise what is implied in being a member of the society by putting him or her during the period of adolescence in an exceptional position . . . outside the society. The youth is no longer a child and may not act as a child; but he is not yet an adult and may not act as adults do. He feels himself cut off, as it were from the ordinary life of the group, having as yet no share in it. As a child he was not yet aware of what it means to be a member of a society, but now, by means of the ceremonies, his attention is directed to the society and its life, by his being placed in a position of isolation outside it. He begins to look forward to the time when he will take his proper place as an adult, and his share in the common life of the camp. At each step of the ceremonies he feels that he is brought a little closer, until at last he can feel himself a man amongst men. Thus he is brought to a consciousness of all that it must mean to him to be a member of the community; he is taught the significance and value of social communion.

Questions for Consideration

1. The excerpts you read concern rites of passage. What rites of passage--whether formal or informal--exist in our contemporary society in the U.S.? Do they involve separation? Incorporation? Discuss an example in one or two paragraphs.

2. Find a person who is much older than you are. Interview the person to find out whether he or she can recall a rite of passage that was significant. You may need to explain what a rite of passage is. Take notes from your interview. Using your notes, write one or two pages about this person's rite of passage.

3. Sometimes, some young men and women in our modern society want to show that they are moving from adolescence to adulthood by choosing behaviors that can be violent, destructive, and even dangerous. What are some examples of such behaviors? Write a paragraph discussing one such example.

USING MODELS TO PRACTICE COMPOSING

Earlier in this chapter, you read about the steps Sienna took as she worked on a writing assignment. Below you will find the essay Sienna wrote. Read the essay, and annotate any of the writing features you think are effective. Circle the transitions you find. Be mindful of the support Sienna used. Note any areas where you think she should have included more support.

Sienna Mendez

INRW 0402

Ms. Cassidy

15 November 2016

Beach Bistro: My Rite of Passage

Waitressing at a restaurant in a tourist town was a rite of passage that changed my life forever. I was from a small town, where my life centered around my high school, my family and friends, and my boyfriend whom I'd been dating for a year. I had a waitressing job at Waffle Barn, but it wasn't challenging, and it didn't seem like part of my identity at all, just a uniform and a paycheck. I had never lived away from home.

When a friend asked me to be her roommate and work at a restaurant on an island with her for the summer, I didn't think about how I'd have to leave behind my family, friends, and boyfriend and separate from my old life. I just said, "Okay." Sara had worked at Beach Bistro the summer before, and she already had an apartment lined up for us to stay in with three other girls, so I didn't plan on being lonely. Besides, my boyfriend promised to drive out soon. However, Sara got so sick the first weekend, she had to go home for the rest of the summer. While I was helping Sara get to the ambulance boat, my boyfriend broke up with me by text message— yes, the first weekend I was gone! My heart was broken, I didn't know anyone in town, and the three other girls in the apartment worked at other places and were hardly ever home.

Things weren't at all how I thought they would be once I got settled in, and the transition period included a lot of learning on my feet. Sara had told me that Beach Bistro was fancier than Waffle Barn, and we wouldn't wear uniforms. I wore a white blouse, black pants, and black high heels the first day. To my surprise, everyone else wore casual clothes—tie dye, tank tops, sarong skirts and sandals. Lang, the kitchen chief, explained to me that I'd need flat shoes to run up and down the stairs from the kitchen, which was in the basement, to the different levels of the restaurant. I was almost broke, but I found a thrift store the next day and got some island wear. I noticed all of the girls wore long, sparkly bead earrings, but I couldn't find any.

The work was very different from Waffle Barn, too. We had to keep all glasses of iced tea refilled without the customers asking for more or even noticing, run up and down stairs with big trays of food, and memorize long lists of specials and all of their ingredients. The restaurant was packed every day of the week. After lunch shift I would feel exhausted. After the second week, my boss asked if I would work a dinner shift after lunch because one of the night waiters couldn't come in. If I thought lunch was crazy, dinner was ten times more crowded. My knees were sore from the stairs and a customer got mad at me for forgetting his dessert. Then I dropped a whole pitcher of tea. Lang found me in the hallway about to cry and told me, "Sienna, we're glad you're helping us tonight. You don't have to be perfect. Just do what you can." I realized that even though I wasn't doing the best job that night, without me they'd be in worse trouble. Then, instead of feeling incompetent, I felt like I mattered. Soon I was working the dinner shift a lot, and I got better at it.

At home, I would ask my parents for help with problems, or my best friend, or my supervisor at work. On the island, however, I was alone, and work time was usually too busy to ask someone what to do, so I had to solve a lot of problems myself. Before shifts, the wait staff would sit on the picnic benches and roll silverware into bundles with the cloth napkins to keep ready at our stations. One guy I worked with a lot would show up late, and our station would run short of silver if I didn't do his bundles for him. I finally told him I didn't mind rolling the silver for him if he would text me and tell me he was running late, and in exchange, he could mop the whole area after our shift for both of us. That was a great trade for me, considering what a nasty chore mopping could be, and it worked for him, too.

By the end of the summer, I felt like a new person, and I looked that way, too. I had a great tan. My style of dress had changed to what we called "island style," and I still like to dress like that. I could handle double shifts, which made me feel good about myself and helped me earn better money. On the last Monday of the summer, the restaurant was closed to the public and we had a big party for the staff. Everyone hugged me and told me they'd miss me. Lang gave me a pair of those long, sparkly

Mendez 3

earrings. It turned out she made them! I felt like I had a new family—my island family. I can't wait to go back there next summer to work again.

In some societies, rites of passage mark a person's transition into adulthood. I feel more adult now. Working double shifts, handling emergencies and difficulties with other people, and having to live on my own made me grow up a bit, and I feel ready to handle the future when I go to college.

A READING AND WRITING ASSIGNMENT

Using Sienna's essay as a model and the material you developed in Practice 6, complete the following assignment:

> Write an essay in which you discuss a rite of passage you have experienced; show readers why this rite of passage was significant.
>
> A rite of passage is usually an event or a short period of time in a person's life that is particularly important and results in personal growth. For example, taking care of a loved one who is dying might trigger a reappraisal of life. For the caregiver, this task may be a rite of passage into new insights and a new way of living. Other rites of passage are more formal, such as getting married, having a child, and getting divorced. Think of an event or time in your life from which you emerged changed in some way: perhaps you became "older and wiser," or maybe you had insights that changed the way you live or that helped you mature. You may structure your paper around the ways this rite of passage has affected you, or you may write about each of the three phases Sienna included in her essay planning.

Use the Quick Start Guide to Integrated Reading and Writing Assignments to help you with this process. Be sure to reread your essay carefully for errors.

⊙ THINKING FROM AN INSTRUCTOR'S POINT OF VIEW

A *rubric* is a detailed grading sheet. Instructors create rubrics to help them grade assignments. One way to create a rubric is to analyze an assignment's instructions and turn them into *objectives* for the rubric. Each objective is then assigned a point value. The process looks something like this.

How Instructors Create Grading Rubrics

1. Analyze the assignment, and take apart the instructions piece by piece as the highlighting here shows.

   Example: Read the article called "Rehab for Bullies." Write an essay in which you argue whether the writer's thesis—that bullies should be put into rehabilitation programs—is a good idea or not. Compose a sound thesis statement, and offer supporting reasons, hypothetical examples, and discussions of how "bully rehabilitation" might affect children who experience it. When you refer to ideas from the article, be sure to use an appropriate method for giving credit to the source.

2. Turn each instruction into a learning objective.

   Examples: Learning objective: The student's essay shows that he or she read the article "Rehab for Bullies."

Learning objective: The student's writing is an essay, and it addresses the topic (whether bully rehab is a good idea).

Learning objective: The student takes a position on the question and writes a sound thesis statement. . . .

3. Assign a point value to each learning objective on the basis of how important the objective is.

Examples: 10 points—Learning objective: The student's essay shows that he or she read the article "Rehab for Bullies."

10 points—Learning objective: The student's writing is an essay, and it addresses the topic (whether bully rehab is a good idea).

15 points—Learning objective: The student takes a position on the question and writes a sound thesis statement. . . .

Here is an example of the first part of an actual grading rubric for a specific essay assignment.

EASY 1 RUBRIC / GRADE SHEET		ENGL 1301 Dr. Herze
Learning Objective/Points Possible	**Comments about Student's Performance**	**Points Scored**
1. Critical reading and understanding as demonstrated in student writing (Instruction from assignment: "Read and analyze the article, 'Light on the Horizon.' Use the article as a starting point for your own ideas on the topic.")	Lydia—You did a nice job showing you understood the main ideas and major supporting details. Work on understanding the writer's tone.	**Possible points: 20** **Score:** 17
2. Student's essay provides an appropriate response to the writing prompt. (Instruction from assignment: Write an essay that responds to this question: "Does 'Light on the Horizon' offer a convincing argument for changing immigration laws?")	Nice job staying on topic and fully considering each of the issues raised in the article.	**Possible points: 20** **Score:** 20

Using the information from the rite of passage essay assignment in Practice 6, create a grading rubric you believe would be an appropriate tool for assessing student essays. When you are finished, write a paragraph explaining what you learned from this activity.

⊙ ADDING TO YOUR VOCABULARY

This chapter's vocabulary words appear below.

initiative	default	accruing	activist
on the cusp	off-the-cuff	aquifer	

Choose five of the vocabulary words from this chapter that you would like to add to your vocabulary, and think about how you can use them this week. For example, one of this chapter's terms is *off-the-cuff*. This term describes something that is said without forethought or preparation. You can often substitute *off-the-cuff* for *unplanned*.

Example: I didn't know my instructor would call on me to explain last night's reading, so I just gave my best *unplanned* answer.

I didn't know my instructor would call on me to explain last night's reading, so I just gave my best *off-the-cuff* answer.

List each of the five words you plan to use this week, and make note of a context in which you could use each word.

Example: *Off-the-cuff.* When I am explaining something to family members but do not have time to get into great depth, I'll let them know my explanation is off-the-cuff.

⊙ ADDITIONAL ASSIGNMENTS

1. Practice audience analysis skills by reading the following paragraph. As a reader, what information would you expect the writer to provide? Has the writer of this paragraph met those needs? Analyze the paragraph, and then write a list of recommendations for how the writer could change or add supporting details to meet readers' needs.

   > You wouldn't believe the kinds of things I've learned working in a nursing home. As an aide, I have had the opportunity to get an inside glimpse into the lives of this isolated world. One patient, whom I will call Diva, changed a perfectly ordinary Monday into a day I will never forget. I am still inspired by that day. Another patient had the most unusual visitors, and from the way she spoke, you would never have guessed that she was from Germany. My experience as a nurse's aide has been exceptional.

2. Choose one of the following thesis statements. If you were writing an essay, what major supporting points would you use to effectively demonstrate the thesis statement you selected? What kinds of supporting details would provide evidence for your major supporting points? Write an informal outline or graphic organizer for the thesis statement you chose.

   a. All US citizens should have to serve two years in the military.
   b. Making US citizens serve a mandatory period of two years in the military is a bad idea.

3. The list of prewriting ideas that follows was generated by Neil, a high school student, in response to the following assignment: Write an essay in which you discuss the high school courses and steps you might take now to help you in determining a future career.

   a. Neil thinks that he might want to be a journalist, so he wrote down all of the things he might consider in exploring this career. Read through Neil's prewriting, and put his ideas into categories.
   b. For each category, determine high school courses or steps that he could take to help him prepare for majoring in journalism in college and to learn more about the field of journalism.

   - Do I want to write for a newspaper

   - I need to know how to write

   - I should find out whether I actually like journalism or not

   - I heard the term "broadcast journalism." What is it?

   - I probably need to develop research skills

   - Maybe I would like to be a reporter on T.V.

   - Some journalists report from around the world

- I would like to travel as a reporter

- Is journalistic writing different from other kinds of writing

- Maybe I should find an internship somewhere

- We have a school newspaper

- My older brother has a friend who works as a photo journalist

- On the radio, I've noticed that reporters seem to specialize in a subject area. Might I want to specialize in a certain subject area?

EMOTIONAL INTELLIGENCE

In some ways, starting college is a rite of passage. Think about the three phases of rites of passage: separation, transition, and reincorporation. Think about the experience of a college student. In what ways does becoming a college student require you to experience separation? What kinds of transitions are required of college students? When you finish college, what kind of reincorporation would you expect? Explain in a paragraph or two.

CULTURAL LITERACY

One part of cultural literacy is having a knowledge of the key issues people are debating today. Two of the issues raised in this chapter—digital footprints and tar sands oil—are in the news often and are important to many people. Choose a reliable news Web site such as CNN, NPR, or *The New York Times.* Browse through the site and skim the articles you find. What are some of the national issues people are discussing today? Make a list of five issues. Next, choose one issue about which you are concerned. It may be one of the five on your list, or it may be a separate issue. Write a paragraph in which you present the issue and discuss your concerns.

CRITICAL THINKING

One of the characteristics of critical thinkers is open-mindedness. Some people are so strongly opinionated that they have difficulty even listening to the views of others. Critical thinkers can also be strongly opinionated, but they have learned how to put their opinions aside and listen—openly and genuinely—to other viewpoints. Critical thinkers are willing to change their viewpoints if another point of view is convincing.

Have you ever thought a particular way about an issue and, having heard convincing information, changed your mind on that issue? If so, write a paragraph explaining how you kept an open mind and the process that led to your changing your position. If not, write a paragraph about a time when your closed-mindedness was not a good thing.

METACOGNITION

Think of a skill you possess that you had to learn. For example, perhaps you know how to work on automotive engines, or maybe you are a great cook, a fabulous guitarist, or a pretty good point guard. Now, think back to a time when you were *not* good at that skill. How did you learn the skill? What did you do in the beginning of the learning process? Did you learn by imitating someone else? Did someone specifically show you what to do? Did you read? Did you talk about the skill? Write a paragraph explaining the way you learned to be good at your skill. Reflect on why that learning method worked for you.

6

Can you identify the animals that made these tracks? Patterns help us know what to expect, not only in the wild, but also in texts.

Text Purposes and Text Patterns

Every text has a purpose. In fact, you could probably think of a long list of writing purposes: to reflect, to memorialize, to define, to entertain, to list, to vent frustration, and to make a plea, just to name a few. Most of the texts you encounter in your college and work life will have one or more of these writing purposes: to inform, to analyze, to evaluate, and to persuade.

To compose texts that effectively fulfill their purposes, writers often use text patterns. **Text patterns**—narration, definition, illustration, classification, comparison-contrast, cause and effect, process analysis, and argument—are modes of thought that communicate ideas. For example, to write an informative article about glaciers melting as a result of global warming, a writer may use a *cause and effect* text pattern. To evaluate alternative forms of energy, a writer may use a *comparison-contrast* text pattern. Writers choose text patterns on the basis of their topics and their writing purposes.

Text patterns help us both as readers and as writers. As readers, we recognize text patterns and expect them to present information in specific ways. As writers, we use text patterns to communicate our thoughts.

In this chapter, we focus on the four writing purposes and learn how text patterns can be used to fulfill these purposes.

CHAPTER OBJECTIVES

After completing this chapter, students will be able to do the following:

- Identify the purposes of texts— to inform, to analyze, to evaluate, and to persuade.

- Connect purposes and text patterns.

- Recognize eight text patterns— narration, definition, illustration, classification, comparison-contrast, cause and effect, process analysis, and argument.

- Analyze these eight text patterns as they appear in readings.

- Use these eight text patterns to compose paragraphs and essays.

- Recognize mixed text patterns in a reading, and use mixed text patterns in writing.

IDENTIFYING THE PURPOSE OF A TEXT

An important part of exploring a text is to ask yourself, "What is the writer's purpose?"

- Does the writer plan *to inform* readers about a particular subject?
- Does the writer plan *to analyze* a particular situation or course of action?
- Does the writer plan *to evaluate* an idea, proposal, or situation?
- Does the writer plan *to persuade* readers of the appropriateness of a particular idea or proposal?

Knowing the writer's purpose helps you determine the text's meaning and decide on the text's effectiveness.

Writing to Inform

Informative texts are straightforward: they tell readers about a subject. Newspaper articles are usually informative, as are textbooks, reference books, travelogues (travel writing), factual magazine articles, reports, and many scholarly journal articles.

You can identify informative writing by its characteristics:

- It exists to deliver information.
- It uses facts and may include data and statistics.
- It often includes citations from sources.
- It does *not* present the author's opinion; thus, it is unbiased.

Writing to Analyze

To **analyze** is to examine a subject, an event, an object, or a possibility very carefully. Analysis requires that we break a subject into its component parts. To analyze the engine of a car, you would look carefully at the individual parts under the hood. The same principle is true of analytical writing: it requires us to look at the individual components of a subject.

We might also use analysis to understand how past events, such as the Civil War, came to be. We might use analysis to examine current events, such as the privacy threats we face when we use the Internet. We might analyze an object, such as a smartphone or a tablet computer. And we might analyze future actions, such as proposals to change voter registration laws or the potential effects of buying oil from a particular country.

You can identify analytical writing by its characteristics:

- It explains or describes the parts of something.
- It explains or describes how something works or could work.
- It explains or describes how something happened or what might happen.
- It uses facts and credible information.
- It presents the topic in a fair and unbiased way.

Writing to Evaluate

Evaluative texts come to a conclusion about the value or effectiveness of a particular thing, idea, or course of action. Evaluation includes analysis. To evaluate the usefulness of a particular smartphone, for instance, you must first analyze it. You can then evaluate its worth. You might even compare it with another smartphone to make your evaluation.

Because evaluation means making a judgment, it usually involves setting up criteria. Suppose you live in a part of the country where tornadoes are common and you have decided to buy a storm shelter. To evaluate the available shelters, you would first analyze them. You might ask questions such as "What is it made of?" "How large is it?" "Is it inside the home or outside?" "Does it have features such as carpeting" and "What does it cost?" After completing your analysis, you would decide which criteria are important to you. You may realize that you want a shelter that is inside your home, costs under $3,000, and is made of steel. In this case, your criteria are location, cost, and material. By using these criteria, you will be able to evaluate your options and choose the shelter that best meets your requirements.

You can identify evaluative writing by its characteristics:

- It is based on analysis.
- It generally presents subjects in a fair and unbiased way.
- It uses a fair and clearly stated appraisal process.
- It uses criteria for weighing choices.
- It makes a judgment.

Writing to Persuade

The goal of a great deal of writing is **persuasion.** Some texts that aim to persuade provide explicit arguments; that is, these texts make it clear that they want readers to buy into the point of view they offer. For example, editorials are brief articles written by newspaper editors. Their purpose—by definition—is to persuade readers of a particular point of view. For example, an editorial may describe an editor's opinion about immigration reform with the goal of persuading readers.

Some texts that aim to persuade are more subtle. For example, a Web site may appear to provide information about a product, but when you analyze the site in depth, you may find that the information is just a means to an end: the site's real purpose is to convince readers to buy the product. Persuasive writing is found in almost every genre of writing: fiction and nonfiction books, magazine articles, some newspaper articles, editorials, Web pages, and so on.

You can identify persuasive writing by its characteristics:

- It attempts to sway readers' opinions on a topic.
- It provides evidence for the writer's opinion.
- It is generally written from a biased (opinionated) point of view.
- It appeals to logic, emotions, and credibility to influence readers.

These four writing purposes—to inform, to analyze, to evaluate, and to persuade—will help you understand the choices writers make in their texts.

PRACTICE ● Determining a Text's Purpose

Read each text description and make an educated guess about the writer's purpose. Each description presents a different purpose: to inform, to analyze, to evaluate, or to persuade.

1. An article in a newsmagazine titled "Fences Won't Stop Illegal Immigration"

Purpose: _____

2. "The iPhone versus the Android: Which One Is Best?"—an article in a computer magazine

Purpose: _____

(continued)

3. An article in a newspaper titled "Entire City Installs Solar Panels on Its Homes"

   Purpose: _____

4. "Current Trends: The Decline of Marriage"—an article in a popular science magazine

   Purpose: _____

CONNECTING PURPOSES AND TEXT PATTERNS

In both oral and written communication, we depend on recognized patterns of thought to communicate ideas. When you read the phrase "for instance," you realize that you are about to be presented with an example that will help you understand another point the writer is making. When you read "Once upon a time," you mentally prepare to hear a story. These patterns that we use to communicate ideas are text patterns.

The most common text patterns are narration, definition, illustration, classification, comparison-contrast, cause and effect, process analysis, and argument. Often when we communicate, we use more than one text pattern. Consider the paragraph that follows, noticing the variety of text patterns that come into play.

An eclipse is an astronomical event that occurs when one object gets in between you and another object and blocks your view. From Earth, we routinely experience two	Definition
kinds of eclipses: an eclipse of the Moon and an eclipse of the Sun. Sometimes, as the	Classification
Earth orbits the Sun, it comes between the Sun and the Moon. When this happens, the	Cause and effect
Earth throws a dark shadow across the Moon. This is known as an eclipse of the Moon, or a lunar eclipse. Sometimes, the Moon passes between the Earth and the Sun. The	Definition
Moon blocks the light of the Sun and a shadow of the Moon is cast on the Earth's surface. This is an eclipse of the Sun, or a solar eclipse.	Definition

Text patterns can be used for single pieces of support, as the paragraph above demonstrates, or they can be used to structure an entire essay. A writer who wants to discuss the causes and effects of eclipses in more depth could devote an entire essay to the subject. In such an essay, the writer could use cause and effect as the basic text pattern for the entire text, elaborating on particular causes and effects in each paragraph, for instance.

In the pages that follow, you will learn how to use text patterns in two ways: as supporting details and as the organizational framework for your writing.

Narration

Narration is simply storytelling. Everyone likes a good story. That's why people who are good at writing speeches or sermons frequently add interesting stories to their texts. Have you ever wondered why we enjoy listening to stories? Sometimes the answer is that the stories themselves are simply fun to hear. Perhaps they are funny, or maybe they retell an event that people enjoy recounting.

Another reason we use narration is to make a point or teach a lesson. Aesop's fables are narratives that communicate moral principles. If you have read "The Tortoise and the Hare," you know that the point of the story is to not give up. Because of his persistence, the slow tortoise wins the race.

When writers use narratives, they often do so to make a point. Even if the writer does not explicitly tell readers the point, the narrative should. The narrative should be such a good story and so well told that readers intuitively understand the writer's point in using it. Writing a good story can be challenging. Not only must the story be compelling, but the writer must choose words carefully so that readers can infer meanings.

THE REPUBLICAN HARE AND THE DEMOCRATIC TORTOISE.
The Tortoise.—If that chap only goes to sleep, I'll win out by a mile.

A political cartoon published on the cover of a July 1908 magazine shows William H. Taft, a Republican hare, racing William Jennings Bryan, a Democratic tortoise, for the presidency. The caption reads, "The Tortoise: If that chap only goes to sleep, I'll win out by a mile." What message was the artist sending with this depiction of a well-known fable? At the time, the artist could not have known that Taft would go on to win the presidential election.

RECOGNIZING THE NARRATION PATTERN IN READINGS

Narrative essays usually present one story that is significant enough to be worthy of its own essay. In a narrative essay, the story *is* the sole content: it speaks for itself.

To identify the narration pattern in a text, look for these characteristics and key words.

CHARACTERISTICS OF THE NARRATION PATTERN

- A meaningful story is told.
- The story has a plot with a beginning, middle, and end.
- The story is told in first-person or third-person point of view.
- Chronological transitions are used to indicate the passing of time.
- Description is used to convey mood, develop characters, create settings, and convey information.

Key Words for the Narration Pattern			
after	as soon as	before	during
finally	first, second, third . . .	following	immediately
initially	later	meanwhile	next
not long after	now	once	soon
then	today	until	when

Narration in Supporting Details

In academic writing, a narrative used as a supporting detail usually takes the form of an *anecdote*—a short, interesting story. Anecdotes are often used as a type of evidence. For example, a veterinarian may write an informative essay about what daily life is like for her. She would very likely use short narratives about different medical cases to help readers get a clear picture of what her days are like.

Narration can also provide a lesson, identify a truth about life, or help readers understand the seriousness of an issue. For example, a writer may tell the story of a soldier who overcomes war injuries to show how success over trauma is possible. Another writer might underscore the dangers of texting and driving with the stories of real people who have lost their lives because of this lethal combination of activities.

Personal stories might also be used as subjects for analysis. For example, researchers often want to analyze personal stories for their research. Hospital researchers may listen to patients' stories to analyze how they can improve their services. These stories can also be used to evaluate hospital programs and make changes. Personal stories and experiences can be valuable bits of research.

In addition to providing material for analysis and evaluation, stories can be persuasive. Suppose the US Congress is considering the passage of a stronger gun control law. Advocates for such a law would be likely to tell their personal stories of tragedy and loss to make their arguments more compelling. These stories can be effective in persuading members of Congress to vote for or against the proposed law.

Finally, short stories are sometimes used to introduce essays. For instance, a writer may use the story of a person who triumphed over obesity to start an essay about effective methods of weight loss. The partial outline that follows demonstrates how narrative can be used as a supporting detail in an essay.

Using Narration as a Supporting Detail

Topic: Why people should work on anger management

Thesis statement: Anger issues should be addressed because they can result in lost jobs, broken relationships, and even death.

INTRODUCTION

Paragraph 1: Introduction

Paragraph 2: How anger issues can result in lost jobs (tell Micah's story) . . .

Narration as a Text Pattern

When a writer has a long story that makes a point, the story becomes the focus of the entire essay. In such an essay, narrative is used as a text pattern.

To write a compelling narrative essay, you will need to find a story worth telling, a story that not only is meaningful to you but that you predict others will find meaningful. Remember that you are writing for a general audience. You may love NASCAR, but your readers may not. Similarly, the story of your sister's wedding is probably not going to capture readers' interest unless something unusual happened. Think about the stories you enjoy hearing. What makes them enjoyable? Often these stories appeal to our curiosity about how other people live, help us imagine what being in a particular situation would be like, or describe events that we can relate to.

To use narrative as a text pattern, writers employ features that are common to all narratives. The **plot,** or structure, of the story usually has these elements:

- A beginning
- Rising action that leads to a **climax,** or high point in the action
- The climax itself (usually a conflict)
- Falling action that leads to a resolution of the conflict
- The resolution itself and the ending

Additionally, the narrative should include the details readers expect. Readers want to know information about the characters involved: how old are they? where do they live? what are they like? Not knowing when an event happened, or not having a clear idea of the order of events in a story, can leave readers confused and dissatisfied. In narrative writing, it is important to include the details that contribute to a story's meaning but to exclude mundane or boring details.

ANALYZING A NARRATIVE TEXT

As you read the narrative essay that follows, "The Chosen One" by Laura Cunningham, see whether you can recognize some of the features of narrative writing. Cunningham's careful choices about plot, time order, details, and wording make her narrative essay particularly effective. As you read, notice the significant features of narrative writing that the annotations point out.

The Chosen One
by Laura Cunningham

A year ago, I boarded a flight to Shanghai during a gale force wind. The plane shivered and taxied back to the hangar twice before takeoff. It is testimony to my anxiety about the purpose of my journey that I felt no fear of flying. I carried with me an empty infant car bed (aptly named the Dream Ride), a three-week supply of diapers, wipes, pediatric antibiotics, bottles and disposable nipples. I was on my way to adopt one of the tens of thousands of baby girls abandoned in China each year.

Today as I write, my 1-year-old daughter sleeps in a crib in the next room. She lies in the position of trust—on her back, her arms widespread, her face tip-tilted as if for the next kiss.

A happy ending, so far, for my darling Chinese daughter, and for me. But the journey to Shanghai has somehow not ended. Many nights, I wake at 3 A.M.—yanked from my dream, my heart hammering alarms. At that silent, moonlit time, I remember my choice.

	Chronological transition: helps readers follow the story
	Plot element: rising action
	Chronological transition
	Foreshadowing: The writer jumps to the end of the story and then returns to tell the story from the beginning.

(continued)

I am embarrassed now to recall the doubt that accompanied me to China. The orphanage had sent a fax (yes, in the new China, orphanages send faxes): "We have a baby for you. We would have taken her picture but it was too cold."

My concern, if I can articulate the chill gut slide of panic as a "concern," was that somehow I would walk into the orphanage and fail to respond to the baby; that somehow she would not feel like "the right one." I would have to go ahead with the adoption out of momentum, some grim sense of decency, but without the hoped-for love at first sight.

The baby, it seemed from the fax, was already chosen. And while I claimed to love all babies, in my secret, cowering heart I had to admit that I was more drawn to some babies than to others. It wasn't beauty or even intelligence that I required of a baby, but some sign of being, well, simpatico.

I could not see her until the orphanage opened Monday morning. I had arrived in Shanghai on Saturday night. The interval was the high tide of my fear—suspense seemed hydraulic; blood rushed through me at unprecedented speed.

Until Monday I had only the ambiguous answers of Ms. Zhang, the orphanage's emissary who had greeted me at the airport. When I asked: "How old is the baby? How big?" Ms. Zhang answered only with another question:

"What size baby clothes have you brought with you?"

Her response raised some possibility of control, or at least influence. Maybe the baby was not yet chosen. In my sneaking secret chicken heart, I could still pick the best and the brightest star of abandoned baby girlhood in Shanghai.

Passing the time until I could meet "my baby," I met another baby at the hotel, already adopted by a single man. (China permits adoptions by foreigners, whether married or unmarried. Its adoption policy is unusual in that citizens, as well as foreigners, must be at least 35 years old to adopt.) She struck me, however, as not meant to be my baby. She did seem just right for her new father, an American psychologist, who carried with him a sitcom's supply of baby paraphernalia.

Next, I went to the nearest tourist attraction, the Temple of the Jade Buddha, where there was said to be a Buddha to whom mothers pray for a good baby.

The Buddha glowed in the dim temple. It wasn't jet lag that sent me reeling to my knees before the Buddha. Half-Jewish, half-Southern Baptist, all doubt, I knelt in truest prayer. Let the baby be one I can truly love.

At 9 sharp the next morning I waited in the orphanage, wearing my winter coat indoors (now I understood the fax). Even in midwinter there was no heat. Vapor rose from the thermoses of hot tea carried by the female employees. The translator announced that the baby was being carried in from the nursery building.

"You will have a choice," she said.

I looked out the window as she pointed across a courtyard filled with dead bamboo and gray laundry. The window itself was grimy, but through it I saw two women in blue smocks, running toward me. Each held a bundle. There were two babies.

They were swaddled in comforters, their heads completely draped in towels. The first baby was unveiled. There was a staccato of Chinese, translated as: "Pick this one. She is more beautiful. She is more intelligent." Baby No. 1 was the nurses' favorite, a 2-month-old of unsurpassed good looks and robust health. She smiled.

Chronological transition

Plot element: The conflict starts to build.

More conflict: expression of anxiety about adopting the right baby

Plot element: Story approaches its climax— seeing the baby and learning whether she has a choice.

Chronological transition

Chronological transition

Plot element: start of the story's climax section. Notice that this very important sentence stands as its own paragraph.

(continued)

But I could not take my eyes from the second baby, who was revealed almost as an afterthought. She was thin, piteous, a green-complexioned elf, with low-set ears that stuck out. She wheezed. In the pocket of my coat, I held a vial of antibiotics, carried on good advice from a friend.

Plot element: another crucial moment in the story's climax

I had no choice. The second baby was sick. I had medicine impossible to obtain here. I accepted the tiny green baby, gasping and oozing, into my arms. I noticed she also had a bald spot, from lying unmoved in her crib.

Climax: The writer makes a choice.

Shame over my earlier indecision blew from the room like the fetid draft of disease and poverty.

Was it love at first sight? I knew in that instant that we were at the start of our life together.

Love overtakes you at odd moments. I was trying to collect a urine sample, required for a medical test. I held her, her little purple fanny over a rice bowl, in my arms all night. I drew the blankets around us both as a tent to keep away the cold. We waited, silently, all night, until she took a literal "tinkle." Her eyes met mine, on the other side of the world, and I knew Little-Miss-Ears-Stick-Out, With-Tears-in-Her-Eyes was mine, all right.

Plot element: Falling action begins.

Within 24 hours, the medicine had taken effect: she turned ivory pink; her eyes cleared. She was beyond my dreams, exquisite, a luminous old soul with contemporary wit. I gazed at her and saw the fatefulness of every mother's choice. It is not the beautiful baby who is chosen, but the chosen baby who becomes beautiful.

Chronological transition

Thesis statement: the moral of the story

To enter a house filled with unwanted babies is to pass through a door that you can never shut. At 3 A.M., I see the others—the aisles of green cribs holding bundled babies. I try to close my eyes to them, but they refuse to disappear. They are lying there. They are cold; they are damp. I see one baby girl especially. She had an odd genetic defect: the skin of her body was coal black, but her face had no color. She looked as if she were wearing the white theatrical mask of tragedy.

Last Christmas, I was able to choose the green, sick baby over the laughing, healthy one. Would I have had the courage to take one of the others? Would someone? I wake up and see the small faces. They are lying there waiting, waiting to be chosen.

Plot element: resolution. Notice that the resolution leaves readers not totally satisfied. This is intentional.

PRACTICE Analyzing a Narrative Text

On a separate sheet, answer the following questions about "The Chosen One" by Laura Cunningham.

1. Do you believe this story would be enjoyed by a wide variety of people? If so, why? What are the features that make it appealing? If not, why not? Explain.

2. The writer does not present the story in straight chronological order. Review the story and describe the order in which Cunningham relates the events.

3. What do you think Cunningham means when she writes that her baby appeared "a luminous old soul with contemporary wit"?

4. Cunningham uses figurative language to make her writing vivid and interesting. For instance, she says she is looking for "the brightest star of abandoned baby girlhood." Find two additional passages that use language in a nonliteral way. For each passage, write a few sentences explaining the effect Cunningham's words may have on readers.

5. In what way does the end of the story *not* present a perfect resolution? Why is the tone at the end of the essay not joyous? Explain in a paragraph.

USING NARRATION IN YOUR WRITING

The following steps can guide you through writing your own narrative essay.

1. **Select a story suitable for your narrative essay.** The story you choose for your essay is the most important element of this assignment. You may use a story in which you were involved, or you may tell a story about someone else. Above all, find a story that a general audience will enjoy. Many stories that we personally find entertaining might make a general audience ready for a good long nap. Here are some examples of the types of stories that may be interesting to a general audience.

   - **Stories about ordinary events (like a graduation ceremony or the birth of a child) if the event is unusual in some way.** *Interesting example:* Your high school graduation night when you had a near-fatal car accident. *Not so interesting:* Your high school graduation night when you went to a party with your friends.
   - **Stories that tap into something most people are curious about.** *Interesting example:* What it is like to live in a house you believe is haunted. *Not so interesting:* How you rented your first apartment.
   - **Stories about something that could happen to the reader but is rare enough to be compelling.** *Interesting example:* What it is like to work in a funeral home. *Not so interesting:* What it is like to work in a clothing store.
   - **Stories that give the reader insight into your unique world.** *Interesting example:* How you learned to live with a disability or chronic disease. *Not so interesting:* How you and your sister fight all the time.
   - **Stories you find compelling enough to remember.** *Interesting example:* Dad's encounter with a crocodile in Australia. *Not so interesting:* How you found a baby bird on a sidewalk.
   - **Stories you yourself would like to read.** *Interesting example:* A story about the variety of cases you have seen in your job as an emergency room technician. *Not so interesting:* A story about how you met and fell in love with your significant other.

2. **Determine the order in which to tell your story.** *How* you tell the story can help readers experience the story in a particular way. Use the order of events to set up tension, anxiety, or any other emotion you would like readers to experience. Sometimes, writers use **foreshadowing**—a hint about events to come in a narrative—to keep readers' interest. Early on in "The Chosen One," the author gives us a clue to how her story resulted in a "happy ending," but we must read to the end of the story to find out what happened.

3. **Create a simple narrative plan, or outline.** Include your thesis statement in your plan. Decide on the major events of the story and the order in which you will tell them, and create a simple outline like the one that follows. Use plot elements—beginning, rising action, climax, falling action, resolution—to structure your narrative.

A Simple Outline for a Narrative Pattern Essay

Thesis statement: Meeting my birth parents was the fulfillment of a dream I have had for a long time. At the same time, it was entirely depressing.

INTRODUCTION: Provide background
Rising action:

- Details about my adoption
- Description of my good life with my adopted family and my persistent longing to meet my birth parents
- Arrangement to meet my birth parents when I turned nineteen
- Anxiety and expectations

Climax: The disappointing encounter with my birth parents

Falling action: The flight back home and the thoughts I had

Conclusion (resolution): Final thoughts

4. **Use creative wording. Figures of speech**—imaginative comparisons between different things—can help readers understand the ideas you wish to convey. For example, instead of just telling readers a room is cold, comparing the room to a meat locker would more effectively convey the same idea. Several figures of speech in particular are useful for writers: personification, metaphor, and simile.

FIGURE OF SPEECH	DEFINITION	EXAMPLE
Personification	Giving human qualities to inanimate things	*Every plant in his yard had seen better days.*
Metaphor	Comparing two unlike things	*Her life is a constant soap opera.*
Simile	Using *like* or *as* to compare two unlike things	*My favorite chair is like a big marshmallow.*

5. **Use descriptive details to create the story's setting.** Descriptive language provides sensory information for readers. By using description, readers can imagine what something looks, sounds, smells, tastes, or feels like. In narrative writing, description helps readers understand characters better. It also helps writers convey a particular mood. For instance, description may convey a sense of eeriness or a sense of peacefulness. Writers also depend on description to create the setting of a story and to render the plot events in a story effectively. In "The Chosen One," Cunningham uses this description, "the tiny green baby, gasping and oozing," to convey the baby's fragility, sickliness, and even lack of appeal.

6. **Make intentional decisions about details and pace.** Cunningham left out details that were mundane so that her story would move at the perfect pace to keep her readers interested. Ask yourself whether the details in your story are necessary. Include details that add value but do not bog down its pace. Use chronological transitions so that readers can keep track of time.

7. **Be very careful about how you word your thesis statement and where you place it.** The thesis statement should not interrupt the narrative. Sometimes placing the thesis statement in the conclusion is an effective strategy for narrative writing since the thesis statement might give away the story's ending if it is placed earlier.

PRACTICE Using Narration in Your Writing

Use the preceding steps to write a narrative essay. Choose one of the following topics, or select your own.

A. Write about a time you witnessed someone acting especially kindly—or especially cruelly—toward another person.

B. Think of an event from your childhood that had an impact on you. Write a brief narrative detailing the event and your feelings about it.

C. Relate a story that your family particularly enjoys retelling. The story might concern something funny that happened, or it might recount a traumatic event that ended well, for example.

If none of these topics appeals to you, come up with your own topic for a narrative essay. Ask classmates or your instructor to give you an honest prediction of how interested (or uninterested) a general audience might be in the story you propose.

Verb Tense Choices

As a writer, you must choose the verb tense you will use to convey information. Verbs express more than the action that happens in a sentence. Verb tenses tell when the action takes place—past, present, or future. For example, in each of the following sentences the tense of the underlined verb expresses the timing of the nurse's action.

Past: Earlier this morning, the nurse examined the patients' charts.

Present: The nurse always examines the patients' charts at 10 a.m.

Future: Tomorrow morning the nurse will examine the patients' charts.

Even without the phrases *Earlier this morning* and *Tomorrow morning*, readers would know which action already happened (past) and which action will happen (future) because of the verb tense.

For the most part, verbs in a text should remain consistent in tense, although there are places where tenses can change. Follow these guidelines to select the best tense for the information you are conveying.

1. USE PAST TENSE FOR NARRATIVE

Most narratives recount events that have happened. So when writers tell a story, they most commonly use past tense. Note this example from Laura Cunningham's "The Chosen One."

Example: "A year ago, I boarded a flight to Shanghai during a gale force wind. The plane shivered and taxied back to the hangar twice before takeoff."

Present tense is less useful for narratives and is best avoided. If we substitute present tense in the Cunningham quote, the passage is confusing. An essential element of the story is expressed in the phrase *A year ago,* but the present tense verbs conflict with that phrase.

Faulty: A year ago, I board a flight to Shanghai during a gale force wind. The plane shivers and taxies back to the hangar twice before takeoff.

For most verbs, we add *-ed* to the present tense to form the past tense. Some verbs, however, have special forms for the past tense: for example, *bring/brought, drink/drank, eat/ate, feel/felt, is/was, think/thought.* Still others keep the same form in the present and past tenses: for example, *cost/cost, cut/cut, hit/hit.* Consult a dictionary if you are unsure of the past tense form for a verb.

2. USE PRESENT TENSE FOR MOST ACADEMIC WRITING

For almost all academic writing, present tense is the correct tense, even when you are writing about the views of a person who died hundreds of years ago. Note the present tense used in this quotation from *Physical Science,* by Bill W. Tillery.

Example: "Newton's first law of motion is also known as the law of inertia and is very similar to one of Galileo's findings about motion."

However, when the goal is to compare historical events or beliefs, use past tense, as in this excerpt from *American Authors in the Nineteenth Century.*

Example: "In the nineteenth century, social changes and the rise of new media revolutionized the way people discovered and read literature. As a result,

(continued)

the audience for American literature <u>grew</u> tremendously, and many authors <u>became</u> celebrities."

Another exception is the use of past tense to describe research processes or studies. Notice the verb tenses in this quotation from "Detroit Exposure and Aerosol Research Study" on the US Environmental Protection Agency's Web site.

Example: "The Detroit Exposure and Aerosol Research Study <u>was</u> a three-year study conducted by the U.S. Environmental Protection Agency (EPA). Its primary objective <u>was</u> to investigate the relationship of select air pollutant concentrations and their sources measured at community air monitoring stations in comparison to those measured in various neighborhoods in Wayne County, Michigan."

3. AVOID UNNECESSARY SHIFTS IN TENSE

Generally, verbs should remain in the same tense throughout a passage. Notice how the shifts in tense in this example are unnecessary and even confusing. In the first sentence, the verbs are in the present tense (*claims, change, processes*), while the verbs in the second sentence are in both the past tense (*wrote*) and the present tense (*act*).

Faulty shift in tense: Margaret Trent <u>claims</u> that social media <u>change</u> the way the brain <u>processes</u> information. She <u>wrote</u> that social media <u>act</u> as "catalysts of neural development."

Corrected: Margaret Trent <u>claims</u> that social media <u>change</u> the way the brain <u>processes</u> information. She <u>writes</u> that social media <u>act</u> as "catalysts of neural development."

Sometimes shifts in tense are acceptable or even necessary, such as when a writer changes from a narrative to another type of writing. Consider this passage from *Physical Science* by Bill W. Tillery. It incorporates the initial sentence we quoted earlier as an example of present tense in academic writing.

Example: "Newton's first law of motion <u>is</u> also <u>known</u> as the law of inertia and is very similar to one of Galileo's findings about motion. Recall that Galileo <u>used</u> the term inertia to describe the tendency of an object to resist changes in motion. Newton's first law <u>describes</u> this tendency more directly."

Notice that the writer uses mostly present tense (*is known, is, describes*) but switches, appropriately, to past tense (*used*) to explain a historical event.

SENTENCE COMBINING

The example that follows shows how to take sentences that use a variety of tenses, combine them to make smoother and longer sentences, and correct the verb tenses for consistency and appropriateness.

Ideas to combine and correct:

- Benjamin Franklin is a scientist and a writer.
- He wrote *Poor Richard's Almanac*.
- He was known for his autobiography.
- Franklin signed the three most important documents of the revolutionary era: the Declaration of Independence, the peace treaty with Britain that ended the Revolutionary War, and the Constitution.
- He is the only person to sign all three.

(continued)

Consistent and appropriate verb tenses: Benjamin Franklin, a scientist and a writer, wrote *Poor Richard's Almanac* and is known for his autobiography. Franklin also was the only person to sign the three most important documents of the revolutionary era: the Declaration of Independence, the peace treaty with Britain that ended the Revolutionary War, and the Constitution.

EXERCISES

Combine each set of sentences to make smoother, longer ones. Change verb tenses as necessary for consistency and appropriateness. You may change the wording as much as you like as long as you communicate the same ideas.

1. Ideas to combine and correct:

    - I stepped onto the train.
    - From the moment I did, I felt something was not right.
    - An older woman was bundled from head to toe in black.
    - She stared at my old suitcase.
    - "That's my suitcase!" she exclaimed loudly.

    Answer: _____

    _____

    _____

2. Ideas to combine and correct:

    - Werner Heisenberg was a German theoretical physicist.
    - He discovered the Uncertainty Principle.
    - The Uncertainty Principle concerns subatomic particles.
    - It claims that we can know the position of a particle or its momentum, but not both.

    Answer: _____

    _____

    _____

3. Ideas to combine and correct:

    - The proposed bill will affect each state.
    - It will require each state to offer free preschool education.
    - According to the bill, any child in a school district will be eligible to attend preschool in the district.

    Answer: _____

    _____

    _____

Definition

To *define* is to express the meaning of a term or concept. In textbooks, you will often come across definitions that briefly explain the meaning of a word. These short definitions are a type of support that enable the writer to continue making a larger point.

Other texts, however, focus primarily on defining a term or concept. As a text pattern, **definition** implies going beyond dictionary explanations and providing a more meaningful or important interpretation. For example, a writer may create an entire essay to explain his personal definition of what it is to be a good parent. Such essays use definition, sometimes called *extended definition*, as a text pattern, not merely as a supporting detail.

RECOGNIZING THE DEFINITION PATTERN IN READINGS

Both uses of definition share some characteristics and key words.

CHARACTERISTICS OF THE DEFINITION PATTERN

- A term or phrase is defined.
- When used as support, a sentence provides a definition. Explanatory sentences may follow.
- When used as a text pattern, the thesis statement concerns the definition in question. Body paragraphs help support the writer's point about the definition.

Key Words for the Definition Pattern		
consists of	define	entails
idea	involves	is characterized by
is known as	meaning of	means
redefine	refers to	term

Definition in Supporting Details

As a type of support, definitions may appear in any paragraph in an essay. Whenever readers may need help understanding a term or concept, a writer may insert a simple definition. For example, a writer may wish to convince readers that the United States needs to invest more time and effort into safeguarding the Internet. One of the writer's reasons may be that cyberterrorism is a real and dangerous threat. Knowing that not all readers will understand what cyberterrorism is, the writer may define the term and provide an example of how cyberterrorism works. The partial outline that follows shows where a writer may use a definition as a type of support.

Using Definition as a Supporting Detail

Topic: Safeguarding the Internet

Thesis statement: The United States needs to invest more time and effort in safeguarding the Internet.

INTRODUCTION
   Paragraph 1

BODY
   Paragraph 2: One of the most serious problems the Internet poses is cyberterrorism.

(continued)

- Definition: Cyberterrorism is . . .
- An example of cyberterrorism is . . .
- Explanation of example

Paragraph 3: The reason cyberterrorism is such a threat is . . .

Definition as a Text Pattern

When definition is used as the focus of an essay, it becomes a text pattern. Writers use the definition text pattern for a variety of reasons. First, definition is helpful in explaining new concepts or terms. For example, not all readers know what urban legends are; thus, a writer may help readers get a clear understanding of urban legends by writing an essay that offers an extended definition.

Second, definition allows writers to create their own, unique meanings for terms or concepts. Phrases such as *common sense* or *the American dream* mean different things to different people. A writer may create his own definition of one of these expressions and present it using the definition text pattern.

Third, definition enables writers to analyze the various ways a particular term or concept has been defined. For example, in the history of law, the term *temporary insanity* has been defined differently over time.

And finally, definition is useful for arguing that an ambiguous or controversial term should be defined in a particular way. Some definition essays focus on defining debatable terms or concepts such as *torture*.

An essay that uses a definition text pattern will have a thesis statement that presents the writer's point about the definition. The body paragraphs will include supporting details that work together to convey the writer's point about the definition. The outline that follows shows definition being used as a text pattern. In the example, the writer is presenting her own definition of *family*, and she wants to persuade readers that her definition is sound.

A Simple Outline for a Definition Pattern Essay

Topic: Defining *family*

Thesis statement: A family is a group of people who are committed to and love one another.

INTRODUCTION

    Paragraph 1: How some people and institutions have defined family narrowly

    Paragraph 2: Thesis statement—writer's definition of *family*

BODY

    Paragraph 3: First characteristic—family members are committed to one another

        Paragraph 4: Additional definition—what *committed* means

        Paragraph 5: Examples of committed families—nuclear family, single-parent family, nontraditional family

    Paragraph 6: Second characteristic—family members *love* one another

        Paragraph 7: Additional definition—what *love* means in a family context

        Paragraph 8: Examples of families that demonstrate love—nuclear family, single-parent family, nontraditional family

CONCLUSION

    Paragraph 9: Why defining the family in a broad way is good for society

In "What I Really Meme Is . . . Anatomy of a Happenin' Thing," author Mary Ann Bell defines a term that is unfamiliar to many people: *meme*. Because the concept of memes is complex, Bell has written an entire essay on the topic. We will examine the components of her essay.

A Definition Text: Introduction and Thesis Statement

Definition texts often begin with an introduction to the term or concept being defined. Bell starts her essay with a definition from *Wikipedia* and then elaborates on that definition.

Introduction Paragraph of "What I Really Meme Is . . . Anatomy of a Happenin' Thing" by Mary Ann Bell

Not long ago, I was relaxing in the den with my daughter and a friend of hers. Out of the blue, my daughter asked, "What is a meme anyway? I keep hearing about them and don't know what they are!" Her friend, a creative writing major, exchanged looks with me. We both knew what the word meant but found it hard to explain. "Well, a meme is, uh," I started. "Never mind!" she replied, "I'll Google it!" Of course, the first hit was from Wikipedia. Also not a surprise, the description there was spot on. Here is what she read to us: A meme is "an idea, behavior or style that spreads from person to person within a culture." It occurred to me that if the three of us with six university degrees between us could not come up with a good definition, then there might be others out there hazy on the concept too—hence, this column.

Thesis statement: The essay starts with a definition from *Wikipedia* and goes on to explain the definition.

A Definition Text: Body Paragraphs and Their Organization

Body paragraphs provide information about the definition the writer is proposing. Writers can include many different types of information in the body paragraphs of definition essays. Here are just a few ways writers can elaborate on and provide support for definition texts:

- Dictionary definition of term or concept
- Competing definitions
- History of term or concept
- Example
- Explanation
- Comparison
- Description
- Characteristics

In her article on memes, Mary Ann Bell writes body paragraphs that provide examples, explanations, additional definitions, and historical information about the term.

Body Paragraphs of "What I Really Meme Is . . . Anatomy of a Happenin' Thing" by Mary Ann Bell

One of the easiest and most tempting ways to define "meme" is to offer examples. The ones most readily recognized are those from popular culture. Here are some recent examples that keep cropping up on social networking sites such as Facebook:

- LOLCats/I can has cheezburger?
- Binders of women [referring to a misspoken phrase by candidate Mitt Romney in a presidential debate in 2012, in which he was referring to notebook binders containing resumes of women job applicants for positions in government when he was Governor of Massachusetts]
- Gangnam-style dancing
- Call me maybe?
- Hey girl (featuring Ryan Gosling)
- Sad Big Bird

Examples: elaboration of the definition

In today's social networking environment, the potential is tremendous for an idea, trend, rumor, meme, or anything catchy to spread very quickly. This is the phenomenon we call "going viral," and it is happening every day. Memes can rise up spontaneously or can be intentionally launched. The day after the second presidential debate in 2012, the phrase "binders of women" and iterations thereof spread overnight across the Internet.

Another meme from the campaign is what I call "Sad Big Bird." During the first presidential debate, Mitt Romney said that PBS's funding should be cut to reduce the deficit, even though he "loved Big Bird" as much as anybody. And so, with lightning speed we were treated to pictures of Big Bird standing in welfare lines, looking dejected with friends, and, in general, tugging at the heartstrings of PBS/Sesame Street fans. People wearing Big Bird suits started showing up at campaign rallies. There were people who admitted they remembered very little from the debate other than the threat to off Big Bird.

Another example

Similarly this past year, Gangnam-style dancing went viral. And it goes without saying that gorgeous pictures of actor Ryan Gosling, a library fan, offering various completions to the line "Hey girl . . ." are loved by librarians. You can see the collection of these pictures on the site called Hey Girl. I Like the Library Too (librarianheygirl .tumblr.com).

More examples

Memes such as these are visual and have a picture or video as the focal point. From these, captions and knockoffs abound. Some hang around for years, such as LOLCats, while others are relatively short-lived. My guess is that "binders of women" will not last far beyond the next months, as the campaign and Mitt Romney's candidacy fade from popular memory. But I am hoping Ryan Gosling does not go away for a very long time.

WHO SAID THAT?

How long has this been going on? The term "meme" is actually a coined one, which makes me think it might make it an example of its own definition. As a matter of fact, this term can be tracked back to its originator, Richard Dawkins, and he is alive and well and following memes to this day.

History of the term and concept

Here is a quotation from an article where he explains: "Our cultural life is full of things that seem to propagate virus-like from one mind to another: tunes, ideas,

(continued)

catch-phrases, fashions, ways of making pots or building arches. In 1976 I coined the word meme (rhymes with cream) for these self-replicating units of culture that have a life of their own." . . .

> Quotation: traces term to its origin and offers another definition

Remembering back to 1976 and forward, I can think of a number of memes that are still lodged in my brain and, perhaps, in yours as well, if your age allows you to remember that far into the past. One example that I remember in particular is the use and overuse of the phrase "Where's the beef?" The meme stems from TV commercials starring a loveable old lady trying to find a decent meat patty in a fast-food hamburger and promoting Wendy's restaurants. Like all good memes, this one has its own Wikipedia article.

> Examples that go further back in history

A Definition Text: Conclusion

Once the definition of the term or concept has been thoroughly explained and supported, writers conclude their essays. Mary Ann Bell concludes by calling attention to the fact that memes are constantly changing and evolving.

Conclusion Paragraph of "What I Really Meme Is . . . Anatomy of a Happenin' Thing" by Mary Ann Bell

Since the advent of the Internet, the sources, subjects, and recipients have increased exponentially. By making it so easy to combine, change, personalize, and otherwise adapt Internet postings, memes now grow and evolve in countless iterations that can go their merry ways, further mutating along the way.

> More explanation: how memes reproduce and mutate

PRACTICE Analyzing a Definition Text

On a separate sheet, answer the following questions about "What I Really Meme Is . . . Anatomy of a Happenin' Thing" by Mary Ann Bell.

1. What is the purpose of the article?
2. After reading her definition of *meme,* do you have a good understanding of what memes are? If so, what type of body content helped you understand the best? Examples? Explanations? History? Explain. If not, what else could Bell have included to help you understand more clearly?
3. What does Bell mean when she says that memes evolve and change over time?
4. Without looking back at Bell's article, define *meme* in your own words. Provide an example that Bell did not include in her article, if you can think of one.

USING DEFINITION IN YOUR WRITING

When your task is to present the meaning of a term or concept, you can use the definition text pattern to structure your writing. The following guidelines can help you through the process of using definition in your writing.

1. Select a topic, and determine your purpose for writing. If you are choosing your own topic for an essay, consider defining a term that may be new to readers, as Mary Ann Bell did when she defined *meme*. Choose a term that will interest readers.

Another approach to finding a topic is to think about terms whose meanings are debated. For example, what does it mean to be *moral*? How do you define *adultery*? You can also choose to define terms that are not necessarily debatable but tend to be defined in personal ways. For example, what does *physical beauty* mean to you? What does *success* mean to you?

If your instructor gives you a term to define, you can move to the next step, determining your writing purpose. Does your assignment tell you whether you are writing to inform, analyze, evaluate, or persuade? Do you want to persuade readers that your definition is the best? Do you want to analyze the way the word has been defined throughout history? Once you are certain about the purpose of the assignment, you can make specific decisions about how you will define the term or concept.

2. Start your prewriting by creating a formal definition that includes term, class, and characteristic. The **term** is the word you are defining, the **class** is the category into which the word fits, and the **characteristic** is simply the quality of the term on which you are focusing, as in the Definition Model diagram.

| [DEFINED TERM] Freedom | is | [CLASS] a right | that | [CHARACTERISTIC] comes with responsibilities |

■ Definition Model

Here are two more examples:

Friendship is a kind of relationship that endures through the ups and downs of life.
<u>term</u>   <u>class</u>   <u>characteristic</u>

A solar panel is a technological device used to generate electricity from the sun's heat.
<u>term</u>   <u>class</u>   <u>characteristic</u>

We can expect that an essay using the definition of *friendship* shown above will give the reader evidence about how friends stand by one another through difficult times.

3. Consider describing the history or background of the term. Unless you are writing a historical analysis, this part of your essay need not be long or extensive. Including a bit of history can make your essay more interesting and can sometimes provide helpful background information. Give credit to any sources you use.

4. Consider using negation in your definition. Negation is a way of defining a term by including an explanation of what the term is *not*. Here is an example from Berkeley's Greater Good Web site:

> Psychologists generally define forgiveness as a conscious, deliberate decision to release feelings of resentment or vengeance toward a person or group who has harmed you, regardless of whether they actually deserve your forgiveness.

Just as important as defining what forgiveness *is*, though, is understanding what forgiveness is *not*. Experts who study or teach forgiveness make clear that when you forgive, you do not gloss over or deny the seriousness of an offense against you. Forgiveness does not mean forgetting, nor does it mean condoning or excusing offenses.

Notice how the definition by negation in the second paragraph of the example helps us understand some of what the author means by *forgiveness*.

5. Determine how you will support your extended definition. Some ideas are providing examples of the way the term has been (or is being) used, citing experts about their definitions of the term, and offering reasons why your definition is appropriate or superior to others. Many types of support can be used to help you make your point. Remember, a definition essay will include a definition, but it will also rely on other support to convey your message.

6. Check your definition for circularity. A **circular definition** includes the term being defined and does not elucidate or clarify meaning.

> **Ineffective:** A Senate committee is a committee composed of members of the Senate.

> **Effective:** A Senate committee is a group of current senators that has specific responsibilities—for example, drafting legislation—regarding a particular area, such as the Armed Services.

7. Write a thesis statement, and construct a simple outline. Remember that although your focus is to define a term, you will need to include support in body paragraphs. The support you choose will help you establish your definition or make your point about the word you are defining.

PRACTICE Using Definition in Your Writing

Use definition as a supporting point in a paragraph and as a text pattern for an essay by completing these two assignments.

1. Write a paragraph in which you define what *social media* are. Provide examples to help readers understand your definition.

2. Use the definition text pattern to write an essay on one of the topics below. Use the Quick Start Guide to Integrated Reading and Writing Assignments for assistance.

   - Define what it means to be educated.
   - Define *egocentrism*. (Note: This definition will require the use of sources. Consult the Quick Start Guide for information about giving credit to every source you use.)
   - Define *freedom of speech*. Provide examples of what the concept means and what it does not mean.

Illustration

Much of the support we use to communicate our thoughts consists of **illustrations**—different types of examples. We frequently use illustrations as supporting details in essays. Occasionally, an essay will present an idea almost exclusively through the use of examples. In such cases, writers support their thesis statement by using illustration as a text pattern.

RECOGNIZING THE ILLUSTRATION PATTERN IN READINGS

Whether used as a supporting detail or as a text pattern, illustration can be identified by its characteristics and key words.

CHARACTERISTICS OF THE ILLUSTRATION PATTERN

- Illustrations are often used with vague, complex, or broad ideas that are hard to understand.
- Illustrations are more concrete and specific than the ideas they explain.
- Illustrations may appear as examples, visual aids, sample quotes, sample statistics, or other concrete samples.
- Illustrations that are examples can be true or hypothetical.
- Illustrations are often followed by explanations.

Key Words for the Illustration Pattern		
consider	for example	for instance
imagine	like	such as
support	to clarify	to explain

Illustration in Supporting Details

Illustrations are commonly used as support in essays of all sorts and for all purposes. Any time a concept could be made easier to understand with an example, a graphic, or a sample of some sort, it is appropriate to use illustration. Here is an example of an illustration (underlined) used in an informative text:

> Having the right tools on hand makes the process of completing a difficult task easier. <u>For example, if you are moving everything you own across town, renting an appliance dolly will make moving day less burdensome.</u>

Illustrations can also be actual visuals—graphs, charts, tables, photos, and drawings. Here is an example of an illustration accompanied by a graph in a persuasive text. Note that an explanation of the graph helps readers understand the illustration's significance.

> One reason for the decline in sales is that a new superstore opened down the street, as the graph below shows. After the competition's superstore was built in 2008, sales profitability dropped from a high of $3.9 million in 2008 to below $2 million in 2013.

The partial outline that follows includes an example (underlined) as an illustration of the writer's point.

Using Illustration as a Supporting Detail

BODY

Paragraph 1: One of the most serious problems the Internet poses is cyberterrorism.

- Definition: Cyberterrorism is . . .
- <u>An example of cyberterrorism is</u> . . .
- <u>Explanation of example</u>

Paragraph 2: The reason cyberterrorism is such a threat is . . .

Illustration as a Text Pattern

Usually, illustration is used as a type of support in an essay rather than as the text pattern for an entire essay. However, writers sometimes depend on illustrations as primary support for their ideas.

When writers attempt to explain a complex idea to an audience with limited knowledge of the subject, illustration can be a useful text pattern. For example, a physics textbook chapter on Newton's first law of motion may use an illustration text pattern. Notice how this excerpt from *Physical Science*, a textbook by Bill W. Tillery, depends heavily on illustration. The illustration in the text has been highlighted, and a diagram used as an illustration has been included.

Newton's First Law of Motion

by Bill W. Tillery

Newton's first law of motion is also known as the *law of inertia* and is very similar to one of Galileo's findings about motion. Recall that Galileo used the term *inertia* to describe the tendency of an object to resist changes in motion. Newton's first law describes this tendency more directly. In modern terms (not Newton's words), the first law of motion is as follows:

> **Every object retains its state of rest or its state of uniform straight-line motion unless acted upon by an unbalanced force.**

This means that an object at rest will remain at rest unless it is put into motion by an unbalanced force; that is, the net force must be greater than zero. Likewise, an object moving with uniform straight-line motion will retain that motion unless a net force causes it to speed up, slow down, or change its direction of travel. Thus, Newton's first law describes the tendency of an object to resist *any* change in its state of motion.

Think of Newton's first law of motion when you ride standing in the aisle of a bus. The bus begins to move, and you, being an independent mass, tend to remain at rest. You take a few steps back as you tend to maintain your position relative to the ground outside. You reach for a seat back or some part of the bus. Once you have a hold on some part of the bus, it supplies the forces needed to give you the same motion as the bus and you no longer find it necessary to step backward. You now have the same motion as the bus, and no forces are involved, at least until the bus goes around a

Hypothetical example: The example starts here and continues through the paragraph.

(continued)

curve. You now feel a tendency to move to the side of the bus. The bus has changed its straight-line motion, but you, again being an independent mass, tend to move straight ahead. The side of the seat forces you into following the curved motion of the bus. The forces you feel when the bus starts moving or turning are a result of your tendency to remain at rest or follow a straight path until forces correct your motion so that it is the same as that of the bus.

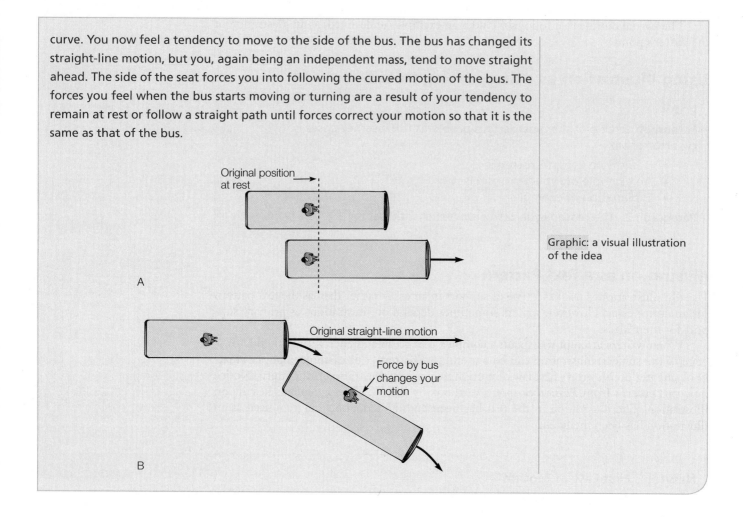

Graphic: a visual illustration of the idea

This textbook selection provides a long hypothetical example. A **hypothetical example** is one that a writer makes up; it is fictional. As an educated guess, a hypothetical example is based on things that could very likely happen. Even though it is fictional, the example must be realistic: it must portray something that would be typical or likely, not something unlikely to happen. In the selection above, the hypothetical example asks readers to imagine being in a bus in motion. Because we can easily imagine standing on a bus, the example—although fictional—is credible and helps the writer make his point.

The type of illustration used depends on the writer's purpose. In an essay whose purpose is to analyze or evaluate, illustrations would likely come from the idea or object being analyzed. For instance, an essay that analyzes a new type of smartphone and evaluates its worth would include examples of the smartphone's features. A writer might analyze the apps built in to the phone and provide an example of one of them, or the writer might include a photo as an illustration of the phone's sleek profile.

In persuasive writing, illustrations can be used as proof. Suppose a writer wants to prove that studying math in college results in real-life benefits. One way to prove this point would be to provide specific examples of how mathematical knowledge benefits us in life.

The outline that follows on the next page demonstrates how a writer can use illustration as a text pattern for an essay by making illustrations (underlined) the primary method for supporting the thesis statement.

A Simple Outline for an Illustration Pattern Essay

Topic: Choosing a career

Thesis statement: One way to choose a career is to find one that is personally interesting, that harmonizes with one's personality, and that fits one's lifestyle.

INTRODUCTION
Paragraph 1: Introduction and thesis statement

BODY
Paragraph 2: In general, the best way to start analyzing careers is to consider personal interests and to find careers that match them.

- Job satisfaction tied to interest
- Chart: shows job satisfaction is tied to interest level
- Anecdote: Leah's choice to quit teaching and open a restaurant
- Need to think creatively about potential jobs
- Example: interest in art, could consider merchandising, industrial painting, even cake decorating or making prosthetics

Paragraph 3: While a satisfying career will be personally interesting, it should also be a good fit for one's personality.

- Consider whether you like working with people.
- Explanation: introvert/extrovert
- Anecdote: Maddie's first job didn't match her personality.
- Examples: good fit for introverts—programmer, writer, chemist
- Examples: good fit for extroverts—activity director, salesperson, trainer

Paragraph 4: Finally, finding a fulfilling career requires choosing a job that matches one's lifestyle preferences.

- Examples of lifestyle issues: traveling, hours of work per week, flexibility
- Anecdote: Andre's story about traveling
- Quote: Andre
- Example of lifestyle fit: Cara's flexible job/parenting

CONCLUSION
Paragraph 5: Concluding thoughts

Notice that the essay will include lots of examples, as well as a chart that illustrates a point, anecdotes used as illustrations, and a quote from Andre, a person whose career choices are used as an illustration.

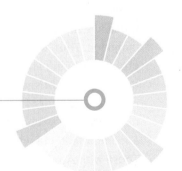

ANALYZING AN ILLUSTRATION TEXT

In the next reading selection, "Life with Asperger's Syndrome," the writer uses illustration as a text pattern. Notice that while illustration is the main method used for evidence, the writer also includes other types of support in the essay.

An Illustration Text: Introduction and Thesis Statement

One way to begin an essay is to use an example followed by an explanation that is tied to the thesis statement, as the writer does in the introduction to "Life with Asperger's Syndrome" on the next page.

Introduction Paragraphs of "Life with Asperger's Syndrome"

Eleven-year-old Paul paced nervously back and forth at the bus stop. His school bus is supposed to arrive every morning at 7:04. Usually Paul could see the bus coming down the street at 7:03, but this morning, at 7:03, there was no bus. A feeling of panic washed over him. When his watch said 7:04, tears began to stream down his face. The bus was not on time. By 7:05, he could not stand it any longer and ran home. If Paul had not been diagnosed with Asperger's syndrome, his mother would probably have been puzzled by this behavior, but she was not shocked. Because he has Asperger's syndrome, Paul is not like other children.	Example Explanation
Asperger's syndrome is a type of autism. Many people have heard of autism before, but not many know about Asperger's syndrome. Autism comes in many forms, some very severe and some quite mild. People who have Asperger's are considered to be on the mild "high functioning" side of the autism range. People with classic autism are often unable to talk and do not like being touched, while many of those with Asperger's can function fairly normally in these areas. However, there are some challenges for those who have Asperger's syndrome, and some of these challenges are significant.	Definition followed by explanation Thesis statement

Examples are often followed by explanations. Readers need to know why they are reading about a particular example, and explanations tie the example to the broader point—the thesis statement or topic sentence—the writer is making.

An Illustration Text: Body Paragraphs and Their Organization

Examples and explanations are the staples of illustration texts. Notice how the body paragraphs below are composed primarily of these features.

Body Paragraphs of "Life with Asperger's Syndrome"

First, those who have Asperger's have a really hard time interacting with other people. While most people can read body language, those with Asperger's cannot. For example, when people are aggravated, they might roll their eyes, cross their arms, or smirk. These are all body language clues that convey a sense of aggravation. When they use this kind of body language, people expect others to step back and proceed with caution. People with Asperger's are often not able to read such body language. Thus, they may respond inappropriately in social situations. Another problem is being able to use body language themselves. One mother recounts how her daughter Chrissy wanted to learn to roll her eyes. Unable to really master the eye roll, and unaware of when eye rolling is an appropriate gesture, Chrissy finally (to her mother's relief) stopped trying to do it. People with Asperger's may cross their arms and impatiently tap their feet, not being aware of the message they are sending. Those with Asperger's can be taught how to read body language; however, social interactions are still often difficult because of this aspect of Asperger's syndrome.	Major supporting point Examples Explanation Example Explanation Example Explanation
Another tendency shared by those with Asperger's is literal thinking. Language meant to be understood literally should be interpreted to mean exactly what the words denote. For example, interpreted literally, the phrase *money talks* would mean that	Major supporting point Example

(continued)

money actually has a voice and audibly speaks. Much of our language is not meant to be interpreted literally. Kevin Leary recounts a moment when Ryan, his eight-year-old son with Asperger's, was playing with cousins. An adult in the family said to one of the children, "You have ants in your pants!" Ryan ran to the boy and started helping him take off his pants, unaware of the non-literal nature of the comment. Young people with Asperger's are especially literal-minded because they have not had enough experience with the world to understand which phrases are meant figuratively. For example, if a person were to tell Ryan that he will get a popsicle "in a minute," Ryan may watch the clock and be upset if he does not receive his treat in 60 seconds. It is a challenge for Asperger's children to learn to be less literal-minded.

A third characteristic of those with Asperger's is inflexibility. People with Asperger's syndrome find comfort in fixed routines and rules. They find it extremely agitating when the rules change or when routines must shift. Suppose you are the parent of a child with Asperger's. Every change you make—such as getting a haircut, putting your car keys in an unusual spot, buying a new pair of shoes—can be the basis for true psychological distress for children with Asperger's. If a tantrum results, the child is not being bratty. Rather, the Asperger brain sends distress signals when routines are broken or change occurs. Not all changes elicit the same reaction, so parents have to learn what sets off their particular child. When presented with such change, the person with Asperger's may throw a fit or may stay awake crying all night. Even making a change that is as minor as moving furniture around may be extremely unsettling for those who have Asperger's syndrome. Learning to be flexible is another of the major challenges those with Asperger's face.

While Asperger's syndrome makes life different and sometimes difficult for those who have it, there are a number of coping mechanisms those with the syndrome can develop in order to function well. Therapists and physicians are becoming more familiar with Asperger's syndrome now as increasing numbers of diagnoses have been made in the last twenty years. (See chart.) Many people with Asperger's syndrome live typical lives. However, being able to adjust to the way neurotypical people think—especially with regard to social interaction—requires effort and diligence.

Sidebar annotations:

Explanation

Example

Hypothetical example

Major supporting point

Examples

Explanation

Example

Major supporting point: discussion of prognosis

Chart used as illustration

Vocabulary Collection Word:
neurotypical

Your in-context definition:
_____
_____

A dictionary definition:
_____
_____

Identified Prevalence of Autism Spectrum Disorders ADDM Network 2000–2008 Combining Data from All Sites				
SURVEILLANCE YEAR	BIRTH YEAR	NUMBER OF ADDM SITES REPORTING	PREVALENCE PER 1,000 CHILDREN (RANGE)	THIS IS ABOUT 1 IN X CHILDREN...
2000	1992	6	6.7 (4.5–9.9)	1 in 150
2002	1994	14	6.6 (3.3–10.6)	1 in 150
2004	1996	8	8.0 (4.6–9.8)	1 in 125
2006	1998	11	9.0 (4.2–12.1)	1 in 110
2008	2000	14	11.3 (4.8–21.2)	1 in 88

Source: Centers for Disease Control and Prevention

Notice that the last body paragraph is a single paragraph of discussion. Because the writer is making a point about increases in autism diagnoses in the United States, the perfect illustration is a chart showing this increase. Not only does the chart illustrate the writer's point, but it also lends credibility to the writer's point since the chart comes from an authoritative source, the Centers for Disease Control and Prevention.

An Illustration Text: Conclusion

The function of any conclusion paragraph is to bring closure to the topic. In this essay, the writer brings closure by ending the story about Paul that began the essay.

Conclusion Paragraph of "Life with Asperger's Syndrome"

> Paul did not get to school on time on the day he walked home from the bus stop. After his mother talked with him about the need to be flexible regarding time, Paul was able to calm down and eventually go to school. With time and maturity, Paul will learn how to deal with such situations. While life with Asperger's will present challenges, many of those who have it have proven that these challenges will not keep them from living happy, productive lives.

Example

Conclusion: presents good news

The conclusion provides the good news about Asperger's syndrome: that those who have it can learn methods for living happily. This ending is intended to leave readers with a feeling of hope and optimism for those who struggle with Asperger's.

PRACTICE Analyzing an Illustration Text

On a separate sheet, answer the following questions about "Life with Asperger's Syndrome."

1. The writer used a character—Paul—as an example. In which paragraphs does the writer mention Paul? Why do you think the writer uses Paul in these particular paragraphs?

2. Paul's case is not the only example the writer uses. Where are other examples used? List the examples used in the essay. Are the other examples of children with Asperger's based on real children, or are they hypothetical examples?

3. Is there a pattern to the writer's organization? For example, does the writer start body paragraphs with examples? When does the writer use explanations?

4. Read each paragraph in the essay but skip over the examples. As a reader, how would you experience the essay if the writer had *not* included examples? Explain your answer.

USING ILLUSTRATION IN YOUR WRITING

The key to using illustration effectively is to consider readers' needs. Has an instructor ever returned to you a writing assignment with the word "Explain" in the margin? If so, you are not alone. Because you already know the point you are communicating, it is easy to make the mistake of thinking your readers also know the point. The best way to guard against this mistake is to put yourself in the place of your readers and ask yourself, "What information might my readers need explained in more depth?" or "What background information do I know that my readers may not know?"

With your audience in mind, you can work through the process of composing an illustration text or selecting illustrations as supporting details. The guidelines that follow can guide you in your illustration writing.

1. Ask yourself how illustration suits your topic and purpose. Some topics lend themselves to illustration more than others do. The key to using illustration as a text pattern is to determine whether illustration will be sufficient support for your point. For example, an essay about how people are judged by their appearances could be developed by providing illustrations. Body paragraphs may include examples of particular ways of dressing or particular hairstyles and the messages those appearances might convey.

On the other hand, an essay explaining how crude oil is refined might not lend itself to the use of examples. Rather, such an essay would more readily be organized by steps or stages.

2. Consider using real examples. If you have access to real-life examples, use them. In "Life with Asperger's Syndrome," the writer uses the examples of Paul, Chrissy, and Ryan. Provide enough information so that readers will know the examples are from real life.

3. Consider using hypothetical examples. Hypothetical examples can be just as effective as real-life examples, but hypothetical examples must be believable and likely to happen.

4. Consider using concrete details. Concrete details help us communicate concepts more clearly. For example, a writer might say that her dorm room is uninviting. She might even explain that an uninviting room is one that a person is not attracted to, a room that does not make a person want to enter it. Yet the term *uninviting* still does not create a clear picture for readers. Concrete details about the room—descriptions of fluorescent lights, gray carpet, gray walls, and a mattress on a simple metal frame—can communicate what *uninviting* means and help readers picture the room more clearly.

5. Consider using an extended example. An extended example is carried through an entire essay. In "Life with Asperger's Syndrome," the writer could have used an extended example by talking about Paul, the boy in the first paragraph, throughout the essay.

6. Consider using visual aids, facts, data, and statistics. You can illustrate a point in a variety of ways. One way is to provide actual visual aids. In many textbooks, visuals such as charts, photos, and graphics are used frequently. Why? One reason is that visuals explain some kinds of information more effectively than words do. A chart or graph is a way to combine data—such as facts and statistics—that can help readers see your point quickly. Remember also that any data you use must come from a reliable source, and you must give credit to the source.

7. Write a thesis statement, and construct a simple outline. Unlike definition essays whose thesis statements are likely to concern a definition the writer is offering, thesis statements for illustration essays vary widely. A writer may use illustration to argue that Ireland is the most beautiful place on earth, or a writer may use illustration to prove that persistent exposure to a certain chemical is associated with cancer. In any case, an illustration essay will primarily be developed by use of examples and presentation of visual illustrations such as charts, graphs, and art.

PRACTICE Using Illustration in Your Writing

Write an essay in which you use illustration as the dominant text pattern. Choose one of the following topics, or select your own.

A. Select an economic principle you believe is important to follow in your financial life. For example, one principle is to not keep a balance on credit cards. Another is to buy only items you can afford to pay cash for. Write an essay in which you use illustrations to show the importance of the economic principle you have chosen.

B. Choose a person you admire, explain why, and give examples to show the person's good qualities or actions. The person can be someone you know, a historical figure, or a well-known contemporary.

C. What are the characteristics of a good employee? Explain your view, and give examples to support your ideas.

Classification

One of the ways we make sense of the world is to use **classification.** To classify is to create categories for groups of items that are similar. For example, scientists would classify a particular volcano as one of several types: cinder cones, composite volcanoes, shield volcanoes, or lava domes. Biologists classify microbes into archaea, bacteria, fungi, protista, viruses, or microbial mergers. Political scientists might put voters into several different categories—gender, race, age, and so on—depending on the needs of a survey or study.

As a text pattern, classification often informs readers about the characteristics of each category of information. An essay about social media, for example, might classify social media into four categories: social networks, blogging Web sites, media-sharing sites, and news-sharing sites. To further explain these categories, a writer might provide the characteristics of each type of social media. While the purpose of such an essay would be to inform, classification is also used to analyze, to evaluate, and to persuade.

RECOGNIZING THE CLASSIFICATION PATTERN IN READINGS

Whether classification is used to present details in a reading or as the basic text pattern for a reading, it can be recognized by its characteristics and key words.

CHARACTERISTICS OF THE CLASSIFICATION PATTERN

- Classification presents information in types, groups, or categories.
- It includes discussion of the features associated with each type, group, or category.
- Classification writing often includes examples of the items of each type or in each group or category.
- Classification writing often includes discussion of the similarities and differences of each type, group, or category.

Key Words for the Classification Pattern			
characteristic	classify	cohort	distinguish
feature	group	identify	kind
quality	section	sort	species
subtype	trait	type	variety

Classification in Supporting Details

Sometimes classification is used to provide helpful information or background knowledge about a subject. Suppose a writer is arguing that adult-onset diabetes can be reversed (an idea that is debatable). One way to begin the discussion would be to provide some background information on diabetes. To do this, the writer might start by classifying diabetes as a metabolic disease. In a body paragraph, she may divide the disease into its two main types: juvenile diabetes and adult-onset diabetes. In this way, classification becomes one of several patterns the writer will use to develop her essay, as this partial outline shows.

Using Classification as a Supporting Detail

Topic: Reversibility of diabetes

Thesis statement: With certain behavioral adjustments, Type II diabetes is reversible for some people.

(continued)

INTRODUCTION
  Paragraph 1
BODY
  Paragraph 2: Classifying diabetes
  - Classification of diabetes as a metabolic disorder
  - Explanation of metabolic disorders
  - Division of diabetes into types:
    ○ Type I diabetes
    ○ Type II diabetes
  Paragraph 3: Weight loss and its effect on Type II diabetes
  - Studies from Centers for Disease Control and Prevention
  - Cause-effect discussion

When classification is used as a supporting detail, the discussion of an item's classification is limited, as this outline demonstrates.

Classification as a Text Pattern

While classification can be used as a supporting detail, it can also be the primary function of a text. Classification is often used to inform or to analyze. Informative texts can employ classification to present information so that readers more easily understand it. For example, an introductory biology textbook might include an informative presentation of biological taxonomy—a ranking system for organisms that includes kingdom, phylum/division, class, order, family, genus, and species. A music education textbook might categorize the different types of instruments in symphony orchestras as woodwinds, brass, percussion, and strings, as in the Classification Model diagram.

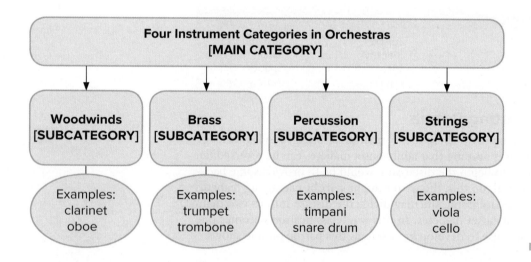

■ Classification Model

While sorting information is a main focus of classification texts, the classification text pattern can also be used to analyze, to evaluate, and to persuade, as these examples demonstrate.

To inform: A magazine article classifying types of financial aid

To analyze: A marketing report presents a breakdown of the types of customers who buy a particular product.

To evaluate: A scholarly journal article on the types of treatment for a psychological disorder evaluates which type helps more people.

To persuade: An essay argues that certain groups of people—such as those with a criminal past or with certain diagnosed mental conditions—should not be allowed to own firearms.

As a text pattern, classification is used to present types, classes, varieties, or groups. Often classification texts are structured so that each type is presented separately, one after another. The discussion of each type or variety includes characteristics that describe the type. The outline below shows how an essay on the types of financial aid available for students might be organized. Notice how each type of financial aid includes a definition, examples, and a discussion of characteristics.

A Simple Outline for a Classification Pattern Essay

Topic: Financial aid available for students

Thesis statement: Three types of financial aid available to college students are scholarships and grants, loans, and work-based aid.

INTRODUCTION
    Paragraph 1: General information about college costs; thesis statement

BODY
    Paragraph 2: First type—scholarships and grants
- Definition of scholarship and grant
- Examples of scholarships and grants
- Characteristic 1: does not require repayment
- Characteristic 2: is usually competitive and more difficult to get
- Characteristic 3: may be awarded to members of a particular group
- Characteristic 4: might have restrictions on how or where one can use it

    Paragraph 3: Second type—loans
- Definition of loan
- Examples of loans
- Characteristic 1: must be repaid
- Characteristic 2: can defer repayment until after college
- Characteristic 3: easy to qualify
- Characteristic 4: can use at any college or university

    Paragraph 4: Third type—work-based aid
- Definition of work-based aid
- Examples of work-based aid
- Characteristic 1: usually does not have to be repaid
- Characteristic 2: sometimes covers more than just tuition and fees
- Characteristic 3: must meet particular requirements to qualify
- Characteristic 4: may be tied to a particular college or university

CONCLUSION
    Paragraph 5: Conclusion

ANALYZING A CLASSIFICATION TEXT

The ideas in a classification text must be presented in an order that makes sense for readers. In the preceding example of the types of financial aid, the essay might present types of aid in the order of how easy (or difficult) each type is to obtain or how relevant each is for most students. The writer of the outline above chose to discuss the most desirable type of financial aid first. In a discussion of communicable diseases, a writer may start with the least serious type and progress to the most serious type. The key to determining the order in which to present types is to consider whether audiences might benefit more from one order than another.

A Classification Text: Introduction and Thesis Statement

In an essay that relies primarily on classification for support, the subject being classified is usually presented in the introduction paragraph, and sometimes the thesis statement contains the categories into which items are placed. In the example that follows, the writers tell readers what they will be classifying (types of workers to fire), but they do not reveal the specific categories until the body of the essay.

Introduction Paragraphs of "Three Types of People to Fire Immediately" by G. Michael Maddock and Raphael Louis Vitón

We (your authors) teach our children to work hard and never, ever give up. We teach them to be grateful, to be full of wonder, to expect good things to happen, and to search for literal and figurative treasure on every beach, in every room, and in every person.	Introduction: leads up to the thesis statement
But some day, when the treasure hunt is over, we'll also teach them to fire people. Why? After working with the most inventive people in the world for two decades, we've discovered the value of a certain item in the leadership toolbox: the pink slip.	
Show of hands: How many of you out there in Innovationland have gotten the "what took you so long?" question from your staff when you finally said goodbye to a teammate who was seemingly always part of problems instead of solutions? We imagine a whole bunch of hands. (Yep, ours went up, too.)	Rhetorical question: shows that authors are not merely coldhearted executives who like to fire employees
These people . . . passive-aggressively block innovation from happening and will suck the energy out of any organization. When confronted with any of the following three [types of] people—and you have found it impossible to change their ways—say goodbye.	Clue that essay will classify types of employees Thesis statement

A Classification Text: Body Paragraphs and Their Organization

Body paragraphs in a classification text present the categories, types, or groups into which the writer divides the subject. In the example that follows, the writers create three types of employees to fire immediately: the victims, the nonbelievers, and the know-it-alls. Notice how the body paragraphs include the characteristics or traits of each type of employee.

Body Paragraphs of "Three Types of People to Fire Immediately" by G. Michael Maddock and Raphael Louis Vitón

1. THE VICTIMS

"Can you believe what they want us to do now? And of course we have no time to do it. I don't get paid enough for this. The boss is clueless."

Victims are people who see problems as occasions for persecution rather than challenges to overcome. We all play the role of victim occasionally, but for some, it has turned into a way of life. These people feel persecuted by humans, processes, and inanimate objects with equal ease—they almost seem to enjoy it. They are often angry, usually annoyed, and almost always complaining. Just when you think everything is humming along perfectly, they find something, anything, to complain about. At Halloween parties, they're Eeyore, the gloomy, pessimistic donkey from the *Winnie the Pooh* stories—regardless of the costume they choose. Victims aren't looking for opportunities; they are looking for problems.

2. THE NONBELIEVERS

"Why should we work so hard on this? Even if we come up with a good idea, the boss will probably kill it. If she doesn't, the market will. I've seen this a hundred times before."

We love the Henry Ford quote: "If you think you can or think you cannot, you are correct." The difference between the winning team that makes industry-changing innovation happen and the losing one that comes up short is a lack of willpower. Said differently, the winners really believed they could do it, while the losers doubted it was possible.

In our experience, we've found the link between believing and succeeding incredibly powerful and real. Great leaders understand this. They find and promote believers within their organizations. They also understand the cancerous effect that nonbelievers have on a team and will cut them out of the organization quickly and without regret.

If you are a leader who says your mission is to innovate, but you have a staff that houses nonbelievers, you are either a lousy leader or in denial. Which is it? You deserve the staff you get. Terminate the nonbelievers.

3. THE KNOW-IT-ALLS

"You people obviously don't understand the business we are in. The regulations will not allow an idea like this, and our stakeholders won't embrace it. Don't even get me started on our IT infrastructure's inability to support it. And then there is the problem of . . . ."

The best innovators are learners, not knowers. The same can be said about innovative cultures; they are learning cultures. The leaders who have built these cultures, either through intuition or experience, know that in order to discover, they must eagerly seek out things they don't understand and jump right into the deep end of the pool. They must fail fearlessly and quickly and then learn and share their lessons with the team. When they behave this way, they empower others around them to follow suit—and presto, a culture of discovery is born and nurtured.

In school, the one who knows the most gets the best grades, goes to the best college, and gets the best salary. On the job, the person who can figure things out the quickest is often celebrated. And unfortunately, it is often this smartest, most-seasoned employee who eventually becomes expert in using his or her knowledge to explain why things are impossible rather than possible.

Type 1: Headings list types of employees. Alternatively, a topic sentence could introduce each type. The presentation of Type 1 is the writer's first major supporting point.

Hypothetical quotation: follows each heading

Characteristic: Victims feel persecuted.

Characteristic: Victims are often angry, annoyed, and complaining.

Characteristic: Victims look for problems.

Type 2: The presentation of Type 2 is the writer's second major supporting point.

Hypothetical quote

Characteristic: Nonbelievers lack willpower.

Characteristic: Nonbelievers are doubters.

Characteristic: Nonbelievers have a negative effect on teams.

Type 3: The presentation of Type 3 is the writer's third major supporting point.

Hypothetical quote

Characteristic: Know-it-alls are not learners.

Characteristic: Know-it-alls do not seek out new information.

Characteristic: Know-it-alls do not want to fail and relearn.

Characteristic: Know-it-alls can be very smart and seasoned yet have a negative effect.

(continued)

This employee should be challenged, retrained, and compensated for failing forward. But if this person's habits are too deeply ingrained to change, you must let him or her go. Otherwise, this individual will unwittingly keep your team from seeing opportunity right under your noses. . . .	Characteristic: Know-it-alls may or may not be able to change.

A Classification Text: Conclusion

In this essay, the writers use a very short conclusion paragraph. The first sentence is a restatement of the main idea.

Conclusion Paragraph of "Three Types of People to Fire Immediately" by G. Michael Maddock and Raphael Louis Vitón

You don't want the victims, nonbelievers, or know-it-alls. It is up to you to make sure they take their anti-innovative outlooks elsewhere.	Conclusion: restatement of main idea

 PRACTICE   **Analyzing a Classification Text**

On a separate sheet, answer the following questions about "Three Types of People to Fire Immediately" by G. Michael Maddock and Raphael Louis Vitón.

1. Read through the paragraphs describing "the victims." Besides providing characteristics of this type of employee, what other information do the writers supply? Examples? Explanations? Comparisons? Statistics?

2. Explain this statement: The description of know-it-alls differs from the other two descriptions in that we have to infer their characteristics.

3. The writers use headings to list the three types of workers. Write a topic sentence for each of these types to replace each heading.

4. What is the purpose of this essay? To inform? To analyze? To evaluate? To persuade? (There can be more than one purpose.) Explain your answer.

USING CLASSIFICATION IN YOUR WRITING

You can use classification as a text pattern for your writing whenever putting information into categories helps you achieve your writing purpose. The guidelines that follow will help you use the classification text pattern in your writing.

1. Ask yourself whether classification suits your purpose. Not all subjects can be classified. If you have been given an assignment, analyzing the assignment will help you determine whether classification will help you organize your text.

A simple way to think of a classification essay topic is to fill in this sentence:

My topic involves types of _____.

Start with a subject area you might be interested in when you go to college. If you are thinking of majoring in nursing, you might choose types of nurses. If you might be an education major, you might consider types of teaching jobs. Alternatively, think of a subject or hobby that interests you, and consider how you might divide it into groups such as types of movies, types of wind instruments, or types of alternative fuel vehicles.

For an even more relevant topic, choose to write about something that will help you solve a problem. For an example, one student, Hector, used the topic of financial aid; you saw the outline he created earlier in this chapter. He chose to write about types of financial aid because he needed to know more about how he could afford his college tuition. If you can find a topic that piques your interest and fits the assignment requirements, use it!

2. Use prewriting to determine the items you will classify and to group them into categories. For his essay classifying financial aid, Hector started by listing the aid that he knew was available. He realized that his list included three types of financial aid—scholarships and grants, loans, and work-based aid—and that these types provided convenient categories for classification. His annotated list is shown here.

Financial Aid Available

Scholarship
- Follow the Dream Art <u>Scholarship</u> at Westview Blayne College
- "Free tuition" <u>work-and-study</u> colleges — Work-based aid
Loan
- The Bill Davenport <u>loan</u>
- Employer-sponsored tuition reimbursement <u>grants</u> for workers — Work-based aid
Work-based aid
- Educators Federation Credit Union <u>Loan</u> for older students
- <u>Work-study</u> funding — Loans
- Federal financial aid <u>loans</u>
- A <u>scholarship</u> at Tennadi University for returning adults ⎤
- The Forty-Plus <u>Scholarship</u> at University of the North ⎥ Scholarships
- Veterans' <u>education</u> benefits ⎦

3. Write a thesis statement that uses the classification pattern. Include the groups or categories in your thesis statement. Be sure to arrange the groups in the same order you plan to use in your essay.

4. Write topic sentences for each group or type you are presenting. Use the body paragraphs to present and discuss the characteristics of each category or type. Plan to devote at least one body paragraph to each type or category. You may even need to use two or more paragraphs for the discussion of characteristics.

As shown in Hector's simple outline for an essay on financial aid, the first body paragraph will be rather long. If he ends up using two paragraphs for the first category, he can consider using two paragraphs for each of the remaining categories. Doing so would make his essay more balanced, but it is not necessary. As a general principle, use the number of body paragraphs required to successfully communicate your point.

As you draft, read back over your essay continually so that you can see your writing from a reader's point of view. Make any changes necessary to clarify your ideas and to make your sentences say exactly what you want them to say. Be certain that, after finishing your essay, readers will be able to correctly list the types or groups you discuss. Make sure your writing is clear enough so that they can easily remember the main characteristics of each type.

PRACTICE Using Classification in Your Writing

Use the preceding steps to write a classification essay. Choose one of the following topics, or select your own.

A. Along with all of the benefits we get from the Internet, we also see that some people use the Internet to harm others. What types of Internet abuse can you think of? Write an essay in which you present them.

B. Write an essay classifying one of the following:

- Types of bosses or managers
- Types of vacations
- Types of child care available in your city
- Types of opportunities for volunteering
- Types of poverty
- Types of diets

⊙ Comparison-Contrast ⊙

Comparing and contrasting are mental activities we do every day. We compare new information we learn in class with information we already know; we contrast a new law with an old law; we take stock of ourselves by comparing and contrasting our qualities with the qualities of others. We also use comparison and contrast to structure our thoughts as we communicate with others in writing.

Technically, to **compare** means to look at the *similarities* between two or more things; to **contrast** means to look at the *differences*. Sometimes, however, people use the term *compare* to mean both: to identify both the similarities and differences. Additionally, comparison-contrast writing always looks at things that are in the same general category. For example, comparing the tourist attractions of one city with those of another is a fair comparison, but comparing the tourist attractions of a city with those of an entire state is not.

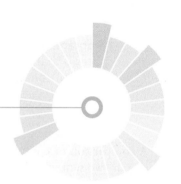

RECOGNIZING THE COMPARISON-CONTRAST PATTERN IN READINGS

To identify the comparison-contrast pattern in a text, look for these characteristics and key words.

CHARACTERISTICS OF THE COMPARISON-CONTRAST PATTERN

- Two or more elements are involved in the comparison and contrast.
- The text presents the differences and/or similarities of these items.
- The text presents an analysis of the items being compared and/or contrasted.

Key Words for the Comparison-Contrast Pattern			
although	but	by the same token	criteria
different	dissimilar	equal	however
in comparison	likewise	nonetheless	on the contrary
on the other hand	otherwise	point	similar

Comparison-Contrast in Supporting Details

We make comparisons so often that we are almost unaware we are making them. Think of the times you have been asked a question and used a comparison to answer.

- Oh, my new job? It's different from my old one because I have to answer phones all day.
- This sandwich tastes as if it's been sitting in a car for hours.

A similarity or a difference can be used as a supporting detail in an essay. Suppose, for example, that you are writing an essay to persuade people that it is morally reprehensible to park illegally in handicapped spots. To bring home your point, you may wish to ask readers to compare their health with the health of someone who needs a handicapped parking spot. You might ask readers to put themselves in the place of a person who uses a wheelchair, a person who just had knee surgery, or an elderly person who cannot walk very far. In an outline like the one on the next page, you might plan to use these kinds of comparisons.

Using Comparison-Contrast as a Supporting Detail

Topic: Respecting handicapped status

Thesis statement: Illegally parking in spaces designated for handicapped people is a reprehensible act; it shows no empathy for those who need handicapped spaces, does not provide much benefit for the person who does the illegal parking, and shows disrespect for the law.

INTRODUCTION

    Paragraph 1

BODY

    Paragraph 2: A person who takes a handicapped parking space without good cause has no empathy for the people who really need such spaces.

    - Types of conditions that merit handicapped parking spaces
    - Comparison: a person in good health vs. a person who just had knee surgery
    - Why people should try to empathize

    Paragraph 3: Another reason no one should illegally park in handicapped spaces is that doing so provides very little benefit to the healthy person and significant hardship to the truly disabled person.

    . . .

A comparison or contrast used as support can take up an entire paragraph or as little as one or two sentences.

Comparison-Contrast as a Text Pattern

Sometimes we write essays that provide extended comparisons or contrasts. For example, a writer may compare and contrast buying a car with leasing a car. In such an essay, the writer is likely to present the factors that are important to consumers, such as monthly payments, mileage limits, warranty considerations, and ownership.

For each writing purpose—that is, to inform, to analyze, to evaluate, and to persuade—comparison-contrast can be an effective choice. Comparison-contrast may be used in a history textbook to inform readers about the different capabilities of the Confederate Army and the Union Army during the Civil War, for example.

The writer of an analysis essay can also use comparison-contrast. For instance, the writer may analyze the differences and similarities between two potential careers. If the writer chooses, she can use her analysis to evaluate the two careers and determine which one is best for her. Thus, comparison-contrast can also lead to making evaluative judgments.

Persuasive writing also makes use of comparison-contrast. Arguments about worker paid vacation time often compare the condition in the U.S. to that in other European countries, for example. However, writers use comparisons only if doing so will help their side of the argument.

An essay that uses comparison-contrast as a primary text pattern can be organized in one of two ways: block (subject-by-subject) arrangement or point-by-point arrangement. Both arrangements depend on having two or more subjects to compare and particular points of comparison for each subject.

In the **block arrangement,** the writer organizes the discussion by subject, covering all the relevant points first for subject A and then for subject B. In the **point-by-point**

arrangement, the writer organizes the discussion by the points of comparison, writing about the first point for both subjects A and B, then about the second point for both subjects A and B, and so on.

For example, we have noted that to compare two subjects—buying a car versus leasing a car—a writer could talk about these points: monthly payments, mileage limits, warranty considerations, and ownership. A circular graphic shows how a block arrangement of ideas would work.

■ In this block arrangement graphic, each subject is in the center of its circle.

The sample outlines that follow highlight the differences between the block and point-by-point arrangements.

Block Arrangement	**Point-by-Point Arrangement**
INTRODUCTION	**INTRODUCTION**
Body	**Body**
Subject 1: Buying	**Point 1:** Monthly payments
• Monthly payments	• Buying
• Mileage limits	• Leasing
• Warranty	**Point 2:** Mileage limits
• Ownership	• Buying
Subject 2: Leasing	• Leasing
• Monthly payments	**Point 3:** Warranty
• Mileage limits	• Buying
• Warranty	• Leasing
• Ownership	**Point 4:** Ownership
	• Buying
	• Leasing
Conclusion	**Conclusion**

The block arrangement can result in some very long body paragraphs if a writer tries to cover all of the points for one subject in a single paragraph. Thus, writers sometimes devote individual paragraphs to each of the points for each subject. Nonetheless, the block arrangement is not always the best choice to discuss subjects that include several points of comparison.

ANALYZING A COMPARISON-CONTRAST TEXT

When you read a comparison-contrast text, clearly identify the subjects being compared and the points of comparison. Sometimes the introduction paragraph will help you identify these elements.

A Comparison-Contrast Text: Introduction and Thesis Statement

Comparison-contrast texts often begin with a discussion of the subjects being analyzed. Each subject is introduced, and enough information is provided so that readers understand why the writer is comparing and contrasting the two subjects. The essay that follows, "Teaching? Or Not," starts with a two-paragraph introduction.

Introduction Paragraphs of "Teaching? Or Not"

The United States is in an educational crisis. We constantly hear about schools that do not make the mark, students who graduate without learning to read, and countries that have far better educational systems than we do. Politicians wring their hands and propose new policies and new laws, but nothing seems to really change.	The first paragraph of the introduction gives readers the broad context: public education is in crisis.
While many issues plague public K–12 education, the problem of attracting talented professionals to pursue teaching careers is a significant problem. One way to understand why is to think like a college student who is deciding whether to major in education. Following Laura—a hypothetical college student—through the process of deciding whether to major in education or accounting will reveal some of the reasons why, for so many college students, teaching pales in comparison with other careers.	The second paragraph narrows the topic to attracting talented students to teaching careers. Thesis statement: The essay compares and contrasts two subjects, (A) majoring in teaching and (B) majoring in accounting.

A Comparison-Contrast Text: Body Paragraphs and Their Organization

The writer has decided to organize her essay using the point-by-point arrangement. What follows are the body paragraphs, each of which addresses a point of comparison.

Body Paragraphs of "Teaching? Or Not" (Point-by-Point Arrangement)

Laura is in her sophomore year and is great at math. She is considering majoring in education and becoming a high school math teacher. Another possibility for Laura is to work in accounting. She aces her accounting classes and finds the work enjoyable.	Background
The first point Laura considers is how many semesters each program—education or accounting—will require before she can graduate. In Laura's state, students who want to teach high school have to complete a degree in their educational field (such as math, English, or science) and then complete the education courses required for teacher certification. What that would mean for Laura is an extra year of college (at a cost of several thousand dollars) to meet the education requirements. In accounting, students have to complete only a four-year degree before going right to work. Also, to	Point 1: educational requirements. Point 1 is a major supporting point for the essay. Subject A (teaching): educational requirements Details Subject B (accounting): educational requirements Details

(continued)

get a teaching degree, Laura would have to spend time in public schools as an intern—in addition to her classes on campus. Accounting requires no on-the-job training, so finishing an accounting degree would be easier than finishing an education degree.

Another issue important for Laura is vacation time and work hours. Teachers' generous vacation time during the summer and holidays is very attractive to Laura. However, she knows that summer vacation time has greatly decreased because of required teacher training activities during the summer break. Laura also knows what the average workday is like for a teacher because both of her parents are teachers. Rising at 5:30 a.m. to be at school for bus duty by 6:45, teaching until 3:30, staying the mandatory one hour after students leave, and then coming home with papers to grade until 8:00 p.m. makes for a long day. Accountants generally get less vacation time than teachers, but at a successful firm, Laura could expect days off for the major holidays and eventually several weeks of vacation. If Laura chose to set up her own accounting practice, she would ultimately be the one to decide her holidays. Laura could likely find a job as an accountant that enabled her to have a typical 8:00 to 5:00 workday. She could go home and not have to think about work until the next morning.

While Laura is not motivated solely by money, salary is an important consideration. The average starting salary for public school teachers is much lower than entry-level salaries for many other professions. In Laura's city, the starting salary for teachers is $28,000. Laura worries that the salary would not enable her to afford a nice apartment, pay off her student loans, and live the way she would like to live. By contrast, people who graduate with a degree in accounting can find entry-level jobs with salaries of about $35,000 where Laura lives. Laura has read that some accountants in her area start at even higher salaries. Potentially, she could start with an entry-level salary of $38,000. That is $10,000 more per year than entry-level teaching salaries in her town, and it would enable her to pay her debts and live the way she would like.

Point 2: vacation time and work hours. Point 2 is the writer's second major supporting point.

Subject A (teaching): vacation time

Details

Subject A (teaching): work hours

Subject B (accounting): vacation time

Details

Subject B (accounting): work hours

Point 3: salary. This is the writer's final major supporting point.

Subject A (teaching): teachers' salaries

Details

Subject B (accounting): accountants' salaries

Details

Suppose the writer had decided to use a block (subject-by-subject) arrangement rather than a point-by-point arrangement. How would the body paragraphs differ? Notice that in the following brief example featuring a block arrangement, the essay includes six body paragraphs—three "point" paragraphs for each subject.

Body Paragraphs of "Teaching? Or Not" (Block Arrangement)

Subject A: teaching major

Body paragraph—point 1: educational requirements

First, in Laura's state, students who want to teach high school have to complete a degree in their educational field (such as math, English, or science) and then complete the education courses required for teacher certification. What that would mean for Laura is an extra year of college (at a cost of several thousand dollars) to meet the education requirements. Because Laura is eager to get out of college and into the workforce, the extra year of education makes an education degree less attractive than an accounting degree.

Subject A: teaching major

Point 1: educational requirements for a teaching major

(continued)

Body paragraph—point 2: vacation time and work hours

Body paragraph—point 3: salary

Subject B: accounting major

Body paragraph—point 1: educational requirements

    The educational requirements for an accounting degree would enable Laura to graduate more quickly than the requirements for an education degree would. For an accounting degree, Laura would need to complete four years of college work with accounting as her major. She could graduate "on time" (after four years) if she were to major in accounting. Also, accounting students are not required to complete internships, so Laura would have to worry only about getting her college work done—not also about working in an internship on the side.

Body paragraph—point 2: vacation time and work hours

Body paragraph—point 3: salary

> Subject B: accounting major
>
> Point 1: educational requirements for an accounting major

A Comparison-Contrast Text: Conclusion

As is true for any text, the writer must bring the essay to a satisfactory conclusion. One way to conclude would be to tell readers the decision Laura made—and that's exactly what the writer of this essay chose to do. Alternatively, comparison-contrast essays may conclude by letting the reader determine which of the compared items is preferable. The conclusion to the sample essay follows.

Conclusion of "Teaching? Or Not"

    Making the choice to teach is not easy. Compared with other jobs, a career in teaching means additional training and a lower paycheck. While those who choose to teach do get a few extra rewards, such as personal satisfaction and summer vacation time, the rewards are just not enough for many people. In the end, Laura decided to become an accountant because, in her words, "I just couldn't afford to be a teacher."

> Conclusion: ends with a quote

PRACTICE Analyzing a Comparison-Contrast Text

On a separate sheet, answer the following questions about "Teaching? Or Not."

1. Which arrangement—point-by-point or block (subject-by-subject)—do you think would work best for an essay comparing two restaurants? Explain your answer.

2. In "Teaching? Or Not" the writer chose three points to consider: educational requirements, vacation time and work hours, and salary. Make a list of four additional points the writer could have used to compare and contrast teaching and accounting.

3. If you were asked to compare and contrast two different homes and then choose the home you liked best, what three points of comparison would be most important to you? Explain why.

4. Remember that one guideline is to compare and contrast things in the same category. Imagine an essay in which a writer claims that Beau's Restaurant—a very expensive steakhouse—is the best place to eat in town. To prove his point, the writer compares Beau's Restaurant with the local McDonald's and Wendy's. Why would such a comparison be unfair?

USING COMPARISON-CONTRAST IN YOUR WRITING

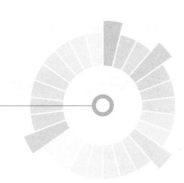

To use the comparison-contrast text pattern in your writing, follow these guidelines.

1. Ask yourself how classification suits your purpose and topic. While classification can be used to accomplish each writing purpose, it must also be appropriate for the topic you select. If showing the similarities and/or differences between two or more subjects is the primary way you will support your thesis statement, comparison-contrast should be the right text pattern to use for your essay.

2. Determine the specific subjects you will compare or contrast. Be precise about the subjects you are analyzing. If you are comparing high school with college, for example, narrow the subjects to make your topic more manageable. Comparing high school students' attitudes with college students' attitudes is a more precise topic and is more easily planned than a broad comparison of high school and college.

3. Make sure your comparison is fair. It is unfair to compare items in two different categories. Suppose a writer attempts to convince readers that children should be encouraged to eat ice cream due to its dairy content as much as they are encouraged to drink milk. Many people would say that ice cream and milk are not in the same category because of the difference in sugar content. To use comparison persuasively, make sure to choose subjects that are in the same category.

4. Determine whether you will compare your subjects (analyze similarities), contrast them (analyze differences), or do both. Very often, comparison-contrast texts include both similarities and differences. Some writing tasks, however, may require you to choose either to compare or to contrast. For example, a geology assignment may require students to write about the differences in the types of rocks found in their hometowns. Because recognizing the differences is the skill the instructor is trying to help students develop, the focus of the assignment will be on contrasting rather than comparing.

5. Determine the points of comparison you will analyze. To determine the points of comparison and contrast, think about your writing purpose. To compare two potential careers, the essay in this section uses the comparative points of educational requirements, vacation time and work hours, and potential salary. The points you choose should be the most pertinent points in the discussion. For example, one could compare the type of clothing teachers can wear to work with the type of clothing accountants can wear to work, but this point would not be as important as other points of comparison.

6. Decide whether to use a block arrangement or a point-by-point arrangement. If you are comparing two subjects and have multiple points of comparison, a point-by-point arrangement will usually be more effective. If you are comparing multiple subjects and have only a few points of comparison, a block arrangement will work well.

Arrangements for a Comparison-Contrast Essay	
Block (Subject-by-Subject) Arrangement: Best for just two subjects with multiple points of comparison	Point-by-Point Arrangement: Best for multiple subjects with only a few points of comparison
Subject A • Point 1 • Point 2 • Point 3 • Point 4	Point 1 • Subject A • Subject B • Subject C

(continued)

Arrangements for a Comparison-Contrast Essay *(continued)*	
Block (Subject-by-Subject) Arrangement: Best for just two subjects with multiple points of comparison	Point-by-Point Arrangement: Best for multiple subjects with only a few points of comparison
Subject B • Point 1 • Point 2 • Point 3 • Point 4	Point 2 • Subject A • Subject B • Subject C Point 3 • Subject A • Subject B • Subject C

NOTE: The actual number of subjects and points will vary, as the arrangements above demonstrate.

7. Write a thesis statement, and construct a simple outline. The thesis statement you write should indicate the two subjects being compared. If you choose to write a closed thesis statement, include the points of comparison, like this:

> Determining whether to buy or lease a vehicle requires considering monthly payment, mileage limit, warranty, and ownership status.

PRACTICE Using Comparison-Contrast in Your Writing

Use the preceding steps to write a comparison-contrast essay. Choose one of the following topics, or select your own.

A. Select two potential career fields. Choose points of comparison that are important to you, such as salary, type of work, job satisfaction, and typical work hours. Write an essay in which you compare both career fields.

B. What are the differences between courses that require you to master a skill—such as a writing or welding course—and courses that require you to think about information, such as history or sociology? Write an essay in which you discuss at least three points of comparison.

C. Write an essay in which you compare and contrast two movies in the same genre. For example, you could compare two horror movies you have seen. Choose appropriate points of comparison, such as the actors' performances, the plot, and special effects.

☉ Cause and Effect ☉

What caused a bridge to collapse? What are the effects of illiteracy? What will happen if the Arctic ice cap melts? These kinds of questions require that we assess causes and effects. Many subjects lend themselves to thinking about cause and effect; thus, it is common to read analyses of *why* something happened or *what will happen if* certain actions are taken. A discussion of causes and/or effects is called a *causal analysis.*

■ Figuring out causes and effects is not always easy. Scientists may agree that climate change is happening, but world governments cannot agree on the actions that will effectively avert its consequences.

RECOGNIZING THE CAUSE AND EFFECT PATTERN IN READINGS

To identify the cause and effect pattern in a text, look for these characteristics and key words.

CHARACTERISTICS OF THE CAUSE AND EFFECT PATTERN

- The text primarily concerns causes, effects, or both.
- The text concerns phenomena or events.
- The text makes predictions or attempts to explain causes of past events.
- The text examines one cause and/or effect, multiple causes and/or effects, or chains of causes and/or effects.

Key Words for the Cause and Effect Pattern			
as a result	at last	because of	cause
consequently	effect	for that reason	if . . . then
since	so	therefore	thus

Cause and Effect in Supporting Details

An analysis of cause and effect often answers the questions "Why?" and "What if?" In some texts, the writer may use the discussion of a cause or effect (or both) as one type of support among others.

Suppose the United States is considering sending troops to the aid of a foreign country in turmoil (let's call this country Otherland). A reporter is writing an article to evaluate all of the options the United States has. The reporter can provide some background about what *caused* the unrest in Otherland so that readers learn why the United States is considering intervening in the first place. After discussing the causes of the unrest, the reporter can describe the effects of the current situation and then discuss the possible types of action the United States could take. Used in this way, the cause and effect discussion becomes a supporting detail in the reporter's article; other details are likely to be other options that the United States should consider. A partial outline for such an article might look like this.

Using Cause and Effect as a Supporting Detail

Topic: Intervening in Otherland

Thesis statement: The United States needs to consider every possible option before intervening in Otherland.

INTRODUCTION
   Paragraph 1

BODY
   Paragraph 2: History of the problem

   - What *caused* the unrest
   - Current situation (effects of the fighting, turmoil, etc.)

   Paragraph 3: Option 1—The United States could wait and do nothing for the time being.

   Paragraph 4: Option 2—The United States could send troops.

The article is structured around a list of possible actions; thus, the reporter will likely discuss the potential effects of each action, along with other information, such as the cost of the action, public opinion about the action, and so on.

Cause and Effect as a Text Pattern

Discussions of causes and effects can be complicated. For instance, what causes a recession? Economists can find so many possible causes that figuring out the most likely ones is truly difficult.

Because cause and effect relationships are so complicated, it is not unusual to see entire essays (and books) devoted to explaining these relationships. Such texts are often organized using cause and effect as a text pattern. The cause and effect text pattern may also be used to explain the *domino effect*, a chain reaction that occurs when one effect causes another effect, which causes another effect, and so on. For example, drought causes the price of hay and corn to increase. The increase in hay and corn prices drives up the cost of beef. The increase in the cost of beef is passed along to consumers, and the net result is that consumers have less money after paying for groceries. An essay that discusses a domino effect might be organized chronologically so that the writer begins with the first cause, moves to its effect, discusses the effect as a new cause, and continues this pattern.

Essays that present causes and effects can achieve a variety of writing purposes. Informative writing often presents causes, effects, or both. For example, a business textbook chapter might explain the positive effects of Internet marketing. An essay on a successful business might present the good decisions that caused the business to succeed.

Analysis is always required for writing about cause and effect relationships, and sometimes analysis is the primary purpose for writing. An essay that presents an environmental problem, such as the rise of sea levels, might present an analysis of its causes and effects.

Sometimes the goal of a causal analysis is to evaluate. For example, a writer may evaluate different options for helping needy children receive free lunches during the summer. In such an essay, the writer will probably evaluate the potential effects of a number of solutions and will determine the solution that would work the best.

Finally, cause and effect is used extensively in persuasive writing. Any time a writer advocates a certain action, a discussion of that action's effects can be used for support. For example, a writer may argue that buying American-made products benefits American workers. To support that argument, the writer would probably present the effects on workers when Americans buy (or fail to buy) American-made products.

Persuasive writing can also focus on causes. What is causing decreases in the honey-bee population? The causes are widely debated; thus, a persuasively focused paper could use a cause and effect text pattern to present a writer's belief—based on evidence—about causes for this phenomenon.

Depending on the number of causes and effects under consideration, a writer can use several different methods of organization, as the cause and effect models show.

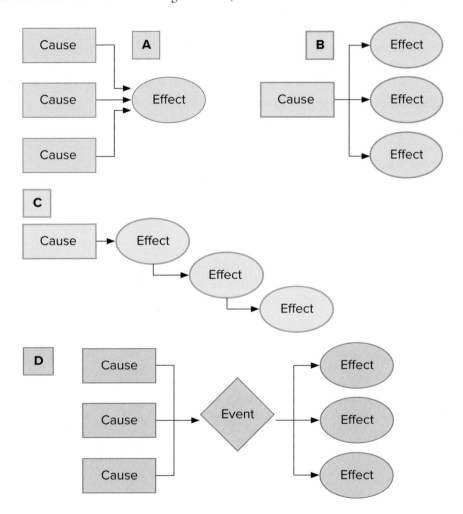

■ Cause and Effect Models (A) Several causes can have the same effect or can combine to create an effect. (B) One cause can have a number of effects. (C) In the domino effect, a cause can start a chain of events. (D) Several causes can come together to produce several effects.

ANALYZING A CAUSE AND EFFECT TEXT

The writers of effective cause and effect essays organize text elements in the way that best suits the subject, purpose, and reader.

A Cause and Effect Text: Introduction and Thesis Statement

In essays developed through a discussion of causes and effects, introductory paragraphs commonly use key words that focus readers' attention on causal analysis. While some writers provide a thesis statement early on, others first demonstrate the causes and/or effects and end their essay with a thesis statement that summarizes the text's information. In either case, the thesis statement will consist of the causes, the effects, or both causes and effects.

The following selection from *Natural Disasters*, a science textbook, demonstrates how the cause and effect pattern can be used to inform. Notice that the writer provides the topic but waits until the conclusion paragraph to offer the thesis statement.

Introduction Paragraph of "US Dust Bowl, 1930s" by Patrick Leon Abbott

Might the worst conditions of the recent past serve as a prologue to the future? One of the greatest weather disasters in US history occurred during the 1930s, when several years of drought turned grain-growing areas in the center of the nation into the "Dust Bowl." Failed crops and malnutrition caused abandonment of thousands of farms and the broad scale migration of displaced people, mostly to California and other western states. This human drama was captured in many articles and books, including *The Grapes of Wrath* by John Steinbeck:	Introduction Causes (failed crops, malnutrition) and effects (abandonment, migration) are summarized.
Now the wind grew strong and hard and it worked at the rain crust in the corn fields. Little by little the sky was darkened by the mixing dust, and the wind felt over the earth, loosened the dust and carried it away.	Note that the thesis statement does not appear in the introduction.

The introduction presents two effects of the Dust Bowl: failed crops and malnutrition. These, in turn, caused additional effects: people abandoned their farms to move West. In the body of the selection, we can expect the writer to elaborate on these causes and effects.

A Cause and Effect Text: Body Paragraphs and Their Organization

In the body paragraphs that follow, the writer first explains a cause in a long paragraph and follows with an explanation of the effects in another long paragraph. In the third body paragraph, the writer presents an alternative explanation of the cause of the Dust Bowl and shows why he rejects the explanation.

Body Paragraphs of "US Dust Bowl, 1930s" by Patrick Leon Abbott

What happened to cause the drought? Recurrent large-scale meanders in the upper-air flow created ridges of high pressure with clockwise flows resulting in descending air. The upper-level high-pressure air was already dry, but as it sank, it became warmer,	First major supporting point (implied): The Dust Bowl was caused by particular weather events.

(continued)

thus reaching the ground hot, dry, and thirsty. As the winds blew across the ground surface, they sucked up moisture, killing plants and exposing bare soil to erosion. Wind-blown clouds of dust built into towering masses of turbulent air and dust called rollers. When they rolled across an area, the Sun was darkened, and dust invaded every possible opening on a human body and came through every crack in a home. Dust even blew as visible masses across East Coast cities and blanketed ships at sea.	Domino effect: One natural event caused another, leading to drought. Effects: Drought affected human life.
The drought began in 1930, a particularly bad time. Only months before, in October 1929, the US stock market had crashed, and the nation's economy began sinking into the Great Depression. By 1931, farmers were becoming desperate. For example, a group of 500 armed farmers went to the town of England in Arkansas to seek food from the Red Cross. They were denied aid, so they went to the town's stores and took the food they needed. The event drew worldwide attention. Here were farmers from the US heartland who had helped feed the world during the early 20th century and through the ravages of World War I; now they could not even feed themselves.	Cause: The drought and the stock market crash made the Dust Bowl events even worse. This is the second major supporting point. Effect Third major supporting point (implied): The cause was not plowing practices.
The dust storms became even worse in 1934 and 1936. Some of the blame for the Dust Bowl was heaped onto the farmers for plowing deeply through drought-tolerant native grasses and exposing bare soil to the winds. The plowed lands were sowed with seeds of plants that could not handle drought and thus died, exposing more soil. The farming practices were not the best, but they did not cause the drought; they just accentuated its effects. Evidence showing that droughts are common is found in the archaeological record. For example, droughts in the past probably led to the downfall of the Anasazi civilization of the southwestern United States and the migration of its people to areas with more dependable water supplies.	Alternative explanation of cause Alternative explanation rejected

Notice that as the writer discusses the causes and effects of the Dust Bowl, he also comments about the events that made the Dust Bowl's effects even worse—the stock market crash and the drought. The last body paragraph rejects a proposed cause of the drought.

A Cause and Effect Text: Conclusion

In this particular text, the writer saves the thesis statement for the conclusion paragraph. Thus, the conclusion serves both to provide the writer's main point and to end the selection.

Conclusion Paragraph of "US Dust Bowl, 1930s" by Patrick Leon Abbott

The Dust Bowl drought affected more than just local agriculture. Combined with the stock market crash, it caused fundamental changes in the economic, social, and political systems of the United States.	Two-sentence thesis statement: summarizes the causes and effects presented and functions as the conclusion

PRACTICE   Analyzing a Cause and Effect Text

On a separate sheet of paper, answer the following questions about "US Dust Bowl, 1930s."

1. What caused the Dust Bowl?
2. What are the relationships among the drought, the stock market crash, and the Great Depression?
3. One body paragraph describes the natural domino effect that created the drought. Was the effect on people part of the domino effect? Why or why not?
4. Think of a weather event that occurred during your lifetime. What were the effects of this event on people and the environment? Write a paragraph to explain.

USING CAUSE AND EFFECT IN YOUR WRITING

Many subjects require that writers address causes and effects. If you are writing a paper and think cause and effect may be a helpful text pattern to use, follow these steps.

1. Ask yourself how cause and effect suits your topic and purpose. Will a discussion of causes and/or effects be the primary focus of your topic? If so, a cause and effect text pattern is appropriate. Events from the past may leave us wondering about their causes, so they are good subjects to consider for such an essay. A topic that prompts us to analyze future effects is also appropriate for the cause and effect text pattern.

While some cause and effect essays consider the past and others consider the future, another option is to think of issues that affect us now and to ask questions about their causes and/or effects. For example, with all of the information available about the harm of smoking cigarettes, many people still smoke them. Why? What causes people to continue a habit they know is dangerous to their health? Find a topic in which you are interested and ask, "Why did this happen?" or "What will be the effects of this event?"

2. Analyze the causes and/or effects of your topic. Use questions to help you determine causes and effects.

- What possible causes (or effects) can you think of for the questions you asked in step 1 above? List them. List as many as you can without censoring your ideas.
- Looking back at the causes (or effects) you have listed, ask, "Which of these are the *least* likely or *least* important causes or effects?" Go back to the list and cross out those that are least likely or least important. If a domino effect is involved, write out each cause and effect in the process.
- Select the most likely causes (or effects) to present in your essay.

3. Analyze the logic of the causes and/or effects you will present. It is, unfortunately, common to make logical errors when you are determining causes and effects. Three common errors are confusing correlations with causes, making faulty predictions, and oversimplifying possible causes.

- **Pitfall 1: Confusing correlations with causes.** A **correlation** is simply a relationship between two things. For example, we have evidence that eating fast food is correlated with having poor health. Imagine, for example, that your friend who eats only fast food (burgers, fries, and shakes, for example) develops a brain tumor. Can we say there is a causal relationship between eating fast food and developing a brain tumor?

Although some research shows that fast food and poor health are related, we do not have enough research to know whether eating fast food specifically *causes* brain tumors. In your friend's case, we see a correlation between eating lots of fast food and developing a brain tumor. However, we cannot prove one caused the other.

The correlation pitfall occurs when we assume that because two things appear to be related, one must have caused the other. If you do not have clear evidence linking a cause to an effect, you cannot assume a causal relationship.

- **Pitfall 2: Making faulty predictions.** When we consider taking an action, being able to make accurate predictions is important. Consider drinking and driving. We cannot say that a person who drinks and drives will definitely be involved in an accident. However, we know from evidence that a high percentage of auto accidents involve a driver who has been drinking alcohol. Thus we *can* say that a person who is driving under the influence of alcohol is *more likely* to be in a car accident than a driver who has not been drinking.

  Sometimes it is tempting to make predictions without much evidence because those predictions might help us win an argument or make a point. For example, someone might claim that if Americans agree to gun control laws, then eventually the government will take away people's guns. This is an *unreasonable prediction* because it is not based on evidence. Often, unreasonable predictions are attempts to make the listener fearful and to thus believe the speaker.

  To avoid making faulty predictions, keep the following questions in mind: "How do you know?" and "Would a reasonable person agree with this prediction?" You can avoid this pitfall by making sure you have sound reasons for your predictions, being certain your predictions would be acceptable to a general audience, and having proof to support them.

- **Pitfall 3: Oversimplifying possible causes.** Failing to consider all the possible causes for an event often results in oversimplification. For example, if you come down with a head cold after flying on a plane, you may blame the head cold on your air travel. This thinking, however, has oversimplified the situation. Touching such objects as doorknobs, grocery carts, and escalator rails can introduce germs that cause illnesses like colds. However, colds take several days to incubate. So if you get a head cold two days after flying, it is likely to have been caused by contact with germs before your flight.

  The best way to determine the cause of an event or phenomenon is to make a list of all the possible causes, cross out the causes that are not applicable to the situation, and try to find a cause that is reasonable.

4. Use very careful language to express causes and effects. After finding a reasonable cause, you will then need to use precise language to express the causal connection you have found. Consider this statement of cause:

Jana's decision to quit her job is probably what made her depressed.

By using *probably*, the writer acknowledges that there may be other causes. Thus, the writer is more accurate, precise, and careful in her language, and this care shows she has thought critically about possible causes.

One way to use more precise language is to use qualifiers, words like *may have, might*, and *likely*. Using qualifiers like these when appropriate will help you make more precise statements about causes and effects.

Common Qualifiers			
a few	most	often	commonly
could	entirely	few	many
may	might	rarely	possibly
seems	seldom	some	sometimes
suggests	the majority	unlikely	usually

5. Write a thesis statement, and construct a simple outline. Determine the best way to present the causes and/or effects you will be discussing. Create an outline in which you detail the specific causes and effects you will address and the order in which you will address them.

PRACTICE Using Cause and Effect in Your Writing

Use the preceding steps to write a cause and effect essay. Choose one of the following topics, or select your own.

A. Write an essay in which you discuss a trend—for example, an increase or decrease in crime in your city or neighborhood—and the causes (or effects) of that trend.

B. Write a cause and effect essay about a good decision you made in life. Explain what caused you to make the decision and the effects of having made the decision.

C. Write an essay in which you discuss the causes or effects of one of the following: alcoholism, faith, a particular disease or condition, worry, a social problem, volunteering, living in a clean (or messy) place.

⊙ Process Analysis ⊙

Perhaps at some point in your life, you struggled to make sense of the driving directions someone gave you. Or maybe you tried following a bread recipe, only to find that the result was an inedible lump of dough. These kinds of experiences emphasize how important it is to explain processes clearly and accurately.

The **process analysis** pattern usually presents the stages, steps, or phases of a process in a particular order. It can also be used to show how a particular historical event or discovery came about. Certain key words and transitions are often used in process analysis texts.

RECOGNIZING THE PROCESS ANALYSIS PATTERN IN READINGS

To identify the process analysis pattern, look for these characteristics and key words.

CHARACTERISTICS OF THE PROCESS ANALYSIS PATTERN

- Process analysis texts provide discussion of a process, procedure, method, course of action, or protocol.
- These texts present a sequence of steps (*first, second, third*, or some other sequencing indicators).
- Process analysis texts provide explanations about how the steps work or how to follow them.

Key Words for the Process Analysis Pattern				
after	before	finally	first, second, third . . .	later
meanwhile	next	now	phase	stage
step	then	to begin	to continue	to end

Process Analysis in Supporting Details

A writer might briefly explain a process in a body paragraph of an essay to give the audience background information. Suppose a writer is composing a narrative essay to tell the story of someone who immigrated to the United States. The writer may devote a paragraph to explaining the process of becoming an American citizen if this information is necessary for readers to understand the immigrant's story. The partial outline that follows shows where a writer may use a brief explanation of a process as a type of support.

Using Process Analysis as a Supporting Detail

Topic: An immigrant's story

Thesis statement: Despite seemingly insurmountable odds, Robbie Kam-Lin realized his dream of American citizenship.

INTRODUCTION
Paragraph 1

BODY
Paragraph 2: Problems in his native land

Paragraph 3: Getting to the United States

Paragraph 4: The long path to citizenship

- The process of becoming an American citizen

What Should I Expect From the Naturalization Process?

Preparing to Apply

- Read *A Guide to Naturalization.*
- Complete the Naturalization Eligibility Worksheet.
- Get an "Application for Naturalization" (Form N-400).
- Visit our website at **www.uscis.gov**.

Completing Your Application and Getting Photographed

- Complete your application.
- Get two passport-style photographs taken.
- Collect the necessary documents.
- Send your application, passport-style photographs, documents, and fee (DO NOT SEND CASH) to the appropriate Lockbox Facility or Service Center.
- Keep a copy of everything you send to USCIS.

Getting Fingerprinted

- Receive an appointment letter from USCIS.
- Go to the fingerprinting location.
- Get your fingerprints taken.
- Mail additional documents if USCIS requests them.
- Wait for USCIS to schedule your interview.

Being Interviewed

- Receive an appointment for your interview.
- Go to your local USCIS office at the specified time.
- Bring state-issued identification, Permanent Resident Card, and any additional documents specific to your case.
- Answer questions about your application and background.
- Take the English and civics tests.
- Receive case status.

Taking the Oath

- Receive a ceremony date.
- Check in at the ceremony.
- Return your Permanent Resident Card.
- Answer questions about what you have done since your interview.
- Take the Oath of Allegiance.
- Receive your Certificate of Naturalization.

Process Analysis as a Text Pattern

Process analysis can be used for a variety of purposes. For instance, when the sole purpose of an essay is to describe how an event came about or to explain how to perform a task, a writer can use process analysis as a text pattern. In *A Guide to Naturalization*, a brochure published by the US Citizenship and Immigration Services, shown above, process analysis is used to outline the steps a person must take to apply for and acquire US citizenship. Process analysis can also be used to explain a process a writer is proposing, such as a new way to handle incoming orders to improve speed and efficiency. Often the purpose of process analysis texts is to inform. An explanation of how global warming works, for example, could be presented using process analysis.

Explaining a process can also be part of an analysis. A scholarly article in an engineering journal might use process analysis to examine the method used to build a bridge that failed. The purpose of such a discussion may also be to evaluate: by examining processes, one can evaluate the best process to use for a given procedure.

Sometimes writers argue about processes to determine which processes are appropriate, which work the best, or which are the most ethical. For example, what is the best process to use to reunite an adopted child with a birth parent? What process should doctors and hospital staff use to determine whether a person is legally dead? What process should hospitals use for organ donation? These are debatable issues that are appropriate for process analysis papers.

Most process analysis papers can be organized by the stages or phases of the process being described. The outline that follows presents an example of how process analysis can be used to structure an informative essay.

A Simple Outline for a Process Analysis Pattern Essay

Topic: Creating a plan to improve customer service

Thesis statement: Any business can improve customer service by using a five-step process.

INTRODUCTION
   Paragraph 1: Introduction and thesis statement

BODY
   Paragraph 2: Stage 1—Examining the situation
   Paragraph 3: Stage 2—Exploring solutions
   Paragraph 4: Stage 3—Implementing a solution
   Paragraph 5: Stage 4—Assessing the solution
   Paragraph 6: Stage 5—Adjusting or creating a new solution

CONCLUSION
   Paragraph 7: Conclusion

ANALYZING A PROCESS ANALYSIS TEXT

Some specific features are typically found in the introduction, thesis statement, body paragraphs, and conclusion of process analysis texts.

A Process Analysis Text: Introduction and Thesis Statement

The introduction paragraph of a process analysis text states the topic and usually includes the thesis statement. The example below is a brief article from the New Jersey Department of Education that presents steps for making schools less violent.

Introduction Paragraph from "School Safety: Three Steps to Make the Peace"

Recent tragic school shootings remind us of the important role each child and each adult has in maintaining the safety of a school. There are three actions children, youth or adults can take to improve the safety of their learning community.	Simple introduction Thesis statement

A Process Analysis Text: Body Paragraphs and Their Organization

The body paragraphs of a process analysis essay describe the steps, phases, or stages of the process in question. Often, each body paragraph presents one particular step, phase, or stage, as in the example that follows.

Body Paragraphs from "School Safety: Three Steps to Make the Peace"

Treat each other with respect. Encourage, teach and above all role model respectful behavior. Identify acts of kindness, give attention to positive and cooperative behavior. Encourage children and youth to "make the peace" in their classroom and hallway. Many districts teach all students conflict resolution skills and train students to be peer mediators to help resolve conflicts. Address name-calling and bullying directly. Both students and staff can say clearly that name-calling and intimidation are not appropriate "in our school." Staff can help to change the climate of harassment by giving positive attention to the person being bullied. Publicly and directly tell the person who has been bullied that what happened to them was not OK, and check to see if there is any assistance you can give them. After an intervention with name-calling, acts of intimidation or harassment, check back in with both the victim and the offender to see if the offending behavior has stopped.	First step (major supporting point 1) Second step (major supporting point 2)
Take threats seriously. If a student or an adult says they are thinking of harming themselves or others, tell a trusted adult. As a student, ask an adult to help you talk with the person who is making threats. As a staff person, work with both student support staff, administration and law enforcement to determine the seriousness of the threat. Work to address the needs of people affected or made fearful by a threat.	Third step (major supporting point 3)
For adults, there is an additional action step: keep weapons away from children and youth. Through newsletters, announcements at PTA/PTSO [parent teacher association/parent teacher student organization] meetings and at parent/teacher conferences, at ball games and concerts, remind adults that if they own a gun, to be sure that the weapon is disassembled, locked away and that the ammunition is locked in a separate place.	An additional step for adults (major supporting point 4)

A Process Analysis Text: Conclusion

The function of the conclusion paragraph is to add any remaining explanations, to comment on the process, and to end the text.

Conclusion Paragraph from "School Safety: Three Steps to Make the Peace"

In spite of incidents like school shootings, schools remain one of the safer places a child or adult can attend in our society. A person is three times more likely to be struck by lightning than to be shot in school. By working together, and supporting one another, parents, students and staff can make the school safe for everyone.	Simple conclusion: provides closure; includes information to help readers

PRACTICE   Analyzing a Process Analysis Text

On a separate sheet, answer the following questions about "School Safety: Three Steps to Make the Peace."

1. What is the writer's purpose? Explain.

2. Do you believe the steps the writer gives for keeping the peace in schools are effectively discussed and explained? Could the writer have presented them in a more convincing way? If so, how?

3. For whom is this article written? How can you tell?

4. How does the fourth step differ from the other steps? Do you think the writer's presentation of the fourth step is effective? Explain.

USING PROCESS ANALYSIS IN YOUR WRITING

You can use process analysis to structure an essay when you want to guide readers through the steps of a process (such as applying for citizenship) or when you want to describe the stages of an event or phenomenon (such as photosynthesis). The guidelines that follow will help you plan a process analysis essay.

1. Determine whether process analysis will fit your topic and your purpose. Process analysis is effective only for papers that present, analyze, evaluate, or make arguments about processes. If you believe your topic is appropriate, determine what you hope to accomplish by presenting the process. Is your goal to present a simple overview of the process? Is the purpose of your writing to teach readers to use the process you will describe? Keep your purpose in mind as you select the types of details to include in your paper.

2. Carefully and critically consider your audience and what your audience needs to know as you explain the process. When explanations of processes go wrong, the reason is usually a failure on the part of the writer to think about the needs of the audience. If you can clearly identify your audience, think about the particular knowledge this audience already has. A general audience cannot be expected to have specific knowledge of specialized subjects. For example, while you can expect a general audience to know that refining oil is an industrial process, you cannot expect such readers to know anything specific about the process.

3. Use prewriting to determine the particular steps of the process you will discuss. Prewriting can help you determine the stages, steps, or phases involved in the process. Read through your prewriting critically to decide the best way to arrange your information. For example, determine whether each step needs its own paragraph or whether some steps belong in a paragraph together. Also, make sure you do not leave out any steps. Thinking like a reader will help you anticipate your readers' needs.

4. Write a thesis statement, and create a simple outline. Choose the best order in which to present each step or stage. Usually, steps or stages are presented in chronological order.

5. Have someone read over your rough draft, looking for missing steps. If you are familiar with the process you are describing, you may forget to include small, but important, steps. For example, a chef knows that to make an omelet, she needs to grease an omelet pan; because she is so familiar with the process, she may leave out this step, thinking readers will certainly know to grease the pan. Make sure you include all the necessary steps in your essay.

PRACTICE Using Process Analysis in Your Writing

Use the preceding steps to write a process analysis essay. Choose one of the following topics, or select your own.

A. Write about a process you have mastered. For example, if you know how to make tamales, you might write an essay explaining the process. If you understand the way an internal combustion engine works, you might write an essay about it. Write with the idea that your essay will be read by someone who knows nothing about the process you are describing.

B. What is the process many people use to find a life partner? Describe the process in steps.

C. Write an essay in which you discuss how parents can build their children's self-esteem. Alternatively, write an essay about the stages teens go through as they become young men and young women.

Recognizing and Using Mixed Text Patterns

Most professional writers use a mixture of patterns as supporting details in their writing. When you read an essay, mark the types of supporting details you find. If most of the supporting details are one particular type, the essay may be written using a single text pattern. For example, an essay that presents primarily causes and effects is likely to be written using the cause and effect text pattern. If the types of supporting details vary, the writer is probably using a mixture of text patterns to support his thesis statement.

In a mixed pattern essay, a writer may devote a few sentences to offering a definition. She may then discuss a cause or an effect or make a brief comparison. The writer chooses the type of supporting detail to use based on her writing purpose.

To analyze mixed pattern essays, ask yourself what the writer is doing in each body paragraph. More specifically, ask questions such as these:

- Is the writer telling a short *story*?
- Is the writer giving an *example* or providing an *illustration*?
- Is the writer *defining* a term or concept?
- Is the writer putting information into a *category*?
- Is the writer explaining a *cause* or *effect*?
- Is the writer making a *comparison*?
- Is the writer explaining the stages, phases, or steps of a *process*?

In addition to finding these text patterns used as support, you may also find other supporting elements, such as *rhetorical questions* (questions to which the writer knows the answer), the use of facts and data, descriptions, summaries of other people's ideas, and explanations. By analyzing each body paragraph and jotting down the type of support the paragraph contains, you will be able to more easily identify the writer's thesis statement and major supporting points. Additionally, you will recognize how writers use mixed patterns and will be able to emulate the strategy of mixing text patterns in your own essays.

What follows is a humorous essay that includes a variety of types of support. As you read it, notice the annotations about the support the writer uses.

Chess Pie— The Making of a Secret Weapon

People where I'm from in Virginia know chess pie, so if I offer them a slice, their only question is, "chocolate, lemon, or pineapple?" When I'm away, though, I frequently run into more questions. *What is a chess pie? Why is it called that?* Both of these questions are difficult to answer exactly. I usually ask my dinner guests to try some and see if they really need more information after that. Usually after one bite, all they ask for is the recipe.	Anecdote
A chess pie is a sort of custard pie characterized by its creamy filling, intense flavor, and the sugary crust that naturally forms on the top as it bakes. No one knows the exact origin of the name, but one theory says that in the old days before refrigeration, this type of pie stored well in the pie chest, thus becoming known as a "ches(t) pie." Chess pies come in a variety of flavors, including pineapple and coconut, but lemon and chocolate are the most common. "Common" is not the right word, though: these pies are phenomenal. Words cannot describe their intense flavor and silky texture.	Definition Definition Category/classification
While most recipes for desserts stress the importance of fresh ingredients, the beauty of chocolate chess pie is that you can keep most of the ingredients—sugar, evaporated milk, vanilla, and baker's chocolate—in the cupboard for months, and the	

(continued)

rest (butter and eggs) you probably have around, anyway. That means that at any given moment, you can make a chocolate chess pie that will impress your toughest food critic friend or win over a special date a lot better than, say, an instant pudding pie with a graham cracker crust. And while the flavor says, "gourmet," chocolate chess pies are easy to make. You don't even need to know how to make your own pie crust: just get the rolled-up kind from the dairy case, give it a fancy edge by pressing it with your fingertips or a fork, and no one will know.

Illustration

Process

Clean up is easy for a chocolate chess pie, since you make the filling all in one pot. All you have to do is melt some butter and baker's chocolate (that's raw chocolate with no sugar added, so don't nibble it) in a pot, stir in the sugar, crack in and stir up the eggs, and then stir in vanilla and evaporated milk. Pour it into pie crusts and bake it. A lemon chess pie is a bit more complicated since you have to juice and grate the lemons, but it's still not very difficult. Just mash together sugar, a pinch of salt, and butter until it's like wet sand, then add eggs, lemon juice, and a drizzle of milk. You have plenty of time while the pies are baking to clean the one pot or bowl you used to make the filling.

Definition

Process

Be aware that different ingredients can produce different—and sometimes quite pleasing—effects. For lemon chess pie, insist on real lemons, not the juice from a squeeze bottle, and get organic lemons if you can—the flavor is much better. You wouldn't play a symphony on a plastic violin, would you? Once you get good at this recipe, you can experiment with Meyer lemons, key limes, and other citrus fruits. The ingredients for lemon chess pie are simple, too—lemons, butter, sugar, eggs, milk, and pie crust—but the flavor will make you legendary at any pot luck. Remember to grate some fresh lemon rind on the top before you bake for a little extra intense lemon flavor.

Cause and effect

Rhetorical question

Cause and effect

I'll leave you with this bit of advice: always choose a recipe that makes two pies. It's just as easy to make two at a time, and you'll want one to keep and one to give away to a new neighbor, someone you'd like to thank, a friend, or someone you'd like to have for a friend. Sharing is part of this pie's tradition. And who would turn down a pie? Let this pie be your secret weapon, too, for making friends and impressing the ones you already have. It's easy as pie.

Rhetorical question

PRACTICE *Analyzing a Mixed Pattern Essay*

On a separate sheet, answer the following questions about "Chess Pie—The Making of a Secret Weapon."

1. The title suggests the essay might present a process. Does it? Explain your answer.
2. The annotations point out some of the major types of support the writer uses. Can you find additional types of support in the essay? If so, explain what they are and where they are used.
3. Could the writer have presented this information using a single text pattern? Why or why not?
4. In what way does the writer use classification? Explain.

MIXING TEXT PATTERNS IN YOUR WRITING

When you plan an essay, consider whether you can best communicate your main idea by using a single text pattern to organize your thoughts or by using a variety of text patterns as support. We will follow the process used by Marcus as he composes an essay using mixed text patterns.

Marcus is writing an essay for his biology class. The instructor has asked each student to write an informative essay about a particular illness. Each student has been assigned a particular disease and has received an information sheet about it. After students submit their work, the instructor will make copies of each student's essay to distribute to the class: the essays must help students learn enough about each illness to be able to answer questions about it on a test. Thus, Marcus's essay needs to include enough information to give his classmates a thorough understanding of the illness.

What text pattern or patterns should Marcus use in his essay on his assigned subject, mononucleosis? Clearly, he will need to *define* the illness because readers will want to know what the disease is. But readers will have other questions as well. Marcus makes a list of the questions readers may have, and then he jots down the kinds of information that will help him answer those questions.

Readers' Potential Questions about Mononucleosis

1. What is it? definition
2. How do people get it? Is it contagious? cause and effect
3. How serious is it? cause and effect
4. What does it "look" like? Can you see it (like measles?) description
5. What does it feel like? illustration
6. What are its symptoms? part of definition, illustration
7. What parts of the body does the disease affect? cause and effect
8. Does the disease have long-lasting effects? cause and effect
9. How long does it take to get rid of it? cause and effect
10. How is it treated? process analysis
11. How can people prevent it? cause and effect

Marcus realizes that his essay does not fit into one text pattern. Rather, he will be using a variety of text patterns as supporting details.

What is the logical way to organize these patterns? To answer this question, Marcus determines what readers need to know first: most likely, they need a definition of mononucleosis. A description of the illness and examples of symptoms will enhance the definition, so he places those items together. Next, Marcus plans to talk about the causes and effects of mononucleosis and the process of treating it. Since understanding causes and effects is yet another way of getting a basic idea of what mononucleosis is, Marcus decides to discuss those as the second major supporting point in the essay. The final major supporting point is the treatment process, so he places that last. He also creates a thesis statement that unifies the major supporting points.

Thesis statement: Mononucleosis is a serious illness, but it is fairly common and is very treatable.

Major supporting point 1: Definition, description, and examples of symptoms

Major supporting point 2: Causes and effects

Major supporting point 3: Treatment process

To finish the outline, Marcus needs to include the supporting details he will use in each section of the body of his essay. At this point, Marcus consults the disease information handout his instructor provided. Using it, he finds specific information to plug into his outline. (He will give credit to the source of this information in his essay.) Here is how he organizes the supporting details (shown in italics).

A Simple Outline for a Mixed Pattern Essay

Thesis statement: Mononucleosis is a serious illness, but it is fairly common and is very treatable.

Major supporting point 1: Definition, description, and examples of symptoms

Definition: "Infectious mononucleosis (IM) is a disease that occurs in older children and adolescents when they develop a primary EBV infection" (Pediatrics).

Description and symptoms:

- *Usually appears in teens*
- *May not look sick but do feel sick*
- *Those infected may seem to simply be tired or lazy*
- *A rash can develop*
- *Pharyngitis*
- *Fever*
- *Profound fatigue*
- *Lymphadenopathy (swollen, enlarged lymph nodes)*

Major supporting point 2: Causes and effects

- *What causes it*
- *What causes it to spread*
- *What body parts it affects*
- *What serious damage it can cause*
  - *Short-term*
  - *Long-term*

Major supporting point 3: Treatment plan (process)

- *Rest (disease resolves on its own)*
- *No contact sports*
- *Over-the-counter medicines for pain and symptom relief*

Marcus can use his simple outline to draft paragraphs for his essay. Additionally, by noting the particular details he will use from his source, Marcus can take these details from his outline and integrate them into his essay, taking care to use the appropriate methods for giving credit to the source.

Complete the practice exercise that follows to try your hand at using mixed text patterns in an essay.

PRACTICE   Selecting Text Patterns for a Mixed Text Pattern Essay

Follow these steps to select text patterns and create an outline for an essay responding to the question, what is a "good parent?" Then write an essay in which you answer this question.

1. Use a prewriting process to create ideas about what makes a good parent.

2. Determine which ideas from your prewriting you would like to include in your essay.

3. Identify the best text pattern to use for presenting each idea.

4. Using the outline for the essay on mononucleosis as a model, write an outline for your essay.

5. Using your outline, compose the essay. Refer to the Quick Start Guide to Integrated Reading and Writing Assignments if you need assistance.

The Basic Elements of Argument

The word *argument* has a bad reputation. When we hear the word, we often think of an unpleasant disagreement or confrontation. We might think of a shouting match or an emotionally charged exchange of words between two angry people. Certainly, these kinds of exchanges are indeed arguments.

However, as the term is used academically, an **argument** is simply an opinion supported by evidence. The word is used in the same way that we use the word *viewpoint*, except that by definition, argument rests on supporting reasons whereas a person's viewpoint may not be as clearly supported. Thus, without any unpleasantness or rancor, a college professor may present her argument on an issue and may ask students to present their arguments on that issue.

IDENTIFYING THE PURPOSE OF ARGUMENT TEXTS

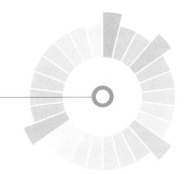

Unlike essays that are written to inform, to analyze, or to evaluate, the goal of an argument essay is to **persuade** a reader to accept a particular position or point of view. In college, you will read many written arguments, and you will also hear many oral arguments. Additionally, you will sometimes be required to write your own argument papers.

As a reader, when you approach argument texts, your goal is to determine the writer's main point and to find the support he uses to back up that point. You should also be able to evaluate the effectiveness of the support the writer uses. For example, a writer claims that Windows-based computers are better than Macs, and he bases that claim on the fact that he had a Mac once and did not like it, whereas he had a Windows-based computer and thought it was great. As a critical reader, you will recognize the weakness of the writer's evidence. He has only one piece of evidence about the quality of Windows-based computers—his own experience! He needs far more evidence to be able to prove persuasively that Windows-based computers are better than Macs. Ultimately, to assess the quality of an argument, you will need to analyze the writer's support and determine the weaknesses and strengths of the writer's argument.

Being able to read arguments critically will help you write better arguments, for you will know where potential weaknesses can lurk in your reasoning and can make sure you present the most convincing case to support your claim. To create a convincing case, you will need to have done enough reading and thinking to form and support a sound argument. Almost always, the grade you receive on an argument paper will be based on the quality of your argument, not on the particular opinion you express. Learning how to construct a sound argument is the aim. Ultimately, the goal of education is for students to think clearly and independently about issues; reading and writing arguments help develop this skill.

RECOGNIZING THE ELEMENTS OF ARGUMENT

In an argument text, the thesis statement puts forth a *claim*—the writer's opinion about a debatable issue. For a thesis statement to be a claim, it has to assert an arguable point. In contrast, the thesis statement of an information or evaluation essay may not be a claim.

> **Thesis statement that is not a claim:** Laws about keeping wild animals as domestic pets vary across the United States. *This is a fact, not an arguable issue. An essay on this topic would present information about the laws in question.*

> **Thesis statement that is a claim:** Keeping wild animals as domestic pets should be illegal. *This statement is an opinion; thus, it is a claim.*

As always, a thesis statement must be supported, and in an argument essay, the support usually consists of evidence in the form of reasons. **Reasons,** then, are the major supporting points of an argument essay. The supporting details for reasons consist of all the information, or **evidence,** a writer needs to back up, explain, illustrate, define, or otherwise defend the major supporting points.

An additional element in argument essays is a **counterargument,** the opposing argument. Writers will often include the opposing argument and then attempt to **refute** it, to show where it is weak and flawed.

STRUCTURING AN ARGUMENT

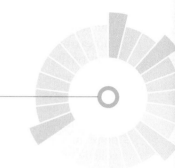

Imagine you are making the claim that parents should not use physical punishment to discipline their children. The following list shows one *reason* (a major supporting point) you might use to support your claim and the kinds of *evidence* (supporting details) you might use.

> **Claim (thesis statement):** Parents should not use physical punishment to discipline their children.

> **Reason (major supporting point):** Children who experience physical punishment act out in physical ways, such as by hitting or biting their peers.

> **Support (supporting details):**

- Explain how children learn behaviors by imitating their parents.
- Use a quote from the psychology textbook to support the point about how children learn.
- Explain the results of a psychological study that showed physical punishment resulted in physically aggressive children.

Notice that the supporting details are very specific. In this case, the supporting details consist of an explanation, a quotation, and the results of a study, and they combine to make the reason believable. If we were to outline the rest of this essay, we would see additional reasons and the supporting details the writer would use to back them up.

IDENTIFYING THREE TYPES OF APPEALS IN ARGUMENTS

Writers generally use three types of support for their claims: logical appeals, ethical appeals, and emotional appeals. An appeal is simply a type of reason.

To support an argument with **logical appeals,** a writer will use reasonable—logical—explanations. For example, if it is raining outside, it is reasonable to argue that your friend should take her umbrella with her when she leaves for work. Another example is to argue that people should avoid getting into debt because debt leads to decreased financial options in life. Logical appeals often make use of text patterns such as cause and effect and comparison-contrast.

In addition to logical appeals, writers also try to assure readers of their good intentions—that they are sincere, honest, and fair and that they have the readers' interests and concerns in mind. They use the testimony of knowledgeable experts to bolster their own credibility and to project self-confidence in their views. An **ethical appeal** consists of support that convinces us of the writer's trustworthiness, impartiality, expert knowledge, and goodwill.

A third type of support appeals to our emotions. Emotions are powerful; they can convince us to believe things and to take actions. For example, advertisements often tap into our emotions to sell products. A pair of name-brand, expensive athletic shoes may be the same quality as a pair of no-name sneakers, but wearing the expensive shoes gives us a *feeling* that the cheap shoes cannot provide. Appealing to our emotions can also mean appealing to our sense of shared values. In a written argument, we might tell the story of a child who is always hungry to make the claim that people should support a government supplemental food program because no child should have to suffer hunger. **Emotional appeals** can provide strong reasons for believing a claim or for taking an action.

PRACTICE ● Identifying the Elements of Argument

Match the term in the left column with the correct definition or example in the right column.

_____ 1. argument

_____ 2. reason

_____ 3. ethical appeal

_____ 4. emotional appeal

_____ 5. logical appeal

_____ 6. counterargument

_____ 7. claim

a. If we don't get enough contributions, kittens like Sadie will be left to live a miserable, lonely life.

b. The thesis statement in an argument essay.

c. I have been a detective for twenty-five years, and I have never seen a defendant more guilty than Mr. Sellers.

d. A major supporting point for an argument essay's thesis statement.

e. The point of view of the opposing side.

f. You should buy the Chevrolet instead of the Ford because the Chevrolet gets better gas mileage.

g. An opinion supported by reasons.

RECOGNIZING ARGUMENTS BY ANALYZING TOPICS

One way to recognize an argument essay is to focus on the essay's topic. Some topics are arguable, and some are not. An arguable topic is one that can be stated as a question whose answer is *debatable*—that is, it can be considered from multiple perspectives. Here are some topic questions whose answers are *not* arguable.

Question: What is the H1N1 flu?

Arguable or not? This question is not arguable because the answer is universally agreed on. Medical professionals know what H1N1 flu is. Thus, a paper that answers this question will simply inform, not argue.

Question: What kinds of college financial aid are available for veterans?

Arguable or not? The answer to this question requires some research, but the answer is easily found and is clear-cut. We do not have to argue about the kinds of financial aid available for veterans because there is an authoritative answer to this question. A paper on this topic will inform, not argue.

Although the questions above are not arguable as they are stated, we can refocus them as arguable issues. To do so, we simply ask, "With what aspects of this topic might people disagree?" Notice how refocusing can result in arguable issues:

Refocus: Should the United States require people to be vaccinated against the H1N1 flu?

Arguable or not? The issue is now arguable. People will disagree on whether the vaccine should be required by law.

Refocus: Should veterans be given more financial aid opportunities than nonveterans?

Arguable or not? Now the issue is arguable. Some people will think the answer is *yes*, and others will disagree.

PRACTICE Recognizing Arguable Issues

Below, you will find a table that lists questions on different topics. If a topic question is arguable, write "arguable" in the right column next to the question. If it is not arguable, then find an issue related to the question that would be arguable. Write the new, arguable question in the right column next to the question. Two examples are given.

Question	Your Response
Example: Should public schools continue to offer summer vacations, or should schooling be year-round?	Arguable
Example: What is text messaging?	Not arguable. Change to this: Why should text messaging while driving be illegal?
1. Should the first two years of college be free?	
2. What does it mean to "drink responsibly"?	
3. Who was Thomas Jefferson?	
4. What is the history of tattooing?	

RECOGNIZING ARGUMENT TEXTS BY THEIR CHARACTERISTICS AND KEY WORDS

In addition to recognizing argument texts by analyzing their topics, you can also use the characteristics of argument texts and the key words associated with argument as clues.

CHARACTERISTICS OF ARGUMENT TEXTS

- Texts that argue have persuasion as their purpose.
- The subject of argument texts is an arguable issue.
- Arguments present the writer's opinion on the issue.
- Arguments present reasons and supporting details to back up the writer's opinion.
- Arguments often use research and analysis as support.

Key Words of Argument Texts			
according to	argues	because	claims
counters	evidence	furthermore	illogical
in fact	logic	reasons	refutes
since	supports	therefore	thus

READING AND ANNOTATING AN ARGUMENT ESSAY

As you read the essay that starts on the next page—"Keep Guns off Campus" by Dennis Henigan—published in the *Huffington Post*, notice the elements of argument as they are pointed out.

Keep Guns Off Campus

by Dennis Henigan

In the wake of the Tucson shooting, Arizona's legislature is considering various bills addressing guns and violence. The legislation with the best chance of passage has nothing to do with strengthening the state's laws to prevent dangerous individuals from easily acquiring the firepower that enabled Jared Loughner to shoot 19 people in about 16 seconds, killing six of them. Incredibly, the bill with the most momentum would force Arizona colleges and universities to allow the concealed carry of guns on campus.

> Background: In February 2011, at a political gathering in Tucson, Arizona, Congresswoman Gabrielle Giffords and several others were shot by a lone gunman. Giffords survived, but six others, including a nine-year-old girl, did not.

The Arizona bill is one of many similar bills being pushed in states across the nation, as the gun lobby seeks to overcome the collective judgment of college administrators, faculty and students that allowing guns on campus is a recipe for disaster. Up until now, sanity has prevailed, as such bills have failed 43 times in 23 states in recent years. But the forces of "guns everywhere" are back, and pitched battles are underway, not only in Arizona, but in Texas and elsewhere.

> Additional background: Expands the essay's scope to show that this is an issue for everyone—not just Arizonans.

It all started with the Virginia Tech mass shooting of almost four years ago, which prompted "gun rights" proponents to argue that the shooting could have been stopped if one of the students in the targeted classrooms had been carrying a gun and could have returned fire. It is revealing that none of the students and teachers who actually were under fire that day have become proponents of concealed carry on campus. Indeed, Colin Goddard, who was shot four times in his French class, has become a crusader for stronger gun laws, as poignantly depicted in the documentary *Living for 32*, now being shown on college campuses coast-to-coast. . . .

> Major supporting point: The argument that having a gun would have stopped the shooter is flawed.
>
> Counterargument: provided by writer

The argument supporting guns on campus is based on a bizarre assessment of relative risks. Its proponents seek to create the remote possibility that a legal gun carrier will be in the right place at the right time when a killer attacks, and will act effectively to stop the attacker, *when the attack itself, particularly a mass attack, is itself a remote possibility*. In order to create the unlikely chance of this "good guy shoots attacker" scenario becoming reality, the proponents of campus concealed carry seek to ensure a proliferation of guns in classrooms, dorm rooms, dining halls, sports stadiums—anywhere where a violent attack may occur.

> Refutation of counterargument starts.
>
> Refutation of counterargument continues.

This necessarily means introducing a broad new array of obvious risks into everyday life on college campuses. Those risks seem anything but remote: that an argument between a professor and a disgruntled student will erupt in gunfire; that an intoxicated student will accidentally discharge his gun while showing it off at a Friday afternoon keg party; that a student's momentary despair over a romantic break-up will turn lethal as he finds a gun and turns it on himself.

> Supporting point for refutation: Allowing guns on campuses actually creates more problems.
>
> Hypothetical examples

The pro-gun crowd assails "gun-free zones" that allegedly invite the violent to attack the unarmed, but the reality is that currently gun-free college campuses are far safer than the gun-saturated communities that surround them. Justice Department figures show that college students aged 18 to 24 experience violence at a 20% lower rate than non-students in the same age group. In addition, 93% of the violence against students occurs off campus.

> Major supporting point (a counterargument): The argument that gun-free zones attract violence is flawed.
>
> Refutation of counterargument
>
> Examples: statistics from an authoritative source, the Justice Department

(continued)

Given that in most states gun owners must be 21 to carry concealed weapons, the "guns on campus" activists question why law-abiding adults licensed to carry in other locations should be barred from doing so on college campuses. Several obvious responses come to mind.

First, the experience of states in making it easier to carry concealed weapons hardly recommends extending concealed carry to college campuses. The evidence is mounting that very dangerous people are being given concealed carry licenses, that they are committing egregious violence with guns, and that liberalized concealed carry is associated with more violent crime, not less. Why should we subject our largely peaceful college campuses to a policy that has led to greater danger outside those campuses? After all, Jared Loughner was a legal concealed carrier under Arizona law until he shot 19 people.

Second, college campuses are particularly hazardous environments for widespread gun possession and carrying. They are populated largely by individuals aged 18 to 24, a highly volatile time of life and the age group with the highest incidence of such behaviors as binge drinking and drug use. Moreover, those young people live in dormitories, group houses and other high-density situations in which it is difficult to ensure that a gun always will be in the possession of the person licensed to carry it.

The pressures of college life itself add to the risk, particularly the risk of suicide. Chancellor Francisco Cigarroa of the University of Texas, in an eloquent letter to Governor Rick Perry opposing concealed carry on campus, cited the concerns of "campus health professionals, who know and deal with the reality of the emotional and psychological pressures of academic life, separation from family, relationships—all pressures that contribute to the harsh reality that suicide is the second leading cause of death among college students."

Finally, don't believe for a minute that the "gun rights" crowd is content to limit campus concealed carry to 21-year-old seniors and grad students. At the same time the gun lobby is pressing the Texas legislature to force Texas universities to allow concealed carry, the NRA is pursuing a lawsuit to strike down, as a violation of the Second Amendment, the Texas law setting 21 as the minimum age to carry concealed. If the NRA gets its way, it will be freshmen and all other students who will be eligible to carry loaded guns on campus.

Students are standing with their professors and administrators in resisting laws forcing campuses to accept guns. The student government at the University of Texas has come out foursquare against such laws. Just this week, 57% of the Texas A&M student body voted against guns on campus. These are young people who have grown up around guns, yet understand they have no place on a college campus.

Ultimately, this is not just a campus safety issue. It also is an issue involving the core values served by institutions of higher education. It is difficult to imagine anything more destructive to an environment of academic freedom—in which controversial issues can be passionately debated free of fear and intimidation—than students or professors "strapped" as they participate in those debates.

Students, faculty and administrators get it. Do our lawmakers?

Sidebar annotations:

Major supporting point: The argument that people who can carry guns should be able to carry them on campus is flawed.

Counterargument

Refutation—reason 1: Concealed carry licenses result in more violence, not less.

Refutation—reason 2: College campuses are more hazardous environments for carrying guns.

Refutation—reason 3: Suicide, in particular, might become more prevalent on college campuses.

Refutation—reason 4: Allowing this action will lead to even more extreme gun laws.

Major supporting point: Students agree that guns on campus won't solve the problem.

Major supporting point: This is an education issue, not a gun rights issue.

Conclusion

PRACTICE ● Analyzing an Argument Text

Using a separate sheet, answer the following questions about "Keep Guns Off Campus" by Dennis Henigan.

1. Is this essay's thesis statement (the writer's claim) stated or implied? If it is stated, write out the sentence, and if it is implied, write it in your own words.

2. Henigan devotes a significant portion of his essay to the opposing argument—that guns should be allowed on campus. Why? Explain your answer.

3. Henigan's major supporting points consist of refutations of the counterargument and his own supporting reasons. Which type of support—refuting the counterarguments or providing his own reasons—do you find most effective? Why?

4. Henigan's conclusion paragraph is extremely short. Do you think it was an effective way to conclude his essay? Why or why not?

USING ARGUMENT IN YOUR WRITING

When you have an assignment to write a persuasive essay, you will need to use the argument text pattern. Follow these guidelines.

1. Make sure your topic is an arguable topic. The primary test is to state the topic in the form of a question and then ask whether the answer to that question is debatable. If the answer is debatable, your topic is probably suitable for an essay employing the argument text pattern.

2. Prewrite to determine what your claim will be, and write a thesis statement. Once you have a thesis statement, you can come up with the best kind of support.

3. Analyze your audience before you construct reasons for your claim. Audience awareness is crucial in determining the kinds of arguments that are likely to persuade an audience and the kinds that are likely to fail. Use these principles to think through your audience's needs and expectations:

- **Write for a diverse audience.** Imagine your audience will contain people who hold a variety of viewpoints, some who agree with you and some who do not. Imagine your audience to be composed of people from various backgrounds, of various ages, of various ethnicities, and so on. For example, if you are trying to convince your audience that women should not serve in active military combat, you should keep in mind that approximately 50 percent of readers will be female. If your thesis is likely to make your audience defensive, it is especially important to word your thoughts carefully and respectfully. It is never appropriate to include profanity or remarks that are racist or sexist or that show disrespect for those who are older or who have disabilities. Showing respect to your audience is key. The technique used by some radio and television hosts of making provocative and biased statements in the guise of "argument" may earn them high entertainment ratings and income, but it is not appropriate or useful in academic argument or in any argument that seeks to find meaningful solutions to problems.

- **Think about the kinds of evidence your audience might find convincing.** Many types of evidence can be used in argument papers: statistics, stories, analogies, facts, studies, explanations of causes and effects, definitions, and predictions. If you are writing an essay for a history professor, it is probably important to use relevant facts, details, and maybe even stories. If you are writing for a general audience, use research that your audience can easily understand. Evidence such as studies, quotes from authorities in the field, and logical explanations of cause and effect can be effective in supporting your thesis. Remember that you will probably have a lot of evidence to choose from as you write your paper. Select only evidence that you think will be effective for your audience.

- **Always imagine that you are writing for a skeptical audience.** Imagine that as they study your paper, your readers are muttering, "Where's the evidence?" or "I disagree" or "Prove it!" Make sure you anticipate the audience's doubts and address them in your paper. Another way to be mindful of your audience's doubts is to be fully aware of the opposing position. If you are arguing for random drug testing in the workplace, for example, you should be fully aware of all the reasons against workplace drug testing. In your paper, you can address the reasons that opponents would offer and then refute them.

- **Keep in mind that your audience is interested in hearing your thesis and your evidence, but your audience also wants to think that you—as a writer—are credible and believable.** Your readers will be judging not only your argument but also *you*. To come across as knowledgeable and competent to a general audience, you must ensure that your paper is written in standard English, conforms to an acceptable format, and demonstrates that you have done the reading necessary to know what you are talking about. Additionally, your argument should show that you are fair to the opposing side. You can demonstrate this fairness by thoroughly understanding the opposing argument and by showing respect to those who advocate it.

4. Identify the reasons you will use to support your claim. List all the reasons you can think of, and analyze each one. Which ones will the opposing side easily refute? Which ones are the most logical? Which, if any, might elicit a positive emotional response from readers? Determine the best reasons and then work on finding support to explain and develop those reasons fully.

5. Analyze counterarguments, and plan how you will refute them. In many argument essays you will find a counterargument (the opposing viewpoint). To show you understand the argument of the other side, your essay can include the arguments of the opposing side and your objections to those arguments.

In professional essays, writers use counterarguments for a variety of reasons. First, by acknowledging the strengths of the opposing argument, they establish goodwill, the sense that they are fair-minded and are giving credit to the valid points of their opponents. Second, explaining a counterargument shows that a writer has carefully listened to the opposing viewpoint. An argument can be fair only when both parties actually listen to each other and consider each other's point of view. Third, knowing the best points of the counterargument enables writers to craft an argument that is effective because they know the points they need to refute. This strategy is similar to the way football coaches and players think. If you can anticipate the play the opposing team will make, you can construct a good counterstrategy.

One way to use argument successfully is to fully understand the *best* arguments of the opposing position. Suppose you strongly believe that gun control laws should be strengthened. When you feel strongly about an issue, it's easy to not really hear the opposing argument. But hearing the opposing argument is not only important; it's absolutely necessary. If you cannot address the opposing argument, point by point, and show why your position is superior, you will not be able to write a convincing essay.

6. Create a simple outline for your argument essay. Determine the order in which you will present each reason and the supporting details needed to develop each reason. If you plan to include counterarguments and refute them, use your outline to note where these elements will occur in your essay.

AVOIDING COMMON LOGICAL ERRORS

It is important to use logical reasons when you construct an argument, but it can be easy to make logical errors. Avoid the following logical errors in your writing.

Faulty Causes or Effects

You cannot say that X caused Y without having some proof. Imagine that your town recently elected a new mayor. In the two years she has been in office, the unemployment rate in your city has increased. It is illogical to claim that X (electing the new mayor) caused Y (the increase in unemployment). Maybe these two things were a coincidence. Unless you have additional information to prove that X caused Y, it is unfair and illogical to make that claim.

You cannot say that if we do action X, then Y will happen, unless you have good evidence. Some people create fear-inducing predictions to convince others of a point of view. For example, a parent who wants her son to go to college might say that if he does not go to college (X), he will end up jobless and homeless (Y). Does she have proof for that prediction? No. She says it to scare her son into believing her point that every successful person goes to college. Making a prediction without enough evidence to do so is a logical error.

Faulty Generalizations

A *generalization* is a statement made about an entire group or class, such as "All horses are animals." Generalizations based on evidence can be fair, but unsubstantiated generalizations are often faulty. For example, consider this statement: women are better chefs than men. Such a generalization is simply not logical. Some women may be better chefs than some men, but it does not follow that all women are better chefs than all men.

Almost any broad statement about a racial, ethnic, socioeconomic, or gender group will result in a generalization that is unfair. Generalizations are commonly used incorrectly in two specific ways: making a statement based on small samples and unfairly representing the opponent's viewpoint.

Generalizations Based on Small Samples

Assume that you had a BXC smartphone and that it performed very poorly. You cannot logically claim that BXC smartphones are low quality because you have only *one* piece of evidence—one phone. Your experience with one sample (one BXC smartphone) is too limited for you to draw conclusions about BXC phones. What if BXC produced two million smartphones and yours was the only one that had problems? Since you do not know the data about the larger group, it is illogical to make a generalization about BXC smartphones.

Unfair Representations of Your Opponent

Imagine reading an argument against gun control in which the writer says people who want guns to be more widely available do not care about human life and want to be able to kill people. This kind of error is unfair because it relies on a stereotype, rather than evidence, about gun rights proponents. It is also unfair because it misrepresents the argument of the group.

Faulty Analogies

One way that people often make a point is by making a comparison. In the study of argument, comparisons are called *analogies.* Here are some examples of analogies.

- Comparing public school education to home schooling to support an argument that home schooling is better
- Comparing the leader of a country to Hitler to support an argument that war against the leader's country is a good idea

- Comparing a current situation—like a recession—to a situation in the past to support an argument that we need to take X or Y action

Analogies can often clarify ideas for readers. It is acceptable to use analogies as long as the two things being compared are similar enough to support the point being made. By definition, the two things being compared in an analogy are different. The critical question is, how different are they?

It would not be fair, for example, for a professor to expect her freshmen writing students to write like students in a senior-level advanced writing course. The analogy between those two groups would be illogical.

PRACTICE Using Argument in Your Writing

1. Consider the following list of topics for an essay using the argument text pattern. For each one, decide whether it is an arguable issue. If it is not an arguable issue, refocus the topic so that it becomes arguable.

   a. The need to make adoptions more affordable

   b. Why people should be organ donors

   c. What diabetes is and how it is treated

   d. Why a missile defense program is a bad idea for the United States

   e. The history of yoga

   f. How we can improve driver's education programs

2. Choose one of the following questions, and use it as the basis for an essay using the argument text pattern.

   a. Do Americans value entertainment more than education?

   b. What are the principles of socialism? Once you learn what they are, judge for yourself: Is socialism an undesirable form of government? Make an argument to prove your point.

   c. Do group projects constitute an effective method for teaching students? Do they really help students learn?

   d. Should all children be required to learn to read music?

   e. Should airline pilots be allowed to carry guns?

   f. Should public school teachers be allowed to carry guns?

   g. Should parents enter their children in beauty pageants?

Passive and Active Voice

Consider this: If you were a prosecutor making the case that a defendant is guilty, which of these sentences would best serve your argument?

A. The defendant <u>threw</u> the woman to the ground and <u>grabbed</u> her purse.

B. The woman <u>was thrown</u> to the ground, and her purse <u>was grabbed</u>.

Sentence A is a direct statement that assigns blame, and it clearly tells us that a particular person (the defendant) did the crime. Sentence B describes the same situation, but it does not tell us *who* did the throwing and grabbing. It does not assign responsibility for the action. Most readers would find sentence A, which is in the active voice, more persuasive than sentence B, which is in the passive voice.

Voice is one way to describe verbs in a sentence. If a verb is in the **active voice,** the verb's subject (underlined in the following example) *performs* the action.

Example: <u>Tasha</u> threw the javelin.

Tasha—the subject of the sentence—is clearly the doer of the action; she was the one who did the throwing.

If a verb is in the **passive voice,** its subject (underlined below) *receives* the action.

Example: The <u>javelin</u> was thrown by Tasha.

The subject, *javelin,* is not doing the action; rather the javelin is being acted upon. It is the recipient of the action. The sentence includes *by Tasha,* so we know who threw the javelin. However, because the doer of the action is not the subject, the sentence has less impact.

Generally, the active voice is best for most writing. Sentences in the active voice are usually more straightforward and lively than those in the passive voice.

There are times, however, when you may want to use passive instead of active voice.

1. USE PASSIVE OR ACTIVE VOICE FOR EMPHASIS

The subject of a sentence is usually the focus of the reader's attention. So, if you want to emphasize a particular element, make that element the subject.

> **Passive voice:** Evidence that hunter-gatherers lived in Texas as far back as 15,500 years ago was recently unearthed by anthropologists.
>
> *Emphasizes the newly discovered evidence about prehistory in Texas.*
>
> **Active voice:** Anthropologists recently unearthed evidence that hunter-gatherers lived in Texas as far back as 15,500 years ago.
>
> *Emphasizes who discovered the new evidence about prehistory in Texas.*

> To decide where to put the emphasis in a sentence, imagine that your sentence is answering a question.

> **Passive voice:** Evidence that hunter-gatherers lived in Texas as far back as 15,500 years ago was recently unearthed by anthropologists.
>
> *Answers this question: What was recently discovered about prehistory in Texas?*
>
> **Active voice:** Anthropologists recently unearthed evidence that hunter-gatherers lived in Texas as far back as 15,500 years ago.
>
> *Answers this question: Who recently discovered new evidence about prehistory in Texas?*

(continued)

2. USE PASSIVE OR ACTIVE VOICE TO EVADE OR INDICATE RESPONSIBILITY

The passive voice can conceal or deemphasize responsibility for an action. For that reason, it is sometimes used in controversial or politically sensitive writing.

Passive voice: During those decades, many Indian children were forcibly removed from their families.

Active voice: During those decades, the federal government forcibly removed many Indian children from their families.

3. USE THE PASSIVE VOICE WHEN THE DOER IS UNKNOWN OR ASSUMED

When readers will presumably know who the doer is, the passive voice allows you to write a more concise sentence.

Passive voice: The new song was written, arranged, recorded, and produced in a matter of months.

Active voice: In a matter of months, the songwriter wrote the new song, the arranger arranged it, the singer recorded it, and the recording studio produced it.

Because it is not necessary to spell out all the doers of various actions, as in the active voice sentence, the passive voice allows the writer to create a more concise sentence.

A RELATED ISSUE: STARTING SENTENCES WITH *There is/was* AND *It is/was*

When writers are composing a first draft, they often resort to using *There is/was* and *It is/was* to begin sentences. Sometimes using these expressions makes it easy to get thoughts down in sentence form. But with few exceptions, these expressions can diminish the quality of the writing. The revision stage is a good time to rewrite these sentences for greater impact. Consider these examples.

Acceptable: There is evidence that high-quality early childhood programs can have a positive effect on the health of adults years later.

Better: Evidence shows that high-quality early childhood programs can have a positive effect on the health of adults years later.

Better: High-quality early childhood programs can have a positive effect on the health of adults years later, according to some evidence.

When you see a sentence in your writing that begins with *There is/are* or *It is/was,* ask yourself, "What is important in this sentence? What do I want to emphasize?"

Sentences beginning with *There is/are* or *It is/was* are grammatically correct, but they are weak. With some effort they can be transformed into sentences that can more effectively communicate your ideas to readers.

SENTENCE COMBINING

In the example that follows, notice how the short sentences are combined into longer sentences that employ active voice.

Ideas to combine:

• That the design was flawed was well known by the company.

• Documentation of the flaw was made before the car seats were manufactured.

• Negligence is what caused the car seats to be manufactured in such a way.

(continued)

Combined using active voice: The company was negligent when it manufactured the car seats. Even though it knew the design was flawed, the company manufactured the car seats anyway.

EXERCISES

Combine each set of sentences into longer, smoother sentences, and use active voice when appropriate.

1. Ideas to combine:

- The old house was inspected by the landlord.

- It was inspected by him after the flood.

- The flooring had been warped by the floodwaters.

- However, the frame of the house had been spared.

- The house was still in good condition.

   Answer: _____

   _____

   _____

2. Ideas to combine:

- Children should be taught problem-solving skills.

- Critical thinking skills can be developed by the teaching of problem solving.

- There is a true sense of accomplishment that can be felt by children who can solve problems.

   Answer: _____

   _____

3. Ideas to combine:

- One serious disease is diabetes.

- An increased risk of heart disease can be a result of diabetes.

- An increase in the risk of stroke can be caused by diabetes.

- Eye problems can be caused by diabetes.

- It is known that nerve damage can occur.

- Foot or leg amputations can be caused by complications of diabetes.

   Answer: _____

   _____

   _____

Skill at organizing documents can transfer directly to the skill of organizing the tasks, events, and materials required in a wide range of careers and is essential in fields such as paralegal work.

Organizing, Drafting, and Summarizing

Have you ever watched a movie that presents plot events in a jumbled order? For example, a movie may start with a dramatic scene—such as a standoff between good guys and bad guys—and then loop back in time to provide the backstory, the information that helps viewers understand the standoff. Or perhaps you have seen a movie that *seems* to be taking place in the present, but at the end of the film you learn that the actions were only a dream. Film-makers make very intentional choices about the order in which they present scenes, and these choices can have dramatic effects on viewers.

Writers also carefully select the order in which they present information. Becoming more aware of the ordering strategies other writers use will help you comprehend the texts you read and will enable you to experiment with these strategies when you write your own essays.

A careful reading of a text can also help you record the writer's ideas in a detailed outline or a graphic organizer, which you can use to write an accurate summary. Many students find that a crucial study skill is to write outlines and summaries of the texts they study. A related skill—writing a paraphrase—also requires a careful, close reading of a text. In this chapter you will have the opportunity to hone these skills.

CHAPTER OBJECTIVES

After completing this chapter, students will be able to do the following:

- Identify common strategies for ordering information.

- Use information-ordering strategies in writing.

- Use outlines and graphic organizers to analyze a text's organization.

- Use outlines to draft essays.

- Use outlines to write detailed and brief summaries.

- Write paraphrases.

IDENTIFYING COMMON STRATEGIES FOR ORDERING INFORMATION

As you analyze texts, notice the choices writers make about the order in which they present information. In general, when we talk about the order of information, we are referring to where writers place the thesis statement and the major supporting points. Three common strategies for ordering information are to use order of importance, chronological order, and spatial order.

Order of Importance

Writers use **order of importance** to organize reasons, concepts, and general information. They consider the effect on readers when deciding whether to place the most important item first or last. Presenting the most important major supporting point first immediately alerts readers to the point's significance for the thesis statement. Placing the most important major supporting point last can also be effective because this point will be fresh in the minds of readers as they finish the text.

In the following example, the writer places the most important major supporting point last to emphasize its value. Note also that placing a major supporting point last in the thesis statement gives it more emphasis than the other points.

Order of Importance Organization in an Essay

INTRODUCTION

Introduction paragraph

Thesis statement: Sibling rivalry is good for children because it promotes better listening skills, better social skills, increased problem-solving skills, and increased self-control.

BODY

Topic sentence for major supporting point 1: One good thing about sibling rivalry is that it promotes better listening skills.

Topic sentence for major supporting point 2: Children who fight with siblings also have better social skills than children who do not.

Topic sentence for major supporting point 3: Even more significantly, sibling rivalry helps children develop problem-solving skills.

Topic sentence for major supporting point 4: Most importantly, children who fight with siblings have greater self-control than children who do not.

CONCLUSION

Conclusion paragraph

Writers also use order of importance to determine where to place information in mixed-pattern essays. The main objective of ordering is to present the information in such a way that readers can more easily follow it. For example, if you are writing an informative essay to help readers understand what a tsunami is and what it can do, starting with a definition of *tsunami* will be helpful. Readers might gain a clearer understanding if you compare tsunamis with other types of destructive natural events, such as hurricanes, tornadoes, and avalanches. This information could be followed by a discussion of the causes and effects of tsunamis, and you might end the essay with the most important supporting point—the most destructive effects of tsunamis—as the simple outline about tsunamis on the next page shows.

Order of Importance Organization in a Mixed-Pattern Essay

INTRODUCTION
Introduction paragraph

Thesis statement: Tsunamis are among the most destructive natural events in the world.

BODY
Paragraph 2: Definition of *tsunami*

Paragraph 3: Comparison of tsunamis with other destructive natural events (use examples)

Paragraph 4: What causes tsunamis

Paragraph 5: Some effects of tsunamis

Paragraph 6: Most destructive effects of tsunamis

CONCLUSION
Conclusion paragraph: Better warning systems are being developed.

Chronological Order

Chronological order uses time or sequence to organize ideas. Events are usually presented in chronological order; steps in a process are presented sequentially. Notice that in the following simple outline, the stages of training for medical doctors are discussed in the order in which they occur—that is, chronologically.

Chronological Order Organization in an Essay

INTRODUCTION
Introduction paragraph

Thesis statement: The three stages of training for medical doctors are medical school, internship, and residency.

BODY
Paragraph 2: Medical school

Paragraph 3: Internship

Paragraph 4: Residency

CONCLUSION
Conclusion paragraph

Spatial Order

Spatial order uses the physical position of objects to organize ideas. Many descriptive passages use spatial organization, as the example on the next page shows. Notice how prepositional phrases (underlined) guide the reader around the cabin's interior.

Spatial Order Organization in a Descriptive Paragraph

The cabin that would be my home for three months needed repair. I walked through the doorway, and to my left I saw an ancient black cookstove. It seemed to be in better condition than anything else in the cabin. Directly above the stove was a hole in the roof about the size of a truck tire. Light streamed in and pooled on the rotted floorboards that had fallen victim to rain, snow, and ice. On the left side of the cabin was an old aluminum cot, its canvas clearly suffering from dry rot. A knee-high pile of trash was heaped in the back corner underneath three shelves next to the only window in the cabin. It would be a long winter.

Transitional Terms for Information-Ordering Strategies

The transitions in the boxes that follow are helpful additions that you can use to identify the order of information in a particular text. You can also use these in your own writing.

TRANSITIONS FOR ORDER OF IMPORTANCE	TRANSITIONS FOR CHRONOLOGICAL ORDER	TRANSITIONS FOR SPATIAL ORDER
first, second, third, significantly, more significantly, most significantly, importantly, more importantly, most importantly, above all, of less significance, of less importance	first, second, third, before, to begin, to continue, during, next, while, until, when, afterward, finally, to conclude	to the right, to the left, above, below, inside, outside, under, beneath, behind, around, beside, next to, adjacent, joining, continuing around, in front of, in back of

By being aware of the ordering strategy a writer uses, you can more effectively understand a passage, the text pattern or patterns being used, and the organization of the content.

PRACTICE ➊ Identifying Ordering Strategies

On the basis of the transitions and content in each passage below, identify the order of arrangement the author has used. Use *OI* for order of importance, *CO* for chronological order, and *SO* for spatial order.

_____ **1.** In April 1952, my father lost his job. He became depressed, and the entire summer, he sat on the front porch smoking cigarettes and barely talking. Mother could do little to console him, for he snapped at anyone who dared conversation. In August of that year, I turned six years old.

_____ **2.** Perhaps the most significant cause of the war was famine and starvation. The people had reached a point of desperation. There was not even enough food to steal from the wealthy. Disenchantment with the priest's advice—while not as significant as the incessant hunger—was prevalent. The priest's assurances of better days to come were hollow utterances in a world of deprivation and despair.

_____ **3.** The top floor of the building was full of windows overlooking the bay. The view was splendid. To the left was the Golden Gate Bridge, resplendent in the morning sun. In the distance was Mount Tamalpais's peak.

USING INFORMATION-ORDERING STRATEGIES IN YOUR WRITING

Making intentional decisions about the order in which you present ideas will help you write more clearly and effectively. To select an appropriate ordering strategy for the type of information you are providing, keep the following factors in mind.

Uses for Organizing Strategies

ORDER OF IMPORTANCE	CHRONOLOGICAL ORDER	SPATIAL ORDER
• Reasons • Classifications (types) • Comparison-contrast information • Causes and effects	• Historical information • Narratives • Processes • Stages or steps • Causes and effects	• Descriptions

In your essay, be sure to present your points in the same order in which they occur in your thesis statement. For example, earlier in the chapter, an example of chronological order contained this thesis statement:

> The three stages of training for medical doctors are medical school, internship, and residency.

In the body paragraphs, the writer should discuss these stages in the order in which they appear in the thesis statement.

PRACTICE ② Using Order of Importance, Chronological Order, and Spatial Order

Complete the following paragraph-writing activities.

1. Order of importance: Write a paragraph in which you present the three most important priorities in your life. Put the most important priority last. Use appropriate transitions.

2. Chronological order: Write a paragraph in which you describe an event, such as what happened during a recent family celebration, or a process that follows a particular sequence, such as how to change a flat tire.

3. Spatial order: Write a paragraph in which you describe your kitchen. Use appropriate transitions.

USING OUTLINES AND GRAPHIC ORGANIZERS TO ANALYZE A TEXT'S ORGANIZATION

An outline can be helpful to you as a reader and as a writer. As a reader, an outline helps you understand the organization of a text and the relationships among ideas in the text. It equips you with everything you need to write a good summary of the reading. As a writer, an outline helps you determine where to place support and how to organize your ideas.

Creating Outlines to Analyze Organization

There is no one-size-fits-all pattern of organization that works for every text. However, most texts do have three components: an introduction, a body, and a conclusion. The number of paragraphs in these three components can vary. Some writers even offer three or four paragraphs of introductory material before getting to the main idea. When you outline a text, be aware that writers do not always place information in the order you expect.

To write an outline for a text you are reading, you need to find the writer's main idea and determine the major supporting points. Sometimes the writer provides clues, such as headings and subheadings. When you see them, notice the differences in size, style, and color. For example, in a textbook on business management and **entrepreneurialism**, chapter titles are large and always appear at the top of a page, main headings appear in green, subheadings are smaller than main headings and appear in blue, and sub-subheadings are in black. As you study the example below, think about what information each section of the text might present.

Vocabulary Collection Word:
entrepreneur

Your in-context definition:

_____

_____

A dictionary definition:

_____

_____

CHAPTER 4

Starting a Business

Entrepreneurialism

PERSONAL TRAITS OF ENTREPRENEURS

Entrepreneurs Are Visionary
Entrepreneurs Are Personable
Entrepreneurs Are Highly Motivated
Entrepreneurs Are Researchers

In a text that does not contain headings and subheadings, you can still distinguish the elements of importance and determine their relationship to one another. The annotations in the following essay identify the elements a reader would use to construct an outline.

How Delaying Gratification Predicts Future Success
by Kari Gardner

"I want what I want, and I want it *now*." We live in a world in which instant gratification is not merely desired: it's expected. If Internet access is delayed for even a few seconds, we are frustrated. If our fast food is not fast enough, we are miffed, and so it goes.

What is required in these circumstances is *delayed gratification*, the ability to postpone the fulfillment of an immediate desire in order to obtain a more substantial reward in the future. To put it more informally, delayed gratification means putting off having something now so you can get something better later on.

Introduction: examples of how people have trouble delaying gratification

Definition

(continued)

Educators and psychologists alike say that being able to tolerate delayed gratification is an extremely valuable skill. People who can put off immediate gratification are more likely to have what it takes to be successful in the important things in life. And there is research to support that opinion.

In the late 1960s and early 1970s, psychologists at Stanford University (led by Walter Mischel) performed a series of studies that came to be known as the Marshmallow Experiment. Young children (from four to six years old) were given a large, fluffy marshmallow and were told they could eat the marshmallow now, or they could wait fifteen minutes and get a second marshmallow.

Many of the kids who were able to delay gratification distracted themselves from the marshmallow by covering their eyes with their hands, turning their backs to the treat, kicking the table, and so forth. Other children who successfully delayed eating the marshmallow used their imaginations to reframe the treat as something else. For example, by thinking about the marshmallow as a cloud or by thinking the marshmallow was just a picture of a marshmallow, children were able to resist eating it immediately.

Of course, a significant number of children simply could not wait. Some nibbled on the marshmallow and eventually popped the whole thing into their mouths, and some ate it almost immediately.

In follow-up studies years later, the psychologists determined that the children who were able to wait longer—to postpone their gratification—tended to do substantially better as adults than those children who were less patient. The psychologists based their assessment on the analysis of the test subjects' levels of behavioral problems, drug and alcohol addiction, educational achievement, SAT scores, and other measures. Although recent studies have suggested that the fundamental issue is more complex than simple self-control, the basic point still stands: it is important to learn to tolerate delayed gratification.

Psychological tests are not the only way to demonstrate the importance of delayed gratification. Proof that it pays to put off pleasure is all around us. People who have the patience and willpower to regularly invest even small amounts of money can easily become very wealthy—if they are willing to wait long enough for their money to multiply. Students who seek college degrees earn them by putting off pleasure today for the reward of a degree tomorrow. And athletes who make it to the top know very well the importance of working hard today so that they can perform well tomorrow.

It will always be easier to eat the marshmallow right away, but doing so may not always be the best choice.

Thesis statement

Major supporting point 1 (implied): The Marshmallow Experiment shows that delayed gratification skills lead to more success in life.

Details: focus on how the experiment was set up (process analysis)

Details: focus on what happened in the experiment (cause and effect)

Details: the conclusion drawn from the experiment (explanation)

Major supporting point 2

Details: people who delay gratification to pursue success (examples)

To outline a text, list the main idea (whether stated in a thesis statement, as in this case, or implied), the major supporting points, and the supporting details that follow the major supporting points. When writing an outline, always use quotation marks if you use actual phrases and sentences from the text, as shown in the outline on the next page. Doing so enables you to remember which words are yours and which came from the source.

Simple Outline of "How Delaying Gratification Predicts Future Success" by Kari Gardner

Thesis statement: "People who can put off immediate gratification are more likely to have what it takes to be successful in the important things in life."

Major supporting point 1 (implied): The Marshmallow Experiment shows that delayed gratification skills lead to more success in life.

Supporting details:

- How the experiment was set up
- What happened in the experiment
- The conclusion drawn from the experiment

Major supporting point 2: "Proof that it pays to put off pleasure is all around us."

Supporting details:

- People who invest
- Students who graduate
- Athletes who train

The preceding outline of "How Delaying Gratification Predicts Future Success" is a simple outline. It includes just the minimum amount of information necessary to map the essay. If you need to remember more of the details than a basic outline allows, you can construct an **enhanced** outline by including additional important information, as this example demonstrates (the added information is in *italics*):

Vocabulary Collection Word:
enhanced

Your in-context definition:

_____

_____

A dictionary definition:

_____

_____

Enhanced Outline of "How Delaying Gratification Predicts Future Success" by Kari Gardner

Introduction: Provides examples of how people have trouble tolerating delayed gratification. **Definition** *of delayed gratification: "the ability to post-pone the fulfillment of an immediate desire in order to obtain a more substantial reward in the future."*

Thesis statement: "People who can put off immediate gratification are more likely to have what it takes to be successful in the important things in life."

Major supporting point 1 (implied): The Marshmallow Experiment shows that delayed gratification skills lead to more success in life.

Supporting details:

- How the experiment was set up: *Children were given the option of one marshmallow now or two later.*
- What happened in the experiment: *Some children waited to eat the marshmallow, and some did not.*
- The conclusion drawn from the experiment: *Children who waited had more success as adults.*
  - *Assessment based on behavioral problems, drug and alcohol addiction, educational achievement, SAT scores*

Major supporting point 2: "Proof that it pays to put off pleasure is all around us."

Supporting details:

- People who invest *(end up wealthy if they wait)*
- Students who graduate *(put off pleasure today for reward tomorrow)*
- Athletes who train *(practice today for performance rewards tomorrow)*

The enhanced outline has more information than the basic outline, particularly in the supporting details. Practice your outlining skills by completing the following assignment.

PRACTICE **3** Outlining a Brief Reading

Read the following passage, and annotate the thesis statement, major supporting points, and supporting details. Then, on a separate sheet, create a simple outline for the reading.

Achieving Optimum Fitness

YOUR ANNOTATIONS

Physical activities play an important role in fitness. Many people participate in endurance exercises, such as walking, running, and swimming, but optimum fitness requires more than endurance activities. Strength training and flexibility development are also important. Maximum fitness can be achieved by performing these three types of exercises regularly.

Exercises such as brisk walking, jogging, and swimming help athletes develop endurance. Endurance training is accomplished by participating in aerobic activities for an extended period of time. Biking, dancing, and yard work (for example, pushing a lawnmower or raking leaves) also qualify as endurance training. These activities involve relatively low-intensity actions performed for extended periods of time. Twenty minutes of continuous activity is typically considered the minimum length of time necessary for significant improvement in endurance. The intensity should be between 60 and 85 percent of maximum heart rate.

Generally speaking, endurance exercises require repeated movement of the large muscles in the arms, legs, or hips. These movements are required to get one's heart pumping rapidly. The principal positive effects of endurance exercise are to the cardiovascular system. (That's why endurance training is also referred to as *cardio*.) Endurance exercise keeps the heart, lungs, and circulatory system healthy and improves overall fitness. As a result, doing cardio helps delay or prevent many diseases that are common in older adults, such as diabetes and heart disease. In addition, building endurance makes it easier to carry out many everyday activities, such as climbing stairs. A bonus of moderate to intense endurance exercise is that the body releases endorphins, natural painkillers that promote an increased sense of well-being.

Strength training is another important activity for fitness. Sometimes called *resistance training*, strength training involves using muscles against a resistant force. The muscles are said to be "under load." Most often the resistance is the function of gravity and weights, although other methods are available (for example, strong elastic bands, and pneumatic/hydraulic cylinders). "Free weights" include barbells and dumbbells with heavy disks attached. Weight machines operate on the same property of gravity.

Lifting weights actually causes microdamage to muscles, which become stronger when they rebuild themselves. At least one day of rest between exercising any particular muscle group is recommended. When properly performed, strength training provides significant benefits in addition to an increase in muscle strength and mass. The connective tissues of the musculoskeletal system—tendons and ligaments—are also strengthened. That is very significant for joint stability, particularly as people age. Weight training also increases bone strength and density, which is very important in

(continued)

the prevention of osteoporosis. An increase in HDL ("good") cholesterol has been linked to resistance training. Increased muscle mass leads to a higher metabolic rate; that means that a person with a muscular body is burning more calories while resting than a person with less muscle mass.

The aspect of fitness people are less likely to consider is flexibility. **Nonetheless,** flexibility is very important for daily life as well as for professional competition. Flexibility exercises stretch the muscles, ligaments, and tendons. The result is that the body becomes more limber. Being flexible gives a person more freedom of movement for other exercises as well as for everyday activities. Stretching exercises, when done properly, assist with posture by balancing the tension placed across the joint by the muscles that cross it. Proper posture minimizes stress and maximizes the strength of all joint movements. Many cases of chronic lower back pain are actually a function of a lack of limberness in the upper legs and in the lower back.

Perhaps the form of exercise most specifically focused on flexibility is yoga. In addition to yoga's obvious contribution to limberness, many practitioners find that it has a positive psychological effect. (Of course, that can be said for the first two types of exercise as well!) Those who regularly practice yoga report that they experience a reduction in anxiety, stress, depression, chronic pain, and sleep difficulties. Put positively, they report a higher general sense of well-being.

A person who engages regularly in endurance exercises, strength training, and flexibility development will become fit. Adding a healthy diet, adequate water intake, and sound sleeping patterns to these three physical activities will result in an optimum level of health and fitness.

Vocabulary Collection Word:
nonetheless

Your in-context definition:
_____
_____

A dictionary definition:
_____
_____

CREATING GRAPHIC ORGANIZERS TO ANALYZE ORGANIZATION

A **graphic organizer** is a visual map that displays much of the same information as an outline. Graphic organizers are designed to show relationships among ideas. Some people find that working with graphic organizers is easier than working with outlines.

Many word-processing programs have a feature, like SmartArt in *Microsoft Word*, that offers templates for graphic organizers. However, you can also draw a graphic organizer by hand.

To create a graphic organizer, begin by drawing a box at the top of the page. The box should be as wide as your sheet of paper because it will form the canopy for all the boxes that follow. As you reread your text, find what you think is the main idea or thesis statement, and write it inside the box. Remember to use quotation marks if you are using a direct quote.

> "People who can put off immediate gratification are more likely to have what it takes to be successful in the important things in life."

Next, look for a major supporting point—an idea that directly proves the main point. Draw a narrower box with this information in it, and connect it to the main box, as shown on the next page.

"People who can put off immediate gratification are more likely to have what it takes to be successful in the important things in life."

The Marshmallow Experiment shows that delayed gratification skills lead to more success in life.

As you come across details, add more boxes, connecting the new boxes to the ideas that they support. When you find new major supporting points that directly prove the main idea, add boxes for those too. Step back and look at the graphic organizer. Does the arrangement of boxes seem logical to you, with lesser ideas supporting greater ideas? If not, rearrange the boxes so that they better reflect a logical organization. As a final step, you might find it helpful to label the boxes that contain the thesis statement and the major supporting point.

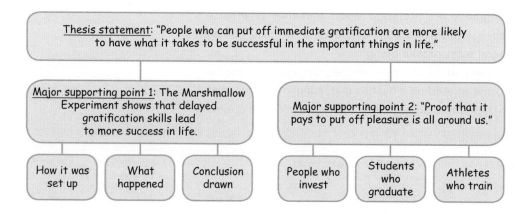

Thesis statement: "People who can put off immediate gratification are more likely to have what it takes to be successful in the important things in life."

Major supporting point 1: The Marshmallow Experiment shows that delayed gratification skills lead to more success in life.

Major supporting point 2: "Proof that it pays to put off pleasure is all around us."

How it was set up

What happened

Conclusion drawn

People who invest

Students who graduate

Athletes who train

Outlines and graphic organizers illustrate the *logic* of a text. Sometimes, though, a writer will jump around in presenting ideas and information. For example, to arouse readers' interest in what lies ahead, a writer may start an essay with a detail for a point that will come later on in the text. In your graphic organizer, be sure to attach the detail to the point that it supports even if the detail appears out of order in the text.

USING OUTLINES TO DRAFT ESSAYS

In addition to serving as a tool to help you understand readings, outlines also make drafting your essay easier. The best kind of outline to use for writing is an enhanced outline. It should contain your thesis statement, your main supporting points, and the supporting details you will use to develop each main supporting point. We will follow the process of Ian, a writing student, as he uses an enhanced outline to draft his essay.

Ian is writing an essay to convince his classmates that investing at an early age is wise. He has already used prewriting to generate ideas, has written a thesis statement, has determined his major supporting points, and has developed the supporting details he will use to develop his ideas. Here is the enhanced outline Ian has created for his essay. Notice that he has indicated the source for each quote he uses—an article entitled "Six Misconceptions about Investing Young" by Jean Folger (www.investopedia.com) and a personal communication from Sean Williams, an investment banker he contacted.

Ian's Enhanced Outline

Title: Start with a Penny

Introduction: I'll tell the story of my grandparents, who came to the United States with nothing and ended up having over a million dollars, simply because they have made small deposits into their investment account each week since they were young.

Thesis statement: One of the most important preparations college students can make for the future is to start investing immediately.

Major supporting point 1: Accruing wealth comes from making small investments over a long period of time.

  Support: Explanation of mathematics

- "A person who starts at age 20 and invests $100 per month until age 65 (a total contribution of $54,000) will have more than $200,000 when he or she reaches age 65 assuming a 5% return" (Folger).
- Example of my grandparents (actual amount they invested)

Major supporting point 2: Almost anyone, even college students, can find small amounts of money to invest.

  Support: Definition—"Discretionary income includes money spent on luxury items, vacations and non-essential goods and services" (Folger).

- How to find discretionary income
- How discretionary income adds up (provide explanation)
- Provide examples

Major supporting point 3: Additionally, investing is easy, and starting to invest at a young age will help you get into the habit of investing.

  Support: Explanation about how easy it is to invest

- Example of setting up an investment account
- Example of buying bonds
- Quote from investment company: "Many people have the idea that investing requires a lot of technical knowledge, but it doesn't. All you need to do is come in and talk with an adviser. The process is similar to setting up a savings account" (Williams).

Major supporting point 4: Finally, college students should start investing because they will most likely need the money.

  Support: Social security and retirement plans may not work.

- Quote: "It is difficult to predict where social security will be in future years, and many investors learned the hard way in the last decade that employee-sponsored retirement plans don't always work out" (Folger).
- As you age, expenses increase.
- Examples of expenses

Conclusion: End by telling readers about the relaxing life my grandparents now enjoy (their travels, nice home, etc.) because of their investments.

Because Ian has a wealth of information in his outline—including quotes, stories, and examples—he can start drafting the body paragraphs by writing sentences for each item on his outline. Using an outline to guide you will make the drafting process easier, but you may still find that your outline is incomplete. Once you start drafting, you may think of additional ideas that would make your essay better. You can always add these ideas to your outline and make sure they fit.

The two columns below demonstrate how Ian uses his outline to draft the sentences in the first body paragraph. Ian had planned to devote only one paragraph for each major supporting point. However, as he began writing, he realized that the explanation of how the math of investing works was requiring a lot of space. Thus, he decided to create a new paragraph for the remaining support he wished to discuss.

Ian's First Draft

Accruing wealth comes from making small investments over a long period of time. My grandfather explained the process so that it was very easy to understand. He told me to imagine loaning a friend $10. Because you loaned him the money, he gives you a 10 percent fee ($1) when he repays the loan. Now you have $11 to loan. Your friend borrows the $11, again paying a 10 percent fee. This time the fee is $1.10. When your friend repays the money, you have $12.10. You haven't done anything but loan money to earn the extra $2.10! Now, imagine you keep doing this until you have $200. When you loan out the $200, you get 10 percent, which is $20. You then have $220 to loan. When you loan it out, you earn $22. The amount of interest goes up as the amount of money you have to loan increases.

The reason to invest at a young age is that if you keep reinvesting your profits, you can accumulate a great deal of wealth over a long time. In fact, "a person who starts at age 20 and invests $100 per month until age 65 (a total contribution of $54,000) will have more than $200,000 when he or she reaches age 65 assuming a 5% return" (Folger). My grandparents started by investing $20 a month, increasing the amount as they were able. They probably never thought they would be millionaires in retirement!

Ian's Enhanced Outline

Major supporting point 1: Accruing wealth comes from making small investments over a long period of time.

Support: Explanation of mathematics

[Explanation of mathematics continues]

- "A person who starts at age 20 and invests $100 per month until age 65 (a total contribution of $54,000) will have more than $200,000 when he or she reaches age 65 assuming a 5% return" (Folger).

- Example of my grandparents (actual amount they invested)

As Ian continues to write body paragraphs, he will make decisions like the one he made regarding creating a new paragraph. Good writers constantly review, revise, and rethink their outlines during the drafting process. Don't be afraid to make changes when you believe those changes would make your essay better. Consider the checklist that follows as you draft your own essays:

- Am I using enough support to fully develop the idea?
- Should I break paragraphs (or combine paragraphs)?
- Should I change the order in which I present information?
- When I reread my essay from the beginning, are there places where the ideas seem not to fit together?
- Are there places where I repeat ideas?

These are only some of the considerations to keep in mind during the drafting process. You will analyze your paper in even more depth as you revise it.

PRACTICE ④ Drafting Body Paragraphs from an Outline

Ian's second major supporting point is that college students can find discretionary income—extra money—to invest. Using Ian's prewriting and outline (both below), draft a paragraph or more for this major supporting point. Use a separate sheet for your draft.

IAN'S PREWRITING

Where college students can find extra money:

- Part-time work
- Not having a cell phone (or having only a basic cell phone)
- Not buying cable TV
- Avoiding debt
- Donating plasma
- Using a portion of birthday gifts to invest

IAN'S ENHANCED OUTLINE

> **Major supporting point 2:** Almost anyone, even college students, can find small amounts of money to invest.
>
> **Support:** Definition—"Discretionary income includes money spent on luxury items, vacations and non-essential goods and services" (Folger).
>
> - How to find discretionary income
> - How discretionary income adds up (provide explanation)
> - Provide examples

USING OUTLINES TO WRITE DETAILED AND BRIEF SUMMARIES

In addition to being a tool for understanding texts and for drafting, outlining assists in writing summaries. In both workplace and academic writing, summarizing is an important skill. As an employee, you may be called on to read a work-related report and summarize it for your boss or coworkers. Or you may be given a thick booklet of guidelines and be expected to follow them. Being able to summarize the booklet and extract the most important information will help you follow the guidelines. In college, you will often summarize textbook chapters and other materials.

The Purpose of a Summary

A **summary** is a shortened version of a source. In a summary, you present the main idea and major supporting points of the source in your own words. A summary must be accurate, appropriately focused, and objective. To ensure the accuracy of your summary, you must correctly understand the text you are summarizing. Thus, it is vital that you read, annotate, analyze, and reread the source until you feel confident you understand it.

To give your summary an appropriate focus, you must carefully choose the points from the original source that you wish to emphasize. Specifically, you need to focus on the main idea (or thesis), the major supporting points for the main idea, and any other important ideas presented after—or in conjunction with—the central idea. If you focus on supporting details and neglect the main idea or the major supporting points, then your summary will not give readers an accurate understanding of the source. One way to choose the most important points to focus on is to write an enhanced outline of the source. An enhanced outline will provide the exact content you will need for a summary.

Finally, summaries must be **objective**. Being objective means that you do not express an opinion on the text you are summarizing. Whether you agree or disagree with the source does not matter in a summary: your goal is to simply present the source's ideas in a brief way.

Vocabulary Collection Word:
objective

Your in-context definition:
_____
_____

A dictionary definition:
_____
_____

Steps for Writing Summaries

The ten steps listed here will help you write an effective summary. You may occasionally quote directly from the text, but most of the summary should be in your own words.

Step 1: Read and annotate the source.

Spend sufficient time reading and annotating the source material. As always, mark the main idea and major supporting details. Look for the information that supports the major supporting details.

Step 2: Create an enhanced outline.

By creating an enhanced outline, such as the one presented earlier in this chapter on "How Delaying Gratification Predicts Future Success," you will have most of the information you will need to write a summary.

Step 3: Start with bibliographic information.

A helpful way to start a summary is to provide bibliographic information about the source. Bibliographic information includes the following:

- Author's name and credentials, if available
- Title of the source (use quotation marks for an article title; italics for a book title)
- Type of publication (specify *book* or *journal*; use italics for a journal title)
- Publisher and place of publication for a book
- Date of publication (add volume and issue numbers for a journal, if available)

We will follow the process that Jason, a college student, follows to write a summary based on the enhanced outline for "How Delaying Gratification Predicts Future Success" on page 229.

In 2005, *Prescott Journal of Ideas* published a brief essay called "How Delaying Gratification Predicts Future Success" by Kari Gardner, a professor of education at Hinton University's Graduate School of Education.

The bibliographic information includes the date, the name of the journal (in italics), the title of the article (in quotation marks), and the author's name and credentials.

We could have worded the bibliographic information differently. Following are two alternative opening statements:

In 2005, Kari Gardner, a professor of education at Hinton University's Graduate School of Education, published a brief essay, "How Delaying Gratification Predicts Future Success," in *Prescott Journal of Ideas*.

"How Delaying Gratification Predicts Future Success," by Kari Gardner, a professor of education at Hinton University's Graduate School of Education, was published in *Prescott Journal of Ideas* in 2005.

Step 4: Write a sentence that tells the reader the topic of the source.

After you read the source, you should have a clear idea of the topic being addressed. Express this topic in one sentence, as Jason did here.

Gardner's essay concerns the issue of delayed gratification.	Source's topic

Step 5: Tell the reader the main idea of the text.

If the thesis statement is explicitly stated in the source, you can quote it directly. If you quote the author's words from the original published source, be sure to note the page on which the words appear. For a source you obtained electronically—such as through your library's online databases—you will usually need only the writer's name. Do not use page numbers from a printout of a source, unless the printout shows an exact replica of the article's pages.

   If the writer's thesis statement is implied—not stated directly—you will need to write a sentence that accurately reflects the thesis statement. In her essay, Gardner includes a thesis statement, so Jason quoted the statement directly.

Vocabulary Collection Word:
database

Your in-context definition:

_____

_____

A dictionary definition:

_____

_____

The essay's thesis statement is clear: "People who can put off immediate gratification are more likely to have what it takes to be successful in the important things in life" (Gardner).	Source's thesis. The author's name is included in parentheses after the quote. Notice where the punctuation is placed.

Step 6: Use the writer's major supporting points and supporting details to summarize the body of the text.

This section will probably be the lengthiest part of your summary. Put all of these ideas in your own words. Here is the main part of Jason's summary.

Gardner proves that people who can delay gratification seem to be more successful in life.	Topic sentence
She discusses the Marshmallow Experiment in which children were given the option of eating one marshmallow immediately or waiting fifteen minutes and getting a second marshmallow.	Source's first major supporting point
The children who waited for the second marshmallow ended up becoming more successful adults.	Summary of supporting details
Another point Gardner makes about delaying gratification is that people who are able to wait sometimes end up getting benefits.	Source's second major supporting point
For example, people who invest and are patient can become wealthy. Students who work hard in college can graduate, and athletes who train hard can succeed in their sports.	Summary of supporting details

Step 7: If any of the points need more explanation, add a sentence or two to provide it.

If your reader might not understand a particular supporting point without an explanation, then you must provide it. Read your summary as if you had never read the original source. Are there places where the supporting details need to be explained in more depth? Keep in mind that a summary should be short, so provide explanations only if they are really needed. Jason added information (shown on the next page) to one of the paragraphs in his summary to explain points that might be unclear to the reader.

She discusses the Marshmallow Experiment in which children were given the option of eating one marshmallow immediately or waiting fifteen minutes and getting a second marshmallow. The children who waited for the second marshmallow ended up becoming more successful adults. They had fewer behavioral problems, less drug and alcohol addiction, greater educational success, and higher SAT scores.

Additional information

Step 8: Discuss any other important points the author makes.

Sometimes sources will include important points that fall outside the main idea and the major supporting points for the main idea. For example, some sources begin by discussing the background of the issue being discussed. Writers sometimes include definitions, alternative points of view, or additional considerations about the topic. If the additional points in a source are important to readers' understanding to the text, include them. In her essay, Gardner provides a definition of *delayed gratification*. Jason decided to include this definition in his summary since understanding this concept is important to the meaning of the text.

Gardner defines *delayed gratification* as "the ability to postpone the fulfillment of an immediate desire in order to obtain a more substantial reward in the future."

Additional information needed for understanding

Step 9: Tell the reader how the source ends.

A simple but effective way to end a summary is to briefly tell the reader how the writer ends his or her article. Here is the end of Jason's summary.

Gardner ends her essay with some advice. "It will always be easier to eat the marshmallow right away, but doing so may not always be the best choice."

End of summary

Step 10: Once you have determined the content of your summary, you are ready to write a draft.

Read Jason's completed **detailed summary** on the next page. Notice not only the content but also the formatting. The summary follows MLA style guidelines.

Example of a Detailed Summary

Alameda 1 — MLA-style heading

Jason Alameda

Dr. Hall

ENGL 1301.33

12 October 2014

A Summary of "How Delaying Gratification Predicts Future Success" — Title, centered

    In 2005, *Prescott Journal of Ideas* published a brief essay called "How Delaying Gratification Predicts Future Success" by Kari Gardner, a professor of education at Hinton University's Graduate School of Education. — Bibliographic information

    Gardner's essay concerns the issue of delayed gratification. The essay's thesis statement is clear: "People who can put off immediate gratification are more likely to have what it takes to be successful in the important things in life" (Gardner). — Source's topic and thesis

    Gardner proves that people who can delay gratification seem to be more successful in life. She discusses the Marshmallow Experiment in which children were given the option of eating one marshmallow immediately or waiting fifteen minutes and getting a second marshmallow. The children who waited for the second marshmallow ended up becoming more successful adults. They had fewer behavioral problems, less drug and alcohol addiction, greater educational success, and higher SAT scores. — Source's first major supporting point and supporting details

    Another point Gardner makes about delaying gratification is that people who are able to wait sometimes end up getting benefits. For example, people who invest and are patient can become wealthy. — Source's second major supporting point and supporting details

Alameda 2

Students who work hard in college can graduate, and athletes who train hard can succeed in their sports.

Gardner defines *delayed gratification* as "the ability to postpone the fulfillment of an immediate desire in order to obtain a more substantial reward in the future."

Additional background information: definition

Gardner ends her essay with some advice. "It will always be easier to eat the marshmallow right away, but doing so may not always be the best choice."

End of summary

Jason's detailed summary above is about half the length of the original text. Sometimes you will want to write summaries that are much shorter. For example, if you need only a brief reference to Gardner's essay in a paper you are writing, you might want only a few lines of summary. In such cases, it is sufficient to include brief bibliographic data and the writer's main point. Here is an example of a **brief summary.**

Example of a Brief Summary

In her essay entitled "How Delaying Gratification Predicts Future Success," Kari Gardner shows that people who can delay gratification end up more successful than those who cannot.

Whether you write a detailed summary or a brief one, your most important task is to provide an accurate representation of the ideas in the text you are summarizing. Try your hand at writing summaries by completing the following exercise.

PRACTICE 5 Writing Detailed and Brief Summaries

In Practice 3, you created an outline for "Achieving Optimum Fitness." Use your outline to write a detailed summary for the reading. When you are finished with the detailed summary, write a brief summary.

WRITING PARAPHRASES

A **paraphrase** is a rewording of a *portion* of a text in your own words to make the meaning of the original text more clear. Paraphrases help you integrate a source's ideas smoothly into your own writing without overusing direct quotations.

While summaries pull out the main ideas and major supporting points from texts, paraphrases focus on clarifying and rewording a particular idea in a text. Another difference between a summary and a paraphrase is that a summary condenses the most important information in a text into a shorter version. A paraphrase, on the other hand, rewords each sentence to help clarify its meaning; thus, a paraphrase will often be as long as the original text.

A paraphrase is similar to a summary in that both must be written in your own words; any wording from the original source must be enclosed in quotation marks and integrated into your own writing. Also, just like a summary, a paraphrase must properly reference the original source.

To write a paraphrase, read the original carefully, and then put it aside. Write what you understand about the original material in your own words. Then check your paraphrase to make sure that it reflects the meaning of the original and that you have not inadvertently used the language of the original without quotation marks. Notice how, in the following paraphrase, the student writer puts into her own words the ideas in the original text, an excerpt from *Selecting a Career in Mental Health*.

ORIGINAL FROM *SELECTING A CAREER IN MENTAL HEALTH* BY CAMILLE ROBERTS	STUDENT'S PARAPHRASE
Psychology is both a science and a profession. As a science, psychology is the study of how people perceive, think, feel, and act; as a profession, it is concerned with predicting how people will act, helping people modify their behavior, and helping organizations, communities, and societies change. Some psychologists focus on research. These professionals conduct experiments and observe human behavior to add to our knowledge about how the mind works. Other psychologists focus on helping people and institutions change their behavior, structure, or functions. They spend time working with individuals and groups of people by analyzing their behaviors and helping them learn to modify their behaviors.	Roberts points out that psychology is a science as well as a profession. The science of psychology covers "how people perceive, think, feel, and act," and it includes research to discover new insights about these elements. Two kinds of psychologists can be identified. First, some psychologists are researchers who spend their time doing experiments and observing people. These psychologists help create information and add to what we already know about how the mind works. The other type of psychologist works directly with people to help them change behaviors that are not working well. This type of psychologist may also work with groups of people to help them change their behaviors.

Remember that you cannot use paraphrased ideas without citing the source. Additionally, if you use any of the source's original language in your paraphrase, you must treat the language as a direct quote and use quotation marks. For example, in the preceding paraphrase, notice that the student includes a direct quotation from the source—in quotation marks—in her second sentence.

PRACTICE (6) Writing a Paraphrase

The following reading about antibiotic resistance is from the Centers for Disease Control and Prevention. Write a paraphrase of this reading.

Antibiotic resistance is a quickly growing, extremely dangerous problem. World health leaders have described antibiotic-resistant bacteria as "nightmare bacteria" that "pose a catastrophic threat" to people in every country in the world. Each year in the United States, at least 2 million people become infected with bacteria that are resistant to antibiotics, and at least 23,000 people die each year as a direct result of these infections. Many more people die from other conditions that were complicated by an antibiotic-resistant infection.

CHAPTER ACTIVITIES

READING AND ANNOTATING

The following passage is from *Mirror for Humanity*, an anthropology textbook by Conrad Phillip Kottak published in 2014. Read and annotate the passage. In particular, identify the thesis statement, the major supporting points, the supporting details, and any other information that would be suitable for an outline, graphic organizer, or summary. If the thesis statement is implied rather than explicit, write it in your own words. When you are finished, answer the questions that follow.

Experiencing Culture: Personal Space and Displays of Affection
by Conrad Phillip Kottak

A few years ago I created and taught a course called Experiencing Culture to American college students in Italy. Students wrote biweekly journals reflecting on the cultural differences they observed between Europeans and Americans. One thing that really struck them was the greater frequency and intensity of PDAs—public displays of affection—between romantic couples in Italy, compared with the United States.

The world's nations and cultures have strikingly different notions about displays of affection and personal space. Cocktail parties in international meeting places such as the United Nations can resemble an elaborate insect mating ritual as diplomats from different countries advance, withdraw, and sidestep. When Americans talk, walk, and dance, they maintain a certain distance from others. Italians or Brazilians, who need less personal space, may interpret such "standoffishness" as a sign of coldness. In conversational pairs, the Italian or Brazilian typically moves in, while the American "instinctively" retreats from a "close talker." Such bodily movements illustrate not instinct, but culture—behavior programmed by years of exposure to a particular cultural tradition.

To what extent are you a product of your particular culture? How much does, and should, your cultural background influence your actions and decisions? Americans may not fully appreciate the power of culture because of the value their culture places on the individual. We have seen that individualism is a distinctive shared value, a feature of American culture, transmitted constantly in our daily lives. In the media, count how many stories focus on individuals versus groups. . . . Certainly we have distinctive features because we are individuals, but we have other distinct **attributes** because we belong to cultural groups.

To return to the cultural contrast that so impressed my American students in Italy, there are striking contrasts between a national culture (American) that tends to be reserved about displays of physical affection and national cultures in which the opposite is true. Brazilians approach, touch, and kiss one another much more frequently than North Americans do. Middle-class Brazilians teach their kids—both boys and girls—to kiss (on the cheek, two or three times, coming and going) every adult relative they ever see. Given the size of Brazilian extended families, this can mean hundreds of people. Women continue kissing all those people throughout their lives. Until they are adolescents, boys kiss all adult relatives. Men typically continue to kiss female relatives and friends, as well as their fathers and uncles throughout their lives.

Do you kiss your father? Your uncle? Your grandfather? How about your mother, aunt, or grandmother? The answer to these questions may differ between men and

Vocabulary Collection Word:
attribute

Your in-context definition:

_____

_____

A dictionary definition:

_____

_____

women, and for male and female relatives. Culture can help us to make sense of these differences. In America, girls typically are encouraged to show affection; this is less true for boys.

However, culture is not static. Sarah Kershaw (2009) describes a recent surge of teenage hugging behavior in American schools. Concerned about potential sexual harassment issues, parents and school officials remain suspicious of such PDAs, even if the younger generation is more tolerant. Even American boys appear to be more likely nowadays to share nonromantic hugs, as such expressions as "bromance" and "man crush" enter our vocabulary. Hugging also has migrated online, where Facebook applications allowing friends to send hugs have tens of thousands of fans.

It's important to note that cultural traits exist because they are learned, not because they are natural or inherently right. Ethnocentrism is the error of viewing one's own culture as superior and applying one's own cultural values in judging people from other cultures. How easy is it for you to see beyond the ethnocentric blinders of your own experience? Do you have an ethnocentric position regarding displays of affection?

Vocabulary Collection Word:
inherently

Your in-context definition:

_____

_____

A dictionary definition:

_____

_____

Questions for Consideration

1. What is the author's thesis statement? If the author expresses it in a sentence, copy the sentence. If not, put the thesis statement in your own words.

2. What are the chief differences between displays of public affection in the United States and Brazil?

3. What does the author identify as some reasons for American attitudes about public affection?

4. Does the author present this information in an unbiased way, or does he present his own opinion?

5. What is ethnocentrism?

USING MODELS TO PRACTICE COMPOSING

Earlier in this chapter, you studied a detailed summary of "How Delaying Gratification Predicts Future Success," which you will use as a model for writing your own summary of Conrad Phillip Kottak's "Experiencing Culture: Personal Space and Displays of Affection."

1. On a separate sheet, construct an enhanced outline or graphic organizer of Kottak's text.

2. Follow your outline and the steps below to write a detailed summary of "Experiencing Culture." Use the detailed summary of "How Delaying Gratification Predicts Future Success" on page 239 as a model.

   • Write a title for your summary.

   • Write an introduction paragraph that provides bibliographic information for the reading. Start with the date, the publication, and the title.

   • Write a paragraph in which you provide the topic and the writer's main idea.

   • Write a paragraph about the first major supporting point the writer uses. Include information about the support used to back up this major supporting point.

   • Write a paragraph for each additional major supporting point the writer uses. Include information about the support used to back up each major supporting point.

- Provide any additional information needed to understand the reading.
- Write a brief ending for your summary by telling readers how the writer ended the text.

A READING AND WRITING ASSIGNMENT

Conrad Phillip Kottak writes about the cultural preferences of most North Americans regarding displays of affection. As Kottak notes, cultural preferences change over time. Write an essay in which you discuss three or four cultural preferences, rules, or traditions that have changed over time. For example, at the beginning of the twentieth century, most middle-class American women did not work outside the home. However, this tradition has changed, and now a majority of women work outside the home. What other preferences, rules, or traditions can you think of that have changed? Here are some areas to consider:

- Child care and child rearing
- Roles of fathers, mothers, grandparents, children
- Rules of etiquette, such as table manners, greetings, rules of politeness
- Traditional activities, such as those involving holiday customs, family meals, birthday parties

Use the Quick Start Guide to Integrated Reading and Writing Assignments to help you with this process.

⊙ THINKING FROM AN INSTRUCTOR'S POINT OF VIEW

Imagine that you have enrolled in a college program that will enable you to become a construction manager. The required book for your first class is thick, and the chapters are long. Your instructor announces that the first major exam will be in two weeks, and it will cover three chapters. When a classmate asks whether the instructor will be handing out a review sheet, he replies that he will not. Your classmate is unhappy and does not understand why the instructor would be so seemingly coldhearted. He asks you to explain the situation to him.

The best way to help your classmate understand the situation is to consider it from the instructor's point of view. Write two or three paragraphs in which you explain the instructor's decision to the best of your ability.

⊙ ADDING TO YOUR VOCABULARY

This chapter's vocabulary words appear below.

entrepreneur	attribute	enhanced	inherently
nonetheless	objective	database	

Choose five of the vocabulary words from this chapter that you would like to add to your vocabulary, and think about how you can use them this week. For example, one of this chapter's words is *nonetheless*. You can often substitute *nonetheless* for *but*, as in the example that follows.

> **Example:** I put bread on my shopping list, *but* I forgot to buy it at the store.
>
> I put bread on my shopping list. *Nonetheless,* I forgot to buy it at the store.

List each of the five words you plan to use this week, and make note of a context in which you could use each word.

> **Example:** *Nonetheless.* I can use this in ordinary conversation with my parents.

⊙ ADDITIONAL ASSIGNMENTS

1. Earlier in this chapter you read about how children in the Marshmallow Experiment who were able to delay gratification turned out to have more successes in life than the children who could not resist temptation. Write three or four paragraphs about times in your life when you decided to either delay gratification or not. What were the circumstances? As you look back, do you think you made the right choice? Explain these situations and reflect on them in your writing.

2. Create a graphic organizer for the essay you wrote in response to "Experiencing Culture: Personal Space and Displays of Affection."

3. Do an Internet search to find information about one of the cultures to which you belong. For example, if you are a horse lover, search for information about equestrian (horse) culture. List some of the cultural beliefs, behaviors, or attributes you find online. Make sure you reference the Web site on which you find the information. Write an essay in which you respond to these attributes by either agreeing that they are part of your culture or disputing them. Explain your reasoning.

4. *Ethnocentrism* results in our believing that our cultural practices are the best ones. What is the problem with ethnocentric thinking? Explain. Think of an example in history when ethnocentrism led to tragedy. Write a paragraph about the tragedy and how it resulted from ethnocentrism.

EMOTIONAL INTELLIGENCE

An important part of emotional intelligence is the ability to understand and deal with your feelings. To be able to do that, you must be able to *name* your feelings.

Sounds easy, right? It's surprisingly difficult sometimes. For example, many people experience periods of unhappiness but cannot quite name what they are feeling. They may feel sad, angry, hopeless, helpless, fearful, or any number of other emotions. By being able to accurately name what you are feeling, you can then find ways to deal with your emotions.

Think of a time you felt very upset. What was the emotion that caused you to be upset? For example, if you have ever come close to being in a car accident caused by another driver, you have probably experienced anger. Underneath that anger, however, would be fear. Write a paragraph about a time you were very upset. What were the emotions responsible for your condition? Work on naming your emotions, and consider writing about your emotions when you experience upsetting (or even joyous) occasions.

CULTURAL LITERACY

As a college student, you will often hear terms associated with higher education. Improve your cultural literacy by learning these terms. Read through the list of words and phrases on the following page. Write definitions for all of them, guessing about the ones that are unfamiliar. Next, compare your answers with a classmate's. Finally, use the Internet or a dictionary to determine what the terms mean. Work on learning the terms you do not know by trying to include them in your daily conversation.

- Higher education
- Associate's degree
- Bachelor's degree
- Master's degree
- Doctorate
- Postsecondary

- Learning objectives
- GPA
- Graduate school
- Undergraduate
- Online courses
- Standardized tests

- Transfer student
- Certificate program
- Syllabus
- Core curriculum
- Matriculation
- College catalog

Are there other words you have heard associated with college that you want to understand? If so, add them to this list.

CRITICAL THINKING

Most of us make predictions every day. If we are stuck in traffic, we predict how late we may be for our appointments. If we are struggling to find the motivation to do an unpleasant task, we predict what will happen if we put the task off or avoid it altogether.

Since predicting is such a common human experience, we should predict as accurately as we can. To predict accurately, we must consider *every* possibility and then choose the most likely one. Failure to think about every possibility can lead to disaster.

Hone your prediction skills by making a list of at least ten possible outcomes for the following scenario: You just took a job as a stocker in a warehouse. The company requires you to work forty hours per week, and you were lucky enough to find a college schedule that enables you to take two courses, requiring six hours per week on campus. In the middle of the semester, you will be moving into your first apartment. How might the semester turn out?

After you make your list of possibilities, determine which possibility is most likely. Next, list actions you could take to minimize any negative consequences you have predicted.

When you finish, answer this question in a paragraph: how can making accurate predictions help you as a student, as an employee, and as a person?

METACOGNITION

Look back at the last few years of your life and assess the major decisions you made. Now, consider your ability to make good predictions. Think about times when you made predictions that turned out to be accurate. Perhaps you predicted you would really like a particular job, so you took the position and you did, indeed, really like the job. Why do you think you made a good prediction in that scenario? Explain.

Now think about a time when you made a bad prediction. Perhaps you were in a failed relationship or did not prepare well enough for a test or assignment. Why do you think you made a poor prediction in that scenario?

On the whole, have you been good at making accurate predictions? Think through your past experiences and reflect on them. How can you make better predictions in the future?

The beginning of a path should be inviting, and the end should make the journey worthwhile. In the same way, as readers we expect texts to invite us in and then end agreeably. In addition, as writers we need to focus on composing engaging introductions and satisfactory conclusions.

Titles, Introductions, and Conclusions

Have you ever picked up a magazine, perhaps while waiting in line at the grocery store, because something on the cover caught your eye? Sometimes a photo gets us curious, or perhaps a title or a description on the cover arouses our interest. Magazine editors depend on intriguing titles and introductions to sell their products. In the same way, good writers create titles and introductions that entice readers.

Titles, introductions, and conclusions frame a text and help readers understand its structure and content. The title is the first clue about a text's content. The introduction often provides background information or uses another method to invite readers to continue reading. The conclusion serves an important function, too. It provides **closure** for readers—the sense that the essay has reached its end.

Mastering the creation of effective titles, introductions, and conclusions is part of writing well. One way to achieve this mastery is to use your reading and analysis skills to determine how successful writers construct these elements.

CHAPTER OBJECTIVES

After completing this chapter, students will be able to do the following:

- **Analyze and create titles.**

- **Read, analyze, and create introductions.**

- **Read, analyze, and create conclusions.**

ANALYZING AND CREATING TITLES

The primary purpose of a title is to give readers an idea about the contents of the essay or to make readers curious about it. Many essays have straightforward titles, as the examples on the next page show.

Essay Content	Straightforward Title
An essay explaining ikebana—the Japanese art of flower arranging	"What Is Ikebana?"
An essay comparing and contrasting nuclear energy and geothermal energy	"A Comparison of Nuclear and Geothermal Energy"
An essay arguing that women's salaries should be equal to that of men's salaries for the same work	"Women's Pay Should Equal Men's Pay"

Titles should be short—ideally, just a few words—although there are no set rules about how many words a title should have. Here are some examples of titles that are unnecessarily long.

- "A Brief Explanation of Ikebana, the Japanese Art of Flower Arranging"
- "A Comparison and Contrast Essay Concerning the Differences between Nuclear Energy and Geothermal Energy"
- "The Debate about Women's Salaries: Why Are Men's Salaries Often Higher than Women's for the Same Job"

Some titles are creative; they provide more than a straightforward glimpse into the text's content. Consider these titles.

Essay Content	Creative Title
An essay explaining ikebana—the Japanese art of flower arranging	"Ikebana: It's Not Just for Japanese Florists"
An essay comparing and contrasting nuclear energy and geothermal energy	"Geothermal: An Alternative to the Nuclear Option"
An essay arguing that women's salaries should be equal to that of men's salaries for the same work	"Equal Work = Equal Pay"

These titles do not explicitly announce what the essay is about. Rather, they give the reader an idea of the topic.

Another feature of two of these titles is the colon (:). Colons introduce lists or explanations. In the case of the examples given above, the colon separates a word (the main part of the title) from a brief phrase that provides more information (the subtitle). In the title "Ikebana: It's Not Just for Japanese Florists," the phrase after the colon explains a bit about the topic, ikebana. The same occurs with this title: "Geothermal: An Alternative to the Nuclear Option." In titles, a colon generally introduces an explanation.

Titles that are not straightforward generally require more creativity to compose. Consider documentary film titles, for instance. Like a written essay, a documentary film has a point to make. A film may have a political message, or it may seek to explain important concepts, such as nuclear proliferation or the health-care crisis, or it may simply document historical events.

Think about some of the documentary films you have seen lately. Did their titles entice you? The documentary film about former Vice President Al Gore's attempts to educate Americans about destructive global climate change is called *An Inconvenient Truth*. The title does not announce the film's subject but rather calls attention to the importance of the film's content. On the other hand, the title of Ken Burns's documentary *The National Parks: America's Best Idea* reveals not only the film's subject but also the filmmaker's view of the subject.

Be aware of titles as you encounter them. Think about how well they accomplish the tasks of indicating the content of the work and making you want to read (or view) it.

PRACTICE ① Analyzing Titles

Read each of the titles that follow, and indicate whether it is a straightforward title or a creative title. Then make a prediction about the text's content.

Title	Straightforward or Creative?	Predicted Content of Text
1. Keys to Passing Algebra		
2. Waking Up: Overcoming Depression and Anxiety		
3. Old McDonald Had a Heart Attack: Fast-Food Perils		
4. How to Reform Immigration Laws		

PRACTICE ② Choosing Titles

Each item below describes an essay. Choose an appropriate title for each essay, and label the title as either "straightforward" or "creative." Construct at least two creative titles.

1. In this essay, the writer argues that race should not be a factor in adoptions.

Title: _____

Type of title: _____

2. This personal essay, by a journalist who survived Hurricane Katrina in New Orleans, concerns his struggle with depression afterward.

Title: _____

Type of title: _____

3. The writer of this essay argues that migrant farmworkers live in terrible conditions.

Title: _____

Type of title: _____

4. In this essay, the writer explains how scientists develop flu vaccines.

Title: _____

Type of title: _____

READING, ANALYZING, AND CREATING INTRODUCTIONS

An introduction serves two functions: it attempts to engage readers, and it offers hints about what the text will concern. Most readers expect an introduction to give them a sense of where the essay will go and what they will learn or experience by reading it. Good readers use the introduction of an essay to develop a set of expectations about what the text will concern.

How Introductions Function

An introduction can consist of one paragraph, or it can have several paragraphs. In the introduction paragraphs, we will often find the essay's thesis statement, but not always. Writers decide where to place the thesis statement based on the content of the essay and on the audience.

Like a first impression at a job interview, an introductory paragraph carries a great deal of weight. It may not be fair to judge an essay by its introduction, but as readers, we all do. The time and effort spent crafting a carefully written, engaging introduction will be worthwhile.

Strategies for Introductions

Writers often use one of these seven strategies to compose introduction paragraphs. The strategies are summarized in the following table and discussed below.

Strategies for Introductions	
Starting with a question	Ask one or more questions that you answer later on in the essay.
Starting with a story	Tell one or more anecdotes, or start a story that you finish later on in the essay.
Starting with background information	Give information about the topic that readers might need—for example, history or definitions.
Starting with a surprise	Begin with one point of view on the topic, and then switch unexpectedly.
Starting with data	Provide relevant statistics on the topic.
Starting with a quotation or adage	Offer a quotation, perhaps from an expert, or an appropriate saying.
Starting with an objective overview	Give both sides of an argument in neutral language before proceeding to focus on a particular point of view.

■ "Once upon a time . . ." is a famous introduction. What does it tell the reader? How do beginnings help us anticipate the content to come?

Each of these strategies is described in more detail below and is illustrated by a professional selection. In addition, an example shows how each strategy could be used to introduce an essay about the benefits of walking. As you study the examples, pay attention to the hints that the introduction paragraphs give regarding the essay content. Also, think about how you can use these strategies in your own writing.

Starting with a Question

Sometimes writers use a question or a set of questions to introduce a topic. The question often presents the topic and leads to the writer's main point. Notice how starting with questions works in the following example.

Introduction from "Campus Diversity and Student Self-Segregation: Separating Myths from Facts" by Debra Humphreys

When students went off to college this fall, they entered more diverse campuses than ever before. For many students, in fact, their college community is the most diverse they have ever encountered. Most students entering college today come from high schools that are predominantly or exclusively one racial or ethnic group. Given this reality, how are students interacting with one another educationally and socially in college? How socially segregated are college campuses? Is campus diversity leading to educational benefits for today's college students or are students too separated into enclaves on campus to benefit from campus diversity?

Three questions introduce the topic. The writer answers these questions later in the text.

Humphreys does not immediately answer the questions she raises in the introduction paragraph. Rather, she uses the questions to focus attention on the issue of self-segregation in colleges. Later in her essay, she answers the questions in her thesis statement.

When you come across texts that start with a question, the *answer* to the question is often the main idea of the reading. Sometimes, though, a question is used simply to get the audience to think about the topic rather than to introduce a specific thesis statement.

Using This Strategy in Your Writing. One way to use this strategy is to make the first sentence of your introduction paragraph a question. If you create a question whose answer will be your thesis statement, you can discuss **conceivable** answers to this question but save *your* answer for last. Your answer to the question will be your thesis statement.

(Make sure to check your instructor's preferences before using the second-person pronoun *you*. While the use of second person is appropriate for *informal* writing, it is generally not acceptable in formal, academic writing.)

Here is an example of an introduction that uses a question at the beginning of the paragraph.

Vocabulary Collection Word:
conceivable

Your in-context definition:

_____

_____

A dictionary definition:

_____

_____

Example: Starting with a Question

Is walking really a legitimate form of exercise? Many people think walking is not strenuous enough to have health benefits. They think that to get in good shape, people must run, do aerobics, kickbox, or participate in another high-intensity exercise. While all of those are good exercises, the reality is that strenuous exercise is not the only way to work out productively. Millions of people who walk for exercise can attest to the power of walking. The truth is simple: walking for exercise results in a variety of health benefits.	A question suggests that the topic is walking for exercise. The question is followed by possible answers. The writer transitions away from what others think. The writer ends with a thesis statement that answers the opening question.

PRACTICE ③ Writing an Introduction That Uses a Question

Imagine you are writing an essay in which you discuss qualities needed in a successful manager. You have decided to use this thesis statement:

> Successful managers must be able to work well with others, solve problems, and manage their time wisely.

On a separate sheet, write an introduction paragraph using this thesis statement. Use the strategy of *starting with a question.*

Starting with a Story

Writers know that everyone likes a good story. One way to create interest is to begin a text with a story. If a writer knows of an anecdote that fits the topic and her point, she may use that story as a starting point. Sometimes writers use **hypothetical stories**—stories that are made up but are realistic enough to be **credible** and likely. A hypothetical story will work only if it relates to your point and comes across as believable to a reasonable audience.

Look at the beginning paragraph of "Life with Asperger's Syndrome." The writer starts by telling a short story about Paul, a child with Asperger's syndrome. Notice that the anecdote is very brief, and it helps the writer introduce the topic. The writer does not present her thesis statement in the first paragraph; she waits until the second paragraph to provide background information on Asperger's syndrome and to state her main idea.

Vocabulary Collection Word:
credible

Your in-context definition:

_____

_____

A dictionary definition:

_____

_____

Introduction from "Life with Asperger's Syndrome"

Eleven-year-old Paul paced nervously back and forth at the bus stop. His school bus is supposed to arrive every morning at 7:04. Usually Paul could see the bus coming down the street at 7:03, but this morning, at 7:03, there was no bus. A feeling of panic washed over him. When his watch said 7:04, tears began to stream down his face. The bus was not on time. By 7:05, he could not stand it any longer and ran home. If Paul had not been diagnosed with Asperger's syndrome, his mother would probably have been puzzled by this behavior, but she was not shocked. Because he has Asperger's syndrome, Paul is not like other children.	A short anecdote about Paul begins.

Transition from the story to the topic: Asperger's syndrome |
| Asperger's syndrome is a type of **autism**. Many people have heard of autism before, but not many know about Asperger's syndrome. Autism comes in many forms, some very severe and some quite mild. People who have Asperger's are considered to be on the mild "high functioning" side of the autism range. People with classic autism are often unable to talk and do not like being touched, while many of those with Asperger's can function fairly normally in these areas. However, there are some challenges for those who have Asperger's syndrome, and some of these challenges are significant. | Background information

Thesis statement |

The story about Paul is much more interesting than a fact about Asperger's syndrome and might encourage the audience to keep reading.

Be aware as a reader that while some texts *are* primarily about a story, others will simply use stories to make a point or to begin the text, as "Life with Asperger's Syndrome" does. When you read a text that begins with a story, first determine whether the story is what the entire essay will be about. If it is not, ask yourself, "What point is the writer making with this story?"

Using This Strategy in Your Writing. Most people like reading a good story, so they will tune in right away. The key is finding a story that is appropriate for your point. For example, if you want to make the point that insomnia is a disorder that affects the quality of life for those who suffer from it, then including a story about a person's experience with insomnia might be a good way to start an introduction. The example that follows shows how you can use a story to introduce an essay.

Vocabulary Collection Word:
autism

Your in-context definition:

_____

_____

A dictionary definition:

_____

_____

Vocabulary Collection Word:
therapeutic

Your in-context definition:

_____

_____

A dictionary definition:

_____

_____

Example: Starting with a Story

In 2007, Felicity Martinez was twenty-four, and she was dying. She had been diagnosed with melanoma not long after she found a suspicious-looking mole on her right shoulder. Felicity got depressed. She knew that depression would not help her put up the strongest fight she could against cancer. Her doctor prescribed a variety of treatments for depression, and they worked. Felicity believes that one of the treatments that especially helped her take control of her life and feel empowered was a **therapeutic** walking routine. Walking helped her become more centered and more determined as she fought and eventually beat the disease. As Felicity's story shows, walking for exercise can result in a variety of positive effects.	The writer starts with a story (narrative) about Felicity Martinez.

The writer uses a transition to move from the specifics of the story to the thesis statement about walking. |

Notice that the writer did not abruptly stop Felicity's story. Instead, after giving Felicity's thoughts about her experience, the writer used a transition ("As Felicity's story shows") to gracefully move to the thesis statement.

When you use a story in an introduction, make sure the story is *entirely* related to your point. In the example above, if Felicity had survived cancer and then incidentally became a walker, her story would not really show that walking can be a life-changing activity.

PRACTICE 4 Writing an Introduction That Uses a Story

Imagine you are writing an essay in which you discuss qualities needed in a successful manager. You have decided to use this thesis statement:

> Successful managers must be able to work well with others, solve problems, and manage their time wisely.

On a separate sheet, write an introduction paragraph using this thesis statement. Use the strategy of *starting with a story.* Consider telling a story about a work experience you had with a good or bad manager.

Starting with Background Information

Some topics are complex enough that audiences need background information. Thus, using background information to lead up to the main point is one way to write an introduction. Notice the annotations in the following example, "Using Media to Make a Difference," from *Introduction to Mass Communication: Media Literacy and Culture* by Stanley J. Baran.

Introduction from "Using Media to Make a Difference: Social Media and the Middle East Democracy Movement" by Stanley J. Baran

Tens of thousands of Iranians from all walks of life took to the streets in the summer of 2009 to protest what they saw as the illegitimate reelection of President Mahmoud Ahmadinejad. The government, already skilled at slowing the Internet and shutting down opposition websites, immediately expelled or placed under house arrest all foreign journalists, closed opposition newspapers, and used its own state-run radio and television stations to first ignore the protests and then blame them on outside Western agitators hostile to Iran. The protesters responded by using the Internet and social media to make a difference for their Green Revolution and democracy.	Topic: using social media for political change The entire introduction paragraph consists of background information about the protest in 2009. The writer reveals his thesis statement in the first paragraph.

As a reader, be careful not to confuse background information with the writer's main idea. As you read an introduction paragraph, ask yourself, "Will the information being presented help me understand this concept or issue more clearly?" When introductory paragraphs provide *a summary of an event* that happened or *a definition of a concept*, that information may be background material.

Using This Strategy in Your Writing. Sometimes, providing background information in the introduction paragraph can help readers more fully understand the context of your thesis statement. Present the background information logically so that it leads to the thesis statement.

Example: Starting with Background Information

Americans have a problem with obesity. According to the Centers for Disease Control and Prevention, to be obese means having a body mass index (BMI) of 30 or higher. Another category of weight management is *morbid obesity*. People who are morbidly obese are at high risk for breathing and walking problems, as well as death. We are a nation that has a high obesity rate, and our children are included in the problem. However, there is something we can do to start making changes: we can walk. If we all began to walk every day, obesity rates in our country would drop dramatically.

The writer starts with background information about obesity.

The sentence forms a transition from the background information to the thesis statement.

In the example above, the background information defines obesity and gives some of its consequences. The writer ends the paragraph with the thesis statement—a solution to the problem.

Be aware that any background information you provide must be true and accurate. Never make up data or statistics. If your instructor allows you to use source material for an assignment, be sure to credit the source properly and provide complete bibliographic information.

PRACTICE 5 Writing an Introduction That Uses Background Information

Imagine you are writing an essay in which you discuss qualities needed in a successful manager. You have decided to use this thesis statement:

> Successful managers must be able to work well with others, solve problems, and manage their time wisely.

On a separate sheet, write an introduction paragraph using this thesis statement. Use the strategy of *starting with background information.*

Starting with a Surprise

Startling a reader with a shocking statement or by using **irony** can be an effective technique in an introduction. One way irony works is for a person to say the opposite of what she means. For example, if a ballpoint pen were to explode in your book bag, you might say "Lovely!" Of course, you don't really think the explosion was lovely, and your tone of voice will certainly convey that.

Irony also can be situational. If a police officer gets a ticket for speeding, we would call the situation ironic. If you get into an accident that wrecks your car the day after you pay off your car loan, the situation would be ironic. The use of irony is one type of surprise that can introduce an essay. Notice how an element of surprise is used in the following example, "Love as a Story," from the textbook *Understanding Human Sexuality* by Janet Shibley Hyde and John D. DeLamater.

Vocabulary Collection Word:
irony

Your in-context definition:

_____

_____

A dictionary definition:

_____

_____

Introduction from "Love as a Story" by Janet Shibley Hyde and John D. DeLamater

When we think of love, our thoughts often turn to the great love stories: Romeo and Juliet, Cinderella and the Prince (Julia Roberts and Richard Gere), King Edward VIII and Wallis Simpson, and *Pygmalion/My Fair Lady*. According to Sternberg, these stories are much more than entertainment. They shape our beliefs about love and relationships, and our beliefs in turn influence our behavior.

The writers explain the effects of love stories.

(continued)

Zach and Tammy have been married 28 years. Their friends have been predicting divorce since the day they were married. They fight almost constantly. Tammy threatens to leave Zach; he tells her that nothing would make him happier. They lived happily ever after.

Valerie and Leonard had a perfect marriage. They told each other and all of their friends that they did. Their children say they never fought. Leonard met someone at his office, and left Valerie. They are divorced.

Wait a minute! Aren't those endings reversed? Zach and Tammy should be divorced, and Valerie and Leonard should be living happily ever after. If love is merely the interaction between two people, how they communicate and behave, you're right—the stories have the wrong endings. But there is more to love than interaction. What matters is how each partner interprets the interaction. To make sense out of what happens in our relationships, we rely on our love stories. A love story is a story about what love should be like, and it has characters, a plot, and a theme.

> The writers give examples of two love stories that are ironic.

> The text makes a transition from the surprise of the stories to the writers' thesis statement.

> The thesis statement appears at the end.

Notice that the writers of this selection use the ironic stories to introduce their thesis statement. The stories clearly serve a function. Sometimes, writers will use facts that are surprising or will make shocking statements as a way to catch the attention of their readers.

Using This Strategy in Your Writing.   One way to use surprise is to employ irony, as the writers of "Love as a Story" do. Another way is to start by offering commonly believed information and to then show that this information is wrong.

Imagine you are writing an essay to argue that homework is *not* a good learning tool for school children. You might begin your essay with all of the common assumptions about homework: that it helps kids learn, that doing homework shows independent thinking, that it fosters discipline, and so on. Close to the end of the paragraph, however, you could tell your readers that this conventional wisdom is actually *wrong*. By making readers think they know what you are going to say, you provide a mild shock when you actually say the opposite. As a result, you may make readers want to know more about your unexpected thesis statement.

This method is tricky to master, but it can be an effective introduction for some essays. Notice how it works in the following example.

Vocabulary Collection Word:
conventional

Your in-context definition:

_____

_____

A dictionary definition:

_____

_____

Example: Starting with a Surprise

Walking is a ridiculous form of exercise. How can people who take leisurely strolls around town call themselves exercise enthusiasts—as if walking counts as a legitimate exercise? We all walk, every day, all the time, yet a large percentage of Americans are still overweight. If people really want to exercise, they need to get serious and train like professional athletes. Does this kind of thinking sound familiar? Anyone who believes such foolish ideas has never tried walking for exercise. People who do walk for exercise tell a different story about walking. They talk about how walking has changed their health, has sharpened their thinking, and has helped them sleep better at night, among other benefits. Anyone who walks regularly knows that walking for exercise results in a variety of positive effects.

> The first sentences present misconceptions about walking. The sentences are italicized to represent overheard speech.

> The question serves as a transition. Then the writer contradicts the italicized ideas.

> The thesis statement makes the *opposite* case from the earlier italicized point of view.

As a reader, notice the important shift from the italicized thoughts to the nonitalicized writer's voice. This is the place where the writer leads to her thesis statement. Not all writers will use italics in this way, but there will likely be a transition between the initial ideas presented and the writer's opposite ideas.

Surprise introductions can be difficult to write. Readers need to "get" the surprise. If you use irony, for instance, readers must be able to identify the irony. If you find surprise introductions too difficult to write well, then choose a more straightforward method.

PRACTICE Writing an Introduction That Uses a Surprise

Imagine you are writing an essay in which you discuss qualities needed in a successful manager. You have decided to use this thesis statement:

> Successful managers must be able to work well with others, solve problems, and manage their time wisely.

On a separate sheet, write an introduction paragraph using this thesis statement. Use the strategy of *starting with a surprise.*

Starting with Data

Data—statistics, percentages, studies, and other types of information—can be incredibly powerful, but this kind of information can also be mind-numbing. Before you consider using data, be sure to check with your instructor about whether source materials can be used for your assignment. Data always come from a source, and you will always need to cite the source if you use data.

Notice the annotations in the following introduction to "Driven to Distraction: Our Wired Generation" by Larry Rosen.

Introduction from "Driven to Distraction: Our Wired Generation" by Larry Rosen

A recent Pew Internet & American Life Project report surveyed 2,462 middle school and high school advanced placement and national writing project teachers and concluded that: "Overwhelming majorities agree with the assertions that today's digital technologies are creating an easily distracted generation with short attention spans and today's students are too 'plugged in' and need more time away from their digital technologies." Two-thirds of the respondents agree with the notion that today's digital technologies do more to distract students than to help them academically.	The source of the data is given, together with details. A quotation is followed by more data.

In this example, the writer does not place his thesis statement in the first paragraph. Rather, the first paragraph gives us data to get us thinking about the effects of digital technologies on students.

Using This Strategy in Your Writing. If you find data that are truly interesting and perhaps even surprising, presenting some of that information can be an effective way to introduce your topic. Keep in mind that using data from a reputable source is crucial, as is making readers aware of the source. Also, remember to ask your instructor whether using a source is acceptable for the assignment. The following example shows how you might use data as a way to introduce a topic.

Example: Starting with Data

According to an article by professional tennis player Martina Navratilova, "Walking 150 minutes a week can reduce the risk of developing diabetes by nearly 60 percent." The benefits of walking also extend to weight loss, she says. She points to a study showing that regular walking resulted in weight loss—primarily in the abdominal area—for the study's participants. Far from being a useless activity, walking for exercise results in a variety of positive effects.

> The introduction starts with the source of the data, as well as a quotation.
>
> Additional data are given.
>
> The thesis statement is a logical conclusion of the data presented earlier.

Notice that statistical information is always used to support a point. The information itself is rarely, if ever, the main point of a text.

PRACTICE ⑦ Writing an Introduction That Uses Data

Imagine you are writing an essay in which you argue that the minimum wage should be raised. You have decided to use this thesis statement:

> The minimum wage in the United States should be raised so that every worker has a chance to escape poverty.

On a separate sheet, write an introduction paragraph using this thesis statement. Use the strategy of *starting with data.* Choose from the data given below to write your introduction.

> Quotation: "Today, the real value of the minimum wage has fallen by nearly one-third since its peak in 1968. And right now, a full-time minimum wage worker makes $14,500 a year, which leaves too many families struggling to make ends meet."
>
> *Source:* The White House Web site at www.whitehouse.gov.

> Quotation: "President Obama took action to lift more workers' wages by requiring that federal contractors pay their employees a fair wage of at least $10.10 an hour."
>
> *Source:* The White House Web site at www.whitehouse.gov.

Starting with a Quotation or Adage

Sometimes, as a writer, you think of the *perfect* quotation or adage (a common saying that states something most people believe to be true). Using a quotation or an adage to start an introduction can be effective.

Since a quotation or adage is likely to be a single sentence, using this method of introduction requires writers to either add an explanation or additional information. In the introduction that follows, Tait Trussell combines an adage with a story to begin his essay "Healing Humor." The adage Trussell uses is actually the main idea he will make in his essay; thus, in this case, the adage is also the thesis statement. Most of the time, a quotation or adage will simply introduce the topic rather than serve as the thesis statement.

Introduction from "Healing Humor" by Tait Trussell

Research is showing that laughter is good medicine.

It was a remarkable case, a generation or so ago. Norman Cousins, the editor and researcher, found laughter to be a cure for a serious disease he had contracted.

Cousins was editor of the *Saturday Review of Literature*. He was diagnosed in 1964 with spondylitis, an acute inflammation of the spine. He was given only a few months to live. Cousins was sure that negative thoughts can cause illness. So, he reasoned that positive thoughts could have the opposite effect.

He left the hospital and checked into a hotel where he watched humorous movies and shows. He found that 10 minutes of hearty laughter resulted in at least two hours of pain-free sleep. He continued this "treatment" until he recovered. He wrote a widely read book about his amazing recovery.

> An adaptation of "laughter is the best medicine," a common adage, this sentence serves as the thesis statement.

An adage like the one Trussell uses is effective because most readers have heard it before but may not have believed it was true.

Using This Strategy in Your Writing. If you find a striking quotation, saying, short song lyric, poem, or any other such item, you can use it to start your introduction paragraph. You must be sure that the item you are using fits the topic *exactly*. If you choose a quote that "kind of" fits, your reader will simply think the introduction paragraph is odd. Notice that the writer of the example below did not have a perfect adage for her thesis. Instead, she chose to adapt a well-known adage.

Example: Starting with a Quotation or Adage

We all know that an apple a day is supposed to keep the doctor away, but eating apples will not necessarily make you fit. A healthier version of the old adage might be "A walk every day keeps illness away." While diet is important for health, it is not the only way to stay healthy. A daily walk for exercise results in a variety of positive effects.

> The writer starts with a well-known adage and then critiques it.
>
> The writer suggests a new adage that acts as a transition to the thesis statement.
>
> The thesis statement appears at the end.

As a reader, any time you see an adage, ask yourself, "What is the general truth the adage presents?" Use the answer to gain understanding about the writer's point.

PRACTICE ⑧ Writing an Introduction That Uses a Quotation or Adage

Imagine you are writing an essay in which you discuss qualities needed in a successful manager. You have decided to use this thesis statement:

> Successful managers must be able to work well with others, solve problems, and manage their time wisely.

On a separate sheet, write an introduction paragraph using this thesis statement. Use the strategy of *starting with a quote or adage*.

Starting with an Objective Overview

Some essays begin with a simple overview of the issue being discussed. If the issue is controversial, an objective overview requires both sides of the issue to be presented. An objective overview can be used to introduce an informative article about the issue, or it can be used at the beginning of a persuasive essay to show that the writer is aware of both sides of the issue.

The following paragraph is an example of an objective overview used as an introduction to an informative article, "Wal-Mart and the Local Economy," by Mitch Renkow.

Introduction from "Wal-Mart and the Local Economy" by Mitch Renkow

With total revenues in excess of $250 billion per year and more than 1.3 million employees worldwide, Wal-Mart Stores, Inc., is the largest corporation in the world. Wal-Mart's staggering—and continuing—growth traces directly to its pioneering of an innovative business model that features sophisticated supply chain management and aggressive cost-cutting. That model, as revolutionary as was that of the Sears & Roebuck Co. in the late 1800s, has profoundly altered patterns of local retail and wholesale trade, as well as the logistics of the transportation and distribution of goods. Wal-Mart sells a wide array of products at lower prices than competing retail outlets. It also hires large numbers of local workers, as well as generating substantial property tax and sales tax revenues for local communities. Nonetheless, Wal-Mart is a frequent target of hostile sentiment, and announcements of plans to build a new Wal-Mart in a given community are often met with considerable protest. Much of the antagonism toward Wal-Mart is rooted in the perceived dislocating effects that new Wal-Mart stores have on competing "mom-and-pop" retail stores.	Pro position: The writer starts with positive info about Wal-Mart and its successes. The writer goes on to give historical info about Wal-Mart's business practices. Con position: The writer gives "the other side": hostility toward Wal-Mart.

In this article, the writer will not take a position on whether Wal-Mart is good for society or the economy. Rather, as the introduction indicates, he will discuss both sides. The objective overview in the introduction paragraph forecasts the discussion to come.

Not much information is provided about either side of the issue in Renkow's introduction paragraph. He will provide more details in the article itself. This is one way to present a very basic overview of the two sides of an issue. Another way is to write one paragraph presenting one viewpoint and a second paragraph for the opposite viewpoint. In the third paragraph, the writer presents the thesis statement.

Using This Strategy in Your Writing.   To use this strategy in your own writing, be sure that you clearly understand both sides of the issue. Provide an overview of both sides, and then present your thesis statement. If you are writing an argument essay, be sure to word your introduction and thesis statement in such a way that readers understand which point of view you are **advocating**.

Vocabulary Collection Word:
advocate

Your in-context definition:

_____

_____

A dictionary definition:

_____

_____

Example: Starting with an Objective Overview

Although we know that exercise is important, very few Americans participate in regular exercise. Realizing this, several national companies have begun to offer their employees 20 minutes per day—in addition to regular breaks and lunch time—to simply take a walk. These employers argue that their companies save money by encouraging daily walks since	Pro argument in favor of time off for exercise at work

(continued)

walkers have lower health-care expenses and higher morale. Some executives, however, say their companies will lose valuable productive time by providing time for daily walks. They believe their employees already have enough time—through scheduled breaks and lunch—to exercise if they really want to. Although both sides make valuable points, companies who have implemented walking programs are beginning to see real benefits from them. A close examination of this issue will show that the potential benefits of giving employees time to walk each day far outweigh any negative consequences.

> Con argument against time off for exercise at work
>
> Transition moves from the two points of view to the writer's thesis statement
>
> Thesis statement

Notice that even though both sides of the issue are briefly mentioned, the writer ends with a thesis statement that shows the position he supports.

PRACTICE 9 Reading, Annotating, and Analyzing Introductions

The introductions from two essays follow. Read and annotate each introduction, and then answer the analysis questions that follow each one.

PASSAGE A: Introduction from "Probing Question: Is 'Just Say No' an Effective Anti-Drug Approach?" by Tom Fitzgerald

YOUR ANNOTATIONS

Many people remember the famous anti-drug slogan coined by former first lady Nancy Reagan: "Just Say No." Critiqued by some for reducing a complex issue to a catch phrase, Reagan's campaign is generally considered to have been unsuccessful. . . .

1. What strategy did the writer use to write this introduction paragraph?

_____

2. What do you predict the essay will be about, based on the introduction and the title?

_____

PASSAGE B: Introduction from "Mark Lepper: Intrinsic Motivation, Extrinsic Motivation and the Process of Learning" by Christine Vandevelde

YOUR ANNOTATIONS

Some years ago, after a lecture, Professor Mark Lepper was approached by a couple who told him about a system of rewards they had set up for their son, which had produced much improved behavior at the dinner table. "He sits up straight and eats his peas and the Brussels sprouts and he is really very well behaved," they reported. Until, that is, the first time the family dined at a nice restaurant. The child looked around, picked up a crystal glass from the table and asked, "How many points not to drop this?" A fine example, says Dr. Lepper, of the detrimental effects of over-reliance on rewards to shape children's behavior.

1. What strategy did the writer use to write this introduction paragraph?

_____

2. Did the writer include his thesis statement in this paragraph?

_____

3. What do you predict the essay will be about, based on the introduction and the title?

_____

PRACTICE ⑩ Choosing Introduction Strategies

Below are three thesis statements. If you were writing an essay for the following thesis statements, which type of introduction paragraph might you use for each one? Why? Explain in one or two sentences.

1. Thesis statement: We need to take action to save our beaches.

   _____

   _____

2. Thesis statement: Instead of punishing students who use smartphones in class, instructors should integrate smartphone technology into their teaching.

   _____

   _____

3. Thesis statement: If you believe a person is having a stroke, there are four actions you can and must take.

   _____

   _____

READING, ANALYZING, AND CREATING CONCLUSIONS

We have all seen movies that end poorly, leaving us with a sense that the movie should not have ended just yet or should have had a different ending. Texts can also suffer from poor endings. The examples that follow will help you understand the function of conclusions and learn how to craft effective endings for your own writing.

How Conclusions Function

The main purpose of a conclusion is to help the reader gain a sense of *closure*—a feeling that it is the right time to bring the writing to an end—and a sense that something has been accomplished, a point has been made, or an idea has been shared.

To **impart** closure, conclusions often re-emphasize the purpose of the essay. Conclusions may also make predictions, emphasize the importance of the issue being discussed, or provide the end of a story that was started in the introduction paragraph.

By analyzing a conclusion, you can sometimes tell whether you fully understand the writer's main point. For example, if the essay is intended to persuade, then the conclusion can serve as a last attempt to get readers to do or believe what the writer is advocating. If the essay presents an analysis and draws a conclusion, the conclusion paragraph is a good place to reiterate the results or findings. While conclusions do not always restate the main point, the content in them should be consistent with the main idea of the essay.

Strategies for Conclusions

Four strategies, summarized in the table on the next page and illustrated in the examples that follow, are commonly used to conclude essays. Keep in mind that regardless of the conclusion strategy employed, an essay can also end with a **proposal**—a suggestion that readers take particular actions in response to what the writer is saying in the essay.

As you read each example, think about whether the conclusion produces a sense of closure. You may notice that conclusion paragraphs often make use of more than one strategy, as the annotations will show. Notice also that the writers do not use "in conclusion" or "to conclude." A good conclusion does not have to announce itself.

Vocabulary Collection Word:
impart

Your in-context definition:

_____

_____

A dictionary definition:

_____

_____

■ In a fairy tale, "happily ever after" tells us the story has come to an end. What do you think readers expect from a satisfactory conclusion?

Strategies for Conclusion Paragraphs	
Concluding by restating and summarizing	Emphasize the thesis or the key points in the essay by restating them in different words.
Concluding by answering an earlier question	Answer a question you asked in the introduction to the essay.
Concluding by finishing a story	Tell the end of a story that you began in the introduction to the essay.
Concluding by speculating	Explain some results, events, or other consequences that *might* occur.

Concluding by Restating and Summarizing

A common method of concluding an essay is to emphasize the thesis statement by restating it. You have read the introduction paragraph Mitch Renkow uses to start his informative essay on Wal-Mart. Now read the conclusion paragraph, and notice how he sums up his informative essay.

Conclusion from "Wal-Mart and the Local Economy" by Mitch Renkow

As is commonly the case with any large shock to the economic system, the coming of a new Wal-Mart to a given community is accompanied by a multitude of different impacts on different individuals and on the local government. Some of these impacts are unambiguously positive for certain groups—lower prices for consumers being an example. Some are unambiguously negative for other groups, such as the loss of business experienced by competing retail outlets. And still others will vary on a case-by-case basis, such as the impacts on local employment and the local government's budget. To a very large extent, whether a new Wal-Mart is a "good" or "bad" thing for an individual depends on which of these varied impacts are most strongly relevant to that individual.

> The writer summarizes positive effects.
>
> The writer summarizes negative effects.
>
> The writer restates the thesis statement.

As a reader, pay particular attention to the conclusion paragraphs. Often, if the writer reiterates a point in the conclusion, that point will be the text's thesis statement. You can sometimes check your knowledge of the thesis statement by studying the writer's closing words.

Using This Strategy in Your Writing.   When you use this method for concluding your writing, be sure to continue composing *new* sentences. It may be tempting to simply insert the thesis statement word for word, but avoid doing so. In the following example, notice that the last sentence adds emphasis to the writer's thesis statement by calling walking "the perfect exercise." Make sure your final sentence wraps up the essay and gives readers a sense of closure.

Example: Concluding by Restating and Summarizing

Walking is clearly an effective form of exercise. Anyone can walk, and very little special gear is needed to participate in a walking program. It is an economical way to exercise, and it pays off in both mental and physical benefits. Walking may just be the perfect exercise.

> The thesis statement is reworded.
>
> The support is briefly summarized.
>
> The short final sentence provides a simple ending for the essay.

PRACTICE 11 Writing a Conclusion by Restating and Summarizing

Read the following student essay on the topic of saving an historic building. Then, on a separate sheet, write a conclusion paragraph for it that uses the strategy of *restating or summarizing.* You will use this essay again for Practices 12 and 14.

SAVE THE GRIFF

In a week, the city will decide whether to slate the historic Griffin Theater for demolition. Should the Griffin Theater be saved? What value does this property have? While some consider this property an eyesore, there are many reasons why it should not be demolished. Instead, we should honor the theater by restoring and repurposing it.

The Griffin Theater, or "the Griff" as it is affectionately known, is a part of local history. George Washington didn't sleep there, and no famous battles were fought over it, but it is historic in the sense that it has been a landmark in this community for generations. Older citizens in the neighborhood remember seeing glamorous movie stars on the screen there, watching newsreels for information, and even skipping school to watch a movie. Many senior citizens have talked about how the Griff was an oasis of air-conditioning for them during hot summers and noted that they still smile when they pass by it at the memory. The Griff has sentimental value to this community and is part of who this community is. People would come from all over the city to visit a restored Griff, just to be able to walk inside it again.

Research shows that historic districts boost a city's sense of identity and are good for tourism. Such areas capitalize on the quaint charm of their historic buildings and are a tourist draw, bringing revenue to shops and restaurants in the district. Simply put, people like to stroll down tree-lined streets and admire the architecture. Who wants all of our community's architectural uniqueness to be replaced by fast-food restaurants, condos, and big box stores? The Griff should be restored because it says "home" to this community.

The Griff's value is not just sentimental. Old buildings were built to different standards and were made with better materials than buildings today. While the plaster work inside the Griff is indeed crumbling in places and in need of repair, the walls are sound and are made of a rare five brick thick construction that will still be standing long after the sheet rock and composite board of the new condos across the street have crumbled. Considering how long older buildings last, restoring the Griff will be more cost-effective to the city than to build a new structure on the same site with today's inferior materials.

Boarded up as it is, the Griff might seem an eyesore. The graffiti spray-painted on it doesn't help. Inside, however, the Griff has many architectural details that are impossible to find elsewhere. The custom-made curving staircase to the balcony includes an elegant, hand-carved walnut handrail. The floor's unique turquoise and gold parquet tile could easily be restored, and many of the stained-glass transom windows emblazoned with the image of a golden griffin are intact. This image could serve as a logo for the building. The main auditorium could easily be converted into office space for a contemporary use, saving the lobby as a reception area full of historic charm. A building like this is too precious to lose.

Concluding by Answering an Earlier Question

Essays that begin with questions can neatly conclude by going back to the question and reminding readers of its answer. Review Debra Humphreys's introduction, which appears earlier in this chapter. She began her essay by asking questions, and she ends it with a summary of the answers. She uses two paragraphs to bring her essay to a conclusion.

Conclusion from "Campus Diversity and Student Self-Segregation: Separating Myths from Facts" by Debra Humphreys

There is little cause for alarm, some cause for celebration and much hope for what lies ahead. The reality is that while there is still a long way to go before American higher education will truly reflect the full diversity of American society, college campuses are becoming much more diverse and their diverse campus environments are having a significant positive effect on this generation of students. College campuses are not dominated by widespread racial/ethnic segregation and the racial/ethnic clustering that does occur isn't impeding intergroup contact. In fact, the existence of racial/ethnic groups and activities, along with other comprehensive campus diversity initiatives, is contributing to the success of today's college students and preparing them to help build a healthier multicultural America for the future.	The essay answers some of the questions posed in the introduction paragraph, and the conclusion sums up the answers. Answer to "How socially segregated are college campuses?" Answer to "Is diversity leading to educational benefits?"

Using This Strategy in Your Writing.   To use this strategy, find new words to repeat the question asked in the introduction. In the example of writing introductions with questions earlier in the chapter, we asked, "Is walking really a legitimate form of exercise?" While the thesis statement provides an answer to the question, the writer can emphasize the answer by repeating the question-and-answer strategy in the conclusion, as shown in the following example.

Notice also that the last sentence is a lighthearted imitation of a television infomercial. This kind of encouragement can be a pleasing way to end an informal essay that advocates an action.

Example: Concluding by Answering an Earlier Question

Is something as simple as taking a daily walk really going to improve your health? The answer is a resounding "Yes!" Not only will walking improve your health and your mood, but it will also make your commitment to an exercise program easier since it requires so little and costs next to nothing. So lace up your sneakers and start your no-risk free trial today!	The introduction question is reworded here. The answer repeats the reasoning used in the essay. The last sentence is a proposal—a call to action for readers.

Notice that both the question and the answer have been reworded for the conclusion paragraph. Never repeat an idea without rewording it.

PRACTICE ⓬ Writing a Conclusion Paragraph by Answering an Earlier Question

Reread the essay "Save the Griff" in Practice 11. The writer uses these questions in the introduction:

- Should the Griffin Theater be saved?
- What value does this property have?

On a separate sheet, write a conclusion paragraph for the essay that uses the strategy of *answering an earlier question*.

Concluding by Finishing a Story

Like returning to an earlier question, another method of concluding is to return to an earlier story. When using stories to introduce essays, writers will sometimes give only a portion of the story and save the story's ending to wrap up the essay. Earlier in this chapter, you read the introduction to "Life with Asperger's Syndrome," an essay that began with a short anecdote about Paul, a child with Asperger's. The writer discusses Asperger's syndrome in the body paragraphs. When she is ready to conclude, she goes back to Paul's story and continues it:

Conclusion from "Life with Asperger's Syndrome"

> Paul did not get to school on time on the day he walked home from the bus stop. After his mother talked with him about the need to be flexible regarding time, Paul was able to calm down and eventually go to school. With time and maturity, Paul will learn how to deal with such situations. While life with Asperger's will present challenges, many of those who have it have proven that these challenges will not keep them from living happy, productive lives.

The writer finishes the story begun in the introduction.

Using This Strategy in Your Writing.   To use this method of concluding, make sure your introduction presents a story. If you have already given readers the ending, you can provide an "update" that bring the readers' attention back to the story.

The example below provides an ending to the story of Felicity Martinez, which was used earlier in this text to start an essay about walking. Notice how the ending provides an update of Felicity's situation.

Example: Concluding by Finishing a Story

> Felicity Martinez credits walking with transforming her life during her battle with cancer, but her story does not end there. Today, Felicity is a fitness and wellness instructor at Lombardy Health Institute. She specializes in exercise therapy for cancer recovery and prevention. Felicity believes, as do many others, that the benefits of a simple activity like walking are not easily grasped, and she is determined to give to others what walking gave to her.

The writer returns to the story begun in the introduction.

The writer gives an update or provides the ending of the story.

The writer uses the end of the story to emphasize the thesis statement.

Going back to Felicity's story helps readers feel that not only has the writer made her point, but also that Felicity's story has been thoroughly told.

PRACTICE 13 Writing a Conclusion Paragraph by Finishing a Story

For Practice 4, you used a story to write an introduction to an essay. Return to that introduction. On a separate sheet, write a conclusion paragraph for the same essay that uses the strategy of *finishing a story.*

Concluding by Speculating

After thinking about an issue, we often speculate about what that issue means to us personally or to the larger world. To *speculate* is to wonder. For example, when we consider how easy it is to take a walk every day and the healthful effects of walking, we may wonder why more people do not do this. We may, in addition, speculate about what life would be like if everyone began to walk more. This speculation might lead to a prediction. Perhaps if more people walked regularly, our health insurance costs would go down. Or perhaps cities would begin to develop more pedestrian-friendly transit routes.

Speculations that predict or that ask "what if" can also be used to forecast dire consequences so that readers will understand the seriousness of an issue or will take action. In "Homo Sapiens RIP," Andrew Gumbel writes about how some people see artificial intelligence used in robots as a serious threat. Notice how Gumbel uses speculation to conclude his essay. (Note: In his conclusion, Gumbel quotes Bill Joy, a computer expert.)

Conclusion from "Homo Sapiens RIP" by Andrew Gumbel

"We have yet to come to terms with the fact that the most compelling 21st-century technologies . . . pose a different threat than the technologies that have come before," Joy writes. "Specifically, robots, engineered organisms, and nanobots share a dangerous amplifying factor: they can self-replicate. A bomb is blown up only once—but one bot can become many, and quickly get out of control. . . .

"I think it is no exaggeration to say we are on the cusp of the further perfection of extreme evil, an evil whose possibility spreads well beyond that which weapons of mass destruction bequeathed to the nation-states, on to a surprising and terrible empowerment of extreme individuals."

> The writer repeats the problem by quoting Bill Joy, an expert.
>
> The writer ends by quoting Joy's speculations about the future.

Using This Strategy in Your Writing.   Carefully consider your thesis statement. If your thesis statement and essay lead you to make speculations and predictions, consider using this strategy. Be careful that these predictions tie directly into your thesis statement's point. Word your predictions in such a way so that your audience understands these things *might* occur, not that they *will* occur.

The following example shows how we might conclude the essay on the benefits of walking with an ending that uses speculation.

Example: Concluding by Speculating

If more people began to walk for exercise, we might see significant changes in the health of our country. These changes might result in lower costs for health insurance, longer lives, and happier people. Cities might begin to accommodate walkers by creating pedestrian-friendly transit routes, thus reducing traffic. The benefits of walking are worth giving it a try.

> The first three sentences speculate about how walking could change the future.
>
> The final sentence proposes an action ("giving it a try").

Note that these predictions or speculations are not part of the writer's support for his thesis statement. They are merely encouragements inserted at the end to motivate readers to try walking. The writer is careful to use the word *might* to avoid saying or implying that these results will definitely occur.

PRACTICE 14   Writing a Conclusion Paragraph by Speculating

Reread the essay "Save the Griff" in Practice 11. On a separate sheet, write a conclusion paragraph for the essay that uses the strategy of *concluding by speculating*.

CHAPTER ACTIVITIES

READING AND ANNOTATING

The following selection is from *The Science of Psychology*, a textbook written by Laura A. King. Read and annotate the selection. Before you read, study the following definitions from the text:

- *Self-esteem* is the degree to which we have positive or negative feelings about ourselves
- *Positive illusions* are rosy views people hold of themselves that are not necessarily rooted in reality
- *Self-serving bias* is the tendency to take credit for our successes and to deny responsibility for our failures when we make attributions about our own behavior
- *Self-objectification* is the tendency to see oneself as an object in others' eyes
- *Stereotype threat* is an individual's fast-acting, self-fulfilling fear of being judged based on a negative stereotype about his or her group
- *Social comparison* is the process by which individuals evaluate their thoughts, feelings, behaviors, and abilities in relation to others

(Note: The selection contains parenthetical references to sources the author has used. Full information about these sources, listed in the author's text, is not given here.)

The Self as a Social Object

by Laura A. King

YOUR ANNOTATIONS

Each of us carries around mental representations of ourselves. We can think of the self as our schema for who we are, what we are like (and not like), and how we feel about these perceptions.

The self is special as well because we value ourselves. One of the most important self related variables is *self-esteem*, the degree to which we have positive or negative feelings about ourselves (Harter, 2013; Kernis, 2013). In general, research has shown that it is good to feel good about oneself (Koch, 2013; O'Brien, Bartoletti, & Leitzel, 2013; Solomon, 2013).

Individuals with high self-esteem often possess a variety of **positive illusions**—rosy views of themselves that are not necessarily rooted in reality (Hansen & Pronin, 2012). Indeed, research shows that many of us think of ourselves as "above average" on valued characteristics, including how trustworthy, objective, and capable we are (Gregg & Sedikides, 2010; Hepper & Sedikides, 2012; Hepper, Sedikides, & Cai, 2013; Sedikides, 2009; Sedikides & Skowronski, 2009, 2012).

Self-serving bias refers to the tendency to take credit for our successes and to deny responsibility for our failures when we make attributions about our own behavior. Think about taking an exam. If you do well, you are likely to take credit for that success ("I'm smart"); you tend to make internal attributions. If you do poorly, however, you are more likely to blame situational factors ("The test was too hard"); you tend to make external attributions.

Self-objectification refers to the tendency to see oneself as an object in others' eyes. Researchers have focused on how women have been socialized to think of themselves and their bodies as objects in the social world (Fredrickson & Roberts, 1997). Chronic feelings of objectification are associated with lower self-esteem and higher levels of depression (Miner-Rubino, Twenge, & Fredrickson, 2002).

Self-objectification can interfere with task performance. For example, in a series of studies, men and women were asked first to try on either a sweater or a swimsuit and then to complete a math test. After trying on a swimsuit, women performed much more poorly on the math test. The researchers surmised that trying on the swimsuit heightened women's experience of self objectification and body shame, reducing their mental resources for completing the math test (Fredrickson & others, 1998).

Stereotype threat is an individual's fast-acting, self-fulfilling fear of being judged based on a negative stereotype about his or her group. A person who experiences stereotype threat is well aware of stereotypical expectations for him or her as a member of a group. In stereotype relevant situations, the individual experiences anxiety about living "down" to expectations and consequently underperforms (Aronson & others, 2013; Hartley & Sutton, 2013; Weger & others, 2012). Claude Steele and Eliot Aronson (1995, 2004) have shown that when a test is presented to African American and European American students who have first simply checked a box indicating their ethnicity, the African Americans perform more poorly. When attention was not drawn to ethnicity, no differences in performance emerged.

Stereotype threat affects performance on math tests by women compared to men, even when both groups have equally strong math training (Spencer, Steele, & Quinn, 1999). European American men, too, can fall prey to stereotype threat; in a study of golf ability, European American men performed more poorly than African American men when they were told the test measured "natural athletic ability" (Stone, 2002).

What factors might help prevent the consequences of stereotype threat? In one study, African American schoolchildren who were asked their race prior to a math test did not perform as well unless the test was presented to them as a challenge, not as a threat (Alter & others, 2010). In addition, self-esteem may help buffer the effects of stereotype threat in women, especially if women are reminded of another aspect of the self (for instance, "college student") that is positively associated with math performance (Rydell & Boucher, 2010).

Have you ever felt great about getting a B on a test, only to feel deflated after finding out a friend got an *A?* Comparing ourselves to other people is one way we come to understand our own behavior. Social comparison is the process by which we evaluate our thoughts, feelings, behaviors, and abilities in relation to others. **Social comparison** tells us what our distinctive characteristics are and aids us in building an identity.

Sixty years ago, Leon Festinger (1954) proposed a theory of social comparison. The theory states that when no objective means are available to evaluate our opinions and abilities, we compare ourselves with others. Extended and modified over the years, Festinger's theory continues to provide an important rationale for how individuals come to know themselves (Brakel, Dijkstra, & Buunk, 2012). Contemporary researchers have focused on *downward* social comparisons, that is, individuals' comparisons with people whom they consider inferior to themselves. People under threat (from negative feedback or low self-esteem, for example) try to feel better by comparing themselves with others who are less fortunate (Caricati, 2012).

Questions for Consideration

1. Give an example of how a positive illusion of oneself might lead to a situation of self-serving bias, and how that might be dangerous or have negative consequences.

2. Give an example of a way in which you might have objectified yourself, fallen prey to a stereotype threat, or comforted yourself with social comparison. Explain how this incident made you feel, and how you feel about it now that you've read this article.

USING MODELS TO PRACTICE COMPOSING

Reggie is a student in an English class and has been given a reading and writing assignment. Here are Reggie's annotations of his assignment.

Reggie's Annotated Assignment

Read, annotate, and analyze "The Self as a Social Object." Make sure you understand the definitions of *self-esteem, positive illusions, self-serving bias, self-objectification, stereotype threat,* and *social comparison.* You will need to use some of these key words in the essay you will write.

> Read, annotate, and analyze the text
>
> Understand definitions (will use some or all of them in the essay)

Write an essay in which you discuss a type of self-objectification, stereotype threat, or social comparison. Plan your essay so that it includes the following elements: an explanation of the behavior and the positive or negative illusions of oneself that help or hurt self-esteem, a discussion of the social factors that might have led to this experience, and an exploration of how someone might, or might not, recover self-esteem afterwards. End your essay by answering an earlier question you've posed about this behavior. You may use examples—either personal or from research—to discuss the behavior.

Give credit to the authors of the reading when you use concepts from their text.

> Write an essay
>
> Select a type of self-objectification, stereotype threat, or social comparison
>
> Do 3 things: explain behavior
> Discuss positive/negative illusions
> Discuss social factors leading to it
> Explore recovery of self-esteem
>
> End by answering question (be sure to ask question earlier)
>
> May use examples
>
> Give credit when necessary

Reggie starts by using simple listing to prewrite about ways people might self-objectify, compare themselves socially, or experience stereotype threat, and whether they are accompanied by positive or negative illusions.

Self-objectification:
- need to make weight for wrestling—negative illusions
- people want to look like movie stars—negative
- selfies on Instagram—positive or negative?
- eating disorders—negative

Stereotype threat:
- dumb jock—negative
- girls and math—negative
- learning disability—negative

Social comparison: (can make people feel positive, even though it's a negative thing to do)
- comparing self to kids who go to worse schools—positive
- comparing self to older brother—negative (or positive)
- racial prejudice—downward comparison, positive illusions

Next, Reggie decides which behavior to discuss in his essay. Reggie's decision is fueled by personal experience—he has Obsessive-Compulsive Disorder or "OCD" and test anxiety, but never thought about it in connection to stereotype threat before. He wants to write about this, and he uses another prewriting activity—freewriting—to generate ideas about the topic. Notice that Reggie uses some of the assignment requirements to guide his prewriting.

OCD and Stereotype Threat

Explanation of behavior—knowing that I might be judged harshly for my disability can lead me to experience stereotype threat—a sudden fear that I won't perform well that paralyzes me

Discussion of social factors—Mrs. Forbes didn't understand my panic, called me a bad student. Doing badly in school before we knew about OCD made me lose confidence in my own abilities. I didn't want to be grouped with learning disabled kids. People made fun of them. The stereotype is that learning disabled kids are dumb.

Recovery of self-esteem—This could be the question I answer: what am I going to do? Relaxation techniques: deep breaths, use positive mantra, picture teacher smiling, remember ways that I have succeeded. If I think hard about it, I can realize that my social threat fears are not based on what's really going on.

Reggie is now ready to create an outline for his essay on his computer.

Reggie's Outline

Title: Stereotype Threat, OCD, and Me

Introduction ideas: Start with an illustration of what it feels like for me to take a test, worrying about what the teacher will think.

Thesis statement: I'm caught in the trap of stereotype threat.

Major supporting point 1: Knowing that I might be judged harshly for my disability can lead me to experience stereotype threat.

- define stereotype threat
- explain what my "group" is (students with disabilities or learning disabilities)
- explain that my fear of being judged negatively due to my disability is a worse distraction than the disability itself

Major supporting point 2: Social factors have led to my awareness of this stereotype and fear of it.

- Mrs. Forbes didn't understand my disability and called me a "bad behaver" and poor student
- I felt misjudged at school (failed tests, meetings with teachers, getting labeled learning disabled)
- other kids called LD kids dumb
- guidance counselor treated me like a toddler

Major supporting point 3: I have found ways to recover my self-esteem and overcome my fears.

- Relaxation techniques my counselor taught me
- remind myself I am smart
- remind myself I am successful at things like debate

Now that Reggie has an outline, he uses the remaining steps in the writing process to draft his essay, revise it, and edit it. What follows is Reggie's final draft. Annotate Reggie's draft for thesis statement, major supporting points, and other important elements. Also, determine the introduction and conclusion strategies Reggie uses.

Chambers 1

Reggie Chambers

Mr. Roberts

ENGL 0402

24 October 2016

Stereotype Threat, OCD, and Me

I've studied for this test all weekend, so it should be a breeze. Then, as my teacher is passing out the tests, she leans down and says to me, "Reggie, you can go out to the hall if you need to." She thinks she's saying this so that only I can hear it, but to me it's as if she's shouting to everyone sitting nearby: "Reggie has a disability!" And suddenly my heart starts pounding and I'm struggling to breathe. *She thinks I'll fail this. Maybe I will, and then I'll never get to prove myself. What if I don't do well? I feel stupid. Maybe I'm really not a good student. I can't focus!* Thoughts like these swarm my head, and what was supposed to be an easy history test looks impossible to start. I'm caught in the trap of stereotype threat. How can I get over these feelings in time to pass this test when all I want to do is run away?

King defines stereotype threat as "an individual's fast-acting, self-fulfilling fear of being judged based on a negative stereotype about his or her group." In my case, the group is made up of those students who have disabilities. I have Obsessive-Compulsive Disorder (OCD), and sometimes it distracts me and interferes with my learning. Sometimes I wonder, though, if the fear that I will be judged negatively due to my OCD isn't a worse distraction. This fear isn't just in my head. I've had some bad experiences in the past that led me to feel this way.

In elementary school, I had a teacher named Mrs. Forbes. That was about the time that my OCD became more noticeable but before it was diagnosed. I was doing things like stacking up my toys at night and refusing to go sleep until I got them perfectly aligned. Mrs. Forbes gave long talks about being a "good behaver" or a "bad behaver" and had everyone's name on a chart with paper clips that got moved if you misbehaved. After four offenses your name got put on the "bad behaver" side of the chart and you got sent to the detention room. I lived in fear that my name would go there. I also lived in fear that my pencil wouldn't line up perfectly on my desk. When another kid knocked my pencil off my desk, I had a panic attack and couldn't stop crying. Sure enough, my name went right into the black box. Later Mrs. Forbes told my parents, right in front of me, that I wasn't a good student, couldn't pay attention, and wouldn't listen.

It took a few years before I had a counselor who taught me ways to resist OCD. Today I have it under control, mostly, but it is still there to distract me, especially when I'm tired or stressed. That means I sometimes need more time than other students to complete a test. My elementary school had a quiet room for learning disabled students to take tests, but it took a lot of work on the part of my parents and my counselor, and a lot of failed tests, before the school realized I needed to go there. I didn't want to be grouped with other learning disabled kids, though. Some of them got teased and called "stupid." I will never forget the way the school counselor talked to me, slowly and carefully like you would to a two-year-old.

Now when I have to take tests, I fear that teachers will think I can't do very well because of my disability. Maybe they will write me off as a poor student before they even see the test. The funny thing is, usually they don't. That means that this fear, this stereotype threat, may not be grounded in my present reality at all.

How do I calm myself down and recover my self-esteem so that I can take the test? I take deep breaths to relax. I recite a positive mantra: "I am smart and I test well." Sometimes it helps to picture my teacher shaking my hand as I graduate, confident in me. Then I remind myself that my disability has led me to do brave things, too. Since feeling awkward in public feels normal to me, public speaking does not cause me as much anxiety as it might other people. I have joined the debate team, and this year we are going to the state championship. Reminding myself that I'm a champion helps me kick social threat fears out the window.

A READING AND WRITING ASSIGNMENT

Now that you have analyzed Reggie's process for completing his essay assignment, write an essay of your own in response to the same assignment. (See "Reggie's Annotated Assignment" on page 269.) Use the Quick Start Guide to Integrated Reading and Writing Assignments to assist you in the writing process.

⊙ THINKING FROM AN INSTRUCTOR'S POINT OF VIEW

Just as a creative title and an interesting introduction can entice you to read an article, you can create titles and introductions that make your instructor look forward to reading your work. Many students are content to write titles and introductions that are "good enough." For instance, a writing instructor assigned a paper on homelessness—what it is, why it exists, and how we should respond to it as a society. Here are the titles from eleven papers she received:

1. Homelessness
2. Homelessness in the United States
3. Homelessness

4. [no title]

5. Why Is There Homelessness?

6. We Are Responsible for Homelessness

7. The Homelessness Cure

8. Homelessness in Society

9. Being Homeless Is Terrible

10. Why Homelessness Matters

11. Homes for All

Clearly, some of these titles are better than others.

Students do not always view their instructors as the audience for their writing. Keeping in mind that your instructors *are* your primary audience will help you design an essay with a title that they may find interesting.

The same is true for introductions and conclusions. The typical introduction paragraph for the students' homelessness essays went something like this:

> Homelessness is a big problem in this day and age. Almost every city in the United States has homeless people in it. However, we can fix the problem of homelessness by talking about what it is and understanding what causes it.

The typical conclusion paragraph went something like this:

> In conclusion, homelessness is a problem that must be fixed. If society used some of the strategies in this essay, no one would have to be homeless anymore.

Not only are the introduction and conclusion paragraphs boring, but they are also inaccurate. The introduction says that we can fix the issue of homelessness by talking about it and understanding it. These are great things to do, but they will not fix homelessness. The conclusion is much too optimistic. Very few solutions are ever universally effective.

Students sometimes write these types of titles, introductions, and conclusions because they do not take the time to think creatively and to consider the needs of their audience. As you construct titles, introductions, and conclusions, work on standing apart from the crowd. Make sure you take the time to be creative. Use strategies in this chapter to your advantage.

Thinking Creatively

1. Which of the titles do you think the instructor found most interesting and impressive? Why? Write a paragraph explaining your choice.

2. Without using any of the titles from the previous list, create a new title for the essay assignment on homelessness.

3. Write a creative introduction for this thesis statement: *Homelessness is a serious problem, but there are some actions we can take to start solving it.*

4. Imagine you have written an essay about steps we can take to solve homelessness. Write a creative conclusion paragraph to end your essay.

⊙ ADDING TO YOUR VOCABULARY

This chapter's vocabulary words appear below.

conceivable	credible	autism	advocate
irony	conventional	therapeutic	

Choose five of the vocabulary words from this chapter that you would like to add to your vocabulary, and think about how you can use them this week. For example, one of this chapter's words is *advocate*. You can often easily substitute *advocate* for *suggest* or sometimes *say*, as in the example that follows.

> **Example:**   I am *saying* that you should obey speed limit laws.
>
> I am *advocating* that you obey speed limit laws.

List each of the five words you plan to use this week, and make note of a context in which you could use each word.

> **Example:**   *Advocating*. I can use this word when I give advice to a family member.

ADDITIONAL ASSIGNMENTS

1. Imagine you are writing an essay with this thesis statement: *Six steps can help you be a more organized person.* The six steps you will discuss are these:
   - Make and use lists.
   - Keep a neat desk.
   - Organize paperwork effectively and daily.
   - Use your smartphone's organizational tools.
   - Identify the obstacles that keep you from being organized, and make a plan to deal with them.
   - Hire help when it is necessary.

   Write an introduction paragraph, a conclusion paragraph, and a title for this essay.

2. Find an essay in this textbook that could benefit from a new introduction paragraph or conclusion paragraph, and write the paragraph.

3. **a.** Scan magazines, textbooks, or other texts. Choose a text with an interesting title. Explain in a paragraph what makes the title interesting.

   b. Do the same for an introduction: find a text that contains a well-written introduction. Write a paragraph explaining why you find the introduction well written.

   c. Follow this same procedure for a conclusion paragraph. Be sure to write down the name of the essay (or textbook chapter) in which you found the interesting or well-written introduction and conclusion.

4. Take out an essay you wrote for this course or for another course. Rewrite the title, introduction, and conclusion using strategies from this chapter. Work on improving the interest and quality of all three elements.

EMOTIONAL INTELLIGENCE

Two types of motivation exist. First, there is *extrinsic motivation*. Something that motivates us extrinsically is something that is outside of us. For example, if my mom says that I will be grounded unless I clean my room immediately, I will clean my room—not because I want to, but because I am being forced to. *Intrinsic motivation* is motivation that comes from inside. If I am building an outdoor fire pit with rocks, I will move the rocks because I want to build the fire pit.

Studies show that students who do work because they are intrinsically motivated to succeed in college *always* do better work than students who do work because they are being forced to. Think of a time when you did a school assignment that you *wanted* to do, not because you were forced to. Now think of an assignment you did because you had to. What was the difference in the quality of those assignments? Explain your answer in a paragraph.

Think about how you can be intrinsically motivated to do school assignments in which you are not personally interested. How can you transform extrinsic motivation to intrinsic motivation—even when the assignments are not ones you long to do? Write a paragraph explaining your ideas.

CULTURAL LITERACY

History is full of books that have been highly influential. From the list below, choose five works that you have not studied, and do an Internet search for each one. Determine why the work is famous. Summarize the work—most are books—in one or two sentences.

The Diary of Anne Frank   *The Origin of Species*
The King James Version Bible   *The Water Margin*
The Iliad and *The Odyssey*   *Romeo and Juliet*
Invisible Man (Ellison)   Aesop's fables
The Quran   *Uncle Tom's Cabin*

CRITICAL THINKING

Ethnocentrism means using your own cultural perspective to evaluate the beliefs and conventions of people from other cultures. For example, a person who lives in the United States may think in an ethnocentric way if he thinks *like an American* and cannot imagine an issue from the perspective of someone who lives in another country.

If you ask many Americans to list the most important documents in the world, they will probably choose works central to American life, such as the U.S. Constitution and the Declaration of Independence. If you ask a Chinese person to list the most important documents, that person is likely to list Chinese books.

Thinking critically requires us to be aware of our tendency to think in ethnocentric ways and to try to think from a broader perspective. Here are some examples of customs and beliefs that have their basis in ethnocentrism:

- Many Muslim women wear head scarves for religious or cultural reasons. Think of an item that people from other religions and cultures might wear. Why do you think people wear these items? What do these items tell others about the wearer's identity and beliefs?

- One delicacy of French cuisine is snails, called *escargot* (pronounced es-car-GO)—a dish that has not gained wide popularity in the United States. Think of other cultural food preferences that you have encountered or read about. Are you adventurous about trying other foods? Or do you prefer to stay with foods you find familiar? Do you think our reactions to people's culinary preferences affect how we feel about their culture or society? Why or why not?

- China, which has a culture of honoring and respecting the elderly, recently passed an "Elderly Rights Law" that makes it illegal for adults to "snub" or "neglect" their elderly parents. What cultural obligations do Americans feel toward their parents? Is there a consistent cultural attitude, or do the expectations vary by region, economic class, or ethnic group? How do cultures respond when changes in society make it difficult to honor long-standing expectations?

Choose one of these topics, and write a paragraph answering the questions given. Alternatively, write a paragraph about your own observations about ethnocentric beliefs.

METACOGNITION

Metacognitive ability means you can see yourself from the outside. Answer the following questions from a metacognitive point of view. Are you an ethnocentric thinker? (An ethnocentric thinker is unable to see things from a different cultural perspective.) Is this something you can change? Explain.

9

An inference is an educated guess. By examining the details of this photo, what inferences can you make? Readers and writers work with inferences in texts as well as in illustrations.

Inferences and Tone

An inference is a conclusion a person draws based on evidence. When we read, we **infer** by examining the information the writer provides. On the other hand, when we speak or write, we can **imply** meanings without stating them outright. For instance, when we need to finish a conversation, we might say something such as "It's getting late." Our words *imply* a deeper meaning—"We need to end this conversation"—and we hope our listeners will *infer* this meaning from what they hear us say.

As readers and observers, we make inferences every day. We might see a restaurant with a paint-worn and disheveled appearance and infer that the food must not be good. Or perhaps we find ourselves in stop-and-go traffic and infer that the freeway will be clogged for a long time, so we take an exit and find an alternative route.

Sometimes our inferences are correct, and sometimes they are totally mistaken. We may learn that the "rundown" restaurant is a fabulous eatery that has been featured on a televised food program, or we may learn that the freeway was not clogged: debris from a tire blowout had simply slowed down traffic temporarily. Being able to make accurate inferences is crucial for good communication.

CHAPTER OBJECTIVES

After completing this chapter, students will be able to do the following:

- **Use details in images and texts to draw accurate inferences.**

- **Analyze the assumptions that influence inferences.**

- **Analyze assumptions to control implications in writing.**

- **Analyze tone in texts.**

- **Recognize first, second, and third person in readings, and make appropriate writing choices concerning person.**

- **Choose an appropriate tone for writing assignments.**

- **Analyze figurative language to make accurate inferences.**

- **Use figurative language in writing.**

- **Draw accurate inferences from graphics.**

USING DETAILS IN IMAGES AND TEXTS TO DRAW ACCURATE INFERENCES

One way to make accurate inferences is to consider details. The details in an image or a text give us information on which we can base our inferences.

Details in an Image

When we observe an image such as a photograph, the details in the photo help us draw inferences. Study the picture shown here. What inferences can you draw from the details in the photo?

Perhaps you noticed the girl in the forefront and the three children in the background. The girl gazing out the window does not have a smile on her face, and her eyebrow is slightly raised. Her intense gaze suggests worry. The children in the background, meanwhile, are running barefoot. All the children have on similar clothing. We might infer that these children are in school because they seem to be wearing school uniforms. We might also infer that the girl looking out the window is not part of the group or that she is not in a playful mood. We may infer that she is lonely or worried or that she wants to be somewhere other than school. These are **sound** inferences because we can support them with the details in the photo.

What would you say to a person who looks at the photo and thinks the girl is nervous and unhappy because she is a new student at the school and misses her old friends? We can see that she is unhappy, but we really cannot see why. The fact that she is not playing with the other children does not give us enough information on which to base the inference that the school is new to her and that she misses her friends. While it would be easy to imagine many different reasons for the girl's posture and facial expression, we can use only the reasons that are supported by evidence to draw correct inferences.

Vocabulary Collection Word:
sound

Your in-context definition:

_____

_____

A dictionary definition:

_____

_____

Details in a Text

To be sound, an inference must be based on the actual information in a text. Read the following passage, and notice the details that are underlined.

> As I <u>walked to my trigonometry class</u> on the <u>first day of the semester</u>, I felt full of hope. <u>Math had never been an easy subject</u> for me, but I knew that with determination, I could do anything. I really believed that.

(continued)

> I found a seat in the middle of the classroom and glanced at the people around me. Most looked nonchalant, as if taking a class in trig were not a big deal. No one spoke.
>
> Five minutes after the class was supposed to begin, a man who looked too young to be a professor walked into the class, slung his gray, worn backpack on the professor's table, and started writing an equation on the board. He muttered something about page 33, so I fumbled through my textbook to find the page. Nothing on the page looked remotely like what the professor had written on the board.
>
> He kept explaining. Something.
>
> "You understand?" he asked the class, turning back to the board before anyone could answer.
>
> I felt that sinking feeling in my stomach that I have felt in so many math classes before. It would be a long semester after all.

We can use the details to make some inferences. We can safely infer that the instructor is young, based on the narrator's description. Some people might be tempted to say the instructor is a teaching assistant, not a professor, but we do not have enough details to make that inference.

Can we infer that the other students are more advanced in mathematics than the narrator? The narrator describes the other students as *nonchalant* (calm, not anxious), but we would need more information to know whether the students are really better at math than the narrator.

Would we be right to infer that, by the end of the passage, the narrator is not optimistic about his ability to do well in the class? Yes, we can make this inference because the last sentence tells us the narrator feels the same way he did in previous math classes, and we know from a detail earlier in the passage that math had never been an easy subject for him.

While we can infer that the narrator has a negative feeling about the class, we *cannot* accurately infer that he will fail. We simply do not have enough information to make that inference. The instructor may turn out to be a wonderful teacher, and even if the instructor is not wonderful, the student may still pass the class.

Base your inferences on the actual details of the passage. Do not add your own assumptions.

Now we will look at a text that is a bit more complex and use it to judge inferences. Read and carefully annotate the following selection from *A First Look at Communication Theory* by Em Griffin. Pay special attention to the details it offers.

What We Can Learn from the *Challenger* Disaster
by Em Griffin

YOUR ANNOTATIONS

[1]On the morning of January 28, 1986, the space shuttle *Challenger* blasted off from the Kennedy Space Center in Florida. [2]Seventy-three seconds later, millions of adults and school children watched on television as the rocket disintegrated in a fiery explosion, and the capsule plunged into the Atlantic Ocean. [3]The death of all seven crew members, and particularly teacher Christa McAuliffe, shocked the nation. [4]For many Americans, the *Challenger* disaster marked the end of a love affair with space. [5]As they learned in the months that followed, the tragedy could have been—should have been—avoided.

(continued)

⁶President Reagan immediately appointed a select commission to determine the probable cause(s) of the accident. ⁷The panel heard four months of testimony from NASA officials, rocket engineers, astronauts, and anyone else who might have knowledge about the failed mission. ⁸In a five-volume published report, the presidential commission identified the primary cause of the accident as a failure in the joint between two stages of the rocket that allowed hot gases to escape during the "burn." ⁹Volatile rocket fuel spewed out when a rubber O-ring failed to seal the joint.

¹⁰The average citizen could understand the mechanics of the commission's finding. ¹¹After all, everyone knows what happens when you pour gasoline on an open flame. ¹²What people found difficult to fathom was why NASA had launched the *Challenger* when there was good reason to believe the conditions weren't safe. ¹³In addition to the defective seal, the commission also concluded that a highly flawed decision process was an important contributing cause of the disaster. ¹⁴Communication, as well as combustion, was responsible for the tragedy.

The details in the passage suggest that the following inferences are sound:

- **The *Challenger* tragedy was thoroughly investigated.** We expect a thorough investigation to include a number of different people who represent different agencies and have different viewpoints. We also expect a thorough investigation to take a significant amount of time. Further, a thorough investigation should be meaningful. The details in the passage show that the investigation met all of these expectations. Thus, we can infer that it was a thorough investigation.

- **After the disaster, teachers and school children discussed the tragedy.** While the writer does not say this explicitly, he does provide details that allow us to make this inference. First, he tells us that "millions of adults and school children watched on television as the rocket disintegrated in a fiery explosion" (sentence 2). It is reasonable to think that children who watched the disaster on television would have been upset by it. Further, since many of these children were watching the disaster from their schools, it is reasonable to infer that their teachers would have discussed the tragedy with them.

One pitfall when drawing inferences is to allow your own personal beliefs, ideas, or biases to influence the inferences you draw. The following inferences are *not* sound. Read each explanation to understand why.

- **The *Challenger* tragedy demonstrated that Americans should not support the space program.** This incorrect inference may be caused by not reading the passage carefully enough, or it may be prompted by the reader's own opinion about the space program. In the passage, we read, "For many Americans, the *Challenger* disaster marked the end of a love affair with space" (sentence 4). Just because many Americans stopped loving space exploration, that does not mean they necessarily wished to end the space program. This inference goes beyond what the details of the text tell us. To make this incorrect inference, the reader has to *add to* the information of the text.

- **NASA engineers did not know how to design flawless O-rings.** This inference is not sound because there are no details in the passage to support it. What we learn in the passage is that the O-ring failed and that communication contributed to this failure. There is no suggestion anywhere that the engineers lacked knowledge. Further, in sentence 5, we read that "the tragedy could have been—should have been—avoided." This suggests that the engineers were perfectly capable of making flawless O-rings but that other factors contributed to the disaster.

As you look for inferences in texts, make sure you use the actual details that the text supplies, not ideas you bring to the text. Be sure you can point to the details that make your inferences accurate.

PRACTICE ➊ Drawing Inferences Based on a Text's Details

Use the passage from *A First Look at Communication Theory* to determine whether the inferences that follow are sound. Write *S* for inferences that are sound and *NS* for those that are not sound. Write a sentence explaining your reasoning for each answer.

_____ **1.** The president at the time was Ronald Reagan.

_____

_____

_____ **2.** The writer believes that school children should not be allowed to watch rocket launches.

_____

_____

_____ **3.** Some people at NASA were probably worried about something going wrong with the launch.

_____

_____

_____

_____ **4.** The panel investigating may not have been qualified to make the investigation.

_____

_____ **5.** Some people involved in the launch knew the shuttle was going to blow up during liftoff.

_____

_____ **6.** Even the most minor details of space flight must be considered for the flight to be safe.

_____

ANALYZING THE ASSUMPTIONS THAT INFLUENCE INFERENCES

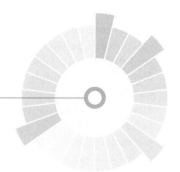

As we interpret the clues in a photo or a text to make inferences, another factor often comes into play: our assumptions. An **assumption** is a belief you hold to be true. For example, because of your experiences, you may have made the assumption that you live in a safe town. You may infer, based on this assumption, that it is safe to leave your doors unlocked at night. Of course, your assumption can be wrong; if it is, your inference—that you can safely leave your doors unlocked—will also be wrong.

It is not always easy to examine our assumptions because sometimes we do not even recognize them. For example, as children, we believed the rest of the world was just like the world in which we grew up. As we matured, we learned this assumption is wrong: other people think very differently and live very differently than we do. Some children grow up with the assumption that they will go to college. Others grow up assuming they will not finish high school. Assumptions like these shape our lives. One of the goals of an education is to help students examine the assumptions they hold and to change those beliefs when it is necessary or helpful to do so.

Assumptions That Affect Our Inferences about Events

Demetria is in her first semester in college. For the first major exam in her history class, she spends thirty minutes before class looking over her textbook. This is the method of studying she used in high school, and she usually passed her tests. When she gets the graded test back, she is astonished to see that she earned a 40. Demetria had incorrectly assumed that college tests would be like high school tests.

Let's imagine that you work for a company that conducts fire drills ten times a year. You are at work and finishing an overdue report. The fire alarm bell rings, and you look around. People are walking toward the exits, chitchatting about the day's events. No one is running out of the building, you don't see smoke, and you don't hear shouting. Your assumption is that a real fire emergency will look different than a fire drill; thus, you infer that there is no danger at hand. Consequently, you continue writing your report—until black smoke starts filling the office.

What went wrong? There were signs that should have guided you to the correct inference. You heard the fire alarm bell, and you knew that it is used to signal fires and warn employees to evacuate. You saw coworkers exiting the building. But your assumption—that a real fire emergency would seem different than a fire drill—led you to make the wrong inference.

Assumptions That Affect Our Inferences about Texts

Readers can make incorrect inferences about texts because their assumptions are faulty. Read the following example to see how assumptions can influence the inferences we make.

> **Text:** I sat in the den glaring at the TV, dumbfounded by what was taking place on the football field. The Colts' quarterback was sacked again—the third time in the game. In disgust, I punched the sofa cushion and sank down into the dilapidated, old couch.

> **Inference 1:** The speaker is a Colts fan.

> **Inference 2:** He is unhappy with the Colts' performance.

The speaker's actions clearly show unhappiness with the events in the Colts' football game, so the idea that the speaker is a Colts fan is a sound inference. Part of the second inference—that the speaker is unhappy with the Colts' performance—is a sound inference. The word *disgust* gives us some proof for the speaker's feelings. However, the pronoun *he* is a problem! Is there any evidence in the paragraph that the speaker is male? Reread the paragraph to see.

In fact, the speaker could be male or female. However, many readers will make the false assumption that the football fan is male, and the stereotype regarding the punching behavior adds to this assumption. In this case, we are incorrect to assume the football fan is a male. The only basis we have for that inference is a stereotype about football fans and male behavior.

Let's consider another example. Read the text below, and analyze the assumptions used to make the inferences.

> **Text:** Positive psychology is, as Dorothy Foltz-Gray defines it, "a discipline that aims not just to relieve suffering but also to increase happiness." The focus of psychology for many years has been to determine what psychological disorders

are and how we can treat them. Positive psychology, a discipline that has gained popularity in the last twenty years, asks different questions. Rather than focusing on disorders, positive psychology seeks to determine what makes us psychologically *well*. What are the stabilizing factors that cause some people to live happy, productive lives? Positive psychology seeks to answer that question.

Inference 1: Dorothy Foltz-Gray is a psychologist.

Inference 2: Psychologists now value positive psychology more than traditional psychology.

Did you infer that Dorothy Foltz-Gray is a psychologist? What assumption might lead a person to make that inference? (See if you can answer this question before reading on to find the answer!)

A reader might also infer that psychologists now value positive psychology more than traditional psychology. Can you figure out the assumption on which that inference might be based?

The first inference—that Dorothy Foltz-Gray is a psychologist—rests on the assumption that a person who defines a term or writes about an issue must be an expert in the field from which that term comes. And sometimes that assumption is true. Textbooks, for example, offer plenty of definitions, and they are always written by professionals in the field. But we might also read articles written by journalists in which we find definitions. Journalists write about a broad range of topics: they are not necessarily experts in a field other than journalism. What's more, students often offer definitions in informative essays, and they are not experts either. Thus, we cannot assume that just because someone proffers a definition or writes about a subject, he or she is an expert in a field.

The second inference—that psychologists now value positive psychology more than traditional psychology—is also based on a false assumption. The assumption is that if something is gaining popularity, it must be better or more valuable than its competitors. In science, however, this assumption is not true. In fact, scientists are often cautious of new theories and are usually slow to change their beliefs. Because the assumption is false, the inference that positive psychology is now valued more than traditional psychology is also false.

As you make inferences, ask yourself, "What assumptions am I making?" While it is very difficult to identify your assumptions, doing so is the first step to thinking more critically and making more accurate judgments.

PRACTICE ❷ Analyzing Assumptions to Make Sound Inferences

Make an inference about each of the situations described below. Determine the assumption on which you based your inference. Finally, evaluate your inference and assumption. Is the assumption reasonable? Is the inference sound? Write a sentence explaining your evaluation.

1. My history class will be an online class.

Inference: _____

_____

Assumption: _____

_____

Evaluation: _____

(continued)

2. Kendra enjoys doing her taxes and volunteers to calculate taxes for her friends and family. She wants to be an accountant.

Inference: _____

_____

Assumption: _____

_____

Evaluation: _____

3. Tom lives in a city known for high crime rates. In fact, Tom's next-door neighbor's apartment was burglarized last week. After buying groceries one evening, Tom arrives home to see his door ajar. Standing quietly at the door, Tom hears shuffling noises inside the apartment.

Inference: _____

_____

Assumption: _____

_____

Evaluation: _____

4. Kaylea had always been shy and bookish, and her hard work paid off when she learned she was the valedictorian of her high school.

Inference: _____

_____

Assumption: _____

_____

Evaluation: _____

ANALYZING ASSUMPTIONS TO CONTROL NEGATIVE IMPLICATIONS IN YOUR WRITING

An important part of writing is considering how a reader will understand your text. One way readers understand texts is by drawing inferences. Thus, good writers think about the potential inferential meanings readers may draw from their writing.

Anticipating Negative Implications in Your Writing

Consider this example. Imelda is writing an essay on why stevia—a very low calorie plant-based sweetener—is better than all the other very low calorie sweeteners on the market. Imelda truly believes in stevia, for she has read reports about its superiority to other sweeteners. It just so happens that Imelda's family owns a stevia production company. Imelda knows that if she mentions her family's business, readers may infer that she believes in stevia only because her family owns a company that produces it. Her awareness of this potential inference will help Imelda make choices about the content to include in her essay and how to word her ideas.

Here is another example. Dawn knows she will miss her English class to study for a biology test, so she writes her English instructor the e-mail message shown here.

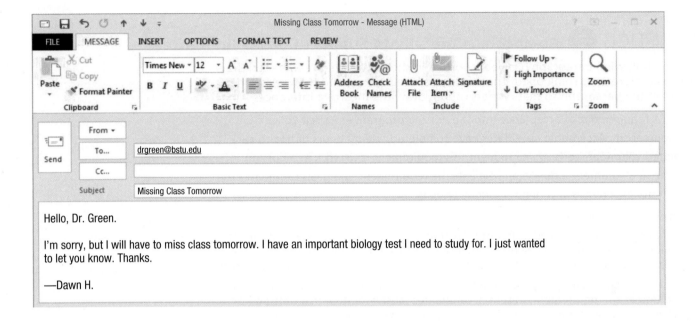

From this note, the instructor may infer that Dawn thinks her biology class is more important than the English class. The rewritten e-mail message that follows is an improvement.

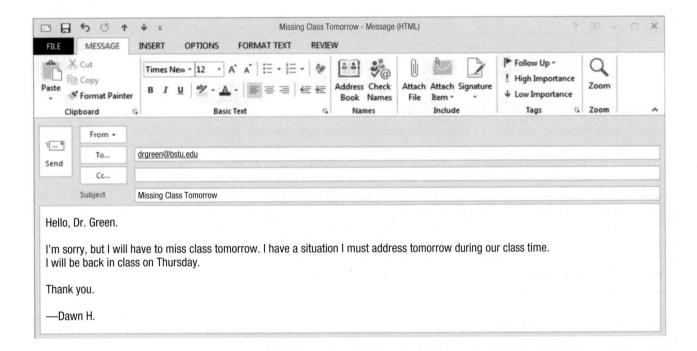

The revised e-mail is not deceptive. It accomplishes the same task—informing the instructor that Dawn will be absent—without implying that another class is more important.

The most effective writers compose their texts with their readers in mind. Anticipating the negative inferences readers might make enables writers to make wording choices that control—to the extent possible—the inferences readers draw from their texts.

PRACTICE ③ Composing Carefully to Support Correct Inferences

The following paragraph has been worded in such a way that readers can draw incorrect inferences. Think about the inferences listed below, and then revise the details in the paragraph so that readers cannot draw the incorrect inferences.

A requirement of acceptance into the nursing program at Farrell College is volunteerism. Acceptable candidates have completed twenty hours of health-care related volunteer work. A way to meet this requirement is to work in a nursing home as a volunteer aide. Doing so meets the requirement and gives candidates the requisite experience in caring for elderly people.

Incorrect inferences:

- From the paragraph, readers might infer that if candidates have twenty hours of volunteer work, they will be accepted into the nursing program. However, volunteer work is only one of the acceptance requirements, so this inference is incorrect.

- The wording of the paragraph might lead some readers to infer that to meet the volunteerism requirement, potential candidates must volunteer in a nursing home. However, volunteering in a nursing home is only one way to meet the requirement, so this inference is incorrect.

Write your own version of the paragraph so that readers cannot make the two incorrect inferences listed above.

_____

_____

_____

_____

Analyzing Assumptions in Your Writing

To be a good communicator, you have to analyze the assumptions in your writing. If you are writing for a general audience, analyze your assumptions about what the audience knows. While you can expect the audience to have general knowledge, such as understanding the major differences between the games of basketball and football, you cannot expect a general audience to know the exact rules of each game. It's important to write in such a way that you explain ideas that a general audience would need to have clarified.

In addition to making assumptions about an audience's knowledge, we are all guilty sometimes of making assumptions based on stereotypes. Many people hold unconscious assumptions about other people related to race or ethnicity, religion, gender, sexual orientation, disability, age, profession or employment, socioeconomic status, political affiliation, or the place where they live or come from. Since it can be hard to recognize our unconscious assumptions, asking ourselves questions about what we have written can help us identify problematic assumptions:

- **Have I avoided making sweeping generalizations about groups of people?**

    Not appropriate: We all know that lawyers cannot be trusted to tell the truth about this issue.

    Appropriate: That attorney has misled the public on a key legal point.

- **Have I referred to a person's gender, race, or other attributes only when doing so was essential to the point I was making?**

    Not appropriate: A woman judge heard the case and rendered the verdict.

Appropriate: Sandra Day O'Connor was the first woman to serve as a justice on the U.S. Supreme Court.

- **Have I avoided ascribing stereotypical characteristics to people, even when the characteristics seem "positive"?**

    Not appropriate: Like most Asian men, he is great at math, which has helped him succeed in computer engineering and programming.

    Appropriate: Patel's extraordinary facility in mathematical thinking has helped him succeed in computer engineering and programming.

- **Have I avoided implying that the "average" person or reader belongs to a specific race, religion, gender, or other group?**

    Not appropriate: Today, the average person looking for a wife may not hesitate to consult an online dating site.

    Appropriate: Today, the average person looking for a spouse may have little reluctance in consulting an online dating site.

- **Have I been as specific as possible in referring to groups of people?**

    Not specific: Native Americans served as coded message senders during World Wars I and II because they could communicate in a language that was not known to America's enemies.

    Specific: Soldiers from the Cherokee, Choctaw, Lakota, Comanche, and Navajo tribes served as coded message senders during World Wars I and II because they could communicate in Native American languages that were not known to America's enemies.

PRACTICE ④ Analyzing Assumptions in Your Writing

A college student has been asked by his former high school to talk to students about his experience in applying to colleges. The paragraph that follows is from the talk he is preparing. Find two problematic assumptions the student is making. Explain why these assumptions are problematic. How do you think the student's listeners will react to this paragraph?

When I got a rejection letter from Monroe Tech, I was pretty upset at first. But when I heard that my classmate John had gotten in, I became really angry. I could see the college taking Lee ahead of me. Everyone knows Asian kids are super smart at math. But John? His major after-school activity was playing for the school's football team. How could he be a better student than I am?

_____
_____
_____
_____

ANALYZING TONE IN TEXTS

If you have spent time around children, you know a disrespectful tone when you hear one. To such a tone, a parent may reply, "Don't take that tone with me!" So, what exactly is tone?

Tone is the attitude with which a message is conveyed. We might use a tone of respect when we speak, or we might use a tone that reveals frustration, anger, or impatience.

Both voice and body language help us discern tone in face-to-face communication. In texts, however, we depend on textual clues to help us identify tone.

Have you ever noticed how difficult it is to determine the tone of a text message or an e-mail? Read the e-mail message that follows. What is its tone?

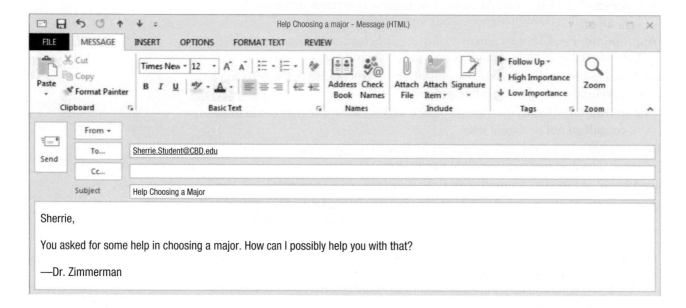

As you read the e-mail message, did you hear a helpful tone in the last sentence, or did you hear a sarcastic tone? Because readers could infer a sarcastic tone, it would be better to write a reply that leaves no room to wonder about the writer's attitude. Compare the following message. Notice how adding a few extra details and making intentional choices about wording help the writer convey a tone that is decidedly positive. Writers must carefully select their words to help readers understand the tone they hope to establish.

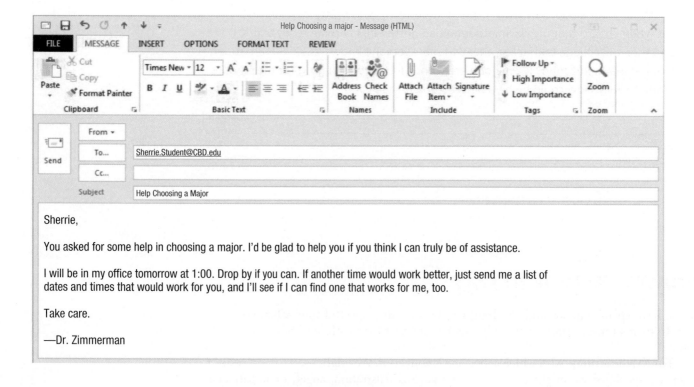

Objective Tone

One way to understand tone is to consider two types: objective and subjective. When a writer attempts to write a text *without* tone or with a neutral tone, we say that the writer uses an **objective tone.** Imagine a news anchor reading the evening news. The anchor's job is to minimize the tone in her voice so that she presents the news in a nonbiased, or objective, manner. The anchor is speaking as a reader, not as an individual. Thus, we are not supposed to focus on the anchor and her particular views. Read the following text for an example of objective tone.

Example of Objective Tone

People who are regularly late for meetings or other appointments can eventually develop a reputation for being less dependable than others. Coworkers and acquaintances rarely know or understand the situations that cause a person to be habitually late, and even if they are aware of such circumstances, they may still come to view the late person as unreliable. In turn, having a reputation as an unreliable person makes it more difficult to receive promotions or be entrusted with high-level tasks.

A few characteristics will help you identify an objective tone.

- **An objective tone is established by avoiding emotionally charged terms.** For example, the passage above refers to a habitually late person as being seen as "an unreliable person," a term that is far less emotionally charged than "a loser" or "a slacker."

- **An objective tone is also established by using impartial, unbiased language.** The passage about habitually late people does not say such people are "poor employees." The writer does not make a judgment; she merely explains a potential effect from being consistently late to appointments.

- **An objective tone is most often associated with formal writing**—writing for professional or academic purposes. For example, if a writer uses slang (such as the word *loser*) to describe a habitually late person, not only does such a word convey an emotional and biased tone, but it also makes the text informal.

When a writer uses an objective tone, we are more likely to infer that the information is reliable. We may not be correct, of course, but we expect reliable information to be delivered in an impersonal, objective way. Thus, when we see the use of an objective tone, we can use it as a clue for making inferences. For example, in the paragraph about people who are habitually late, it would be wrong to make the inference that the writer has disdain for such people. The writer does not reveal her own attitude toward the subject.

We would also be wrong to infer that the writer is never late for her own appointments. She reveals nothing about her behaviors or her attitudes. For all we know, the writer might be a habitually late person herself! Thus, when you identify an objective tone, you cannot make inferences about the writer's attitude toward the topic.

Vocabulary Collection Word:
disdain

Your in-context definition:

_____

_____

A dictionary definition:

_____

Subjective Tone

A **subjective tone** is used when a writer is not trying to present information in a neutral way. We have shown how news anchors attempt to use an objective tone so that they do not reveal their personal biases about issues. Political commentators, on the other hand, discuss news events but do so in a subjective, biased way. They are paid to offer their opinions on current events, so using a subjective tone is appropriate. A few characteristics will help you identify a subjective tone.

- **A subjective tone makes use of emotional clues.** Sometimes writers use a subjective tone to convey anger or to convey delight; or they may use a subjective tone to write sarcastically, to express surprise, or to convey warmth and friendship.
- **A subjective tone can express bias**—a person's preferences or particular point of view. If a person is biased, that simply means the person has an opinion about a subject.
- **Unlike objective writing, subjective writing is often informal.** That is, writers may use everyday language, slang, contractions, and a conversational tone, as if they were having a chat with their readers.

Sometimes we hear the term *biased* and think it means "unfair." However, a person who is biased about a subject is not necessarily unfair. When you write an essay on a controversial topic, such as immigration reform, and submit it for grading, you can expect that your instructor will be biased about the issue, but he or she can still grade your paper fairly.

We see bias in texts when writers reveal their personal opinions or points of view. Writers seeking to be objective try to present a topic in a neutral manner. The use of a subjective tone is appropriate when writers want to present their personal views or reveal information about themselves. A subjective tone will often allow readers to infer the writer's bias or attitudes toward a subject. It can also reveal the writer's emotions about the subject.

The use of a subjective tone is intentional: writers hope readers will come to share the same emotions or opinions as they do. Read the following example to become familiar with subjective tone in texts and the inferences we can draw from such texts.

Example of Subjective Tone

I work with a poor colleague who is always late. He's not only late to meetings, but he's late to work every single day. The variety of excuses he uses when he stumbles through the door each morning is always amusing. He cannot help but utter some lame excuse. "I was caught in traffic. Darn freeway!" or "I can't believe my alarm clock failed me again!" It would be so much better—and so much more appropriate—for him to creep over to his office and slink into his chair like the clueless **buffoon** he is.

Vocabulary Collection Word:
buffoon

Your in-context definition:
_____
_____

A dictionary definition:
_____
_____

In the example, the writer uses *I* (first person), as well as contractions, both of which are characteristics of informal writing. The writer does not attempt to hide his own attitude about his coworker. Indeed, he calls his colleague a "clueless buffoon," just in case readers did not pick up on his **contempt**.

If we carefully examine the writer's word choices, we can get a better idea of his tone and his attitude.

- "Poor colleague." The term *poor* reveals the writer's disdain or contempt.
- "Stumbles through the door." A person who stumbles through a door is clumsy, a detail that is consistent with the name used in the last sentence, *buffoon*.
- "Some lame excuse." The adjective *lame* suggests that the coworker cannot even think of a good reason for his tardiness. And *excuse* suggests that the reason is not legitimate.
- "Creep over to his office and slink into his chair." The verbs *creep* and *slink* are generally used to describe how animals move; such words **dehumanize** the coworker and add to the tone of disdain.
- "Clueless buffoon." Any time a writer engages in name-calling, you can be sure the tone is not objective. Besides adding to the subjective tone, this detail adds an element of condescension and meanness to the writer's tone.

Vocabulary Collection Word:
contempt

Your in-context definition:
_____
_____

A dictionary definition:
_____
_____

Vocabulary Collection Word:
dehumanize

Your in-context definition:
_____
_____

A dictionary definition:
_____
_____

Because a subjective tone reveals a great deal about the writer's thoughts and attitude, you can create accurate inferences by analyzing the tone. Notice how the inferences that follow are based on the writer's subjective, **condescending** tone.

Accurate inference: The writer has contempt for his colleague.

Accurate inference: The writer does not think his colleague's reasons for being late are legitimate.

Accurate inference: The writer feels superior to his colleague.

Complete the following exercise to try your hand at distinguishing between objective and subjective tones, and then use your analysis of tone to make accurate inferences.

PRACTICE (5) Identifying Tone to Make Accurate Inferences

Read each of the following passages, and answer the corresponding questions.

PASSAGE A: Excerpt from *Business Now* by Amit Shah

An entrepreneur has several potential sources of capital: personal savings, relatives, former employers, banks, finance companies, venture capitalists (a person or investment company that loans money to businesses), and government agencies such as the SBA [Small Business Administration], the Farmers Home Administration, and the Economic Development Authority. Isabella Capital, LLC, is a venture capital firm that focuses on woman-owned businesses.

There are also angel investors, usually wealthy people who invest their own money in a business in return for a share of the company. Angel investors are different from venture capitalists, in that venture capitalists usually invest other people's money, while angel investors invest their own funds. The Angel Capital Association operates in North America and works to bring together angel investors and entrepreneurs.

1. What is the tone of this passage?

   _____

2. On the basis of the tone, is it accurate to infer that the writer approves more highly of angel investors than the other kinds of investors mentioned in the paragraph? Explain your answer.

   _____
   _____
   _____

PASSAGE B

So-called authorities urge everyone, every year, to get the flu shot. Almost all the people I know seem to go for the hype and rush to the local clinic or local drugstore, stand in line, and pay for this vaccination. What they don't realize is that they're paying for a mixture of vaccine and toxic chemicals—such as mercury and thimerosal—that is not even guaranteed to work. In fact, when my neighbor got a flu shot, she became so ill with a flu-like sickness that she could barely get out of bed. When ignorance meets fear, people make extremely bad decisions. You won't see me in line for a flu shot, and I've never had the flu yet!

(continued)

Vocabulary Collection Word:
condescending

Your in-context definition:

_____

_____

A dictionary definition:

_____

_____

1. What is the tone of this passage?

_____

2. On the basis of the tone, is it accurate to infer that the writer thinks she is smarter than people who get flu shots? Explain your answer.

_____

_____

_____

_____

Formal Writing

The kind of writing you will do for college assignments is formal writing. Business reports, letters, legal documents, and many other professional texts consist of formal writing. The characteristics of formal writing include the following:

- Use of third person (*one*); avoidance of first person (*I*) and second person (*you*)
- Avoidance of slang
- Avoidance of contractions
- Use of proper grammar
- Use of higher-level sentence structure (more complex sentences) and vocabulary

Save informal writing for correspondence—such as e-mail and text messages—between friends and for other informal occasions. Do not use it in your academic writing. Even though many people think of e-mail as an informal mode of expression, it is better to use formal rather than informal writing for e-mail messages to employers and professors. Above all, do not use the informal language of text messaging in academic or job-related e-mail messages.

 GRAMMAR FOCUS | **Point of View**

Writers have the choice of using first-, second-, or third-person point of view. The point of view is conveyed by the pronouns a writer uses.

First-person pronouns: I, me, my, mine, myself; we, us, our, ours, ourselves

Second-person pronouns: you, your, yours, yourself

Third-person pronouns: he, him, his, himself; she, her, hers, herself; they, them, their, theirs, themselves; it, its, itself; one, oneself

The point of view a writer uses contributes to establishing a subjective or objective tone. The key is to choose the correct point of view for your writing purpose.

1. USE FIRST-PERSON POINT OF VIEW FOR A SUBJECTIVE TONE

First-person point of view is the writer's voice, so it draws attention to the writer and conveys a more intimate and subjective tone than second- or third-person point of view. Sometimes such a tone is desirable, as in a narrative essay, autobiography, or personal letter. At other times, using first person may detract from the authority of your voice. Consider the difference in these two statements.

(continued)

Uses first person: In my opinion, using physical punishment to teach children lessons is not wise.

Does *not* use first person: Using physical punishment to teach children lessons is not wise.

The example using first person (*In my opinion*) weakens the impact of the idea that is presented by implying that it is simply a matter of the writer's belief. While the second example is still an assertion of a belief, it is more confident and objective and therefore seems to be universally true.

2. USE SECOND-PERSON POINT OF VIEW TO GIVE INSTRUCTIONS

Second-person point of view addresses readers directly, so it can convey a personal tone. However, statements in second person can sound demanding. At its worst, the use of second person can result in writing that is the equivalent of wagging one's forefinger, as these examples show.

Uses second person: You need to stop playing on your cell phone and start listening in class.

Does *not* use second person: Students need to stop playing on their cell phones and start listening in class.

Notice how the first example (*You . . . your*) sounds like a personal scolding. The second example gets across the same idea without scolding the reader.

Second-person writing can be used effectively in business letters, in instructions and how-to or process texts, and in speeches. For example, in a how-to text, a writer may use second person to personalize instructions, as follows.

Uses second person: When you calculate your income taxes, you will need your W-2 forms from the previous year, as well as any other forms that show the income you earned during the tax year.

Remember also that command statements are implicitly in second person.

Uses a command: To calculate your income taxes, use your W-2 forms from the previous year, as well as any other forms that show the income you earned during the tax year.

The word *you* is implied as the subject of *use* (*To calculate your income taxes,* [*you*] *use . . .*). Notice how terse a command can be; because of their no-nonsense tone, commands are best employed sparingly.

3. USE THIRD-PERSON POINT OF VIEW FOR ACADEMIC WORK AND OTHER FORMAL WRITING

Third person helps create an objective tone. The writing sounds more authoritative because the information in the text is not tied to the writer's voice. Note the following example.

Uses third person: Several educators have studied issues associated with higher education. They believe that the most significant problem in higher education is affordability.

(continued)

Compare this with the following example, which uses first person.

Uses first person: I believe that the most significant problem in higher education is affordability.

Using third person—and avoiding *I think* or *I believe*—de-emphasizes the writer and puts the focus on the idea, which is presented as a significant view that can be supported by evidence, and not just as the writer's personal opinion.

As a general rule, use third person for all academic writing. Formal business writing and government reports also require third-person point of view.

SENTENCE COMBINING

The examples that follow show how to take ideas expressed in one point of view, combine them, and change them into third-person point of view.

Ideas to combine and express in third person:

- I believe we should move up the voting date of the presidential primaries in our state.

- Other states vote earlier.

- You might think it doesn't make a difference.

- That is not true.

- The states that vote earlier get to whittle down the field of candidates, leaving us with only their choices to vote on.

Combined sentences using third person: Our state should move up the date it holds its presidential primaries. The states that vote earlier have a larger voice in the elections, because their earlier votes often whittle down the candidate field before the elections even reach our state.

Try your hand at converting first and second person into third-person texts.

EXERCISES

You will find three sets of sentences below. Combine the sentences to make smoother, longer ones, and change all first- and second-person pronouns into third person. You may change the wording as much as you like as long as you communicate the same ideas.

1. Ideas to combine and express in third person:

   - You should use three guidelines to control credit card spending.
   - You will avoid getting into financial difficulty if you do.
   - You should not charge more than you can afford.
   - You should always pay more than the minimum amount due each month.
   - You should use cash for luxury items.
   - Luxury items are things like iPads, expensive purses, and car stereos.

   Answer: _____
   _____
   _____
   _____

2. Ideas to combine and express in third person:

   - One education law was called the No Child Left Behind Act.
   - Under this act, you had more options for your children's education.

(continued)

- You could choose a public school other than the one in your district.
- You could do this if the school in your area was not performing well.
- You could do this if your local school was unsafe.

Answer: _____

_____

_____

3. Ideas to combine and express in third person:

- The flu and the common cold have symptoms.
- These symptoms are similar.
- I can tell you that the flu is worse than the common cold.
- You have symptoms such as fever, body aches, tiredness, and cough.
- Your flu symptoms are more intense than your cold symptoms.

Answer: _____

_____

_____

CHOOSING AN APPROPRIATE TONE FOR YOUR WRITING ASSIGNMENTS

If your purpose in writing is to inform, you should strive to create an objective tone. Doing so will help readers understand that you are writing to inform them, not persuade them. To create an objective tone, write on a formal level by avoiding contractions, slang, and conversational-style language. Avoid emotional language and bias, also. Notice the differences between the two examples that follow:

Subjective tone: People who make the mistake of getting the flu shot aren't the sharpest tools in the shed.

cliché used in conversational-style language

contraction

Objective tone: People who choose to get the flu shot may not be properly informed about the dangers and **efficacy** of the vaccine.

When you are writing a text in which you want to reveal your own opinion or set a particular tone, be sure to choose language carefully to reveal the *type* of subjective tone you wish to communicate. For example, a text written with a subjective tone can be worded in such a way as to communicate different feelings.

- **Subjective tone communicating anger:** People who avoid the flu shot are ignorant fools. They are so selfish that they don't care that their choice might result in a major flu epidemic.

     Potential inference: The writer is angry and feels threatened by those who resist the flu shot.

- **Subjective tone communicating compassion:** People who avoid the flu shot are simply unaware of the tragic results that can follow their decision. They want the

Vocabulary Collection Word:
efficacy

Your in-context definition:

_____

_____

A dictionary definition:

_____

_____

best for their families, but their lack of information leads them to make choices that, sadly, may result in more harm than good.

> **Potential inference:** The writer feels sorry for people who resist the flu shot and thinks they are simply misinformed.

If you choose an appropriate tone for your writing, your potential readers will be more likely to make correct inferences about the content you are communicating.

PRACTICE ⑥ Writing to Convey a Particular Tone

Write three paragraphs, each with a different tone. In each paragraph, explain the same content. Specifically, write about one reason why some people make the decision to drive when they are legally intoxicated. In the first paragraph, convey your idea using an objective tone. In the second, use a subjective tone that communicates anger. For the third paragraph, use a subjective tone that communicates compassion.

ANALYZING FIGURATIVE LANGUAGE TO MAKE ACCURATE INFERENCES

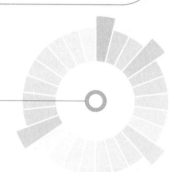

Figurative language is language that creatively suggests meanings beyond the literal meanings of the words. A word's **literal** meaning is its *actual* meaning. For example, the literal meaning of the word *star* is a celestial body made of gases. However, we also use the word *star* in a figurative way to suggest a person who is a celebrity. Similarly, we frequently use adjectives in nonliteral ways: a *sweet* car is not one made of sugar; a *crabby* customer does not have an exoskeleton and pincers; and a *chilling* reminder does not change a room's temperature. These adjectives are used figuratively: they convey meanings that are not literal.

One way figurative language works is by tapping into the connotations of words. Words have both connotations and denotations. The **denotation** of *rock*, for instance, is a mass of solid material from the earth. A husband who says that his wife is "his rock" does not mean she is a mass of solid material. He is using the qualities of a rock to describe his wife: she is unchanging, dependable, and solid. These positive qualities are **connotations**: they are ideas that go beyond the word's denotation to suggest additional meanings.

Recognizing when a word is used in a nonliteral way can help you make correct inferences. For example, consider the following passage, from sports reporter Tom Orsborn's blog on the Web site of the *San Antonio Express-News*. Note especially the figurative language, some of which is underlined.

> Nicknamed "The Brick Layer" by defensive line coach Rod Marinelli, Dallas Cowboys end George Selvie is ready to do some heavy lifting with Anthony Spencer out for the year.
>
> "It's just going out there and working hard every day, <u>just laying bricks</u>," Selvie said, when asked about his moniker. "That's what we say, '<u>Brick layer, go lay some bricks today.</u>' I just go out there and do my job and, hopefully, a couple of times I <u>get thrown a bone</u> and <u>get a sack</u>."

You probably figured out that George Selvie is a football player, not a brick layer. Calling him a "brick layer," however, adds meaning to Selvie's role on the team. Laying bricks, in this context, is an ordinary kind of job that takes a particular skill. Readers can infer that Selvie is not playing a flashy role in his position. They can also infer that being a brick layer is a positive thing. The coach's instruction to "go lay some bricks today" is matter-of-fact and reveals that this activity is a necessary element for team success.

We can find additional figurative expressions in the passage. For example, Selvie says he will occasionally get "thrown a bone." Obviously, no one really throws bones at him, but just as getting a bone is a treat for a dog, getting "a sack" is a treat for Selvie. "Sacking" a quarterback does not mean putting the guy in a big bag; it means tackling him to prevent a pass or a play. The passage contains one more figurative expression. If you examine the paragraph closely, you will find it. Metaphors and similes are commonly used types of figurative language. A **metaphor** is the use of a word in a nonliteral way to suggest a comparison. Calling Selvie a "brick layer" is using a metaphor. The metaphor works because we attribute to Selvie the characteristics of brick layers. Here are some additional examples of metaphors:

- "Our copy machine is a *fossil* that, surprisingly, still functions." This metaphor works by transferring a characteristic of a fossil—its old age—to the copy machine. We can infer that the copy machine is old.

- "I found a *gem* at the garage sale—a signed photograph of Martin Luther King, Jr." A photograph is not a gem, but in the same way that a gem is rare and valuable, the signed photograph is also. We can infer that the signed photograph may be worth significant money.

Similes function the same way metaphors do, but they draw attention to themselves as figurative language because they are used in conjunction with the words *like* or *as*. Here are a few examples of similes:

- "When I opened the dishwasher door, water gushed out *like a tidal wave*." By comparing the water to a tidal wave, the writer leads readers to infer that a large quantity of water quickly rushed out of the dishwasher.

- "The policy was *as clear as mud*." Since mud is not clear, we can infer that the policy was not clear either.

A third type of figurative language is **personification,** the use of human (and sometimes animal) qualities to describe an inanimate object. Notice how personification works by studying the examples that follow:

- "The table *groaned* with the weight of years of unopened mail, packed boxes, and old office supplies." A table cannot groan, but a human or an animal can. Using the term *groan* to describe the table helps readers think of the table as a person under too much stress.

- "My old iPhone *drew its last breath* yesterday. I will be shopping for another one today." The personification of the iPhone as a kind of living creature is a creative way to imply that the iPhone is irreparably broken.

Carefully analyzing the figurative language in readings can help you gain a better understanding of the writer's point, the writer's attitude toward that point, and the inferences you can draw from the text.

PRACTICE 7 Drawing Inferences from Figurative Language

Analyze the following passage. Underline each of the figurative words or phrases you find, and answer the questions that follow.

Alaska is a land of extremes. There is no other way to say it. It's extreme in temperature—from 50° below zero to close to 100°F within a single year. It's extreme in landscape—from valleys so wide that you can't see across them to mountains that reach to the sky. It's extreme in population density—from Anchorage with its bustling 300,000 people to the hundreds (or perhaps thousands) of people who live alone in cabins as isolated as desert islands. It's extreme in the amount of sunlight it receives. Above the Arctic Circle, the sun hides in winter, peeking out only occasionally. But in the summer, the sun is a constant companion, sometimes brightening the sky for twenty-four hours at a time. Regardless of these extremes—or perhaps because of them—Alaska is irresistible to many.

1. Where is personification used in this paragraph?

   _____

   _____

2. Based on the figurative language in this passage, what can you infer about Alaska?

   _____

   _____

USING FIGURATIVE LANGUAGE IN YOUR WRITING

One of the functions of figurative language is to suggest meanings by the use of comparisons. Metaphors and similes suggest that one thing is like another, and personification takes the qualities of something that is alive and attributes them to something that is inanimate. By suggesting meanings, figurative language adds to how readers understand texts. For example, a writer could describe a restaurant in a literal way.

   Literal description: My Bánh Mì is a Vietnamese restaurant that features freshly
      baked bread and traditional bánh mì sandwiches.

But the use of figurative language to describe the restaurant helps readers infer what makes the restaurant special.

   Figurative description: Stepping into My Bánh Mì *is like* stepping into a bakery
      tucked away on a side street in Saigon.

While both sentences are well written, the use of figurative language in the second sentence suggests that the restaurant has a certain ambience; the first sentence does not make the same suggestion.

   In the following sentences, notice how the figurative description suggests meanings that the literal description does not.

   Literal description: The neglected lodge had old carpeting and smoke-stained wall-
      paper. It was not a good location for the reception.

   Figurative description: The neglected lodge looked *like* a smokers' lounge from the
      1960s. The *walls barely held on* to their *tired* and peeling wallpaper, and the thick shag
      carpet under our feet *seemed to crawl* with bugs. It was no place for a reception.

While the literal description may be accurate, it does not provide the reader with the details needed to really visualize the lodge. The figurative description, on the other hand, helps the reader more clearly understand what the lodge was like in its state of disrepair. The second description allows the reader to make accurate inferences.

When possible, use figurative language to suggest meanings. Instead of *telling* readers what things are like, use figurative language so that readers will have a more active role in imagining and making correct inferences. When you use figurative language, readers may find your writing more enjoyable and richer in meaning than they would otherwise.

Be careful about overusing figurative language. A text with too many metaphors or too much personification may end up sounding silly. Also, be careful about mixing metaphors. A **mixed metaphor** is a sentence or set of sentences that makes use of more than one metaphor and, as a consequence, results in confusion (or laughter), as these examples show:

I'm grasping at the last straw. (*Grasping at straws* is combined with *the last straw*.)

I was out on a limb without a leg to stand on. (*Out on a limb* and *without a leg to stand on* are both metaphors, but they don't belong together.)

We'll burn that bridge when we come to it. (Combines *Don't burn your bridges* and *We'll cross that bridge when we come to it.*)

PRACTICE 8 Experimenting with Figurative Language to Suggest Meanings

Use figurative language—metaphors, similes, and personification—to complete each writing task. When you finish writing each description, reread your writing and ask yourself, "What inference could a person make from this writing?"

1. Write two or three sentences in which you use figurative language to describe a dog that looks vicious.

2. Write two or three sentences in which you use figurative language to describe a memorable meal.

3. Write two or three sentences in which you use figurative language to describe a particular quality of a boss, a friend, a coworker, or a family member. For example, you could describe a friend's constantly positive attitude.

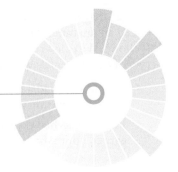

DRAWING ACCURATE INFERENCES FROM GRAPHICS

Many texts are accompanied by visuals, such as charts, graphs, artwork, cartoons, and photos. Often visuals are not explained: they are simply presented alongside other information. Thus, readers must infer their meanings.

General Guidelines for Reading Graphics

At the beginning of this chapter, you saw how readers can make inferences based on the details in an image. When photos are not accompanied by a caption, readers must infer their meaning. Just as the details of a photo can help you make inferences, the same is true for the details of graphics—graphs, charts, and illustrations. You can make accurate inferences from graphics by following these guidelines.

Step 1: Read the graphic's title.

Because charts, graphs, and illustrations contain so few words, it is crucial to start by reading the title. From the title you can often determine the type of information offered. In the graphic below, for example, the title helps us understand the three elements that make up the graph: unemployment, weekly earnings, and education.

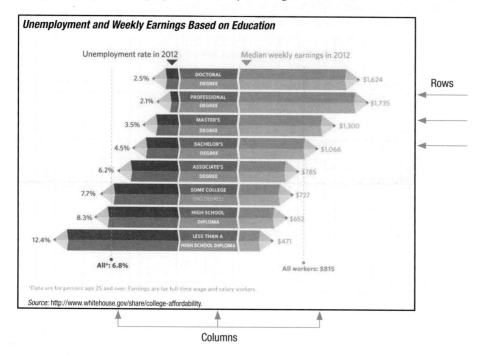

Step 2: Read the descriptions in the graphic.

Often, graphics use colors to code particular pieces of information. In the graph shown above, red depicts the unemployment rate in 2012. Gray presents education level, and yellow depicts median weekly earnings in 2012. Like tables, graphs often present information in columns and rows. Rows are always horizontal, and columns are vertical.

Step 3: Write sentences based on a graph's details.

By putting graphic information into your own words, you can more easily understand the meaning of the information. For example, start with the bottom row of information. It tells us that in 2012, the people who had less than a high school diploma (gray) experienced an unemployment rate of 12.4 percent (red) and made approximately $471 a week (yellow). We can write sentences expressing the data for each row in the graph. Here are two of the sentences we can construct.

- People who had a bachelor's degree had an unemployment rate of 4.5 percent and earned approximately $1,066 a week.
- People who had a doctoral degree had an unemployment rate of 2.5 percent and earned approximately $1,624 a week.

Step 4: Draw inferences from your sentences.

What conclusions can you draw from the content of your sentences? In the case of the graph, we can analyze the sentences listed above. From these sentences, we can infer the following.

Inference: In general, the more education a person has, the less likely he or she is to be unemployed and the more money per week the person will make.

Note that there is one exception. People with doctoral degrees had slightly more unemployment and made slightly less money per week than people with professional degrees. Notice how the inference contains the phrase *in general*. When wording inferences, be careful to use qualifiers such as *most*, *some*, *on the whole*, and *usually*.

PRACTICE (9) Drawing Inferences from Graphics

The graphic entitled "Conditions Treated by Most Commonly Used Drugs" is from the Food and Drug Administration. Use the four-step process to analyze the graphic. After completing your analysis, make two inferences.

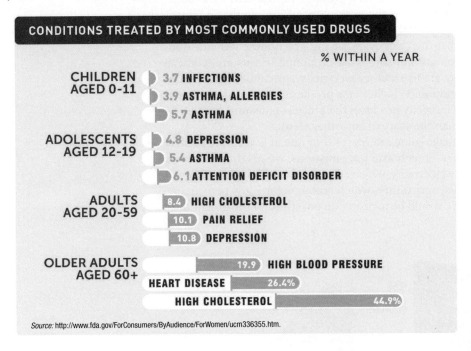

Special Considerations for Reading Line Graphs, Pie Charts, and Maps

A **line graph** shows relationships between data by plotting points. You may be familiar with line graphs from math courses. A line graph has a vertical axis and a horizontal axis. Each axis represents different values—such as years, amounts, and so on. In the example that follows, the horizontal axis indicates years, and the vertical axis indicates the percentage of increase. The graph measures two things: the increase in the miles people travel and the increase in population. The legend indicates what the different-colored lines represent.

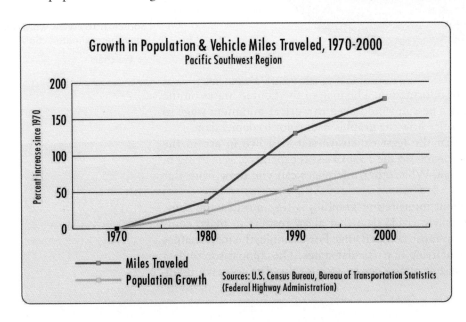

Line graph.

Notice that the distance traveled (depicted by the purple line) increases at a faster rate than the population (green line). One inference we can make from this data is that people are traveling more than they used to.

In addition to line graphs, you will encounter graphs that are round—often called **pie charts.** These graphs divide data into groups, and each group is represented by a "slice" of the pie chart. The size of each slice indicates the percentage of the pie that it constitutes. Added together, they generally total 100 percent. The title, given in the middle of the pie chart shown here, indicates that the chart is displaying greenhouse gas emissions categorized by economic sector. If you are not sure what economic sectors are, you can look at the pie pieces and see that there are five sectors: electricity, agriculture, commercial and residential, industry, and transportation. Which sector produces the most greenhouse gas emissions? The chart shows that electricity produces the greatest emissions because its share of the pie is 33 percent, larger than the share of any other sector.

By analyzing this chart, you can make some inferences. For one, it is accurate to infer that if we want to substantially reduce greenhouse gas emissions, we need to put more emphasis on transforming sectors like electricity, which accounts for a high percentage of total emissions, rather than sectors like agriculture, which accounts for a low percentage. By addressing electricity emissions, we would be focusing on one-third of the greenhouse gas emissions in the country.

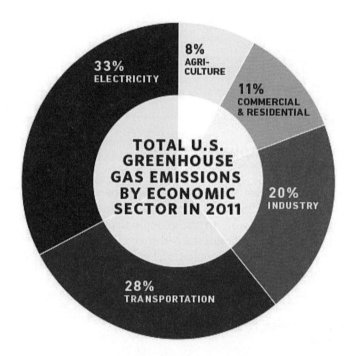

Source: http://www.whitehouse.gov/share/climate-action-plan.

■ Pie chart.

Maps are another way to present information. The map of the United States on the next page depicts the hours per week a person would need to work at minimum wage to afford an apartment in each state. Notice how the graphic uses color to depict data.

From this map, we can infer that the least expensive states to live in are in the southern and middle United States. Living on the East Coast is expensive, as is living in California, Florida, Alaska, and Hawaii. What other inferences can you draw from this graphic?

Another thing to remember about interpreting graphics is that most of the time, graphics are comparative. That is, they provide data that allow readers to make comparisons and to create inferences from those comparisons. For example, the map enables readers to compare the affordability of living in particular states. The comparison of data makes the graphic meaningful because it allows readers to use the data to make inferences and decisions.

2014 HOURS AT MINIMUM WAGE NEEDED TO AFFORD RENT

In no state can minimum wage workers afford a two-bedroom rental unit at Fair Market Rent, working a standard 40-hour work week, without paying more than 30% of their income.

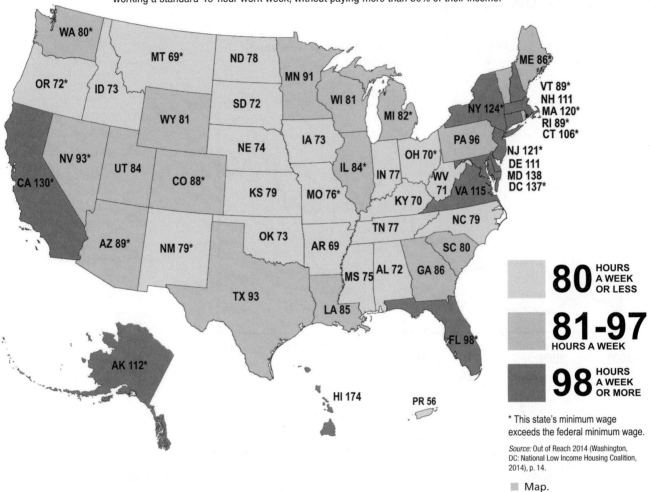

WA 80*
MT 69*
ND 78
MN 91
ME 86*
OR 72*
ID 73
VT 89*
NH 111
SD 72
WI 81
MA 120*
WY 81
MI 82*
NY 124*
RI 89*
CT 106*
NV 93*
NE 74
IA 73
PA 96
UT 84
OH 70*
NJ 121*
CA 130*
CO 88*
IL 84*
IN 77
WV 71
DE 111
MD 138
KS 79
MO 76*
KY 70
VA 115
DC 137*
AZ 89*
NM 79*
OK 73
AR 69
TN 77
NC 79
SC 80
MS 75
AL 72
GA 86
TX 93
LA 85
FL 98*
AK 112*
HI 174
PR 56

80 HOURS A WEEK OR LESS

81-97 HOURS A WEEK

98 HOURS A WEEK OR MORE

* This state's minimum wage exceeds the federal minimum wage.

Source: Out of Reach 2014 (Washington, DC: National Low Income Housing Coalition, 2014), p. 14.

▩ Map.

PRACTICE ⑩ Analyzing Inferences Drawn from Graphics

These numbered statements are followed by a line graph, on the next page. Study the line graph, and then determine whether the statements and inferences are accurate.

Accurate or inaccurate?

_____ 1. Statement: In January 2008, fewer than three hundred rigs were operating in the United States, and the price of gas was a little more than $1.00.

_____ 2. Statement: In 2011, gas prices reached their highest point.

_____ 3. Statement: Every time the number of rigs operating is increased, gas prices increase.

_____ 4. Inference: For the most part, gas prices have increased over time, even though the number of oil rigs has generally increased during the same period.

_____ 5. Inference: A dramatic increase in the number of oil rigs will result in a dramatic decrease in the cost of gasoline. ("Inaccurate" should be the answer.)

_____ 6. Inference: Factors other than the amount of drilling we do in the United States affect the cost of gasoline.

(continued)

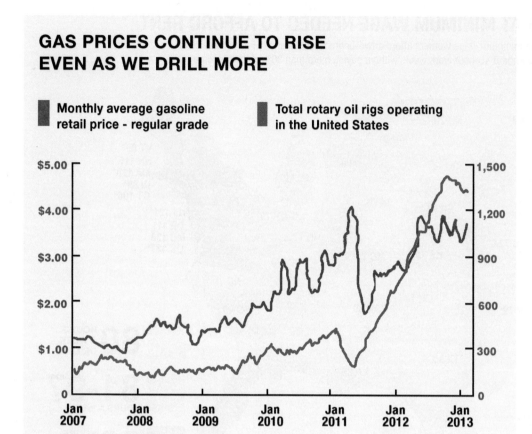

GAS PRICES CONTINUE TO RISE EVEN AS WE DRILL MORE

■ Monthly average gasoline retail price - regular grade

■ Total rotary oil rigs operating in the United States

CHAPTER ACTIVITIES

READING AND ANNOTATING

The following discussion of biases and heuristics is excerpted from a textbook, *The Science of Psychology*, by Laura A. King. Read and annotate the text, and then answer the questions that follow.

(Note: The selection contains parenthetical references to sources the author has used. Full information about these sources, listed in the author's text, is not given here.)

Biases and Heuristics

by Laura A. King

In many cases, our decision-making strategies are well adapted to deal with a variety of problems (Nisbett & Ross, 1980; Tversky & Kahneman, 1974). However, at times, reliance on heuristics can lead to biased decisions and outright errors. Here we look at a few biases and heuristic errors.

Confirmation bias is the tendency to search for and use information that supports our ideas rather than refutes them (N. W Jackson, 2012; Mendel & others, 2011). Our decisions can also become further biased because we tend to seek out and listen to people whose views confirm our own while we avoid those with dissenting views.

Confirmation bias is sometimes also referred to as "myside bias," as it involves seeking our and believing information that supports one's own beliefs. For instance, during

YOUR ANNOTATIONS

the 2012 U.S. presidential elections, many polling experts agreed that President Obama would win reelection. Nevertheless, pundits who supported former Governor Mitt Romney argued forcefully that the polls were wrong and were quite surprised by the outcome. Members of Romney's staff were described as "utterly 'shellshocked'" (Firestone, 2012). Avoiding confirmation bias means seeking out disconfirming information and applying the same rigorous analysis to both sides of an argument, even when the information seems to point in a direction we dread.

Hindsight bias is our tendency to report falsely, after the fact, that we accurately predicted an outcome. It is sometimes referred to as the "I knew it all along effect." With this type of bias, people tend to view events that have happened as more predictable than they were and to represent themselves as being more accurate in their predictions than they actually were (Yopchick & Kim, 2012). For instance, at the end of a long baseball season, fans might say they knew all along that a particular team would win the World Series.

Although the hindsight bias might sound self-serving in the sense that it means remembering ourselves as having known more than we really did know, cognitive psychologists recognize that this bias may be based on new learning and on updating our knowledge about the world (Nestler, Blank, & Egloff, 2010; Pezzo, 2011). One reason for hindsight bias is that actual events are more vivid in our minds than all those things that failed to happen, an effect called the availability heuristic.

The **availability heuristic** refers to a prediction about the probability of an event based on the ease of recalling or imagining similar events (McDermott, 2009). Essentially, this heuristic means we think that events that are *cognitively available* are more likely to happen. Have you ever experienced a sudden fear of flying right after hearing about an airplane crash? Shocking events such as plane crashes stick in our minds, making it seem as if such disasters are common. The chance of dying in a plane crash in a given year, however, is tiny (1 in 400,000) compared to the chance of dying in a car accident (1 in 6,500). Because car accidents are less newsworthy, they are less likely to catch our attention and remain in our awareness.

The availability heuristic can reinforce generalizations about other people (Chou & Edge, 2012). Imagine, for instance, that Elvedina, a Mexican American girl, tells her mother that she wants to be a doctor. Her mother, who has never seen a Latina doctor, finds it hard to conceive of her daughter's pursuing such a career and might suggest that she try nursing instead.

Also reflective of the impact of vivid cases on decision making is **base rate neglect**, the tendency to ignore information about general principles in favor of very specific but vivid information. Let's say that as a prospective car buyer, you read *Consumer Reports* and find that a panel of experts rates a particular vehicle exceptionally well. You might still be swayed in your purchasing decision, however, if a friend tells you about her bad experiences with that car. Similarly, imagine being told that the average exam score for a test in your psychology class was 75 percent. If you were asked to guess a random student's score, 75 percent would be a good answer—the mean tells us the central tendency of any distribution. Yet if the student provided just a little bit of information, such as how many hours he studied, you might give too much weight to that specific information, losing sight of the valuable base rate information you have, namely, the class mean.

To experience another heuristic in action, consider the following example. A psychologist tells you she has assembled 100 men, all in their 20s, in the hallway outside your classroom. The group consists of 5 members of the U.S. National Swim Team and 95 engineers. She is going to randomly select one man and bring him into the room, and you can win $100 if you accurately guess whether he is an engineer or an

Olympic-caliber swimmer. The man stands before you. Tall and lanky, he is wearing a tight T-shirt, jeans, and flip-flops. He has sunglasses perched on his clean-shaven head. Is he an engineer or an elite swimmer? If you guessed Olympic swimmer, you have just fallen victim to the representativeness heuristic.

The **representativeness heuristic** is the tendency to make judgments about group membership based on physical appearances or the match between a person and one's stereotype of a group rather than on available base rate information (Nilsson, Juslin, & Olsson, 2008). Essentially, a stereotype is the use of concepts to make generalizations about a group of people. In the example just described, the base rate information tells you that, 95 times out of 100, the man in your class is likely to be an engineer. The optimal approach to winning the $100 is simply to shut your eyes and guess engineer, no matter what the man looks like.

The representativeness heuristic can be particularly damaging in the context of social judgments. Consider a scenario where a particular engineering corporation seeks to hire a new chief executive officer (CEO). Lori, a top-notch candidate with an undergraduate engineering degree and an MBA from an outstanding business school, applies. If there are few women in upper management at the firm, the company's board of directors might inaccurately view Lori as "not fitting" their view of the prototypical CEO—and miss the chance to hire an exceptional candidate.

Heuristics help us make decisions rapidly, but to solve problems accurately and make the best decisions, we must sometimes override these shortcuts and think more deeply, critically, and creatively. Now that you have learned about heuristics and their potential to lead to biased and inaccurate conclusions, you might be wondering if this learning will pay off. Will you be less likely to be influenced by such biases in the future? Some people seem more likely to use heuristics whereas others are more likely to apply careful thought to decisions, overriding the influence of these shortcuts. Intelligence, interest in thinking through complex problems carefully, and maintaining an open mind are associated with less susceptibility to the biases promoted by heuristics (Chiesi, Primi, & Morsanyi, 2011; Toplak, West, & Stanovich, 2011). However, even very smart deep thinkers may not recognize their own vulnerability to cognitive biases.

Questions for Consideration

1. In a paragraph, describe how the availability heuristic and base rate neglect are related.

2. Is there a situation in which confirmation bias could be good for the person who holds it? Give an example and defend your answer.

3. Discriminating against someone due to racial prejudice would fall under the category of which bias or heuristic? Explain your answer.

4. Maria is vacationing on a bay where no sharks have ever been sited. She likes to watch old movies, though, and one night she watches *Jaws*, a movie about a giant killing shark. The next day, she decides not to go swimming, for fear a shark will bite her. What heuristic or bias is guiding her decision? Explain.

USING MODELS TO PRACTICE COMPOSING

Leticia is a student in a writing class. She has been given a writing assignment, which she has annotated. Read through the assignment instructions Leticia's instructor provided, and note how Leticia annotated the assignment. Did she neglect to annotate a key point? If so, add your own annotation.

Leticia's Annotated Assignment

Essay Assignment: Read and annotate "Biases and Heuristics," paying particular attention to the types of biases and heuristics that sometimes guide people when they are making decisions.

Select three of the heuristics and/or biases mentioned in the reading, and think of an example of each that could have disastrous results in the context of school. For example, consider how a student might fall prey to confirmation bias when thinking about his grade in Chemistry. There's a study session for the mid-term and a big soccer game he wants to go to on the same night. He might be tempted to go to the game, and tell himself that he's doing well in the class; after all, the teacher always smiles at him, the experiments in class are fun and easy to do, and he got good grades on the few quizzes they've had. This student is making a dangerous error. If he searched for information that refuted his choice, he would easily find in the course material that quizzes are not worth much toward his final grade, and if he doesn't study hard for the mid-term, which counts for 40% of his final grade, he might fail the class.

After you've selected three biases and/or heuristics to analyze, use a method of prewriting to think about how using these biases and heuristics to make decisions in school can have negative consequences. Write an essay in which you present each bias or heuristic and the examples you have found or created. (You may use hypothetical examples.) Use your examples to show how the bias or heuristic is misleading. Be sure to discuss the potential negative effects of decision-making in school guided by your chosen biases or heuristics. Your essay should be written in formal language and have an objective tone.

Annotations (right margin):

Read and annotate article

Select 3 heuristics or biases

Example

Figure out how using these biases/ heuristics = negative consequences

Formal language, objective tone

Annotations (left margin):

Prewrite

In essay, present biases or heuristics, use examples to show how bias or heuristic is misleading, and present negative effects.

After annotating her assignment, Leticia was ready for prewriting. She started by re-reading the chart explaining the biases and heuristics, then freewriting—writing without stopping for 15 minutes—to think about how each might lead to disastrous results in school. Here's Leticia's freewriting—done on computer—on one of the heuristics.

Hindsight bias—well, Arturo and Angela are perfect for each other. They always have been, and I always told him to ask her out, and now that they finally started dating when they went to college, I feel like I knew all along that it would happen, but is that really hindsight bias? Sort of, because they could have gone to different colleges and never had a chance to date. I didn't know it for sure. So even if it is hindsight bias, is it disastrous? Not them getting together, that's great. And it's not a big disaster if I feel like I predicted them being a couple even if I didn't really. So, can I think of another example that might show how hindsight bias could lead to negative consequences? Ok what if I want to be an engineer in my career but I'm afraid I'm not very good at math. And then I fail a final test in math class. I could say that I knew that would happen and then I'd believe I just wasn't cut out for engineering. If I really want to be an engineer, I should work harder in math class. I shouldn't let a bias get in my way.

After freewriting about several ideas, Leticia chose three biases and/or heuristics as the topic to be discussed in her essay. She created a thesis statement and a simple outline.

Leticia's Simple Outline

INTRODUCTION PARAGRAPH

Thesis statement: In school, making decisions based on biases and heuristics can have disastrous effects.

Body paragraph 1: Base rate neglect can lead a student to make decisions in school that could badly impact that student's future.

Body paragraph 2: A student who makes decisions based on the representativeness heuristic might suffer socially and academically.

Body paragraph 3: Students should remember to do their research before making a decision based on the availability heuristic.

CONCLUSION PARAGRAPH

At this point, Leticia started drafting her essay. What follows is one of the body paragraphs from her essay. Read and annotate the paragraph to identify the bias or heuristic she is discussing and the negative effects she identifies. Annotate passages that help you identify the tone Leticia is using.

Leticia's Paragraph

> It's easy to see how the representativeness heuristic could hurt a student socially. If she judges people who could become her friends only by stereotypes of their appearance or a single aspect, she might miss out on a lot of good friendships, and people will probably think she is prejudiced or snobby. She could miss out on romance, too. For example, in college my older sister thought art majors were just slackers, so she was shocked to learn that a guy she had a crush on was a painting major. She was able to put aside her stereotypical ideas about art majors long enough to get to know him, and now they are married, and he is a successful graphic designer. But could the representativeness heuristic be applied academically, too? Certainly. If we judge our teachers by our stereotyped ideas about their race, body type, gender, country of origin, or even their area of academics, we'll be blind to what they are really like. That's disrespectful, and it could lead to bad study habits as well.

YOUR ANNOTATIONS

A READING AND WRITING ASSIGNMENT

Now it is your turn to write an essay about biases and heuristics in response to the assignment Leticia's instructor gave her (page 307). Follow these steps, using Leticia's work as a model.

1. Reread Leticia's assignment and any additional annotations you made.
2. Use freewriting to think about how different biases and heuristics can have negative effects when used to make decisions in school.
3. Choose three biases and/or heuristics; if you need to, use additional prewriting to develop more ideas about the negative consequences.
4. Write a thesis statement.

5. Create a simple outline that contains your thesis statement and topic sentences for your body paragraphs. Write as many body paragraphs as you need to support your thesis statement.

6. Using your outline, draft the introduction, body paragraphs, and conclusion for your essay.

7. As you revise and edit your writing, look for words and phrases that express the tone of your essay. Make any necessary changes to achieve an objective tone.

Use the Quick Start Guide to Integrated Reading and Writing Assignments for assistance.

THINKING FROM AN INSTRUCTOR'S POINT OF VIEW

Do you ever make inferences about your instructors? You might think some are brilliant, some are just putting in their time, and so on. To make such inferences, you probably made mental notes about your instructors' strengths and weaknesses, not intentionally, but unconsciously. These judgments contributed to an overall impression, and on the basis of that impression you made inferences.

Instructors sometimes make inferences about students, and employers may make inferences about their employees. Imagine you are an instructor. Consider the scenarios that follow. What inference would you make about each student? Write your inferences on a sheet of paper.

1. Reynaldo is ten minutes early to every class meeting.

2. Melissa texts under her desk most days in class.

3. Rachel works in the tutoring lab with tutors almost every day after class.

4. Jonathan often borrows a pen and paper from his classmates.

5. Carolyn does not show up on the first day, even though she has registered for the course.

6. Li helps other students in class when she is finished with her work.

7. Donnie puts his head down and sleeps most days in class.

8. Ahzab greets his instructor most days by asking, "How are you doing?"

ADDING TO YOUR VOCABULARY

This chapter's vocabulary words appear below.

sound	contempt	efficacy	condescending
buffoon	dehumanize	disdain	

Choose five of the vocabulary words from this chapter that you would like to add to your vocabulary, and think about how you can use them this week. For example, one of this chapter's words is *buffoon*. You can often substitute *buffoon* for *clown* or *joker*, as in the example that follows.

Example: Some *joker* thought it would be funny to push all of the buttons on the elevator.

Some *buffoon* thought it would be funny to push all of the buttons on the elevator.

List each of the five words you plan to use this week, and make note of a context in which you could use each word.

Example: *Buffoon.* When one of my friends is acting silly at an inappropriate time, I can call him a buffoon.

⊙ ADDITIONAL ASSIGNMENTS

1. Write an essay in which you analyze how social cues lead us to form inferences. For example, if you are in a conversation with someone and the person starts looking away, nodding, and saying "uh-huh" but is obviously not listening to you, you are likely to infer that the person is not interested in talking to you. In your essay, discuss four or five inferences we can make from social cues.

2. Write a paragraph in which you explain how people might draw false inferences about someone else based on a heuristic or bias.

3. Write a list of inferences you can draw from the following infographic, which appears on the Environmental Protection Agency's Web site.

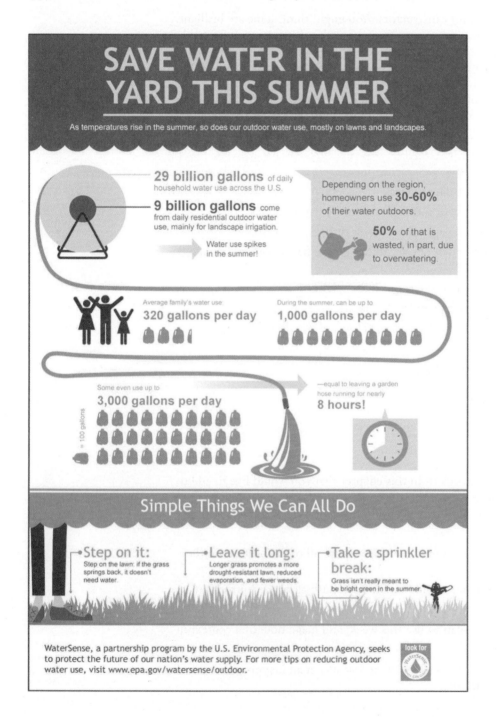

EMOTIONAL INTELLIGENCE

Good emotional intelligence requires that we make sound inferences about other people and about social situations. Have you ever misinterpreted another person's actions? If so, you have made an incorrect *social* inference. For example, we might infer that a quiet person is a snob. After getting to know the person, however, we may discover the person is not a snob at all but is shy. Think of a time when you made an incorrect social inference. What caused you to make this mistake? What can you learn from the experience? Explain in a paragraph.

CULTURAL LITERACY

Student exchange is a wonderful way to immerse yourself in another culture. Typically, a student goes to stay in another country for a semester. Before going, students should study the other culture as much as possible. Even so, they may not be able to find much information about the day-to-day life. Imagine scenarios in which students could make bad decisions in another culture based on biases or heuristics they might bring with them. Next, imagine biases or heuristics about Americans that American students might encounter while abroad. Write a paragraph or two about how a bias or heuristic could lead a student on exchange to make bad decisions, and what the student could do to prevent others from judging her negatively due to their own biases or heuristics.

CRITICAL THINKING

The following dialog demonstrates how using a heuristic or bias can result in an incorrect inference. Study the dialog and determine the heuristic or bias that was used to draw the incorrect inference.

Mac: My best friend wants to join a fraternity when he goes to college, but I don't. I don't want my weekends to be taken up with a bunch of social events—most of them will probably be loud, too. I don't want to wear a toga. I want to study and get into medical school.

Casey: Don't you know they're not all like that? My brother's fraternity at college is centered on community service and studying together. Only honors students are allowed to stay at the house, and most of them get into prestigious med schools.

Write a paragraph explaining your analysis.

METACOGNITION

One way to have more metacognitive awareness is to think about how your thinking can be affected by biases and heuristics.

To do this, spend a moment considering what your life would be like if you made decisions based on each of the biases or heuristics below. Write a sentence or two explaining possible outcomes of these kinds of decision-making.

- Hindsight bias convinces you that you are almost always right about the outcomes of things. You feel you have predicted many economic upswings and decide to become an investor.

- You let the availability heuristic guide your decisions about how to pack for a vacation: you've never had a flat tire before, so why bring a spare? It's not usually cold where you're going, so why pack a sweater? You've always gotten in to restaurants you liked before; why make a reservation?

- You let the representativeness heuristic guide your decisions about who to make friends with and who to hire: you will only make friends with or hire people who look like the people you already know and trust.

Making a clay pot involves a series of modifications. Sometimes the potter even has to start anew. Writing is a similar craft: successful essays require thoughtful reshaping and revising.

Revising and Editing

Have you ever painted a room in your house or apartment? If so, you know that while painting can start out as an enjoyable project, it quickly becomes hard work. As you get closer and closer to finishing the painting job, you begin to long for the moment when you can stand back and look at what you have accomplished. What happens if you stand back, sighing in relief, only to notice that one half of the room needs another coat, and paint dripped onto the baseboard, and you see a spot on the ceiling? Even worse, what happens if you realize that the color is just not right?

If you really want the room to look perfect, you will have to make some revisions. Some revisions will be major, such as changing the color of the paint. Other revisions may be less difficult, such as adding another coat or cleaning up areas where the paint went out of bounds. In writing, too, you will find that you must make revisions even after you thought you were done. How well you focus on making minor as well as major changes will determine the quality of your finished work.

The purpose of revising is to make sure your writing communicates its message as well as it can. For a text to communicate successfully, it must be well organized and unified, well developed, and clearly presented. Additionally, writing should be edited so that it is free from grammatical and mechanical errors.

CHAPTER OBJECTIVES

After completing this chapter, students will be able to do the following:

- **Revise for better organization and unity.**
- **Revise for better development.**
- **Revise for better clarity.**
- **Connect pronouns to unambiguous antecedents.**
- **Make revisions during drafting.**
- **Revise with an audience in mind.**
- **Edit and format an essay.**
- **Create agreement between subjects and verbs.**

REVISING FOR ORGANIZATION AND UNITY

If you use a well-planned outline, you will be able to create texts that follow a logical plan of presentation. One hallmark of an organized paper is **unity.** A text has unity if the paragraphs are appropriately related to the main idea.

Paragraphs have unity when the sentences within them are related to the paragraph's topic sentence. No random thoughts or "stray" ideas occur in unified writing.

One way to revise with unity in mind is to analyze the organization of your essay. Ask yourself whether each body paragraph clearly supports the thesis statement. Then examine the sentences in each paragraph. Do the sentences support the paragraph's topic sentence? Every sentence in your essay should be related to the ideas around it. If you see a sentence with information that is unrelated to the main idea of the paragraph, either revise it so that it supports the information in the paragraph or omit the sentence altogether.

Another task in revision is to determine whether changing the organization of the ideas will make your writing easier to follow. The following example, featuring a paragraph from an article on opening a bakery, demonstrates how changing the organization of sentences can result in much better writing. Here is the original paragraph, which discusses one major supporting point of the article.

¹One of the most demanding parts of owning a bakery is cleaning up. ²Most bakeries are small operations, and their owners cannot afford to hire custodial staff. ³Thus, the bakers themselves are responsible for cleanup duties. ⁴Whenever flour, sugar, cocoa, and other powdery foods are used in a kitchen, there will be a mess, regardless of how careful kitchen staff are. ⁵Cleaning up requires a great deal of time, and the process is physically demanding. ⁶Potential bakery owners should be aware of the time and effort that must be expended to simply keep the kitchen clean. ⁷Perhaps the most important part of cleanup is keeping the floor clean. ⁸Oils are always involved in the baking process and present a true hazard if they end up on the floor. ⁹And because oil is an expensive ingredient, bakers should be especially careful with it.	Sentence 1: major supporting point (topic sentence) Sentence 4: examples of foods that make a mess Sentences 5 and 6: details about time and effort needed for cleaning up Sentences 7 and 8: details about keeping floors clean and hazards of oil Sentence 9: detail about cost of oil

Only one sentence is truly out of place. Can you tell which one? Most of the sentences support the topic sentence, sentence 1. They give examples of messy foods, discuss the time and effort needed for cleaning up, and point out the particular importance of dealing with spilled oil.

Sentence 9, however, does not belong in the paragraph. Although the sentence deals with oil, which is discussed in the paragraph, the information it gives—the high cost of oil—has nothing to do with the task of cleaning up a bakery kitchen. We can see why the writer included the sentence while drafting the paragraph; it seems to be linked to the discussion of oil. But if the writer takes the time to revise, she will see that the cost of oil is not really important to the point she is making in the topic sentence.

The writer had planned to end her paragraph with the most **precarious** aspect of a messy kitchen—the floor. However, by ending her paragraph with a discussion of the hazards of oil, she has separated the mess caused by oil from the messes caused by powdery foods. It would be more logical to put the specific *causes* of a messy kitchen together. Thus, the paragraph would be improved if sentences 7 and 8 were nearer to the sentences about powdery foods. Here is the revised paragraph.

Vocabulary Collection Word:
precarious

Your in-context definition:

_____

_____

A dictionary definition:

_____

One of the most demanding parts of owning a bakery is cleaning up. Most bakeries are small operations, and their owners cannot afford to hire custodial staff. Thus, the bakers themselves are responsible for cleanup duties. Whenever flour, sugar, cocoa, and other powdery foods are used in a kitchen, there will be a mess, regardless of how careful kitchen staff are. Perhaps the most important part of cleanup is keeping the floor clean. Oils are always involved in the baking process and present a true hazard if they end up on the floor. Cleaning up requires a great deal of time, and the process is physically demanding. Potential bakery owners should be aware of the time and effort that must be expended to simply keep the kitchen clean.	Major supporting point (topic sentence) Cause: powdery foods Cause: oils

Complete the practice exercise that follows to improve the organization and unity of a paragraph.

PRACTICE ① Improving the Organization and Unity of a Paragraph

Read the paragraph that follows, annotating it to determine how its organization can be improved. Using sentence numbers, note the order in which you would place the sentences. If any sentences detract from the paragraph's unity, reword or delete them. Next revise the paragraph on a separate sheet. Reword sentences, if necessary, to write a clearer, more organized paragraph.

YOUR ANNOTATIONS

^{1}While a wide variety of majors and minors exist for college degrees, four primary types of degrees are common. ^{2}The associate's degree requires roughly sixty hours of college credit, approximately two years of full-time college course work. ^{3}The doctorate requires approximately four years of course work beyond the master's degree. ^{4}Not many people wish to be in college long enough to earn doctorate degrees. ^{5}A master's degree requires two years of course work beyond a bachelor's degree, approximately six years of course work from the start of college. ^{6}The time spent on a master's degree usually pays off. ^{7}A bachelor's degree requires approximately four years of college: two years to earn an associate's degree plus two more years to obtain the bachelor's degree.

REVISING FOR BETTER DEVELOPMENT

Development refers to the quantity and the quality of supporting details you use to back up your ideas. To judge the development of your writing, first think about the main idea you are communicating. Without looking at your draft, make a list of the questions your audience would need to have answered in order to fully understand or accept your main idea. Next, read your paper. Have you included enough information for readers to understand or accept the main idea? Is the information the *right kind* of information?

In the following paragraph, the writer's main idea is to explain one method for financial decision making. Read the annotations to see the kind of development this paragraph needs.

^{1}One way to make smart fiscal decisions is to use the Internet for research. ^{2}Almost any topic can be thoroughly researched with an Internet search. ^{3}Many consumers have questions about their finances. ^{4}Using Internet sources can help consumers make smarter decisions.

Sentence 1 is the topic sentence.

Sentences 2 and 3 provide no new information.

Sentence 4 repeats the information in the topic sentence.

A reader interested in learning how to use the Internet for financial research will need more specific information than the writer offers. Notice that sentences 2 and 3 do not contribute new information to develop the idea of using an Internet search. Also, sentence 4 simply repeats the information in the topic sentence. Repeated information detracts from a paragraph's development and takes up space that should be given to useful information.

By thinking of some of the questions readers may have, the writer can revise the paragraph to make it much more detailed and helpful. Here are some questions the writer could answer:

- *For what kinds of financial decision making is the Internet helpful?* The Internet provides advice for getting a mortgage, figuring out the most economical transportation options, and finding the credit cards with the lowest interest rates, as well as information on many other financial topics.

- *Can you give me an example of how a financial Web site might help me?* For example, www.bestccsaround.com offers information to help consumers find credit cards with low interest rates.

- *How can I put the knowledge I gain from such Web sites to use?* Many of the Web sites even contain links that will take consumers to sites where they can apply for low-interest financial products. For example, www.creditcarddreams.com links consumers to credit cards that fit their needs.

Thinking through readers' potential questions allows the writer to revise the paragraph so that it is much more fully developed. Notice how the writer has used the answers to these questions to revise the paragraph, providing major supporting points and details that improve its development.

One way to make smart fiscal decisions is to use the Internet for research. Web sites	Topic sentence
provide advice for getting a mortgage, figuring out the most economical transportation	
options, and finding the credit cards with the lowest interest rates, as well as information	Major supporting point 1
on many other financial topics. For example, *Best Credit Cards Around* (www.bestccsa round.com) offers information on the interest rates of loans and credit cards available	Supporting details
to consumers. Many of the Web sites even contain links that will take consumers to	Major supporting point 2
sites where they can apply for low-interest financial products. For example, Credit Card Dreams (www.creditcarddreams.com) links consumers to credit cards that fit their needs.	Supporting details

Complete the practice exercise that follows to improve the development of a paragraph. As you complete the exercise, try to think like a reader. What information would a fully developed paragraph give readers?

PRACTICE ❷ Improving the Development of a Paragraph

The following paragraph's main idea needs better development. List questions readers might ask, and use the answers to make changes to the paragraph. Rewrite the paragraph on a separate sheet.

Some people opt to purchase smartphones instead of laptop computers because the apps on smartphones can do almost everything one expects from a computer. While reading the screen may be a bit more difficult with a smartphone, the computer capabilities are quite amazing.

Readers' questions:

_____

_____

_____

_____

_____

_____

_____

REVISING FOR BETTER CLARITY

Writing clearly starts at the level of word selection. It is important to choose the very best word to communicate a thought. The suggestions in this section will help you express your ideas clearly.

Look for Awkward or Vague Expressions

In an essay about whether college education should be free, a student, Sandra, wrote this sentence:

> People that went to college and got stuck in big loans that they now have to pay back with interest and they are being crushed by can't leverage those funds elsewhere by buying things, and that endangers the American way of life.

Can you spot places where the student's expression could be clearer? Think about these points:

- The phrase "People that went to college and got stuck in big loans that they now have to pay back with interest and they are being crushed by" is awkward to read. "People that went to college" are more simply "College graduates," and describing them as "saddled with huge debt" saves many words while saying the same thing clearly. "Debt" implies that it has to be paid back, and "saddled" keeps some of the sense of being "crushed." "College graduates saddled with huge debt" is a clear, easy-to-read replacement that only uses six words.

- While the words might sound impressive at first, the phrase "leverage those funds elsewhere" is ambiguous—what does it mean, really, to "leverage," and what does she mean by "funds?" Sometimes simpler language does the trick to clear up **ambiguity**. The "funds" she mentions here are "the money they send to banks every month," and by "leverage," Sandra simply means "spend." It would be much clearer to say "spend the money they send to banks every month" rather than "leverage the funds elsewhere."

- The phrase "buying things" is vague. What kinds of things? Sandra could paint a clearer picture of what she means with concrete, specific examples, such as "consumer goods like cars and houses."

- The expression "the American way of life" is not exactly what the writer means. What part of the American way of life would be affected if people don't have money to spend on things? Perhaps she means the national economy. Is the national economy "endangered," or does that sound too dramatic? Perhaps "hurt" would be closer to what she means.

Here is Sandra's sentence revised for clarity:

> College graduates who have significant debt cannot buy consumer goods such as cars and houses. As a result, the national economy is affected, since these graduates cannot make such purchases.

Restate Complicated Ideas Out Loud

Later in her paper, Sandra wrote this passage:

> Everyone deserves the **incentive** to go to college free, so to make Americans fine with using taxes on college, you can put in certain rules such as making a certain amount of tries at one class before you have to pay and things like that to push them even more would be in place.

Sometimes when students write sentences like these, if an instructor asks them to explain their ideas aloud in their own words, they will construct much clearer sentences. Consider this exchange.

Vocabulary Collection Word:
ambiguity

Your in-context definition:

_____

_____

A dictionary definition:

_____

_____

Vocabulary Collection Word:
incentive

Your in-context definition:

_____

_____

A dictionary definition:

_____

_____

Revision Questions	
Organization and unity	• Are my ideas organized in a logical and convincing way? • Does my writing have a successful introduction and conclusion?
Clarity	• Is my main idea clearly stated or implied? • Have I made the relationship between the support and my main idea clear?
Development	• Have I provided enough support (definitions, examples, comparisons, causes, effects, and so on) for the main idea? • Have I answered readers' potential questions?
Tone	• Is the tone of my paper appropriate?
Assignment requirements	• Does the paper meet assignment requirements?

Student Example of Preparing to Revise a Draft

To demonstrate the essay revision process, we will observe the revision process used by Maria, a student in a college reading and writing class. Maria has drafted an essay for her English class. To begin the revision process, she reviews the assignment instructions, which she had annotated at the start of the assignment.

Maria's Annotated Assignment

Write an essay to be published in our college newspaper. (You do not really have to publish your essay, but imagine that your audience will be the student body and anyone else who reads our newspaper.) Your topic is this: Should instructors assign group projects? Some students dislike group projects because not everyone in the group does the work, so these projects unfairly reward slackers. Other students love group projects because they learn from their peers and enjoy working with them. What is your point of view on this topic? Select one of these views:

- Group projects are good assignments.
- Group projects are good assignments only if they include certain conditions.
- Group projects should not be assigned.

Discuss at least three reasons for your position.

Write a college newspaper essay.

Audience = student body

Topic

Provide my opinion

Looks good! Use this.

Need 3 reasons.

After rereading the assignment instructions, Maria thinks about each particular assignment element:

- Write for a student audience.
- Choose one point of view.
- Give three reasons.

Maria also figures out her instructor's unstated expectations:

- Write a thesis statement.
- Write an introduction, body, and conclusion.
- Make sure the paper is developed enough.
- Use correct grammar and spelling.

Student Example of a Draft Annotated for Revision

Now that Maria has reviewed the assignment, she can start the revision process. She begins by printing out a copy of her draft. Having a paper copy to write on is the best way to revise. It is easier to skip over mistakes when you read a computer screen, so revise with a pen in your hand.

To begin, Maria consciously shifts her thinking so that she is reading her paper not as herself but as her readers—the student body and others who read the newspaper. As she reads, she makes notes about what her readers might think. She looks for places where organization and unity, clarity, and tone can be improved.

Maria's Annotated Draft

Intro is too short.	I do not understand why every instructor at Marquez College seems to love group projects. Group projects are truly a waste of time, to be honest.	Sounds rude.
I didn't state my thesis: Group projects should not be assigned.		
	I clearly remember my speech class here at Marquez College. The most difficult assignment I ever did in my life was in that class, and it was a group assignment in which we had to choose a controversial issue, find the best research we could on that issue, and use that research to make an argument for or against the issue. It was a horrible experience.	This sentence is too long!!!
I didn't explain why it was so horrible. Need more details.		This para is all negative. Need a more positive tone.

(continued)

A bit rude. Need to say how great that prof's lectures actually were!

In my speech class, our professor sat at her desk and read a book while we struggled to make sense of the assignment in groups. Instead of reading, she could have been really teaching us. I want to learn from my professor, not my classmates.

Reorganize this para so it doesn't start with the example.

Readers may not get what I mean by "terrible decisions." Needs more explanation. Seems random—cut.

In another class, the professor assigned the group project and made some ⟨terrible decisions⟩ about due dates and announcements. Most of the groups were scrambling at the last minute to throw something together for a grade. ~~The topic was global warming.~~

But not all instructors handle group projects in this way. I should say that.

Another reason to not assign group work is the issue of time. Groups spend so much time just figuring out how to work together that little time is available for the project. It is usually impossible for all group members to meet at the same time, so there are lots of e-mails and texts we have to send. And even wasted time in personal meet-ings make group projects unpleasant. People feel awkward, so we end up talking about our lives and getting to know each other. Getting to know my classmates is fine, but it's not why I enrolled in the course.

Grammar? Revise.

Maybe profs could tell us how to get to know one another quickly and then move on to the assignment.

An instructor might say the purpose of a group project is to teach time management. If they would give some guidelines or ideas about time management, maybe group projects wouldn't be so horrible.

Maybe this is a rude tone.

Sounds whiny.

Give more details about the slacker. Use term "slacker"?

Unrelated—delete.

The way group projects are graded is simply unfair. For example, I did most of the work in my group, but the other group members got the same grade I did. A ⟨slacker⟩ got the very same grade I got. ~~He was actually a jerk I knew from high school.~~ What did he learn from this project? He learned that he can get away with being a slacker.

Maybe give an idea about how projects could be graded more fairly?

Sounds so snobby!

I can tolerate working with students, but do not base my grade on that work. Instructors can assign group projects, but they should also teach students how to work in groups.

Last sentence doesn't fit thesis statement. Do I want to say group projects are OK if instructors do certain things, or do I want to stick with idea that group projects should never be assigned? Revise.

Student Example of a Revised Draft

Maria has come up with a variety of ideas for improving her paper when she revises. What follows is Maria's revised essay. Notice that Maria changed her point of view from the one she initially highlighted in the assignment. So she changed her thesis statement to reflect her new point of view. As you read it, annotate the areas where you see other changes. Do you see any other places where Maria could make more improvements?

Maria Colonio

Prof. Liu

English 110

4 April 2014

Professors: Just Say "No" to Group Projects

Group projects are popular assignments at Marquez College and probably at many other colleges. I understand why teachers use group projects. They want students to learn to work together, and they want us to help one another in the learning process. However, I do not think these goals are met very well by group projects as most instructors assign them. For group projects to really work, professors need to include specific information about how the groups should function and how individual student grades will be determined.

I clearly remember my speech class here at Marquez College. The most difficult assignment I ever did in my life was in that class. It was a group assignment. We had to choose a controversial issue, find the best research we could on that issue, and use that research to make an argument for or against the issue. It was not a good experience. My group was dysfunctional. As a student concerned about grades, I was the one who did the calling and e-mailing to beg group members to contribute to the project. In the end, I alone did the work. I learned quite a bit, but it simply was not fair that the other group members received the same grade of "A" that I did.

One reason to not assign group work is the issue of time. Groups spend so much time just figuring out how to work together that little time is available for the project. It is usually impossible for all group members to meet at the same time, so there are lots of e-mails and texts we have to send. This could be time we spent on the task, not on coordinating meetings with our fellow students. And even meetings include a lot of wasted time. People feel awkward, so we end up talking about our lives and getting to know one another. That is fun, but it is not exactly the kind of learning I want to be doing in college. If instructors would give groups instructions to spend five minutes on introductions, five minutes to exchange information, and so on, groups would function better.

The second reason group projects should not be assigned is that the way they are graded is sometimes seen as unfair by students. I am sure my professors all try to be fair, but group projects sometimes make it impossible. For example, I did most of the work in my group, but the other group members got the same grade I did. I researched the issue along with another student, while three of our classmates sat in the library and talked. One guy never attended the group meetings, and he only did a small portion of what he was assigned to do. He turned in a paragraph the day before our paper was due, but he got the very same grade I got. What did he learn from this project? He learned that he can get away with being a slacker. That is not the kind of message professors are trying to send to their students. A better way to grade group projects would be to give students individual grades based on the quality of the project and the participation level of the student. That way, even if the project is an "F," the student who worked the hardest has a chance to pass.

Another reason why I dislike group projects and think they should not be assigned is that I want to learn from my professor, not my fellow

Colonio 3

students. No offense, fellow students, but you guys do not have the master's degree or doctorate that our professors have. I get much more out of a good discussion or lecture than a group project. Teachers have lots of knowledge and expertise. Finding a way to share this knowledge would be much more valuable than assigning a group project.

I know that some professors value group projects because of the cooperation required to do them. I do not mind working with my fellow students, but please do not base my grade on the classmates in my group. If Marquez College faculty use group projects, I hope they will consider helping the groups function better and assigning individual grades to individual students. These steps will make group work something students can really use for learning.

Maria's essay changed dramatically through the revision process. Examine the important changes Maria made by completing the following exercise.

PRACTICE ⑤ Determining a Student's Revision

List three changes Maria made in her revised draft on pages 326–328, and explain the effect the change might have on the reader.

1. _____
   _____
   _____

2. _____
   _____
   _____

3. _____
   _____
   _____
   _____
   _____

REVISING WITH AN AUDIENCE IN MIND

As Maria revised her essay, she tried to see her writing as the college newspaper readers would see it. Keeping an audience in mind as you revise is crucial. More important, however, is understanding what particular audiences need and expect from your texts.

Let's consider an essay directed at a different audience. Pauline works at a **marketing** company, Imperial KRC Brands, as a receptionist. She has learned that her company offers a "Back to College" incentive plan. This plan allows employees six hours off work per week to attend college classes. Additionally, the plan pays for any college expenses that management has approved. The company awards only two such scholarships per department, and other employees in Pauline's department are also applying. Applicants must each write an essay to make their case. Here are the essay instructions that Pauline's company has issued.

Vocabulary Collection Word:
marketing

Your in-context definition:

_____

_____

A dictionary definition:

_____

_____

Back to College Incentive Plan

Applying for College Tuition Payment: As part of Imperial KRC Brands' interest in professional development, we have set aside funds to pay for college tuition for select employees. Because these funds are limited, employees need to request these funds and fully explain why such funds should be granted to them. To apply, please follow these instructions:

1. Write an essay of no more than 500 words in which you discuss the following:

   - Your employment history with Imperial KRC Brands
   - The college program or degree you are pursuing
   - The reason you are pursuing this program or degree
   - How this program or degree will help you be a better employee at Imperial KRC Brands
   - Where you are in your studies or graduation plan
   - Specific details regarding the amount of funding you will need for the academic year

2. Submit this essay to your supervisor by the deadline: April 12.

Example of an Essay Draft Written for an Employer

Pauline is nervous about writing this essay. She has written essays for college instructors, but she has never written any major documents for work purposes. Nonetheless, she has produced a draft of her essay, and she now needs help revising it for her particular audience. Here is Pauline's draft. As you read it, annotate any places you believe need revision.

Pauline's Draft

I have worked here at Imperial KRC Brands for four years as a receptionist, it has been a great career for me so far. I want to go back to college to get my degree. You cannot make that much as a receptionist, I know that I could get more secretarial skills, but my real goal is to get a bachelor's degree in accounting.

I think accounting would be a good career choice for me because I am good with numbers and I love math and I am extremely organized. All important for accountants. I know this because my brother is an accountant and I have helped him on the weekends. I have also talked with Stacy McMann in the Accounting Department, she thinks my aptitude for accounting is strong.

YOUR ANNOTATIONS

(continued)

I would like Imperial KRC Brands to cover my tuition expenses because if I get my accounting degree, I will continue to work for Imperial. I will give back to the company.

I want to start back in the fall semester, approximately on August 27th. I would need to leave early two days a week in order to make it in time for class. I can train someone to take my place during the times I would be gone.

Thank you.

YOUR ANNOTATIONS

We are now going to compare Pauline's draft with the instructions she received.

FROM THE INSTRUCTIONS	WHAT PAULINE WROTE	HOW PAULINE MIGHT REVISE FOR IMPROVEMENT
"Write an essay of no more than 500 words."	Pauline's essay is 211 words, so it is well below the maximum of 500.	Pauline meets this requirement but misses an opportunity. She could add almost 300 words to strengthen her case.
Discuss "your employment history with Imperial KRC Brands."	Pauline offers only one sentence about her employment history: "I have worked here at Imperial KRC Brands for four years as a receptionist, it has been a great career for me so far."	Pauline does not fully meet this requirement. When a person is asked to "discuss" something, we usually expect more than one sentence. Pauline could have talked about how she has mastered new tasks on this job, how she has advanced (if she has), how she has made positive contributions to the company, and so on. Additionally, this passage contains a comma splice, an error she should correct when editing.
Discuss "the college program or degree you are pursuing."	Pauline writes, "My real goal is to get a bachelor's degree in accounting. I think accounting would be a good career choice for me because I am good with numbers and I love math and I am extremely organized. All important for accountants. I know this because my brother is an accountant and I have helped him on the weekends. I have also talked with Stacy McMann in the Accounting Department, she thinks my aptitude for accounting is strong."	Pauline did a much better job here but could still improve. She could have elaborated more on her organizational abilities as a receptionist. It was a good idea to include the work she has done for her brother because it shows she has an idea what accounting will entail. Also, she uses the endorsement of a coworker, Stacy McMann. If Stacy has a good reputation, this endorsement will be helpful. In the editing process, Pauline should correct the grammatical errors in these sentences.
Discuss "the reason you are pursuing this program or degree."	Pauline makes it clear that financial concerns are part of her decision.	This passage meets the requirement but could be improved. While it is true that a paycheck is important, a letter requesting college funding may not be the place to talk about salary. We like to think that people get college degrees because they are cut out for a particular line of work, not just because they want more money.
Discuss "how this program or degree will help you be a better employee at Imperial KRC Brands."	Pauline writes, "If I get my accounting degree, I will continue to work for Imperial. I will give back to the company."	Pauline does not fully meet this requirement. One thing she needs to reconsider is the word *if*. Pauline's essay would be much stronger if she used the word *when* instead of *if*. Also, Pauline did not give her audience many reasons to invest in her.
Discuss "where you are in your studies or graduation plan."	Pauline does not answer this question at all. Perhaps she simply overlooked it.	Pauline needs to address the issue of her status in college.
Include "specific details regarding the amount of funding you will need for the academic year."	Pauline writes, "I want to start back in the fall semester, approximately on August 27th. I would need to leave early two days a week in order to make it in time for class. I can train someone to take my place during the times I would be gone."	Pauline does not fully meet this requirement. It is helpful that she provides the start date and has a plan for the days she will be gone, but she must include the amount of funding she needs since the assignment clearly asks for that information.

Example of a Revised Draft Written for an Employer

By comparing Pauline's writing to the assignment instructions, we found a number of places where her essay could be improved. In the next box you will see how Pauline revised her essay. Her revisions are underlined and appear in blue ink. As you read her revised essay, annotate the areas of improvement. In your annotations, explain why you think the particular passage shows improvement.

Pauline's Revision

I have worked here at Imperial KRC Brands for four years as a receptionist. It has been a great career for me so far. When I began here four years ago, I did not know much about clerical work. My experiences as a receptionist have taught me many things, such as how to use software programs like *Excel* and *Microsoft Word*, how to keep an organized calendar of appointments, and how to assist management in a variety of tasks, including phone work and file organization. I have also become more aware of my own interests in life. I am writing because one of my interests is accounting, and I am asking Imperial to help me achieve my goal of a B.S. in Accounting.

I think accounting would be a good career choice for me. I am good with numbers, and I love math. Additionally, I am extremely organized. All of these qualities are important for accountants. I have had some experience with accounting work. My brother is an accountant, and I have helped him update records on the weekends. I have also talked with Stacy McMann in the Accounting Department. She has commented on my organizational abilities, and she thinks my aptitude for accounting is strong.

I am asking Imperial KRC Brands to cover my tuition expenses. Specifically, I will need $9,250.00 for the 2014–2015 academic year. I plan to continue to work for Imperial even after I finish college. This has been a wonderful work environment for me, and I want to give back to the company.

I have about 62 hours in college credit at this point, making me almost a junior. I want to start back in the fall semester, which begins on August 27. I would need to leave early two days a week in order to make it in time for class. I can train someone to take my place during the times I would be gone, if that would be helpful.

Finally, I want to thank Imperial KRC Brands for caring so much about its employees. The opportunity to go back to college is an opportunity I will not squander.

YOUR ANNOTATIONS

Pauline's essay changed dramatically during the revision stage. It is now 357 words compared with the original 210, and it is better developed. Furthermore, she addresses each of the requirements listed in the essay instructions. Her audience will read a polished, carefully revised essay, and Pauline's chances for getting the tuition scholarship are now much greater.

EDITING AND FORMATTING AN ESSAY

The best way to distinguish editing from revising is to think of revising as re-visioning ideas, and editing as finding mistakes in specific grammatical and stylistic details. Editing helps you prepare your revised text for submission.

People who are employed as editors are trained to find *every* error in a text. The range of errors one could look for is very wide. When you edit, it is important to focus on the most common areas of difficulty that you have in writing. If you know that you have particular trouble with a certain grammatical concept, such as subject-verb agreement, make sure that you take extra time during the editing stage to check the agreement of each subject and verb.

Using SMART TRACS to Edit Your Essay

In addition to checking for the specific errors you tend to make, use the **acronym** SMART TRACS to remember ten issues to check for in your paper.

Vocabulary Collection Word:
acronym

Your in-context definition:

_____

_____

A dictionary definition:

_____

_____

SMART TRACS Editing Plan

Use the SMART TRACS editing plan to check your work for common writing errors.

S = Spelling
M = Missing words
A = Accurate punctuation
R = Repeated words
T = Terminal punctuation
T = Tense consistency
R = Rhythm
A = Active voice
C = Confusing words
S = Sources

S = Spelling. The good news is that the spelling of many words can be checked with the spell-checker in your word-processing program. However, words that sound the same but are spelled differently need special consideration. A spell-checker will not catch the incorrect use of *their* for *there,* for example. If you are writing by hand and come to a word you are unsure about, take a guess at its spelling, and then look up the word in a dictionary. Do not yield to the temptation to skip over it and hope you have spelled it correctly. Keeping a list of words you often misspell will help you learn to spell them properly.

M = Missing words. Have you ever read a with a missing word? (Read that again: did you see that it should have included the word *sentence?*) We sometimes leave out words because we think more quickly than we write. Additionally, our brains can compensate for left-out words. For example, you were probably able to understand the first sentence in this paragraph because your brain uses context clues to think about what the word likely is. We can even figure out words with missing letters. See whether you can understand this sentence: *I wld lke to hve a stk for dinnr.* Our minds are able to add in the missing letters, missing words, and misspellings. Thus, it is important that you read your paper very carefully when looking for missing words. Read each sentence aloud very slowly. Better yet, have a friend read your paper aloud to you.

A = Accurate punctuation. Inaccurate punctuation, especially involving commas and semicolons, can result in major sentence errors, such as these:

Run-ons (sentences joined without any punctuation)

Comma splices (sentences joined with only a comma)

Fragments (sentences lacking a subject, verb, or both)

(continued)

Check all commas to make sure you are using them correctly. Check semicolons to be sure that you are using them only to separate two related, complete sentences.

R = **Repeated words.** It is very easy to use the same word repeatedly. Read this paragraph for an example of repeating the same word repeatedly. If you repeatedly use the word *repeat,* for example, readers may not take your writing seriously. You may need to repeat a writing assignment if you repeatedly repeat the same word. One way to avoid repetition is to use synonyms. Additionally, read your paper out loud and listen. You are sometimes more likely to *hear* repeated words than to see them.

T = **Terminal punctuation.** Have you ever written a question and ended it with a period instead of a question mark. (We just did!) Be sure to check all of the sentences in your paper to make sure you use the appropriate *terminal* (ending) punctuation. Use a period—the most common terminal punctuation mark—only with a complete sentence. Use a semicolon only at the end of one complete sentence and the beginning of another. A comma is *not* a terminal punctuation mark. Do not use it to join two complete sentences. By analyzing each punctuation mark in your writing, you will be better able to spot sentence fragments and run-ons. To find comma splices, read sentences aloud to determine where they should end. Use appropriate punctuation between two complete sentences.

T = **Tense consistency.** In general, if you start your essay or paragraph in past tense, stay in past tense. If you start in present tense, stay in present tense. There will be times when you will need to shift tense, such as when you refer to something in the past. Be very mindful of verb tenses during the revision process. Circle each verb, and check to make sure you have chosen the appropriate tense.

R = **Rhythm.** If you read your paper out loud, you will be able to hear the rhythm of your sentences. Good writing usually consists of sentences of different lengths and different types. Read the two passages below out loud to hear the differences in their rhythms:

> **Passage A:** The ceremony started. We recited the Pledge of Allegiance. We sang the national anthem. The guest speaker talked. She delivered a speech. The speech was about giving back to society. The graduates stood up to be recognized. Their names were called. The graduates walked up to the stage. They received their diplomas. They walked back to their seats.

> **Passage B:** The ceremony started with the Pledge of Allegiance and the national anthem. Next, a guest speaker delivered a speech to the graduates about giving back to society. Soon, the graduates stood up to be recognized. As their names were called, they walked to the stage, received their diplomas, and walked back to their seats.

Use variety in sentence length and sentence type to create writing that is more rhythmically appealing.

A = **Active voice.** To use active voice, structure the sentence so that the agent (subject) doing the action (verb) is presented in the proper place. Start by

(continued)

analyzing the main verb of the sentence. In the example below, *broke* is the main verb. To write the sentence in active voice, put the agent—the person who did the breaking—first, as the example shows:

Active voice: John broke the window.

Passive voice: The window was broken by John.

Sentences written in passive voice are often wordier and more complicated than they would be if they were written in active voice. In addition, many writing instructors characterize sentences in active voice as being "stronger" than those in passive voice. Thus, from a stylistic perspective, using active voice is often (though not always) preferable.

C = **Confusing words.** A large number of words in the English language are commonly misused. Examples include *their, they're, there; its, it's; two, too, to; affect, effect; loose, lose;* and *desert, dessert.* To improve this aspect of your writing, start by reading through a list of the most commonly confused words. Mark those that you have trouble with. Make note cards for those words, and include their meanings and rules for use. As you read and write, refer to your note cards so that you learn the correct usage of the problem words. When you revise, look for the specific words on your note cards by using your word processor's "Find" function. Check each of the words to make sure you have used it correctly, and make changes where necessary.

S = **Sources.** If your writing contains sources, make sure that you have (a) integrated the source material grammatically; (b) used a proper attribution convention; (c) created a works cited or references list; and (d) correctly formatted your paper.

In the exercise that follows, you will use the SMART TRACS editing plan to make changes to the first two paragraphs of a student's essay.

PRACTICE ⑥ Editing a Text

Read the two paragraphs that follow from a student's essay on how to raise healthier children. Use SMART TRACS to look for specific types of errors. When you find errors, annotate them. When you finish, rewrite the student's paragraphs on a separate sheet to correct the errors.

Parents do want the best for their children. To have a good education, strong morals, respectful to others, and to grow up to be strong and healthy. So parents always thinking of ways to protect the future of their kids and to do that is making sure they're healthy.

First, parents need to consider the healthy foods they will feed their children. When their toddlers parents shouldn't give up them alot of sweets try to balance it out by giving them plenty of healthy fruits and vegetables. For instance healthy foods like carrots, apples, grapes, sweet peppers, and oranges should be given to the children. These healthy foods are much healthier than the junkfood most children crave. Even though its hard to get kids to eat healthy vegtables. The best kinds of vegtables are

(continued)

the healthy leafy green vegtables like collard greens, spinach, and green beans These are the foods that have positive health affects. As far as healthy snacks for them I would give them gram crackers, yogurt and popcorn but not soda, you could switch that out with a healthier drink such as natural juice, milk or some water.

 Subject-Verb Agreement

A common and significant error is a lack of agreement between a subject and its verb. If you know that you are prone to make this error, focus on it while editing, and take a moment to review the basics of subject-verb agreement.

A singular subject must be matched with a singular verb, and a plural subject must be paired with a plural verb. In the following examples, the sentence's subject is in italics, and the sentence's verb is underlined.

Examples: An *animal* releases hormones as a response to stress.

Animals release hormones as a response to stress.

You may notice that nouns ending in *-s* (plural nouns) often agree with verbs that *do not* end in *-s*. While there are exceptions, it can be helpful to check subject nouns and verbs for their *-s* endings and to make sure the subject and verb agree.

Examples: hawk flies (singular)   hawks fly (plural)

psychologist listens (singular)   psychologists listen (plural)

she is   they are

As the last example above shows, even irregular verbs (*is*) have an *-s* ending in the singular.

The guidelines that follow show how to think about particular subject-verb agreement situations that can be confusing.

1. IF A SUBJECT CONTAINS TWO OR MORE NOUNS OR PRONOUNS JOINED BY *AND*, USE A PLURAL VERB

Often a subject contains two or more nouns or pronouns joined together. If *and* is used to connect the parts of the subject, then the verb should usually be plural.

Example: An *evaluation* and an *analysis* are **included in the report.**

A rare exception occurs when the two nouns are typically thought of as a single unit.

Example: *Steak and eggs* is my favorite breakfast.

2. IF A SUBJECT CONTAINS *OR* OR *NOR*, MAKE THE VERB AGREE WITH THE PART OF THE SUBJECT CLOSEST TO THE VERB

If two nouns or pronouns in a subject are joined by *or* or *nor*, the subject is not necessarily plural. The part of the subject that is nearest to the verb determines

(continued)

whether the verb is singular or plural. When a singular subject noun is connected by *or* or *nor* to a plural subject noun, place the plural noun closer to the verb, and use a plural verb, as in the following examples.

Examples: The *awl* [singular noun] **or** the *bits* [plural noun] belong in the bin.

Do the *bits* **or** the *awl* belong in the bin?

In the question example above, the helping verb (*do*) shows that the verb is plural.

3. WATCH OUT FOR WORDS THAT COME BETWEEN THE SUBJECT AND THE VERB

Sometimes a phrase or a clause that comes between the subject and the verb can cause confusion about subject-verb agreement. Remember that the verb should agree with the subject, not with a noun or pronoun in the phrase or clause.

Examples: The *computers* **in the new lab** are easy to use.

The *diagram* **that came with the instructions** identifies the parts.

To determine the right agreement, mentally strike through intervening words to identify the correct subject.

4. DETERMINE WHETHER SUBJECTS INDICATING QUANTITIES ARE SINGULAR OR PLURAL

Words such as *fraction, majority, part,* and *percent* are typically followed by a prepositional phrase. In those cases, the **object of the preposition** determines whether you should use a singular or plural verb. If the object of the preposition is singular, use a singular verb. Likewise, if the object of the preposition is plural, use a plural verb.

Examples: *Forty percent* **of the hay** has been distributed.

Forty percent **of the bales** have been distributed.

5. FOR NOUNS THAT CAN BE PLURAL OR SINGULAR, USE THE VERB FORM THAT REFLECTS THE MEANING OF THE SENTENCE

Many nouns that refer to groups of people can be either singular or plural. Some examples are *audience, board, committee, council, family, group, set,* and *team.* In a sentence describing the action of the entire group, a singular verb is needed. In a sentence describing the actions of individuals in a group, a plural verb is logical.

Example: The *committee* has voted in favor of the proposal.

The *committee* have different views on the proposal.

If a plural verb sounds awkward, try inserting a plural noun into the subject, as follows.

Example: The *committee members* have different views on the proposal.

6. DETERMINE WHETHER PRONOUN SUBJECTS ARE SINGULAR OR PLURAL

Pronouns that include the word *one* or *body* are singular and need singular verbs. Some pronouns—for example, *both, few, many,* and *several*—are plural and need

(continued)

plural verbs. A few pronouns—*all, any, more, most, some*—can be singular or plural depending on the meaning of the sentence. As with nouns indicating quantities, a prepositional phrase may determine whether the pronoun is singular or plural.

Examples: *More* is known today about effective urban planning strategies.

More [strategies] are used by planners to resolve overcrowding issues.

All of the study **participants** have been paid a nominal fee.

All of the study's **cost** has been covered by a grant.

7. USE SINGULAR VERBS FOR MONEY, TIME, AND TITLES

A sum of money, a period of time, or a title of a work is thought of as a single unit and so takes a singular verb.

Examples: *Twenty years* is a long time to spend in college.

Seventy-five dollars is the price of the ticket.

Bury My Heart at Wounded Knee is the assigned reading.

SENTENCE COMBINING

The examples that follow show how to combine sentences and select the appropriate verb to create subject-verb agreement.

Ideas to combine using correct subject-verb agreement:

• Nearly half the electricity created in the United States results from burning coal.

• Soot is a by-product of burning coal.

• Toxic air emissions are a by-product of burning coal.

• There are other by-products of burning coal.

• These by-products include acid rain.

• They include smog.

Combined sentences with subject-verb agreement: Nearly half the electricity created in the United States results from burning coal. Soot and toxic air emissions are by-products of burning coal. Other by-products include acid rain and smog.

Try your hand at combining sentences and selecting the appropriate verbs to create subject-verb agreement.

EXERCISES

You will find three sets of sentences below. Combine the sentences to make smoother, longer ones, and make sure subjects and verbs agree.

1. Ideas to combine:

• Genes probably influence the development of autism spectrum disorders.

• The environment seems to influence the development of autism spectrum disorders.

(continued)

- The disorders are usually diagnosed in children rather than adults.
- The cause is being researched.
- Methods for treating autism spectrum disorders are being researched.

Answer: _____

_____

_____

2. Ideas to combine:

- Contracts are signed by people.
- The people who sign them are called "parties" to the contract.
- One party signs the contract.
- Another party signs the contract.
- The agreement is between both parties.

Answer: _____

_____

3. Ideas to combine:

- Nanoscience is a relatively new scientific interest.
- Nanoscience is the study of very small things, such as atoms.
- Nanoscience involves using small things for inventions.
- Agricultural practices are affected by nanoscience.
- Computer technology is affected by nanoscience.
- Certain fields of study use nanoscience.
- One field is chemistry.
- Another field is physics.

Answer: _____

_____

_____

_____

Formatting Your Essay

In addition to being revised and edited, the final draft of your paper should meet the formatting requirements specified by your instructor. If your instructor has not given you specific information about how to format your paper, use the formatting specifications from the Modern Language Association. See the Quick Start Guide to Integrated Reading and Writing Assignments for basic information about MLA style.

Important formatting considerations include these:

- Setting the correct margins and tabs
- Using a correct header and page number system
- Using an appropriate heading
- Knowing whether to use a cover sheet, binder, staple, or paper clip for submitting your paper

- Using appropriate line spacing
- Using the appropriate font and font size
- Using the appropriate method for documenting sources

Using the correct format for setting up and submitting your paper is one of the easiest parts of writing. Make sure you get credit for this easy task by following instructions perfectly.

CHAPTER ACTIVITIES

READING AND ANNOTATING

The following essay is about revising. The writer, Benjamin Percy, teaches creative writing at Iowa State University and has published novels and short stories. As you read and annotate Percy's essay, think about the comparisons he is making.

Home Improvement

by Benjamin Percy

The Realtor said, "It's got good bones." That's what people say about ugly houses— and this was an ugly house. No one had done a thing to it since 1965, the year it was built. Every inch of the place was plastered with flocked or floral-patterned wallpaper, even the insides of the cabinets. All the light fixtures were white orbs collared by thin brass rings. The outside of the oven grew as hot as the inside. The master bedroom had curtains that matched its shaggy carpet that resembled in its color nothing so much as a mint green urinal puck. The roof was rotten and sagging. The furnace and gutters were rusted out.

But my wife and I walked through the backyard, a quarter acre of rich grass bordered by shade plants and mature ash trees whose branches came together overhead like a cathedral's roof. And we stood before the river-rock fireplaces and sat on the three-season porch and laid our hands flat along the walls and smiled as you would when rubbing a belly ripe with pregnancy. And bought the place.

This was April 2008, and we were shoving books into boxes, packing up the moving truck, when the phone rang with good news: I had sold my novel, *The Wilding*. My editor at Graywolf Press, Fiona McCrae, told me how excited she was about the manuscript, but wondered if I might be **amenable** to some changes. Of course, I said. What did she have in mind? "How about let's start with the point of view?" she said. "Might we shift it from first to third? And in doing so, with the freedom afforded to the characters, perhaps we could add five interlocking plotlines all coming to a head at once?" The book had good bones, in other words, but it needed some renovation.

Fiona has a British accent and somehow this makes everything she says sound reasonable. So I said, "Sure, no problem." And I meant it. I recognized the narrative as less of a novel and more of an extended short story, a shnovel. Here was the architectural solution, a new blueprint delivered from the contractor to the carpenter. I felt fired up, ready to flip open my toolbox and get to work. It wasn't until later, when I printed the manuscript and began to riffle through its pages, that I shuddered at the job ahead of me.

I'm no stranger to starting over. I wrote three failed novels before selling *The Wilding*. They were not a waste of time, not at all. I learned from them the humility that comes from watching something you've spent years working on turn to dust in your hands.

YOUR ANNOTATIONS

Vocabulary Collection Word:
amenable

Your in-context definition:

_____

_____

A dictionary definition:

_____

_____

And I discovered—by dissecting their cold carcasses—the many ways I might rob their organs and bones, their images and characters and settings and metaphors, and rearrange them, reimagine them, as short stories.

"Refresh, Refresh" is a good example. For my graduate thesis I wrote a (wretched) novel called "King of the Wild Frontier" (panned by students, faculty, agents, and editors alike). The fight scenes that appear in "Refresh, Refresh" are almost directly lifted from it, though their context couldn't be more different. Neither could the early and late drafts of the short story. Originally "Refresh, Refresh" was supernatural—my agent helped me transform it into scorched-earth realism. Originally it was forty pages—the Paris Review helped me winnow it down to eighteen. Originally the grandfather played a much larger role, and his subplot involved an amputated foot preserved in a bucket of formaldehyde—he ended up getting his own story, "The Killing" (which also recycles a number of scenes from "King of the Wild Frontier"). I could go on about the axed weight-lifting scenes, the three boys who became two, the brain-damaged vet, Floyd, who every night set up his karaoke machine outside the Dairy Queen and served as a kind of Greek chorus. Gone.

So much of revision, I've discovered, is about coming to terms with that word: gone. Letting things go. When revising, the beginning writer spends hours consulting the thesaurus, replacing a period with a semicolon, cutting adjectives, adding a few descriptive sentences—whereas the professional writer mercilessly lops off limbs, rips out innards like party streamers, drains away gallons of blood, and then calls down the lightning to bring the body back to life.

Revision doesn't come easy. That's why I used to resist it. When I received comments on my work, my eyes skimmed over the criticism and homed in on the compliments. That's no way to be. You've got to write every day as if you were clocking in for a job. Or if not every day, then damn near it. If you're not disciplined in your production—if you're writing only when the mood strikes or when a deadline looms—then naturally you'll be more protective of your work so that when it comes time to cut, your saw will tremble with hesitation. But if you're producing reams of pages you'll be less resistant to revision, because you know it won't be long before another load of timber comes down the road.

I discovered this in grad school, when writing became a full-time job and when critiques became sharp toothed, long nailed. One time a professor handed me back a manuscript with every single page slashed through with an enormous black X. There were no comments except a single word scrawled over the title: Don't.

When I later spoke to the professor, I pushed him further, asking what he meant, exactly. Don't what? Don't bother? Was the story no good? No, he said. That wasn't it. He liked the story—"Just don't write it that way." His advice served as an eraser. I pretended the original document no longer existed, and when I began another draft, it filled up a clean white screen unchained from the rusted-out sentences written previously.

I have thrown away thousands of pages—and sometimes you need to do that—sometimes you have to start over. But sometimes you don't. Sometimes your story needs some serious renovation—the walls are full of mold, the roof is leaking—and sometimes it simply needs some cosmetic work, a little paint splashed on the walls.

I've learned that revision is far less intense and traumatic when I begin a story with its end in mind. I used to be an organic writer, who had no game plan, who followed tooth-and-claw instinct, who considered writing an act of discovery. I let the garden grow and returned to it later to trim back the tangles, rip out the weeds.

Vocabulary Collection Word:
organic

Your in-context definition:

_____

_____

A dictionary definition:

_____

_____

Dan Chaon—the author of such dynamite collections as *Among the Missing*—is such a writer. For every fifteen-page short story, he produces more than a hundred pages. His stories "Big Me" and "The Bees" went through so many drafts that he "would have probably been better off writing a novel," he says. Sometimes he lays the pages down on the floor and wanders among them, rearranging them, isolating some scenes, crumpling up others and tossing them aside, until finally he decides what the story is about and returns to his desk to realize the piece in a shorter form.

On the other end of the spectrum is the Lego-block writer. He has his design in mind and snaps each piece into place and takes pleasure in how tidily everything comes together. I've tried this, too, and though it might work for some, for me it made the act of writing feel lifeless, boring.

I now fall somewhere between these two categories. I know my ending—maybe not everything about it, but generally where things will end up, what will happen—and I know one or two scenes that occur in the middle. In aiming toward them, I take far fewer wrong turns.

I used to consider editing something you did once a story was completed. I now begin each day by reading what I have already written. If it's a short story, I mean from the first line forward. If a novel, I mean from the start of the chapter I'm working on. I sometimes spend hours editing before I shift to an imaginative mode and begin to punch out new material. So I'm essentially in a constant state of revision, and by the time I finish the story, I might have edited it two dozen times, turning it over and over in my hands, sanding it until it's free of slivers.

Faulkner said, "Kill your darlings," and in that tradition I created a cemetery folder. In it I have files—tombstones, I call them—with titles like "Images" or "Metaphors" or "Characters" or "Dialogue." Into these I dump and bury anything excised from a story. For some reason, having a cemetery makes it easier to cut, to kill. Perhaps it's because I know the writing isn't lost—it has a place—and I can always return to the freshly shoveled grave and perform a voodoo ceremony.

It took me a year to rewrite *The Wilding,* to move from first to third person, to free up those characters and braid together their stories. And when I handed it in to Fiona in March 2009, she said—again, with a British accent—"Fantastic. Exactly what we wanted. Now would you mind cutting several of these subplots? And maybe we could add another in a female perspective? And while we're at it, how about let's rethink the ending?" And, and, and.

And then I got back to work.

I was hammering at the keyboard all week, and hammering at my house all weekend. I ripped out the carpeting and wrenched out the thousands of tacks and staples, to reveal gleaming hardwood. I scored the wallpaper and sprayed it with hot, soapy water and scraped—and scraped—and scraped away damp bits of paper, leaving the drywall beneath pitted. So I mudded and sanded and textured and painted. I tossed out the oven. I tossed out the curtains. I unscrewed the cracked, yellowing outlets and light switches and replaced them with white plates and once shocked myself so badly that my thumbnail bled and turned black. I pulled out the brass and shoved in wrought-iron light fixtures. We had a new roof thrown on, new gutters hung.

Not long ago, our Realtor stopped by to check on us. He shook my hand—a hand yellowed with calluses and crosshatched with scrapes, colored with bruises. He hardly recognized the house just as I hardly recognize the novel as it has moved from first to final draft. "You've been working hard," he said, and I said, "Yes."

Questions for Consideration

1. In his essay, Percy compares revising to several other activities. List the comparisons he uses.

_____

_____

2. What is his attitude toward revising his work?

_____

_____

3. What advice would Percy likely give college freshmen about academic writing?

_____

_____

4. Percy mentions several of his writing projects that were not good. For example, he writes, "One time a professor handed me back a manuscript with every single page slashed through with an enormous black X. There were no comments except a single word scrawled over the title: Don't." He does not seem to be embarrassed by these "failures." Why do you think he lacks embarrassment? Why do you think he shares these events from his past?

_____

_____

5. What process have you used to revise your writing in the past? Has your process been effective? What have you learned from Percy's essay about an effective revision process?

_____

_____

USING MODELS TO PRACTICE REVISING AND EDITING

Below you will find a list of specific revision and editing strategies, followed by a student paragraph, "The Case for City Chickens," on the next page. As you read the paragraph, look for opportunities to make the changes listed, and then revise or edit as appropriate.

Revision and Editing Strategies

1. Find two short sentences, and combine them to make a longer sentence.

_____

2. Find a sentence that could be followed with an example. Write a sentence providing the example.

_____

3. Consider how the order of the sentences could be improved. List the sentence numbers in the order in which you would place them.

_____

4. Find an error in word choice by considering commonly confused words. Change the misused word to the appropriate one.

_____

5. Find a phrase that is vague. Revise it so that its meaning is clear by using more specific, concrete terms.

_____

_____

The Case for City Chickens

Should our city's present laws be changed to allow citizens to keep chickens in their yards? As a teenage city chicken owner in Richmond pointed out, keeping chickens gives you more than just eggs. Long ago, laws were established in most cities to keep chickens and other livestock away from where people lived in houses because at that time, even pigs ran wild in the street. Many of our citizens aren't even aware that chickens are illegal here. Cities like Portland, Denver, Seattle, and even New York now allow backyard chickens, usually with a limit of one chicken per household member. Some cities have restrictions on how close to houses a chicken coop can be. Others say chickens have to be in an enclosed chicken run. Even still, these cities allow chickens. One city chicken owner gives all of the eggs her foul produce to the local homeless shelter.

A READING AND WRITING ASSIGNMENT

Below, you will find an essay assignment and a rough draft written by Jalyn Martin, a student in an English class. First, read and annotate the assignment, and then read through Jalyn's rough draft. Revise his rough draft, and use SMART TRACS to edit it. Produce a final copy of Jalyn's paper in a correctly formatted document.

Essay Assignment for English 1301

	YOUR ANNOTATIONS
Write an essay in which you provide a single change or a variety of changes parents can make to help their children be healthier. Imagine you are writing to have your essay published in a parenting magazine. Be sure to take the audience into consideration as you write. In addition, follow these instructions: • Offer at least three reasons for your position. • Include topic sentences for each of the body paragraphs. • Make sure that each body paragraph is well supported. • Use standard English grammar, correct spelling, and appropriate punctuation. • Do not include the use of any sources. • Format your essay using MLA style.	

Jalyn's Draft

	YOUR ANNOTATIONS
An old saying is *the work of a child is to play.* This adage is absolutely true, but it does not specify the type of play children need. More and more, children are abandoning the good, wholesome play that occurs in backyards and on sidewalks. Play is becoming an inside activity, and it is becoming solitary. Is sitting in front of a video game really the kind of play that should be *children's work*? There is nothing wrong with inside play, but children need more outside play than they get. Parents can help their children be healthier by making them play outside.	

(continued)

First, Children need sunshine. Playing outside means children will get the Vitamin D they need. Our bodies need vitamin D. You may know that vitamin D comes from milk, but it also comes from being in the sun. Without it, children are more susceptible to diseases. Additionally, being in the sun seems to have an affect on your mood. Who can be sad or grumpy on a beautiful sunny day?

Second, Video games make our kids lazy, so people need to send their kids outside. People debate whether violent video games make children more violent. Too much staring into a tv screen can't be a good habit. Besides, when you are playing video games, they are sitting down all day. Everybody needs to play some video games, but playing too much can turn you into a couch potato.

Third, There are things kids can do outdoors that they can never do indoors. Exploring nature, building forts, doing mischievous things like graffiti, getting to know the kids that live around them. Outdoor play makes kids be more creative. They have to come up with their own games. They can also get to know the children who live around them. They can ride bikes. They can explore parts of their neighborhood they would never see if they were in front of a tv all day.

Parents who care about their children's health need to consider sending their kids outside, a healthy kid is a kid who comes in totally wiped out and filthy from a wonderful day playing cowboys and Indians or hiking through the woods with their buddies. If we want our children to not be overweight and to get the vitamins they need, we should encourage them to play outside. The way we all did when we were children.

YOUR ANNOTATIONS

⊙ THINKING FROM AN INSTRUCTOR'S POINT OF VIEW

Carol Sweedler-Brown, an English professor, wondered whether handwriting ability has an effect on the grades students receive. Samuel Miller, another researcher, explains in the following passage what Sweedler-Brown did to answer this question.

> One example of the research is Sweedler-Brown's 1992 study in which 27 original essays were graded in three graphic modes: typed, nicely handwritten, and poorly handwritten. Nicely handwritten copies of the essays received significantly higher scores than the poorly handwritten or typed versions. There was no difference in the scores between the typed and poorly written versions, revealing a strong grader bias toward good handwriting.

As Sweedler-Brown's research shows, handwriting *does* have an effect on one's grade. While it may not be fair that handwriting matters, it does.

As a student, it is important to know that every assignment you submit produces an impression. What factors other than handwriting can you think of that can help you make a good impression when turning in assignments? List at least three ways to submit work that produces a favorable impression. Is there anything that might prevent you from putting into practice the items on your list? Write a paragraph explaining your answer.

⊙ ADDING TO YOUR VOCABULARY

This chapter's vocabulary words appear below.

precarious	acronym	incentive	organic
marketing	ambiguity	amenable	

Choose five of the vocabulary words from this chapter that you would like to add to your vocabulary, and think about how you can use them this week. For example, one of this chapter's words is *amenable*. You can often substitute *amenable* for *open to* or *OK with*, as in the example that follows.

Example: Marcus is *OK with* having the party at his house.

                Marcus is *amenable to* having the party at his house.

List each of the five words you plan to use this week, and make note of a context in which you could use each word.

Example: *Amenable.* I can use this with my parents when they propose going somewhere or doing something.

⊙ ADDITIONAL ASSIGNMENTS

1. Revising and editing enable you to improve your writing. People who restore automobiles or houses participate in a kind of revision process. Even cooking makes use of revision. Chefs, for example, might alter a recipe five or six times before they consider it perfect. Write an essay in which you compare the process of revising a text to the revision process of some other creative activity. In what ways are the processes similar?

2. Write an essay about a time when you "revised" a product or a process repeatedly. Describe the process you used. Explain what motivated you to keep revising until the product was nearly perfect.

3. One of the most common writing errors is to use particular words incorrectly. Many writers struggle with commonly confused words such as *affect* and *effect*. One way to master confusing words is to intentionally study them and use them. Make a list of ten words you commonly confuse. Write an essay, story, letter, or e-mail in which you use each of these ten words correctly. When you are finished, use the revising and editing process to refine your work.

4. The word *revision* includes two word parts with which you are familiar: *re* (again) and *visi* (to see or view). *Revision*, then, means "to see again." At right are two photographs. Choose one photograph. Imagine you are an artist and a client has asked you to revise her house or her old truck. Envision what the house or truck *could* look like. What particular features would you change to make it more beautiful or more appealing? Explain your vision in one or two paragraphs. Revise and edit your paragraphs when you are finished.

5. Find an essay you wrote for this writing class or for another class, and print out a copy. Read your paper out loud, imagining yourself reading it for the first time. Use the processes in this chapter to revise and edit your paper. When you are finished with your revision, repeat this entire process. See if revising the paper a second time makes a difference in the quality (and quantity) of your writing.

EMOTIONAL INTELLIGENCE

What is *netiquette*? If you are unsure, do an Internet search, and read about the topic. Write two or three paragraphs in which you define *netiquette* and explain some common netiquette guidelines. Be sure to give credit to any sources you use.

CULTURAL LITERACY

Every culture has its artifacts—songs, art, literature, activities, traditions—that are meaningful in a special way. Spend a moment and think about artifacts from your culture that are important to you. Perhaps you and your family are very patriotic and celebrate July 4th by raising the flag. Perhaps making tamales at Christmas or on other occasions is a cultural tradition that your family cherishes. Find three artifacts from your culture and explain in a few paragraphs what they mean to you.

CRITICAL THINKING

One element of critical thinking is being imaginative and creative enough to think about options. Often, the more options you consider, the better your decision. Practice thinking creatively by considering career choices. First, make a list of three things you want in a career. Here is an example of such a list:

1. A salary of at least $15 an hour
2. The ability to work during the day (no night shifts!)
3. A career that involves the use of a computer

Using your list, think creatively about the various careers that meet these criteria. See if you can come up with twenty potential careers. Push yourself and think hard. If you cannot come up with twenty potential careers, ask your friends and classmates to help you. Once you make your list, circle the careers on it that you had not thought of before. Do any interest you? Write a paragraph in which you discuss a few of the new ideas you thought of.

METACOGNITION

Think back to a group project in which you participated. Imagine that you can see yourself—and all of the other group members—from the outside. Evaluate your role in the group. Did you contribute in a positive way? Were you the leader? How important a role did you play? If you were an instructor, how would you evaluate the role you played in the group project? Explain in one or two paragraphs.

PART 3

Additional Skills

11 Using Sources

**Strategies for Reading
and Writing Exams**

Professionals know that for the best outcome, they must use good sources and position their materials with care, whether they are building a house, catering a party, or writing an essay.

Using Sources

Many—if not most—of the writing assignments you will do in college and at work will include the use of source materials. What should be the connection between a source's ideas and your own ideas? When should you refer to sources in your writing? How do you use sources without plagiarizing? How do you integrate quotes and source references smoothly? These are a few of the questions we will consider in this chapter to help you use sources accurately, ethically, and effectively.

CHAPTER OBJECTIVES

After completing this chapter, students will be able to do the following:

- **Prepare to use source materials.**
- **Work with readings for a source-based essay.**
- **Develop a source-based essay.**
- **Create in-text references in MLA and APA styles.**
- **Format an MLA paper and prepare a works cited list.**
- **Format an APA paper and prepare a references list.**
- **Check an essay for plagiarism.**

GETTING STARTED: PREPARING TO USE SOURCE MATERIALS

The best way to start any reading and writing task is to analyze and annotate the assignment itself. In the simple example that follows, the student's annotations point out the significant verbs that will help him determine exactly what to focus on when reading the sources.

English 0301 Reading and Writing Project

Most cities have recycling programs of some sort. In the essays that follow, you will learn about the cities with the best recycling programs in the United States. <u>As you read</u> about these cities, <u>determine the factors</u> that help them rank high in their recycling initiatives. Once you have determined these factors, <u>think about the recycling program in your own city</u>. How does it <u>compare with the cities you have read about</u>? <u>Write an essay</u> in which you <u>use the factors</u> you have identified <u>to compare</u> your city's recycling program to those you have read about. <u>Evaluate how good a job your city is doing</u> with its recycling program, and <u>provide your evaluation</u> in your essay. Your essay should have <u>two parts</u>: <u>an analysis</u> of your city's recycling program based on the factors you have read about, and <u>an evaluation</u> of the quality of your city's recycling program.

Read sources.

Determine factors used to judge recycling programs.

Compare my city's recycling program with the programs of cities in the articles.

Write an essay and use the factors for the comparison.

Evaluate my city's program.

Essay should have an analysis and an evaluation.

By annotating the assignment, the student has identified the tasks he must focus on when he reads the source material. He is clear about his purpose: to figure out what makes the recycling programs of particular cities good. He must also figure out the factors that are used to judge the recycling programs (such as percentage of waste recycled, public awareness and participation, and so on). With these things in mind, the student can read in a more focused way.

WORKING WITH READINGS

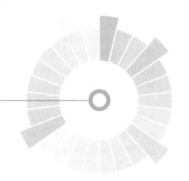

When you are ready to start reading the sources, use a previewing process to guide your work. Start by considering who wrote the source, for whom it was written, and when and where it was published. After previewing, read and annotate the sources. Next, create an outline, a summary, and an information sheet for each source. As you work with sources, keep in mind the information that follows.

Examining Authors for Bias and Credibility

One way to assess the credibility of a source is to evaluate the author: her position, her reputation, and the subjects she often writes about. A quick Internet search will help you obtain this information. Knowing the writer's background will help you understand her authority on the subject—as well as her biases. For example, if a writer has a reputation as an advocate of prison reform, you can expect her article to reflect that point of view. If she teaches criminology at a university or is a prison warden, her position lends credibility to her writing. Researching the writer's background will enable you to refer to her credentials later when you draft your essay. Doing so will tell your readers that the source you are using is credible.

Reputable Web sites go to some trouble to be transparent about who runs them and who writes for them. If you cannot find information about the source of the information on a Web site, be wary about using it for research. If you learn only that an article on a site is authored by Millard Wentworth, for example, you have not really learned anything (unless the name Millard Wentworth is meaningful to you!). If author biographies are provided, you have a bit more information and can rank the site a bit higher in terms of credibility. To determine more about a site's author or sponsoring organization, conduct a search using *Google* or another search engine.

Examining Audience

Examining the potential audience for a source will add to your understanding. Consider an article about diabetes that appears in a journal for doctors. The writer has made certain assumptions about the medical knowledge of the audience. When you read the article, you may need to consult dictionaries or other sources to understand it. An article that appears on the Web site of People for the Ethical Treatment of Animals (PETA) will be written for an audience that, for the most part, shares PETA's views. Knowing the beliefs of the audience will help you more accurately understand the writer's point.

Examining Date and Historical Context

Another aspect of the source to consider is when it was published. If the source is not current, consider its historical context. Suppose you are reading an article about the oil industry, and you notice that it was written in 1976. If you know that the United States experienced an energy crisis in the mid-1970s, you will better understand the issues discussed in the article. If you notice that an article about preparing for disaster was written in 1999 and you know that some people were anxious about entering the next millennium, you will have additional insight into the piece. The historical context can affect your understanding of a piece of writing. In general, unless a source is important or ground-breaking in its field (for example, a work on psychology by Sigmund Freud), use sources written within the last five years.

Examining the Source for Bias and Credibility

A source is *biased* if it advocates or promotes a particular view on an issue. For example, suppose you want to determine whether high-fructose corn syrup is good for you. If you look at the Web site of a company that produces high-fructose corn syrup, you would expect to find information that is biased in favor of the product and the many ways it improves foods and beverages. Likewise, it is unlikely that you would find arguments against the product. Therefore, you would be unwise to base your determination solely on the evidence of that biased Web site.

At times, reading biased sources might suit your writing task. For instance, in a persuasive essay, you might want to present the viewpoint of the corn syrup company as well as the viewpoint of those opposed to the wide use of corn syrup as a sweetener (a viewpoint that will also be biased). Comparing these two biased sources may be helpful in such a paper. Often, however, writers are best served by looking for sources that are neutral and do not have an interest in promoting a particular point of view.

Examining the Source for Bias

Sources may come from general magazines, scholarly journals, Web sites, and a variety of other publications. Knowing a source's origin will help you predict potential biases. Some journals and magazines directly reveal their biases. For example, just the name of *The American Conservative* gives you a clue about the magazine's political orientation. If you go to the magazine's Web site, you will find a definitive statement of the magazine's biases. The magazine says, "To solve the country's seemingly intractable—and, in the long-term, lethal—strategic, economic, and socio-cultural problems requires a rediscovery of traditional conservatism. That's the mission of *The American Conservative.*" Similarly, if you do an Internet search on book publishers, you also may be able to detect biases. Ignatius Press, for example, describes itself as the "primary publisher in U.S. of Pope Benedict XVI's books." We can expect books from Ignatius Press to have a Roman Catholic bias.

Determining the bias of Web sites can be a bit trickier. One way to do so is to examine its **domain name**—the last part of its Web address. Common domain names are *.com*, *.gov*, *.edu*, and *.org*. If a Web site address ends in *.com*, it is a commercial Web site, and you should suspect it will contain biases in favor of the product or service it is selling. Web sites whose domain is *.org* (meaning that it represents an organization) may be less biased, but *.org* sites often promote ideas. For example, PETA has this on its home page (www.peta.org): "Animals are *not* ours to eat, wear, experiment on, use for entertainment, or abuse in any other way." The bias of PETA's organizational Web site is clearly stated. Note that having a bias does not mean a source is disreputable; it simply tells you the source is not neutral.

Web sites sponsored by federal, state, and local governments have the domain *.gov*. Much of the information on government Web sites—in particular, statistical information—is simply factual. However, the Web site of a particular agency or department (for example, the US Environmental Protection Agency) may advocate for activities such as conservation and more regulation, which other organizations (for example, energy companies) do not favor. Additionally, individual senators and congressional representatives have Web sites that end in *.gov*. These sites will be biased because they will present the senator's or representative's point of view.

Web sites that end in *.edu* are educational—that is, associated with colleges, universities, and other recognized educational institutions. While these sites are likely to be less biased than *.com* sites, it is important to remember that professors and even students often have personal Web sites sponsored by their institution. Those personal Web sites often present points of view about issues. Thus, these sites will also present bias.

In the end, you—as a consumer of information—must always be the one to make a careful choice about the bias of a particular Web site or source. Bias is not necessarily a bad thing, but as a researcher, you must know whether your sources are biased or take a neutral point of view.

Examining the Source for Credibility

In general, you can determine the **credibility** of a source—its trustworthiness—by examining its origin. For example, we expect articles in *The New York Times* to be written ethically and credibly. Similarly, we expect articles that appear in **peer-reviewed** journals (journals that have a stringent process for selecting what they publish) to be credible. On the other end of the credibility spectrum are tabloids that present celebrity gossip and news items that are often unverifiable—ranging from accounts of alien landings to reports of six-headed babies. You can often do an Internet search of a source's name to learn more about its reputation and credibility.

To assess a source that comes from a Web site, you must assess the Web site itself. Study the Web site shown below and the clues that are pointed out as you review the following factors. First, a professional Web site will be well edited and will not contain

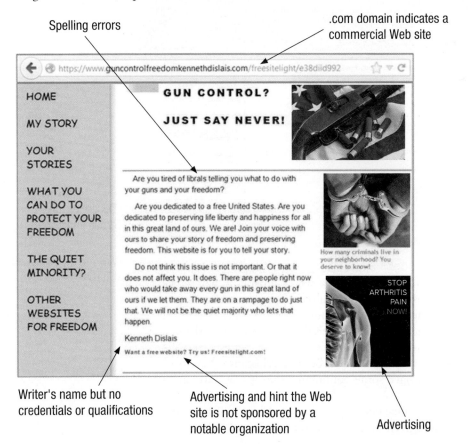

A Web site that is biased and is *not* credible.

errors in spelling or grammar. Ideally, it should not carry advertising. Some credible Web sites do allow advertising, but as a rule, look for those that do not. Advertising is a sign that the owner of the Web site wants to make money by luring people to the site; thus, the owner may decide to post the content that draws in the most people, which may not necessarily be the most authoritative content on a subject. Additionally, a credible Web site will offer support for the information it posts. For example, some Web sites provide bibliographies to show the sources the authors consulted, a practice that allows readers to evaluate the credibility of the information.

Clearly, the Web site shown on the previous page is biased, but its bias is not the problem. The real question is whether we should regard its writer, Kenneth Dislais, as a credible or qualified source for information about gun control. He offers no biographical information about himself; in fact, we have no information about the sponsors of the Web site either. The only information we have is that it was created by means of a free Web site generator. Why should we believe that Kenneth Dislais knows *anything* about the issue of gun control? We do know one thing: he did not use a spell-checker to proofread his Web site! Further, the site includes advertisements that are not related to the content. In summary, when you encounter sites like this one, question the value of the information. Can you verify that it is anything other than a mouthpiece for one unknown individual? If not, the site lacks credibility and is a poor source.

Now, take a look at another Web site for an organization that opposes gun control. Notice that this site, sponsored by Citizens for Responsible Gun Ownership, is biased but credible.

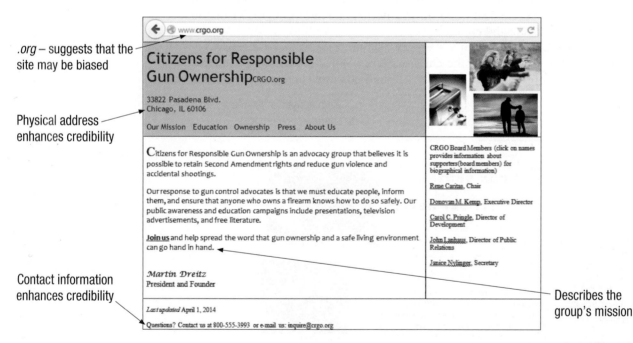

▪ A Web site that is biased but is also credible.

The Web site goes to some trouble to let viewers know who sponsors it, where the organization is located (its physical address), and the group's philosophy and mission. Also, the clear identification of the site's founder and president and easy availability of information about its supporters (board members) lend it credibility. Moreover, the site provides ways for the sponsoring organization to be contacted, which suggests that the group is well-established. While we know that the site will be biased because it exists to promote the rights of gun owners, we can have some confidence that it may ultimately prove to have trustworthy information.

Finally, let's examine a Web site that is credible but is not biased on the issue of gun ownership. Notice the characteristics of this objectively oriented site, www.yesnovote121015.org.

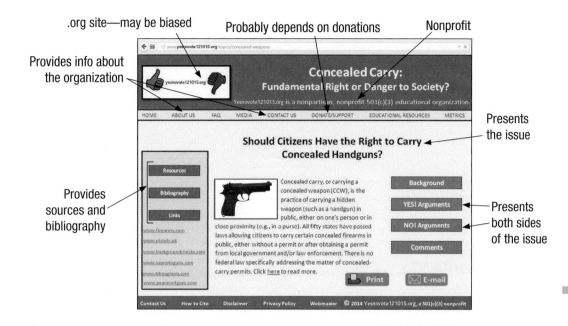

The following labels point to parts of the website:

- .org site—may be biased
- Probably depends on donations
- Nonprofit
- Provides info about the organization
- Provides sources and bibliography
- Presents the issue
- Presents both sides of the issue

■ A Web site that is *not* biased and is credible.

The site provides numerous clues that it is credible and seeks to be objective. Its name suggests that we will learn about both sides of issues. The site confirms this idea by providing a neutral introduction to the issue of carrying concealed guns and then offering both sides of the argument. Also, the Web site enhances its credibility by giving resources and bibliographies. We can see that www.yesnovote121015.org is a nonprofit educational organization that depends on donations and is not funded by people on a particular side of an issue. These facts help establish the site as both credible and objective.

PRACTICE ❶ Examining Sources

Bibliographic information is given below for two textual sources and a Web site. All of these sources concern the effects of aspartame, the artificial sweetener used in many products, including NutraSweet. Using this information and an Internet search engine to look up information about the publication and the writers, answer the questions that follow each source.

1. Author: Joe and Teresa Graedon

Title: "How Safe Is Aspartame?"

Source: *The Buffalo News*

Date: 4 January 2006

a. How credible are these writers?

_____

_____

b. Does anything about the publication (*The Buffalo News*) suggest bias?

_____

_____

2. Author: John Briffa

Title: "Aspartame and Its Effects on Health: Independently Funded Studies Have Found Potential for Adverse Effects"

Journal: *BMJ* (*British Medical Journal*), vol. 330, no. 7486, pp. 309–10

(continued)

Publisher: BMJ Publishing Group

Date: February 2005

   a. How credible is this writer?

_____

   b. Does anything about the publication (*British Medical Journal*) suggest bias?

_____

   c. For what audience was this written?

_____

3. http://www.aspartame.org

   a. How credible is this Web site?

_____

   b. Does anything about this Web site suggest bias?

_____

_____

   c. What did you learn about the authors of this Web site?

_____

Reading and Annotating Sources

The best way to work with sources is to print them out and have a pen, pencil, and highlighter ready. Read the source, using a pencil to annotate the ideas that seem to be important. It is difficult to recognize the most important ideas in a text the first time you read it, so using a pencil will enable you to go back and make changes.

Read the source a second time, this time using your pen and highlighter to annotate the text. Mark the major supporting points, the thesis statement, nuggets of information you find interesting or useful, potential quotes, and any passages about which you have questions. Write questions and comments in the margin. If you are reading more than one source, annotate any connections you notice between the sources.

If, after you have read the source several times, you are confused or unsure about its meaning, read it again. There is nothing wrong with reading a source several times; in fact, doing so is quite common and always useful. Another idea to help with your comprehension is to write down the topic on a piece of paper. Next, write down the main point the writer is making about the topic. Put this information into a sentence. What you have written *should* be the writer's thesis statement. Work with your course instructor or a lab instructor if you need additional help comprehending a text.

As you search for potential quotes, think about the assignment. If you keep in mind the kind of paper you will be writing, you are more likely to select appropriate quotes. You cannot be totally certain about which parts of your sources you will actually use in your paper until you create an outline and work on a draft. To select quotes you think you may use, look over your annotations. You should have noted the main idea, major supporting points, and particularly interesting minor supporting details. These are potentially useful passages to use as quotations. It is vitally important to copy these passages *word-for-word*. A quote must include the exact words you find in the original source.

Outlining, Summarizing, and Preparing Information Sheets for Sources

Once you have read and understood a source, prepare a brief outline and a brief summary. Create an *information sheet* that includes the outline and summary and enough information to render the source useful as a reference as you write your essay. Under the heading "General Notes," write all the bibliographic information you have (author, title, publication, date of publication, city of publication, publisher or sponsoring organization, and pages or URL if you are using a Web source) and comment on any points of interest to you. For example, you could note an essay idea that the source suggests to you. Here's a sample format for an information sheet.

Model for an Information Sheet

INFORMATION SHEET :

GENERAL NOTES
- Authors:
- Publication:
- Date:
- [Interesting points]

SIMPLE OUTLINE
  Thesis statement:
  Major supporting point 1:
  Major supporting point 2:
  Major supporting point 3:

BRIEF SUMMARY

ISSUES AND KEY WORDS

POTENTIAL QUOTES

When you have created an information sheet for each source, you are ready to start the next phase of the integrated reading and writing process: developing your essay.

PRACTICE ② Selecting Information to Use from Sources

What follows is one of the articles referred to in Practice 1.
- Read and annotate the article.
- On a separate sheet, use the format shown above to prepare a page of notes. Include bibliographic information, a simple outline, a brief summary, and three quotes.

How Safe Is Aspartame?
by Joe Graedon and Teresa Graedon

People love to hate artificial sweeteners. Starting with saccharin in the late 1950s, some have enthusiastically embraced the idea of sweets without calories. Others have warned that saccharin, cyclamate and aspartame are too dangerous for human consumption.

The debate is often intensely emotional. Cyclamate was removed from the market in 1969 when animal studies showed an excess of tumors in rats exposed to the sweetener. This remained controversial for the next 20 years, but the Food and Drug Administration did not reverse itself.

The FDA proposed pulling saccharin off the market in the mid-1970s, also on the suspicion that it might cause cancer. The agency let those plans drop due to public outcry and congressional outrage.

YOUR ANNOTATIONS

Saccharin is the sweetener most often sold in pink packages. A common brand is Sweet'n Low. Cyclamate is approved for use in many countries but is banned in the United States. Aspartame, most often sold in blue packages, was initially marketed as NutraSweet. Its health effects are widely debated.

(continued)

The most popular noncaloric sweetener for the past few decades has been aspartame. This artificial sweetener was introduced with great fanfare in 1981 as one of the safest alternatives to sugar ever created. The FDA announced when it approved aspartame, "Few compounds have withstood such detailed testing and repeated, close scrutiny, and the process through which aspartame has gone should provide the public with additional confidence of its safety."

That's their story, and they're sticking to it. Through the years, though, frightening tales of aspartame toxicity have circulated on the Internet.

One reader wrote: "I know from firsthand experience that there are very serious problems with aspartame. In 1996 I was diagnosed with epilepsy. At that time I was trying to lose weight and eating a lot of products with aspartame.

"I became suspicious and stopped eating aspartame-laced products. Even though my neurologist was skeptical, I was able to discontinue my seizure medicine and have not had further seizures."

Others have blamed aspartame for a wide variety of health problems including headaches, dizziness, confusion, memory loss, depression, blindness, ADD, ALS, lupus and multiple sclerosis.

With dozens of symptoms attributed to aspartame, it is easy to discount the diatribes. We were skeptical about the more exaggerated claims, especially regarding links to cancer.

Recent research by a European foundation has forced us to look at aspartame in a new light, however. A study published online in the journal *Environmental Health Perspectives* (Nov. 17, 2005) involved 1,800 rats and six dosage levels of aspartame in their chow.

The rats in this study were not sacrificed but lived out their natural lives and were examined upon death. The authors report an excess of leukemias, lymphomas and malignant tumors among rats fed aspartame at several dosage levels.

Critics charge that the researchers did not follow standard protocols for this type of study. The investigators respond that "the findings speak for themselves."

Source Information

Author: Joe Graedon and Teresa Graedon

Title: "How Safe Is Aspartame?"

Publication: *The Buffalo News*

Date: 4 January 2006

URL: Accessed on Web in a database titled *HighBeam Research,* at https://www.highbeam.com/doc/1P2-22974920.html

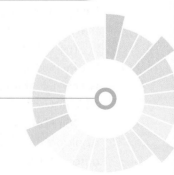

DEVELOPING YOUR SOURCE-BASED ESSAY

Once you have read, annotated, analyzed, and prepared information sheets for all your sources, you are ready to start thinking about your own essay. It is wise to go back to the assignment and reread it before going on. You should look frequently at the assignment during the reading and writing process to stay on track. After you have reviewed the assignment, follow these steps to start developing your essay.

Synthesizing Sources

Begin by categorizing your sources according to focus or point of view. For example, assume you are reading about the changing definition of the family in the United States. Some of your sources discuss types of families (such as single-parent families and multi-generational families). Others discuss why our definitions of the family are changing. You could categorize your sources into "types" and "explanations."

Or imagine you are reading about a controversial topic, such as the effects of violent video games. Some sources claim that such games enhance problem-solving skills and hand-eye coordination. Others claim that these games have little to no effect on participants. Still others claim that there is a direct relationship between playing violent video games and being violent in real life. You might put these sources into the groups "pro," "con," and "neutral/other." Once you have a clear picture of the points of view of your sources, you can choose the best categories. If you categorize your sources, you will more easily be able to locate the source you need to support a particular point while writing.

Another way to synthesize your sources is to create a table that is designed specifically for your assignment. For instance, if you were working on the recycling assignment, you would need to know details about the various recycling programs from each city. You would also need to know which factors the writers analyzed to judge the effectiveness of the programs. Thus, you could make a table like the one that follows to synthesize your information.

	SOURCE 1: MATTAVILLE, WASHINGTON	SOURCE 2: WESTERSON, FLORIDA	SOURCE 3: RIO TERRA, CALIFORNIA
Percentage of community that participates in recycling program	81	88	84
Percentage of trash recycled	78	82	82
Recycling of glass?	Yes	No	Yes
Recycling of paper and plastic?	Yes	Yes	Yes
Recycling of furniture?	Yes	No	No
Recycling of wood?	Yes	Yes	Yes

This kind of table will help you see how each recycling program compares to the others, and it will help you determine the criteria (in the left column) you can use in your analysis of your own city's recycling program. Of course, the content of the chart you create will depend on the content of the sources you are analyzing.

Prewriting to Develop Your Ideas

As you read your sources, make notes, and synthesize the source material, you will start to have an idea of what you want to communicate in your thesis statement. Use a prewriting method to generate ideas about the topic. One way to start is to prewrite about each of the elements you need to include in your paper. For example, in the assignment we analyzed earlier, these are the required elements:

- Factors used to judge recycling programs
- Comparison of my city's recycling program with the programs of cities in the articles
- Analysis of my city's program using factors for comparison
- Evaluation of my city's program

Use prewriting to generate ideas for each of the elements that will be in your essay.

Constructing a Thesis Statement and Support

Once you believe you understand the issues well enough to know what point you would like to make, construct a thesis statement. Make sure your thesis statement is grammatically correct and that it communicates the main message you want to express in your paper.

After writing a thesis statement, you will choose your major supporting points. Let's take the example of Krystal, a student who is writing an essay about the dangers of concussions from playing football. She has read a number of sources on the topic, and her prewriting has led her to compose this thesis statement.

> The effects of concussions sustained while playing football are so serious that players should demand changes or refuse to play the game.

On the basis of her reading and thesis statement, Krystal lists the information she needs to support her position. What will her readers need to know? As she determines her readers' needs, she jots them down in the left column. Then she writes a complete sentence for each need in the right column, making sure the sentence supports her thesis statement.

Thesis statement: The effects of concussions sustained while playing football are so serious that players should demand changes or refuse to play the game.

TO SUPPORT MY THESIS STATEMENT, I WILL NEED TO . . .	MAJOR SUPPORTING POINTS
Explain the effects of concussions	Scientists have learned that concussions have serious long-term effects on the brain. [List effects.]
Suggest changes that can decrease these negative effects	Players and those who care about them should demand changes. • The first thing that can be done is to reduce the number of concussions by changing some of the rules in football. • A second solution is to require the use of a new type of helmet. • Third, football coaches, trainers, physicians, players, and the families of players must be trained to identify concussions and consult the appropriate health-care professionals so that concussions are treated correctly.
Convince players to not play if such changes are not made	Players must educate themselves about the realities and then stand up for themselves—if necessary, by refusing to play—for the sake of their long-term health and for those who care about them.

Notice how the major supporting points in the second column are directly related to both the thesis statement and to the readers' needs.

Creating an Outline

Krystal is now ready to create an outline. An outline does not have to be formal to be effective, but it does need to be written with care. The thesis statement and the major supporting points must be included in the form of well-written, complete sentences. Ideally, Krystal should be able to simply copy those sentences from her outline and put them directly into her paper.

As Krystal creates her outline, she determines how many body paragraphs she will need for each major supporting point. Some major supporting points can be expressed in a single paragraph, but others may need more than one body paragraph. Krystal's outline, which follows, demonstrates this idea.

Outline for a Source-Based Essay

Topic: Concussions in football

Thesis statement: The effects of concussions sustained while playing football are so serious that players should demand changes or refuse to play the game.

INTRODUCTION

Paragraph 1: Explain why so many people are talking about this issue these days. Start with the story of Dave Duerson. End with thesis statement.

BODY

Paragraph 2 (major supporting point 1—effects): Scientists have learned that concussions have serious long-term effects on the brain.

Paragraph 3 (major supporting point 2—changes): Players and those who care about them should demand changes. The first thing that can be done is to reduce the number of concussions by changing some of the rules in football.

Paragraph 4 (major supporting point 3—changes): A second solution is to require the use of a new type of helmet.

Paragraph 5 (major supporting point 4—changes): Third, football coaches, trainers, physicians, players, and the families of players must be trained to identify concussions and consult the appropriate health-care professionals so that concussions are treated correctly.

Paragraph 6 (major supporting point 5—refuse to play): Players must educate themselves about the realities and then stand up for themselves—if necessary, by refusing to play—for the sake of their long-term health and for those who care about them.

CONCLUSION

Paragraph 7: Explain how this issue affects not only NFL players but also kids across the country. Urge a solution.

Adding Source Material and Details to Your Outline

Now that she has an outline, Krystal can start adding minor supporting details, including source materials. She has to consider carefully when and where to use quotes from her sources. She will not want to overuse her research by including too many quotes or by merely summarizing a variety of sources. The result would be a paper that jumps from quote to quote or from summary to summary without tying the information together in a way that represents her perspective and insights. Professors want to see *your* writing. So remember that quotes are best used sparingly and only when they truly support the point you are making.

Remember that when you use specific ideas from *any* source, even if you put them into your own words, you *must* give credit to the author of those ideas. Many students wonder whether they need to cite sources for well-known ideas, or **common knowledge**. Krystal may write, for instance, that football is a dangerous sport. Because many others have said the same, she does not have to cite other people who have made this general statement. In contrast, a statistic on the number of head injuries in football *would* need to come from a cited source because a statistic is not common knowledge. In her paper, Krystal will include specific information about the effects of concussions and solutions to the concussion problem that she learned about from her sources, and she will cite these sources when she uses them.

As Krystal considers how best to support her thesis statement, she selects several sources that will be advantageous and adds them to her outline. She uses the last name of the writer to refer to the source materials she will incorporate in her essay.

Essay Outline Annotated to Include Sources

Topic: Concussions in football

Thesis statement: The effects of concussions sustained while playing football are so serious that players should demand changes or refuse to play the game.

INTRODUCTION

Paragraph 1: Explain why so many people are talking about this issue these days. Start with the story of Dave Duerson. End with thesis statement. Use Jackson source for Duerson's story.

BODY

Paragraph 2 (major supporting point 1—effects): Scientists have learned that concussions have serious long-term effects on the brain. Use Monroe source and CDC source for quotes and statistics.

Paragraph 3 (major supporting point 2—changes): Players and those who care about them should demand changes. The first thing that can be done is to reduce the number of concussions by changing some of the rules in football. Use Davidson source to explain possible rule changes.

Paragraph 4 (major supporting point 3—changes): A second solution is to require the use of a new type of helmet. Use Jackson source and Monroe source for new helmet innovation information.

Paragraph 5 (major supporting point 4—changes): Third, football coaches, trainers, physicians, players, and the families of players must be trained to identify concussions and consult the appropriate health-care professionals so that concussions are treated correctly. Use quotes from CDC source.

Paragraph 6 (major supporting point 5—refuse to play): Players must educate themselves about the realities and then stand up for themselves—if necessary, by refusing to play—for the sake of their long-term health and for those who care about them. Use the story of the Melville City League as an example—Monroe source.

CONCLUSION

Paragraph 7: Explain how this issue affects not only NFL players but also youth football players across the country. Urge that a solution be found.

PRACTICE 3 Choosing Source Materials

The following paragraphs about anger management are from "Controlling Anger before It Controls You," which appears on the Web site of the American Psychological Association. Following the paragraphs you will see an outline for a student's essay on anger management. Read the source paragraphs and the outline. Choose two passages that provide helpful information and would make good quotes for the essay. Underline each quote, and note where you would put it in the outline.

Source Paragraphs

According to Jerry Deffenbacher, PhD, a psychologist who specializes in anger management, some people really are more "hotheaded" than others are; they get angry more easily and more intensely than the average person does. There are also those who don't show their anger in loud spectacular ways but are chronically

YOUR ANNOTATIONS

(continued)

irritable and grumpy. Easily angered people don't always curse and throw things; sometimes they withdraw socially, sulk, or get physically ill.

People who are easily angered generally have what some psychologists call a low tolerance for frustration, meaning simply that they feel that they should not have to be subjected to frustration, inconvenience, or annoyance. They can't take things in stride, and they're particularly infuriated if the situation seems somehow unjust: for example, being corrected for a minor mistake.

What makes these people this way? A number of things. One cause may be genetic or physiological: There is evidence that some children are born irritable, touchy, and easily angered, and that these signs are present from a very early age. Another may be sociocultural. Anger is often regarded as negative; we're taught that it's all right to express anxiety, depression, or other emotions but not to express anger. As a result, we don't learn how to handle it or channel it constructively.

Source: © 2005 by the American Psychological Association.

Outline for a Student's Essay

Introduction
    Thesis statement: People who have trouble controlling their anger can learn techniques to manage it.

Body
    Major supporting point 1: What are anger disorders?

    Major supporting point 2: What causes anger disorders?

    Major supporting point 3: How is anger management disorder diagnosed?

    Major supporting point 4: How is anger management disorder treated?

    Major supporting point 5: What is the outlook for people who go through anger management programs?

Conclusion

Writing a Complete Draft of Your Essay

Once you have an outline ready, you can use it to compose a first draft. Keep in mind that an outline is a plan, and as such it is changeable. If you write a body paragraph and find that you have not planned for enough support, change your outline by adding more examples or perhaps an anecdote or a comparison.

Use a recursive process when you draft. To *recur* means "to happen again." Recursive drafting means that you go back and reread what you have written, make changes, and resume drafting. After completing each paragraph, read your essay from the beginning. You will find areas that need more development, are unclear, and so on. Make changes as you draft.

Integrating Ideas and Quotes from Sources Correctly

As you draft your paper, integrate source material carefully. The key to using quotes effectively is knowing *when* to use them and *how* to integrate them. During the process of reading source materials, you annotated your sources and identified significant passages. You also wrote down possible quotations on your information sheets. Keep in mind that because you wrote your notes before you knew exactly what you would be saying in your paper, the quotes you chose may not be the best ones to support your points. Be willing to go back to the source to choose the most appropriate quotes for your purpose.

A **quotation** consists of the exact words of a source. Even if the writer of the source made a grammatical error, you must reproduce the source exactly, errors included. You must acknowledge the source in the body of the text as well as in a list of references or works cited, which you will learn about later in this chapter.

Determining When to Use Quotations

Using quotations carefully can help you write an impressive, well-researched paper. However, if you use quotes like seasoning salt—sprinkling them here and there at random—you will have a paper that makes little sense. Use quotations only in the following situations.

- **You need to support your point of view with authoritative information.** The most common reason for using a quote is to back up your own ideas by citing professionals or experts who agree with you.

    Example: Some serious psychological disorders show up during the early adult years. Ian Christopher points out that "schizophrenia, generalized anxiety disorders, and bipolar disorder commonly manifest in early adulthood."

- **You wish to provide complex or technical explanations.** Sometimes only experts can explain complex phenomena. Carefully select quotes when an expert can offer a better explanation than you can.

    Example: According to the Center for Genetic Origination, mutation consists of "the moment when a nucleotide sequence of the genome of an organism or related being undergoes change."

- **Using your own wording of a concept or idea would not be as effective as quoting the source's wording.** When you find a source that words an idea perfectly, it is fine to quote that source as long as you give credit.

    Example: George Orwell writes, "Doublethink means the power of holding two contradictory beliefs in one's mind simultaneously, and accepting both of them."

- **The source has used a particularly important phrase, and you do not want to change the wording of that phrase.** In the following example, the last name of the source's writer is provided in parentheses.

    Example: The detective refers to himself as "the lone ranger of the casino industry" (Cavanaugh).

Let's consider Krystal's project and her decision to quote from experts. Krystal is arguing that football players must demand changes to the game because the effects of concussions are so serious. Since she is not a doctor or a medical researcher, she needs support from experts to prove that concussions are truly as bad as she says. She has chosen a source written by a doctor who is an authority, but now she must choose the actual quote to use. Here is the source, along with Krystal's reasoning process.

Commentary: Concussions in Football
by Michael Craig Miller

Consider what happens to the brain on impact. It accelerates very quickly, then decelerates just as quickly as it bangs into the skull. Nerve cells get stretched, connections between nerve cells get disrupted or sheared. Neurologists dispute the definition of a concussion, but terminology aside, all of this causes a short-term disturbance in brain function. It's no wonder that victims feel dazed, assuming they remain conscious.

But there is growing evidence that professional football players are prone to the kind of brain damage common in boxers, a condition that used to be called

Have this in my notes, but I need more detail.

Good information, but doesn't show how serious concussions are.

(continued)

dementia pugilistica, but is now referred to as chronic traumatic encephalopathy (CTE). Postmortem analyses of the brains of players who died relatively young have revealed signs of neurodegeneration similar to that found in Alzheimer's disease.

More recently, researchers have focused attention on the effect of *repetitive* impacts, which are common in football. One concern is that of "second-impact syndrome." If two head injuries occur in relatively rapid succession, such as within the course of one game, the outcome can be catastrophic, with brain swelling and death. So players are at great risk if they return to the field too soon.

Excerpted from the *Harvard Mental Health Letter*. © 2010, Harvard University. Note: Harvard Health Publications does not endorse any products or medical procedures.

Source Information
Author: Michael Craig Miller
Title: "Commentary: Concussions in Football"
Publication: *Harvard Mental Health Letter*
Date: January 2010
ISSN: 1057–5022
Volume: 26
Issue: 7
Page: 8

> Excellent information because it shows how serious the damage is and refers to "evidence." Clearly written from medical perspective; don't want to use this whole passage, though. I've underlined best parts.

> Can show how concussions can be even <u>more</u> serious by using this passage.

After thinking carefully, Krystal decides the quote will work best if it reveals the source's authority on the subject *and* supports the point that concussion effects are serious. Krystal decides against using a quote she had previously identified in order to find one that perfectly fits her ideas.

Effective writers are selective about using quotations. The following guidelines will help you make decisions about when and what to quote.

- **Do not use a quote just to use a quote.** Always have a good reason for quoting a source.

- **Avoid using quotes too often.** If you pepper your essay with too many quotes, your voice will be lost, and you will not communicate your message effectively.

- **Use a lengthy quote only when you have a very good reason to do so.** Quotations—especially those that are more than two or three sentences long—take up a lot of space. You may be tempted to fill your paper with long quotations (and thus more easily reach a required word count), but do not yield to this temptation.

- **Avoid starting a paragraph with a quote.** Take ownership of the paragraphs in your paper by starting them with your own words. Use quotes very selectively to supplement your voice and your ideas; *your* voice should be the dominant voice heard in an essay.

- **Avoid using dialogue-style quotations.** Instead of repeating the dialogue as you might in a story, use a single quotation or your own words, as in the following example.

Dialogue: Colleen said, "You're always making irresponsible choices."

"Maybe you're right," I replied.

Better: Colleen told me I am always making irresponsible choices. Maybe she was right.

PRACTICE ④ Determining When to Use Quotations

The following paragraphs are from a student's essay about the positive effects of learning to play an instrument. Rihanna has used research to support her ideas. Each direct quote is shown in bold and numbered. Read through these paragraphs, and determine when her use of research is appropriate and when it is not appropriate. Use the guidelines in this chapter to help you decide.

Rihanna's Paragraphs

[1]**"Learning piano taught me persistence," claims Benjamin Briggs.** Briggs is a classical pianist living in Chicago. Many musicians who have achieved an impressive level of mastery find that their practicing habits have influenced their ability to persist in other tasks. Some musicians become adept at other skills, such as cooking, painting, or writing poetry. For Briggs, the persistence skills he gained as a musician have affected other parts of his life:

[2]**I have used the same persistence techniques in other areas of my life. When I began running, I didn't even think about giving up after that first, awful day of heavy breathing and sweating. I simply got up the next morning and did the same thing: ran three miles that nearly killed me. I think my persistence at piano kind of taught me not to give up in anything. I am always surprised when my children give up so easily after a failed attempt at something. I remember my first time working through a Rachmaninoff piece. It was futile, I thought. But some months later, I was playing the piece decently, and by the end of a few more months, I got it.**

Not all musicians begin their musical careers enjoying practice time. Jan-Lin Chu has also benefited from the persistence required to master her instrument, the cello, but she did not always enjoy the process. Chu says that her hours of practice each day at first made her feel trapped, but she had little control over her time: her mother strictly required three hours of practice daily (Chu 15). [3]**Chu eventually became "a happy little prisoner," as she says in her journal, when she made peace with her practice responsibilities and grew to even enjoy the time (15).** She credits her persistence in practicing cello with her recent mastery of Spanish, a language she had hoped to learn for a long time. [4]**Learning Spanish, says Chu, "is much like learning pieces for cello. It requires persistence, daily work, patience, and practice" (17).**

Assess Rihanna's use of quotes. Which quotes should she leave in? Which should she take out? Explain your answers.

1. Quote 1: _____

_____

2. Quote 2: _____

_____

3. Quote 3: _____

_____

4. Quote 4: _____

_____

Determining How to Use Quotations

As you might have gathered by now, good writing requires authors to integrate quotes smoothly. You can quote in two ways. The first is to use the actual words from a source. The second is to put the source's ideas into your own words.

Whether you use a **direct quotation** (the exact words from a source enclosed in quotation marks) or an **indirect quotation** (the ideas of a source put into your own words), you must follow these guidelines.

Represent the Source Fairly

When you quote, you are providing readers with another person's ideas, and you must do so accurately. Be thoroughly familiar with the entire source—the main idea, major supporting points, minor supporting details, examples, and so on—so that you do not misrepresent the writer's ideas.

Present the Source Accurately

When you use the ideas of a source in a direct quote, you must restate the words *exactly as they appear* in the original source. Check and double-check to make sure your transcription is accurate.

Even if the author has made a spelling or grammatical error in the words you are quoting, you must include it in your quote. You can indicate that the error was in the original source by using the Latin adverb *sic*, which means "that's how it was written."

Example: Trenton Wiley writes that coaches still "fail to take concushins [sic] seriously enough."

Use Attributive Tags

An **attributive tag** gives credit to the author of the quote you are using in your essay. These tags can be used to introduce a quote, to interrupt a quote, or at the end of a quote. In addition to giving credit to the author, attributive tags can provide information about the source or about the author's credibility or viewpoint, as the examples in the table show.

Attributive Tags for Quotations

LOCATION OF ATTRIBUTIVE TAG	EXAMPLE	EXPLANATION
Before the quote: According to	According to Michael Craig Miller, MD, editor in chief of the *Harvard Mental Health Letter,* "Postmortem analyses of the brains of players who died relatively young have revealed signs of neurodegeneration similar to that found in Alzheimer's disease."	The attributive tag goes before the name, and the name is followed by a comma. The writer's degree (MD) and his position or affiliation are also included to lend credibility to his words. Since the quote is a complete sentence, the first word is capitalized. The period at the end of the sentence goes inside the quotation marks.
Before the quote: As . . . writes, As . . . says, As . . . notes, As . . . claims, As . . . states, As . . . remarks, As . . . shows, As . . . contends,	As Michael Craig Miller, MD, writes in the *Harvard Mental Health Letter,* "Postmortem analyses of the brains of players who died relatively young have revealed signs of neurodegeneration similar to that found in Alzheimer's disease."	This attributive tag emphasizes where the doctor's writing was published.
After the quote: —claims . . . —according to . . . —as . . . writes	"Postmortem analyses of the brains of players who died relatively young have revealed signs of neurodegeneration similar to that found in Alzheimer's disease," claims Michael Craig Miller, MD, an advocate of stronger safety guidelines for football.	The sentence begins with the quote. At the end of the quote, a comma and then quotation marks are used. These are followed by the attributive tag (*claims*) and the writer's credentials. Notice that the attributive tag is followed with a comment about the doctor's viewpoint, which further helps the reader understand Dr. Miller's position.

Use Indirect Quotes Correctly

When you want to briefly summarize a source or refer to an idea from a source, you can create an indirect quote by using your own words. When you put ideas in your own words, you do not use quotation marks. However, you still have to give credit to the source. One way to create an indirect quote is to use attributive tags.

Example: According to Samara Johnston, those who voyaged to the Americas had to learn methods for dealing with illness and death.

Another way is to state the idea and follow it with a reference in parentheses.

Example: Those who voyaged to the Americas had to learn methods for dealing with illness and death (Johnston).

Note that the period goes *after* the parenthetical reference. Later in the chapter, you will find an explanation of when and how to use parenthetical references in your writing.

Avoid Run-on Sentences and Sentence Fragments When Using Quotes

You know that run-on sentences and sentence fragments are all errors. But did you know that if you use quotes incorrectly, you can create these kinds of errors?

For example, this quote is a complete sentence: "Postmortem analyses of the brains of players who died relatively young have revealed signs of neurodegeneration similar to that found in Alzheimer's disease." If you joined this quotation to another complete sentence without appropriate punctuation, you would create a type of run-on sentence known as a *comma splice*. To avoid run-ons and sentence fragments when using quotes, follow these guidelines.

- **When the quote is a complete sentence, do not add it to another complete sentence. Use correct punctuation to separate the two complete sentences.**

  Incorrect, with comma splice: Michael Craig Miller, MD, would like to see stronger regulations in place to prevent concussions in football, "Postmortem analyses of the brains of players who died relatively young have revealed signs of neurodegeneration similar to that found in Alzheimer's disease."

  Corrected by creating two complete sentences: Michael Craig Miller, MD, would like to see stronger regulations in place to prevent concussions in football. According to Miller, "Postmortem analyses of the brains of players who died relatively young have revealed signs of neurodegeneration similar to that found in Alzheimer's disease."

  Note: When you quote complete sentences, capitalize the first word of the quoted sentence.

- **When a quote is *not* a complete sentence, it cannot stand on its own, even with an attributive tag. Add your own words to the fragment to make it into a complete sentence. Clearly identify the source's words by using quotation marks around the quote.**

  Incorrect, with fragment: Michael Craig Miller, MD, cites evidence of serious damage from concussions. "Neurodegeneration similar to that found in Alzheimer's disease."

  Corrected by adding words to make a complete sentence: In the brains of people who have suffered concussions, researchers have found "neurodegeneration similar to that found in Alzheimer's disease," according to Michael Craig Miller, MD.

  Note: Do not capitalize fragments that you quote.

- **You can interrupt a quote with an attributive tag, but you cannot put a complete sentence on one side of the attributive tag and a complete sentence on the other side.**

  Incorrect, with a comma splice: "If two head injuries occur in relatively rapid succession, such as within the course of one game, the outcome can be catastrophic, with brain swelling and death," states Dr. Michael Craig Miller, "So players are at great risk if they return to the field too soon."

Corrected by inserting attributive tags: "If two head injuries occur in relatively rapid succession, such as within the course of one game, the outcome can be catastrophic, with brain swelling and death," states Dr. Michael Craig Miller. "So players are at great risk if they return to the field too soon," Miller explains.

Apply Correct Punctuation Rules for Quotations

Most of the time, punctuation goes inside the quotation marks.

> **Example:**   A more effective form of punishment, writes Dr. Brennan, "is intentional exclusion."

If a question mark is part of the quotation, put it inside the quotation marks.

> **Example:**   She asked, "Why should we bother to learn this?"

When you have a quote within a quote, use single quotation marks for the internal quote, and double quotation marks for the outer one.

> **Example:**   According to Marilyn Jackson, "County officials called the new ordinance 'a necessary evil.'"

Learn to Use Ellipses

An ellipsis is a mark made up of three spaced dots (. . .) that indicates the omission of words from quoted material. Study the list that follows to see how to use ellipses correctly. If you have additional questions about the use of ellipses, refer to a style manual such as the *MLA Handbook*, 8th Edition, or the *Publication Manual of the American Psychological Association*.

- **Original source:** On the voyage to the Americas, illness was a common cause of death.

  > **Material to omit from the middle of the sentence:** On the voyage ~~to the Americas,~~ illness was a common cause of death.

  > **Use an ellipsis to show omission:** "On the voyage . . . illness was a common cause of death."

- **Original source:** With little to no medicine available, not much could be done for those who became ill.

  > **Material to omit from the end of the sentence:** With little to no medicine available, not much could be done ~~for those who became ill~~.

  > **Use an ellipsis to show omission:** "With little to no medicine available, not much could be done. . . ."

  Note: The ellipsis follows the period at the end of the sentence.

- **Original source:** On the voyage to the Americas, illness was a common cause of death. With little to no medicine available, not much could be done for those who became ill. Consequently, mariners had to solve the problem of disposing of the dead.

  > **Entire sentence to be omitted:** On the voyage to the Americas, illness was a common cause of death. ~~With little to no medicine available, not much could be done for those who became ill.~~ Consequently, mariners had to solve the problem of disposing of the dead.

  > **Use an ellipsis to show omission:** "On the voyage to the Americas, illness was a common cause of death. . . . Consequently, mariners had to solve the problem of disposing of the dead."

Give Credit to the Source to Avoid Plagiarism

As you learned earlier, *plagiarism* is using someone else's words or ideas without giving that source proper credit. To avoid plagiarism, you must make sure every source you use in your essay is credited both in the text itself and in a list of sources at the end of the essay. Neglecting to properly credit sources is plagiarism, even if you do not intend to plagiarize.

Just as with quotations, every time you use a writer's idea—even when you put it into your own words—you must give the writer credit by using an attributive tag or by putting the writer's name in parentheses after the idea.

Example: Christa Brennan writes that children who have to earn video gaming privileges are better equipped for hard work later in life.

Example: It may be true that children who have to earn video gaming privileges are better equipped for hard work later in life (Brennan).

If you continue to use information from the same source, make sure that you consistently give credit to the source. Do not move between your own ideas and the source's ideas without making it clear where the source's ideas start and end. Here is an example.

UNCLEAR	CLEAR
Christa Brennan writes that children who have to earn video gaming privileges are better equipped for hard work later in life. Children who earn those privileges begin to associate leisure time with work. By making this connection, children come to expect that they will have to earn certain recreational privileges. As a result, these children have a less difficult time accepting the hard work that is required in college and in the workplace. Parents should consider having children earn privileges such as video gaming by completing some kind of work or chore.	Christa Brennan writes that children who have to earn video gaming privileges are better equipped for hard work later in life. According to Brennan, children who earn those privileges begin to associate leisure time with work. By making this connection, children come to expect that they will have to earn certain recreational privileges; as a result, these children have a less difficult time accepting the hard work that is required in college and in the workplace (Brennan). Clearly, parents should consider having children earn privileges such as video gaming by completing some kind of work or chore.

PRACTICE 5 Constructing Accurate and Effective Quotations

Below are four paragraphs about anger management from an article, "Controlling Anger before It Controls You," on the American Psychological Association's Web site. The paragraphs discuss one method for managing anger called *cognitive restructuring*. After the source, you will see a student's paragraph about cognitive restructuring. Unfortunately, the student has not credited any sources in his paragraph. He needs to do so, not only to show where he learned about cognitive restructuring, but also to improve his writing. On a separate sheet, rewrite the student's paragraph and use at least two quotes (direct or indirect) to improve the writing and to show where the student's ideas came from.

Source Paragraphs

Cognitive Restructuring

Simply put, this means changing the way you think. Angry people tend to curse, swear, or speak in highly colorful terms that reflect their inner thoughts. When you're angry, your thinking can get very exaggerated and overly dramatic. Try replacing these thoughts with more rational ones. For instance, instead of telling yourself, "oh, it's awful, it's terrible, everything's ruined," tell yourself, "it's frustrating, and it's understandable that I'm upset about it, but it's not the end of the world and getting angry is not going to fix it anyhow."

(continued)

Be careful of words like "never" or "always" when talking about yourself or someone else. "This !&*%@ machine never works," or "you're always forgetting things" are not just inaccurate; they also serve to make you feel that your anger is justified and that there's no way to solve the problem. They also alienate and humiliate people who might otherwise be willing to work with you on a solution.

Remind yourself that getting angry is not going to fix anything, that it won't make you feel better (and may actually make you feel worse).

Logic defeats anger, because anger, even when it's justified, can quickly become irrational. So use cold hard logic on yourself. Remind yourself that the world is "not out to get you," you're just experiencing some of the rough spots of daily life. Do this each time you feel anger getting the best of you, and it'll help you get a more balanced perspective. Angry people tend to demand things: fairness, appreciation, agreement, willingness to do things their way. Everyone wants these things, and we are all hurt and disappointed when we don't get them, but angry people demand them, and when their demands aren't met, their disappointment becomes anger. As part of their cognitive restructuring, angry people need to become aware of their demanding nature and translate their expectations into desires. In other words, saying, "I would like" something is healthier than saying, "I demand" or "I must have" something. When you're unable to get what you want, you will experience the normal reactions—frustration, disappointment, hurt—but not anger. Some angry people use this anger as a way to avoid feeling hurt, but that doesn't mean the hurt goes away.

Source: © 2005 by the American Psychological Association.

Student's Paragraph

One way to master anger is to use cognitive restructuring. The key to doing this is recognizing the negative ways our minds think when we are angry and replacing negativity with logical thoughts. Sometimes by changing the words we use to describe events to ourselves, we can become calmer and more rational. Certain terms are not only unhelpful to think of, but they are also illogical. An example of cognitive restructuring is to reword a negative event. For example, if you get cut off in traffic, instead of calling the act *unfair* or *unjust,* think of it as *an unfortunate incident.* You can even make up hypothetical reasons for the event. Tell yourself the person may be going to the hospital to meet a loved one who was in an accident. This kind of restructuring can make frustrating events more tolerable.

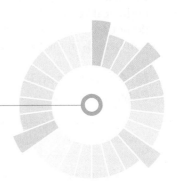

CREATING IN-TEXT REFERENCES IN MLA AND APA STYLES

Giving proper credit for sources involves (1) creating in-text references at the places in your essay where you use sources and (2) supplying complete information about each source in a list at the end of the essay. Both the Modern Language Association (MLA) and the American Psychological Association (APA) have published guidebooks with instructions on how to properly credit sources—the *MLA Handbook*, 8th Edition, and the *Publication Manual of the American Psychological Association*, respectively. Your instructor will very likely have you use one of these style guides. Following are basic guidelines for creating in-text references.

Using MLA Style for In-Text References

Parenthetical documentation is the term given to the MLA's method for giving in-text credit to sources. The parenthetical reference (information in parentheses) gives the reader enough information to locate full bibliographic information for the source in the list of works cited at the end of the essay.

Let's say that one of your sources is an article by Jeanette LeFarve titled "Understanding Anorexia." Because you found this article in a magazine in the library (not in a computer database), you can see the article's original page numbers. You wish to quote this passage from page 15 of the article: "Anorexia is actually a mental disorder that manifests in physical symptoms." To use this quote, you would find an attributive tag that fits into your sentence. The first time you use a source, you should give the writer's first and last name in the attribution. If you use the source again, you can use only the last name, since readers have already been introduced to the source. Here is an example.

MLA Style for an In-Text Reference (When Author's Name Is in the Sentence)

> According to Jeanette LeFarve, "Anorexia is actually a mental disorder that manifests in physical symptoms" (15).

Notice that the end quotation marks appear *before* the parenthetical reference and that the period follows the parenthetical reference. Notice also that LeFarve's name does not appear in the parentheses because it is used in the attributive tag. Thus, readers will understand that the quote comes from LeFarve and that it appears on page 15 in the source. If readers want to find the original source, they can look at the list of works cited at the end of your essay, find Jeanette LeFarve's name, and use the bibliographic information to look up the article.

If you refer to LeFarve's article without using her name in an attributive tag, you will need to put her name in the parenthetical reference. Here is an example.

MLA Style for an In-Text Reference (When Author's Name Is Not in the Sentence)

> "Anorexia is actually a mental disorder that manifests in physical symptoms" (LeFarve 15).

Notice that the parenthetical reference follows the end quotation mark and is followed by a period. Notice also that there is no comma between the writer's name and the page number.

Sources obtained from a Web site or from an online database often do not include the original page numbers, so when using those sources, you will not be able to include page numbers in your in-text reference. Do not use the page numbers from a printout of an article from the Web; they are not the original page numbers. If you use a source that does not have page numbers, you can either include just the writer's name in a parenthetical reference or simply use an attributive tag to credit the writer. When readers do not see a page number, they will know that the source you used did not contain page numbers, as in the following examples.

MLA Style for an In-Text Reference to a Source without Page Numbers

> One scientist claims that anorexia can be cured by behavioral therapy (Mallin).

or

> Mallin claims that anorexia can be cured by behavioral therapy.

Remember that you should not use quotation marks when you are putting an idea into your own words. Notice that at the end of the first example, the period follows the parenthetical reference.

If you use an article that has no author listed, use the full title of the work, if brief, in quotation marks, in place of the author's name. If the title is long, use the first few significant title words. For example, for a quote on page 25 of an anonymous article entitled "Fighting Anorexia," you would refer to the source as in the following example.

MLA Style for an In-Text Reference to a Source with No Author

"The clinics that specialize in anorexia often treat the disorder with a variety of treatment modalities" ("Fighting Anorexia" 25).

Finally, you will sometimes want to use a source that is quoted by another source. For instance, imagine that in Mallin's article about anorexia, she quotes this statistic from a treatment center: "approximately 1% of female teenagers have anorexia." If you would like to use this quote in your paper, you may do so, but you will need to add *qtd. in* (for "quoted in") to your parenthetical reference, as shown in the following example.

MLA Style for an In-Text Reference to a Source Quoted in Another Source

Few people realize that "approximately 1% of female teenagers have anorexia" (qtd. in Mallin).

In the list of works cited, you will include an entry for Mallin's article. Readers can then locate Mallin's article if they wish to find information about the original source.

For more information on MLA style for in-text references, consult the latest edition of the *MLA Handbook*.

Using APA Style for In-Text References

When you cite sources in APA style, two pieces of information are essential: the name of the author and the date of the source. As with MLA style, you use parentheses to show where quotes and ideas came from.

When you use a writer's idea and include the writer's name in the sentence, put the date of the source in parentheses; in another set of parentheses, include the page number where the information was found, as in the following example.

APA Style for an In-Text Reference (When Author's Name Is in the Sentence)

According to Heinmann (2004), the prevalence of anorexia nervosa among girls in grades 7 and 8 rose by 5% from 1998 to 2002 (p. 21).

Because the author of this essay is using her own words rather than quoting from Heinmann directly, she does not use quotation marks. The date of Heinmann's article (in this case, a year) follows his name in parentheses. The end of the sentence contains a parenthetical reference with the page number. Note that in APA style, you use the abbreviation *p.* for "page" (or *pp.* for "pages") and then insert the number. The sentence period follows.

If you do not mention the name of the writer in your text, include the writer's name in the parenthetical reference with the date and the page number, as in the following example.

APA Style for an In-Text Reference (When Author's Name Is Not in the Sentence)

The prevalence of anorexia nervosa among girls in grades 7 and 8 rose by 5% from 1998 to 2002 (Heinmann, 2004, p. 21).

Notice that the writer's name is followed by a comma, the date of publication, another comma, and the page number.

If no author is indicated in the source, cite the first significant word or words of the title instead, as shown below.

APA Style for an In-Text Reference to a Source with No Author

Several girls reported feeling uneasy with their bodies ("Why Girls," 2006, pp. 31–32).

Notice that the abbreviated title is in quotation marks to indicate that the source is an article (or other short work) with no author indicated. The comma goes inside the end quotation mark, and the date and the page numbers follow.

Page numbers should be included only when you have the original page numbers from the source. If you are looking at a book, you can see the original page numbers. If you are looking at a journal article online, you will probably not see page numbers, so you cannot use them in your parenthetical references. For more information on APA style for in-text references, consult the latest edition of the *Publication Manual of the American Psychological Association*.

The differences between the MLA and APA citation systems may seem minor—whether you need a comma, whether you use *p.* before the page number, and so on. However, using these systems properly shows your instructor that you take your research seriously and that you are good at following instructions.

Setting Off a Long Quotation

Both MLA and APA give guidelines for setting off long quotations so that they stand out in the text of an essay.

In MLA style, set off a quotation of more than four lines by indenting it a half inch from the left margin (the same number of indentation spaces required by a new paragraph). Do not use quotation marks and do not indent the first line of the long quote. Follow the quote with a period and then the parenthetical reference, as in the following example.

MLA Style for a Long Quotation

Educational researchers are calling for innovative ways to deal with misbehaving children in public schools:

> There are alternatives to meting out punishment that treats our school children like criminals. Instead of sending students to the principal's office or worse—calling police into classrooms to deal with disorderly conduct—schools can equip their teachers with tools proven to create safe, supportive learning environments and defuse disruption. The very things that mitigate student stress and bad behavior make a school what it's supposed to be: a healthy and productive place to learn. (Cantor 341)

In APA style, set off a quotation of forty words or more by indenting it a half inch from the left margin (the same indentation required by a new paragraph). Omit the quotation marks, and after the period at the end of the quoted passage, insert a parenthetical reference that includes the writer's last name, the date, and any page numbers.

APA Style for a Long Quotation

Educational researchers are calling for innovative ways to deal with misbehaving children in public schools:

> There are alternatives to meting out punishment that treats our school children like criminals. Instead of sending students to the principal's office or worse—calling police into classrooms to deal with disorderly conduct—schools can equip their teachers with tools proven to create safe, supportive learning environments and defuse disruption. The very things that mitigate student stress and bad behavior make a school what it's supposed to be: a healthy and productive place to learn. (Cantor, 2013, p. 341)

MLA STYLE: FORMATTING A PAPER AND PREPARING A WORKS CITED LIST

For a source-based paper in an English class, most instructors require the use of MLA style. The following section covers a few of the basic MLA style requirements. For complete information about how to use MLA style, see the latest edition of the *MLA Handbook*. Your library or writing center is likely to have a copy.

Formatting a Paper in MLA Style

Most instructors who require MLA style can immediately tell whether a paper adheres to the MLA guidelines just by glancing at it. MLA style requires the following formatting elements:

- One-inch margins on all sides
- A header in the top margin area that includes the student's last name and the page number (with no *p.* abbreviation)
- On the first page of the paper, an additional header includes the student's full name, instructor's name, course information, and date
- The date in this format: 12 February 2012
- A centered title—regular text font, not bold or underlined
- Double-spacing throughout, with no additional space between the heading, title, or body of the paper
- Left-justified text, with no end-of-line hyphenation
- Half-inch indentions to begin new paragraphs

If you are unfamiliar with word processing and think you may have trouble formatting your paper, ask for assistance from someone in your library or writing center. A staff member there should be able to help you learn how to format your paper using word-processing software. See also the student paper later in this chapter for an example of MLA formatting.

The second and following pages of a source-based essay in MLA format must also conform to MLA requirements. These pages should (a) have the same header as the first page (your last name and page number), (b) have the same one-inch margins on all sides, and (c) be double-spaced. Only the first page of an essay should have the heading and title.

In general, do not use folders, plastic binders, or any sort of cover for source-based essays. A source-based essay should not have a title page unless your instructor directs you otherwise. Use black ink and a simple 12-point font such as Times New Roman. If your instructor has not given you specific directions regarding how to bind your paper, use a staple or a paper clip. And always keep a copy of your paper.

Creating Entries for an MLA Works Cited List

For each source you refer to in your essay, full bibliographic data must appear in a works cited list. Only sources you used within your paper for ideas or quotes should be included. If you read a source but did not refer to it in your paper, do not add it to your works cited list.

The sources on your works cited list are called *entries*. If you have referred to five sources in your paper, you will have five entries on your works cited list. Each type of source has its own format. The following sections present a few of the most common formats for entries. If you use other types of sources than those listed here, consult the latest edition of the *MLA Handbook* for guidance.

An Article in a Scholarly Journal

Last name, first name. "Title of article." *Title of publication*, vol. and volume number, no. and issue number, month or season (if available) and year of publication, p. or pp. and page numbers (for print articles).

Martin, Louise. "The Nature of Anorexia." *Journal of Disease Therapies*, vol. 255, no. 3, 2005, pp. 13-21.

Note: The specific punctuation *counts*! Do not forget the period after the writer's name, after the article's title, and at the very end of the entry. Also, notice where the commas appear in the example above. In addition, pay attention to which words are capitalized. In MLA style, the first and last words of titles are capitalized, as are all principal words.

If you accessed the journal article in a database, then see how to cite a periodical in an online database on the next page. If you accessed an online-only journal, then see how to cite a work found only on the Web on the next page.

An Article in a Newspaper

Last name, first name. "Title of article." *Name of newspaper* [city], day month year of publication, p. or pp. and page numbers (for print articles).

Hernandez, Simon. "What You Need to Know about Your Teenage Daughter." *Daily News* [Marysville], 13 June 2007, pp. D1+.

Note: If the newspaper title includes the city's name (for instance, *The New York Times*), there is no need to supply the city in the works cited entry. Also, if a newspaper article extends beyond one page, use a plus sign (+) to indicate this fact. If you accessed the article on the Web, then include the publication date provided online and use a URL in place of page numbers, like this:

Ellin, Abby. "In Fighting Anorexia, Recovery Is Elusive." *The New York Times*, 25 Apr. 2011, nyti.ms/1ONQc4y.

An Article in a Magazine

Last name, first name. "Title of article." *Name of magazine*, month (abbreviated) and year of publication, p. or pp. and page numbers (for print articles).

Washington, Misa. "Not Eating?" *Good Housekeeping* Dec. 2007, pp. 35–37.

Note: When listing a month as part of the publication date for a source, abbreviate all months except for May, June, and July. A magazine differs from a journal in that magazines usually publish less scholarly items.

A Book

Last name, first name. *Title of book.* Name of publisher, year.

Durmond, William. *Clinical Studies of Anorexia.* Tranham Press, 2006.

Note that if the publisher's name includes the words *University Press*, then abbreviate those words as *UP* (with no period after *UP*).

If there are two or more authors, list the first author's name in reverse order (last name first), and then give the subsequent authors' names in regular order (first name first), as shown below:

Durmond, William, and Martina McDaniel. *Clinical Studies of Anorexia.* Tranham Press, 2006.

A Work in an Anthology

Last name, first name. "Title of the specific work." *Title of the anthology*, edited by and editor's name, name of publisher, year of publication, p. or pp. and page numbers of the specific work.

Capps, Li. "Brooklyn's Story." *Stories of Girls in Crisis*, edited by Ann-Marie Tillich, Chicago Media Publishers, 2000, pp. 90–95.

Note: An anthology is a collection of writings.

An Article in a Reference Book

"Title of article." *Title of reference work*, number or type of edition (if available), name of publisher, year of publication.

"Anorexia Nervosa." *Taber's Cyclopedic Medical Dictionary*, 22nd ed., F. A. Davis, 2013.

Note: If a reference book has entries or articles organized alphabetically, then you do not need to include a page number in your citation.

A Work Found Only on the Web

Information from Web sites can be difficult to document, especially if the item is not from an online newspaper, journal, or database. For these other kinds of items, provide as much of the following information as you can:

1. Name of the author or editor of the work
2. Title of the work (if the work's title is the same as the title of the Web page, skip this step)
3. If the work is a Web page, title of the Web page (italicized)
4. Version or edition used (if you can find this information)
5. Publisher or sponsor of the site; if the publisher or sponsor is the same name as the title of the Web site (as in the example below), then skip this element
6. Date of publication or date the Web page was last updated (day, month, and year); if unavailable, then you can add the date you retrieved the work at the end of the entry, like this: Accessed 1 May 2016.
7. A URL; do not include *http://* and *https://* when you list the URL into your works cited entry

Here is an example of an article from the Cleveland Clinic's Web site:

"Anorexia Nervosa." *Cleveland Clinic*, 29 Mar. 2012, my.clevelandclinic.org/services/neurological_institute/center-for-behavioral-health/disease-conditions/hic-anorexia-nervosa.

A Periodical in an Online Database

Use the same format you would use for an article obtained in print, except conclude the entry with the following information:

1. Title of the database (italicized)
2. A URL or a DOI for the article. A DOI (digital object identifier) is an alphanumeric code assigned by some publishers to online scholarly texts. If your source has a DOI, then use that in your entry instead of a URL.

Here is a source you saw previously (for an article in a newspaper). It has been converted to the format used for an online database:

Ellin, Abby. "In Fighting Anorexia, Recovery Is Elusive." *The New York Times*, 26 Apr. 2011, p. D5. *General OneFile*, go.galegroup.com/ps/i.do?id=GALE%7CA254713336&v=2.1&u=nysl_me_wls&it=r&p=GPS&sw=w&asid=9305cab421f0450c61419847a4863acf.

A Sample Paper in MLA Style

What follows is a source-based essay that uses MLA style written by a student, Meg Almond. You can use this model to format your own papers in MLA style. Note that your works cited list should start on a new page and should be the last item in your paper. It should include the same header as the rest of the paper (your last name and the page number). The list should be double-spaced and alphabetized. The first line of each entry should start at the left margin, and subsequent lines in the entry should be indented one-half inch.

Almond 1

Meg Almond

Dr. Hoeffner

English 0301

26 May 2014

Causes of Anorexia Nervosa

 In a land with an overabundance of food, some people starve themselves to death. These people are victims of anorexia nervosa, defined by the Mayo Clinic as "an eating disorder that causes people to obsess about their weight and the food they eat." Anorexia, as it is often called, is usually seen as a mental disorder that affects the body. People who have it tend to "equate thinness with self-worth" ("Anorexia"). While the Mayo Clinic's description is correct, it is not complete. The causes of anorexia are more complex than most people realize.

 To begin, some researchers think there might be a medical basis for anorexia. Swedish researchers have learned some interesting things from studying people with anorexia. According to Thea Jourdan of the *Daily Mail*, a London newspaper, "The Swedish research showed that sufferers of anorexia and bulimia have unusually high levels of certain antibodies in their blood. These antibodies are produced by their own immune system in response to infections." Jourdan goes on to explain that the antibodies have an effect on brain chemicals, and a by-product is that one's appetite is affected. Jourdan points out that it may be wise to reclassify anorexia "as an auto-immune

---

Margin annotations:

Double-spacing throughout; 1-inch margins; 1/2-inch paragraph indent

Title centered

Introduction

Quotation as part of a sentence

Parenthetical reference to a Web source without page numbers

Thesis statement

Transition ("To begin") to major supporting point 1

Attributive tag giving author and source

Quotations as evidence

1"

½"

Almond 2

disease (a bit like rheumatoid arthritis)." If anorexia is found to be

caused by a virus or if it is classified as an autoimmune response,

the treatment of sufferers would change dramatically.

    Another possible cause for anorexia is genetics. A

National Institutes of Health study called the Genetics of

Anorexia Nervosa is designed to research the role genetics

plays in anorexia ("Researcher"). The genetic theory is that

certain people have a set of genes that work together to create

a genetic tendency toward anorexia. These genes are often

found in more than one person in a family, according to the

genetic theory ("Researcher"). Craig Johnson directs the

eating disorders unit at Laureate Psychiatric Hospital in Tulsa,

Oklahoma. He claims that "if a person has a family member

who has had anorexia nervosa, she or he is 12 times more at

risk of developing the illness." In his words, "Genetics loads

the gun. Environment pulls the trigger" (qtd. in "Researcher").

    Understanding that researchers are not sure about the

causes of anorexia is very important. When a person develops

anorexia, she is often blamed for the disease. She is told "Just eat!"

as if she had complete control over her destiny. Since people think

anorexia is a disease that is only in the mind, they think anorexia

sufferers must *want* to be sick, or they must want to be thin.

    A friend of mine (anonymous, for privacy reasons) from

high school has suffered from anorexia for three years and is

desperate to get better. She has been

Major supporting point 2

Parenthetical reference to a source listed by title (no author name)

Quote integrated into a sentence with *that*

Major supporting point 3

Personal example as evidence

Almond 3

in and out of treatment for the disorder. "It's frustrating when people say things like 'She just wants attention.' They really don't know what it's like. I mean, if I eat two or three french fries, I feel guilty all day" (Anonymous). At 5 feet 4 inches and 101 pounds, my friend is very thin, but she cannot look at herself without feeling disgusted. "I know it's not rational, but I can't control my feelings" (Anonymous). People like my friend do not want attention. They simply cannot control the irrational thoughts that flood their minds.

Many disorders and conditions are caused by brain chemistry problems. People who are depressed take medicines to help the brain work right, and people who have other disorders such as autism or ADHD also have medicines to help change their brain chemicals. Maybe someday researchers will discover a medicine that will help change the brain chemicals responsible for anorexia. If people learn that the causes of anorexia are more complex than they realized, those who suffer from the condition, as well as their families, will have an easier time fighting it. As Robert Finn says, "Rethinking the purely psychoanalytic model has a number of implications. For one thing, parents can quit blaming themselves, family dysfunction, or careless comments for causing their children's anorexia." Research and science may someday give us the answer, but until we have it, blame is not the solution.

Conclusion

Ending with a quote and a speculation

Almond 4

Works Cited

Anonymous. Personal interview. 3 Mar. 2014. ◄——— Personal interview

"Anorexia Nervosa: Overview." *Mayo Clinic*, Mayo Founda- ◄——— Organization as author

    tion for Medical Education and Research, 5 Jan. 2012,

    www.mayoclinic.org/diseases-conditions/anorexia/

    home/ovc-20179508.

Finn, Robert. "Fallacies about Anorexia Undermine Treat-

    ment." *Clinical Psychiatry News*, vol. 33, no. 8, Aug. 2005, ◄——— Article in a journal found online

    doi:10.1016/S0270-6644(05)70609-3.

Jourdan, Thea. "Anorexia Is a Real Disease." *Daily Mail*, 27 ◄——— Article in a newspaper found online

    Sept. 2005, www.dailymail.co.uk/health/article-363643/

    Anorexia-em-real-em-disease.html.

"Researcher Says Anorexia May Be Genetic." *AP Online*. 21 ◄——— Listed by title (no author)

    Feb. 2007. *HighBeam Research*, www.highbeam.com/

    doc/1Y1-103448899.html.

Right-margin annotations:

Works cited list starting on a new page; title centered

Entries alphabetical and flush left with subsequent lines indented 1/2 inch

APA STYLE: FORMATTING A PAPER AND PREPARING A REFERENCES LIST

Professors of sociology, psychology, and other social science disciplines often prefer APA style to MLA style. As you saw earlier for in-text citations, the two styles are similar, but there are a few differences. We will look at the basic principles of APA style here. For a more comprehensive explanation, consult the latest edition of the *Publication Manual of the American Psychological Association*.

Formatting a Paper in APA Style

In APA style, source-based essays must conform to the following formatting guidelines:

- The paper starts with a separate title page that includes a running head, the page number, the complete title of the work, the writer's name, and the writer's affiliation (such as a university or a company), if any. See the sample paper later in this chapter for an example.

- A running head (the title in shortened form) appears at the top left of each page. On the first (title) page, the words *Running Head* and a colon precede the title. Subsequent pages have just the shortened title.

- A page number appears in the upper right corner on all pages, including the title page.

- An abstract appears on the second page. An abstract is a 150- to 250-word summary of your paper. It is often easiest to write this brief summary after you are finished writing the paper. Type "Abstract" on the top line of page 2. On the next line, without indenting, start writing the abstract.

- The body of the paper begins on the third page. It starts with the title centered on the top line of the page, followed by a double space.

- The paper must be double-spaced.

- All margins are one inch.

- Paragraphs are indented a half inch (except for the abstract, which is not indented).

Do not use folders, plastic binders, or any sort of cover for your source-based essay. Use a simple 12-point font such as Times New Roman, and print in black ink. If your instructor has not given you specific directions regarding how to bind your paper, use a staple or a paper clip. Remember always to keep a copy of your essay. See the sample APA paper later in this chapter for an example of APA formatting.

Creating Entries for an APA References List

A paper in APA style ends with a list of references, which are the sources you have used in the paper. A reader should be able to flip to the references page of your essay and easily find information for every source mentioned in your paper. The list of references should be organized alphabetically by author or, if the work has no author, by the first significant word of the title. If you used several works by the same author, they should be listed in chronological order of publication date.

The sources you include on your reference page must be formatted correctly. A few of the APA guidelines differ in significant ways from the MLA guidelines. In particular, in APA, the author's last name is spelled out, but initials are used for the first and middle names. Additionally, APA capitalization guidelines differ from those for MLA. For titles of journals, magazines, and newspapers in a references list, capitalize the main words, as usual. But for article and book titles, capitalize only the first word and any proper nouns. The titles of articles are not italicized and are not put in quotation marks, but the titles of books, journals, magazines, and newspapers are italicized.

The information below provides only a few of the many types of source formats specified by the APA. For complete information, consult the latest edition of the *Publication Manual of the American Psychological Association*.

An Article in a Scholarly Journal

Last name, initial. (Date of publication). Title. *Periodical title, volume*(issue), page numbers.

Martin, L. (2005). The nature of anorexia. *Journal of Disease Therapies, 255*(3), 13–21.

As in MLA style, the details *matter*! Use periods and commas correctly. Notice the rules regarding spacing—for example, there's no space between the volume and issue numbers. Also notice what is and is not italicized here and in the following examples.

An Article in a Newspaper

Last name, initial. (Date). Title of article. *Name of newspaper*, page numbers.

Hernandez, S. (2007, June 13). What you need to know about your teenage daughter. *New York Times*, pp. B11–12.

An Article in a Magazine

Last name, initial. (Date). Title of article. *Name of magazine*, page numbers.

Krantz, M. (2007, December). New solutions for daycare. *Good Housekeeping*, 35–37.

A Book by a Single Author

Last name, initial. (Date). *Title of book.* City of publication, state abbreviation: name of publisher.

Durmond, W. (2006). *Clinical studies of anorexia.* New York, NY: Tranham.

A Book with More Than One Author

List each additional author (up to seven total); use an ampersand (&) before the last author.

Williams, W., O'Connell, T., & Rouch, M. (2006). *Environmental factors in eating disorders.* Chicago, IL: United Medical Publishers.

A Work in an Anthology

Last name of article author, initial. (Date). Title of work. "In" editor of the anthology (Ed.), *title of the anthology* (page numbers). City of publication, state abbreviation: publisher.

Kennedy, D. (2002). Sustaining thought in brain injury patients. In J. T. Crasch (Ed.), *The brain and regenerative transformation* (pp. 332–335). Washington, DC: Collman Brothers.

A Work Found Only on the Web

APA requires an entry to include retrieval information—either a Web page or, preferably, a DOI designation. A **DOI (digital object identifier)** is an alphanumeric code that identifies a specific online reference. Most articles in databases are assigned a DOI. If you can find the DOI of a source, follow the instructions here for referencing that source.

An Online Article with DOI

Author's last name, initial. (Date of publication). Title of article. *Title of periodical, volume*(issue), page numbers. doi: unique identifier

Martin, J. (2003). Toward a theory of consciousness. *Journal of Neuroscience, 112,* 313–321. doi: 10.1033/0005-022X.30.8.750

An Online Article without DOI

If an article retrieved from an online source does not have a DOI, use the URL for the site from which you retrieved the item:

Braggar, B. (1997). A view from the top. *Journal of Progress, 31,* 244–247. Retrieved from http://jopd/archives/ava

Research from a Web Site

Start with the name of the Web site and the date the Web site was last updated—if available (and if not, use *n.d.*). Then give the name of the document and the URL, as in the following example.

Brady Center to Prevent Gun Violence. (2008, November 30). *Brady background checks: Fifteen years of saving lives* [Report]. Retrieved from http://www.bradycampaign.org/sites/default/files/brady-law-15years.pdf

A Sample Paper in APA Style

The references page should include a running head and page number, and the title *References* should be centered at the top. Each of the entries should be double-spaced and formatted with hanging indentation, as seen in this sample paper in APA style.

Title Page

Running Head: CAUSES OF ANOREXIA NERVOSA   1

Causes of Anorexia Nervosa
Megan Almond
Marshall Community College North

Title, writer's name, and institution centered top to bottom and left to right

Paper

1-inch margins all around; double-spacing throughout

CAUSES OF ANOREXIA NERVOSA   2

Running head and page number

Causes of Anorexia Nervosa

Title centered

In a land with an overabundance of food, some people starve themselves to death. These people are victims of anorexia nervosa, defined by the Mayo Clinic (2012, para. 1) as "an eating disorder that causes people to obsess about their weight and the food they eat." Anorexia, as it is often called, is usually seen as a mental disorder that affects the body. People who have it tend to "equate thinness with self-worth" (Mayo Clinic, 2012, para. 2). While the Mayo Clinic's description is correct, it is not complete. The causes of anorexia are more complex than most people realize.

Paragraph number in a parenthetical reference for a source without page numbers

Source, date, and para-graph number in a parenthetical reference after integrated quote

To begin, some researchers think there might be a medical basis for anorexia. Swedish researchers have learned some interesting things from studying people with anorexia. According to Thea Jourdan (2005) of the *Daily Mail*, a London newspaper, "The Swedish research showed that sufferers of anorexia and bulimia have unusually high levels of certain antibodies in their blood. These antibodies are produced by their own immune system in response to infections" (para. 6). Jourdan goes on to

Date of publication after attributive tag

explain that the antibodies have an effect on brain chemicals, and a by-product is that one's appetite is affected (para. 7). Jourdan points out that it may be wise to reclassify anorexia "as an auto-immune disease (a bit like rheumatoid arthritis)" (para. 7). If anorexia is found to be caused by a virus or if it is classified as an autoimmune response, the treatment of sufferers would change dramatically.

Another possible cause for anorexia is genetics. A National Institutes of Health study called the Genetics of Anorexia Nervosa is designed to research the role genetics plays in anorexia ("Researcher," 2003, para. 2). The genetic theory is that certain people have a set of genes that work together to create a genetic tendency toward anorexia. These genes are often found in more than one person in a family, according to the genetic theory ("Researcher," 2003, para. 4). Craig Johnson directs the eating disorders unit at Laureate Psychiatric Hospital in Tulsa, Oklahoma. He claims that "if a person has a family member who has had anorexia nervosa, she or he is 12 times more at risk of developing the illness." In his words, "Genetics loads the gun. Environment pulls the trigger" (as cited in "Researcher," 2003, para. 4).

Understanding that researchers are not sure about the causes of anorexia is very important. When a person develops anorexia, she is often blamed for the disease. She is told "Just eat!" as if she had complete control over her destiny. Since people think anorexia is a disease that is only in the mind, they think anorexia sufferers must *want* to be sick, or they must want to be thin.

Parenthetical reference for a source listed by title

CAUSES OF ANOREXIA NERVOSA   4

      A friend of mine (anonymous, for privacy reasons) from high school has suffered from anorexia for three years and is desperate to get better. She has been in and out of treatment for the disorder. "It's frustrating when people say things like 'She just wants attention.' They really don't know what it's like. I mean, if I eat two or three french fries, I feel guilty all day" (personal interview, March 3, 2014). At 5 feet 4 inches and 101 pounds, my friend is very thin, but she cannot look at herself without feeling disgusted. "I know it's not rational, but I can't control my feelings" (personal interview, March 3, 2014). People like my friend do not want attention. They simply cannot control the irrational thoughts that flood their minds.

      Many disorders and conditions are caused by brain chemistry problems. People who are depressed take medicines to help the brain work right, and people who have other disorders such as autism or ADHD also have medicines to help change their brain chemicals. Maybe someday researchers will discover a medicine that will help change the brain chemicals responsible for anorexia. If people learn that the causes of anorexia are more complex than they realized, those who suffer from the condition, as well as their families, will have an easier time fighting it. As Robert Finn (2005) says, "Rethinking the purely psychoanalytic model has a number of implications. For one thing, parents can quit blaming themselves, family dysfunction, or careless comments for causing their children's anorexia" (para. 16). Research and science may someday give us the answer, but until we have it, blame is not the solution.

> Parenthetical reference for a personal communication (APA does not require an entry in the references list)

CAUSES OF ANOREXIA NERVOSA   5

References

Anonymous. (2014, March 3). Personal interview.

Finn, R. (2005). Fallacies about anorexia undermine
    treatment. *Clinical Psychiatry News, 33*(8), 50.
    doi: 10.1016/S0270-6644(05)70609-3

Jourdan, T. (2005, September 27). Anorexia is a real
    disease. *Daily Mail.* Retrieved from http://www.
    dailymail.co.uk/health/article-363643/Anorexia-
    em-real-em-disease.html

Mayo Clinic. (2012, January 5). Diseases and conditions:
    Anorexia nervosa. *Mayo Clinic Patient Care and
    Health Info.* Retrieved from http://www.
    mayoclinic.org/diseasesconditions/anorexia/
    basics/definition/con-20033002

Researcher says anorexia may be genetic. (2007,
    February 21). *AP Online.* Retrieved from https://
    www.highbeam.com/doc/1Y1-103448899.html

Annotations (right margin):

References list starting on a new page; title centered

First line of entry at left margin with subsequent lines indented 1/2 inch

Entry for a personal interview, if required by instructor

Scholarly article with a DOI

Newspaper article retrieved from a Web site

Organization as author

Article listed by title (no author given)

CHECKING YOUR ESSAY FOR PLAGIARISM

Plagiarism—using another person's words or ideas without giving proper credit—is a serious offense in academic writing. It can lead to a failing grade and even to dismissal from college. Certainly, submitting a paper you have not written and claiming it as your own work is plagiarism—and professors can recognize such intentional plagiarism right away. But plagiarism can also be unintentional; it can result from paying insufficient attention to how you credit your sources. To make sure you have properly credited your sources, use the following checklist.

Checklist for Documentation

1. Reread your entire paper. Underline each section where you used an idea or a quote from a source. Now, for each of these underlined sections, answer the following questions:
   - Have you provided the necessary attribution so that it is clear to readers where the quotation or idea came from?
   - Have you provided a parenthetical reference for the source that will enable readers to find the corresponding entry in your works cited or references list?
2. Compare the amount of source information to the amount of your own writing. What is the ratio? Aim to have no more than 30 percent of your paper come from source information.
3. Make a list of the sources you used in your paper. Is there an entry with complete information for each source on the works cited or references list?
4. Proofread each works cited or references entry. Do the entries conform to the appropriate style—MLA or APA?

Remember that if you have trouble understanding either MLA or APA style, you can seek assistance from tutors, learning center instructors, librarians, your instructor, and online resources.

PART 4

Well-Crafted Sentences

Sentence Combining: Phrases and Clauses

Have you ever been amazed at how eloquently some people write? Some people put together sentences in such a way that their writing is a rhythmic, flowing cascade of thoughts. These people have a wealth of tools at their fingertips when they write, and many of these tools include strategies for combining sentences. Combining sentences not only adds variety and clarity to writing but also helps guide the reader in following the writer's course of ideas.

Look at the following paragraph, which does not make use of any sentence-combining strategies.

Paragraph A: Our planet is composed of four different layers. These layers have varying physical and chemical properties. The outer layer is called the *crust*. It averages about fifty miles in thickness. It consists of about a dozen large, irregularly shaped sections. These sections are called *tectonic plates*. The plates slide over one another. They slide under one another. They slide past one another. These sliding events take place on top of a second layer of the Earth called the *mantle*.

The sentences in the paragraph above are complete sentences, and they express the writer's thoughts adequately. But they are boring! Notice how similar they are in length. Combining some of the sentences results in a much more eloquent (and more pleasing to read) version.

Paragraph B: Our planet is composed of four different layers that have varying physical and chemical properties. The outer layer, which is called the *crust*, averages about fifty miles in thickness, and it consists

UNIT OBJECTIVES

After completing this unit, students will be able to do the following:

- **Combine sentences using prepositional phrases (and punctuate correctly).**

- **Combine sentences using verbal phrases (and punctuate correctly).**

- **Combine sentences using coordinating conjunctions (and punctuate correctly).**

- **Combine sentences using dependent words (and punctuate correctly).**

- **Combine sentences using conjunctive adverbs (and punctuate correctly).**

of about a dozen large, irregularly shaped sections. These sections, referred to as *tectonic plates*, slide over, under, and past one another on top of a second layer, known as the *mantle*, that lies beneath the crust.

Can you tell the difference between the two paragraphs? To write the second paragraph, the writer did three things.

- Combined short, choppy sentences into longer ones. Paragraph A has ten sentences; paragraph B has three.
- Changed wording so that fewer sentences start with *it* or *they* (words the author repeated too frequently).
- Created sentences of varying lengths. The first sentence in paragraph B is considerably shorter than the two that follow it.

These changes made the paragraph *much* easier to read and greatly improved the writing style.

The explanations and exercises in this unit present sentence-combining strategies that will help you learn new ways to create sentences. The goal of this section of the text is to give you additional tools to use as a writer. If you like a particular sentence-combining strategy, annotate it or put a sticky note on the page. Intentionally use the strategy in your next writing assignment. Experiment with these strategies. The more adept you become at combining sentences, the more impressive, eloquent, and effective your writing will become.

COMBINING PHRASES TO CREATE NEW SENTENCES

Phrases are sets of words that function as a group but do not include both a subject and a verb. Because phrases lack either a subject or a verb or both, they cannot stand alone as complete sentences. Two important types of phrases are prepositional phrases and verbal phrases.

Combining Sentences Using Prepositional Phrases

Prepositions are words that connect a noun or a pronoun to other elements in a sentence. A preposition is always a part of a *prepositional phrase*. In the following example, the prepositional phrase is underlined, and the preposition is in bold print.

> **In** the textbook, a chart illustrates important terminology.

Prepositional phrases are useful because they enable writers to communicate more information in a sentence than would be possible otherwise. For example, consider the information presented by the following sentences:

- Many monarch butterflies spend each winter in the same particular location.
- They winter in Mexico.
- They live in huge colonies.
- They stay all winter in trees.
- These trees are located in the mountains.
- The mountains are in southern Mexico.

These sentences convey a great deal of information. The problem is that reading them is cumbersome. These choppy little sentences require the reader to start and stop repeatedly. What if all of these ideas could be combined into one single, smooth sentence? By taking the prepositional phrases (underlined) out of the short sentences and joining them together, the writer can produce a longer, smoother sentence that conveys the same ideas:

> Monarch butterflies spend each winter in huge colonies in trees in the mountains of southern Mexico.

By combining prepositional phrases, we can create a much more compact, interesting sentence.

Common Prepositions

The chart below lists some of the most common prepositions. Notice that some prepositions are single words, and some are made up of two words.

Common Single-Word Prepositions					
about	as	by	in	on	to
after	at	during	into	out	under
against	before	for	like	over	with
around	between	from	of	through	without

Common Double-Word Prepositions			
according to	close to	inside of	out from
ahead of	due to	instead of	out of
aside from	except for	near to	outside of
because of	far from	next to	regardless of

A prepositional phrase contains *at least* a preposition and its **object,** which is a noun or pronoun. In the example that follows, you will see four prepositional phrases. The prepositions are in bold print, and the objects are underlined and identified.

Examples: **at** the <u>dance,</u> **over** the <u>moon,</u> **with** <u>Timothy,</u> **because of** the <u>storm</u>

object   object   object   object

Prepositional phrases function like adjectives and adverbs. They typically answer questions such as these: *What kind? Which one? When? Where? How?* Using prepositional phrases effectively makes writing more descriptive, more precise, and more interesting.

Examples of Prepositional Phrases

SENTENCE WITHOUT PREPOSITIONAL PHRASE	A READER'S QUESTION	ANSWER	EXPANDED SENTENCE USING PREPOSITIONAL PHRASE
My favorite reading materials are books.	What kind of books?	books about science	My favorite reading materials are books <u>about science.</u>
The truck is for sale.	Which truck?	the truck by the fence	The truck <u>by the fence</u> is for sale.
The shopping rush will end.	When?	after the holiday season	The shopping rush will end <u>after the holiday season.</u>
They need to show up on time.	Where?	at the worksite	They need to show up on time <u>at the worksite.</u>
She paid for the calculator.	How?	with cash	She paid for the calculator <u>with cash.</u>

How to Use Prepositional Phrases

First, use prepositional phrases to add interesting and pertinent details to your writing. Read the following paragraph, which has two prepositional phrases (underlined). As you read, can you think of details a reader might want to know that would make the passage more interesting and informative?

Paragraph A: We have all seen litter accumulate. It ends up as <u>marine debris</u> and is deposited ashore. Indeed, take a walk <u>along any beach</u> and you are likely to encounter ocean garbage.

Perhaps a reader would want to know exactly *where* litter accumulates and exactly *how* it gets deposited on the shore. We can add details such as these in individual sentences, as in paragraph B below. Notice that these added sentences have prepositional phrases (underlined).

> **Paragraph B:** We have all seen litter accumulate. It accumulates in cities. It accumulates along roadways. Much of it collects together. It collects in storm drains. It collects in canals. It flows through streams. It flows through rivers. It flows into our oceans. It is driven by currents—sometimes thousands of miles from its origin. It ends up as marine debris and is deposited ashore. It is driven by wind and tide. Indeed, take a walk along any beach in the world and you are likely to encounter ocean garbage.

The additional sentences give the reader much more information. However, because all the new sentences are short and constructed in the same way, the writing is very choppy and repetitive. Glance back at all of the uses of *it*. The writer can use sentence-combining strategies to write less repetitive, choppy sentences. Notice how in paragraph C, the writer combines prepositional phrases to create an effective and detailed passage.

> **Paragraph C:** We've all seen litter accumulate in cities and along roadways. Much of it collects in storm drains and canals and eventually flows through streams and rivers and into our oceans. Driven by currents—sometimes thousands of miles from its origin—some marine debris is deposited ashore by wind and tide. Indeed, take a walk along any beach in the world and you are likely to encounter ocean garbage.

The power of prepositional phrases lies in their ability to add meaningful descriptive information to passages.

PUNCTUATION TIP   **Prepositional Phrases**

Generally speaking, a prepositional phrase that begins a sentence should be followed by a comma, especially if the phrase contains three or more words.

Examples: Before the flood, our house was in beautiful condition.

Around the first of each year, tax preparers become busy.

Note that commas are *not* used when prepositional phrases appear in the body of sentences, even if one prepositional phrase follows another one.

Examples: The hands on the clock on the wall seemed to move incredibly slowly.

Monarch butterflies winter in huge colonies in trees in the mountains of southern Mexico.

PRACTICE ❶ Adding and Combining Prepositional Phrases

A. Add prepositional phrases to the simple sentences that follow. Add at least three prepositional phrases to each sentence. Underline each prepositional phrase.

Example: The chapter was short.

The chapter about podiatry in my medical textbook from 1972 was short.

1. Students eat.

_____

2. The class will travel.

_____

(continued)

3. Moving was difficult.

_____

4. Diana passed.

_____

5. Women can vote.

_____

B. Combine each group of sentences below into one sentence using prepositional phrases. Be sure to follow the punctuation guidelines. Underline each prepositional phrase.

Example:

- She found her wallet.
- It was in her jacket.
- Her jacket was on the washing machine.

  She found her wallet in her jacket on the washing machine.

1. Some people enjoy hunting for coins.

They do their searching on weekends and holidays.

Hunting for coins is a hobby for these folks.

_____

2. Caches of coins are sometimes buried in open fields or forests.

Usually, coins buried in such locations are hidden near landmarks.

Landmarks are features like tall trees or boulders.

_____

3. Coins are sometimes hidden underground but merely stashed unburied.

Treasure hunters have found hoards of coins in caves.

A deserted mine could be the location of a treasure trove.

Old, abandoned cellars have been known to be the spot where hidden coin stashes were located.

_____

_____

4. Coin hoards have been found in old, unused sheds and barns.

Ghost towns are filled with buildings that would make good hiding places for a trove of coins.

Any structure can be a location for a hidden coin cache.

_____

_____

5. Even a house can potentially be a hiding place for hidden treasure.

Within a house, coins can be hidden in the walls.

They can be hidden under floorboards or in an attic.

Attics are full of nooks and crannies.

_____

_____

(continued)

6. Metal detectors can facilitate locating hidden coins.

Treasure seekers use metal detectors in searching the ground in fields and forests.

Metal detectors are used when treasure hunters explore underground sites.

They are useful even within structures for scanning inside walls, floors, and attics.

_____

_____

Combining Sentences Using Verbal Phrases

A **verbal** is a verb form that functions in a sentence as a noun, adjective, or adverb. In a sense, a verbal is both a verb and some other part of speech. It may have its own modifiers and objects, and the verbal plus the words that accompany it together form a **verbal phrase.** Three types of verbal phrases occur in English:

- *to + verb* phrases
- *-ing* phrases
- *-ed/-en* phrases

Verbal phrases provide you with a tool for creating sentence variety, one of the characteristics of good writing. Learning to use the three types of verbal phrases will expand your sentence-writing ability. In addition, verbal phrases help you accomplish other writing goals.

to + verb Phrases

Form a *to + verb* (also known as an **infinitive**) by putting the word *to* in front of a verb stem.

> to + write = to write
> to + sleep = to sleep
> to + speak up = to speak up

A *to + verb* phrase is composed of the *to + verb* itself together with any accompanying words. In the following examples, the verbal is in bold print and the *to + verb* phrase is underlined.

> **To acquire** the entire collection is a worthy goal.
> He is the man **to call** about a job.

-ing Phrases

To form an *-ing* verbal, add *-ing* to the end of the verb. Sometimes the final *-e* of a verb must be deleted (as with the verb *leave* in the example below) or the final letter of a verb must be doubled (as with *plan* in the example below) before the *-ing* is added.

> find + ing = finding
> leave − e + ing = leaving
> plan + n + ing = planning

An *-ing* verbal phrase consists of the verbal together with its accompanying words. In these examples, the *-ing* verbal is in bold print and the verbal phrase is underlined.

> **Finding** the lost keys made her day.
> **Planning** efficiently, Luis was able to complete his work on time.
> The hardest part of beginning college for some teenage students is **leaving** home.
> The **winding** path disappeared into the woods.

-ed/-en Phrases

An -ed/-en phrase consists of the -ed/-en form of a verb together with the words that accompany it. (The -ed or -en form of a verb, sometimes called the **past participle,** appears in verbs such as *has written* and *will have talked.* Occasionally, the form is irregular; for example, *buy* becomes *bought* in *has bought* and *do* becomes *done* in *have done.*) In the following examples, the verbal is in bold print and the verbal phrase is underlined.

> The young widow, **supported** lovingly by her family, worked through her grief.
> A drain **clogged** with hair is one of a plumber's most common problems to solve.
> **Done** with the assignment, the children were free to play outside.
> She could work any sudoku puzzle **given** enough time.

How to Use Verbal Phrases

Verbals of all three types can be used for a variety of purposes. The explanations and exercises that follow will walk you through the process of identifying when to create verbal phrases to accomplish particular purposes.

Using Verbal Phrases to Add Information Verbal phrases can perform some of the same functions as prepositional phrases. The questions *what kind, which one,* and *how* are often addressed using verbals of the *-ing* and *-ed* varieties. For example, consider this sentence:

> Chenille Café is an unusual restaurant.

It's a complete sentence; nothing is wrong with it. However, you may wish to say more about how the restaurant is unusual. You could add these sentences to do so.

- The restaurant offers specialty desserts.
- It has French toast cheesecake.
- It offers banana meringue cookies.
- It sells caramel pie.

Now the reader has more information, but the string of short sentences makes for choppy and crude writing. Using a verbal enables you to write one sentence combining all these ideas. Note how the underlined verbal phrase below incorporates the ideas into the sentence.

> **Offering** specialty desserts such as French toast cheesecake, banana meringue cookies, and caramel pie, the Chenille Café is an unusual restaurant.

The following chart shows ways in which verbal phrases can answer questions.

SENTENCE WITHOUT VERBAL PHRASE	A READER'S QUESTION	ANSWER	EXPANDED SENTENCE USING VERBAL PHRASE
My favorite reading materials are books.	What kind of books?	books by athletes books about investigations	My favorite reading materials are books **written** by athletes. My favorite reading materials are books **involving** investigations.
The truck is for sale.	Which truck?	the truck on the lot the truck our family once owned	The truck **sitting** on the lot is for sale. The truck once **owned** by our family is for sale.
She paid for the calculator.	How?	with a credit card	She paid for the calculator **using** a credit card.

■ PRACTICE **2** Using Verbal Phrases to Add Information

Combine each group of sentences below by creating a verbal phrase that answers *what kind, which one,* or *how.* An example has been provided.

Example:

- Margie was touched by the generosity of her coworkers.
- She could not speak without crying.

Margie, touched by the generosity of her coworkers, could not speak without crying.

1. Children of undocumented immigrants live in the United States.
   They need the chance for a college education.

   _____

   _____

2. The children of undocumented immigrants are affected by their parents' legal status.
   The children often believe they cannot be admitted to a college in the United States.

   _____

   _____

3. Undocumented students are not legally prohibited from enrolling in college.
   No such federal law exists.

   _____

4. Colleges write their own policies about the admission of undocumented students.
   These policies vary from college to college.

   _____

   _____

5. Many undocumented students hope to obtain a college education in the United States.
   Opportunities exist for them to do so.

   _____

   _____

Using Verbal Phrases to Express Purpose Verbal phrases allow you to explain a reason concisely. Consider these sentences:

- Building a new house takes time.
- It also requires a lot of planning.
- It is often more expensive than buying an existing house.
- It is wasteful.
- Buy an existing home rather than build a new one!

These sentences convey the writer's reasoning, but they take a lot of space, repeat words, and offer no sentence variety. A more effective alternative is to combine the sentences using verbal phrases (underlined below, with verbals in bold).

   To save time and money and **to reduce** planning and waste, potential homeowners should buy an existing home rather than build a new one.

   Notice that *to* + *verb* phrases are often used to express purpose or, as shown in the chart on the next page, to answer the question *why*.

SENTENCE WITHOUT VERBAL PHRASE	A READER'S QUESTION	ANSWER	EXPANDED SENTENCE USING VERBAL PHRASE
The deer scrambled up the embankment.	Why?	because of the rising floodwaters	The deer scrambled up the embankment **to escape** the rising floodwaters.
Lori locked the door.	Why?	for some peace and quiet	Lori locked the door **to get** some peace and quiet.
We went to the market.	Why?	We needed some fresh vegetables.	We went to the market **to buy** some fresh vegetables.

PRACTICE ③ Using *to + verb* Verbal Phrases to Express Purpose

Combine each group of sentences below by creating a *to + verb* phrase to answer the question *why.* An example has been provided.

Example:

- Searle-Gorley Industries will produce a new kind of radar.
- They will use space-related technology as the basis for this production.

To produce a new kind of radar, Searle-Gorley Industries will use space-related technology.

1. The Supplemental Nutrition Assistance Program (SNAP) was created by the federal government.
   It reduces hunger in America.

   _____

   _____

2. SNAP provides food resources for struggling Americans.
   It helps them while they are between jobs or unemployed.

   _____

   _____

3. SNAP needs continued government funding.
   Approximately fifteen million children live in food-insecure households.

   _____

   _____

4. The program expands and contracts.
   It responds to the ebb and flow of the economy.

   _____

5. SNAP assists the food banks that so many people depend on.
   More people can be helped that way.

   _____

Using Verbal Phrases to Name Activities Verbals can act as nouns to name activities or actions: *singing, hoping, lifting, thinking.* The verbals most commonly used as nouns are *-ing* and *to + verb* verbals. Notice how the *-ing* verbal (in bold print) acts as a noun in the following example.

Plowing is a basic task of most farmers.

Because *plowing* is a verbal and not an ordinary noun, an object (such as *field*) and other words can be included as a part of a verbal phrase, as in the sentence below.

Plowing <u>a field on a hot summer day</u> is an unpleasant task at best.
object

The following example shows that *to + verb* verbal phrases can also function well as nouns.

To plow <u>a field on a hot summer day</u> is an unpleasant task at best.
object

Verbals that function as nouns often answer the question *what*.

What is the greatest human endeavor?

To pursue <u>wisdom</u> is the greatest human endeavor.

The writer could just as well use an *-ing* verbal:

Pursuing <u>wisdom</u> is the greatest human endeavor.

PRACTICE ❹ Using Verbal Phrases to Name Activities

Combine each group of sentences below by creating a verbal phrase that names an activity. Use either *-ing* or *to + verb* verbal phrases.

Example:

- People who counsel others must be sensitive.
- People who counsel others must have good listening skills.

To counsel others, a person must be sensitive and have good listening skills.

1. Veterans return from military service.
   They look for jobs.
   However, they find that landing a job is difficult.

   _____

2. In the civilian world, a veteran may not qualify for the same type of job she held in the military.
   That is the case when the veteran lacks the civilian certifications or licenses needed for employment in a given field.

   _____

   _____

3. Veterans often must repeat education or training.
   Doing so provides them with the "piece of paper" needed for employment.

   _____

   _____

4. We should find a method for officially certifying veterans' skills in the civilian setting.
   We should make veterans' transition to civilian life as smooth as possible.

   _____

   _____

5. We should show our appreciation to veterans for their service.
   One way to show our appreciation is to facilitate their re-entry into the workforce.

   _____

   _____

Using Verbal Phrases to Replace Unclear Pronouns Sometimes writers use words such as *it, that, this, these,* and *those* without making clear what these words refer to. Consider this example:

> The students planned to survey the freshman class. However, it would take time.

Readers are left confused. What would take time—the planning, the survey, or both? Replacing *it* with a verbal phrase (underlined) can eliminate this confusion. Note the differences in meaning in the following sentences.

> The students planned to survey the freshman class. However, **planning** the survey would take time.

> The students planned to survey the freshman class. However, **conducting** the survey would take time.

> The students planned to survey the freshman class. However, **planning** and **conducting** the survey would take time.

In all these sentences, the verbal phrase acts as a noun, replacing the pronoun *it* as the subject of the sentence.

Even when pronoun reference is not a problem, using verbal phrases to replace pronouns can make for clearer and more precise writing—a goal of every good writer. Look at the following example:

> Mika hopes to make it through the shift without incident. **That** is her only goal.

What is Mika's only goal? *To make it through the shift without incident.* The following sentence replaces the vague pronoun *that* with a verbal phrase.

> **To make** it through the shift without incident is Mika's only goal.

Combining the two sentences in this manner both clarifies and condenses.

PRACTICE ⑤ Using Verbal Phrases to Clarify Pronoun Reference

Combine each group of sentences below. Use verbal phrases to replace the unclear pronouns. An example has been provided.

Example:

- Mark would rather read than mow the lawn.
- He sometimes neglects it for a long time.

Mark would rather read than mow, so he sometimes neglects mowing the lawn for a long time.

1. Many students put off selecting a major and starting a degree program.
   They say it is too stressful.

   _____

   _____

2. After a year or two of dabbling in different courses, students may feel comfortable about selecting a major.
   They are more confident about it.

   _____

   _____

3. Of course, many students later change their majors.
   They should not feel bad about this.

   _____

   _____

(continued)

4. College is a good time to consider career options.

It will affect a person's future happiness.

_____

_____

5. Fortunately, career exploration workshops can help in the process.

Attending them can help students make better decisions.

_____

_____

Using Verbal Phrases to Create Variety in Sentence Structure Knowing how to use verbal phrases gives you a way to vary the structures of sentences but keep their meanings. We have seen in the preceding examples how verbal phrases can introduce variety into a series of short, simple sentences. In addition, verbal phrases can introduce variety into any paragraph dominated by one type of sentence structure. Consider these sentences:

- Jill, who had to be taken to the hospital against her wishes, was upset.
- Her car, which had been totaled in the wreck, had to be towed away.
- The emergency room doctor, who reassured Jill's family, quickly explained that Jill would be fine.
- Jill's father, who sat in the waiting room, chattered incessantly.
- Jill's mother, who was satisfied with the care her daughter was receiving, read the newspaper.

Notice that every sentence has the same basic structure. Listed in sequence, the sentences make for tedious reading. Using verbal phrases in some sentences makes the passage easier to read and more interesting. The verbal phrases are underlined in the following examples.

- Jill, who had to be taken to the hospital against her wishes, was upset.
- Her car, **totaled** in the wreck, had to be towed away.
- **To reassure** Jill's family, the emergency room doctor quickly explained that Jill would be fine.
- Jill's father sat in the waiting room, **chatting** incessantly.
- **Satisfied** with the care her daughter was receiving, Jill's mother read the newspaper.

PRACTICE ⑥ Using Verbal Phrases to Create Variety in Sentence Structure

Combine the sentences in each sentence group below using a verbal phrase to replace all or part of one of the sentences, as the example illustrates.

Example:

- ECON 101 was the course about which I knew the least.
- ECON 101 was required for graduation.

ECON 101, required for graduation, was the course about which I knew the least.

1. A ceremonial blessing of the fleet, which is given by a local Catholic priest, is a custom in Biloxi, Mississippi.

It marks the beginning of shrimp fishing season.

_____

_____

(Continued)

2. The Blessing of the Fleet is a tradition that has its origins in Europe.
   Its purpose was to transmit God's grace for a safe and bountiful fishing season.

   _____

   _____

3. Fishermen travel long distances to reach Biloxi.
   They want to participate in the blessing.

   _____

4. A procession that passes by the anchored "Blessing Boat" begins.
   More than thirty shrimp boats are in the procession.

   _____

5. The priest, who stands on the "Blessing Boat," sprinkles holy water.
   He sprinkles it on each of the passing shrimp boats.

   _____

   _____

PUNCTUATION TIP   **Misplaced Modifiers**

A modifying phrase should be located as close as possible to the word it describes. Descriptive phrases that are not properly positioned are called *misplaced modifiers* and can create confusion for the reader. This issue is of special concern with regard to verbal phrase modifiers. In the following examples, the verbal phrases are underlined and the words that the phrases modify are in bold print.

Correct:	Driving home, **Jim** saw the old tree swing.
Misplaced modifier:	**Jim** saw the old tree swing driving home. (The swing was not driving home.)
Correct:	Coming down the stairs for dinner, **Rita** smelled the oysters.
Misplaced modifier:	**Rita** smelled the oysters coming down the stairs for dinner. (The oysters were not coming down the stairs.)

Similarly, if the modified word is missing from the sentence, the result, called a *dangling modifier,* can create confusion and even misreading.

Dangling modifier:	Walking down the street, a car hit a bicyclist. (The car was not walking down the street.)
Correct:	Walking down the street, **they** saw a car hit a bicyclist.

COMBINING CLAUSES TO CREATE NEW SENTENCES

A **clause** is group of words containing a subject and a verb. Here are some examples:

- the engineer is drawing a blueprint
- that the intersection is busy
- when a coyote howled at the moon

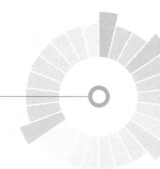

Some clauses are also sentences. A **sentence** has at least one clause, starts with a capital letter, has end punctuation, and can stand alone as a complete thought.

Sentence with one clause: The engineer is drawing a blueprint.

capital letter   end punctuation

A sentence can have more than one clause. In the following example, the two clauses (underlined) are joined by a connecting word (*so*).

Sentence with two clauses: The intersection is busy, **so** traffic is moving slowly.

clause   connecting word   clause

Imagine an entire paragraph made up of single-clause sentences. What would the effect be? Read paragraph A, which is made up of single-clause sentences.

Paragraph A: Registered nurses spend much of the day walking and standing. They also bend and stretch quite a bit. They must often lift and move patients. They are vulnerable to back injuries. Registered nurses work closely with people. The people may have infectious diseases. Nurses often come in contact with hazardous drugs. They often come into contact with other dangerous substances. Registered nurses must follow strict, standardized guidelines.

Now read paragraph B, in which some single-clause sentences have been joined together. The connecting words are underlined.

Paragraph B: Registered nurses spend much of the day walking and standing, and they also bend and stretch quite a bit. They must often lift and move patients, so they are vulnerable to back injuries. Registered nurses work closely with people who may have infectious diseases. Because they often come in contact with hazardous drugs and other dangerous substances, registered nurses must follow strict, standardized guidelines.

The variety in sentence length and type make paragraph B more interesting to read. Also, the ways in which the sentences are connected give the reader more information. In paragraph A, the cause and effect relationships are only implied. The causes are listed separately and are not tied to their effects, as they are in paragraph B. In the revised paragraph, the second sentence uses *so* and the fourth sentence uses *because*. These words clarify the cause and effect relationships.

Paragraph A:

- Registered nurses spend much of the day walking and standing.
- They also bend and stretch quite a bit.
- They must often lift and move patients.

In this paragraph, the causes are listed separately and not tried to the effect.

- They are vulnerable to back injuries.

Effect

Paragraph B:

- Registered nurses spend much of the day walking and standing, and they also bend and stretch quite a bit.
- They must often lift and move patients, so they are vulnerable to back injuries.

The combined sentences do a better job at helping readers notice the causes and effect.

Additionally, combining the following two sentences with the word *who* emphasizes the fact that nurses work with certain types of people.

Paragraph A:	Presenting these ideas separately makes the second sentence seem unimportant.
• Registered nurses work closely with people.	
• The people may have infectious diseases.	
Paragraph B:	Combining the sentences shows readers why the information is important: nurses work with such people.
• Registered nurses work closely with people who may have infectious diseases.	

By carefully selecting clauses to connect, writers can produce texts that are clearer and that convey meaning more effectively.

Combining Sentences Using Coordinating Conjunctions

One way to join two or more clauses to create a sentence is by using a **coordinating conjunction (CC).** You may already be familiar with the seven coordinating conjunctions. They are often referred to using the acronym FANBOYS: *for, and, nor, but, or, yet, so.*

Think of these seven coordinating conjunctions as sentence connectors. In the same way that physical tools such as hammers and crowbars have specific purposes, coordinating conjunctions do also. For example, *but* is used to join two clauses to show that the clauses (underlined below) mean opposite things, as this example shows:

Some Americans believe extreme measures should be taken for airport security, **but** others believe the measures violate their privacy rights.

The first clause (*Some Americans . . . security*) expresses agreement with the use of extreme measures. The second clause (*others believe . . . rights*) expresses disagreement with extreme measures. Using *but* enables the writer to alert readers to the contrasting information in the two clauses.

PUNCTUATION TIP **Comma Splices and Run-ons**

When combining two complete sentences with a coordinating conjunction (CC), use a comma after the first clause, and then add the conjunction and the second clause.

Correct:

Fossils are plentiful in central Texas, so paleontologists are drawn there.
complete sentence   , CC   complete sentence

Mammoth fossils have been found, and a camel fossil was discovered there.
complete sentence   , CC   complete sentence

Joining two complete sentences using a comma alone, without a coordinating conjunction, results in a **comma splice error.**

Comma splices:

Fossils are plentiful in central Texas, paleontologists are drawn there.
complete   [comma]   complete   =   error:
sentence   sentence   comma
splice

(continued)

> Mammoth fossils have been found, a camel fossil was discovered there.
> complete   [comma]   complete   =   comma
> sentence   sentence   splice
>
> Joining two complete sentences by running them together without punctuation and without a coordinating conjunction results in a **run-on sentence error.**
>
> **Run-on sentences:**
>
> Fossils are plentiful in central Texas paleontologists are drawn there.
>
> no comma or CC = **run-on sentence**
>
> Mammoth fossils have been found a camel fossil was discovered there.
>
> no comma or CC = **run-on sentence**

What follows are explanations of when to use coordinating conjunctions and guidelines for using them, followed by practice opportunities.

Using *for*

When to Use *for*: When you want to provide an explanation.

Why to Use *for*: To make clear which sentence is being explained.

Example: Solar technology works well in Arizona, for Arizona has very few cloudy days.

For tells the reader *why* solar technology works well in Arizona. If the sentences are separated, readers might see them as two unrelated facts:

- Solar technology works well in Arizona.
- Arizona has very few cloudy days.

When the sentences are combined using *for*, readers can see that the second clause is an explanation of the first.

How to use *for*: Find sentences that are related because one sentence explains the other. Use *for* to join the sentences.

PRACTICE **7** Using *for* to Join Sentences

Read each pair of sentences. Does one sentence answer the question *why* about the other sentence? If so, use *for* to write a single sentence that combines the two sentences. If not, explain why combining the sentences would not be appropriate.

1. One hazard of a volcano is a lahar. A lahar is a mixture of volcanic ash, rock, debris, and water.

_____

_____

2. A lahar can be incredibly destructive to people who live nearby. It occurs quickly and can travel down the slopes of a volcano.

_____

_____

(continued)

3. Lahars are generated when a high volume of hot or cold water mixes with ash and rock and starts downslope. When most people think of volcanoes, they envision a mountain with a lahar.

_____

_____

4. Rainfall or melting snow can be hazardous during a volcanic eruption. The combination of water and the eruption produces a lahar.

_____

_____

5. When moving, a lahar looks like a mass of wet concrete. As a lahar rushes down the sides of a volcano, the speed at which it moves as well as the amount of water and rock debris it carries constantly change.

_____

_____

6. The beginning surge of water and rock debris is forceful. It often erodes rocks and vegetation from the side of a volcano and along any river valley it enters.

_____

_____

7. If a lahar enters a river, the hazards will increase. The eroding rock debris and additional water can cause the lahar to grow to more than ten times its initial size.

_____

_____

8. As a lahar moves farther away from a volcano, it will eventually begin to lose its heavy load of sediment. It will also decrease in size.

_____

_____

Using *and*

When to Use *and*: When you want to add information or to join two sentences that are related in meaning.

Why to Use *and*: To put together clauses that contain related information.

> **Example:**   Geothermal heat is a major source of energy in Iceland, <u>and</u> it is used there both to produce direct heat for homes and businesses and to generate electricity.

And allows us to combine two related facts: that geothermal heat is a major source of energy in Iceland and that it is used there both to produce direct heat for homes and businesses and to generate electricity.

Writing often requires us to provide related pieces of information. Technically, we could write complete sentences for each separate piece of information, but doing so would result in very choppy writing, such as this:

> Wind technology works well in western Texas. It has been used there extensively since 1975. In certain parts of western Texas, wind turbines are visible as far as the eye can see.

Combining information that is related in meaning reduces choppiness and shows that the elements joined together are related. We can revise the previous sentences as follows. (Notice that the last sentence was *not* added to the combined sentence because it is not closely enough related in meaning to the previous sentences.)

Wind technology works well in western Texas, and it has been used there extensively since 1975. In certain parts of western Texas, wind turbines are visible as far as the eye can see.

How to Use *and*: Find sentences that each provide related pieces of information about the same subject. Use *and* to combine them.

PRACTICE (8) Using *and* to Join Sentences

Read each pair of sentences. Does one sentence provide additional related information about the other sentence? If so, use *and* (preceded by a comma) to create a single sentence that combines the two sentences. If not, explain why combining the sentences would not be appropriate.

1. Africanized honeybees get part of their genetic code from European honeybees. They get another part from African honeybees.

   _____

   _____

2. Many questions about Africanized bees remain a mystery. Researchers have learned about some of the traits of Africanized bees.

   _____

   _____

3. Beekeepers are especially concerned about the traits of Africanized bees. Manageability of the bees is a necessary condition for the productivity of a hive.

   _____

   _____

4. Beekeepers want to know whether Africanized bees produce as much honey as European bees. They want to know whether Africanized bees require more care than European bees.

   _____

   _____

5. Africanized bees have a combination of African and European traits. It appears that African traits are showing themselves to be the dominant ones.

   _____

   _____

6. Both types of bees share some characteristics. Six biological and behavioral factors set Africanized bees apart from European bees.

   _____

   _____

7. One of these factors is especially significant. European queen honeybees mate disproportionately with African drones.

   _____

   _____

8. Thus, more of the genes in the colony are from African honeybees. The genetic makeup of the entire bee population is slowly affected.

   _____

   _____

Using *nor*

When to Use *nor:* When you want to connect negative statements in a series, or, in conjunction with *neither,* when you want to connect two equally negative possibilities.

Why to Use *nor:* To avoid stringing together clause after clause of similar—but negative—statements *and* to show that two or more alternatives are equally negative.

> **Example:**   The bureaucrat was not very kind, <u>nor</u> was he particularly helpful.

1. Use *nor* to link two negative statements. *Nor* functions like *and* except that the two statements being joined are both negative. In the example above, we have two negative statements:

- The bureaucrat was not very kind.
- The bureaucrat was not particularly helpful.

These statements are similar because they both point out things the bureaucrat was *not.* Thus, we can use *nor* to link them.

2. Use *nor* together with *neither,* as in the following example.

> **Example:**   The committee members will <u>neither</u> phone Mark, <u>nor</u> will they
>   interview him.

The *neither/nor* combination negates two different options. In the case of the example, the options are phoning and interviewing. By joining these ideas together in one sentence, the writer emphasizes that each option is equally rejected.

How to Use *nor:* Find two or more negative statements in a series. Use *nor* to join the clauses. Also, find two options that are equally negative, and use *neither/nor* to join them.

PRACTICE ⑨ Using *nor* to Join Sentences

Read each pair of sentences. Are they both negative statements? If so, use *nor* or *neither/nor* to write a single sentence that combines the two sentences. If not, explain why combining the sentences would not be appropriate.

1. In democratic societies like the United States, the voting process is protected by federal laws. The Federal Bureau of Investigation (FBI) is responsible for analyzing all cases of suspected election crimes.

   _____

2. The FBI does not investigate all potential election crime cases. They investigate only cases involving potential violations of federal law.

   _____

   _____

3. For example, an individual may not give more than $4,600 to a federal candidate. Committees and groups may not exceed the limits set by law when making donations to federal candidates.

   _____

   _____

4. A donor may not ask a friend to give money to a federal candidate and then reimburse the friend. To do so is a federal election crime.

   _____

   _____

(continued)

5. A voter may not intentionally give false information when registering to vote. A voter may not cast more than one ballot in a federal election.

_____

_____

6. When civil rights are alleged to have been violated in an election, the incidents are investigated by the FBI. For example, a scheme designed to keep minorities from voting would be under FBI jurisdiction.

_____

7. While many federal election offenses exist, some common actions are not against the law. For instance, giving voters a ride to the polls is not illegal. Encouraging friends, neighbors, and acquaintances to cast a ballot is not against the law.

_____

_____

8. Offering stamps to voters does not violate any law. Giving voters time off from work is not illegal.

_____

Using *but*

When to Use *but*: When you want to show a difference in two ideas; when you want to indicate a change of direction.

Why to Use *but*: To help readers understand that one sentence is different (and perhaps opposite) in meaning from another sentence.

Example: Senators and representatives love the idea of a law to make college education free, but they will not vote for one.

But indicates a complete change in direction in this sentence. Readers see *but* and are notified that the meaning of the sentence is about to change direction. In the example, *but* functions to join two contradictory statements:

- Senators and representatives love the idea of a law to make college education free.
- They will not vote for a law to make college education free.

When *but* is used, readers can see that it is possible for two contradictory conditions to exist. Also, *but* leads readers to the more important point. The clause that follows *but* reflects the actual case, the truth of the matter.

How to Use *but*: Find two sentences that are related to each other because the idea in one *opposes* the idea in the other. Use *but* to show this opposition.

PRACTICE 10 Using *but* to Join Sentences

Read each pair of sentences. Are the ideas in these sentences related but opposed to each other? If so, use *but* to write a single sentence that combines the two sentences. If not, explain why combining the sentences would not be appropriate.

1. Most people in the United States live in cities. They depend on the agricultural production of the countryside.

_____

_____

(continued)

2. Fifty percent of the United States, 907 million acres, is cropland, pastureland, or rangeland. This land is owned and managed by farmers and ranchers and their families.

   _____

   _____

3. This 50 percent of the United States is owned and managed by less than 2 percent of US citizens. We rely on them to produce the food on which the American consumer depends.

   _____

   _____

4. Most of the time, our agricultural systems work. Shortages do sometimes occur.

   _____

5. California, for example, provides a steady supply of strawberries to the United States and beyond. Diseases such as Fusarium wilt threaten the strawberry supply.

   _____

   _____

6. When diseases affect large areas of cropland, supplies become limited and prices go up. Chemists and biologists work diligently to determine the causes of crop diseases.

   _____

   _____

7. In general, crops are planted in areas where the climate is favorable to growth. In recent years, extreme weather changes have threatened crops and made shortages inevitable.

   _____

   _____

8. Many people around the world depend on the United States to meet their food demands. Farmers, ranchers, and food scientists are determined not to let these people down.

   _____

   _____

Using *or*

When to Use *or*: When you want to offer clear alternatives.

Why to Use *or*: To indicate to readers two or more options from which to choose.

> **Example:**   Geology students must participate in a field trip, or they must create a project.

Or reveals options to the reader. In the example, the use of *or* makes it clear that two alternatives are available: a field trip or a project.

The term *or* is very specific in its meaning. Read the menu item below carefully, noticing what *or* tells you about the entrée:

> The grilled salmon can be served on a bed of rice pilaf, or it can be served atop grilled asparagus.

The use of *or* means diners will have to choose between rice pilaf and grilled asparagus.

Sometimes the combination *either/or* is used to present the alternatives in a sentence:

> Either the law should be repealed, or it should be changed.

Either/or puts a stronger emphasis on the fact that only two choices exist.

How to Use *or* and *either/or:* Find two sentences with related content, each of which provides an alternative to the other. Use *or* to connect them, or use *either/or* to connect them.

PRACTICE ⓫ Using *or* or *either/or* to Join Sentences

Read each pair of sentences. Are these sentences related, and do they also provide different alternatives? If so, use *or* or *either/or* to write a single sentence that combines the two sentences. If not, explain why combining the sentences would not be appropriate.

1. One reason Congress created the Affordable Care Act was to make sure anyone who wants health care can get it. The Affordable Care Act improves existing insurance in a variety of ways.

   _____

2. In the past, consumers could get affordable insurance if their employers offered it. If they did not have employer-sponsored insurance, they would have to purchase insurance on the open market if they were to be insured.

   _____
   _____
   _____

3. Under the Affordable Care Act, workers can continue to participate in their employer's plans. Alternatively, virtually all consumers can purchase affordable insurance plans on the open market.

   _____
   _____

4. Before the Affordable Care Act became law, insurance companies could use consumers' premiums for administrative costs. They could use consumers' premiums to provide health-care services.

   _____
   _____
   _____

5. Now, insurance companies must use consumers' premiums exclusively to provide health-care services. They will be out of compliance with the new law if they do not.

   _____

6. Preventive care is now covered at no cost to the consumer. In the past, consumers had to pay for portions of preventive care.

   _____

7. The new plan allows consumers to choose their own doctors. Those who want a doctor to be assigned can request one.

   _____
   _____

8. Many old plans prohibited people from using emergency services out of their area health-care networks. Now, health-care plans cover the use of emergency services outside of network areas.

   _____

Using *yet*

When to Use *yet:* When you want to strongly emphasize a contrast between two ideas.

Why to Use yet: To focus readers' attention on the contrast itself rather than the ideas being contrasted.

  Example: Jared is a pilot, <u>yet</u> he is afraid of heights.

Yet emphasizes the irony of the contrast in this example. *Irony* means the use of words that mean the opposite of what a reader would ordinarily expect, typically for humorous or emphatic effect. Compare the sentence above with the sentences that follow:

* Jared is a pilot.
* He is afraid of heights.

While these two sentences communicate the same ideas as the single sentence that uses *yet*, the ideas do not seem as connected as they do when they are joined in a single sentence using the conjunction *yet*. Additionally, readers cannot see the intentional irony as easily when the construction used involves two sentences rather than one.

  We could use *but* instead of *yet*. If we used *but*, the sentence would not emphasize the irony of the situation as clearly as if we used *yet*:

  Jared is a pilot, <u>but</u> he is afraid of heights.

Using *but* makes the sentence sound much more ordinary than using *yet*.

How to Use yet: When you can join two sentences with *but*, try using *yet*. Be aware that *yet* provides a special emphasis on how the sentences offer contrasting information. Save the use of *yet* for those occasions when you want to draw attention to that contrast.

PRACTICE 12 Using *yet* to Join Sentences

Read each pair of sentences. Does one sentence contrast with the other, and does the contrast emphasize irony? If so, use *yet* to write a single sentence that combines the two sentences. If not, explain why combining the sentences would not be appropriate.

1. Hackers are computer experts who are able to penetrate secure computer systems to get access to data. Some people who hack into computers use the information they find for illegal activities.

   _____

   _____

2. Most Americans know that hackers pose real threats to online activities. People continue to use the Internet for very important financial transactions.

   _____

   _____

3. Ironically, private companies and government institutions have spent billions of dollars trying to outsmart the hackers. The hackers continue to break into even the most secure systems.

   _____

   _____

4. Some people classify hackers into two groups, crackers and hackers. Crackers are the bad guys, the ones who hack for personal gain, and hackers are those who hack for fun or to show where weaknesses in "the system" can be found.

   _____

   _____

(continued)

5. Hackers may think they do no harm. Their activities can result in serious damage.

   _____

6. Suppose, for example, that a hacker is able to break into a particular bank's computer system. If word gets out that the bank's system is vulnerable, crackers may begin to hack into it immediately.

   _____

   _____

7. Hackers acknowledge this possibility. They typically say that the good they do by alerting companies to their security vulnerabilities outweighs any possible negative consequences.

   _____

   _____

8. Perhaps the best thing a hacker can do is to take a job with a company that needs rigorous computer security. Such a position would be the perfect opportunity for an expert hacker.

   _____

   _____

Using *so*

When to Use *so*: When you want to show a cause and effect relationship.

Why to Use *so*: To join two clauses that are directly related by cause and effect.

> **Example:** The cost of living increased this year, <u>so</u> employees are asking for a 2 percent raise.

So brings together a cause (the increase in the cost of living) and an effect (employees' request for a raise). Joining together the two clauses with *so* makes it clear that the first clause is a reason for the second.

Sometimes it is difficult to see the cause and effect relationship between sentences without joining the ones that are related, as this example shows.

- The new manufacturing facility was completed.
- The company held a grand opening ceremony.
- Factory workers marched in protest.

Was the grand opening related to the completion of the new facility? We cannot be sure. Did the workers protest the completion of the facility or the ceremony or something else? We have no way of knowing. When some of the sentences are linked together, we can more clearly see the cause and effect relationships.

- The new manufacturing facility was completed, <u>so</u> the company held a grand opening ceremony.
- Factory workers marched to protest the lavishness of the ceremony.

How to Use *so*: Find sentences in which one sentence expresses a cause and the other sentence expresses its effect. Use *so* to combine them.

PRACTICE ⓫ Using *so* to Join Sentences

Read each pair of sentences. Does one sentence express a cause and the other sentence express its effect? If so, use *so* to write a single sentence that combines the two sentences. If not, explain why combining the sentences would not be appropriate.

1. Child labor has been tolerated in every country on earth. It still exists in many countries.

   _____

   _____

2. The United States has strict labor laws protecting children. All children have the opportunity to go to school.

   _____

   _____

3. Companies cannot put children in jobs that involve conditions detrimental to a child's health and well-being. Teenagers younger than eighteen cannot be employed as coal miners or hazardous cargo handlers, for example.

   _____

   _____

   _____

4. In general, teens must be sixteen or older to engage in most nonfarm work. Minors aged fourteen and fifteen may work outside of school hours in certain occupations under certain conditions.

   _____

   _____

5. Minors of any age may be employed in certain jobs. They may deliver newspapers; perform in radio, television, film, or theatrical productions; or work in nonhazardous, nonfarm businesses solely owned by their parents.

   _____

   _____

6. The laws that govern agricultural work differ from those that cover nonfarm work. Teens who work on farms may have different rights than those who work in nonfarm jobs.

   _____

   _____

7. The federal government allows children over the age of fourteen to work on farms after school hours. Each state has particular laws governing farm work.

   _____

   _____

8. Child labor laws protect children and teenagers. Teens who want to work can do so without exploitation.

   _____

   _____

Now that you have used each coordinating conjunction individually, complete the exercise that follows to try your hand at joining clauses using a variety of coordinating conjunctions.

PRACTICE **14** Using Coordinating Conjunctions to Combine Sentences

Some of the following groups of sentences can be combined using a conjunction from the FANBOYS list (*for, and, nor, but, or, yet, so*). Combine the sentences you believe should be joined. Keep in mind the reasons for joining sentences: to show how one sentence relates to another sentence; to avoid lists of short, choppy sentences; and to emphasize some ideas over others. Not all sentences need to be combined. For each set of sentences you join, be prepared to explain why you chose to join them. Be sure to combine at least five sets of sentences, but join more if you believe doing so would be effective.

1. In the summertime, especially, dehydration can become a serious health risk.
    It can be a health risk all year long.

    _____

    _____

2. Dehydration occurs when your body has lost too much water.
    You have not drunk enough water to keep the fluids in your body replenished.

    _____

    _____

3. Dehydration is dangerous.
    When you lose too much water, your body's systems do not have enough fluids to carry out their functions.

    _____

    _____

4. Playing sports and doing other vigorous work in hot weather makes summer especially a time to be aware of dehydration.
    The excessive sweating from the heat and the activity can cause your body to lose fluids rapidly.

    _____

5. Being thirsty is not always a reliable way to sense whether you are dehydrated.
    You should be aware of other signs of dehydration.

    _____

    _____

6. Drinking more water will usually take care of mild dehydration in healthy people.
    Severe dehydration, even for healthy people, requires immediate medical attention.

    _____

    _____

7. Drink water before, during, and after exercise or other hard work.
    You can reduce your chances of becoming dehydrated.

    _____

    _____

8. Do not fail to drink plenty of water or a reliable sports drink outdoors during hot weather.
    Do not fail to take dehydration seriously, when you do feel symptoms.

    _____

    _____

(continued)

9. Symptoms of mild dehydration can be a sticky mouth, dry skin, headache, and lightheadedness.

   Symptoms of severe dehydration can be extreme thirst, dry skin that doesn't "bounce back" when pinched up, and rapid heartbeat or breathing

   _____

10. People generally have some awareness of dehydration as a health risk.

    Awareness on the part of people needs to be better.

    _____

    _____

11. Not just excessive sweating can cause dehydration.

    Having diarrhea or vomiting can also cause dehydration.

    _____

    _____

12. You can lose water not only through sweating.

    You can also lose water through rapid breathing, due to exhaling more water vapor as you breathe faster.

    _____

    _____

Combining Sentences Using Dependent Words

The use of coordinating conjunctions (FANBOYS) is not the only way to join sentences. Another method is to use dependent words. Remember that a clause is a group of words containing a subject and a verb. A clause that can stand alone as a complete thought is sometimes called an **independent clause**. When an independent clause begins with a capital letter and has end punctuation, it is a sentence.

Independent clause: Accounting majors must take several math classes.

We can weaken the ability of a clause to stand alone by adding a dependent word, such as *although*, to it.

Dependent clause: <u>although</u> accounting majors must take several math classes

        dependent word

When we add a dependent word, the clause—now a **dependent clause**—can no longer stand alone because it is now an *incomplete* thought. After reading a dependent clause, we wonder about the writer's point; we need more information.

Writers can use dependent clauses effectively by combining them with independent clauses. In the following example, the dependent clause is underlined and the dependent word is in bold print.

<u>**Although** accounting majors must take several math classes</u>, they do not need many English classes.

Dependent words have a variety of functions, as the following chart shows. (Be aware that many of these words can also function as prepositions or as other parts of speech.)

Functions of Dependent Words

TO REVEAL CAUSES AND EFFECTS	TO SHOW COMPARISONS	TO SHOW CONTRASTS	TO SHOW POSSIBILITIES	TO PROVIDE TIME INFORMATION	TO MODIFY A NOUN OR ACT AS A NOUN
because for in order to since so that	as in the same way just as like that	although even though in spite of the fact regardless of the fact that that though whereas	if in case in the event once unless until whether (or not)	after as as long as as soon as before now that once since until when whenever while	that what whatever which whichever who whoever whom whomever whose

Using Dependent Words to Show How Ideas Are Related

As the chart demonstrates, dependent words can help readers more accurately decipher the relationships between the ideas in sentences. Consider these sentences:

- Art history is interesting to Shawna.
- She enjoyed taking the art history class.

If we want to show that Shawna's interest in art history was the cause of her enjoyment in the class, we can use the dependent word *because* to combine the sentences. The word *because* signals readers to look for a cause and effect relationship.

> **Because** art history is interesting to Shawna, she enjoyed taking the art history class.
>
>   dependent clause (cause)   independent clause (effect)

Notice that the dependent clause (*because art history is interesting to Shawna*) provides the *cause*, and the independent clause (*she enjoyed taking the art history class*) provides the *effect:* the fact that art history is interesting to Shawna *caused* her to enjoy the art history class.

You can use dependent words to combine sentences to show different relationships. In these examples, the dependent clauses are underlined and the dependent words are in bold print.

- **To show cause and effect**

  Candidates rarely spend campaign time at schools **since** minors cannot vote.

        effect   cause

- **To show comparison**

  Just as college is expensive, life without a college degree is also expensive.

        situation A   (compared to)   situation B

- **To show contrast**

  We prepared for war **although** Congress had not authorized military engagement.

        situation A   (contrasted with)   situation B

- **To show possibility**

  A student cannot graduate **unless** he or she passes an English course.

        possibility   (related to)   condition

- **To show time**

  When they are young, children are often afraid of monsters.

  time information   (related to)   situation or action

- **To modify a noun or act as a noun**

  The final exam, **which** was given yesterday, covered the semester's work.

                   modifies *exam*

  Whoever leaves the room last should turn out the light.

             acts as a noun

PUNCTUATION TIP   **Nonessential and Essential Modifier Clauses and Phrases**

A dependent clause that modifies a noun can be either essential or nonessential. Use commas around nonessential clauses only.

Nonessential modifier clauses: A nonessential clause adds interesting, but not necessary, information about the noun it modifies and should be set off with commas. Clauses beginning with *which* are always nonessential. In the following example, the nonessential dependent clause (underlined) modifies the word *form*. Notice the commas around the clause.

> The personnel form, which is required for all applicants, can be completed online.

Essential modifier clauses: A clause is essential when it identifies the noun it modifies. If the meaning of the sentence would not be clear without the modifying clause, then the clause is essential and should *not* be set off with commas. Modifier clauses beginning with *that* are always essential. In the following example, the essential dependent clause (underlined) modifies the word *class*.

> The English class that is required for graduation is offered only in the spring.

Essential and nonessential phrases: Like clauses, phrases can also be essential and non-essential. In the following example, the underlined phrase is not set off by commas.

> **Example:**   The compass displayed in the glass case is the oldest one.

If a customer asks, "Which compass is the oldest?" the phrase *displayed in the glass case* tells the customer which compass is being discussed. Therefore the phrase is essential to the meaning of the sentence and is not set off by commas. Consider, however, the following sentence.

> **Example:** The compass, battered by years of use at sea, guided us home.

In describing the compass as *battered by years of use at sea*, the writer is not identifying this particular compass as compared with some other compasses. Rather the writer is just providing extra information. Notice the commas around the verbal phrase. If a phrase merely provides additional information, then it is nonessential and should be set off by commas.

When a proper noun is used, any phrase that describes the person or thing cannot be *identifying* because its identity has already been provided by its name. So, phrases modifying proper nouns are always nonessential and are thus set off by commas.

> **Examples:**   Abraham Lincoln, born in Kentucky and raised in Indiana, is claimed by both states as a "native son."
>
>   Lincoln, hoping to avert war, modified the content of his first inaugural address.

Using Dependent Words to Emphasize Ideas

Besides showing relationships, dependent words are used to emphasize the relative importance of one idea as compared to another. The separate clauses that follow do not give readers any clues about whether one idea is more important than the other.

- Sue had never missed a day of training.
- She could not finish the marathon.

Notice how the meaning of the sentences changes when we use the dependent word *although* to join the clauses.

> **Although** Sue had never missed a day of training, she could not finish the marathon.
>
> dependent clause = less important   independent clause = more important

The most important point in the combined sentence is that Sue could not finish the marathon.

We can change the emphasis of the sentence and suggest a different meaning by making the second clause dependent.

> **Although** she could not finish the marathon, Sue had never missed a day of training.
>
> dependent clause = less important   independent clause = more important

The emphasis in this sentence is on the fact that Sue had never missed a day of training. The point we might infer is that Sue is to be commended for her faithfulness to her training schedule.

PUNCTUATION TIP   **Fragments**

A dependent clause that stands alone is a sentence fragment. A dependent clause must be combined with an independent clause.

> **Fragment: After** I began to use a graphing calculator.
>
> dependent clause

When you make one clause dependent, join it to an independent clause.

> **Correct: After** I began to use a graphing calculator, I scored higher on math tests.
>
> dependent clause   independent clause

In general, if the *dependent* clause comes first, put a comma after it.

> **Correct: After** I began to use a graphing calculator, I scored higher on math tests.
>
> dependent clause   comma   independent clause

If the *independent* clause comes first, a comma is not necessary and usually should not be used.

> **Correct:** I scored higher on math tests **after** I began to use a graphing calculator.
>
> independent clause   (no comma)   dependent clause

When to Use Dependent Words to Combine Sentences

Making clauses dependent is a way for you, as a writer, to help your writing more clearly convey your thoughts. Use dependent word clause constructions in these cases:

- When showing the relationship between clauses will help readers better understand your ideas
- When two sentences are related and you wish to emphasize the importance of one over the other

PRACTICE 15 Using Dependent Words to Reveal Relationships

For each group of independent clauses, follow these steps to practice using dependent words to combine sentences.

A. Read each group of sentences.

B. Determine whether the sentences in a group share one of these relationships:

Cause and effect

Comparison

Contrast

Conditionality

Time

Noun or Noun Modifier

C. If the clauses do share a relationship, choose a dependent word that expresses that relationship. Refer to the Functions of Dependent Words chart for a list of dependent words.

D. Check the punctuation rules, and make sure your combined sentences follow them.

1. People today from all walks of life have tattoos.
   The general public might believe that tattoos are completely safe.
   Relationship: _____
   Combined sentence: _____
   _____

2. Tattoo artists are, generally speaking, conscientious about their work.
   They take measures to make sure their practice is safe and hygienic.
   Relationship: _____
   Combined sentence: _____
   _____

3. Tattooists try to maintain a sanitized work environment.
   Not all risks can be eliminated.
   Relationship: _____
   Combined sentence: _____
   _____

4. A particular type of bacteria has been found in hospitals and has caused infections in patients after catheterization and minor surgeries.
   The bacteria is named nontuberculous mycobacteria (NTM).
   Relationship: _____
   Combined sentence: _____
   _____
   _____

5. NTM has been found in hospitals.
   NTM has been found in certain tattoo inks.

(continued)

Relationship: _____

Combined sentence: _____

_____

6. Some of these contaminated inks caused serious infections in tattoo recipients in at least four states in late 2011 and early 2012.

   The FDA is reaching out to tattoo artists, ink and pigment manufacturers, and public health officials to warn them of the potential for infection.

   Relationship: _____

   Combined sentence: _____

   _____

   _____

   _____

7. Getting the word out to tattooists is particularly critical.

   They are on the front lines.

   Relationship: _____

   Combined sentence: _____

   _____

8. A tattoo artist may diligently follow hygienic practices.

   The tattooist may not be aware that an ink itself is contaminated.

   Relationship: _____

   Combined sentence: _____

   _____

9. Tattoo artists can minimize the risk of infection.

   They can use inks that have been processed to ensure they are free from disease-causing bacteria.

   Relationship: _____

   Combined sentence: _____

   _____

10. Awareness of the problem involving tattoo inks becomes widespread among tattoo parlor operators.

    The problem of infection related to tattoos will be greatly reduced.

    Relationship: _____

    Combined sentence: _____

    _____

    _____

Now that you have practiced using dependent words to show relationships between sentences, try your hand at using dependent words for emphasis.

PRACTICE **16** Using Dependent Words to Emphasize the Importance of Ideas

Below are eight groups of sentences. Add dependent words to combine the sentences in each group if you believe emphasizing one of the clauses over the other is important. Here are the specific steps to follow:

A. Read each group of sentences.

B. Determine which sentence you would like to make the most important in the group, and circle it.

(continued)

C. Select an appropriate dependent word, and use it to combine the two sentences.

D. Check the punctuation rules, and make sure your combined sentences follow them.

1. European immigrants colonized North America. The forests were thick, game was abundant, the water teemed with life, and the air was pure and clean.

_____

_____

2. The settlers had a pioneering spirit. The natural bounty of the land was what really invited them to push westward in the early eighteenth century.

_____

_____

3. They explored and built cities in the Southwest. They built cities in the Ohio Valley and Great Lakes regions.

_____

4. Railroads were built to create easy passage across the country. Cities in the West and Midwest grew.

_____

_____

5. Forests were logged, and plains and prairies were devoted to grain production and livestock. The environment began to suffer.

_____

_____

6. Freshwater resources were threatened. Large sewer systems were needed for the collection of wastewater.

_____

_____

7. More and more coal was being burned. City skies were darkening.

_____

8. People began to realize that the environment is fragile. It became less acceptable to continue to abuse the environment.

_____

_____

Combining Sentences Using Conjunctive Adverbs

Conjunctive adverbs (CA) are another type of sentence connector. Conjunctive adverbs are words such as *consequently, however,* and *finally.* In the examples that follow, the words in bold print are conjunctive adverbs. Notice the punctuation that sets off the conjunctive adverbs.

Separate clauses:

Robotics is a rapidly developing field. Job opportunities are increasing.

Combined using a conjunctive adverb:

Robotics is a rapidly developing field; **consequently,** job opportunities are increasing.

        clause   CA   clause

Separate clauses:

The flu vaccine is effective. Not everyone chooses to receive it.

Combined using a conjunctive adverb:

The flu vaccine is effective; **however,** not everyone chooses to receive it.

       clause   CA   clause

The chart below lists the most common conjunctive adverbs for each of six different functions.

Functions of Conjunctive Adverbs

ADDITION	ALTERNATIVE	CAUSE AND EFFECT	CONDITIONALITY	CONTRAST	TIME
additionally also besides equally furthermore moreover similarly	alternatively instead otherwise	consequently hence therefore thus	otherwise	conversely however nevertheless nonetheless rather	afterward finally meanwhile previously subsequently

Like coordinating conjunctions and dependent words, conjunctive adverbs help you show the relationship between two clauses. They are also effective methods of combining short, choppy sentences so that a text flows more smoothly.

However, conjunctive adverbs often have one attribute that other methods of combining clauses do not have: they elevate the diction of a sentence. **Diction** refers to the level of formality a writer establishes through word choice. In the example that follows, notice how the diction is affected by the use of a conjunctive adverb (in bold print):

Slang: Some people don't recycle 'cause it's a pain in the neck.

Casual diction: Some people think recycling is too difficult, so they don't do it.

Formal diction: Some people perceive recycling as a burden; **consequently,** these people do not participate in recycling.

The use of the conjunctive adverb *consequently* helps raise the diction level of the sentence.

Conjunctive adverbs are used more frequently in texts written on a formal level, such as scholarly articles, research papers, and legal and medical documents. Academic writing is formal writing, so using conjunctive adverbs is a perfectly acceptable—and often desirable—strategy to use in writing for college courses.

PUNCTUATION TIP   **Conjunctive Adverbs**

When you use a conjunctive adverb to connect two clauses, you must also use a semicolon before the adverb and a comma after it.

Correct:

Green tea is full of antioxidants; **thus,** many people drink it for their health.

    independent clause;   CA,   independent clause

White tea also has health benefits; **however,** it is not used as commonly as green tea.

    independent clause;   CA,   independent clause

Commas alone may not be used with a conjunctive adverb to join two clauses. If a writer uses commas alone, the result is a comma splice.

Comma splice:

Green tea is full of antioxidants, **thus,** many people drink it for their health.

    independent clause,   CA,   independent clause

(continued)

A conjunctive adverb cannot join two sentences without any surrounding punctuation or with just a comma. The result is a run-on sentence.

Run-on error:

Green tea is full of antioxidants **thus** many people drink it for their health.

(missing punctuation)

Green tea is full of antioxidants **thus,** many people drink it for their health.

(insufficient punctuation)

Using conjunctive adverbs correctly:

1. Make sure you are joining two independent clauses (complete sentences).

   Children need protection. Parents must provide it.

   independent clause   independent clause

2. Select a conjunctive adverb appropriate for the meaning of the sentences.

   Children need protection. therefore Parents must provide it.

3. Insert the correct punctuation marks around the conjunctive adverb, and use appropriate capitalization.

   Children need protection. ; therefore, pParents must provide it.

   Children need protection; therefore, parents must provide it.

When to Use Conjunctive Adverbs to Combine Sentences

As you know, combining sentences can help writers avoid using the same single-clause sentences over and over. Using conjunctive adverbs to combine sentences, when appropriate, contributes to sentence variety and more eloquent writing. When you see that you have written many simple sentences, consider using conjunctive adverbs to combine some of them.

In addition to providing sentence variety, conjunctive adverbs help you more clearly communicate meanings. A simple example is using a conjunctive adverb to help readers understand time relationships. Read the sentences that follow:

- Matthew was in an auto accident.
- Matthew was seen texting someone.

The sentences may result in confusion about time order. Was Matthew texting someone when he was in the auto accident? Was Matthew texting someone before or after the auto accident? Using a conjunctive adverb can clarify the confusion:

Matthew was in an auto accident; **afterward**, he was seen texting someone.

Matthew was in an auto accident; **previously**, he was seen texting someone.

The use of either *afterward* or *previously* clears up the confusion about when Matthew had the accident in relation to when he was seen drinking.

As you practice using conjunctive adverbs, find sentences that could be confusing to readers. Determine whether a conjunctive adverb might help clarify the meaning of the sentences or even make the relationships between sentences clearer. Practice using conjunctive adverbs to link clauses together when appropriate.

Using Conjunctive Adverbs to Show How Ideas Are Related

As the Functions of Conjunctive Adverbs chart demonstrates, each conjunctive adverb indicates a particular relationship. The sentences that follow provide an example for each of the types of relationships conjunctive adverbs can demonstrate.

- **To add information**
  Videos can help explain concepts; **additionally,** online sites can be effective tools.
  <u>statement A</u>   added to   <u>statement B</u>

- **To reveal alternatives**
  Students can study in the library; **alternatively,** they can study at home.
  <u>option A</u>   compared with   <u>option B</u>

- **To indicate cause and effect**
  The sun emits radiation; **thus,** using sunblock provides important protection.
  <u>cause</u>   <u>effect</u>

- **To indicate conditionality**
  Children must be taught manners; **otherwise,** they will behave like animals.
  <u>condition</u>   related to   <u>result</u>

- **To show contrast**
  The flu shot is supposed to be effective; **however,** its effectiveness is never universal.
  <u>idea A</u>   contrasted to   <u>idea B</u>

- **To indicate a time relationship**
  The jurors filed out of the courtroom; **meanwhile,** the defendant sat anxiously.
  <u>time information showing simultaneous events</u>

PRACTICE **17** Using Conjunctive Adverbs

Read each of the following groups of sentences. Use conjunctive adverbs to join the sentences when doing so will clarify meanings, show relationships, or eliminate choppiness. Using the Functions of Conjunctive Adverbs chart, select the appropriate conjunctive adverb for each group. Remember to use correct punctuation for each sentence you compose.

1. Millions of Americans are looking for jobs online.
The Internet has become fertile ground for phony business opportunity schemes.

_____

_____

2. These schemes sound like excellent opportunities.
The company names sound legitimate.

_____

_____

3. The wages promised by some of the employers are too good to be true.
Desperate job seekers hold out hope that the jobs are real.

_____

_____

4. Unfortunately, most of these jobs are not good opportunities at all.
They are actually schemes to swindle, not help, job applicants.

_____

_____

(continued)

5. Often, to apply, one must provide a great deal of personal information.

   Applicants routinely give out their driver's license number or social security number.

   _____

   _____

6. People who are "hired" by these companies receive a paycheck from a company outside the United States.

   The explanation is that the employer does not have any banking set up in the United States.

   _____

7. The amount of the check is significantly more than the employee is owed for salary.

   The employee is instructed to deposit the check and wire the overpayment back to the employer's bank.

   _____

   _____

   _____

8. The employee does as instructed.

   The employer's check is found to be fraudulent, and the swindled "employee" loses his or her money.

   _____

   _____

COMBINED PRACTICE

Use coordinating conjunctions, dependent words, and conjunctive adverbs to combine the sentences in at least ten of the following groups. Be prepared to explain why you decided to combine the sentences and why you chose the method and the particular combining word that you used.

1. Cybersecurity, phishing, worms, Trojan horses, hackers, and viruses seem to be in the news every day.

   Are these threats really serious?

   _____

2. Internet experts say that these threats are serious.

   You should take steps to protect yourself from being a victim of online privacy theft.

   _____

   _____

3. The first step in protecting yourself is to recognize the risks.

   Become familiar with some of the terminology associated with cybersecurity.

   _____

4. Hackers are everywhere.

   The goal of most of them is to exploit weaknesses in software and computer systems for their own gain.

   _____

   _____

(continued)

5. Their intentions are sometimes fairly benign and motivated primarily by curiosity.
   Their actions are typically in violation of the intended use of the systems that they are exploiting.

   _____

   _____

6. Their meddling often creates problems for users.
   These problems can include the downloading of malicious code such as viruses, worms, and Trojan horses.

   _____

7. Some people use the terms *viruses, worms,* and *Trojan horses* interchangeably.
   Each has unique characteristics.

   _____

   _____

8. A virus is a type of malicious code.
   A virus requires the user to actually do something before it infects a computer.

   _____

   _____

9. One action that could activate a virus is opening an e-mail attachment.
   Going to a particular Web page is another action that could trigger the downloading of a virus.

   _____

   _____

10. A worm is similar to a virus by design and is considered to be a subclass of a virus.
    Unlike a virus, worms have the capability to spread without any human action.

    _____

    _____

11. The victim computer becomes infected.
    The worm will attempt to locate and infect other computers.

    _____

    _____

12. Worms can spread through your entire computer and others' computers.
    Viruses cannot spread from one computer to another.

    _____

    _____

13. A Trojan horse program is software that appears to be legitimate and useful.
    It will actually do damage once installed or run on a computer.

    _____

    _____

14. Users on the receiving end of a Trojan horse are frequently tricked into opening the program.
    They believe that they are receiving legitimate software or files from a legitimate source.

    _____

    _____

15. For example, a program may claim to be speeding up your computer.
    It may actually be sending your confidential information to a data thief.

    _____

    _____

(continued)

16. Spyware is sneaky software.

It piggybacks on downloadable software like screen savers, games, and music files.

_____

_____

17. Spyware sends information about what you are doing on the Internet to a third party.

The third party can then target you with pop-up ads and other pesky intrusions.

_____

_____

18. Browsers enable you to block pop-up ads.

You can also install anti-spyware programs to stop other threats to your privacy.

_____

_____

19. Viruses, worms, and Trojan horses are collectively referred to as malware.

The word _malware_ is derived from a combination of _malicious_ and _software_.

_____

_____

20. Having effective antivirus and spyware-removal software on your computer is a good start to protecting yourself from these intruders.

A practical protective step to take is to stay away from disreputable and unknown sites.

_____

_____

_____

COMBINED PRACTICE 2

What follows is the first draft of an essay. It contains very choppy sentences, many repeated words, and very few sentence connectors. Improve the draft by doing the following:

- Use coordinating conjunctions, dependent words, and conjunctive adverbs to combine some of the sentences in the essay.
- Make additional wording changes to clarify ideas.
- Make additional wording changes to avoid repetition.
- Rearrange ideas, if necessary.
- Make any other changes that will produce more eloquent writing.

Be sure to make at least six combined sentences. Write the finished draft on a separate sheet of paper.

True College Prerequisites

College students know what prerequisites are. They are courses. Students must take prerequisite courses before certain other courses. For example, English Composition I is a prerequisite. It must be taken before English Composition II. Other types of prerequisites exist as well. These other types of prerequisites are abilities that students should have

(continued)

developed even before starting college. They include a strong work ethic. The ability to be goal-oriented is a prerequisite. The ability to be organized is a prerequisite.

Not all college students are used to studying. Some high schools are not academically demanding. Others are. Some students enter college with a strong work ethic. Other students do not. *Work ethic* refers to a student's willingness to work hard. Passing college classes requires a work ethic. The work ethic should be strong. For example, learning a foreign language requires daily work. Some students have never studied on an every day basis. This requirement will be a change for those students. The same requirement is true of other courses. Math requires daily study. Some fast-paced courses require daily study. Students will need a strong work ethic. It will be required of them each week. It may be required each day.

Another prerequisite for college is to be goal-oriented. Students who are goal-oriented are good at setting goals. They set goals that are attainable. They create strategies to reach their goals. They troubleshoot their strategies to make sure their plans are working. For instance, goal-oriented students often plan out their semester class schedule far in advance of the registration period. They like to see what is coming. They like to plan for the future. Keeping the future in mind helps them be more motivated with the daily difficulties of college.

The ability to be organized is a prerequisite that can really be helpful in college. Organization alone can help students pass classes. Not being organized can cause students to miss due dates. It can cause students to misplace important papers. It can cause students to fail to set aside enough time for studying. Not being an organized thinker can also cause problems. Some students cannot organize their notes. They cannot organize the information presented in class. They cannot organize the information they read. Being able to organize course materials is important. It helps students manage the materials. It helps students condense the materials. It makes the materials easier to think about. It makes the materials easier to memorize.

Yes, some skills are prerequisites for college success. Students need these skills to succeed. Starting college with a strong work ethic is indispensable. Staying goal-oriented is vitally important. Being able to organize one's life is essential. Being able to organize one's course materials is crucial. These prerequisite skills are vital. They may make the difference between success and failure.

UNIT

2

"The travelers were ready for the desert/dessert."
Choosing the right word can make a difference in
how well you communicate your ideas.

Spelling and Word Choice

Easy access to software and smartphone apps that check spelling as we write
has made spelling a much less crucial skill than it once was. Even so, spelling
remains significant. Indeed, the fact that technological tools have made correct spelling more commonplace makes it all the more important that writers
get it right! Today's readers simply expect correct spelling.

In this unit we emphasize the aspects of spelling that computers cannot
fix for us. First, we consider some broad strategies for improving spelling
and look at a few spelling rules. Then, we present some specific words that
are frequently confused. The unit concludes with a discussion of the use of
clichés and slang.

UNIT OBJECTIVES

*After completing this unit, students
will be able to do the following:*

- **Use four strategies for improving
  spelling.**

- **Apply four basic spelling rules.**

- **Use homophones and commonly
  confused words correctly.**

- **Avoid using clichés and slang
  in professional and academic
  writing.**

USING SPELLING STRATEGIES

Here are four useful strategies for improving your spelling.

- **Read.** Reading has a huge impact on spelling. If you see a word over and
  over, your mind grips that visual representation of the word.
- **Use a spell-checker.** Virtually all word-processing software packages
  include a spell-checker.

- **Use a dictionary.** No longer do you need to lug around a twenty-pound dictionary. Free, excellent, and easy-to-use dictionaries are available online and as mobile apps. Three good online dictionaries are *Merriam-Webster*, *Oxford Dictionaries*, and the *American Heritage Dictionary*.
- **Make a list of words you commonly misspell.** You will be surprised how quickly you will remember the correct spelling of a word once you make a point of learning it.

APPLYING SPELLING RULES

The spelling of a great many words follows specific rules. These four basic spelling rules will help you improve your spelling.

The Order of *i* and *e*

You probably remember the little rhyme about spelling words that contain *-ie* or *-ei*:

Write *i* before *e*,

Except after *c*,

Or when it sounds like an *a*,

As in *neighbor* and *weigh*.

Examples: *i* **before** *e*: relief, believe, niece, chief

except after c: receive, ceiling, conceit, deceit

when it sounds like an *a*:   vein, sleigh, weigh, neigh

Several exceptions to the rule do exist. The list below contains virtually all of the exceptions that you are likely to use in your writing.

ancient	deficient	glacier	science
atheism	efficient	height	seize
caffeine	either	heist	society
codeine	feisty	leisure	sovereign
conscience	foreign	neither	sufficient
counterfeit	forfeit	protein	weird

Final -e and Suffixes

Drop the final *-e* before a suffix that begins with a vowel, but retain the final *-e* before a suffix that begins with a consonant.

Examples: arrive + ing = arriving   brave + ly = bravely

guide + ance = guidance   achieve + ment = achievement

date + ing = dating   like + ness = likeness

Final -y and Suffixes

Change a final *-y* that is preceded by a consonant to *-i* before a suffix (with one exception, as noted).

Examples: rely + -ance = reliance   study + -ed = studied

supply + -er = supplier   carry + -es = carries

beauty + -ful = beautiful   ugly + -est = ugliest

Exception: If the suffix begins with -*i* (as with -*ing*), then the final -*y* is retained:

rally + -ing = rallying   deny + -ing = denying

If the word ends in a -*y* that is preceded by a vowel, then add the suffix without making any change to the root word.

Examples: annoy + -ance = annoyance   destroy + -ed = destroyed

betray + -er = betrayer   monkey + -s = monkeys

joy + -ful = joyful   delay + -ing = delaying

Final Consonant and Suffixes

When adding a suffix that begins with a vowel, double a final single consonant if both of these criteria are met:

- A single vowel precedes the consonant.
- The word has only one syllable, or the last syllable is accented.

Examples in which both criteria are met:

grab + -ing = grabbing   submit + -ed = submitted   refer + -al = referral

Examples in which both criteria are *not* met:

pool + -ed = pooled (The final consonant is preceded by more than one vowel.)

mourn + -ful = mournful (The final consonant is preceded by another consonant.)

benefit + -ed = benefited (The last syllable is not accented.)

MASTERING COMMON USAGE ERRORS

Sometimes writing mistakes occur because a writer confuses one word for another; these kinds of missteps are called *usage errors*. Some spelling errors are usage errors; in other words, knowing which word is the proper one to use can often enable you to avoid a spelling mistake.

Frequently, the kind of confusion involved is a function of two words that sound the same (or almost the same) but are spelled differently (and are two entirely different words). Each of the words in such a pair is called a **homophone.** (We will include in this category "near homophones"—words that are not properly pronounced in an identical manner but are close enough to create usage problems.) However, not all usage mix-ups happen because words have similar pronunciations; we will address those other kinds of usage difficulties separately.

Homophones

Spell-checkers will, at best, detect only a few homophone errors. That is why learning common homophones is crucial.

accept/except

accept = (verb) to receive; to take in

except = (preposition) other than

Examples: I *accept* your apology.

I will buy everything on this table *except* the vase.

Quick Check   Fill in the blanks with the correct words.

_____ criticism! Doing so, while difficult, can pay huge dividends. If your boss tells you that everything in your performance is great _____ your punctuality, take that as encouragement to be on time rather than as condemnation of the job you are doing.

advice/advise

advice = (noun) a recommendation as a guide to action; words of counsel

advise = (verb) to give advice; to counsel; to offer a suggestion

Examples: I strongly recommend that you take his *advice*.

The attorney will *advise* you regarding this matter.

Quick Check   Fill in the blanks with the correct words.

How would you _____ me to proceed? What is your _____? No matter what your instructions are, I will follow your _____.

affect/effect

affect = (verb) to influence or change

effect = (noun) result

Examples: The dark weather *affects* my moods.

Sunshine has a positive *effect* on me.

Quick Check   Fill in the blanks with the correct words.

The sun can _____ different people in different ways. One _____ that the sun has on some people is to contribute to their being in a good mood. Another _____ it can have is to cause sunburn.

allot/a lot

allot = (verb) to provide

a lot = (noun) a group of items; many

Note: *Alot* is an incorrect spelling of *a lot* and is not a word.

Examples: The professor will *allot* the students one hour for the exam.

A lot of items are in the lost and found bin.

Quick Check   Fill in the blanks with the correct words.

The judge will _____ each person six jars. The contest requires that we fill those jars with as many pennies as we can. Without question, each of the jars will hold _____ of pennies!

---

all ready/already

all ready = (adverbial phrase) entirely prepared; set to proceed

already = (adverb) has occurred previously

Examples: The kids were *all ready* for the trip. (Better: All of the kids were *ready* for the trip.)

I have *already* read this book.

Quick Check   Fill in the blank with the correct word.

We have _____ learned this material.

---

bare/bear

bare = (verb) to reveal

    (adjective) to be in a revealed state

bear = (verb) to support or carry (both literally and figuratively)

    (noun) a very large mammal with stocky legs, a long snout, and shaggy fur

Examples: My *bare* arms were cold in the auditorium.

The old *bear* is literally starving; I cannot *bear* to see it suffer so.

Quick Check   Fill in the blanks with the correct words.

The refrigerator is _____, but the pantry shelves are so loaded with dry goods that I'm not sure that they can _____ the weight. However, I simply cannot _____ going to the grocery store during the weekend, so we will just need to make do with canned food for now.

---

brake/break

brake = (noun) the part of a vehicle that causes slowing and stopping

    (verb) to slow or stop something, such as a vehicle

break = (noun) a recess period; a fracture (as in a bone)

    (verb) to split into pieces; to interrupt; to take a recess

Examples: The *brakes* in his jalopy were dangerously worn.

When approaching a stop sign, you should *brake* smoothly.

We should probably take a fifteen-minute *break*.

The kids will *break* the glass figurines if they play with them.

Quick Check   Fill in the blanks with the correct words.

I was afraid that my car would _____ down. I took it to the shop to have the _____

checked. They said it would be an hour before anyone could look at the car because

all of the mechanics were on _____.   The shop boss said that before they do any

work, they will drive the car and _____ hard to test the system.

breath/breathe

breath = (noun) a single inhalation and exhalation of air
breathe = (verb) to inhale and exhale air

Examples: She took a *breath* of air.

She needs to *breathe* the fresh air.

Quick Check   Fill in the blanks with the correct words.

The bus was so hot that it was hard to _____.   I felt as though I could not take

even a single _____.

cite/sight/site

cite = (verb) to make reference to; to create a *citation*
sight = (noun) the faculty of vision; something seen
   (verb) to see something; to adjust the aiming apparatus (as of a gun)
site = (noun) a location; a piece of land

Examples: You should always *cite* the sources used in an academic paper; in addition, you need to use the proper form for all of your *citations*.

The Christmas tree with all of its ornaments and lights was quite a *sight*.

The home is located at a very convenient *site*—near a bank, a pharmacy, and a grocery store. (The house is in a convenient *situation*.)

Quick Check   Fill in the blanks with the correct words.

The _____ where the mammoths were found is a riverbed. It was quite a _____ to see so many people working to uncover the fossilized bones. The articles that the paleontologists write about the work being done there will no doubt frequently be _____ (past tense) in scholarly journals in the future.

clothes/cloths

clothes = (plural noun) attire, apparel, garments
cloths = (noun, plural of *cloth*) pieces of fabric, such as those used for cleaning

Examples: Back-to-school time means that we get to shop for *clothes*!

Cloths work far better than paper towels for some tasks.

Quick Check   Fill in the blanks with the correct words.

When I am ready to clean the house, I put on some old _____, find some _____ to dust with, get out the vacuum cleaner, and line up all of my cleaning products on the table.

coarse/course

coarse = (adjective) rough; vulgar; unsophisticated (as in *coarse* humor)
course = (noun) route; sequence; an academic class
    (verb) to run through (as in blood coursing through a person's veins)

Examples: The *coarse* sandpaper was perfect for the job.

Which *course* of action should we take?

I am taking a *course* at the local community college.

The river *courses* through the lush valley.

Quick Check   Fill in the blanks with the correct words.

In one of my nursing _____, I learned something that pertained to my own health! I will need a _____ of antibiotics to get rid of a persistent rash. The rash dries out my skin and makes it feel _____.

complement/compliment

complement = (noun) something that completes or makes perfect
    (verb) to provide an addition that fits well or is appropriate

compliment = (noun) an expression of approval, esteem, or acknowledgment

(verb) to offer praise, admiration, or respect

Examples: Some people think milk is a perfect *complement* to cookies in the same way that ice cream exquisitely *complements* apple pie.

I never expected to receive a *compliment* from my boss, so I was shocked when she said to me in front of the entire work group, "I'd really like to *compliment* you on your performance this quarter."

Quick Check   Fill in the blanks with the correct words.

I couldn't wait to _____ the host on the reception, which was such a nice

_____ to the lecture. I was delighted to receive several _____ for the

dip and crackers I brought to the reception. Raspberry preserves are a wonderful

_____ to cream cheese in a dip.

conscience/conscious

conscience = (noun) a person's intuitive sense of right and wrong

conscious = (adjective) awake; intentional

Examples: My *conscience* tells me that I really should donate blood.

The hockey player was *conscious* after his fall.

I made a *conscious* decision to contribute more to charity this year.

Quick Check   Fill in the blanks with the correct words.

The defendant was _____ of the crowd of angry people behind him. Even so, his

_____ did not prompt him to confess.

decent/descent/dissent

decent = (adjective) proper; appropriate; satisfactory

descent = (noun) downward movement; downward slope

dissent = (verb) to disagree; to differ in opinion

(noun) the expression of an opposing view

Examples: The dress code required everyone to wear *decent* clothing.

The airplane began its *descent* into Chicago.

The senator expressed her *dissent* regarding the proposed bill.

Quick Check   Fill in the blanks with the correct words.

The used book of mythology that I bought recently is in _____ condition. It

includes my favorite myth—the story of Hercules's _____ into the underworld.

Although almost all of the reviews were glowing, I did read a couple that expressed

_____ as to its being a great collection of stories.

desert/dessert

desert = (noun) a dry, arid area, typically with a very warm climate

dessert = (noun) a sweet treat, usually the last course in a meal

Examples: Many types of cactus thrive in the *desert*.

I'd like strawberry cheesecake for *dessert*.

Quick Check   Fill in the blanks with the correct words.

A restaurant in the _____ would probably earn more revenue from selling cold

drinks than from serving coffee and _____.

fair/fare

fair = (adjective) impartial or just; not cloudy (with reference to weather)

(noun) an exhibition or exposition, such as a county *fair*

fare = (noun) a fee

(verb) to experience good or bad fortune or treatment

Examples: Professor Hendricks is tough but *fair*.

The children want to go to the state *fair* because they love the rides.

I have money enough for train *fare*, but I don't have enough for an airline ticket.

Amy did not win a medal, but she did not *fare* too badly at the tournament.

Quick Check   Fill in the blanks with the correct words.

Having the _____ occur right after school starts in the fall is not _____! School kids

want to be able to attend. Moreover, for the city to raise the standard bus _____

during this time of the year is also not _____.

farther/further

farther = (adjective, adverb) to a greater length or distance (literally)

further = (adjective, adverb) to a greater degree (figuratively)

Examples: Soldier: "We marched *farther* today than you told us we would."

Sergeant: "If you complain *further*, I'll make you do it again!"

Quick Check   Fill in the blanks with the correct words.

I had to drive _____ to get to the college library than to the public library.

However, going to the library on campus will enable me to go much _____ with

my research than I could have gone at the public library.

forth/fourth

forth = (adverb) onward; forward

fourth = (adjective) something that is number four in a series

Examples: She stretched *forth* her hands as she offered a blessing on the couple's marriage.

The sprinter did not receive a medal because he finished *fourth*.

Quick Check   Fill in the blanks with the correct words.

Although this campaign would represent their _____ attempt, the emperor

exhorted his army: "Go _____ and conquer the enemy!"

hear/here

hear = (verb) to perceive sound

here = (adverb) in or at this place

Examples: Her ability to *hear* was compromised by ear infections.

We will have the trial *here* in our city.

Quick Check   Fill in the blanks with the correct words.

The rafting guide said, "Look, someone drowns _____ every summer. So, it's vitally

important that you let me know if you can't _____ the instructions I'm giving."

hole/whole

hole = (noun) gap; opening

whole = (adjective) entire; complete

Examples: Some people like to wear jeans with *holes* in them.

We have to read the *whole* book for this class.

Quick Check   Fill in the blanks with the correct words.

The _____ house needed repair. The walls needed painting. The plumbing leaked.

The roof even had a huge _____ in it.

its/it's

its = (adjective) possessive form of *it*

it's = (contraction) *it is*

Examples: The tree dropped *its* (possessive) leaves in a matter of a few days.

The grass is suffering from the drought; *it's* (*it is*) turning brown.

Quick Check   Fill in the blanks with the correct words.

The house for sale looked promising, but ____ roof was in bad shape. I thought,

"I don't know if ____ the house for us."

lead/led

The usage of these two words is especially complicated, so we will lay out the variations in a chart.

Word	Part of Speech	Rhymes with	Definition
lead	verb, present tense	bead, deed, feed	to guide, especially by going in advance
lead	noun	head, dead, red	a type of metal; a pencil's marking substance
led	verb, past tense	head, dead, red	past tense of the verb *lead*

Examples: You can *lead* a horse to water.

The pencil required for standardized tests is one with a No. 2 *lead*.

They *led* the donkeys to the feed trough.

Quick Check   Fill in the blanks with the correct words.

The art teacher said, "Watch as I _____ you through this exercise. Sketch lightly so

you don't break your pencil's _____. After I have _____ you through it once, you will

be able to do it on your own."

loose/lose

loose = (adjective) not tight

lose = (verb) to not retain; to fail to win

Examples: The *loose* shoestring caused Andrea to trip.

We did *lose* the game, but we enjoyed ourselves anyway.

Quick Check   Fill in the blanks with the correct words.

Some school districts are making rules prohibiting the wearing of clothing that is too

_____ . Students who violate these rules will _____ privileges.

passed/past

passed = (verb, past tense) proceeded; happened; exceeded

past = (adjective) a time ago

(noun) a time before the present

Examples: The runner who leads the marathon *passed* the halfway point
minutes ago.

The old man told delightful stories taken from his colorful *past.*

Quick Check   Fill in the blanks with the correct words.

Once the deadline had _____ , it was too late to apply for the grant. I'd like to

put that lost opportunity out of mind and leave it entirely in the _____ .

peace/piece

peace = (noun) tranquility; a sense of calm

piece = (noun) a part of something

Examples: Spreading *peace* throughout the world is a noble goal.

A *piece* of the jigsaw puzzle was missing.

Quick Check   Fill in the blanks with the correct words.

Those kids made so much noise that no one had any _____ all night. I'd sure like to

give them a _____ of my mind!

plain/plane

plain = (adjective) simple; unadorned

(noun) a vast area of mostly level land

plane = (noun) a flat surface; an airplane; a woodworking tool
    (verb) to smooth or shape a wood surface by using a *plane*

Examples: While *plain*, Shaker furniture is nonetheless beautiful.
    The open *plain* before us stretched as far as the eye could see.
    In geometry, circles, squares, and triangles are figures that exist in a *plane*.
    A carpenter can *plane* the uneven edge of a door.

Quick Check   Fill in the blanks with the correct words.

From up in the _____ I could see the _____ below us. The landscape was _____

yet beautiful. The countryside was so flat that I was reminded of a _____ in my

geometry textbook.

principal/principle

principal = (adjective) first; most important; highest in rank or degree
    (noun) leader of an elementary or secondary school; headmaster
principle = (noun) a law, rule, truth, or guideline

Examples: The *principal* reason I stayed home was my broken leg.
    Ms. Williams is the new *principal* of the high school.
    There are five *principles* of good citizenship.

Quick Check   Fill in the blanks with the correct words.

This morning, the high school _____ discussed the _____ of civility, which she

said should govern the way students treat one another.

quiet/quit/quite

quiet = (adjective) noiseless
quit = (verb) to stop
quite = (adverb) completely; wholly

Examples: A *quiet* evening was just what I needed after my stressful day.
    I plan to *quit* eating sweets after New Year's Day.
    The dinner was *quite* wonderful.

Quick Check   Fill in the blanks with the correct words.

The woman is _____ a conversationalist. She wouldn't _____ talking long enough

for anyone else to say anything. The rest of us were _____ all night while we just

listened to her.

right/rite/write

right = (adjective) correct; opposite of *left*

   (noun) a just claim (as in civil rights or human rights)

rite = (noun) a ritual

write = (verb) to put words and ideas into a visual form

Examples: Maria wants to do the *right* thing about her mistakes.

   One *rite* our culture observes is the celebration of birthdays.

   Anyone can learn to *write* with practice and diligence.

Quick Check   Fill in the blanks with the correct words.

The _____ of fasting is part of many religions. Some believers like to _____ poetry

to express their experience and understanding of God. Each person chooses a way

to honor God that he or she believes is _____.

sale/sell

sale = (noun) an event where items are offered for purchase

sell = (verb) to offer for purchase

Examples: The electronics store is having a huge *sale*.

   Rachel is going to *sell* her condo.

Quick Check   Fill in the blanks with the correct words.

I need to post a sign that says, "Tomatoes for _____." We have so many tomatoes this

summer that if we don't _____ some soon, I'm afraid that they will rot.

set/sit

set = (verb) to place something down; to fix or arrange something

sit = (verb) to rest the body on the buttocks

Examples: The grandfather *set* the groceries on the counter.

   The children will *sit* together at a separate table at the party.

Quick Check   Fill in the blanks with the correct words.

We will _____ the food on the counter and put all of the drinks in the refrigerator.

After we eat, we can all _____ around and talk.

tail/tale/tell

tail = (noun) the often elongated appendage attached to the rear portion of an animal's body; something that resembles an animal's tail

(verb) to follow for surveillance purposes

tale = (noun) a story or fable (typically, a fictional story)

tell = (verb) to make known by speech or writing; to express (as a story, a lie, and so on)

Examples: Unfortunately, the car ran over our dog's *tail*.

FBI agents have been known to *tail* suspects for months.

Before beginning the fairy *tale*, the teacher will *tell* students about its historical background.

Quick Check   Fill in the blanks with the correct words.

I want to _____ you one of Aesop's fables. It's the _____ about the fox that lost its _____ in

a trap.

their/there/they're

their = (adjectival pronoun) possessive form of *they*

there = (adverb) in or at that place (as opposed to *here*)

they're = (contraction) *they are*

Examples: *Their* insurance policy covered the cost of the wrecked car.

She drove the car *there* and then walked back here.

The children are hoping that *they're* (*they are*) going to the zoo today.

Quick Check   Fill in the blanks with the correct words.

My parents are visiting Colorado this month. They drove in _____ motor home, and

they are planning to stay _____ for several weeks. However, _____ definitely

planning on leaving before the snow starts to fall.

threw/through

threw = (verb) past tense of *throw*

through = (preposition) in one side and out the other side of something

Examples: The pitcher *threw* the ball over 100 miles per hour.

We took the subway *through* the tunnel under the San Francisco Bay.

Quick Check   Fill in the blanks with the correct words.

_____ his mask, the umpire clearly saw that the pitcher _____ the ball with the intention of hitting the batter.

to/too/two

to = (preposition) indicates movement toward something

too = (adverb) also; in addition to

two = (noun, adjective) the number 2

Examples: I decided to go *to* the mall.

Maria wanted to go *too*, so she rode with me.

Two eagles circled overhead.

Quick Check   Fill in the blanks with the correct words.

The man was _____ tired to continue hiking. He walked over ____ a tree, where he slumped down, took out all the food he had left—just _____ cupcakes—and slowly ate them.

want/won't

want = (verb) to desire

won't = (contraction) *will not*

Examples: We all *want* to see the film.

We *won't* (*will not*) pay $20 per movie ticket.

Quick Check   Fill in the blanks with the correct words.

I know you don't _____ to wait for the supervisor, but if you _____ to take your luggage with you, you must wait. We _____ allow your luggage on the plane otherwise.

wares/wear/where

wares = (plural noun) things that are being sold by someone

wear = (verb) to use a particular garment as clothing

where = (adverb) at; in what location (*Where* can also be used as an interrogative, a word used to ask a question, in the same manner as *who*, *what*, and *why*.)

Examples: The peddler showed his *wares* to the crowd.

She will *wear* that coat until the sleeves fall off!

The restaurant *where* the crime occurred is close to our neighborhood.

Where can we find another coat like it?

Quick Check   Fill in the blanks with the correct words.

"_____ can I find something special to _____ to the party?" I wondered. At that moment, an advertisement popped up on my computer screen.

"Take a look at our _____!" the retailer's ad said just as I was struggling with the question as to _____ I could find a unique dress for the reception. It seems that everyone _____ the same traditional designs.

weak/week

weak = (adjective) not strong

week = (noun) a period of seven days

Examples: He felt *weak* after skipping both breakfast and lunch.

Next *week* is going to be a very busy time at work.

Quick Check   Fill in the blanks with the correct words.

She felt _____ after having been sick in bed for a full _____.

weather/whether

weather = (noun) the condition of the atmosphere during some period of time

(verb) to endure (as in *to weather a storm*)

whether = (conjunction) function word that introduces two alternatives

Examples: The bad *weather* meant we had to delay the shopping trip.

I didn't know *whether* (or not) you wanted cream in your coffee.

Quick Check   Fill in the blanks with the correct words.

It doesn't matter _____ the _____ is nice. The postal service always delivers the mail.

we're/were

we're = (contraction) *we are*

were = (verb) a past tense form of the verb *to be*

Examples: I hope *we're* (*we are*) going to get coffee after the play.

The children *were* glad to go outside to play.

Quick Check   Fill in the blanks with the correct words.

_____ going to the movies. We had planned to go yesterday, but we _____ held up

by the traffic.

---

who's/whose

who's = (contraction) *who is*

whose = (adjective) indicates possession (*Whose* can also be used as an interrogative, a word used to ask a question, in the same manner as *who*, *what*, and *why*.)

Examples: I live near Mr. Carter, *who's* (*who is*) my dad's best friend.

The donor, *whose* name will not be announced, deserves credit nonetheless.

Whose scarf was left in the break room?

Quick Check   Fill in the blanks with the correct words.

She is the woman _____ husband won the raffle. She's the same woman _____

going to be in charge of the fund-raiser.

---

your/you're

your = (adjective) indicates possession

you're = (contraction) *you are*

Examples: I'd like to borrow *your* car.

If *you're* going to sleep over, we will need to locate a cot.

Quick Check   Fill in the blanks with the correct words.

I'm sorry that _____ not feeling well. Would you like me to pick _____ children up

from school?

Other Commonly Confused Words

Sometimes as writers we face word choice challenges that are not related to the matter of homophones. We will address several cases in this section.

among/between

among = (preposition) used when referring to a group of three or more

between = (preposition) used when referring to a group of two

Examples: The workers began to talk *among* themselves.

Between you and me, I think Macy is the best candidate.

Quick Check Fill in the blanks with the correct words.

The class members discussed the ideas _____ themselves. Meanwhile, Gabriella and

I devised a plan _____ the two of us.

amount/number

amount = (noun) the quantity of something that *cannot* be counted

number = (noun) the quantity of something that *can* be counted

Examples: We received a large *amount* of rain over the weekend.

A large *number* of suggestions were submitted to the management staff.

Quick Check Fill in the blanks with the correct words.

We saw a great _____ of floats in the parade. The _____ of cold drinks that

people drank that day was astounding.

believe/feel

believe = (verb) to be convinced by logic or reason

feel = (verb) to experience an emotion; to touch

Examples: I *believe* that the defendant is guilty.

I *feel* sad for the victim's family.

Quick Check Fill in the blanks with the correct words.

My view of the accident causes me to _____ that the driver of the green car was at

fault. I _____ a great deal of concern for all those who were injured.

can/may

can = (verb) to be able to doing something

may = (verb) to be permitted to do something

Examples: Coach, you know that I *can* run the entire distance without hurting

myself, so *may* I please enter the marathon?

Quick Check   Fill in the blanks with the correct words.

_____ I swim in your pool? I _____ swim like a fish. I _____ dive well, too!

casual/causal

casual = (adjective) informal

causal = (adjective) responsible for causing

Examples: *Casual* dress will be appropriate for the meeting.

A *causal* factor in the fire was the use of a space heater.

Quick Check   Fill in the blanks with the correct words.

Her attitude toward the interview was far too _____.   In fact, her attitude was a

_____ element in the company's decision to decline to offer her the job.

fewer/less

fewer = (adjective) not so many; smaller in number

less = (adjective) not so much; smaller in amount

Examples: *Fewer* shoppers made major purchases this season than last season.

The tank actually has *less* gasoline in it than the gauge indicates.

Quick Check   Fill in the blanks with the correct words.

If we can make the vaccine readily available, the result will be _____ disease, _____

deaths, and consequently a much happier society.

lay/lie

Determining how to use these two words is particularly complicated, so we will lay out the variations in a chart.

Word	Part of Speech	Definition	Past Tense
lay	verb	to set something down	laid
lie	verb	to recline	lay

Examples: I *lay* the logs on the back porch every autumn.

I *laid* the logs on the back porch last year but not this year. (past tense of *lay*)

The cat *lies* on the rug every afternoon.

The cat *lay* on the rug for an hour, but then it got up. (past tense of *lie*)

Quick Check   Fill in the blanks with the correct words:

I need you to ____ down in your bed and rest. Children who are ill must ____ aside

other activities until they are healthy. I know that yesterday you ____ down most of

the day, and I know that you ____ aside all of the things you wanted to do, but you

still must ____ in bed and rest today.

AVOIDING CLICHÉS AND SLANG

Most of us use clichés and slang in everyday speech. Thus, it is easy for these expressions to slide into our writing. Avoiding clichés and slang in your writing will make your writing more professional and will keep it in line with the standards of academic writing.

Clichés

A **cliché** is a phrase or sentence that is commonly used and often overused. For example, "better safe than sorry" is a common cliché, as is "peace of mind." There is nothing wrong with using clichés in casual conversation; we all do it. The primary complaint against clichés is that using them does not require us to think critically about language choices. Sometimes we reach for a cliché simply because it is handy, not because it fits our purpose better than other phrases. Thus, the writer who depends on clichés may be seen as lazy and considered less creative than the writer who does not.

Even worse than using a cliché is *misusing* a cliché. Here are just a few examples of how clichés are misused—and consequently do not make sense!

Standard Cliché	Confused Form of Cliché
It's not rocket science. (It's not brain surgery.)	It's not rocket surgery.
tough row to hoe	a tough road to hoe
dog-eat-dog world	doggy-dog world

You can avoid making mistakes with clichés simply by avoiding their use. Instead of using a cliché, create your own unique phrase. A common type of cliché is a simile—a comparison using *as* or *like*. By creating your own original expressions, you will avoid making embarrassing mistakes by misusing clichés, but just as importantly, you will be able to convey your thoughts more creatively and precisely.

Cliché (in Standard Form)	New Formation of the Cliché
as dry as a bone	as dry as a rock in the desert
as happy as a clam	as happy as a mouse in a grain silo
like a fish out of water	like a cat at the Westminster Dog Show

When you use a cliché, your readers will understand the meaning of the phrase, but you will have missed an opportunity to write in a fresh, original way. A much better option is create a new phrase.

Slang

Humans are very imaginative when it comes to language. Every culture and each new generation finds a way to bend linguistic rules a bit, and what results from that bending is *slang*. Slang is simply language used in a nonstandard way. For example, *croak* is a standard word when it refers to the sound a frog makes; however, when it is used as a synonym for *die*, the word is slang. (Example: "The old buzzard finally croaked.") Other slang words have no standard meaning; they are directly created as slang words. The word *scuzzy* is an example; its only use is as a slang word meaning "dirty" or "shabby in condition or character." (Example: "If you don't shave and do something with your hair, you'll just look scuzzy.")

Linguists, people who study language, will be quick to tell you that there is nothing wrong with slang. Most English professors agree. Slang wording becomes a problem when people use it in the wrong places. Most employers, for example, expect their employees to avoid slang in written communication and, in some work settings, in spoken communication also. Additionally, academic writing should never contain slang, and e-mails and other correspondence between students and instructors should be slang-free. In general, anytime you wish to establish a tone of seriousness, avoid slang.

So, what fits into that category we call *slang*? In "What Is Slang?" Robert Beard, a linguist, calls slang

> a code in which one vaguely related or unrelated word or phrase is substituted for a more common one. The words that are replaced in slang are the most common ones: good (*cherry, boss, phat, da bomb*), bad (*icky, yucky, jankety*), crazy (*nuts, bananas, crackers, bonkers*), smart (*brainy, savvy, sharp*), fast (*scream, tear out, fly, like greased lightning*), slow (*dragging, poky, crawling, creeping*).

One point Beard makes about slang is that it functions as a code: it separates the in-crowd from the outsiders. Because slang is a cultural code, its most appropriate use is within a particular cultural context. If you are hanging out with friends, using slang is probably not only common but actually expected.

If you are unsure whether a term is considered slang, look it up in a dictionary. Almost every dictionary will identify slang words in some fashion.

3

> Punctuation marks are like road signs. They prepare people for what is ahead and point them in the right direction.

Punctuation and Mechanics

Punctuation is a tool that helps writers communicate their thoughts. End punctuation signals the end of a complete thought and comes at the end of a complete sentence. Commas group sets of words together so readers can grasp the meaning of a sentence as well as the importance of certain elements in the sentence. In this unit, we will discuss the various types of punctuation available to writers, when to use each type, and how to use each type correctly.

UNIT OBJECTIVES

After completing this unit, students will be able to do the following:

- **Use end punctuation correctly.**
- **Use commas correctly.**
- **Use apostrophes, colons, and semicolons correctly.**
- **Use hyphens, parentheses, dashes, quotation marks, and ellipses correctly.**

USING END PUNCTUATION CORRECTLY

A sentence is a complete thought. End punctuation shows readers where one thought ends and where the next thought begins. Sentences can end in periods, question marks, or exclamation marks.

TYPE	EXPLANATION	EXAMPLES
Period	A declarative (ordinary) sentence ends with a period.	*The sky is deep blue* *She cooks lunch daily.*
Question mark	A question is a sentence that asks something and ends with a question mark.	*How are you?* *What time is it?*
Exclamation mark	A sentence that emphasizes a point or strongly expresses an emotion ends with an exclamation mark. An interjection or command also ends with an exclamation mark.	*My way is right!* *I am so happy!* *Wow! That's cool.* *Clean your room!*

Particular situations pose special problems for each of the three types of end punctuation, as the chart below illustrates.

TYPE	TROUBLE SPOTS	EXAMPLES
Period	Two complete thoughts that are combined without proper punctuation between them are called *run-on sentences*. This form is grammatically incorrect.	*The workers are <u>drained they</u> <u>have labored all night.</u>* (Period needed between *drained* and *they*.)
Question mark	Sentences in which the subject is wondering or asking about something should not end with a question mark. A question mark is only used when a question is being asked directly.	*I wonder if it will rain today. Ty asked whether the mail had come.* (No question mark needed.)
Exclamation mark	A sentence that is merely *reporting* strong emotion does not need an exclamation mark.	*Mira was excited about the news. Indeed, she was ecstatic.* (No exclamation mark needed.)

PRACTICE ① Using End Punctuation Correctly

Read the paragraph below, adding the appropriate end punctuation to each sentence. (Capital letters indicate where new sentences begin.)

Close the door How many times do I have to tell you that Whether it's cold or hot outside doesn't matter You need to close the door regardless Have you ever looked at our utility bills Do you realize how much of our income goes to pay for heating and cooling Think If you would just think before you act, things would be so much better around here

USING COMMAS CORRECTLY

Commas are primarily used to separate or to join elements within a sentence.

Commas after Introductory Elements

A comma should follow several types of words, phrases, and clauses that are used to begin a sentence.

USE	EXAMPLES
After a prepositional phrase of 3 + words	After the Saint Patrick's Day parade (,) we had lunch at a pub. On my birthday (,) my mom always bakes a special cake.
After an introductory verbal phrase	Talking rapidly (,) the agent described every detail about the house. Tired to the bone (,) the rangers collapsed in the cabin.
After some single words to clarify meaning or insert a useful pause	Yes (,) I did think her apology was sincere. However (,) I have enjoyed staying at this hotel.
After a dependent clause that begins a sentence	Although my family was out of town (,) I still enjoyed the holidays. Until he left (,) no one realized how much of a pest he had been.

Note that when a dependent clause is placed at the *end* of a sentence, no comma is needed.

Examples: I still enjoyed the holidays <u>although my family was out of town.</u>

No one realized how much of a pest he had been <u>until he left.</u>

PRACTICE ② Adding Commas after Introductory Elements

Read the paragraph below and consider the introductory elements in each sentence. If commas are needed, add them. Circle each comma you add.

By 4:00 p.m. the town was deserted. Across from Seawall Boulevard businesses had boarded up their windows and doors. Although the storm was not supposed to make landfall until the next day most people were not waiting around. However a few people intentionally remained on the island. Seeking one last bit of adventure before heading for the mainland the surfers stayed to ride the waves a last time. Scared though they were their excitement trumped their common sense.

Commas with Conjunctions

If two sentences are joined together with a FANBOYS conjunction (*for, and, nor, but, or, yet, so*), a comma is needed before the conjunction.

CONJUNCTION	EXAMPLES
for	The parrot chattered constantly ⟨,⟩ for it hoped that a cracker would be presented.
and	The two boxers shook hands ⟨,⟩ and then they returned to their corners.
nor	The windows were not locked ⟨,⟩ nor were the curtains drawn shut.
but	Mr. Li wants to go the beach ⟨,⟩ but Ms. Li prefers taking a trip to the mountains.
or	He must do the assignment ⟨,⟩ or he will surely suffer the consequences.
yet	The heat was intense ⟨,⟩ yet the firefighters continued to battle the fire all night.
so	Tissa completed her homework ⟨,⟩ so she decided she could take time for some fun.

PRACTICE ③ Using Commas and Conjunctions to Join Sentences

Guided by the examples in the chart above, write two sentences using each conjunction. Add commas appropriately.

for   1 a. _____

    b. _____

and   2 a. _____

    b. _____

nor   3 a. _____

    b. _____

but   4 a. _____

    b. _____

(continued)

or	5	a.	_____
		b.	_____
yet	6	a.	_____
		b.	_____
so	7	a.	_____
		b.	_____

Commas in a Series

Use commas to separate elements in a series.

TYPE OF SERIES	EXAMPLES
adjectives	The cake is moist (,) sweet (,) and delicious.
nouns	The Broncos (,) the Panthers (,) the Redskins (,) and the Cowboys are the best teams in the league.
verbs	The mayor ran for reelection (,) won the race (,) and continued his political career.

Note that omitting the comma before the word *and* or *or* in a series is grammatically acceptable in journalism and other types of writing. However, because leaving out the comma can sometimes cause confusion, many writers include it. In academic writing, a comma is always used before *and* or *or.*

Commas between Dual Adjectives

Sometimes a noun is preceded by two adjectives that modify the noun separately. A comma between such dual adjectives is required.

Examples: The grand (,) glorious staircase makes the home seem regal.

Sweet (,) sticky cakes were served with the tea.

She freely offered advice to the sincere (,) curious girl.

PRACTICE ④ Using Commas in a Series and between Dual Adjectives

Read the paragraph that follows, and add commas where necessary. Circle each comma you add.

I needed to take three science courses in college, so I chose to take anatomy physiology and microbiology. The intriguing stimulating courses provided me with information I use to this day. I learned about the bones in the human body the major body systems and the principal types of diseases. My interesting witty professor for all three courses was a retired cardiologist. He had years of surgical experience from which to draw wonderful stories, so he made the classes very entertaining. His classes convinced me that I would love to become a certified nursing assistant a licensed vocational nurse or a registered nurse, and so I am very glad that I took those courses.

Other Uses of Commas

Some commas are required simply as technical punctuation details based on rules developed by printers, who desired consistency in producing published works.

FUNCTION	EXAMPLES
To separate elements in addresses	811 Martin Drive (,) Richmond (,) VA
To separate the day of the month from the year and the year from whatever follows (when needed)	Wynn was born on May 16 (,) 1887 (,) and he died on May 17 (,) 1989. The battle on March 3 (,) 1777 (,) was especially brutal.
To separate the day of the week from the month	I arrived on Tuesday (,) April 18.
To set off dialogue	Jayne said (,) "I wish I knew how to ice skate." "I took a year of lessons and then dropped out (,) " Ashley replied.
To introduce a quotation from a written source	In the words of Enrique Marquez (,) "An epidemic is a disease gone rogue."
To separate a person's name from a title that follows it	Soo Kim (,) mayor of Yuma (,) is the host for the week. Carrie Garza (,) MD (,) was the speaker at the conference.

Several situations involving comma usage require special attention, as the chart below illustrates.

TYPICAL USAGE	TROUBLE SPOT
To separate the day of the month from the year **Example:** Wynn was born on May 15, 1887.	Do *not* use a comma to separate the month from the year. **Example:** He died in May 1989.
To set off dialogue **Example:** Jayne said, "I wish I knew how to skate!"	Do *not* use a comma when dialogue is described but not quoted directly. **Example:** Jayne said that she wished she knew how to skate. (Note the use of the word *that* and the absence of quotation marks.)
To introduce a quote from a written source **Example:** The CDC report stated, "No significant outbreak of the virus has occurred."	Do *not* use a comma when the word *that* is used to transition into a quotation. **Example:** The CDC report stated that no significant outbreak of the virus had occurred. (Note the use of the word *that* and the absence of quotation marks.)

PRACTICE 5 Using Commas Correctly

Read the paragraph below, and add commas where necessary. Circle each comma you add.

Selena walked hurriedly into the classroom. She quickly took the nearest seat quietly unzipped her backpack and noiselessly removed her textbook. Opening her book she sighed anxiously. The test would be extremely difficult and she knew that she had not studied enough. Throughout the entire semester Biology 101 had been a tough course for her. Her professor Sue McGee MD was a retired surgeon and she was very demanding. Professor McGee had told the class that the exam would be challenging and Selena knew that she meant it.

Selena glanced backward and saw classmates studiously reading their notes. Her heart slowly sank as she realized that she had put herself into a very difficult situation. Nevertheless she summoned her inner strength closed her eyes and said to herself "Sellie you can do this. You know you can."

USING APOSTROPHES, COLONS, AND SEMICOLONS CORRECTLY

Apostrophes, colons, and semicolons play important roles in sentences.

Apostrophes

Apostrophes are used for two principal reasons: to create contractions and to show possession by a noun.

Apostrophe Use in Contractions

A **contraction** is a word formed by the merging of two other words. When the words are merged, one or more letters are dropped. An apostrophe's role is to stand in the spot that the dropped letters have vacated. The key to forming contractions correctly is to use the apostrophe in *the very place* that the omitted letters once stood. Generally speaking, contractions should be used sparingly in academic or formal writing.

ORIGINAL WORDS	LETTERS OMITTED	CONTRACTION
do + not	*o* (in *not*)	don't
should + have	*ha*	should've
he + will	*wi*	he'll

Apostrophe Use to Show Possession

For a singular noun, simply add -'s to the noun in order to show possession. Names are treated in the same manner as other nouns.

SINGULAR NOUN	POSSESSIVE
the coach	the coach's cap
a truck	a truck's tires
a New York Yankee	a New York Yankee's hits
the scientist	the scientist's graph
a city	a city's schools

For a plural noun, follow these rules to show possession:

1. If the plural noun ends in -*s*, add only an apostrophe.
2. If the plural noun does not end in -*s*, add -'*s*.

PLURAL NOUN	POSSESSIVE
coaches	coaches' caps
scientists	scientists' graphs
New York Yankees	New York Yankees' infield
children (no -*s*)	children's toys
women (no -*s*)	women's vote

PRACTICE ⑥ Using Apostrophes Correctly

Read the paragraphs below, and add apostrophes where necessary. Circle each apostrophe you add.

Men s involvement in the construction industry is long established. However, women s participation is on the rise, so much so that some people have replaced the word *tradesmen* with *tradesworkers* because they don t want to suggest a gender bias.

Various members of the workforce are involved in the construction of a house. They specialize in various areas, and workers tools vary from trade to trade.

Concrete finishers principal role in building a house is pouring a foundation. Driveways and sidewalks are also the fruit of their labor. A concrete finisher has a tool called a "screed"; he ll use that to level and smooth poured concrete.

Carpenters tasks primarily involve the "framing" of a house. Carpenters build the wooden structures that support the house s walls, ceilings, and roof. Hammers, saws, and measuring tapes are probably the most important tools for carpenters.

Masons lay brick and do other kinds of stonework. Masons use mortar as a type of adhesive between the bricks. A mason s number one tool is a trowel.

Wiring houses is electricians assignment. An electrician relies on a special kind of pliers that can be used to cut, strip, and crimp wire; she ll never go to a job site without this special tool.

The responsibility of carpet layers is evident in the name of their trade. Carpet layers use a special tool called a "knee kicker" to stretch carpet for wall-to-wall installation.

A plumber s job in a house s construction is to install the pipes that carry water and the fixtures that provide outlets for water. Plumbers carry with them a set of tools that includes a propane torch, a hacksaw, and various wrenches.

Colons and Semicolons

Colons and semicolons help writers create interesting and varied sentences.

Colons

A colon's function is to introduce an explanation, a list, or a long quotation.

FUNCTION OF COLON	EXAMPLES
To introduce explanations	I decided to stay home for one good reason ⚬:⚬ the roads were frozen and the bridges icy. The result of the survey was clear ⚬:⚬ students want more parking.
To introduce lists	Campers will need the following ⚬:⚬ a flashlight, a backpack, and a knife. The car certainly had problems ⚬:⚬ bent frame, bad brakes, and bald tires.
To introduce long quotes	Mark Twain had this to say about books ⚬:⚬ "In a good bookroom you feel in some mysterious way that you are absorbing the wisdom contained in all the books through your skin without even opening them."

Semicolons

A semicolon is used to connect two complete sentences. Its function is similar to that of a FANBOYS conjunction (*for, and, nor, but, or, yet, so*): it joins two complete thoughts that are equally weighted in the mind of the writer. The two most common situations in which semicolons are properly used are described below.

FUNCTION OF SEMICOLON	EXAMPLES
To connect clauses that are clearly related in meaning or content	The plane was delayed ⓢ the airport was packed. The judge looked at the defendant ⓢ the defendant looked at his attorney.
To connect clauses using a conjunctive adverb	I took a wrong turn ⓢ <u>consequently</u>, I arrived at the party late. We slowly learned the truth ⓢ <u>thus</u>, we began to take action.

Note that each clause connected with a semicolon must be an *independent clause*—a complete thought capable of standing alone as a sentence. A comma used in place of a semicolon results in a *comma splice error.*

PRACTICE ⑦ Using Commas, Colons, and Semicolons Correctly

Insert the appropriate punctuation—comma, semicolon, or colon—in the sentences below. If no punctuation is needed, write *NP* in the blank.

1. We went to eat after the play __ we went home after we ate.

2. The instructions indicated ____ that each piece needed to be thoroughly cleaned before assembly.

3. Even though the theater company's interpretation of *Hamlet* was highly unusual__ I found the performance to be superb.

4. The types of art that could be submitted in the contest were strictly limited __ oil paintings, watercolors, pastels, or charcoal sketches.

5. We sailed for a day on rough seas ____ because a storm had just passed through our sea route.

6. The restaurant specializes in ham and beans __ buttermilk pie __ and grits casserole.

7. The play lasted for two hours __ consequently, we didn't get home until late.

8. The surgeons continued the operation ____ even though the outlook for the patient seemed grim.

9. This is one of my favorite lines from Jack Kerouac's *On the Road* __ "Why think about that when all the golden lands ahead of you and all kinds of unforeseen events wait lurking to surprise you and make you glad you're alive to see?"

10. The surface of the road ahead is smooth enough __ however, the curves and the ice and the wind will make it treacherous indeed.

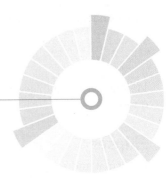

USING HYPHENS, DASHES, PARENTHESES, QUOTATION MARKS, AND ELLIPSES CORRECTLY

Hyphens, dashes, parentheses, quotation marks, and ellipses are used less frequently than the punctuation marks covered above.

Hyphens

The hyphen, which is a small horizontal mark, has three main uses, as shown in the following table.

USE	EXAMPLES	TIP
In some compound nouns	mother-in-law six-pack	The rules about when to use hyphens with compounds are inconsistent, so check a dictionary if in doubt.
In fractions and numbers that consist of two words	two-thirds twenty-seven	Numbers higher than one hundred are usually written with numerals: 101, 237, and so on.
In ranges of numbers or years	pp. 25-32 1920-2011	Do not use a hyphen to replace *to* in a construction with *from*: "The civil unrest took place *from* 2010 *to* 2014."

Dashes and Parentheses

A dash is a horizontal mark that is longer than a hyphen. Both dashes and parentheses set off material that interrupts a sentence but adds to its meaning. The principal difference between dashes and parentheses is how they focus the reader's attention. Dashes highlight an interruption; parentheses deemphasize it.

PUNCTUATION TYPE	FUNCTION	EXAMPLES
Dash	To set off emphasized information	The tiger—furious and roaring—leaped toward the tourists. The song—wistful and tender—touched his soul.
Parentheses	To set off understated information	The bus (which had seen better days) rolled along. Sammy (who had never liked school) joined the army.

Note that with word-processing software, you create a dash by typing two hyphens (--) without any spaces between them or on either side of them. Some word-processing software will automatically change the two hyphens into a dash (—). Both styles (two hyphens and a long dash) are acceptable, so there is no need to worry about this detail.

Quotation Marks

Double and single quotation marks serve different purposes.

TYPE	FUNCTION	EXAMPLES
Double quotes	To indicate a word-for-word quotation	According to Confucius, "Everything has beauty, but not everyone sees it."
Double quotes	To indicate dialogue in a narrative	They asked, "So what are you?" The Buddha simply replied, "I am awake."
Double quotes	To set off special terms	The term "scientific method" refers to a specific procedure used for investigation in the natural sciences.
Single quotes	To indicate a quote *within* a quote	The patient complained, "I told the doctor I was ill, but he muttered, 'It's probably all in your head.' Then he just walked away."

When you write, place periods and commas *inside* quotation marks, even inside single quotes.

Ellipses

In formal and scholarly writing, an ellipsis consists of three spaced periods that indicate the omission of words from quoted material. As a student writing academic papers, you may want to shorten a long quotation by using ellipses to show where you have omitted words. When the omission is at the end of a quoted sentence, the ellipsis is preceded by a period.

In informal writing and in some forms of literature, an ellipsis indicates a pause. Although you may never use an ellipsis for that purpose as a writer, you should be aware of this use as a reader. Why does the author want the reader to pause at the designated place? How does the pause affect the meaning being conveyed?

The chart below provides examples of different uses of ellipses.

FUNCTION	EXAMPLES
To show that words have been omitted from quoted material	"On the voyage(. .)illness was a common cause of death." "With little to no medicine available, not much could be done.(. .)The captain decided to head for port."
To show a pause in thinking or to show hesitation or uncertainty	I was wondering if maybe you'd be willing to loan me ten bucks(. .) I was dreaming of a time long ago(. .)

PRACTICE Using Hyphens, Dashes, Parentheses, Quotation Marks, and Ellipses Correctly

In the sentences below, insert the appropriate punctuation.

1. Rock climbing and horseback riding   although it burns fewer calories than rock climbing   both exercise muscles you might not typically use in your daily activities. [dashes]

2. Some exercise physiologists that is, health professionals who analyze and help people maintain physical fitness discount the value of horseback riding as exercise. [parentheses]

3. Many health conscious people have increased their level of physical activity. [hyphen]

4. I wonder whether I might enjoy either horseback riding or rock climbing   [ellipsis]

5. Rock climbing is excellent exercise can burn 500-900 calories per hour . [parentheses]

6. The Equestrian Medical Safety Association recommends all riders wear properly fitted helmets. The association states on its Website,   Head injuries account for approximately 60% of deaths resulting from equestrian accidents. [quotation marks]

7. A person could ride a horse all day and not get tired   couldn't do that rock climbing, I'm pretty sure   [dash and ellipsis]

CREDITS

Text Credits

Chapter 2

Page 27: Larry Roberts, John Janovy, Jr., and Steve Nadler, *Foundations of Parasitology*, 9th ed. New York: McGraw-Hill, 2013, p. 2; p. 29: William Cunningham and Mary Ann Cunningham, *Principles of Environmental Science*, 7th ed. New York: McGraw-Hill, 2013, pp. 267–268; p. 30: Fish Consumption Advisory from William Cunningham and Mary Ann Cunningham, *Principles of Environmental Science*, 5th ed., Figure 10.17 (p. 246). Copyright © 2009 by McGraw-Hill Education. Reprinted with permission; p. 46: "the ability to perceive . . . " is from *Managing Stress*. MTD Training and Ventus Publishing, 2010, p. 48.

Chapter 3

Page 51: Textbook chapter headings from William Cunningham and Mary Ann Cunningham, *Principles of Environmental Science*, 5th ed. New York: McGraw-Hill, 2009, pp. 25, 36; p. 51: Food Chain figure from William Cunningham and Mary Ann Cunningham, *Principles of Environmental Science*, 5th ed., Figure 2.2. Copyright © 2009 by McGraw-Hill Education. Reprinted with permission; p. 53: Chapter Outline and caption from Charles R. Swanson, Neil Chamelin, and Leonard Territo, *Criminal Investigation*, 11th ed. New York: McGraw-Hill, 2012, from Chapter 4; p. 64: Eldon D. Enger and Bradley F. Smith, *Environmental Science: A Study of Interrelationships*, 13th ed., pp. 382–383. Copyright © 2013 by McGraw-Hill Education. Reprinted with permission.

Chapter 4

Page 81: Paragraphs A-C in Practice 5 are from Judith A. Boss, *THINK: Critical Thinking and Logic Skills for Everyday Life*, 2nd ed. New York: McGraw-Hill, 2012, p. 277; p. 89: Kathryn Rentz, Marie E. Flatley, and Paula Lentz, *Lesikar's Business Communication: Connecting in a Digital World*, 12th ed., p. 3. Copyright © 2011 by McGraw-Hill Education. Reprinted with permission; p. 101: Peter J. McDonnell, MD, "Adapting to the Situation." Reprinted with permission from *Ophthalmology Times*, January 15, 2010. *Ophthalmology Times* is a copyrighted publication of Advanstar Communications Inc. All rights reserved. This article was originally published with the title "Viewpoint:

Key Is Learning To Be Successful Wherever You Land in Your Profession."

Chapter 5

Page 111: Bryce Covert, "Four Ideas for How Obama Could Really Transform the Cost of College." This article was published by ThinkProgress, August 21, 2013. Reprinted with permission; p. 126: Excerpt from Brittany Horn, "Recovery Is Slow in Rural China's 'Cancer Villages'." © 2013 by Brittany Horn. Reprinted by permission of the author. From McClatchyDC.com, August 19, 2013; p. 136: Richard T. Schaefer, "The Life Course" from *Sociology*, 13th ed., p. 89. Copyright © 2012 McGraw-Hill Education. Reprinted with permission; p. 137: "The Interpretation of Andamanese Customs and Beliefs: Ceremonial" from A. R. Brown, *The Andaman Islanders: A Study in Social Anthropology*, London: Cambridge University Press, 1922, pp. 276–279

Chapter 6

Page 148: Adapted from http://starchild.gsfc.nasa.gov/docs/StarChild/questions/question6.html; p. 151: Laura Cunningham, "The Chosen One." © 1994 by Laura Cunningham. Reprinted by permission of the author. From *New York Times Magazine*, April 17, 1994; p. 161: Mary Ann Bell, "What I Really Meme Is. . . Anatomy of a Happenin' Thing," *Internet@Schools*, vol. 20, Issue 2 (March/April 2013), p. 24. © Copyright 2013 Information Today, Inc. Reprinted with permission; p. 167: Bill W. Tillery, *Physical Science*, 9th ed., excerpt and Figure 2.19 from p. 41. Copyright © 2012 by McGraw-Hill Education. Reprinted with permission; p. 171: Table "Identified Prevalence of Autism Spectrum Disorders" from U.S. Centers for Disease Control and Prevention, http://www.cdc.gov/ncbddd/autism/data.html#prevalence; p. 178: Excerpts from G. Michael Maddock and Raphael Louis Vitón, "Three Types of People to Fire Immediately," Businessweek.com, November 8, 2011. © 2011 Bloomberg L.P. All rights reserved. Reprinted with permission; p. 194: Patrick Leon Abbott, *Natural Disasters*, 8th ed., pp. 338–339. Copyright © 2012 by McGraw-Hill Education. Reprinted with permission; p. 200: *A Guide to Naturalization*. Washington, DC: U.S. Citizenship and

Immigration Services, M-476 (rev. 03/12), p. 31; p. 213: Dennis Henigan, "Keep Guns Off Campus." Reprinted by permission of the author. From *Huffington Post*, March 3, 2011.

Chapter 7

Page 241: *Antibiotic Resistance Threats in the US*. Atlanta, GA: Centers for Disease Control and Prevention, September 16, 2013. www.cdc.gov; p. 242: Conrad Phillip Kottak, *Mirror for Humanity*, 10th ed., pp. 35–36. Copyright © 2016 McGraw-Hill Education. Reprinted with permission.

Chapter 8

Page 250: Reprinted with permission from "Campus Diversity and Student Self-Segregation: Separating Myths from Facts," by Debra Humphreys. Copyright 1999 by the Association of American Colleges and Universities; p. 253: Stanley J. Baran, *Introduction to Mass Communication: Media Literacy and Culture*, 8th ed., p. 394. Copyright © 2014 by McGraw-Hill Education. Reprinted with permission; p. 254: Janet Shibley Hyde and John DeLamater, *Understanding Human Sexuality*, 11th ed., p. 275. Copyright © 2011 by McGraw-Hill Education. Reprinted with permission; p. 256: From Larry D. Rosen, "Driven to Distraction: Our Wired Generation." © 2012 Larry D. Rosen, Ph.D. Reprinted by permission of the author. From *St. Paul Pioneer Press*, November 12, 2012; p. 258: Tait Trussell, "Healing Humor." © 2008 by Tait Trussell. Reprinted by permission of the author. From *Saturday Evening Post*, vol. 280, no. 4 (July/August 2008); p. 259: From Mitch Renkow, "Wal-Mart and the Local Economy," *NC State Economist*, November/December 2005. Reprinted by permission of the author; p. 260: From Tom Fitzgerald, "Probing Question: Is 'Just Say No' an effective anti-drug approach?" *Penn State News*, January 23, 2006; p. 260: From Christine VanDeVelde Luskin, "Mark Lepper: Intrinsic Motivation, Extrinsic Motivation and the Process of Learning," *Bing Times Online*, Stanford University, 2003; p. 262: From Mitch Renkow, "Wal-Mart and the Local Economy," *NC State Economist*, November/December 2005. Reprinted by permission of the author; p. 264: reprinted with permission from "Campus Diversity and Student Self-Segregation: Separating

Myths from Facts," by Debra Humphreys. Copyright 1999 by the Association of American Colleges and Universities; p. 266: Andrew Gumbel, "Homo Sapiens RIP," *The Independent*, March 15, 2000. Reprinted with permission. © independent .co.uk. http://www.independent.co.uk; p. 267: "The Self as a Social Object" from Laura A. King, *The Science of Psychology*, 3rd ed., pp. 435-436. Copyright © 2014 by McGraw-Hill Education. Reprinted with permission.

Chapter 9

Page 279: Em Griffin, *A First Look at Communication Theory*, 1st ed. New York: McGraw-Hill, 1991; p. 282: From Dorothy Foltz-Gray, "What Really Makes Us Happy," *Prevention* 58.2 (2006): 156–163; p. 291: Passage A is from Amit Shah, *Business Now*. New York: McGraw-Hill, 2011, p. 79; p. 296: From Tom Orsborn, "'Brick Layer' Ready to Replace Spencer Full-Time," MySanAntonio. com, September 25, 2013; p. 303: Map from Althea Arnold et al., *Out of Reach 2014*. Washington, DC: National Low Income Housing Coalition, p. 14. © 2014 National Low Income Housing Coalition. Reprinted with permission; p. 304: "Biases and Heuristics" from Laura A. King, *The Science of Psychology*, 3rd ed., pp. 261–263. Copyright © 2014 by McGraw-Hill Education. Reprinted with permission.

Chapter 10

Page 339: Benjamin Percy, "Home Improvement: Revision as Renovation," *Poets & Writers Magazine*, May/June 2010. Reprinted with permission of the publisher, Poets & Writers, Inc., 90 Broad Street, Suite 2100, New York, NY 10004, www.pw.org

Chapter 11

Page 355: Joe and Teresa Graedon, "How Safe Is Aspartame?" The People's Pharmacy®, January 9, 2006. Reprinted with permission. www.peoplespharmacy .com. Appeared in *Buffalo News*, January 4, 2006; p. 360: This content is excerpted with permission from *Controlling Anger Before It Controls You*, http://www.apa .org/topics/anger/control.aspx. Copyright © 2005 by the American Psychological Association. No further reproduction or distribution is permitted without written permission from the American Psychological Association; p. 362: "Commentary. Concussions in Football," by Miller, Michael Craig. Excerpted

from the *Harvard Mental Health Letter*, vol. 26, no. 7 (January 2010). © 2010, Harvard University. For more information visit: http://www.health.harvard.edu/ Note: Harvard Health Publications does not endorse any products or medical procedures; p. 368: This content is excerpted with permission from *Controlling Anger Before It Controls You*, http://www.apa .org/topics/anger/control.aspx. Copyright © 2005 by the American Psychological Association. No further reproduction or distribution is permitted without written permission from the American Psychological Association; p. 372: From Pamela Cantor, "Police and Punishment: Strategic Alternatives for Schools," *District Administration*, August 2013. http://www .districtadministration.com

Photo Credits

Part Openers

1: © Doug Steakley/Lonely Planet Images/ Getty Images; 2: © Radius Images/Corbis RF; 3: © Dean Uhlinger/Corbis RF; 4: © Digital Vision/Getty Images RF

Chapter 1

Opener (top): © Blend Images/Getty Images RF; (middle): © BananaStock/PunchStock RF; (bottom): © Stockbyte/Getty Images RF; (right): © Purestock/SuperStock RF; p. 3: © Margie Hoeffner; p. 4 (left): © Granger Wootz/Blend Images/Corbis RF; p. 4 (right): © Barry Howe/Corbis RF; p. 6: © Jose Luis Pelaez Inc/Blend Images LLC RF; p. 8 (top): © Halfdark/Getty Images RF; p. 8 (bottom): © Hero/age fotostock RF

Chapter 2

Opener: © Hero Images/Getty Images RF

Chapter 3

Opener: © Ana Abejon/E+/Getty Images RF; p. 52: CDC; p. 53: © Dr. Richard Souviron; p. 56 (left): © Dieter Melhorn/ Alamy RF; p. 56 (top right): © Stockbyte/ Getty Images RF; p. 56 (bottom right): Walt Jennings/FEMA

Chapter 4

Opener: © Michael Babwahsingh; p. 97: Photographs in the Carol M. Highsmith Archive, Library of Congress, Prints and Photographs Division; p. 108: © Image Source/Digital Images/Getty RF

Chapter 5

Opener: © Calle Montes/Photononstop/ Corbis

Chapter 6

Opener: (left): © Design Pics/Bilderbuch RF; (middle): © Ingram Publishing RF; (right): © Creatas/PunchStock RF; p. 149: Library of Congress Prints and Photographs Division LC-DIG-ppmsca-26286; p. 191: © Digital Vision/PunchStock

Chapter 7

Opener: © ZUMA Press, Inc./Alamy

Chapter 8

Opener: © Felix Behnke/Cultura/ Getty Images RF; p. 250: © The Palma Collection/Getty Images RF; p. 261: © Comstock Images RF

Chapter 9

Opener: © Terry J. Alcorn/Photodisc/ Getty Images RF; p. 278: © Roy McMahon/Corbis RF

Chapter 10

Opener: © Stockbyte/Getty Images RF; p. 324: © Ocean/Corbis RF; p. 344: © John Lund/Sam Diephuis/Blend Images LLC RF; p. 345 (top): © The John B. Lovelace Collection Photographs in Carol M. Highsmith's American Project, LOC; p. 345 (bottom): © Radius Images/Getty Images RF

Chapter 11

Opener: © McGraw-Hill Education/ Christopher Kerrigan, photographer; p. 351 (top): © C. Sherburne/PhotoLink/ Getty Images RF; p. 351 (middle): © Brand X Pictures/Getty Images RF; p. 351 (bottom): © Purestock/SuperStock RF; p. 352 (top): © Rich Legg/E+/Getty Images RF; p. 352 (bottom): © Andrew Penner/E+/Getty Images RF; p. 352 (left): © Laurent Hamels/PhotoAlton/Corbis RF; p. 353: © Jupiterimages RF

Grammar Units

Unit 1 p. 388: © Digital Vision/Getty Images RF; Unit 2 (left) p. 428: © Imagestate Media (John Foxx)/Image State RF; Unit 2 (right) p. 428 © Dusty Pixel photography/Getty Images RF; Unit 3 p. 450: © Image 100/Corbis RF

INDEX

Note: Page numbers in italics refer to illustrations; page numbers in boldface refer to plates; page numbers followed by a "t" refer to tables.